———————≫—————

Utah's Black Hawk War

John Alton Peterson

The University of Utah Press
Salt Lake City

Printed on acid-free paper

Library of Congress Cataloging-in-Publication Data

Peterson, John Alton, 1957–
    Utah's Black Hawk War / John Alton Peterson.
        p.   cm.
    Includes bibliographical references (p.   ) and index.
    ISBN 0-87480-583-X (alk. paper)
    1. Black Hawk War (Utah), 1865–1872.   I. Title.
E83.867.P47   1998
973.8'2—dc21   98-21752

For Linda,
Jeff, Jaren, Jennifer, Kerstin, and Derek,
who, like some of their ancestors,
temporarily gave up husband and father
that he might chase
Black Hawk.
And for Betty,
who gave me life,
and Chas,
who gave me a love for History.

I have made a ceaseless effort not to ridicule, not to bewail, nor to scorn human actions, but to understand them.

—Spinoza

Contents

Acknowledgments

My SINCERE THANKS to professors Robert A. Trennert, Peter Iverson, and Albert L. Hurtado of the Department of History at Arizona State University, who read early drafts of *Utah's Black Hawk War* and made helpful recommendations. Special mention goes to my father, Dr. Charles S. Peterson, whose interest, insights, and suggestions, in this project *and throughout my life*, have been profound and have had lasting impact. Grateful appreciation is hereby tendered to the various librarians and archivists at Archives and Manuscripts and at Special Collections, Harold B. Lee Library, Brigham Young University, Provo, Utah; the Department of Special Collections, Manuscript Division and Western Americana, Marriott Library, University of Utah, Salt Lake City, Utah; Special Collections and Archives at Utah State University, Logan, Utah; the Family History Library of the Church of Jesus Christ of Latter-day Saints, Salt Lake City, Utah; the Manuscript Division of the Library of Congress, Washington, D.C.; the National Anthropological Archives, Washington, D.C.; the National Archives, Washington, D.C.; Utah State Archives, Salt Lake City, Utah; and the Utah State Historical Society, Salt Lake City, Utah.

Special thanks go to my friends and former colleagues at the Church Historical Department, the Church of Jesus Christ of Latter-day Saints, Salt Lake City, Utah, whose interest and service have been exceptional, especially Ronald Barney, Jay Burrup, Randall Dixon, Linda Haslam, Gordon Irving, James L. Kimball, Jr., Chad Orton, Bill Slaughter, Steve Sorensen, and Ronald Watt. Walter Jones of the Department of Special Collections at the University of Utah displayed a level of helpfulness and kindness that went far beyond the call of duty. Similarly, local historian Marva Loy Eggett of Spring Lake, Utah, rendered extraordinary assistance. Charmaine Thompson, Archaeologist, Uinta National Forest, Provo, Utah, made available files relative to the repatriation and reburial of Black Hawk's remains. Gordon Irving read the manuscript in its entirety and made insightful suggestions. Brian Flammer designed and produced the maps.

I also express appreciation to various members of the Ute Tribe, who shared oral tradition and research, particularly Arlene M. Appah, Thomasina Appah, Sylvia M. Cornpeach, Clifford H. Duncan, and Richard Mountain. Thanks also to the Max Millet family of Phoenix, Arizona, whose contribution made possible an extended visit to the National Archives and other repositories in Washington, D.C. Finally, and most importantly, I express my thanks and devotion to my wife, Linda Israelsen Peterson, without whose patience, support, and steady cheerfulness this book would not have been possible.

List of Abbreviations

AGO   Records of the Adjutant General's Office, NA.

BIA   Records of the Bureau of Indian Affairs, NA.

BYC   Brigham Young Collection, CHD.

BYUA&M   Archives and Manuscripts, Harold B. Lee Library, Brigham Young University, Provo, Utah.

BYUSC   Special Collections, Harold B. Lee Library, Brigham Young University, Provo, Utah.

CHD   Church Historical Department, the Church of Jesus Christ of Latter-day Saints, Salt Lake City, Utah.

CR   "Record of Provo Military District Command 1857–1858 and Campaign Record of Expedition to Sanpete and Piute Military District 1866–1867, under command of William B. Pace," BYUSC.

DUP   Daughters of Utah Pioneers.

DN   *Deseret News.*

FHL   Family History Library, the Church of Jesus Christ of Latter-day Saints, Salt Lake City, Utah.

GAS   George A. Smith Collection, CHD.

HOJ   Historian's Office Journal, CHD.

HOLB   Historian's Office Letter Book, CHD.

JD   *Journal of Discourses.*

JH   Journal History of the Church of Jesus Christ of Latter-day Saints, CHD.

MS	*Millennial Star.*
NA	National Archives, Washington, D.C.
RSI	*Report of the Secretary of the Interior.*
RUSA	Records of the U.S. Army Continental Commands, 1821–1920, NA.
SDTP	State Department Territorial Papers, USA.
TAS	Theodore Albert Schroeder Papers, CHD.
TEP	Territorial Executive Papers, USA.
TMR	Territorial Militia Records, USA.
UHQ	*Utah Historical Quarterly.*
USHS	Utah State Historical Society, Salt Lake City, Utah.
USA	Utah State Archives, Salt Lake City, Utah.
UUWA	University of Utah, Western Americana, Marriott Library, Salt Lake City, Utah.
WBP	William B. Pace Collection, CHD.

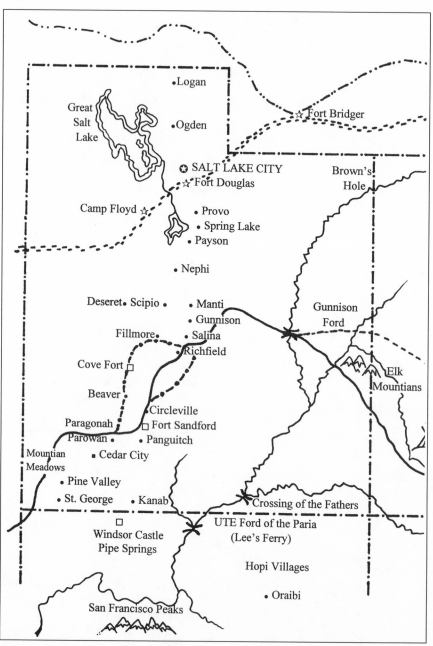

Areas of the Black Hawk War, 1865–1872

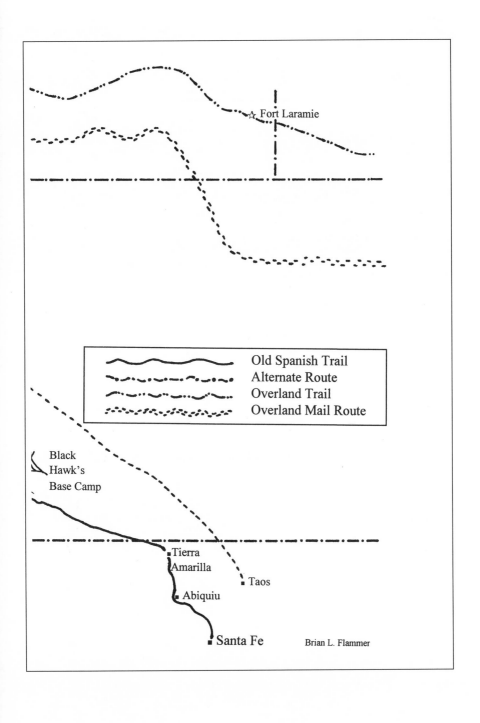

Fort Laramie

Old Spanish Trail
Alternate Route
Overland Trail
Overland Mail Route

Black
Hawk's
Base Camp

Tierra
Amarilla

Taos

Abiquiu

Santa Fe   Brian L. Flammer

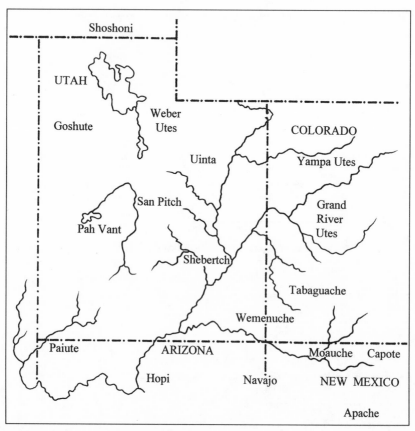

Indians of Utah and Surrounding Areas

Utah Counties in 1866

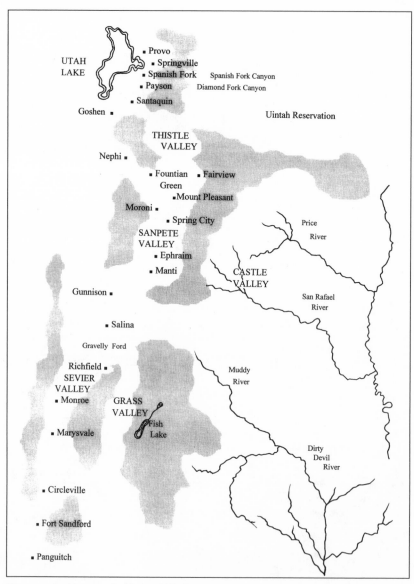

Morman Settlements in Central Utah in 1866

———————— ≫ ————————

Introduction

If we are going to tell the whole story of Indian-white relations, we must make an all-out attempt to picture the clash of cultures so that there will be an understanding of both cultures, not just one. . . . What we are seeking, . . . is a wider basis of truth, a better understanding of what has happened in the past. We may then have a truer account of what actually happened to both Indians and whites and of the emergence of a new culture that formed on the frontier at the point of contact.

. . . at some future time it may be that even Old Posey, an intrepid, determined Ute and the leader of a local war in Utah, as well as Tecumseh, Pontiac, Blackhawk, Sitting Bull, and Chief Joseph, will be recognized as truly national figures in our history. As much as the heroic figure of the scout, the plainsman, the mountain man, and the cowboy himself, these courageous Indians deserve our respect and admiration. For they and all their Indian brethren may have made contributions to our life-style which may ultimately bring about a better America.

—Wilbur R. Jacobs, 1973[1]

RELATED ONLY IN NAME to the more widely known Sac-Fox war that raged in Illinois a generation earlier,[2] Utah's Black Hawk War represents a complex and interesting anomaly in the history of the American West. Beginning in 1865, certain Northern Utes and their allies were led by a brilliant Indian leader named Antonga (called Black Hawk by the whites) in a series of intense and successful raids on livestock owned by the Mormon settlers of Utah. From 1865 to 1872, literally thousands

---

[1] Wilbur Jacobs, "The Indian and the Frontier," 43, 54.
[2] For information regarding the 1832 Black Hawk War in Illinois see Ford, *History of Illinois*, 102–65; Armstrong, *The Sauks and the Black Hawk War*; Eby, *"Disgraceful Affair"*; and Nichols, *Black Hawk*.

of horses and cattle were run off and marketed in a complex Native American trading system involving white and Hispanic middlemen and covering a huge piece of country including most of Utah as well as parts of Colorado, New Mexico, Arizona, Nevada, and Wyoming. Meanwhile, Brigham Young and his followers (members of the Church of Jesus Christ of Latter-day Saints, commonly called Latter-day Saints or Mormons) responded with vigorous but ineffective military operations conducted by the Nauvoo Legion, a church-run militia.

The three-year period from 1865 to 1867, when Black Hawk personally directed Native American military activities, was by far the most intense part of the conflict. Over one hundred daring stock raids punctuated by frequent killings and pitched battles caused Latter-day Saints in central and southern Utah to consider themselves in a state of open warfare. They built scores of forts and abandoned dozens of settlements while hundreds of local militiamen chased their elusive adversaries through the wilderness with little success. Although livestock (and not Mormon lives) was usually the raiders' primary object, at least seventy whites were killed. Perhaps twice that many Native Americans lost their lives in acts of violence as the settlers of Utah took measures to protect their property and avenge their losses. Though actual fatalities were low when compared with other major conflicts in the region (in part because federal troops were not employed), the war had tremendous impact on both societies.

Late in the summer of 1867, Black Hawk made peace with the Mormons. Without his leadership, the war that bore his name waned dramatically and a treaty of peace was signed in 1868. Related raiding and killing continued, however, until 1872, when a Ghost Dance crisis finally forced Latter-day Saint leaders to call for the deployment of federal soldiers. With the appearance of the U.S. troops, the seven-and-a-half-year-old conflict abruptly ended.

While the Black Hawk War was unquestionably an expression of the general Indian unrest in the trans-Mississippi West during the 1860s and 1870s,[3] one important factor unique to Utah made it an anomaly in Western history. The war was played out against the backdrop of an exceedingly complex set of political conditions involving Mormons, Indians, and gentiles[4] that enabled Black Hawk and others to carry on

---

[3] For a general discussion of the causes and expressions of this unrest see Utley, *Indian Frontier*, 1–98.

[4] Gentile is a scriptural term adapted by Latter-day Saints to refer to non-Mormons and will be used throughout this study to mean non-LDS whites. For a brief description of the

their raiding for almost eight years with little threat of the bloody federal military reprisals Native Americans experienced on all sides of the Mormon heartland during the period. The Utes' neighbors to the west felt the wrath of federal troops in Nevada's Paiute War of 1860, while their Shoshoni relatives to the north lost 250 of their number in the Bear River Massacre at the hands of Colonel Patrick E. Connor in January 1863. To the south, the Navajos were forced by Kit Carson's brutal campaigns to leave their homelands and make the "Long Walk" to a new reservation at the Bosque Redondo in New Mexico in 1864, hundreds perishing in the process. Little over three months before the beginning of the Black Hawk War, hundreds of the Utes' neighbors to the east, the Cheyenne and Southern Arapahos, were destroyed in the infamous "Sand Creek Massacre" by a combined force of Colorado militia and federal soldiers.[5]

As evidence of his political acumen, Black Hawk launched his assault on the Mormon settlements at a time of intense political struggle between Latter-day Saint Utah and the federal government. Polygamy and Brigham Young's theocratic rule and isolationist policies had long been a source of tension between Utah Territory and Washington. In 1857 President James Buchanan sent U.S. troops to install a replacement to Young as Utah's territorial governor, precipitating the so-called Utah War. In 1862 several hundred California and Nevada Volunteers, led by a cabal of rabidly anti-Mormon officers, occupied Utah to guard overland routes and bind the territory to the Union. Friction between the church hierarchy and the soldiers' commander, Colonel Patrick E. Connor, nearly broke out in violence several times in 1864. Quite aware that Mormon and gentile leaders distrusted each other more than they did the Indians, Black Hawk gambled that the Latter-day Saints would not call in U.S. troops against him, or that, if they did, Connor would refuse to send them.

Black Hawk read the political situation astutely. As the Civil War came to a close (officially ending the very day the Black Hawk War began), eastern politicians were again turning their attention to the last

---

political contest between Mormons and the United States government during these years see Dwyer, *The Gentile Comes to Utah*; and Lyman, *Political Deliverance*, 7–40.

[5] For a general description of the cataclysmic misfortunes inflicted on Indian communities by whites during this period see Utley, *Indian Frontier*, 65–98. For more specific descriptions of the challenges white expansion posed to the Utes' nearest neighbors see Egan, *Sand in a Whirlwind*; Brigham Madsen, *Shoshoni Frontier*; Trafzer, *Carson Campaign*; and Hoig, *Sand Creek Massacre*.

surviving sibling of the Republican party's loathed "twin relics of barbarism."[6] With slavery successfully snuffed out, polygamy and "un-American" governmental practices in Utah increasingly became hot items on the national agenda. Fearing that war with the Indians would give Washington a needed pretext to send more troops to Utah and thereby increase federal power in the territory, Young directed his followers to keep quiet about the raiders' activities and to deal with them on their own. Pursuing a policy of military self-sufficiency in Indian matters, which endured until 1872, Mormon Utah repressed comprehensive newspaper reports of the fighting and carefully concealed information from unsympathetic federal officials. An interesting break with American tradition, this move tended to make the conflict a nearly secret war as far as the federal government and the American public were concerned.

Mormons were unable to keep officials totally in the dark; however, Connor (who much to Brigham Young's chagrin was occasionally petitioned by Mormons to chastise Black Hawk) set a precedent of his own by simply choosing to ignore the war. For more than seven years the United States military pursued a unique hands-off policy that allowed the raiders to operate without federal interference. In short, then, the Black Hawk War erupted and was sustained as the result of an uneasy, dynamic, and often times volatile triangle which formed as Mormons, gentiles, and Indians jockeyed for position in the Territory of Utah.

Seeking to further their own interests, each group played the other two off against one another. Reminiscent of Indian wars waged during the colonial era of American history, the Black Hawk War was, at least in part, one front of a political battle fought by whites against whites. Indeed, to a certain degree, the war was the result of incipient national efforts to "Americanize Utah for Statehood," which would not come to fruition until even after Utah became the Union's forty-fifth state in 1896. As such, it was an early expression of the anti-polygamy crusades that vexed Mormon Utah during the 1880s.[7]

This said, it must be understood that the Indians were not simply casual observers or mere pawns employed in a "whites only" contest. Just as the Iroquois and Cherokees had earlier played opposing European empires off against each other, the Utes exploited the political situation

---

[6] Gustive Larson, *Americanization of Utah*, 22.
[7] See ibid.; and Lyman, *Political Deliverance*.

as best they could. They displayed deft political capacity and turned Mormons and gentiles into pawns of their own, often manipulating whites as successfully as they were exploited by them.

There are other ways in which the war highlights interesting anomalies in the history of the West. A central tenet of Latter-day Saint religion was that the Indians were descendants of Israel and eventually would be restored to the fold of Jehovah's covenant. The Book of Mormon taught that the Indians would rise from their fallen and "cursed" condition to become "white and delightsome," once again enjoying all the blessings (and culture) of God's chosen people.[8] Believing the Latter-day Saints were to be the agents of this regeneration, Brigham Young (who until 1857 also served as Utah's superintendent of Indian affairs) constantly urged his people to be kind and generous to the territory's natives while systematically appropriating their lands to themselves. Missions were established and hundreds of Native Americans were baptized while Young sought to inspire his people with his oft-quoted maxim that it was "better to feed the Indians than fight them."[9]

In comparison with most of their frontier contemporaries, Mormons got along so well with their Indian neighbors that much of the nation developed grossly exaggerated notions of the Saints' extraordinary influence over the western tribes. This in turn spawned a powerful and abiding paranoia that Brigham Young would one day lead a pan-Indian army against the United States. In reality, as the Black Hawk War ultimately demonstrated, the Latter-day Saints wielded nowhere near the influence with Native Americans they themselves claimed or were generally given credit for by others. In fact, as a result of the fighting, they lost much of the influence they actually had. Nonetheless, a study of the war provides great insight into the distinctive Latter-day Saint religious ideals and practices that directed Indian-white relations over an immense tract of country in the nineteenth-century American West.

Within months of the organization of the Church of Jesus Christ of Latter-day Saints in 1830, Joseph Smith, the church's first prophet, optimistically sent Parley P. Pratt, Oliver Cowdery, Peter Whitmer, Jr., and Ziba Peterson on the first formal LDS mission.[10] Not surprisingly, Indians, or "Lamanites" as the Book of Mormon called them, were the

---

[8] 2 Nephi 12:12 in the Book of Mormon, 6th European ed., (London: Brigham Young, Jr., 1866).

[9] For example, see *JD*, 10:231–32.

[10] Jennings, "The First Mormon Mission to the Indians."

object. Dazzled by visions of the destiny of the Lamanite in the last days, these first Latter-day Saint missionaries turned their faces westward and ultimately drew their church with them, securing for the Mormon people a vital role in the settling of the American West. Mormons essentially became the first group of white settlers in the interior West, extending their dominion over a huge area. Latter-day Saint Indian relations, therefore, should be of prime concern to students of the history of the western United States.

A result of Latter-day Saint theology and the forceful leadership of Brigham Young, much of the eighteen-year period preceding the Black Hawk War was characterized by symbiotic relationships between Mormons and Indians, which were generally intimate, peaceful, and friendly associations extraordinary to the history of the region. This was greatly enhanced by the facts that Indian title to the land was not extinguished for years after settlement and that both societies lived side by side. Each Mormon village had its known set of Indian neighbors who spent seasons living nearby, surviving increasingly by begging as settlement destroyed the ecosystems upon which they had formerly relied. Furthermore, the mobile nature of native subsistence patterns and the Latter-day Saints' own peripatetic colonization practices caused some Indians to be well known to the white community throughout the entire territory. The converse was equally true, creating a condition of remarkable personal interaction between the two peoples. As intertwined as the two societies had become, the Black Hawk War, unlike most Indian wars of the era, was a war fought between acquaintances. In a very real sense it was a war between neighbors.

The fact that many of the Indians and Mormons involved knew each other intimately and had enjoyed former, albeit sometimes strained, relationships, contributed a tragic and uncommon quality to the conflict. Friendships maintained between certain members of both groups continued to play important conciliatory roles throughout the period of hostility. More often, however, deep animosity of the sort developed between former friends in relationships gone awry caused Mormon-Indian relations to sour. Despite Latter-day Saint doctrines, a *comparatively* positive shared past, and the efforts of peace-minded leaders in both groups, interaction between the groups took on violent dimensions more characteristic of the era's general Indian-white relations.

In this sense, the Black Hawk War was especially tragic. It represented the failure of a people whose very spiritual life was closely focused on Indian relations to live in peace with their native neighbors.

Often conducting themselves more like conquerors than missionaries, the Latter-day Saints displaced native societies and colluded with federal officials to place them on reservations. In fact, from the Utes' point of view, the Black Hawk War was largely fought to resist displacement and removal to the Uintah Reservation and the Mormon expansion that had caused such exigencies in the first place.

The incredible irony of this is the fact that the Mormons were in Utah because they had been displaced themselves. Pushed from frontier settlements in New York, Ohio, Missouri, and Illinois, the white participants of the Black Hawk War undoubtedly knew as much about displacement, persecution, and injustice as any other group of whites Native Americans ever encountered. The Mormon experience tended to temper, but by no means eradicate, the traditional white response to the Indian dilemma. Despite the bloody evidence provided in this study, compared to their gentile counterparts throughout the West, the Latter-day Saints displayed exceptional restraint, a product of Mormon doctrine and the constant preaching of Brigham Young. Unfortunately for both the Indians and the whites, however, the settlers of Utah in practice fell far short of their Latter-day Saint ideals.

Despite the modern tendency to castigate whites out of hand as aggressors and to represent Indians always as innocent victims, the Utah setting calls for understanding and compassion towards the positions of both groups. The simple fact was that two honorable peoples were hopelessly trapped not only by their own cultures, goals, and interests but also by the larger political and national forces of their time. Both were victims of violent demographic and political changes that threatened their very existences as communities. While religious issues usually get the credit, Mormons were pushed to Utah by the same expanding North American population system that eventually settled the country by whites and drove Indians in Utah and throughout the West onto reservations. Part of an even larger demographic tragedy, a considerable number of the whites involved in the Black Hawk War were poverty-stricken emigrants cast from exploding European populations. Their land invaded by more than 100,000 Latter-day Saints, the Indians themselves became part of a vicious demographic catastrophe that forced men like Black Hawk to take desperate action or starve. At the same time, Mormons were forced by contingencies nearly as desperate to fight back.

The object here is not to use presentist values to condemn or exonerate a particular group; it is, rather, to understand and chronicle an intense struggle between two intelligent, resourceful, but threatened peoples in the context of the political and demographic world in which they found themselves. What emerges is perhaps Utah's most tragic story, which in turn is part of an even larger American story laced with blood and bitter agony.

Ultimately much larger in scope and impact than the Mountain Meadows Massacre (where a relatively small number of Mormon frontiersmen and Indians brutally killed more than a hundred gentile emigrants in 1857),[11] the Black Hawk War touched in crucial ways literally every contemporary Mormon and Indian in Utah. Massacres and murders on the part of both groups left lasting scars on both communities. Representative of others, the Thistle Valley, Ephraim, and Glenwood massacres on the part of the Indians, and the Squaw Fight, Circleville Massacre, and the brutal slayings of Sanpitch and other Indian leaders at the hands of the Mormons, all carry the classic elements of tragedy. While the memory of them has faded, such incidents inspired animosities that have had enduring influence.

The war not only has escaped the consciousness of modern Utah society, it also has largely been ignored by students of Mormon, Utah, Western, and Indian history.[12] While most modern Utahns, for example, know something of the Mountain Meadows Massacre, at this writing perhaps less than 1 percent have even heard of the Black Hawk War let alone know what it was fought for or the general meaning it had for

---

[11] See Brooks, *Mountain Meadows Massacre*; and Wise, *Massacre at Mountain Meadows*.

[12] Until now, no comprehensive history of the Black Hawk War has ever been written. The only published volume dealing exclusively with the subject is Culmsee, *Utah's Black Hawk War*. Based on a series of newspaper articles written by Carlton Culmsee in 1933 and 1934 for the *Deseret News*, the book is a collection of dramatic and embellished stories bereft of historical context. Utah's classic work on Indian-white relations is Gottfredson, *Indian Depredations*. A poorly organized collection of reminiscences relating to general Indian-white conflict in nineteenth-century Utah, this book was edited by a participant of the Black Hawk War and contains numerous documentary and oral accounts obtained from veterans that are preserved nowhere else. While it is an important source book for the war, it contains no analysis and many errors. Prior to my own work, three graduate studies were written on the subject: Barton, "Black Hawk War"; Spencer, "Black Hawk War"; and Metcalf, "A Reappraisal of Utah's Black Hawk War." As is to be expected from master's theses, each is somewhat shallow in research and incomplete in scope and analysis. My own doctoral dissertation was the first in-depth and critical study of the Black Hawk War; see John A. Peterson, "Mormons, Indians, and Gentiles and Utah's Black Hawk War." No published work representative of what has been called "the New Mormon History" deals at any length with the Black Hawk War, but several earlier historians included chapters or even shorter sections regarding it in general histories. For examples see Whitney, *History of Utah*, 2:187–214; Roberts, *Comprehensive History*, 5:146–71; and Neff, *History of Utah*, 398–409. See also Richard Young, "The Nauvoo Legion," 441–52.

the Indians, the Mormons, and the history of the state. The truth is, nineteenth-century Mormons failed to implement the humanitarian teachings, policies, and examples of both Joseph Smith and Brigham Young and in practice rejected a founding tenet of their faith. Undoubtedly motivated by shame, the Latter-day Saints, who are generally known for their extraordinary historical consciousness, have successfully dropped this episode from their folklore and historical canon. It is therefore time the story is retold.

As has been mentioned, the Mormons worked hard to keep information regarding the war from the federal government and the public media. Simultaneously, other forces unique to the Utah situation kept the conflict outside the scope of normal military and newspaper reporting practices. These anomalies, combined with the fact that the Indians themselves left no records, have necessitated a disproportionate reliance on Latter-day Saint documents. Due to the Saints' singular proclivity for record keeping, however, these last-named sources are extraordinarily rich. It therefore goes without saying that available sources have naturally produced a lopsided Mormon narrative. I have, however, extensively searched U.S. Indian Office, U.S. War Department, and Utah territorial papers in an attempt to understand and document the gentile perspective.

To a surprising degree, the feelings, attitudes, actions, and desperate frustrations of the Indians of Utah were captured and preserved by the white record. Reports of speeches and numerous letters dictated by Indian leaders to white interpreters are of special importance among the thousands of letters, official reports, military dispatches, newspaper and journal accounts, and reminiscences I have consulted. Understandably, such white sources are tainted with serious racial biases which tend to skew the vision of unwary readers. Since Native American participants kept no records and handed down very little through oral tradition, the modern historian has no choice but to seek to reconstruct Indian feelings, motivations, and actions from records left by whites. While such an approach is precarious, at least some picture of the Indian perspective is preserved.

Significantly, Indians emerge in this study as people of face and personality. Black Hawk, Mountain, Sanpitch, Tamaritz, Tabby, Kanosh, Sowiette, and Toquana influenced the flow of events as profoundly as did Brigham Young, Daniel H. Wells, Orson Hyde, and Warren S. Snow for the Mormons, or as Patrick E. Connor, Orsemus H. Irish, and Franklin H. Head did on the part of Utah's gentile federal officials.

As dynamic figures in history, the Indians of Utah acted intelligently and energetically in dealing with the challenges that faced them. Like the whites, they responded individually, each operating in ways best suited to his or her own unique nature, world view, and self-interest. Tabby, Sowiette, and Kanosh, for example, were acquiescent before the onslaught of Mormon expansion; on the other hand, Black Hawk, Jake Arapeen, Mountain, Tamaritz, and their followers risked (and sometimes lost) their lives to oppose it. Most of the Indians of Utah found themselves somewhere between the two extremes. Unfortunately, many who did not resort to violence were severely punished for the actions of those who did.

Along with Brigham Young, Black Hawk (Antonga) himself emerges as one of the most dynamic and effective figures involved in the conflict. Actually siding with the Latter-day Saints in the first major Ute-Mormon conflict, the 1850 Fort Utah Fight, Black Hawk enigmatically led Mormon patrols in attacks against his own people. Witnessing first-hand the effects of "chain and ball" fired from a Mormon cannon on his own camp, he later saw the decapitated heads of scores of his tribesmen displayed at the Mormon fort. Rewarded by being appointed head chief of what was left of the Timpanogos band (and by being held in confinement for weeks of winter weather under the settlers' cannon platform), Black Hawk, like hundreds of his people, evidently was baptized into the Mormon church. Witnessing the agony his association with settlers had brought to his band, however, quickly (and thoroughly) transformed him from the Latter-day Saints' leading Ute ally to one of the most truculent and outspoken leaders of Ute resistence to Mormon settlement. For more than a decade before the beginning of the Black Hawk War, Antonga Black Hawk, along with Wakara, Tintic, and Squash-Head, was one of the four most important native opponents of Mormon colonization.

Latter-day Saint writers have accorded Black Hawk a certain significance but more as the fiendish leader of a cruel and costly outbreak than as a Native American leader with remarkable vision and capacity. Given the circumstances under which he operated, he put together an imposing war machine and masterminded a sophisticated strategy that suggests he had a keen grasp of the economic, political, and geographic contexts within which he operated. Comparable to Cochise, Sitting Bull, and Geronimo, Black Hawk fostered an extraordinary pan-regional movement that enabled him to operate in an enormous section of country and establish a three-front war. Like Tecumseh, though admittedly on a smaller scale, he sought to turn the conflict into a pan-Indian war and succeeded in involving Utes from many bands as well as significant numbers of Navajos, Paiutes, Piedes, Goshutes, Apaches, Hopis, and Shoshonis. Interestingly, Black Hawk's efforts to export the war initiated a major Navajo-Mormon war that eventually took on a life of its own. Like his close relative Wakara, Black Hawk ran stock incredibly long distances over the Old Spanish Trail and dozens of other ancient Indian trails through what is arguably the roughest country in North America. As Wakara's heir to leadership of the Shiberetch band, Black Hawk funneled thousands of stolen animals to Taos and Santa Fe markets in what can be viewed as the grand finale of the glory days of Ute raiding. Similar to Tenskwatawa, the Shawnee prophet, the Ute war chief was inspired by dreams and visions, and his entire movement was colored by mystical and nativistic nuances barely recognized by the whites he confronted.

Like other Indian leaders, Black Hawk worked to establish a barrier to white expansion and actually succeeded in collapsing the line of Mormon settlement, causing scores of villages in over a half dozen large counties to be abandoned. For almost a decade the tide of white expansion in Utah came to a dead stop and in most of the territory actually receded. Like other defenders of Indian rights, though, Black Hawk found that he could not hold his position, and his efforts eventually crumbled. Seriously wounded in a pitched battle with the Nauvoo Legion and suffering from deadly diseases brought by white men, in a curious twist, Black Hawk returned to his former alliance with the Mormon people. Obviously dying, he accepted Brigham Young as his shaman, prophet, and spiritual advisor and sought to make peace with the Mormon god by working to reconcile his people to their conquerors. Weak and emaciated, the former war chief rode hundreds of miles in attempts to stop what he had started. On Young's cue, he visited virtually every major village and hamlet he had raided, meeting his former enemies face to face and humbly begging their "forgiveness." The war had swept beyond even his control, however, and it did not end until nearly two years after his death in 1870.

Despite his ultimate failure, it is unquestioned that Black Hawk was an Indian leader of singular importance. As a result of Brigham Young's policy of concealing Black Hawk's activities from the federal government and the American public, as well as the government's own hands-off policy regarding the conflict, Antonga Black Hawk's name has not been attached to the list of key Native American leaders to which it rightly belongs.[13] Perhaps symbolic of what his resistance meant to his followers, however, the Ute war chief was honored by receiving the appellation of his tribe to replace his own given name— even after his capitulation, his partisans affectionately called him "Nu-ints" or "Noonch," the very name by which the Northern Utes knew themselves.[14]

Brigham Young emerges as the most forceful and effective figure involved in the Black Hawk War. There are few surprises in this. He was in command not only of his own people but of the political situation, the strategies used, and, at times, even of the Indians themselves. Years of kind treatment of Indians had won him tremendous influence with Native Americans, and he occupied a niche of almost mythic proportions in their world view. He earned the image of a symbolic "father" at least as powerful to the native mind as "the Great White Father" who lived and ruled in distant Washington.

As Antonga Black Hawk's 1869 "Peace Path" and the 1872 Ghost Dance crisis that ended the Black Hawk War demonstrated, Indians also cast Young in a certain prophetic role as a holy man and seer. Lamentably, despite his influence and efforts for peace, the prophet alone could not avoid war. The simple truth is that, try as he might, he could not induce his people to follow his policies. Significantly, throughout the conflict, the raiders did not consider themselves at war with Young or even with the Mormons generally. From their perspective, the war was largely a personal affair, focused primarily on Sanpete and Sevier County Latter-day Saints who through their mistreatment and abuse of Indians had demonstrated themselves to be enemies.

It was not totally understood by the Indians, however, that Brigham

---

[13] Neither Black Hawk nor his war are so much as mentioned in such surveys of Indian history, studies of Native American leaders, and biographical lists as Brown, *Bury My Heart at Wounded Knee*; Dillon, *North American Indian Wars*; Dockstader, *Great North American Indians*; Edmunds, *American Indian Leaders*; Hoxie, *Indians in American History*; Josephy, *The Patriot Chiefs*; Malinowski, *Native North American Biography*; Utley, *Indian Frontier*; Carl Waldman, *Who Was Who in Native American History*; Harry Waldman, *Dictionary of Indians*; or Wilcomb Washburn, *The Indian in America*. In the massive multivolume *Handbook of North American Indians* his name appears only twice, and then he is only mentioned cursorily as the leader of a band; see volume 11:365, 547.

[14] John Wesley Powell, "Government," 2–3, in idem, "Life and Culture of the Ute"; idem, "Indian Life," 4–5; and *RSI*, 1873: 424. Most references to *RSI* in this study are taken from various *Report(s) of the Commissioner of Indian Affairs* reprinted in *RSI*.

Young himself was the primary planner of the military operations the Mormons launched against them. Although one of his counselors in the church's ruling First Presidency,[15] Daniel H. Wells, was ostensibly the leading officer of the Nauvoo Legion, Young secretly played the role of commander in chief. Shrewdly distancing himself from involvement in military affairs, he was largely held guiltless by the Indians, while the outstanding implementor of his policy, Brigadier General Warren S. Snow, commander of the Sanpete Military District of the Nauvoo Legion, became their archenemy and symbolic nemesis.

Aside from the Indians, Brigham Young had other reasons to obscure his leadership of the Nauvoo Legion. Nothing less than an ecclesiastical army, the legion involved the Mormon church in a function of state and was the ultimate expression of the theocracy's power. As such it was a major point of contention between the Latter-day Saints and the United States government. An anomaly in the post–Civil War era, the Nauvoo Legion, which was repeatedly proclaimed to be illegal by Utah's federal officials, was a direct breach of the limitation on states' rights the Civil War was fought to enforce. Earlier, during the 1853–54 Walker War and the so-called 1857 Utah War, Brigham Young was territorial governor of Utah (or, in the case of the latter, he at least had some legal claim to the position) and thus employed the Legion as a bona fide and legitimate function of state. By the time of the Black Hawk War, however, the Latter-day Saints had elected him "governor" of an extralegal shadow government known as the "Ghost State of Deseret." Viewed by his people as the titular head of a government in waiting, as far as the laws of the United States were concerned, however, Brigham Young was no more than a private citizen.

Throughout the period, Mormon watchers in and out of Utah were convinced Young was preparing to deploy the Nauvoo Legion against the United States Army as he had done during the Utah War. There is no question he utilized the Indian war to bring the Nauvoo Legion to the highest state of effectiveness and organization in its history. The Black Hawk War provided the opportunity to purchase weapons, obtain uniforms, levy drafts, polish field operations, and streamline

---

[15] The Prophet and President of the Church of Jesus Christ of Latter-day Saints is usually assisted by a pair of advisors or counselors (though during Young's time sometimes there were more). Modeled after the New Testament apostolic triumvirate of Peter, James, and John, together they constitute the First Presidency, the highest governing body of the church. Next to them in authority is a council of twelve apostles.

organizational structures. All the while, as far as the church president and his followers were concerned, protecting Latter-day Saints from Indians was *not* the principal reason the Nauvoo Legion existed.

Mormon historians have long looked at the 1840 Nauvoo City Charter under which the Nauvoo Legion came into being as an extraordinary grant of power. In contrast to Joseph Smith's use of the Nauvoo Legion in the 1840s, which at least had a basis in powers legally granted by the State of Illinois,[16] during the Black Hawk War Brigham Young assumed even greater powers with absolutely no legal grant from any state, territorial, or federal government. Indeed, the church leader's mobilization and personal direction of the Nauvoo Legion during the Black Hawk War is perhaps the most outright case of church invasion in the issues of state that can be cited in post–Civil War United States history. Interestingly, the 1872 Ghost Dance crisis, which produced the circumstances that ultimately brought the Black Hawk War to an end, enabled the federal government to disable and effectually disband the Nauvoo Legion, thus once and for all destroying Young's military power.

Military force, it can be argued, is the ultimate expression of human power. The emasculation of the Nauvoo Legion near the close of the Black Hawk War, while it was clearly not the undoing of Brigham Young, signaled a major loosening of the prophet's grip on the territory. A complete picture of Young's involvement in the Nauvoo Legion during the post–Utah War period has not fully been presented in the literature of Mormon history, and thus an important understanding of his actual power emerges in a study of the Black Hawk War.

As has been pointed out, the Black Hawk War has largely been ignored by Utah, Mormon, Western, and Indian historians. It has been viewed as an obscure "side ring" action. In truth, the Black Hawk War and its related racial, religious, political, and national issues are of prime importance to Utah and Mormon history. It ranks in significance with the creation of the territory, the Mountain Meadows Massacre, the Utah War, the coming of the transcontinental railroad, the antipolygamy raids, the Manifesto, and statehood. It should be considered one of the major topics in nineteenth-century Mormon and Utah history.

---

[16] See Flanders, *Nauvoo*; Hallwas and Launius, *Cultures in Conflict*; Quinn, *Mormon Hierarchy: Origins*, 105–6; James Kimball, "Study of the Nauvoo Charter"; idem, "Nauvoo Charter: Reinterpretation"; idem, "A Wall to Defend Zion"; Bailey, "The Nauvoo Legion," in *Armies of God*, 79–138; and Sweeney, "Nauvoo Legion in Illinois."

These fields have been dominated by three major historical approaches. Interpreted largely through studies of spiritual affairs, economic affairs, and political affairs, the body of historical literature is like a three-legged bench wanting a fourth leg for stability. Shorted by our limited vision of Indian affairs because no complete examination of the Black Hawk War has been made, this analysis fills important voids in Mormon and Utah studies. Admittedly, it is just one component of a comprehensive evaluation of Mormon-Indian relations that remains to be completed.[17]

For the larger fields of American, Western, and Indian history, this study also fills important gaps. It not only provides insight into the peculiar Latter-day Saint notions regarding Indians that directed Indian relations over a huge portion of the American West but also introduces and chronicles the life of Antonga Black Hawk, a key nineteenth-century Indian leader, who, through white manipulation of the historical record, has been forgotten—until now.

[17] For a discussion noting the "short shrift rendered to Indian studies" in Mormon historiography see Walker, "Toward a Reconstruction of Mormon and Indian Relations, 1847–1877." For a historiographic essay and listing of what had been written on the issue until 1985 see Whittaker, "Mormons and Native Americans."

CHAPTER ONE

Beginnings and the Uneasy Triangle

The Redskins continue on the rampage on the Plains. There is
little doubt that they receive encouragement and supplies from
the Mormons. Both will have to be dispossessed or exterminated,
before a great while.

—San Francisco Flag, 1867[1]

The Altercation in Manti

ON SUNDAY, 9 April 1865, Ulysses S. Grant and Robert E. Lee met in
the parlor of Wilmer McLean's brick home in Appomattox Court
House, Virginia, to negotiate the conclusion of the Civil War. That
same day, far to the west, a handful of Mormons and Northern Utes
met in the central Utah town of Manti in an attempt to achieve a peace
of their own. Unlike the negotiations at Appomattox, however, those at
Manti failed, and the events that transpired there are viewed as the beginning of Utah's Black Hawk War, the longest and most serious
Indian-white conflict in Utah history.

The meeting between Ute leaders and Manti frontiersmen was
informal. Representatives from several bands that wintered near the
Latter-day Saint settlements in Sanpete Valley met on horseback with
John Lowry, a hotheaded interpreter employed by the United States
Indian Office. Native spokesmen included Sow-ok-soo-bet, An-kar-
tewets, Toquana, Black Hawk, and Jake Arapeen. Lowry had called the
meeting a few weeks earlier when he discovered hungry Indians had
butchered fifteen head of cattle owned by the settlers. The winter of
1864–65 was particularly severe, and Utes drawn to the settlements by
the prospects of begging were desperately hungry. Added to this,

---

[1] *San Francisco Flag*, as quoted in *DN*, 26 June 1867.

measles and other diseases brought by whites had ravaged their numbers and bewildered tribesmen blamed the settlers for the fatalities,
believing their neighbors used their influence with God to send death
upon them. These and other factors induced what originally was a very
small party led by Black Hawk and Jake to not only help themselves to
cattle but to determine to fight the Mormons in the spring.

As early as February, Black Hawk boasted that as soon as the snow
melted his band would kill settlers and eat "Mormon beef." Lowry informed local church leaders of the threat, but they concluded it was
"just Indian talk." Not until he found the slaughtered remains of one of
his own animals did Lowry begin to take Black Hawk seriously. In
March he confronted the Utes and arranged the 9 April meeting hoping that more peacefully disposed Indians would force Black Hawk to
stop slaughtering livestock and threatening whites.

That some of the Utes hoped to settle the affair amicably is clear.
Sow-ok-soo-bet, known to whites as "Joe," delivered a horse sent by
Chief Sanpitch to pay Lowry for an ox Black Hawk had killed. Still not
satisfied, Lowry, who reportedly had been drinking, angrily harangued
the Indians. Jake Arapeen, described by settlers as "a small saucy Indian," was the most vocal of the delegates. Arguing passionately, he
cited numerous Ute grievances with both the Mormons and the federal
government. Trying to soothe his embittered friend, Joe reminded him
of the settlers' frequent gifts of food and supplies. Toquana, the son of
Sowiette, the aged head chief of the Northern Ute tribe, also defended
the Latter-day Saints and raised his voice for peace.

Black Hawk and Jake, however, refused to be pacified. As Lowry
launched into them with another tirade, Jake set an arrow to his bow.
Grabbing the Indian by the hair, Lowry yanked him from his horse and
the two scuffled on the ground until separated by peace-minded associates from both sides. Wild with rage, Lowry started home to get a pistol, while the entire Ute delegation rode out of town, Black Hawk and
Jake hurling threats over their shoulders as they went.[2]

---

[2] Jake Arapeen was an Indian of high status. His father, Chief Arapeen, was a brother of
Sanpitch and Wakara (commonly known as Walker). These three, along with Sowiette, were
the most powerful Ute chieftains encountered by the Mormons; by the time of the Black
Hawk War, however, both Wakara and Arapeen were dead. For the description of Jake see
Olsen, "Life Story," 7. For information regarding the failed negotiations at Manti see Warren S. Snow to Brigham Young, 22 April 1865, BYC; Kearnes, "Statement as to Indian Difficulties"; Peacock, Journal, 9 April 1865; idem, "Indian difficulties," 1; Bean, Autobiography,

First Blood

Outwardly, the altercation between Jake Arapeen and John Lowry was not unique and raised little concern among Manti's settlers. In fact, when fifteen young herdsmen left to investigate the extent of the stock killings the following morning they took no weapons. At Twelve Mile Creek (so named because of its distance from Manti) they saw sixteen Indians riding towards them. When within firing distance, the Indians, led by Black Hawk, began to shoot. The herdsmen continued, however, supposing the Utes were just "fooling." Not until they heard bullets whistling past their heads did they wheel their horses. As they did, Peter Ludvigsen toppled from his horse with a bullet hole in the back of his head. Leaving their dead compatriot where he fell, the surprised herdsmen fled back to Manti. Meanwhile, the raiders stripped the dead man of all but his socks, viciously smashing his face into a prickly pear. They then cut a large piece of skin from his back, which they reportedly ate as some sort of ceremonial opening of hostilities.[3]

Unwittingly, the Manti youths had stumbled onto a major cattle raid already in progress. Immediately following the unseating of Jake Arapeen in Manti, Black Hawk and his followers had ordered their women and children to strike their camp located at a defunct Indian reservation on Twelve Mile Creek. Tepees were hurriedly dismantled and dragged behind horses with other camp gear towards the safety of Salina Canyon. The following morning, as the herdsmen were leaving Manti, Black Hawk and his men began to gather the Mormons' cattle. By the time the whites reached Twelve Mile Creek, the raiders had collected fifteen head. Fearing that the herdsmen would spoil their plans, they attacked, sending the terrified youths bolting back towards town. After brutalizing the remains of Ludvigsen, the raiders made a sweep of the Manti range, increasing the size of their herd to forty. They then drove their booty towards Salina, gathering even more cattle en route.

As they made their way south, runners carried word of the raid to several Ute bands encamped near Salina. These immediately struck their lodges and moved into Salina Canyon, where they were followed

1897, 68–69; "Proceedings of a Council with the Utah Indians," 37–38; and Gottfredson, *Indian Depredations*, 335–38.

    [3] Kearnes, "Statement as to Indian Difficulties"; Peacock, Journal, 10 April 1865; Orson Hyde to Brigham Young, 14 April 1865, BYC; Warren S. Snow to Brigham Young, 22 April 1865; Merrill, "A Veteran of the Black Hawk War," 59; and DUP, *Our Pioneer Heritage*, 9:176.

after dark by Jake, Black Hawk, and their new herd. These bands re-inforced Black Hawk's original sixteen raiders with seventy more men.[4]

During the day, the people of Salina were unaware of the trouble and went about their business, hardly noticing the removal of the In-dian families into the canyon. Earlier, two Salina residents went up the canyon to check on some lost stock. One was Barney Ward, a mountain man who had converted to Mormonism and had lived in the Rocky Mountain area for over thirty years. Despite the fact that he spoke the Ute language fluently and had fathered several mixed-blood children by a Shoshoni woman,[5] Ward and a young Danish companion, James Anderson were killed by Black Hawk's party.[6] That night the raiders came back down the canyon with a force of about fifty men. Still unde-tected, they succeeded in driving off most of Salina's horses and cattle, swelling the size of their stolen herd to more than 125 animals.[7]

When Ward and Anderson failed to return, the townspeople became worried; but not until 1:00 A.M. the next day, 11 April, were they ap-prised of the fight in Manti and of Ludvigsen's death. After daybreak a small group of Salina horsemen gingerly made their way up the canyon in search of the missing men. About five miles up the canyon they dis-covered Barney Ward "striped of his clothing[,] scalped[,] and shot in several places." Following tracks from the place of Ward's killing, they came upon the body of James Anderson. Evidence at the site convinced Hamilton Kearnes, the LDS bishop of Gunnison, that the young Dane had been "scalped while yet alive." Horrified at what he saw, Bishop Kearnes reported to Brigham Young that Anderson's "head was split open and his brains scattered around and his body otherwise very much mangled."[8]

The Salina Canyon Fight

Throughout 11 April, bands of mounted militiamen began arriving in Salina. Called out by Nauvoo Legion Colonel Reddick N. Allred, they

[4] One Salina resident recalled that the raiders' messengers reached Indians there about 1:00 P.M. Their evacuation was so quick that by 3:00 P.M. there was "no sign of an indian to be seen." Rasmussen, "Life of Peter Rasmussen."

[5] Ward is believed to have come to the West with Nathaniel Wyeth in 1834, as he partici-pated in the construction of Fort Hall that summer. See Hafen, "Elijah Barney Ward," 343–51.

[6] Warren S. Snow to Brigham Young, 22 April 1865; and Rasmussen, "Life of Peter Ras-mussen."

[7] Orson Hyde to Brigham Young, 14 April 1865, BYC; Reddick N. Allred to Brigham Young, 11 April 1865, BYC; and Hamilton Kearnes to Brigham Young, 15 April, 1865, BYC.

[8] Kearnes, "Statement as to Indian Difficulties"; and Rasmussen, "Life of Peter Ras-mussen."

came from Gunnison and such Sanpete Valley settlements as Manti, Ephraim, and Spring City.[9] The following morning, 12 April, Allred started up Salina Canyon with a force of eighty-four men.[10] Hoping the cattle could not be taken over the canyon's summit on account of the snowpack, they planned to chastise the raiders and recover the stock. About fourteen miles up they came across freshly killed beeves, which apparently had just been abandoned in the process of being butchered. Certain the fleeing Indians must be just ahead, the troopers urged their horses through a narrow defile through which only one rider could pass at a time. Sometime after the last man had made it through the gap, and while they were strung out in a narrow gorge surrounded by steep canyon walls, they were attacked by a large native force concealed on the cliffs. Horses bolted and reared as their riders dismounted and sought cover in the rocks and willows along the creek bottom. Still the troopers saw no Indians, only smoke rising from the rocks and trees above them.

Black Hawk's men poured down a "murderous fire" while the militiamen searched in vain for adequate cover or targets to shoot at. Sizing up their precarious position, Allred ordered a retreat. Immediately a panicked stampede of frenzied men and horses raced down the canyon "through Showers of balls like hail." In the confusion coats, saddles, blankets, and weapons were scattered as frantic horses threw their riders and went crashing through the brush. Once the untrained mass of men and horses started down the path, Allred found it virtually impossible to assemble them. He considered a rally necessary, however, because a number of his men were still up the trail under heavy fire. Jens Sorensen, a young Dane from Ephraim, broke his ankle when he was thrown from a mule, and he was shot in the hip as he hobbled towards his comrades. Several others near him struggled to free terrified horses whose bridles had become entangled in the brush.

The militia's retreat brought an estimated eighty attackers out of hiding. Simultaneously, Allred managed to rally twenty men, who for the first time returned effective fire, killing "two or three" Indians. By the time most of their straggling comrades reached the small collection of militiamen who remained with Allred, Ute cross fire dictated a second headlong dash for safety. As they fled, William Kearnes, the son of Gunnison's bishop, was shot in the head and died instantly. Meanwhile,

[9] Reddick N. Allred to Brigham Young, 11 April 1865. As in the case of Spring City, the names of some settlements have changed since the time of the Black Hawk War; to avoid confusion, I will use modern designations.
[10] Kearnes, "Statement as to Indian Difficulties."

the wounded and horseless Jens Sorensen called on his fellows for help, but he was left to be killed, as "none had the hardihood to stay another minute under such fire."[11]

The shooting during the ambush was so intense and the trap so well laid that most of the Mormons considered it a miracle that any of them escaped.[12] One militiaman attributed their deliverance to two facts. First, Black Hawk's men "over-shot" their targets: "Had the Indians known how their guns were carrying they could have shot us down fast," he declared. Second, the raiders for some reason did not anticipate the legionnaires' uncontrolled flight back to the gap and had stationed none of their men there. The panicked withdrawal of the majority of Allred's troops preserved their lives, and some of them later reminisced (with good reason) that had they not taken the pass so swiftly the outcome might have been similar to that suffered by Custer's men in 1876.[13]

Once the militiamen had all cleared the pass they made the long ride back to Salina "feeling pretty blue." Near the mouth of the canyon they met Bishop Kearnes, and more than one writer chronicled the doleful feelings expressed as the bishop learned of his son's death.[14] Apparently the Indians followed the soldiers back down the canyon far enough that at night their defeated foes in Salina could hear them celebrate with dances, exultant shouts, and the discharging of weapons.[15]

Black Hawk, Jake, and their band of raiders had reason to celebrate. In the three days that had passed since they argued with John Lowry in Manti, they had made good on their promise to kill settlers and steal "Mormon beef." Five Latter-day Saints were dead and the raiders were in possession of about 125 head of cattle as well as a substantial number of horses. Added to this, they had scored a tremendous moral victory by routing the Nauvoo Legion. In a society that extolled cunning in raiding, daring in war, and prized horses, guns, and meat as symbols of power and wealth, Black Hawk and Jake had considerably strengthened

---

[11] Ibid.; Reddick N. Allred to Major Tuttle, 12 April 1865, BYC; Orson Hyde to Brigham Young, 14 April 1865; Warren S. Snow to Brigham Young, 22 April 1865; Gottfredson, *Indian Depredations*, 132–37; "Gunnison Ward Historical Record," 14–15; Peacock, Journal, 12 April 1865; Sylvester, "Indian Wars," 1–2; Ahlstrom, "Biography," 5; and Cox, "Biographical Sketch," 15–16.

[12] Warren S. Snow to Brigham Young, 22 April 1865; Orson Hyde to Brigham Young, 14 April 1865; and Cox, "Biographical Sketch," 15.

[13] Sylvester, "Indian Wars," 1–2.

[14] For example, see ibid.

[15] Hamilton Kearnes to Brigham Young, 13 April 1865, BYC.

their positions. This initial success undoubtedly played a major role in inaugurating the series of stock raids that persisted from 1865 to 1872 and was almost immediately named "the Black Hawk War." Their forces would soon be reinforced by recruits from various bands of Utes from as far away as Colorado and New Mexico, as well as by Goshutes, Paiutes, Piedes, Weber Utes, Navajos, and even a few Shoshonis, Hopis, and Jicarilla Apaches.

The Uneasy Triangle

As pointed out in the Introduction, Black Hawk's initial raids, and in fact the whole conflict, must be viewed against the backdrop of the uneasy and oftentimes volatile triangle that formed as Mormons, Indians, and gentiles struggled for position in the Territory of Utah. Although a lengthy discussion of this incredibly complex and fascinating phenomenon is not possible here, some review of its nature and development is essential.

Even before he formally organized the Church of Jesus Christ of Latter-day Saints in 1830, Joseph Smith, Jr., the founder of Mormonism, had great interest in Native Americans. Indeed, they were the focal point of his earliest-known written revelation, wherein the Lord told him that "the very purpose" ancient records preserved on gold plates were brought forth through him was that the Indians, or "Lamanites" as the Lord called them, "might come to the knowledge of their fathers [Ancient Israel], and . . . believe the gospel and rely upon the merits of Jesus Christ."[16] Smith's translation of these plates, the Book of Mormon, accepted by Latter-day Saints as scripture, prophesied that when Native Americans were "restored unto the knowledge of . . . Jesus Christ, . . . their scales of darkness shall begin to fall from their eyes; and many generations shall not pass away among them, save they shall be a white and a delightsome people."[17] Not long after Smith published his translation of the gold plates as the Book of Mormon in

---

[16] While Smith received other revelations earlier, section 3 of current editions of the *Doctrine and Covenants* was apparently the first revelation he wrote down. The manuscript revelation was first published in 1833. See Bushman, *Beginnings of Mormonism*, 93; [Joseph Smith, Jr., et al.,] *Book of Commandments*, 7–9; Cook, *Revelations of Joseph Smith*, 8–9; and modern editions of the *Doctrine and Covenants*, section 3.

[17] Book of Mormon (1830), 117. Compare 2 Nephi 30:3–6 in modern editions, where "they shall be a *white* and a delightsome people" has been changed to "they shall be a *pure* and a delightsome people" to "bring the material into conformity with prepublication manuscripts and early editions edited by the Prophet Joseph Smith." Italics mine. See "A Brief Explanation About the Book of Mormon" in front matter of 1981 and later editions of the Book of Mormon.

upstate New York in 1830, Latter-day Saint assertions of the book's prophecies of the destruction of wicked gentiles by Native Americans spawned rumors that Smith's fledgling church hoped to incite Indians to violence against non-Mormon whites. "But if the Gentiles will not repent," the Book of Mormon prophesied,

> I will suffer my people, O house of Israel [Mormons and Indians], that they shall go through among them, and tread them down, and they shall be as salt that hath lost his savour, which is thenceforth good for nothing, but to be cast out, and to be trodden under foot of my people, O house of Israel. . . . ye shall be among them as a lion among the beasts of the forest, and as a young lion among the flocks of sheep, who, if he goeth through, both treadeth down and teareth in pieces, and none can deliver. . . . I will make thy horn iron, and I will make thy hoofs brass. And thou shalt beat in pieces many people; and I will consecrate their gain [the gentiles' property] unto the Lord, and their substance unto the Lord of the whole earth. . . . [for] Thus has the Father commanded me, that I should give unto this people [Mormons and Indians] this land for their inheritance.[18]

Charges of Mormon "tampering with the Indians" were sharpened by the fact that other revelations directed the first formal Latter-day Saint mission to be among the Lamanites and indicated that Zion, the New Jerusalem of Biblical promise, was to be located "on the borders by the Lamanites" in Independence, Missouri, to facilitate the Native Americans' mass conversion.[19] Significantly, one early revelation of Joseph Smith made the "restoration" of the Indian a precursor to the Second Coming of Christ. "But before the great day of the Lord shall come," it read, "Jacob shall flourish in the wilderness, and the Lamanites shall blossom as the rose." As a result, the conversion of the Lamanite was connected to early Mormonism's intense millenarian impulse.[20] Proselytizing Native Americans became a primary focus of the

---

[18] The Book of Mormon (1830), 488, 496–97. Compare with 3 Nephi 16:10–16, and 20:15–21 in current editions.

[19] The Indian Removal Act of 1830 established a "permanent" line between Indian lands to which Eastern tribes were driven and the area of white settlement. Independence, Missouri, was the frontier outpost of white society nearest that line. See *Book of Commandments*, 67–70; and [Joseph Smith, Jr., et al.,] *Doctrine and Covenants of the Church of the Latter Day Saints*, 154–55. Compare with modern editions of the *Doctrine and Covenants*, sections 28 and 32.

[20] *Book of Commandments*, 116–19, especially 118; compare with modern editions of the *Doctrine and Covenants*, 49:24.

millennialistic "Saints of the Latter Days." Hence, as early church historian and apostle George A. Smith pointed out, "In the early years of
the Church, there was a *great anxiety among the brethren to travel and
preach the Gospel among the Lamanites.*"[21]

Meanwhile, another early revelation dictated by Joseph Smith
prophesied that "the remnants who are left of the land [the Indians]
shall marshal themselves, and shall become exceedingly angry, and shall
vex the gentiles with a sore vexation."[22] Despite revelations counseling
them not to speak of such things "before the world,"[23] rank and file
Latter-day Saints continued to call attention to their belief that Native
Americans would be used as "the battle axe of the Lord" in cleansing the
American nation of iniquity. Throughout the 1830s and 1840s, as the
church was embroiled in a series of devastating civil wars with its neighbors in Missouri and Illinois, such boasts and the rumors they spawned
flourished and in fact fostered a false but widely held and persistent no-
tion that the Latter-day Saints wielded great influence with Indians.
This growing paranoia was coupled with the more substantial threat to
American society that the Mormons were building an independent
"Kingdom" in the heart of the American democracy that they believed
would eventually "break in pieces all Nations" and fill the whole earth.[24]

Perhaps the ultimate expression of the American notion of "Manifest
Destiny," the importance of what can be termed the Latter-day Saint
"Doctrine of Kingdom" cannot be overstated. It simply is the key to understanding Mormon history in the nineteenth century and the key to
understanding the acute persecution the Latter-day Saints suffered at
the hands of other Americans during the period. Put succinctly, Mormons believed that God had commissioned them to build the kingdom
spoken of in the second chapter of Daniel, which the God of Heaven
promised to set up in the Last Days. Essentially, it was the kingdom the
resurrected Christ, the King of Kings, was to take possession of at His
coming. In the meantime, this latter-day kingdom, like a stone rolling
down a mountain (to use the scriptural image), was to expand and eventually "smite," "break in pieces and consume" all other worldly kingdoms, after which it would "fill the whole earth," and "stand for ever."[25]

---

21 *JD*, 3:28. Italics mine.
22 Joseph Smith, Jr. [et al.], *History of the Church*, 1:301–2.
23 For example, see *Doctrine and Covenants*, 105:23–24.
24 See LeSueur, *1838 Mormon War in Missouri*, especially 71–72; and Hallwas and Launius, *Cultures in Conflict*, especially 103–7.
25 See Daniel 2:31–45.

Dead serious about their own calling to bring about the fulfillment of this prophecy, and never prone to keep quiet about their beliefs, Latter-day Saints boldly declared it to their non-Mormon neighbors. The doctrine obviously ran counter to the ideals of the American Revolution, which had only recently "declared independence" from kings and kingdoms. The belief naturally was viewed by others as sinister and threatening, if not blatantly seditious.[26] Apostle and later church president John Taylor, who was with Joseph Smith when he was killed in an Illinois jail in 1844, and who himself was brutally shot four times during the assassination, recognized the relationship between his people's suffering and the Doctrine of Kingdom. "Why is it that we are persecuted?" he once asked as a federal army threatened Mormon Utah in 1857. Answering his own question, he declared, "It is because we believe in the establishment of the kingdom of God upon the earth—because we say and know that God has established his kingdom."[27] Languishing in a Missouri prison in 1839 after the Mormons had been forcibly driven from that state, Hyrum Smith, Joseph's brother and a high church leader in his own right, penned the following in his journal:

"... after a long trial by the inquisitors I was with Several others committed to Jail for my religion beleving as I do that the church is the one Spoken of by the prophet Daniel[,] the Stone that was to rowl [*sic*] that should strike at the feet of the image & brake down the Hole Image & become a grate Mountain & fill the hole Earth[.] therefore my persicutors pretended that I had Committed treason[.] the same acquisations was [made] against the Son of god[,] this be cause of the iniquity of the world."[28]

Later, Governor Thomas Ford justified the State of Illinois in driving the Latter-day Saints into the wilderness by stating that "the Mormons openly denounced the government of the United States as utterly corrupt, and as being about to pass away, and to be replaced by the government of God, to be administered by his servant Joseph."[29]

One of Joseph Smith's revelations, already cited above, clearly

---

[26] Much excellent work has been done on the role of the Doctrine of Kingdom in Mormon history. For example, see Andrus, *Joseph Smith and World Government*; Flanders, *Nauvoo*; Hanson, *Quest for Empire*; Hill, *Quest for Refuge*; and Hallwas and Launius, *Cultures in Conflict*.

[27] *JD*, 6:21.

[28] Hyrum Smith, "Dayly [*sic*] Record," 1.

[29] Ford, *History of Illinois*, 321–22.

connected the Lamanites to the work of sweeping the wicked from the earth in order that the Kingdom of God might expand. The Indians were to "vex the Gentiles with a sore vexation . . . until the consumption decreed, hath made a full end of all nations."[30] A powerful example of the apprehension Mormon kingdom building and related rumors of their planned military use of Native Americans instilled in the hearts of their gentile neighbors appeared in print on the heels of Joseph Smith's murder at the hands of an enraged Illinois and Missouri public:

The great aim of Joseph Smith was evidently to cloth[e] himself with the most unlimited power, civil, military and ecclesiastical, over all who became members of his society. . . . He stated that Emma his wife, was of Indian descent, in a line from one of the tribes of Israel. That he (Joseph) was a descendant from Joseph of old through the blood of Ephraim. And that God had appointed and ordained that he, with his descendants, would rule over all Israel, meaning the Latter Day Saints or the Mormons, the Indian tribes and ultimately the Jews and Gentiles. . . . Joe further stated, that God had revealed to him, that the Indians and Latter Day Saints, under Joe as their King and Ruler, were to conquer the Gentiles, and that their subjection to this authority was to be obtained *by the sword!* From this revelation . . . Joe was accordingly crowned KING under God, over the immediate house of Israel. . . . It is also a fact, ascertained beyond controversy, that the Indian tribes of Sacs and Foxes, Siouxs and Potowattamies, were consulted, and their assent obtained previous to the *mock* crowning of this unmitigated Impostor, and that delegations were sent to Nauvoo from each of the above tribes about the time of the [coronation] ceremony . . . These delegations of Indians were seen by hundreds and hundreds at Nauvoo [the Mormon capital in Illinois].[31]

After Smith's death, the growing myth of colossal Indian influence was transferred to his successor, Brigham Young, who was shrewd enough to use it for political advantage. Chased from Nauvoo by writs

---

[30] [Richards], *Pearl of Great Price*, 35. Compare with current *Doctrine and Covenants*, 87:1–8.

[31] George T.M. Davis, as quoted in Hallwas and Launius, *Cultures in Conflict*, 103–7. Italics in original.

charging him with treason ("for colleaguing with the Indians, building an arsenal, and making Cannon" to use against the United States, among other things[32]), Young, while directing his people's historic trek to the Great Basin, established a host of temporary settlements on Indian lands near the Omaha, Oto, Pottawattami, Sioux, and Pawnee Indians and privately treated with some of these tribes on behalf of the Mormon kingdom. Simultaneously, Latter-day Saints were openly instructed by their leaders that "The Lamanites have to be taught. They have to be baptized and a great army organized and prepared to redeem Zion and avenge the blood of [Joseph Smith and his brother Hyrum,] which mighty work shall be accomplished as the Lord liveth." In Washington, the commissioner of Indian affairs, the secretary of war, and the president of the United States naturally viewed these developments with great suspicion, while Young openly declared that his church had "more influence with the Indians than all other nations on the earth *and if we are compelled to, we will use it.*"[33]

Finally settling in Utah in 1847, Young's followers immediately commenced cultivating the good graces of the Utes, Shoshonis, Navajos, and other powerful western tribes among whom they settled. Their boasts of influence backfired, however, as they were blamed by gentiles for virtually every non-Mormon death at the hands of Indians on the Overland Trail and elsewhere in the interior West. The most notable example was the death of Captain John W. Gunnison, a government explorer who was killed with seven of his surveying party by Pahvant Indians on Utah's Sevier River in 1853. Highly publicized in the national press, Gunnison's murder was laid at the door of the Latter-day Saints and became, in the view of one recent writer, "seminal to the history of the American West" in that it led to the 1857 Utah War and the related Mountain Meadows Massacre.[34] While the Saints were innocent of most of the Indian atrocities charged to them, (including the Gunnison Massacre), there is no question that they actively worked to incite Indians to violence against whites in both of the last-named Mormon-gentile conflicts.

The "Utah War" was precipitated in the tense years immediately

---

[32] Clayton, *Intimate Chronicle*, 182.

[33] Bennett, *Mormons at the Missouri*, especially chapter 5; Trennert, *Alternative to Extinction*, 145–48; Coates, "Cultural Conflict," especially 283–84; and Hallwas and Launius, *Cultures in Conflict*, 321–22. For the Young quotation see, Bennett, 103. Italics mine.

[34] Fielding, *Unsolicited Chronicler*, dust jacket; and Ronald Walker, "Gunnison Massacre."

preceding the American Civil War, as the newly created Republican party attached Mormon polygamy to the slavery issue as one of the "twin relics of barbarism" it was pledged to destroy. It occurred when a federal campaign to curb Brigham Young's theocratic leadership as Utah's territorial governor, as well as his supposed "tampering with Indians" as ex officio superintendent of Indian affairs, ended in impasse. As a result, President James Buchanan dispatched over 2,500 soldiers to Utah in 1857 to ensure the removal of the church leader as governor and superintendent and to install his newly appointed non-Mormon successor, Alfred Cumming.[35] The role gentile beliefs regarding Mormon Indian affairs played in engendering the conflict in the first place can be seen in speeches delivered on the floors of Congress during the period. For example, Stephen A. Douglas, senator from the Latter-day Saints' former home state of Illinois, thundered that

> the Mormon government, with Brigham Young at its head, is now forming alliances with Indian tribes in Utah and adjoining Territories—stimulating the Indians to acts of hostility—and organizing bands of his own followers, under the name of Danites, or Destroying Angels, to prosecute a system of robbery and murders upon American citizens who support the authority of the United States, and denounce the infamous and disgusting practices and institutions of the Mormon government.[36]

In actuality, however, the coming of the army inspired far more "tampering with Indians" (on the parts of both the Mormons and the government) than had ever occurred in the territory before. As the army neared Utah, church leaders and federal military officers alike employed Indian spies and scurried to secure promises of native help for the armed conflict that both sides expected. Dangerously approaching actual bloodshed, a successful guerilla campaign on the part of the Nauvoo Legion (with the help of winter snows) stalled U.S. troops near Fort Bridger long enough for cooler heads to orchestrate the bloodless entrance of the soldiers and new governor into the Mormon community. But tragically, in the tense months that led up to the peaceful set-

[35] See Gustive Larson, *Americanization of Utah*, 22; Furniss, *Mormon Conflict*; Bailey, "The Utah War," in *Armies of God*, 185–255; idem, *Holy Smoke*; and Poll and Hansen, "Buchanan's Blunder."

[36] Richard Young, "The Nauvoo Legion," 249. The Danites were loosely organized Mormon vigilantes who most often acted independently of church leaders. Though there is no question that they actually existed, in the minds of the American public their activities took on mythic qualities which exceeded reality by gargantuan proportions.

tlement of the crisis, Mormon frontiersmen and Indians massacred over one hundred gentile emigrants at Mountain Meadows in southwestern Utah.[37]

As governor, Alfred Cumming took the path of compromise, often standing between the Saints and the fiercely anti-Mormon federal judges and military officers who accompanied him to Utah. Despite his efforts, continued attempts by Washington to bring Utah to heel strengthened Mormon apprehension of official gentile violence against the church hierarchy. "As to the Congress of the United States," declared George A. Smith to his fellow apostles at a prayer meeting in 1859, "their is not ten men [among them] but what want to Cut the throats of the [First] presidency & the Twelve Apostles." Smith prayed God "to Curse them & give them No power over us," and expressed the desire of his quorum saying, "I want to pray for the removal of the armey."[38] The hierarchy felt their prayers were miraculously answered two years later when the Civil War called both Governor Cumming and the U.S. Army back to the States.

Even before the passage of the organic act that created the Territory of Utah in 1850, the animosity between the United States government and the Mormon settlers in Utah impacted virtually every aspect of territorial policy, including important matters of U.S. Indian Office procedure. Most notable among these was the reluctance of the federal government to extinguish Indian land title for fear that native rights to the soil would be usurped by the Latter-day Saints, thereby strengthening the church's position. Normally moving quickly to extinguish title through formal treaties before or in the early stages of white settlement, the federal government, as a result of Utah's unique situation, purposely allowed nearly eighteen years to pass before extinguishing native title and providing for Indian removal to reservations. Even then, Congress authorized the move only because of an expected massive influx of gentiles into the territory. A conspicuous anomaly in the history of the American frontier experience, these unusual circumstances allowed the settlers and the Indians to occupy the same lands for nearly two decades, providing an uncommon opportunity for developing extraordinarily intimate Indian-white relations.

This perceived "neglect" was not lost on the Mormons, who repeat-

---

[37] See Brooks, *Mountain Meadows Massacre*; and Wise, *Massacre at Mountain Meadows*. See references in note 35 for information on the Utah War.

[38] Woodruff, *Journal*, 6:293–94.

edly petitioned Congress and the commissioner of Indian affairs for the much more rapid "extinguishment and removal" process they saw taking place in areas of gentile settlement. "This Territory presents the only instance of the organization of a Territorial Government by Congress," they once provocatively declared, where the land had been "thrown open to settlement, without measures being first adopted to extinguish the Indian title." The settlers were told that the policy resulted from the fact that "the country was obtained from Mexico" and, as that "nation never recognized the Indian title, the United States would adopt the same policy." Such arguments fell on deaf ears, however, and the Latter-day Saints continued to see themselves as the victims of federally supported religious persecution.[39]

In the minds of the Saints, the Civil War was God's promised retribution upon their persecutors—the nation that had killed their prophets, driven them into the wilderness, and had sent "the flower of the American army" against them. As early as 1832 Joseph Smith received a revelation prophesying that "the Southern States shall be divided against the Northern States," and that war would break out "beginning at the rebellion of South Carolina, which will eventually terminate in the death and misery of many souls."[40] In 1833 Smith prophesied that unless the president of the United States helped the church retrieve lands it was driven from in Jackson County, Missouri, the Lord would "arise and come forth out of his hiding place, and in his fury vex the nation, and in his hot displeasure, and in his fierce anger, in his time, . . . cut off these wicked, unfaithful, and unjust stewards, and appoint them their portion among hypocrites and unbelievers; even in outer darkness, where there is weeping, and wailing, and gnashing of teeth."[41] Similarly, after the Latter-day Saints were driven from Illinois following the martyrdom of Joseph and Hyrum Smith, Brigham Young himself dictated a revelation in which he prophesied,

Thy brethren have rejected you and your testimony, even the nation that has driven you out; and now cometh the day of their

---

[39] George A. Smith and James Lewis to Hon. Milard Filmore [*sic*], President of the United States, undated, but received at the Indian Office 20 August 1851, BIA, M234, 897; and "Petition of Gov. and Judges &c of Utah Territory in relation to the Indians" to Hon. A. B. Greenwood, 1 November 1860, BYC.

[40] Joseph Smith, Jr., [et al.], *History of the Church*, 1:301–2; compare with current editions of the *Doctrine and Covenants*, section 87.

[41] [Joseph Smith, Jr., et al.,] *Doctrine and Covenants of the Church of the Latter Day Saints*, 239; compare with current editions of the *Doctrine and Covenants*, 101:86–92.

calamity, even the days of sorrow, like a woman that is taken in travail; and their sorrow shall be great, unless they speedily repent; yea, very speedily; for they killed the Prophets, and they that were sent unto them, and they have shed innocent blood, which crieth from the ground against them.[42]

As reports of casualties in the East poured in to Utah by way of the recently completed transcontinental telegraph line, the Mormons generally rejoiced that "the words of the Prophets are rapidly being fulfilled" in the calamitous war that was ravaging the country.[43] Interestingly, even some of the great eastern newspapers knew of these prophecies and published some of them, the *Philadelphia Sunday Mercury* frankly raising the question, "Have we not had a prophet among us?"[44] Meanwhile, Young exulted that "this thing is coming to pass, just as Brother Joseph said, thirty years ago; that the South would rise against the North, and the North against the South, and that they would fight until both parties were destroyed." "And for my part," he added, "I give it God speed, for they have spilt the blood of the prophet."[45]

Viewing himself as Smith's legal successor, since his arrival in Utah Brigham Young had used all his powers to build a Mormon theocracy in the interior West. Even when the Utah War effectively deposed him as legal governor of the territory, without skipping a beat he continued on as the de facto chief of state. Mormons rejoiced that Governor Cumming had been forced to admit that although on paper he was "governor of the Territory," Brigham Young was still "governor of the people."[46] From 1860 on Young had himself "elected" governor of the "State of Deseret," described by historian Dale Morgan as "a ghost state" that tacitly existed beside the official territorial government authorized by Washington. During the period, Mormons were taught that "the Priesthood is the Standard and the Priesthood is greater than

---

[42] Brigham Young, "The Word and Will of the Lord, Given at the Winter Quarters of the Camp of Israel, Omaha Nation, West Bank of the Missouri River, near Council Bluffs, January 14th, 1847," *MS* 14 (1 May 1852): 150–52; compare with modern editions of the *Doctrine and Covenants*, 136:34–36.

[43] For examples of Latter-day Saint reaction to the Civil War see Charles Walker, *Diary*, 1:154, 233, 245.

[44] *Philadelphia Sunday Mercury*, 5 May 1861, photocopy in author's possession.

[45] Thomas J. Drake and Charles B. Waite, Associate Justices, Supreme Court Utah Territory, to His Excellency Abraham Lincoln, 6 March 1863, in Abraham Lincoln Papers, series 1863, March 5–28, reel 50, #22251-7, Library of Congress, Washington, D.C.

[46] Manuscript History of Brigham Young, 28 January 1864.

the law."[47] Brigham Young even instructed his people to pray "three times a day for the reins of government to be taken out of the hands of the wicked and placed in the hands of the righteous."[48] War with the United States was viewed as a looming possibility, while Young repeatedly prophesied that the Saints would yet see the day when the Indians would "be a shield to this people."[49]

With the U.S. troops recalled to fight in the east, the church's political power was momentarily unchecked, and the Latter-day Saints, who had unsuccessfully applied for statehood a number of times, boldly proclaimed the existence of their "State of Deseret" early in 1862.[50] The *Deseret News*, the official church newspaper, declared that the new state superseded "the Territorial form of rule, unconstitutionally imposed [upon them] by Congress." Moreover, the paper announced that, should the government fail to admit Deseret into the Union, the Saints were prepared to throw off "the Federal yoke" and assume the right of self-government by force.[51]

Eastern presses portrayed Utah's so-called "declaration of Independence" in its worst possible light, and national leaders felt constrained to send volunteers from California to keep the church in line.[52] By the fall of 1862, the troops from California arrived in Utah, where their commander, Colonel Patrick E. Connor, established Camp Douglas (named after Stephen A. Douglas) on a bench overlooking Salt Lake City. Ostensibly in the territory to "guard the overland trail" from rebel attacks and Indian raids, among themselves gentiles admitted that the troops were kept there "to see that the Mormons did not inflate the minds of the Indians and cause an outbreak while the Union was in danger."[53] Connor trained his howitzers on Brigham Young's mansions and took it upon himself to destroy the Mormon theocracy.

---

[47] Weibye, "Journal," 2 September 1866 (in Danish); and Morgan, *State of Deseret*, 91–119.

[48] Hansen, *Autobiography*, 144.

[49] Coombs, Diary, 28 July 1866.

[50] This was actually a *reorganization* of Mormon state government. This time, however, the Saints proposed to operate "a ghost government" independent of the territorial government set up by Congress. During the entire period spanned by the Black Hawk War, Brigham Young made annual speeches to the territorial legislature as "Governor" in spite of the fact that he *was not* the federally appointed and legally recognized governor of the territory. See Morgan, *State of Deseret*, 91–119.

[51] *DN*, 29 January 1862.

[52] Acting Governor Francis H. Wooton to Secretary of State William H. Seward, 5 September 1861, SDTP.

[53] "Mrs. Burlingame's Journal," in Waite, *Adventures*, 117.

Arriving just before the California Volunteers was newly appointed gentile governor Stephen Harding. At least as opposed to the theocratic nature of Mormon society as Connor, Harding wrote numerous letters to President Lincoln and other powerful eastern officials depicting the Mormon church as being guilty of gross treason.[54] To Lincoln and his secretary of state he wrote, "There is no more loyalty amongst the leaders [of the church] than in the states south of [the] Potomac," and he warned that "if the North shall fail . . . this Territory will renounce us openly."

Well aware of contemporary Mormon teachings regarding the Kingdom of God, Harding was convinced that Brigham Young was secretly procuring guns and cannons and manufacturing shells and cartridges in order to establish "a universal empire" to first embrace the territory and then the entire continent. Furthermore, the governor was disgusted that the polygamous church president was "about every week adding to his Harrem," and this in violation of anti-polygamy laws recently passed by Congress! Finally, he alleged that certain Mormons were trading with Indians for goods stolen from murdered victims on the Overland Trail.[55]

Filled with alarm, Harding repeatedly called for the establishment of martial law and worked with Connor to upset Mormon political plans. When Indian raids increased on sections of the Overland Trail and telegraph line in Utah, Harding told the president and secretary of state that church authorities instigated them as part of a plan to draw the military out of Salt Lake City so they could run out the governor. Harding even blamed Connor's slaughter of several hundred Shoshonis in the January 1863 Battle of Bear River on the Saints' meddling with the Indians.[56] Other gentiles continued to circulate the old rumors of Danites, or "in plain English, assassins in the name of the Lord," who reportedly assumed "savage disguises" and took vengeance on the church's enemies.

According to Sir Richard Burton, British aristocrat and world traveler who visited Utah in the early 1860s, such stories became so widespread in the western states and territories that the phrase "he has met the Indians," became a proverb "meaning that a Gentile ha[d] fallen

---

[54] See correspondence of Stephen S. Harding to Secretary of State William H. Seward, Secretary of War Edwin M. Stanton, General W. Julian, and others, for 1862 and 1863, SDTP.

[55] Stephen S. Harding to William H. Seward, 3 February 1863, SDTP.

[56] Ibid.; and Stephen S. Harding to William H. Seward, 11 April 1863, SDTP.

into the power of [Young's] destroying angels." With due skepticism, Burton acknowledged that "not a trader could be scalped, nor a horse-stealer shot, or a notorious villain of a Gentile knived without the deed of blood being attributed to Danite hands directed by prophetic heads." Similarly, rumors continued to run rampant that in a war with the U.S. Army Young and his coreligionists "would be assisted by 30,000 or 40,000 Indians."[57]

Despite Harding's proud claims of early involvement with Joseph Smith during the publication of the Book of Mormon in 1829, considering his staunch opposition to their theocracy, Mormons had few good feelings towards him. Disrespectfully designating Harding as "that thing that is here that *calls himself* Governor," Young worked to rid the territory of his influence.[58] At a mass meeting held in March 1863, Utahns drafted official documents addressed to Abraham Lincoln calling for the removal of their governor and two federally appointed district judges. Private messages were also sent calling for the removal of the troops stationed at Camp Douglas.[59] While refusing to vacate the military base (even though it was named for his political nemesis Stephen A. Douglas), Lincoln obliged the Saints by recalling Harding and appointing Utah's moderate superintendent of Indian affairs, J. Duane Doty, as governor. Despite such efforts to get along with Utah, Lincoln was depicted by the hierarchy as "a damned old scamp and villain," whose wickedness was not even eclipsed by "Pharoah of old." Characteristic of his "with malice towards none" spirit, however, Lincoln instructed Doty not to "provoke difficulties" with the Mormons, especially since war in Utah would compromise Union efforts to defeat Confederate forces in the South. In accordance, Doty followed a pacific course. "There are three powers governing this [territory]," he wrote in 1864, "The Mormon Church; the Military; and the Civil. It is difficult to prevent collisions, but they are to be avoided, if possible."[60]

Preventing collisions proved to be impossible, however, as Doty soon discovered. Colonel Connor, a Catholic and a passionately patriotic Irish-American, viewed Young's theocracy with abhorrence, and,

[57] Burton, *City of the Saints*, 395, 398.

[58] Miscellaneous Minutes, 30 October 1862, BYC. Italics in original.

[59] *DN*, 4 March 1863; and Stephen S. Harding to William H. Seward, 15 March 1863, SDTP.

[60] Miscellaneous Minutes, 23 August 1863, BYC; and J. Duane Doty to Isaac Newton, 20 December 1864, SDTP.

finding himself in a position to do something about it, he solemnly vowed to destroy it. Like most other government officials cognizant of Utah affairs, Connor believed the people of the territory were "ignorant dupes" entirely under the control of an "ecclesiastical monarchy." "The most of them are foreigners," he wrote, "gathered from the lower classes of Europe—men and women who know nothing about the American Government or its institutions." He found the whole community "bitter and unrelenting in their hostility to the Government," an attitude fostered by the "so-termed sermons" delivered in their tabernacles, which, according to him, were "models of obscenity and treason." "It is part of their creed," he wrote his superiors, "that the Government and people of the United States are the enemies alike of God and his chosen people, the Latter day Saints." He firmly believed that church leaders "incited" Indians "to acts of hostility" in hopes of driving gentiles out of the territory. Like others, he felt that his massacre of several hundred Shoshonis in the 1863 Battle of Bear River (also known as the Bear River Massacre) was necessary to wean the Indians from the Mormons.

Upon learning that his superiors in the military (most notably the Commander in Chief, Abraham Lincoln) would not support his bringing the Mormons to heel "at the point of the bayonet," Connor's strategy took a more subtle two-pronged approach. First, Connor hoped to end Utah's isolation by creating circumstances that would bring large numbers of gentiles to the territory. "The secret" of the hierarchy's power, he wrote, "lies in this one word—isolation." By sending hundreds of soldiers on prospecting missions, he hoped gold and silver discoveries would bring thousands of gentiles flocking to the area. Supporting any plan that would attract gentile interest, Connor became an energetic booster of mining, commerce, and industry in Utah. The second prong of Connor's strategy, which in the long run proved even more effective than the first, was to commence a propaganda campaign to "educate" the rest of the nation and the world about what was going on in Utah, hoping that enough political pressure could be generated to topple the Mormon government.[61]

---

[61] Long, *Saints and the Union*, especially 259. For contemporary descriptions of Connor's policy see Patrick Edward Connor to Major J. W. Barnes, 6 April 1865, U.S. Department of War, *War of the Rebellion*, series 1, vol. 50, pt. 2: 1184–86; C.D. Waudell to General Connor, 20 June 1865, District of the Plains, Register of Letters received, Jan.–Sept. 1865, in vol. 781, District of Missouri, 525–26, RUSA, pt. 2, entry 3257; and P. Edw. Connor, Brig. Genl. to

Connor set about accomplishing this by establishing a newspaper in Salt Lake City, which ostensibly served gentiles in Utah but whose real purpose was to convey news of "Utah issues" to the rest of the nation through the newly established transcontinental telegraph line. The masthead of Connor's paper, both in its name and motto, provides insight into how Connor viewed his role in Utah. The name, *The Daily Union Vedette*, denoted "a mounted sentinel, stationed in advance of the pickets, to watch an enemy, and give notice of danger." The motto read, "A Champion brave, alert and strong . . . To aid the right, oppose the wrong." The *Vedette* repeatedly stated that it was devoted exclusively "to an unyielding and unrelenting warfare against . . . Polygamy and the one man power of Utah until both are overthrown and *completely destroyed.*"[62] Its pages were filled with stinging editorials and vitriolic articles possessing a rancor that shocked even the Latter-day Saints, who had seen much yellow journalism before. What was not immediately clear to the Mormons, however, was the extent to which Connor was able to disburse the paper's articles throughout the English-speaking world.

Charles Wentworth Dilke, a gentile newspaperman from Great Britain making an epic journey through "the English-speaking countries" in 1866 and 1867, stopped in Salt Lake City and described the nature of the *Vedette* and the extent of its influence:

> The attack upon Mormondom has been systematized, and is conducted with military skill, by trench and parallel. . . . General Connor, of Fenian fame, sets up the *Union Vedette* in Salt Lake City, and publishes on Saturdays a sheet expressly intended for Eastern reading. . . . From this source it is that come the whole of the paragraphs against Brigham and Mormondom which appear in the Eastern papers, and find their way to London. The editor has to fill his paper with peppery leaders, well-spiced telegrams, stinging "facts." Every week there must be something that can be used and quoted against Brigham. . . . It must not be supposed that the *Vedette* does the Mormons no harm; the perpetual reiteration in the Eastern and English papers of three sets of stories alone would suffice to break down a flourishing power. The three

---

Major W.W. Barnes, A.A. Genl, U.S. Forces Kansas and the Territories, 30 November and 5 December 1865, District of Utah, 1865–1866, Letters Sent, Oct. 1865–June 1866, no. 345/1st 850 District of Missouri, 11–13, 18–19, RUSA, RG 393, pt. 3, entry 824.

   [62] For example, see the *Salt Lake Union Vedette*, 5 April 1866.

lines that are invariably taken as foundations for their stories are these—that the Mormon women are wretched and would fain get away, but are checked by the Danites; that the Mormons are ready to fight with the Federal troops with the hope of success; that robbery of the people by the apostles and elders is at the bottom of Mormonism—or, as the *Vedette* puts it, "on tithing and loaning hang all the law and the profits."

Calling the *Vedette* anti-Mormon "trash," Dilke postulated that "the constant teasing" and "wasp-like pertinacity of the *Vedette* has done some harm to liberty of thought throughout the world." Dilke noted that the "mere fact of the existence of the *Vedette* refutes the stories of the acts of the Danites in these modern days." Were the Mormon assassins as real and ubiquitous as the newspaper said they were, the newspaper would have been silenced long ago. Its very existence, "disposes of the first set of stories," Dilke continued, "and the third is equally answered by a glance at its pages." Sheet after sheet of gentile advertisements attempting to attract Mormon money in Dilke's mind "testified" to freedom and prosperity enjoyed by rank and file Latter-day Saints.[63]

The *Vedette's* stories, however, were taken as gospel in much of the United States, especially in Washington, D.C. The growing federal anti-Mormonism the *Vedette* contributed to inadvertently had serious negative repercussions for the Indians of Utah. One salient example was an unprecedented reduction of congressional appropriations to feed the territory's Indians. Undoubtedly believing reports of Mormon instigation of violence on the Overland Trail, Congress reduced Utah's Indian Office appropriation by 92 percent, replacing the usual $60,000 annual appropriation with a meager $5,000.[64] These problems were compounded by the fact that Mormons, as a result of their animus towards federal officials, refused to allow Indian Office field officers to buy beef and flour for the Indians on credit. When the superintendent and agents did have cash, they were often charged exorbitant prices. Hence, they found themselves unable to feed their desperately hungry Indian wards.[65]

Unfortunately, many Utah bands for years had been forced to depend upon supplies provided by the Indian Office to sustain them

---

[63] Dilke, *Greater Britain*, 1:157, 169–70, 172.

[64] Amos Reed, Clerk Utah Superintendency, to William P. Dole, Commissioner of Indian Affairs, 20 December 1862, BIA, M234, 900.

[65] J. Duane Doty to William P. Dole, 22 April 1863, BIA, M234, 901; and Agent F.W. Hatch to William P. Dole, 15 January 1864, BIA, M234, 901.

through the territory's fierce winters. Mormons had long since occupied most of Utah's fertile, sustenance-producing valleys and had killed or driven off much of what little game remained. Brigham Young urged his people to help support the Indians.[66] Some, however, used the Indians' hunger as an opportunity to turn them away from the government by claiming that the Great Father in Washington had deserted them and did not intend to give them any more presents. "These, with other mischievious stories," wrote Superintendent Doty to the commissioner of Indian affairs, "entirely destroy the influence of the Superintendent over them."[67]

Mormon influence over the Indians, however, originally much stronger than that of the government, was also on the wane. The occasional beeves and sacks of flour Mormon bishops dealt out to local Indians were little more than token efforts when it came to sustaining the lives of entire bands. The conflict between the church and the government was actually driving the Indians from both groups of whites. Left on their own, individual bands were forced to play both ends against the middle, stroking for the moment the side from which they expected to get the most sustenance.

Sometimes it was a dangerous game. In the spring of 1863 Black Hawk himself led several attacks against gentiles and apparently directed the plundering of government property within gunshot of large numbers of armed Mormons, who reportedly watched gleefully as the natives despoiled their enemies. Patrick Connor, now a brevet brigadier general in consideration of his victory at the Battle of Bear River, sent troops up Spanish Fork Canyon after the offenders. But Mormons, including one Isaac Potter, a cattle thief who would later figure prominently in encouraging and even planning some of Black Hawk's raids, alerted the Indians and thus thwarted Connor's plan for a surprise attack. In spite of the warning, several Utes still lost their lives in the fight that ensued.[68]

The following year, when the Spanish Fork Indian Agency was more fully stocked than it had been for years, native allegiance went the other way. Local Indians butchered settlers' cattle, shot at Latter-day Saints,

---

[66] For example, see Brigham Young to Orson Hyde, 18 June 1864, BYC.

[67] F.W. Hatch to William P. Dole, 14 March 1863, BIA, M234, 901; and J. Duane Doty to William P. Dole, 4 April 1863, BIA, M234, 901.

[68] Don Carlos Johnson, *History of Springville*, 61–62; Stephen S. Harding to William H. Seward, 15 April 1863, SDTP; and U.S. Department of War, *War of the Rebellion*, series 1, vol. 50, pt. 1: 204–8.

and allied themselves to Connor.[69] It was a particularly good time for the Indians to exploit the Mormons. Twice during the spring and summer of 1864 Connor had tried to capture Young and other church leaders and to put Salt Lake City under martial law. But the Nauvoo Legion was mobilized in each instance and thousands of armed Saints rallied to protect their leaders. On the verge of actual warfare, Mormons could not afford to give Connor a pretext for attack by punishing Indians for depredations.

When the U.S. War Department got word of Connor's activities, however, he was sternly ordered not to meddle with the Latter-day Saints for fear that war in Utah "might prove fatal to the Union cause." In July 1864 Connor was reminded that the object of troops being in Utah was to protect the Overland Trail "and not to endeavor to correct the evil conduct, manifest as it is, of the inhabitants of that Territory." He was therefore instructed to remove his troops in order that their presence not trigger an outbreak in Utah. Consequently, Connor and the majority of his men moved to Denver in November 1864, thus allowing Black Hawk to start his raids with most of the federal troops out of the territory.[70]

Within days of the initial raids and killings that inaugurated the Black Hawk War in April 1865, "friendly" Indians informed settlers that before Connor left Utah for Colorado he told Black Hawk "that it was all right for him . . . to help kill the mormons."[71] Whether the general himself actually urged Black Hawk to attack the Saints is unknown, but other military men during the period certainly informed the chief that they planned on "fighting the Mormons" and clearly hoped he would join them when they did.[72] In any case, it was generally believed by Utahns that Connor "on the sly was inciting the Indians to further depredations against us."[73] As shall be seen, however, the Utes had plenty of their own reasons to make war on the settlers of Utah. Similarly, they recognized the antipathy existing between the Saints and the government as a unique opportunity to attack Mormons without incurring the army reprisals experienced by the Navajos, Shoshonis, Cheyennes, and Arapahos. In this they judged perceptively, and for more than seven years they were able to raid Utah's settlers without

---

[69] Orson Hyde to Brigham Young, 10–16 June 1864, BYC.
[70] *Records of California Men*, 517–18.
[71] Orson Hyde to Brigham Young, 15 April 1865, BYC.
[72] A. Milton Musser to Brigham Young, 25 August 1869, BYC.
[73] See Milas Johnson, "Life Review of a Mormon," 18.

provoking the deployment of U.S. troops, a situation unheard of in any other territory or state with similar Indian hostilities.

On the day after the Salina Canyon fight, the grieving Hamilton Kearnes sent a rider towards Salt Lake City with two dispatches. One informed Brigham Young of Black Hawk's ambush, while the other requested the commander at Camp Douglas to bring soldiers and howitzers to shell the Indians out of their position near the mouth of the canyon. A misunderstanding in instructions to his courier almost cost Kearnes his bishopric. Both dispatches were to go to Young first, and, *if he approved*, the second was to be sent to the remnant of Connor's troops at Camp Douglas. By mistake, however, the second message went straight to the post commander.[74]

Brigham Young was outraged. "It would have been far better to have the Indians to war with and to deal with," the church president wrote, than to invite gentile soldiers into the southern settlements.[75] When the local Nauvoo Legion commander learned of the mix-up, he expressed the typical Mormon reaction, writing, "Had I of Known that [Kearnes] had sent direct to our enemies, I should at once have sent an express for the stoping of the application, for every man should know that such a course would bring the deepest sorrow upon the Israel of our God."[76] This attitude originated from Young's frequent instructions to upper-level ecclesiastical and militia leaders that the federal installation at Camp Douglas near the heart of Salt Lake City was "the best place [the troops] can be in for doing the least injury." The church president could clearly see that near the Saints' largest population center and Nauvoo Legion headquarters the soldiers could not "do much hurt," while if they were located away from the Mormon center of strength "they would go unrestrained" in their efforts to upset his plans. As a result, after Kearnes's message was mistakenly sent to Camp Douglas, the policy was rigorously reaffirmed that Young "should be the first" and "only one" informed of such "critical subjects" lest Indian depredations become "the excuse or pretext for more powerful enemies to occupy the country."[77]

Once the call for troops had been made, however, church leaders

---

[74] H.H. Kearnes to Brigham Young, 13 April 1865; Warren S. Snow to Brigham Young, 22 April 1865; Orson Hyde to Brigham Young, 23 April 1865, BYC; and Affidavit of Joshua Sylvester, Josiah Simmons, Jonathan Lemister, and P.P. Brown, 3 May 1865, BYC.

[75] Brigham Young to Orson Hyde, 16 April 1865, BYC.

[76] Warren S. Snow to Brigham Young, 22 April 1865.

[77] Miscellaneous Minutes, 30 October 1862, BYC; and George A. Smith to Orson Hyde, 5 November 1865, HOLB, 2:510–11.

nervously watched to see how the military would react. Apostle Orson Hyde felt that the way the troops responded, or, rather, failed to respond, would demonstrate the military's involvement in the attack. "If Conor has set the Indians on us," he speculated, "it will not be within his province to chastise them for it. Some excuse will be offered for non intirferance."[78] When Connor sent word that the raids did not affect the Overland Trail or telegraph line and therefore were outside his jurisdiction, the apostle undoubtedly felt his hunch was confirmed.[79] Almost eight years later, Orson Hyde still maintained his position. "The Indians," he stated from the podium in the Salt Lake Tabernacle, "had an idea that they could do with us as seemed them good—prey upon our substance and murder our men, women and children whenever they felt like it, and the military of the Government would wink at it, because they thought the Government wanted to get rid of us."[80]

Utah's Black Hawk War in many respects was characteristic of other Indian troubles in the West during the period. The uneasy triangle that was formed between Mormons, Indians, and gentiles, however, made the war a distinct and important anomaly in Western history. In an era remembered for quick and bloody military reprisals against Indians, the animosity between Mormons and the government allowed the Utes to raid the settlers of Utah for more than seven years without federal interference. Like Indian wars waged during the colonial era of American history, the Black Hawk War was one front of a political battle fought by whites against other whites. Much as groups like the Iroquois and Cherokees had played off whites representing opposing European empires against each other, the Utes exploited the political situation as best they could. Like Indians in colonial times, they were in turn exploited by opposing groups of whites and employed as tools by one against the other. From start to finish, the Black Hawk War was profoundly influenced by the uneasy triangle that formed as Mormons, Indians, and gentiles grappled for position in the Territory of Utah.

[78] Orson Hyde to Brigham Young, 15 April 1865.

[79] U.S. Congress, House, *Memorial of the Legislative Assembly of Utah Territory*, 21 February 1868.

[80] "Discourse by President Orson Hyde, Delivered in the New Tabernacle, Salt Lake City, Sunday Morning, October 5, 1873," *JD*, 16:229.

CHAPTER TWO

Antonga's Agony

Great leaders become great and they become leaders precisely because they themselves have experienced the identity struggle of
their people in both a most personal and a most representative
way.

—Erik Erikson[1]

BECAUSE OF THE IMPORTANCE of the personal tragedy Mormon settlement brought to the man who from its beginning was the prime moving force behind the Black Hawk War, it is necessary to examine the
forces that molded Antonga Black Hawk himself. This chapter examines his life before the war against the backdrop of the appalling experience of his family members and friends at the hands of the white
invaders. It is at once the account of Black Hawk's immense personal
tragedy and the almost unspeakable familial and tribal anguish his own
story represented for his people. Because of his understandably forceful reaction to his personal calamity, Antonga as war chief eventually
carried his pain to all the peoples of Utah, in the end tremendously
compounding his own agony, as well as that of all those around him,
Indian, white, and Hispanic.

Multiple Black Hawks

Black Hawk's pre-war years have been almost totally obscured from
historical interpretation. His Indian name hardly grasped by historians,
even the faintest picture of his early life has entirely eluded us, until
now. The swirl of conflicting accounts left by his white contemporaries
has made a study of his life nearly impossible, and, while some of what
emerges here is tenuous, it is still tremendously useful in understanding

---

[1] As quoted in Fawn M. Brodie, *Thomas Jefferson: An Intimate History* (New York: W.W.
Norton & Company, 1974), 104.

the war itself as well as Black Hawk's role in Mormon-Indian relations generally.

Besides the fact that neither Black Hawk nor his people left any written record whatsoever, the confusion arises from two prominent types of historical sources left by whites. First, white records made before 1865, and even during the war itself, consistently demonstrate that very little effort was made to preserve information of substance relative to the lives of individual Indians. This undoubtedly stemmed from the fact that, despite their claims to the contrary, to the Latter-day Saints in general Native Americans were of little personal interest. Clearly demonstrating their writers' primary objective, contemporary Mormon sources focused on the colonization and pioneering of kingdom building, and Indians were usually mentioned only when they impeded such processes. Although scant references are made to powerful multiband headmen like Sowiette, Antero, Tabby, Wakara, Arapeen, and Peteetneet, single band leaders (or "petit chiefs," as the Saints sometimes called them) such as Black Hawk was in the 1850s and early 1860s were rarely mentioned by name in official or private correspondence, journals, or Nauvoo Legion reports. It goes without saying that rank and file Indians were almost never individually mentioned either by name or otherwise.

A second, and even more problematic type of source was left by Antonga's white contemporaries in the form of reminiscences and autobiographies written, in most cases, many years after the war. In the waning years of the nineteenth century, and especially in the first three decades of the twentieth, after the passing of the frontier period of American history was beginning to be articulated and romanticized, literally hundreds of Latter-day Saint men and women left narratives of their personal experience during Utah's Indian wars. In an effort to pass on to posterity their connection with the Black Hawk conflict (or, for some, in hard-fought attempts to claim pensions in a movement that began before the turn of the century and continued into the 1920s), many left personal descriptions and anecdotes relating to Black Hawk, which, judging from repeated and gross inconsistencies, obviously cannot all be true. The problem was highlighted in a 1915 letter from William Probert to Peter Gottfredson, both of whom were Black Hawk War veterans, at a time when the former was helping the latter collect information for what was to become the classic source book on the Black Hawk War, *Indian Depredations in Utah*, first published in 1919. "There are probably a dozen men in Utah who claim the honor of killing Black Hawk, *none of which is true*," Probert caustically wrote, correctly citing the fact that Black Hawk passed away peacefully at Spring Lake in 1870 near the place of his birth on Summit Creek.[2] Some writers, obviously partaking of the same penchant for exaggeration and misinformation that Probert deplored, offered conflicting reminiscences variously describing Black Hawk as a very young man at the time of the war, while others referred to him as middle-aged, or even as an "old" man. He is sometimes represented as springing directly from adolescence to chieftainship with the initial killings that started the war; in other accounts he is portrayed as a family man long tried in the arts of leadership.[3] Almost every aspect of his life was contradictorily chronicled. He was variously estimated in height from over six feet to barely more than five and a half feet. He is described as a Ute from a number of diverse Northern Ute bands, as a Paiute or Pi-ede, or even as being a mixed blood of Navajo or Sioux ancestry.[4] Dozens of

---

[2] William Probert to Peter Gottfredson, 1 July 1915, in Gottfredson, *Indian Depredations*, 227–29. Italics mine.

[3] Milas E. Johnson, for example, who was only thirteen at the time he describes, tells of a twenty-year-old Black Hawk fighting white Spring Lake youths for possession of a favorite swimming hole in 1864. Milas Johnson, Autobiography, 8. Johnson's relative, Benjamin F. Johnson, referred to "the *young* Indian Blackhawk," yet described him at the time the war commenced as having "a squaw." Benjamin Johnson, *My Life's Review*, 227–28. Francis G. Wall describes "Young Black Hawk" playing ball "with the boys" in Glenwood on the eve of the war. Francis G. Wall, Autobiography, in DUP, *Our Pioneer Heritage*, 7:366. Similarly, the family of Jesse W. Fox claimed Black Hawk, "when a boy, had been a pupil" in Fox's Manti school. Whitney, *History of Utah*, 4:347–48. Eliza M. Munson estimated Black Hawk's age at "about 18 or 19 when he started his first depredations." Munson, "Questions concerning the Black Hawk War." William Probert, on the other hand, referred to Black Hawk as being an "*old warrior*," in 1869, just four years later. Gottfredson, *Indian Depredations*, 228. Eli Day reported that Black Hawk started his war in the first place because his "wives and children had died from evil diseases from mingling with wicked white men." Day, "History of Eli A. Day," 10. Mary Goble Pay wrote that before the war Black Hawk would bring his "three nice looking squaws" in at harvest time "to get us to hire them to husk corn. He would come with them but he would not work. He would make the bargain for us to pay them so much corn and the best dinner we could get them. Which was not very rich I assure you. . . . It was fun to see them try to use their plates and knives and forks like the whites." Pay, Life History, 11. Lorena W. Larsen described seeing Black Hawk in 1869 when she was nine years old. "The school children had the privilege of passing by in single file," she remembered, "to take a last look at *that old warrior* who had made the people of that section tremble with fear during the past years." Lorena Larsen, "Black Hawk War," 1. Italics mine.

[4] Springville's local chronicler, Don Carlos Johnson, for example, wrote, "Black-Hawk was a renegade chief and was the principal leader of the war which bears his name. He was a lithe, active man, about 5-10 and appeared to have sprung from some other tribe, probably the Navajoes. His eyes were rather brown than black. He sported a fine mustache, and was rather dudified in appearance." Don Carlos Johnson, "The Indians of Utah Valley," 5 March 1908. Josiah Rogerson, on the other hand, wrote that Black Hawk "was fully Six Feet one and A half; straight as an Arrow, . . . he said that his Father, was a renegade from the SIOUX, tribe

differing accounts are recorded of how the war broke out.[5] The list of inconsistencies in these later written sources goes on and on. Such confusion in contemporary testimony has led more than one writer to conclude that Mormons encountered at least two different Ute chieftains named "Black Hawk" during their first two decades of settlement in Utah.[6] Considering the fact that many settlers had previously lived in Illinois and elsewhere in the Old Northwest (many of

---

of Indians, that lived on the North-Platte, and in the vicinity of Ft' Laramie. . . . his Mother, A daughter of one of the most distinguished Chiefs of the Ute tribe." Rogerson, "Ending of the Black Hawk War," 3. Eliza Munson reported that Black Hawk "was of the tribe of the low San Piches," a Paiute/Piede-like band living in Sanpete Valley. Eliza Munson, "Questions Concerning Black Hawk War." Mary Goble Pay described Black Hawk as "a fine looking chief" but wrote that he "looked different from the other [Ute] chiefs. He was tall and had long feathers. His nose was long and he had a small moustache. He looked like he had Jewish blood in him. He could talk English quite well. He had three nice looking squaws." Pay, "History," 11.

[5] Peter Rasmussen, for example, wrote that the "cause of the Blackhawk war was that John Lowery [*sic*] of Manti caught an Indian killing a beef belonging to him [Lowry] for which he whiped him with a rope which is a disgrace with an Indian so they proceded to take vengence on the Whites." Rasmussen, "Life of Peter Rasmussen." Oluf Larson wrote that it started when "the dispute between a white man of Manti and an Indian over shirt led to blows." Oluf Larson, "Biographical Sketch," 45. Amasa Porter affirmed that "some Indians stole a few brass kettles from the Indian Farm north of Payson and went through that city with these kettles tied on a pony. When near the Potter home, a man from the Farm overtook the indians and smashed one of the kettles over the head of one of the thieves. These few Indians proceeded to the camp up the canyon southeast of the city. Fearing trouble, some of the whites followed and attempted to pacify them, but failed. Soon after, the war opened." Barton, "Black Hawk War," 27. Jesse W. Fox apparently told his children that the Indian beaten with the bucket was none other than Black Hawk. Whitney, *History of Utah*, 4:348. Callie Morley wrote that "there were a number of opinions as to the direct thing that set [the war] off," one being that "Abner Lowery slapped an Indian Chief when he tried to steal flour from the mill, [while] another source said Chief Jake had been ignonimously yanked from a horse by a white man and a quarrel resulted in which he swore vengence on the settlers." Morley, "Daniel & Amanda Henrie," 17. John Codman wrote that "the notorious Black Hawk, went to a person at St. Peter's, with whom some flour had been left for him by the Indian agent. The man was drunk, and whipped Black Hawk." Codman, *Round Trip*, 244–45. Superintendent Irish was told by Indians that the war started when John Lowry ("a man who drinks whiskey") and An-kar-tewets (who was "mourning the death of his father") quarreled in Manti. "Proceedings of a Council with the Utah Indians," 37–38. Francis Wall wrote that Black Hawk stole one of Lowry's horses and rode into Manti on it. "When John Lowry saw him on his horse, he pulled the Indian off and slapped him," Wall remembered. "This made Black Hawk mad," and, as a result, he "and his brother left and went to Twelve Mile Creek" where "they met two Manti men with loads of wood. The Indians shot the white men and that's what started the war." Francis Wall, Autobiography, in DUP, *Our Pioneer Heritage*, 7:366. Even the well-informed Indian interpreter George W. Bean recorded that it was Black Hawk himself Lowry attacked and beat "severely" despite the fact that Lowry's own testimony (and that of dozens of others) was that it was Jake Arapeen he fought with. George Bean, Autobiography, 1897, 68–89; and Gottfredson, *Indian Depredations*, 335–38.

[6] "History of Provo City," 239; and Sonne, *World of Wakara*, 95.

whom would have been well versed in the lore of Illinois' own Black Hawk War), it is not hard to acknowledge that the name could have been used for more than one Ute, it being perhaps an especially fitting name to denominate natives with a particular penchant for opposing white settlement. Laden with contemporary racial overtones, the name was given by whites during the same period to a host of individuals, including a Winnebago, an Ogallalah Sioux, a Kiowa-Apache, and perhaps to a White Knife Western Shoshoni as well.[7]

A perusal of Ute genealogical records and consultation with present-day tribal members does indeed confirm that there was more than one Ute "Black Hawk." Undoubtedly a source for some of the above-mentioned confusion is the fact that Antonga Black Hawk had a nephew of the same English name who was living at the time the war commenced but who was much too young to have taken a leading part in the war and who was later mistaken by some reminiscence writers as his older and more prominent war-chief uncle. This second Black Hawk, sired by Antonga's brother "Quibits,"[8] or "Mountain," was born in 1851 and would have been only fourteen years old at the time the war broke out. Perhaps he was the "young" Black Hawk some writers later remembered playing ball, attending school, and fighting with whites over swimming holes. Considering his father's and uncle's leading roles in the war, however, it is likely this second Black Hawk also participated in the fighting as a teenager.[9]

Be this as it may, primary contemporary sources (that is, those written from 1847 to 1865) make it abundantly clear that Black Hawk, war chief of the 1865 conflict, is the same man repeatedly referred to as "Chief Black Hawk" as early as 1850, throughout the 1850s, and into the early 1860s. This is in accordance with vehement assertions by the war chief's present-day relatives and modern Ute elders that "the Black

---

[7] Taylor and Sturtevant, *Native Americans,* 237; Hoig, *Western Odyssey,* 83; Nye, *Plains Indian Raiders,* 382–83; and William C. Penney [or Tenney], Kanosh, Millard Co., U.T. to Mr. John J. Critchlow, 29 October 1875, enclosed in J.J. Critchlow, U.S. Ind. Agt., Salt Lake City, to Hon E.N. Smith, Com. Ind. Affairs, Washington, D.C., 18 November 1875, in BIA, M234, 905.

[8] Also appearing as Kibets or Kibe in the sources.

[9] This second Ute Black Hawk, nephew of Antonga Black Hawk and son of Mountain, was listed nearly seven years after his uncle's death in "List of Indians entitled to rations at Uintah Agency," in J.J. Critchlow, U.S. Ind. Agent, Uintah Valley Agency, Utah, to Hon. J.L. Smith, Com. Ind Affairs, Washington, D.C., 15 July 1877, in BIA, M234, 905. He apparently lived until 1942. See "Vital Records of the Ute Indians to 1946"; Martineau, *Southern Paiutes,* 274–75; and Duncan, *Official Memorandum.*

Hawk of the war of that name was a chief from the earliest time of Mormon settlement."[10]

Antonga and the Fort Utah Carnage

Black Hawk was born at Spring Lake near the south end of Utah Valley, probably between 1824 and 1830. Reportedly named by whites after the "old [Sac-Fox] warrior of that name" who fought white settlement so aggressively in the Illinois and Iowa area from whence the Mormons came, Black Hawk may have come by his name by right of his own resistance to white settlement early on.[11] Just as likely though, his English name may have been derived from the "A-vick-a-ba" (meaning "crow" or "blackbird") clan of the Timpanogos Utes, who claimed "the neighborhood of Summit Cr." in which Black Hawk was born and later came to die.[12] Whatever the origin of his English name,

[10] There are no known living descendants of Antonga Black Hawk. Family lore is preserved, however, through the posterity of his brother Mountain. In a 29 December 1995 interview, three great-great-grandchildren and a great-great-great-granddaughter of Mountain made the following statement through their spokesman Richard Mountain:

> Our Father told us that Black Hawk was Chief from the beginning. From the time that the Mormons first came to the Salt Lake Valley. Black Hawk was a negotiator for his people. He attended meetings with Brigham Young and told him, "We would appreciate it if you would leave our land and go somewhere else. Move on to California." Yes, Antonguer was Black Hawk. We don't know that name, but we know that what you describe of him was done by the same Black Hawk that fought in the Black Hawk War. We grew up knowing that our ancestor Mountain was the brother of Black Hawk. We have heard many stories of Black Hawk. One I can remember was when we would drive to Provo, there at Deer Creek near the mouth of Provo Canyon where the mountains come together, steep on both sides, Father would point up at those rocks and say "Black Hawk used to fight on those cliffs, and he would escape through those rocks."

Interview of Richard Mountain and his sisters Arlene M. Appah and Sylvia M. Cornpeach, and niece Thomasina Appah, all of Fort Duchesne on the Uintah and Ouray Reservation, conducted by the author and Bret Anderson, in the home of Thomas and Arlene Appah, Fort Duchesne, Utah, 29 December 1995, notes in author's possession; interview of Clifford H. Duncan, Native American consultant, conducted by the author and Bret Anderson in the home of Clifford H. Duncan, Roosevelt, Utah, 30 December 1995, notes in author's possession; and Duncan, Official Memorandum.

[11] Daniel Jones, *Forty Years Among the Indians*, 164.

[12] "List of the Treibes [*sic*] and Bands of the Ute Nation commonly called Utahs, Inhabiting the Eastern portion of the Great-Basin," c. 1855, BIA, M234, 897. The Spring Lake area was also known as Summit Creek. A week following Black Hawk's death, Brigham Young wrote, "Black Hawk, the Indian Chief who took so conspicuous a part in our last Indian wars, died on the 27th of last month near Spring Lake Villa, and in a small ravine near by his tribe buried him. That locality, I understand, was the place of his birth, there he commenced his depredations, and thither he went to die." Brigham Young to Horace S. Eldredge, 4 October 1870, BYC.

it is clear it was not the name by which he was known to his people. During the 1850s, his Indian name appears in white sources as "An Tonga," most often spelled "An-ton-guer."[13] Since modern Utes do not recognize the name as being of Ute derivation, it is possible that even this name was given to him by whites, perhaps by French trappers.[14] His name also appears in the white record as "An-ker-an-kage," perhaps a transliteration closer to his original Ute name.[15]

No photograph or contemporary artistic rendering of Black Hawk has as yet been authenticated.[16] The most reliable verbal description found to date also appears to be the *only* such caricature to have been made during his lifetime. On 8 May 1859, Captain James H. Simpson, a U.S. Army Corps of Topographical Engineers explorer, led a team of artists, photographers, and scientists across the deserts of Utah and Nevada and inadvertently encountered Black Hawk. In his extraordinarily precise and "scientific" journal, Simpson made these comments after a professional artist sketched the Ute leader[17]:

[13] For examples of "An-ton-guer" see George A. Smith to the Editor of the *Deseret News*, 12 June 1855, BIA, M234, 897; and George W. Armstrong to Brigham Young, 30 June 1855, BIA, M234, 897. For "An Tonga," see "A List of Names of persons who were summoned into a posse on the 17th day of Feby A.D. 1856. By Thomas S. Johnson U. S. Deputy Marshal to assist him in arresting certain Indians . . . ," TMR, #1391. The name An-ton-guer/Antonga must not be confused with Anton, the English name of another Indian leader in early Utah history who was a brother of Wakara and who is clearly a separate individual, as he is mentioned in correspondence *along with Black Hawk*. For example, see Brigham Young to Wakara, 14 April 1853, BYC.

[14] Interview of Richard Mountain et al., by the author and Bret Anderson, 29 December 1995; and interview of Clifford H. Duncan by the author and Bret Anderson, 30 December 1995. For evidence that French traders were closely associated with the Utes (and sometimes gave them French names) see Ferris, *Life in the Rocky Mountains*, 349; Dimick B. Huntington to President Young, 18 May 1849, BYC; and Stephen B. Rose to Brigham Young, 30 June 1853, BIA, M234, 897.

[15] JH, 8 June 1855, 1. For evidence that An-ker-an-kage is Black Hawk see George A. Smith to the Editor of the *Deseret News*, 12 June 1855; and George W. Armstrong to Brigham Young, 30 June 1855.

[16] A photograph commonly believed to be Utah's Black Hawk exists in the files of the USHS (970.2, P. 1, #15189). This photograph has been published in Utah as being Black Hawk from as early as 1947 to as recently as 1995; see J.N. Washburn, "Black Hawk," 154; and *DN*, 4 September 1995. My thanks to Charmaine Thompson, Archaeologist, Uinta National Forest, Provo, Utah, for confirming the fact that this photo was *not* the Ute Black Hawk but rather the image of a Kiowa-Apache of the same English name photographed by William S. Soule between 1867 and 1875; see Nye, *Plains Indian Raiders*, 382–83, and xiv. See also Paula Richardson Fleming, Photo Archivist, National Anthropological Archives, National Museum of Natural History, Smithsonian Institution, Washington, D.C., to Marva Loy Eggett, 2 October 1997, in author's possession and in John A. Peterson, Black Hawk Collection, UUWA.

[17] Unfortunately, while Simpson's *Report of Explorations* was published with many artistic sketches, this one was not included.

Just before dinner a Parvan [Pahvant] (Ute) Indian (Black Hawk) came into camp. This is the first Indian we have seen on our route. His squaw is a Go-shoot woman, and he lives among that people. Gave him his dinner and some tobacco. Had a sketch of him taken. He wears his hair tied up at the temples and behind; carries a buckskin pouch and powder-horn; a bow and quiver swung on his right side; wears a pink checked American shirt, buckskin leggins and moccasins, and a blanket around his loins; an old black silk handkerchief is tied about his neck. He has one huge iron spur on his right heel, and rides a sorrel pony. His height is 5 feet 7½ inches; has a stout square frame; *age, probably, 35*; carries a rifle. His bow is 3 feet long, and is made of sheep's horn; arrow, 25 inches long, feathered, and barbed with iron. His countenance is ordinarily sardonic, but lights up in conversation, and shows as much intelligence as Indians do ordinarily.[18]

If Simpson's estimation of an age of thirty-five in 1859 is correct, Antonga Black Hawk was in his early twenties when the first Mormons arrived in 1847. Interestingly, his name is connected with the very first bloodshed between Mormons and the Northern Utes.

When the Mormons first settled the Great Salt Lake Valley, they settled in a no-man's-land of sorts claimed by both the Utes and Shoshonis but securely held by neither. Thus located on the periphery of both tribes, the Latter-day Saints were able to commence their first colonies with little native interference. But the herds of cattle and horses the newcomers brought with them were a constant temptation to the large number of Timpanogos Utes who lived in nearby Utah Valley to the South. On 1 March 1849 a Nauvoo Legion company was sent south with orders "to take such measures as would put a final end" to Ute stealing of Mormon stock. Overawed by the large body of armed whites, a leader named "Little Chief" directed his son, perhaps Tintic, to lead the legionnaires by night to a small camp of offenders.

---

[18] Simpson, *Report of Explorations*, 51–52. Italics mine. Modern Utes believe that Black Hawk was associated with the Pahvants as well as with the Timpanogos; see the Uintah-Ouray Tribe, *Ute Government*, 25. That Black Hawk was listed as a Pahvant rather than a Timpanogos is undoubtedly to be understood in context of the facts that the Timpanogos spent much time with and intermarried with the Pahvants, that whites were usually unconcerned with exact band affiliation of individual Indians, and, most importantly, that band affiliation was constantly in a state of flux as individuals and families frequently changed band associations. See Dimick B. Huntington to Brigham Young, 11 November 1853, BYC.

The Mormon troops surrounded the lodges near dawn, and Brigham Young's Indian interpreter (and brother-in-law) Dimick Huntington told the Indians they "had not come to fight but . . . to see about [the] cattle that had been stolen." Considering the fact that there were "13 beef hides" in their camp as evidence of their activities, four adult Ute males and their families took cover in a creek bottom and opened fire on the much larger white force. Fighting "with the most determined resolution to die rather than yield," one by one the drastically outnumbered men were killed, and thirteen women and children surrendered, including "a lad" who "looked to be about eighteen years of age." The youth, later believed by some contemporaries to have been Black Hawk, "had fought manfully" during the engagement but now "shook with fright . . . expecting to be killed any minute." Anxious not to harm the young prisoner, the militiamen took him and his family to Salt Lake City, where they were "cared for" until spring. Meanwhile, Little Chief condemned the militia for "not killing the lad," prophesying that he "would kill a white man yet for revenge."[19] Whether or not this youth was indeed Black Hawk cannot be conclusively documented. It is interesting to note, however, the tradition among modern Utes that Black Hawk's family was murdered by Mormons.[20] One thing is certain, however: the results of this skirmish, which became known as the fight on Battle Creek, initiated decisions by Latter-day Saint leaders that within months would bring Black Hawk to the forefront.

On 10 March 1849, just four days after the victorious militiamen returned with their young prisoner to Salt Lake City, the need for range for famished cattle and settlement sites for land-hungry Saints induced Brigham Young to initiate plans for the colonization of Utah Valley—the single most important Northern Ute stronghold. Dimick Huntington and two other men were designated as the presidency of the "Provo Branch" of the Church of Jesus Christ of Latter-day Saints and within

---

[19] Stout, *Diary*, 2:344–47; Utah Stake Manuscript History; JH, 6 March 1849; Driggs, *Timpanogos Town*, 14–21; and John Brown, *Autobiography*, 103–5. Black Hawk himself reportedly affirmed to Mormon mountain man Joshua Terry that he was indeed the youthful survivor of the Battle Creek fight and "could never understand why the whitemen had shot down" his relatives. "It put bitterness in his heart; and though he lived for some time with the white people, his mind was ever set on avenging the wrong" and was the principal reason "he later made war against them." John Brown, a participant in the fight, repeatedly denied this. See Driggs, 19–20; and John Brown, 105.

[20] Duncan, Official Memorandum.

days were leading a company of thirty men and their families, along with wagons, household goods, and livestock, to a proposed settlement site on the Provo River not far from Utah Lake. An-kar-tewets, who fifteen years later would witness the beginning of the Black Hawk War and become "one of Black Hawk's most active raiders,"[21] boldly placed himself and his pony on the trail in front of the newcomers and loudly told them to go back where they came from. Huntington reasoned in the Ute language for over an hour with An-kar-tewets and other angry Indians who gathered there, pleading with them to give the Saints a chance to show they could live together in peace. Lured by promises of trade, the Indians finally relented, but only after making Huntington "raise his right hand and swear by the sun that [the Mormons] would not drive the Indians from their lands, nor take away their rights."[22]

Fully aware of the hazardous nature of their undertaking, the new colony immediately commenced building Fort Utah just west of the present city of Provo. With log cabins arranged in a large "parallelogram," the fort was simply made by filling the spaces between cabins with twelve-foot pickets. Inside the enclosure they built a large platform on which they mounted a cannon. Before the fort was completed, however, they discovered that the very site they had settled on "was the great annual gathering place for all the Ute bands of the valleys for two hundred miles, east and south." The Indians assembled annually to feast on trout and suckers, which at the peak of their yearly spawning run filled the Provo River "from bank to bank as thick as they could swim." The Mormon fort obviously was a source of irritation, but it also instantaneously became the center of native trade and gambling, which only worked to increase tensions.[23] Near the first of August 1849, an Indian the Mormons named "Bishop" (because his appearance and gestures resembled those of Presiding Bishop Newel K. Whitney) apparently stole a shirt. Confronted by three Mormons, including Richard Ivie, a struggle ensued in which Bishop was killed.

Anxious to hide the deed from the Utes, Ivie and the others ripped out the dead man's entrails, filled his abdominal cavity with rocks, and sank the body in the Provo River. Ute fishermen eventually

---

[21] Daniel Jones, *Forty Years Among the Indians*, 170.

[22] "History of Provo," 234; Utah Stake Manuscript History; and Bean, *Autobiography*, 46, 50.

[23] Utah Stake Manuscript History; Bean, *Autobiography*, 46–52; and Gottfredson, *Indian Depredations*, 20–22.

discovered their mutilated tribesman and apparently also learned the identity of at least one of the killers.[24] Understandably provoked, Bishop's kin took shots at members of the Ivie family and wantonly killed cattle.[25] In an attempt to overawe the increasingly aggressive Timpanogos, the Mormons occasionally fired their cannon, but in the process a tragic accident occurred in which one man lost his life and George W. Bean, later an important negotiator in the Black Hawk War, lost an arm.[26] When the cannon failed to intimidate the natives, Mormon leaders worked to restrain a growing desire among their people to make war on their neighbors. While "friendly" Indians continued to visit the fort, others viewed the Saints' restraint as cowardice, boasting that they would soon "kill the men and take the women."[27]

As winter came on, the Indians belligerently helped themselves to Mormon cattle, and by January 1850 sixty head had been taken. When a party of settlers visited the Indian encampment to discuss the problem, the Utes angrily raised "the war whoop" and prepared for battle. At last, frustrated local leaders wrote to President Young begging for permission to chastise the Timpanogos militarily. Though unaware as yet of Bishop's murder, Young generally recognized his people's role in the growing conflict, and tersely stated that "there was no necessity for fighting and killing Indians, *if the brethren would act wisely in their intercourse with them.*" Flatly denying them the permission they sought, Young warned the brethren that "if they killed Indians for stealing they would have to answer for it."[28]

At the same time, Young counseled the settlers not to allow any of the Indians into the fort. Shortly, "Old Elk," a Timpanogos war chief and the Saints' most outspoken antagonist, came into the fort seeking medicine, as a measles epidemic had settled in on both groups. Rashly acting on Young's counsel, Alexander Williams grabbed Old Elk, who was already weakened by the disease, and "kicked him out of the Fort."[29] The sick and indignant chief immediately directed the creation of rude but effective breastworks around the strategically located Tim-

---

[24] JH, 31 January, 7–8; Gottfredson, *Indian Depredations*, 22–23; and Bean, *Autobiography*, 50.

[25] Isaac Higbee to Brigham Young, 15 October 1849, BYC.

[26] Bean, *Autobiography*, 57–61.

[27] Isaac Higbee to Brigham Young, 15 October 1849, BYC.

[28] Alexander Williams and J.Y. Willis to "Prests Young & Higbee," 7 January 1850, BYC; Utah Stake Manuscript History, and variant version in JH, 9 January 1850. Italics mine.

[29] JH, 31 January 1850, 7–8.

panogos encampment on the Provo River bottoms about a mile from the fort. As a result, the frightened Saints sent riders to Salt Lake City with news of more stock thefts, insults, and threats, along with word that local Mormons were unanimous in their desire to attack the Indians before they were attacked by them. Brigham Young, characteristically "extremely averse to the adoption of harsh measures," was urged by Captain Howard Stansbury and Lieutenant George W. Howland, the only U.S. military officers in the area, that, considering the circumstances, a punitive strike was "not only of good policy, but one of absolute necessity [for] self-preservation." Though he later acknowledged that he acted against his own better judgement and felt misled because he was not informed of the whites' provocation of the trouble by the killing of Bishop, Young finally relented and ordered out 150 militiamen. At Young's request, Stansbury sent Howland along to indicate that the action was sanctioned by United States military authority.[30]

In the tense days immediately preceding the Mormon attack "Antonguer, sometimes called Black Hawk, and several other Indians came into the fort asking peace for themselves and families, and offering service to aid the settlers."[31] It can be speculated that Antonga had come to trust the Mormons during his stay in Salt Lake City as a prisoner the year before, if he indeed was the "lad" who survived the fight at Battle Creek. Lore among later generations of Utahns was that "*in his youth*, he visited the homes of the pioneers, played games with their children; *and with members of his family, enjoyed their hospitality.* Their kindness he never forgot and he was known among them as a *good Indian.*"[32] In any case, 1850 military correspondence repeatedly refers to him as "the friendly Indian Black Hawk,"[33] and he was inside the fort early on the morning of 8 February 1850 when the Mormon troops from Salt Lake City arrived under the cover of darkness.

Joined by the Fort Utah militia, the now-sizable frontier army marched later that morning through two feet of snow and intense cold to the Indian encampment, where an estimated seventy warriors and their families were ensconced behind their fortifications. Dimick

---

[30] Utah Stake Manuscript History; "History of Provo," 235–36; JH, 31 January 1850, 7–8; Richard Young, "Nauvoo Legion," 122; and Stansbury, *Exploration*, 148–49.

[31] "History of Provo," 239.

[32] DUP, *Our Pioneer Heritage*, 3:423–24. Italics mine.

[33] Peter W. Conover, William McBride, Commanding Capts. and John McEwan Commissary, to Major General D.H. Wells, 20 February 1850, TMR, #1313; and Daniel H. Wells to Capt McBride, 23 February 1850, TMR, #49.

Huntington met with Stick-in-Head, the band's civil chief, in a last-ditch effort to avoid bloodshed.[34] Old Elk, however, commenced firing and the negotiations broke into serious fighting. Thus commenced the bloodiest week of Indian killing in Utah history, and Antonga Black Hawk was a firsthand witness.

Stick-in-Head and Old Elk's forces were well armed and well positioned, and fought bravely for two days, killing one and wounding some eighteen Mormons. At least four factors, however, led the Timpanogos to desert their stronghold during the night following the second day of fighting. First, Old Elk, already suffering from measles, was severely wounded, leaving Stick-in-Head, who was less inclined to fight, in charge. Second, the Mormons had employed their cannon using "chain shot," which had ripped off the legs of one Indian woman and apparently killed and maimed others, which naturally horrified the Utes. Third, using an ingenious portable barricade, the Mormons had secured an elevated position from which their cannon could be used to much greater advantage. Fourth, the Indians had nearly exhausted their supply of gunpowder and knew that their arrows would be no match for their adversaries' cannon. Early on the morning of the third day, a Sunday, Black Hawk was sent from the fort to scout out the Indian position. We can only imagine his feelings as he walked through the deserted camp, finding the bodies of nine band members he certainly knew along with "signs of many more being killed or wounded."[35]

Antonga returned to the fort with word that the Indians had trudged off through the snow in several directions during the bitterly cold night, their bloody trails witnessing that casualties were high.[36] Considering it was the Sabbath day, General Daniel H. Wells, who had just arrived from Salt Lake City, pronounced a day of rest. In the following days, however, the militia separated into groups to track their prey. "The friendly Indian Black Hawk" himself served as "pilot" of one of

[34] Their orders were to stop the "operations of all hostile Indians, exterminating such as do not separate themselves from their hostile clans and sue for peace." Characteristic of all Nauvoo Legion battle orders during the period, the instructions contained this postscript: "In carrying out the above order you will Keep in exercise every principle of humanity, compatible with the laws of war, and see that no violence is permitted to women and children. . . . The Utah Indians have been notified repeatedly of the consequences . . . if they did not cease to molest the white inhabitants and their herds." Special Order No. 2, Head Quarters Nauvoo Legion, Major General's Office, G.S.L. City, 31 January 1850, Daniel H. Wells, Major General, Nauvoo Legion, TMR, b1, f2.

[35] "History of Provo," 239; Stout, *Diary*, 2:362; Utah Stake Manuscript History; Richard Young, "Nauvoo Legion," 122–23; and Gottfredson, *Indian Depredations*, 28–35.

[36] "History of Provo," 239.

these groups, which followed a bloody trail into Rock Canyon, an incredibly steep and treacherous box canyon which now overlooks the Provo LDS Temple and Brigham Young University.[37]

White sentries scaled huge rocks at the mouth of the canyon from which they could command the canyon floor while Black Hawk, followed at some distance by other whites, made his way up the trail. Near the mouth of the canyon he found a few tepees. After "a general scattering of the squaws and children," Black Hawk entered the lodges, discovering the frozen corpses of Old Elk and about a dozen others, "including Squaws and children," some of whom had died of wounds, but most having expired "through want, fatigue and exposure" in the lethal cold. As the militiamen gathered up some twenty-three prisoners, Old Elk's wife, described as "the handsomest squaw in the Ute nation," sought to escape by scaling the mountain's almost perpendicular cliffs but plunged to her death before the eyes of her pursuers. Whether she slipped or purposely jumped was debated by witnesses. Rock Canyon's "Squaw Peak" evidently took its name from this tragedy. Farther up the canyon, additional lodges were found and in a number of small engagements several more Indians were killed. Bloody trails convinced Black Hawk and white trackers, however, that Stick-in-Head and others had previously escaped on snowshoes.[38] In the aftermath of the Rock Canyon fight the militiamen pillaged the dead for souvenirs, and one of them, William Hickman, went so far as to sever Old Elk's head from his body because Jim Bridger had once offered a hundred dollars reward for it.[39]

While Black Hawk's white associates were at work in Rock Canyon, men under General Wells chased other Utes out onto the ice on the south end of Utah Lake, where they killed twenty-nine more Indians

---

[37] Ibid.; Peter W. Conover, Wm. McBride, Commanding Capts., John McEwan, Commissary, to Major General D.H. Wells, 20 February 1850; and "Hunting trails Battle grounds etc. Peter W. Cownover [*sic*], Samuel Ewing, Thomas Willis, Robert Egbert, Edwd C Holden, Abram G. Cownover, 'Black Hawk,'" 20 February 1850, TMR, #33.

[38] Daniel H. Wells, Major Genl., Head Quarters Fort Utah, Comdg. to Prest Brigham Young, Governor & Commander in Chief, GSL City, 18 February 1850, TMR, #44; Utah Stake Manuscript History; and "History of Provo," 239–40.

[39] Hickman, *Brigham's Destroying Angel*, 68. John W. Gunnison wrote that "'Old Elk,' the terror of the mountains . . . had long boasted that no single [white] person or trapper could live with him in the valleys, and numbers are supposed to have fallen under his rifle." Gunnison, *The Mormons*, 146–47. Similarly, Howard Stansbury wrote that Old Elk was a "crafty and blood-thirsty savage, who had been already guilty of several murders, and had openly threatened that he would kill every white man that he found alone upon the prairies." Stansbury, *Exploration*, 149.

and took even more women and children prisoners. Figures of the total Indian casualties vary, but it was later estimated that only thirteen escaped of the "seventy or eighty warriors who had engaged in the Provo battle."[40] Only one Mormon life was lost. A single Timpanogos warrior was taken captive, An-kar-tewets, before whom, it will be remembered, Dimick Huntington, with raised hand, had given his solemn oath that the whites would not usurp the Indians' land.[41] An-kar-tewets and an estimated "26 women & children prisoners" were temporarily confined at Fort Utah, where they, along with Black Hawk, used the cannon platform as a crude shelter to protect themselves from Utah's winter gales. Eventually, the women and children were taken to Salt Lake City where they were to be taught the "arts of civilization."[42] Some of them soon died, however, only intensifying native torment. Within months, most of the survivors had slipped away one by one to carry their bitterness to their people.

A final and gruesome indignity occurred while Black Hawk and the other prisoners still sought refuge from the bitter cold under their captors' cannon at Fort Utah. Perhaps inspired by the sight of Old Elk's head being treated as a trophy of war, Dr. James Blake, a gentile army surgeon accompanying the Stansbury expedition, commissioned several Mormons to return to the battlefields to decapitate the corpses that still lay frozen in the snow. Blake planned to send the heads "to Washington to a medical institution" for scientific examination. Abner Blackburn, hired with another Mormon to help Blake obtain the heads, wrote this grisly account of the affair:

> A few days after the last batle with the Indians, a government surgeon wanted James Or and me to take a sley [and] cross over on the ice and secure the Indians heads, for he wanted to send them to Washington to a medical institution. [We] hired a sley [and] crost over on the ice. The weather was bitter cold. The surgeon to[o]k out his box of instruments and comenced. It took him a quarter of an hour to cut off one head. The sun was getting low and [it was] frezing cold. Jim and me took the job in our own hands. We were not going to wait on the surgeons slow motion. Jerked our knives out and had them all off in a few minutes. They

---

[40] "History of Provo," 240; and Richard Young, "Nauvoo Legion," 123–24.
[41] Bean, *Autobiography*, 62.
[42] Ibid.; and Stout, *Diary*, 2:362.

were frozen and come off easy in our fassion. The surgeon stood back and watched us finish the job.[43]

Reportedly "40 or 50" heads were boxed up and taken to the fort, where for several weeks they were openly viewed as curiosities by the settlers. Before the grisly contents of the boxes could be delivered to the doctor in Salt Lake City, however, "the weather turned warm" and "the indian heads smelt loud" and turned "green with rot."[44] The heads were probably not concealed from the Indians held at the fort, for tradition among the Utes was that the gruesome decapitations were "held up as a warning to other Indians." It is difficult to conceive the impact that the viewing of the severed heads of clansmen, friends, and kin had upon Antonga Black Hawk and the others huddled under the cannon platform. More than half a century later tribal elders still bitterly spoke of it, understandably complaining that "such things cannot be erased from the Ute memory. The witnesses still live, and the spirit of revenge will not soon die in the Indian breast."[45]

The Fort Utah campaign and its butchery has great significance for the Black Hawk War, which erupted fifteen years later. Many key personalities of the later conflict were involved, one way or the other, in the former. On the part of the Mormons, Brigham Young, Daniel H. Wells, Dimick Huntington, George W. Bean, Robert T. Burton, William B. Pace, and scores of others all took some part in both. Like Black Hawk and An-kar-tewets, who later became leading raiders, Tabby, Sanpitch, and Antero, who discovered the decapitated bodies of their tribesmen abandoned on various battlefields, would carry the emotional scars of the earlier conflict into the later war.[46] By far the bloodiest single week of Indian killing in Utah history (within Utah's present borders), considering tribal notions of vengeance, the defeat of the Utes in 1850 naturally became the backdrop against which all later Mormon-Ute relations must be viewed. That the Black Hawk War's first raid culminated in the death of Barney Ward, the mountain man who "helped defeat the Indians in the Provo war for which they ever after held a grudge against him" exemplifies the two conflicts'

---

[43] Blackburn, *Frontiersman*, 170.

[44] Ibid., 170–71; and Workers of the Writers' Program, *Provo*, 58–59.

[45] "Hatred of Utes for the Mormons . . . Alleged Atrocities of Early Days Recalled and Claims that Cruelty Was Practiced by the Church Apostles and Disciples," in *Denver Daily News*, 14 September 1905, 6; and Martineau, *Southern Paiutes*, 54.

[46] "History of Provo," 240.

interconnectedness.[47] Not surprisingly, bitterness over the killings at Fort Utah was still being expressed in peace talks at the close of the Black Hawk War in 1872 and has in fact persisted to our own time.[48]

Black Hawk undoubtedly learned valuable lessons regarding the strategies of warfare at Fort Utah. The failure of the Timpanogos Utes to withstand a frontal Mormon attack was not lost on the future war chief, whose own strategy of strike, pillage, and run, and of avoiding pitched winter engagements at all cost, would never open his people up to a similar disaster again. For his people generally, the once-powerful Timpanogos band was thrust well on its way to extinction; by the beginning of the Black Hawk War, it had effectively ceased to exist. Just what possessed Black Hawk to side with the whites during this early conflict is unknown. If he indeed was the teenage survivor of the Battle Creek fight, he had spent a significant amount of time interacting with, and perhaps coming to trust, Mormons, or, perhaps more likely, becoming overawed by their power. Whatever his reasons for originally siding with the Mormons, it can be safely surmised that he would never forget the grisly images of seeing his relatives and acquaintances shot down, their bloodied corpses frozen in the snow, and their amputated heads displayed in the Mormon fort. Also, the agony of An-kar-tewets as he huddled over the captive widows and orphans struggling to keep warm and held at gunpoint under Fort Utah's cannon platform were scenes that would never leave Black Hawk. Within four years of the battle, "the friendly Indian Black Hawk" would rise to become one of the Latter-day Saints' most recalcitrant antagonists, and, in the words of Brigham Young, he eventually became "the most formidable foe amongst the red men that the Saints have had to encounter."[49]

Chief Black Hawk

Initially Antonga's involvement at Fort Utah seems to have profited the young Ute. On 23 February 1850 Daniel H. Wells released An-kar-

---

[47] *Deseret Evening News,* 6 June 1906, 10. As has been pointed out, Elijah Barney Ward came to Fort Hall as early as 1834. A companion of Jedediah Smith, Kit Carson, Jim Bridger, and others, he "established a trading post at Provo" in 1837 "and kept it until 1848." Having traded and lived among the Utes of Utah Valley for more than a decade, Ward's siding with the Mormons embittered his former friends. Interestingly, Ward was baptized a Latter-day Saint within days of the Fort Utah victory. See LeRoy Hafen, "Elijah Barney Ward," 343–51.

[48] Daniel Jones, *Forty Years Among the Indians,* 211–14; "Hatred of Utes for the Mormons . . . ," *Denver Daily News,* 14 September 1905, 6; and Martineau, *Southern Paiutes,* 54.

[49] Brigham Young to President H.S. Eldredge, 4 October 1870, BYC.

tewets "to apprize the *Survivors* of his nation" that they could now safely "return and dwell in peace *if* they cease[d] their depredations." The general also directed the messenger to inform the decimated Timpanogos that "The friendly Indian Black Hawk *must be their chief and they must obey him.*" "If they will do this we will return them their horses and become again their friends," Wells promised, earnestly stating, "We do not wish to continue to war with them, but merely teach them to do right."[50] Clearly, the devastation of the Timpanogos did not mean a change in Latter-day Saint dreams of what their gospel could do for the Indians, but their means of "teaching the Indians to do right" in this instance was disastrous. Gentile Army lieutenant John W. Gunnison, who witnessed the Mormon reaction to the Fort Utah conflict firsthand, noted the irony of the Saints' position when he wrote, "It is a curious matter of reflection, that those whose *mission* it is to convert these aborigines by the sword of the spirit, should thus be obliged to destroy them—but they stoutly affirm that these people will yet, under their instruction, fulfil the prophecy that 'a nation shall be born in a day;' and when they have completed the destined time, will listen to the truth and become 'a fair and delightsome people.' "[51]

Elevating "the friendly Indian Black Hawk" to chieftainship was clearly part of the plan for unfolding the prophecy Gunnison described. There is no firm evidence that Black Hawk held any position of authority before being placed in one by the Latter-day Saints. Until his death twenty years later, contemporary documents repeatedly refer to him as "chief," although the exact nature of his leadership clearly changed from year to year in the constant metamorphosis of a besieged and failing Ute political system. That Black Hawk was accepted by his people as a leader at all is remarkable. Not only was he elevated to tribal authority by white men, but he could be viewed also as a traitor for having sided with the settlers at Fort Utah and for guiding them in what turned out to be their greatest single Ute slaughter. Perhaps Black Hawk's family relationships hold the key to this interesting enigma.

As the Fort Utah debacle unfolded, Brigham Young referred to Black Hawk as "Walker's relative."[52] One source even averred that Black Hawk was a "half brother to the famous war chief Walker."[53]

---

[50] Daniel H. Wells to Capt. McBride, 23 February 1850, TMR, #49. Italics mine.

[51] Gunnison, *The Mormons*, 147. Italics in original.

[52] "I propose that the friendly Indian, (Walker's relative) that is with you, live at the Fort, as heretofore, . . ." Brigham Young to Daniel H. Wells, 14–15 February 1850, BYC.

[53] "History of Utah," 239.

That he could have been is possible, but it is not unequivocally demonstrable from white sources, even though Young referred to him in an 1853 letter as Wakara's brother.[54] Before his death at the hands of the Utes in 1853, John W. Gunnison offered a curious piece to the puzzle when he emphasized that among the Northern Utes "chieftainship descends from father to son" and described that "a late chief, acting on the plurality law [polygamy], left above thirty sons, most of whom have small clans under them."[55]

Whether brother, nephew, or cousin, Black Hawk as "Walker's relative" was part of the single most powerful family in the Northern Ute conglomerate—a family consistently described in white sources as being at the very apex of the Ute aristocracy.[56] Wakara himself, long the prestigious war chief of the confederated Northern Ute bands, was second only to the civil head chief Sowiette, who, incidentally, was variously listed in contemporary sources as being Wakara's "half brother" and uncle.[57] Brigham Young called Wakara's own band, the Shiberetches, "the chivalry of the Utahs." Virtually every other major band in the Northern Ute confederacy was led by close relatives of Wakara. Arapeen, Sanpitch, Ammon, Grosepeen, and Tabby, all important headmen, were said to be his brothers.[58] Antero was reportedly his cousin,[59] Peteetneet his uncle,[60] and So-ok-sow-bet, or "Joe," his "relative." Family connection to Wakara was no small matter, for among Indians from California to Colorado and south into

[54] In a letter to Wakara, Young wrote, "When I see you, and your braves, I shall also expect to see arrowpin, Grospin, Taba, Peteetneet, Blackhawk, Anton, and all of your Brothers . . ." In spite of the fact that multiple sources indicate that at least five of the seven listed (all but Peteetneet and Black Hawk) were Wakara's actual brothers, Young throws serious doubt on his literal use of the word "brother" when he continued the above sentence with "and I will be your Brother, and you will be my Brother. . . ." Brigham Young to "Captain Wacher [*sic*], Chief of Utahs," 14 April 1853, BYC.

[55] Gunnison, *The Mormons*, 149.

[56] Sonne, "Royal Blood of the Utes."

[57] Gunnison, *The Mormons*, 149; and Anonymous statement containing "Weight, size &c of Indians," 2 August 1852, BYC, r92, b58, f18.

[58] The first four were, without question, Wakara's actual brothers. Tabby's relationship with Wakara is not always clear in the Mormon sources. Dimick Huntington, the foremost Latter-day Saint authority on the Utes, confirmed that he was "a brother," as do some other respectable sources. The fact that cousins and other close relatives were often "considered as a brother," however, confuses these relationships. Huntington, *Vocabulary*, 28; "History of Provo," 240; Sidwell, "Reminiscences of Early Manti," 3–4, 6; and Martineau, *Southern Paiutes*, 75.

[59] "History of Provo," 240.

[60] Anonymous statement containing "Weight, size &c of Indians," 2 August 1852.

Mexico his reputation for military prowess and raiding ability was unsurpassed.[61]

Lest Black Hawk's youth be construed as prohibiting real chieftainship, it should be noted that when the Mormons arrived in Utah, Wakara was little over thirty and Antero was in his mid-twenties and that both had been chiefs for some time.[62] Two of Black Hawk's contemporaries, who became chiefs at about the same time, were also very young. Kanosh was already head chief of the Pahvants in 1851 at age twenty-three, while Ouray, of the Tabaguache Utes of southwestern Colorado, was a chief in 1855 at the age of twenty-two.[63]

From the Saints' perspective, their victory at Fort Utah initially had a positive effect upon the Northern Utes. Wakara, Arapeen, Antero, and Tabby anxiously reasserted their "friendship,"[64] the former two "receiving baptism" within weeks of the fight, and Wakara begging to be ordained to the Latter-day Saint priesthood in order to "spread the gospel to others." By July 1850 Sowiette, Antero, Tabby, Grospeen, Jake Arapeen, Showan, and hundreds of Utes of lesser note had joined the Mormon church.[65] Eventually Sowiette, Wakara, Arapeen, and a chief named Unhoquitch were ordained to the office of Elder in the Melchizedek Priesthood.[66] Isaac Morley, the presiding church official in Sanpete Valley (which was settled shortly after Utah Valley in 1849) expressed the hoped-for connection between colonization and Lamanite conversions when he rejoiced following Wakara's baptism "that no mission to the scattered sons of Joseph, was ever attended with brighter prospects." "The door is opened," he exulted, "and they are coming in." As "a stone from the quarry needs polishing to become useful," he

---

[61] Brigham Young to Luke Lea, Commissioner of Indian Affairs, 13 August 1851, BYC; Sonne, "Royal Blood of the Utes"; idem, *World of Wakara*; Bailey, *Walkara*; and Gustive Larson, "Walkara's Half Century."

[62] Anonymous statement containing "Weight, size &c of Indians."

[63] Bean, *Autobiography*, 70; and P. David Smith, *Ouray*, 43, 49. Brigham Young called Kanosh "quite young" in 1855. Brigham Young to George Manypenny, Commissioner of Indian Affairs, 26 June 1855, BIA, M234, 897. In 1865 Kanosh referred to himself as "only a boy." "Proceedings of a Council with the Utah Indians," 8.

[64] "History of Provo," 241.

[65] For Walker and Arapeen's baptism see Isaac Morley to Brigham Young, 17 April 1850, BYC. JH, 7 July 1850, 5–6 contains a list of 126 Indian baptisms (108 males and eighteen females), illustrating the rush of Northern Ute baptisms following the Fort Utah fight. The list shows Antero's name in its common variation "An, ter, ope"; Sowiette appears as "Sow,a,att"; Tabby, as "Tab, ah"; Grospeen, as "Grow,sa,pene"; Jake Arapeen by his Indian name "Ye, na, wood"; and Showan, as "Show,er,won."

[66] JH, 9 June 1851, 1.

continued, "we believe there are some here that may be made, (with watchful care) to shine as bright gems in the Temple of the Lord, yes, stars that may spread their twinkling, light to distant tribes."[67] We have no record of Black Hawk's baptism; but it is likely that he was baptized, for Daniel H. Wells arranged for him to be escorted to the semiannual general conference of the church in Salt Lake City in April 1850.[68]

It is clear that the Mormons initially treated Black Hawk as head chief of the defeated Timpanogos. Indian horses captured during the fighting were delivered to "Chief Black Hawk" at general conference, and he was directed to return them "to the rightful owners, or nearest of kin."[69] In mid-May, General Wells addressed a letter to "Petete nete[,] Walker[,] Sowaette[, and] Black Hawk," headmen of the Northern Ute Nation, expressing peace, friendship, and an eagerness to meet with the Ute leaders.[70] Ten days later, Brigham Young and other top church officials held a meeting with key Ute leaders "in Walkers tent in Utah Valley" at which Black Hawk played a leading role. In addition to Black Hawk and Wakara, Sowiette, Antero, Arapeen, Sanpitch, Grospeen, Ammon, Tabby, and Stick-in-Head (a survivor of the Fort Utah fight) were present. After shaking hands with hundreds of Utes who came to meet him personally, the church president addressed the huge native gathering that circled about him outside Wakara's lodge.

Young told the Indians that he and his coreligionists had come to their lands to stay, and, though strangers now, he expected shortly to become "intimately acquainted." "Our Father the Great Spirit has plenty of land for you *and for the Mormons,*" he assured them. Referring to the Fort Utah problems, he said, "If any of you have esteemed us to be your enemies, it is because you have been enemies to us, and what has passed this last winter we want forgotten." "We have many things to say to you when you [are able to] understand them, to tell you of your forefathers, who they were," he promised them, prophesying that when they became like their fathers they would "not have any enemies" at all.[71] Peace seemed to have been restored, and the defeated Indians invited their conquerors to settle freely on their lands.[72]

---

[67] Isaac Morley to Brigham Young, 17 April 1850.

[68] Daniel H. Wells to Bishop Higbee & Conover, 21 March 1850, TMR, #57.

[69] Ibid.

[70] Daniel H. Wells to Petete nete, Walker, Sowiette, and Black Hawk, 13 May 1850, TMR, #61.

[71] "A meeting in Walkers tent in Utah Valley, between B. Young, H. C. Kimball, and the brethren, with Walker, [et al.,]" 22 May 1850, BYC, r92, b58, f14. Italics mine.

[72] For example, see Dimick B. Huntington to Brigham Young, 30 January 1851, BYC.

Black Hawk, the Slave Trade, and the Walker War

Little is known of Black Hawk for the next three years, although he is occasionally mentioned in contemporary sources as "chief" of the "Timpanagoos, or Lake Utes." In 1851, for example, as thousands of immigrants poured into Utah, Juab, and Sanpete valleys, Stick-in-Head, Peteetneet, and Black Hawk were listed by Brigham Young in official Indian Office correspondence as being the major "chiefs of bands" of the Timpanogos, whom he described as being "broken up into small bands."[73] That the new leader was personally affected by the stream of new settlers is certain.

While Young had assured Black Hawk and other Indian leaders in 1850 that "the Great Spirit has plenty of land" for both the Latter-day Saints and the Utes and that he expected their respective peoples to become "intimately acquainted," the following year Apostle George A. Smith, on behalf of the legislature of the newly established Territory of Utah (and presumably under the direction of Governor Young himself), petitioned President Millard Fillmore to see that Congress extinguish Indian title to the territory, and "*provide measures for the removal of [the] Indians from Utah.*"[74] This evidence suggests that the ambivalence between the church's stated mission regarding the Lamanites and its actual practice came directly from the top.

By 1852 the Utes generally were "becoming very much excited by the encroachments of the Mormons," complaining that they were settling "all the most valuable lands, extending three hundred miles" from Salt Lake City. The Utes told gentile Indian agents that the Saints "at first, conciliated the Indians by kind treatment, but when they once got a foothold, they began to *force their way*—the consequence was a war with the Indians, and in many instances a most brutal butchery." This same end, the Utes feared, would "be the result, wherever the Mormons may make a settlement." Once "driven from their lands and their hunting ground destroyed, without any compensation," many Utes were "reduced to a state of suffering, bordering on starvation," causing "some of the most daring and desperate to approach the settlements, and demand compensation for their lands, when upon the slightest pretexts they are shot down or driven to the Mountains" by the Mormons.

[73] Brigham Young to Luke Lea, Commissioner of Indian Affairs, 13 August 1851, BYC; and Brigham Young to Henry R. Day, Indian Sub-agent, 21 July 1851, BIA, M234, 897.

[74] George A. Smith and James Lewis to Hon. Milard Filmore [*sic*], President of the United States, undated, received by the Indian Office 20 August 1851, BIA, M234, 897. Italics mine.

"These scenes frequently occur," one agent charged, reporting that "the other day, an Indian was found dead, in the vicinity of the city, [anonymously] shot through the body."[75]

"Sub-agent" H.R. Day wrote the Commissioner of Indian Affairs in 1852 that in repeated councils held with the "different [Utah] Chiefs and Braves . . . the Indians complained bitterly of the treatment they had received from the Mormon settlers, from the time they first entered the Territory up to the present." Day wrote further:

> I can perhaps convey their Ideas better by giving you the language of the Old chief Sow-er-ette, who raising himself up to his full height said to me, American—good! Mormon—No good! American—friend —Mormon—kill—steal[!]
>
> The Chief said they claimed all the lands upon which were settled the Mormons, and that they were driving them further every year, making use of their soil and what little timber there was, and expressed a wish If there [*sic*] Great Father [the President of the United States] was so powerful, that he would not permit the Mormons to drive them out of the vallies into the Mountains, where they must starve.[76]

These problems were greatly compounded by the fact that late in 1851 Brigham Young moved to end the illegal Indian slave trade in Utah. For years before the arrival of the Latter-day Saints, the Northern Utes had carried on a brisk, lucrative, and far-reaching slave trade with Spaniards, Mexicans, Americans, and other Indians throughout the West. Extending this trade from California to the Great Plains, and from at least as far north as Idaho to the Mexican provinces of Sonora and Chihuahua, Wakara and key "relatives," including Black Hawk, were kingpins in an imposing market that involved virtually all of the Northern Utes.[77] The powerful mounted Ute bands sometimes traded for, but more often simply kidnapped Shoshoni, Goshute, Weber-Ute, Paiute, Pi-ede, Pahvant, and even other Ute children and teenagers, whom they most often took directly to Taos or Santa Fe. The Utes told Mormons that "for a young Indian the Spanish and Mexicans will pay

---

[75] J.H. Holman to Luke Lea, Commissioner of Indian Affairs, 28 November 1851, BIA, M234, 897. Italics in original.

[76] H.R. Day to Luke Lea, 2 January 1852, BIA, M234, 897.

[77] Heap, *Route to the Pacific*, 92; and Brigham Young to "Captain Wacher [*sic*] Chief of Utahs," 14 April 1853, BYC.

$300 to $500," and that in Colorado, New Mexico, and Sonora these slaves "labor as negroes do in the States."[78] Even a decade and a half after Young had outlawed the Ute slave trade in Utah, General James Carleton estimated that there were four thousand Indian slaves in New Mexico alone.[79]

Wakara's wealth and power, as well as that of his relatives and the Northern Ute conglomerate in general, was to a large extent based on this trade, and, as a result, Young's attempts to terminate it were nearly as threatening to the Utes as was Mormon settlement in the first place. The slave trade permeated all aspects of Northern Ute life and constituted their main source of income. During this period, Utes spoke Spanish much better than they spoke English, and they frequently decorated their clothing with pesos and Spanish cloth. Their horses were often caparisoned with ornate Spanish bridles and saddles, and the slave trade provided them with their most important source of guns, lead, and powder. Captured stock also played a major part in this Santa Fe trade, and, although the Mormons were not yet fully cognizant of it, and would not be even during the Black Hawk War, much of the stock the Utes stole from them was driven along the Old Spanish Trail with the slaves to southern Colorado and northern New Mexico.[80] The fact that Northern Utes, and Black Hawk personally, were involved in this "Santa Fe trade" would have important repercussions during the Black Hawk War, when an older and wiser Black Hawk, without the help of Wakara, would drive thousands of stolen cattle down the Old Spanish Trail towards the Taos and Santa Fe markets.

By 1853, Mormon expansion and the attempted abolition of the slave trade had set the stage for another general outbreak of armed conflict between the Utes and the settlers, and again Black Hawk was in the middle of it. Sometime during the spring of that year, Wakara and his men leveled their rifles at Latter-day Saints in the Cedar City region in southern Utah who were attempting to capture white and Hispanic slave traders for not obeying Young's mandate. Wakara held the

[78] Thomas D. Brown to Brigham Young, 22 December 1854, in Sonne, *World of Wakara*, 214–15.

[79] Meline, *Two Thousand Miles on Horseback*, 120.

[80] For general information regarding the Old Spanish Trail and the Indian slave trade in early Utah see Hafen and Hafen, *Old Spanish Trail*, especially "Slave Catchers: Traffic in Indian Women and Children," 259–83; Crampton and Steven Madsen, *Spanish Trail*; and William J. Snow, "Utah Indians and Spanish Slave Trade." See also "B. Young's Testimony [in] U.S. v[s.] Pedro Leon, Libel," BYC, r92, b58, f14.

Mormons up long enough for the slavers to escape, openly praising the traders while he berated the Saints for their interference.[81]

On hearing of Wakara's forceful complicity in the escape of the traders and of his plans to "throw the Saints away," Young wrote the war chief, affirming, "I have been friendly with you, and still wish to be, . . . and intend to do you all the good I can." Establishing a pattern of negotiation through his brother-in-law and interpreter that he would repeatedly employ throughout the Black Hawk War, he wrote: "I send Dimick [Huntington], our old friend to you, that you may see him, and hear him talk; you know him and know that he tells you the truth. I want you to hear him, for the Great spirit loves Dimick, and will love you, if you hearken unto him." Then, in a clear reference to Black Hawk's involvement with Wakara, Young closed his letter with this hope: "When I see you, and your braves, I shall also expect to see arrowpin, Grospin, Taaba, Peetetneet, Blackhawk, Anton, and all of your Brothers, and I will be your Brother, and you will be my Brother."[82] In a much more resolute moment, Young directed a messenger to "tell Walker" that if he and "the Utahs will do right the time will come when they will become a 'white and delightsome people,' but if they continue to sell their children into slavery, and rob other Indians of their children . . . *they will continue to decrease until they become extinct, until there is no man of them.*"[83] That Wakara died after a blood vessel burst in his head during a gambling match less than two years later appears not to have been lost on Black Hawk, who eventually came to see "Brigham" as a holy man whose prophecies came true.

Though there is some evidence that Black Hawk participated in the 1853 "Walker War," because his movements cannot be tracked the conflict will only be mentioned cursorily here to give some idea of that war's role in compounding native suffering and in training the young chief and others for the much longer and more substantial 1865–1872 conflict.[84] Although the Walker War has received much more attention at the hands of historians than has the Black Hawk War, Brigham

---

[81] Brigham Young to Captain Wacher [*sic*] Chief of Utahs, 14 April 1853, BYC.

[82] Ibid.

[83] Brigham Young to Isaac Morley, 7 May 1853, Edyth Romney Typescripts, b18, f1. Italics mine.

[84] A year following the Walker War, Black Hawk was listed as being one of the "ringleaders" of a belligerent band of Utes encamped in Utah Valley who were described as "the ones that done the most of the mischeaf last summer." See Peter W. Conover to Daniel H. Wells, 18 June 1854, TMR, #445; Alexander Williams to Brigham Young, 22 September 1854, BYC; and George W. Bean to Brigham Young, 24 September 1854, BYC.

Young referred to the 1853–1854 conflict simply as "a slight disturbance" in which a handful of whites and about a score of Indians lost
their lives.[85] Once again the Timpanogos and the settlers of Utah Valley were involved in the outbreak of hostilities. The trouble started in
July 1853 when James Ivie, whose son Richard had helped touch off the
1850 Fort Utah conflict by killing Bishop, knocked a Ute senseless for
beating his "squaw" for making what the Indian felt was an unfair trade
with the Ivie family. In the throes of death, the Indian was brought by
tribesmen to the camp of Wakara, who, considering Ute grievances relative to Mormon expansion and Young's attempted closure of the slave
trade, was simply waiting for a pretext to commence hostilities. After
making several punitive strikes in which a number of whites were
killed, Wakara's people retreated to the mountains, running off what
livestock they could. For the remainder of the 1853 season occasional
stock raids, not frontal attacks on Mormon villages, characterized the
Walker War. As he later would during the Black Hawk War, Brigham
Young counseled his people to build forts, guard their stock, obtain
arms, and seek to conciliate the Indians by friendly gestures.[86]

Evidence that Black Hawk took part in the war is not extensive;
however, the fact that most Northern Utes did participate and that his
own later strategy consistently mirrored that of Wakara suggest that
Black Hawk probably learned the arts of war personally from the older
man. Certainly many of Black Hawk's raiders did, not the least of
whom was Sanpitch, who for more than a quarter century rode with his
brother Wakara.[87] In any case, native strategies used during both conflicts were almost exactly the same. Wakara used Shiberetches, or "Elk
Mountain Utes," from the Four Corners region of Utah, Colorado,
New Mexico, and Arizona to form the central core of his raiding band,
as did Black Hawk after him. The Shiberetches, described as being "a
mixture" of Ute, Navajo, and Hopi blood who had "considerable intercourse" with all of these tribes, allowed both Wakara and Black Hawk
to involve Navajos in their war with the Mormons and provided both
leaders with important connections for moving stolen stock to the
Santa Fe market.[88] The fact that the Shiberetches were repeatedly referred to as "Walker's Band" during Wakara's lifetime, and then as

---

[85] Brigham Young to "Dear Brother Hosea," 30 September 1853, BYC.
[86] Christy, "The Walker War."
[87] Codman, *Round Trip*, 233–34.
[88] Brigham Young to George Manypenny, 27 May 1856, Governor's Letter Book, BYC.

"Black Hawk's Band" during the later conflict, is strong evidence of a more than casual relationship between the two "relatives."[89]

In addition to involving Navajos in the hostilities, both Wakara and Black Hawk led "allied troops of Utahs, Pahutes, Parvains, and Payedes."[90] Both war chiefs made stealing stock, and not killing Saints, their primary focus. But on this point arises an issue of gradation. When Wakara learned that the Mormons were abandoning villages (as they did during both conflicts), he wrote George A. Smith telling him that "the Mormons were d— fools for abandoning their houses and towns, for he did not intend to molest them there, as it was his intention to confine his depredation to their cattle, and that he advised them to return and mind their crops, for, if they neglected them, they would starve, and be obliged to leave the country, which was not what he desired, for then there would be no cattle for him to take."[91] Having suffered an additional decade of difficult experiences with the Mormons to build up their frustrations, Black Hawk's raiders tended to be much more violent than Wakara's, though they still rarely assaulted villages.

One of the most interesting aspects of Wakara's strategy later emulated by Black Hawk was the driving of stolen stock for great distances over rugged mountain and desert terrain. Wakara's long rides earned him fame among his contemporaries and later historians.[92] On the other hand, Black Hawk's similar feats were hardly grasped by his contemporaries and have been understood and chronicled by virtually no modern scholar, despite the fact that he and his raiders moved much more sizable numbers of stolen Mormon herds. Interestingly, Wakara's disposal of Mormon cattle in Colorado and New Mexico during the

---

[89] For reference to the Shiberetches (who also appear in the sources under the similar names of Cheveritts, Cheverets, Shiverits, Sheverts, Ashivorits, among others) as "Walker's band" see Brigham Young to Henry R. Day, 21 July 1851, BIA, M234, 897; and Brigham Young to Luke Lea, Commissioner of Indian Affairs, 13 August 1851, BYC. That the Shiberetches made up the core of Black Hawk's raiders is well documented. The first report of the outbreak of the Black Hawk War to reach Brigham Young contained this sentence, "I am informed that Black Hawk is at there [*sic*] head and is joined by the Shiveretts." R.N. Allred to Brigham Young, 11 April 1865, BYC. John Wesley Powell later wrote, "There was another band usually called Red Lake Utes and sometimes Shib-e-ritches that held their allegiance to Black Hawk or as he was known in Indian Language Nu-ints . . ." John Wesley Powell, "Government," 2, in "Life and Culture of the Ute."

[90] Carvalho, *Incidents of Travel*, 187.

[91] Heap, *Route to the Pacific*, 92.

[92] For examples see Codman, *Round Trip*, 233–34; Lieut. E.G. Beckwith, *Report of Explorations for a Route for the Pacific Railroad* (Washington, 1855), 1 October 1853, as quoted in Sonne, *World of Wakara*, 170; *Los Angeles Star*, 25 December 1852, as quoted in Sonne, 150; Bailey, *Walkara*; Sonne, *World of Wakara*; and Gustive Larson, "Walkara's Half Century."

Walker War drew the attention of Indians throughout the whole region to Utah beef, which in turn eventually allowed Black Hawk to involve raiders from several tribes and many bands over a huge tract of country that today comprises parts of seven large western states.

From 1854 to the Beginning of the Black Hawk War

Due to Brigham Young's strenuous efforts to make peace with Wakara, the Walker War can be said to have ended by the early spring of 1854. Black Hawk returned to Utah Valley that summer with about thirty warriors, identified as some "of the ones that done the most of the mischeaf last summer." They camped adjacent to old Fort Utah, which had now become the flourishing city of Provo. It was said that "the ringleaders of this band were Tintick[,] Peteteneat [,] Highforehead[,] Black Hawk[,] and Quieah." A truculent sub-chief the settlers pejoratively named Squash-Head was also there; soon there was trouble. Convinced by Young's quickness to resolve the Walker War that "Brother Brigham wont fight," the Indians broke into houses, scared women and children, stole "anything they [could] get their hands on" and threatened to drive off stock.[93] As usual, Young was petitioned for permission to chastise the Indians militarily. Convinced by the Fort Utah tragedy that giving in to such requests would only bring disaster, the church president's response typified the attitude regarding Mormon-Indian relations that would characterize him for the rest of his life:

> Your letter by yesterdays express is received, from which I learn that the Indians in your vicinity are getting quite saucy, are pilfering &c. You very naturally inquire "shall we bear it?" Now what would you do if you did not bear it? Would you wrangle and quarrel with them when you know that that would only make matters worse, and lead on to even [further] hostilities[?] *Nine cases in ten where such outrages are complained of which have fallen under my observation, the parties complaining are partially to blame; a great majority of the people never receive such treatment, nor even insults from them, but those are generally abused the most who have little wisdom, patience, or forbearance. I can scarce remember an instance where an Indian was civilly treated, that he abused a family.* Tis true it sometimes becomes a little burdensome to comply with all of their require-

---

[93] Peter W. Conover to Daniel H. Wells, 18 June 1854, Brigham Young Letter Books, Edyth Romney Typescripts; and George W. Bean to Brigham Young, 24 September 1854.

ments, but they are not generally very extensive, and it is much better to do so when a person can and do it with a good grace too, as tho' they were willing. *I tell you the spirit of the [Latter-day Saint] people instead of holding them [up] by their faith, is against [the Indians], for the least aggravation or offence, damn them, kill them, is the first thing you hear, the boys set the dogs on them and threaten them; now until the people can get a better spirit in themselves towards them, how can you expect that the Indians will have a better....* The brethren must consider, are the Indians not Israel, and are not this people Israel also, and must Israel be at war with each other[?] Do we not know that we have been driven into these mountains, amongst these wild creatures by the gentile world with whom we could not live, and must it now be said that we cannot live with Israel either? *Let us be wise and consider our relations towards them and be diligent by faith, prayer and practice, also to gain an ascendency over them and save as many of them as we can to exercise a genial influence over them and gradually lead them from their savage propensities....* I do not feel in the least discouraged in regard to these Indians. We must be friends, and have peace with them, and although we may have to pass through difficulties with them before we can attain our object, yet it must, and will be attained. Israel must be at peace with each other, and if we do not consider our ways, and so order our feelings, and our course and conduct toward them, we may yet see the time, when we will be obliged to live with them for the simple reason that we can live no where else.[94]

As a result of Young's leadership, instead of a fight, the settlers held feasts for the Indians, such as one held on 15 August 1854 in which "over 200 partook." It was reported that "Three beeves were killed, 4 barrels of biscuits furnished, together with a large quantity of vegetables." Black Hawk and the others also received "a large amount of clothing," all "contributed" by the residents of Provo.[95]

The attempt to live in peace with the Utes brought serious challenges, however. While they were still camped near Provo, Black Hawk and his associates were attacked by eighty Shoshonis, or Snakes, taking vengeance for a Ute raid on their horse herd. Three of the Utes were

---

[94] Brigham Young to Col. P.W. Conover, 18 June 1854, Brigham Young Letter Books; and Brigham Young to Major Geo. W. Bradley and Brethren at Nephi, 18 June 1854, Brigham Young Letter Books. Italics mine.
[95] JH, 15 August 1854, 1.

killed and Squash-Head, also known as Squash, was wounded. The Snakes had come to Provo under the pretense of visiting Barney Ward, who was married to a Shoshoni woman. After the battle, a wounded female relative of the mountain man's wife took refuge in Ward's Provo home, and within an hour Black Hawk and forty Utes entered the city in a frenzy, demanding "that the squaw should be delivered to them"— a demand that was flatly refused.

In accordance with the peace treaty that ended the Walker War, Black Hawk and the others considered the Mormons bound as allies to help them chase and chastise the Snakes. Learning that such help would not be forthcoming, the Indians beset Ward's house (whose occupants had been led away by armed whites), destroying almost all of his personal effects. In his wrath, Peteetneet, head chief of the band Black Hawk was now most closely associated with, angrily alleged "that he had heard that Brigham told the Snakes to come on them" and that if "he could find out that was the case the Utahs would then know what to do." "The whole drift of the Indians," one report read, "is that if they do not obtain revenge of the Snakes they will have it of the Mormons." Fortunately for the Mormons, Peteetneet, Black Hawk, Tintic, Squash, and the others subsequently attacked the Shoshoni party, killing several, though they were again bested by the larger force. Still, they made threats against the lives of the Provo authorities and even Young himself, and they killed Mormon stock as they headed for the mountains in a rage.[96]

The following year, 1855, there was yet more trouble between the Utes and the people of Provo, and once again Black Hawk was involved. For generations the Northern Utes had come each spring to Utah Valley to take trout from the Provo River during the fishes' annual spawning run. The city of Provo was built on the traditional fishing grounds, however, and, as the number of homes and fences increased, the native fishermen had less space for themselves and their horses. In May 1855 forty lodges of Utes with hundreds of horses made their annual visit to the river. Still upset over the episode the previous fall, Black Hawk, Tintic, and Squash tore down Mormon fences and let their animals into enclosed fields, destroying hundreds of acres of crops. They also chased whites fishing with nets from the river.

---

[96] Alexander Williams to Brigham Young, 22 September 1854, BYC; Alexander Williams to Brigham Young, 24 September 1854, BYC; and George W. Bean to Brigham Young, 24 September 1854.

To show their own displeasure, whites killed a mare owned by Tintic and a colt owned by Black Hawk, who in turn killed Mormon cattle. Again the Utes and the people of Provo came dangerously close to actual warfare. However, as he was wont to do under such circumstances, Brigham Young sent Dimick Huntington, this time accompanied by Apostle George A. Smith, to make whatever concessions were necessary to avert bloodshed. "Those first disposed for peace were Tabba [Tabby], Sanpitch and Grosepine," the official report of the parley read, while "the principal leaders of the disaffected were Tintick, Squash and An-ton-guer (Black Hawk)." Tintic, Squash, and Black Hawk, since Wakara's death clearly the dominant leaders of resistance to white settlement, passionately voiced their grievances regarding whites depleting fish supplies by the use of nets, the fencing off of grazing lands traditionally used during the fishing festival, and the killing of their horses.

Implementing Young's instructions, Smith, Huntington, and Mormon Indian agents quietly listened, paid the chiefs for their dead horses, and agreed to keep whites off the river during the fishing festival. They also gave the chiefs gifts of flour, shirts, and tobacco and promised to fence off hundreds of acres exclusively for Indian grazing purposes both in Provo and in the Spanish Fork area. This last move soon evolved into a system of establishing "Indian Farms," where Young's agents reserved and fenced thousands of acres of grazing lands and raised crops for native use. Through these efforts, bloodshed was avoided, and, after whites with nets helped the Indians make a sizable catch, Black Hawk and his comrades left the area.[97]

Associating with Tintic and Squash was dangerous business for Black Hawk. Along with Black Hawk himself, these Timpanogos petit chiefs were coming to be viewed as the most dangerous and belligerent Indians in Utah. It was generally believed that Squash, described as "the terror of the neighborhood," had killed and cannibalized a Mormon child, and the peculiar shape of his head (for which he was named) convinced many settlers that he and his relatives were subhuman. Both Tintic and Squash had participated in the Walker War, and Tintic had broken with Wakara when the war chief made peace with the Mormons

[97] George W. Armstrong to Brigham Young, 4 June 1855, BYC; George A. Smith to Editor of the *Deseret News*, 12 June 1855, in BIA, M234, 897; George W. Armstrong to Brigham Young, 30 June 1855, BIA, M234, 897; JH, 8 June 1855, 1, and JH, 9 June 1855, 1; and Beeton, "An Experiment with Indian Farms."

early in 1854. By the winter of 1855, Tintic and Squash had drawn off a "small band of disaffected Utes" west of Utah Lake, where they stole stock, threatened settlers, and belligerently spoke of Indian "grievances from the first Settlement of the Territory until the present time."[98]

By early 1856 rank and file Latter-day Saints had had enough of such Indians, and because Indian Superintendent Brigham Young was wont to ignore petty thefts in order to keep the peace, they went behind their church leader's back and complained to gentile federal judges. Yet another outbreak of hostilities, known as "the Tintic War," was provoked when "on the oath of James Ivie of Provo" Associate Justice W.W. Drummond sent a 100-man posse to bring Squash in to face murder charges, while Tintic and several others were indicted for "stealing cattle and horses."[99] Certain that it could result only in trouble, Brigham Young as governor and superintendent of Indian affairs countermanded Drummond's writ and issued orders disbanding the posse.[100] In a rare act of ecclesiastical disobedience in theocratic Utah, the LDS deputy marshal leading the posse ignored Young's directives, captured Squash, and precipitated a major gun battle in attempting to take Tintic. Tintic was wounded and several other Indians, including a woman, were killed. Meanwhile, Squash, who was shackled and held prisoner in Bishop Aaron Johnson's house in Springville, mysteriously had his throat slit "from ear to ear," his guards claiming he committed suicide with a common table knife with which he had been breakfasting. Even among the Mormons "it was darkly hinted at the time that some white person had done the bloody deed."[101] Tintic, who had fled to Goshute country in the Cedar Valley area west of Utah Lake, made war with a vengeance. In addition to killing several herdsmen, he and his followers drove off hundreds of sheep, horses, and cattle and worked hard to

[98] Don Carlos Johnson, *History of Springville*, 28; idem, "The Indians of Utah Valley," 20 February 1908; JH, 1 March 1856; George W. Armstrong to Brigham Young, 19 February 1856, BYC; Thomas Smith Johnson to the Editor of the *Deseret News*, 10 March 1856, TMR, #509; and Brigham Young to George W. Manypenny, Commissioner of Indian Affairs, 31 March 1856, Governor's Letter Book, BYC.

[99] George W. Armstrong to Brigham Young, 31 March 1856, BIA, M234, 898. For general information relative to "the Tintic War" see Lynn Carson, *Tintic War*; and Gottfredson, *Indian Depredations*, 100–107.

[100] Brigham Young, Ex Officio Superintendent of Indian Affairs, to the Inhabitants of the Territory, 22 February 1856, TMR, #485.

[101] Thomas Smith Johnson to the Editor of the *Deseret News*, 10 March 1856; George W. Armstrong to Brigham Young, 31 March 1856; Don Carlos Johnson, *History of Springville*, 28; and idem, "Indians of Utah Valley," 27 February 1908.

encourage the Goshutes and "White Knife" Shoshonis of western Utah and eastern Nevada to join him in all-out war against the settlers.[102]

Black Hawk also was involved in a dangerous Indian-white encounter when the Mormon posse surrounded several excited Timpanogos camps searching for Tintic's "hostiles." Aware of their connection with Tintic and Squash, Black Hawk, Peteetneet, and several of the latter's sons were forced to show they were "good Indians" by joining the Mormon posse as guides in a winter campaign against the raiders.[103] It is not hard to imagine that Black Hawk viewed his forced participation in the expedition against his friends as just one more indignity foisted upon him by the white invaders. Luckily for Tintic, though, before the posse could capture him, Young regained control of the situation, called off all operations against the Indians, and instead "punished" the leaders of the "disobedient" posse by calling them on foreign missions.[104] His policy remained one of not provoking Indians to violence by prosecuting them for petty theft, despite the ardent cries of his people. With tensions increasing between Mormons and the federal government, Young needed peace in Utah, and he would soon have need for Indian allies.

The coming of large numbers of federal troops to the territory during the 1857–58 Utah War has been discussed elsewhere. Suffice it to say, by the spring of 1858 most of the Timpanogos Utes, and therefore presumably Black Hawk, had been drawn to the banner of the United States Army, which promised "a price for Mormon scalps." Not surprisingly, Tintic sided with the federal government against the Latter-day Saints, but apparently so too did Sowiette, Antero, Sanpitch, Ank-a-walk-ets, and many of "the other chiefs" from Utah Valley.[105] When federal arbitrators later that year worked out peace terms and offered Brigham Young and other church leaders amnesty, Peteetneet's

---

[102] Thomas Smith Johnson to the Editor of the *Deseret News*, 10 March 1856; Gottfredson, *Indian Depredations*, 100–107; and George W. Armstrong to Brigham Young, 30 September 1856, BIA, M234, 898.

[103] "An Tonga" is specifically mentioned in "A List of Names of persons who were summoned into a posse on the 17th day of Feby. A.D. 1856. By Thomas S. Johnson U.S. Deputy Marshal to assist him in arresting certain Indians . . . ," TMR, #1391. See also Thomas Smith Johnson to the Editor of the *Deseret News*, 10 March 1856.

[104] Thomas Smith Johnson to the Editor of the *Deseret News*, 10 March 1856, and related correspondence, TMR; Lucius N. Scovil to George A. Smith, March 1856, GAS; JH, 24 February 1856, 3–4; and JH, 16 July 1859, 1.

[105] Charles B. Hancock to Aaron Johnson, 26 September 1857, BYC; Arrapene to Brigham Young, 28 February 1858, BYC; JH, 8 February 1858, 2, 14 April 1858, 11 May 1858, 1, and 30 May 1858, 1; and George A. Smith to T.B.H. Stenhouse, 7 June 1858, HOLB.

Timpanogos at the Spanish Fork Indian Farm (the group Black Hawk was most closely associated with) were understandably chagrined that a United States rout of the Mormons was not forthcoming, "as they had anticipated a fine time plundering the Mormons, while their Allies the U.S. Troops, were killing the people."[106]

Many Timpanogos and other Utes, however, flocked to army head-quarters at Camp Floyd in Cedar Valley west of Utah Lake, and by 1859 they were sometimes employed by gentile federal judges to catch Saints charged with polygamy, treason, murder, and a host of other al-leged crimes related to the Utah War and the Mountain Meadows Massacre.[107] That Black Hawk cast his lot with the soldiers is likely, for in May 1859 Captain James H. Simpson recognized Black Hawk as an Indian with whom the troops were familiar and noted in his journal that the chief was then living with the Goshutes not far from Camp Floyd.[108] Actually marrying a Goshute woman, Antonga Black Hawk would later capitalize on his Goshute connections and lead some of the Goshutes against the Mormons during the Black Hawk War.[109]

Little is known of Black Hawk's movements over the next four years. By 1861 Peteetneet, headman of Black Hawk's band, was dead and was succeeded by Black Hawk's brother Mountain. By 1862 Mountain's band of Timpanogos Utes had "permanently" settled on the Spanish Fork Indian Farm. In addition to being described as "the remains of the two once powerful bands of Warker [*sic*] and Pee-tee-neete," they were characterized as being the most truculent Indians in Utah. "As a whole," their agent wrote, "I think they are the most depraved, super-stitious, adicted to all manner of crime, [and] under the least restraint, of any of the Indians within this agency." Highlighting a problem that would figure prominently during the Black Hawk War, he pointed out that they were influenced "in a great measure" by "white desperadoes who infest this country and furnish them whiskey."[110] It is unknown whether or not Black Hawk made his home with Mountain's band during this period. Perhaps he remained with the Goshutes or was part of the Timpanogos band the agent called "rambling Indians," who "roamed" from Salt Lake City to Denver to Santa Fe, receiving

---

[106] George A. Smith to T.B.H. Stenhouse, 23 June 1858, HOLB.

[107] For example, see Arapeen to Brigham Young, 28 February 1858; and JH, 18 April 1859, 2.

[108] Simpson, *Report of Explorations*, 51–52.

[109] Ibid. For an example of Goshute involvement in the Black Hawk War see Cropper, "Life and Experience," 57.

[110] F.W. Hatch to J. Duane Doty, 16 September 1862, in *RSI*, 1862:350.

presents "from ten or more agents the same year."[111] It is certain, however, that at least as early as the spring of 1863 Black Hawk was war chief of the remnant of Peteetneet and Wakara's Timpanogos, still the most bellicose of Utah bands.

In part a response to Patrick Connor's massacre of hundreds of Shoshoni on the Bear River in January 1863, later that spring Black Hawk, Sanpitch, Tabby, and Little Soldier led war parties in several forays against gentile traffic on mail roads in northwestern Utah. However, these Indians articulated another reason for their violence, telling government agents that they believed that "unless they kill some white persons they will never get any presents." Black Hawk was repeatedly seen leading small parties of warriors to and from the mail road; fresh scalps were seen dangling from their lances and they openly displayed stolen goods.[112] Black Hawk and one such raiding party reportedly were tracked by Connor's troops into Spanish Fork Canyon, where the soldiers surprised a large gathering of Utes, killing several Indians with their howitzers.[113] The attack got the attention of the Indians, and, afraid that Connor intended to massacre them as he had the Shoshonis, they met him in formal treaty talks at the Spanish Fork Indian Farm on 14 July 1863. In his official report of the peace conference, which was attended by "every leading Chief of the tribe, except San Pitch," who was sick, Connor noted that Black Hawk was one of six "Chiefs of separate bands" with whom he treated. The others included such notables as Antero, Tabby, Kanosh, and Ank-a-walkets. These men, along with Sanpitch and Black Hawk, were "the principal men" of the hostile bands, according to the superintendent of Indian affairs.[114]

Connor's treaty secured general peace for over a year and a half, until the outbreak of the Black Hawk War in April 1865. But it was

[111] *RSI*, 1862:352.

[112] George Bradley to Brigham Young, 23 June 1863, BYC; JH, 1 July 1863, 4–5; "Report of H.M. Vaile, on his expedition from Denver, Colorado, to Great Salt Lake City, and back, under instructions from Wm. Gilpin, governor, and ex officio superintendent of Indian Affairs, Colorado Territory," 5 July 1862, in *RCIA*, 1862:236. For examples of Black Hawk's own involvement see Henroid, "Biography," 11; Benjamin Johnson, *My Life's Review*, 229; and Don Carlos Johnson, *History of Springville*, 61.

[113] The soldiers claimed they killed thirty Utes, but local Mormons reported that only three or four were killed. See Don Carlos Johnson, *History of Springville*, 61–62; Brigham Young Manuscript History, 16 and 17 April 1863; U.S. Department of War, *War of the Rebellion*, series 1, vol. 50, pt. 1: 204–8; and Thurber, "Journal," 304–5.

[114] Patrick E. Connor, Brig. Genl. U.S. Vols., Great Salt Lake City, to Lieut. Col. R.C. Drum, 18 July 1863, AGO, RG 94, M619, 204; and James Duane Doty to William P. Dole, 18 July 1863, BIA, M234, 901.

clear that men like Black Hawk, Sanpitch, and Jake Arapeen were un-happy with both the military and the Latter-day Saints and were simply waiting for an auspicious time to recommence hostilities. Following his 1863 parley with Connor, Black Hawk almost immediately began hold-ing councils with Shiberetch, Tabaguache, Weeminuche, and Mouche Utes from eastern Utah, Colorado, and New Mexico in an attempt to enlist them in a war with the whites.[115] When hostilities commenced on 9 April 1865, some of these recruits were with Black Hawk, Jake, and their men.

As discussed, there are some reminiscences that seem to indicate that Black Hawk was a young Indian who rose overnight from obscurity to renown when his acts of violence started the war that now bears his name. It has been shown, however, that Antonga Black Hawk had long been involved in the fierce struggle between whites and the Indians of Utah. In the first dispatch sent to Brigham Young the day after the first killings of the war, Black Hawk was referred to by name as a person the church president would be acquainted with.[116] In the days and weeks that followed, many letters poured in, all speaking of "Black Hawk" as a well-known Indian leader.[117] The following month (May 1865), when the entire John Given family was killed in the second raid of the war, Traveling Bishop A. Milton Musser confided to his journal that "the *Notorious* Blackhawk Chief" was responsible.[118] A Salt Lake City news-paper also referred to Black Hawk as the leader of a band "*long known* as a desperate gang of robbers and murderers."[119] Federal military cor-respondence later in 1865 alluded to "*the noted* chief, Black Hawk, and tribe, who have been committing depredations."[120] In his first official report of the Black Hawk War, Utah Superintendent of Indian Affairs Franklin H. Head referred to Black Hawk as a "*somewhat prominent* chief of the Utah Indians."[121]

In his late thirties or early forties when he commenced his war in 1865, Antonga was no boyish upstart. "Black Hawk" had long been

---

[115] O'Neil, "History of the Ute Indians," 56; Uintah-Ouray Tribe, *Ute Government*, 8; and Jorgensen, "Ethnohistory of the Northern Ute," 78.

[116] R.N. Allred to Brigham Young, 11 April 1865, BYC.

[117] For examples see Orson Hyde to Brigham Young, 15, 23, and 26 April 1865, BYC.

[118] Musser, Journal, 27 May 1865. Italics mine.

[119] Undated *Salt Lake Daily Telegraph* article copied into Manuscript History of Brigham Young, 1865: 322–27, especially see 322 and 325. Italics mine.

[120] Captain John H. Dalton, presumably to Commander of Camp Douglas, 14 December 1865, Register of Letters Received, Oct. 1865–June 1866, District of Missouri, 103, RUSA, RG 393, pt. III, entry 827. Italics mine.

[121] Franklin H. Head to D.N. Cooley, 30 April 1866, *RSI*, 1866:128. Italics mine.

"prominent," and as one of the top three or four leaders of Ute resistance for over a decade before he inaugurated the conflict, from the settlers' viewpoint he had certainly been "long known" as "notorious." Black Hawk died and was buried east of Spring Lake in 1870. His remains were unearthed by miners in 1917 and displayed for decades in an LDS museum on Temple Square in Salt Lake City. His skeletal remains were examined in 1995 and 1996 by a number of anthropologists and historical archaeologists. Under the Native American Graves Protection and Repatriation Act of 1990, Black Hawk's remains were reinterred in a Spring Lake park by his next of kin on 4 May 1996, and a permanent marker was dedicated by them on 27 September 1997. Based on scientific methodologies, anthropological estimates of his age vary, the lowest suggesting he was from "35 to 39 years in age" at the time of his death, while the highest concluded he was "at least fifty." Another placed his age in 1870 at "perhaps 45 years old."[122] I have tentatively accepted this last figure because it is best supported by contemporary written white sources as well as oral tradition among Black

---

[122] Black Hawk died 26 September 1870. See Benjamin F. Johnson to the Editor of the *Deseret News*, 27 September 1870, in *Deseret Evening News*, 30 September 1870, also in JH, 26 September 1870, 1; and Brigham Young to H.S. Eldredge, 4 October 1870, BYC. For information regarding the opening of Black Hawk's grave see JH, 22 September 1917, 2, 29 September 1917, 5, 20 September 1919, 3–4, and 21 September 1919, 4. Several erroneous stories relative to Black Hawk's death and burial continue to be related; they variously give the place of his burial as Spanish Fork and Hobble Creek canyons in Utah County, as well as the Uintah Reservation. For example, see JH, 15 February 1926, 3; and Culmsee, 157–58. Because the Spring Lake burial site is on national forest land, Uinta National Forest Historical Archaeologist Charmaine Thompson headed up an in-depth historical, archaeological, and anthropological investigation that confirmed the location of Black Hawk's grave, identified his remains, and supervised their reburial in Spring Lake on 4 May 1996. Thompson was assisted by the staff of the Brigham Young University Museum of Peoples and Cultures, including physical anthropologist Shane A. Baker, Staff Archaeologist, Office of Public Archaeology, Brigham Young University. Also involved were forensic anthropologist Shannon A. Novak, Anthropologist for the Utah Museum of Natural History at the University of Utah, Everett J. Bassett, archaeologist at the University of Utah, physical anthropologist and historical archaeologist Donald D. Southworth of Sagebrush Archaeological Consultants, Ogden, Utah, and Native American consultant Clifford H. Duncan. See *Salt Lake Tribune*, 1 May 1996; files relative to the repatriation of the remains of Black Hawk, U.S. Department of Agriculture, Uinta National Forest, Provo, Utah; Duncan, Official Memorandum; Novak, "Skeletal Analysis of the Remains of Black Hawk"; "Chief Blackhawk's Legacy Now Set In Stone," *Provo Daily Herald*, 28 September 1997; Charmaine Thompson to John Peterson, 1 October 1997, in author's possession (copy also available at UUWA); Conversation with Shannon Novak and Everett Bassett while examining Black Hawk's remains at the Museum of Peoples and Cultures, Brigham Young University, 8 March 1996, recorded in author's personal journal, 8 March 1996, in author's possession; multiple conversations with Charmaine Thompson during the years 1995 to 1997; and telephone conversations with Shannon Novak, Everett Bassett, Shane Baker, and Donald Southworth, 10 October 1997.

Hawk's next of kin, who, as has been pointed out, strongly aver that he was an adult when the Mormons arrived in 1847.[123]

A close relative of Wakara, Black Hawk was a member of the most important family in Northern Ute society and by birth was positioned at the very peak of his people's aristocracy. Recognized by Mormons as an important leader as early as 1850, he was rewarded for his non-aggression during the Fort Utah fight by being appointed by the white conquerors as head chief of the Timpanogos Utes. Closely involved with Wakara's slave trading and related warfare, Black Hawk gained valuable experience he would use later in his own crusade against the Latter-day Saints. As early as 1854 and 1855 he had emerged, with Squash-Head and Tintic, as one of the three most outspoken champions of Northern Ute rights. While he was obviously enraged at the white invaders and occasionally came out in open hostility against them, until 1865, as the episode at Fort Utah demonstrated, he most often sought conciliation and participated in peace parleys with both Mormons and gentiles.

The incredible anguish that white settlement brought to his own life, however, along with that produced by the collective misfortune of his people, eventually compelled him to violence. From the decapitation of kinsmen on Utah Valley's blood-soaked battlefields and his subsequent winter incarceration under his conquerors' cannon platform, to the continual abuse, hunger, and disease that followed in the wake of expanding Mormon settlement upon his lands, Antonga Black Hawk's story is characterized by the deepest sort of human suffering. Beginning in April 1865 Antonga carried his agony to all the peoples of Utah, eventually intensifying his own, as well as that of all those around him—Indian, white, and Hispanic. Truly, as Erik Erikson has suggested of great leaders in general, Black Hawk became the leader he was precisely because he experienced the struggle of his people "in both a most personal and most representative way."[124]

---

[123] In a telephone conversation 10 October 1997, forensic anthropologist Shannon A. Novak told me that determining age from skeletal remains "is still an imprecise science" and that a "ten year margin of error is assumed." She said that it is easier to report only that a man was either a "young adult, a middle-aged adult, or an older adult." She said that at the time of his death, Black Hawk was definitely "a middle-aged adult" and that, based on her analysis, given the standard margin of error, he easily could have been in his early forties when the war commenced. Novak originally estimated Black Hawk's age at death between 35 and 39 in her "Skeletal Analysis of the Remains of Black Hawk"; this was the lowest estimate by any examiner.

[124] See note 1.

Chapter Three

Setting the Stage For War

We have a large number of Indians with us, [camped near Manti,] presenting the appearance of two cities side by side, with entirely different manners and customs.

—George Peacock, Manti[1]

Here is the father of all the Utes, Sow-e-ett. He used to be the great chief and father of us all, but now he is very old, poor and blind. He has no flesh on his bones, he is going down. . . . In past times, the Washington chiefs that came here from the United States would think and talk two ways and deceive us: they always talked and thought different from Pres. Young. They have been liars, two tongues and two hearts. . . . In former times, this land, where I laid my father, was very poor, but now it is not poor, it has got to be a good land since Pres. Young and the Mormons came here. All their children have plenty to eat, and they have plenty of property. I have but few brothers and friends, and do not see what use it would be to trade the land where there are so few of us. Whatever we would trade for would be all gone soon, whether blankets, or hats, or shirts, or money. . . . If the Americans buy the land, where would the Mormons, who live here go to? Will the Lord take them up to his country? I think this is the Mormons' land, the Bishops' land, with the Utahs: let them all live here together. I do not want to cut the land in two. Let it all remain as it is.

—Kanosh, treaty talks at Spanish Fork, 1865[2]

---

[1] George Peacock, Manti, to the Editor of the *Deseret News*, 12 August 1854, in *Deseret News*, 24 August 1854, 3.

[2] "Proceedings of a Council with the Utah Indians," 7–9.

You have all agreed you can see [the Indians] here are poor, but we are all the same flesh and blood. The land used to be good here and we were all plentiful, but it has been bad lately. There has been blood spilt on it; but through this treaty I hope it will be good again. I hope the children of those who have them will grow up and live and be good. But for me, I have no children. When you see me you see all my flesh. My children have all died and gone into the ground. The earth takes them all.

—Sow-ok-soo-bet (Joe),
treaty talks at Spanish Fork, 1865[3]

The Indians of Utah

AT THE TIME the Black Hawk War started in 1865, the Indians of Utah probably numbered around 10,000 individuals loosely organized in several hundred constantly changing bands that were parts of three major tribal divisions—Ute, Shoshoni, and Navajo. Since all of these Indians wandered over "vast extents," and frequently shifted from one band to another, most white observers concluded that it was "impossible to tell with any degree of accuracy their numbers."[4] The fact that most of these Indians spent part of each year outside the territory, while others lived principally elsewhere and only occasionally visited Utah, presented a major problem to whites attempting to arrive at reliable population figures. Unfortunately, those who attempted to estimate the size of native populations often counted all groups that spent any time in Utah, thus producing much higher numbers than would actually have been in the territory at any one time.

Dimick B. Huntington, for example, without question the best-qualified Mormon to make such a calculation, estimated in 1865 that there were 23,000 Indians in Utah.[5] Despite the fact that he neglected to take the Navajos into account, Huntington's figure, which was undoubtedly based on guesses made by Indians who had little concept of territorial boundaries, was unquestionably high. He estimated that

[3] Ibid., 23.
[4] Brigham Young to George W. Manypenny, Commissioner of Indian Affairs, 30 June 1855, Governor's Letter Book, BYC; and J.F. Collins to William P. Dole, Commissioner of Indian Affairs, 8 October 1861, *RSI*, 1861:733.
[5] In 1869 LDS Church Historian and Apostle George A. Smith wrote that Huntington was "better acquainted with the language, habits, manners, customs, antiquities and history of the Utahs and other numerous tribes in this and contiguous territories than any other living man." See George A. Smith to N.S. Elderkin, 14 October 1869, HOLB, 2:910.

there were 7,000 Shoshonis; 1,000 Goshutes and Weber Utes; 4,000 Paiutes; 2,500 Pahvants, Timpanogos, and Sanpitches; 3,000 Uintas and Shiberetches; 3,000 Yampa and White River Utes; and 2,500 Tabaguache and Weeminuche Utes. An obvious problem with these figures is that the Shoshoni spent the largest part of the year in Idaho and Wyoming, while the Timpanogos, Uinta, Yampa, and Shiberetch Utes traditionally spent almost as much time in Colorado and New Mexico as they did in Utah. Many of the Goshutes counted by Huntington spent much of their time in Nevada, while both the White River Utes and the Tabaguache spent very little time in Utah. Although Huntington's overall figure may be a good guess for how many Indians crossed Utah's borders sometime during the year, the number in the territory at any given time was undoubtedly much smaller.[6]

Another problem in understanding Native American demographics is that neither Ute, Shoshoni, and Navajo tribal divisions, nor the bands within them, had rigid boundaries, and lines of distinction blurred where one group met another. The Weber Utes, for example, occupied lands where Ute and Shoshoni territories met, and were a crossbreed created by intermarriages between both tribes. While their practices and dress caused most whites to consider them Utes, they spoke the Shoshoni language. Claimed as tribesmen by both groups, however, it was as common for them to hunt buffalo on the plains with Washakie's Shoshonis as it was to associate with Sowiette's Utes to the south. When Utes and Shoshonis fought each other, whites noted with interest that the Weber Utes were often excluded from the conflict and harmed by neither side.[7] Similar mixed groups characterized the Four Corners area where Apache, Hopi, Navajo, and Ute lands met. Especially in the case of the two last-named tribes, such hybrid groups greatly facilitated the spread of Black Hawk's influence. The Utes were "so mixed up by marriage" with Indians of other major tribal stock, that, as one white observer correctly prognosticated, "when one band will begin the war it will involve [them] all."[8]

The Utes and Shoshonis were very closely related as far as lifestyle, religion, language, and many other cultural motifs were concerned. While their dialects had become so different that they could not un-

---

[6] Dimick B. Huntington, "Tribes of Indians in Utah reported by Dimick Huntington", 26 April 1865, BYC.

[7] For example, see *MS*, 59:396–97.

[8] W.F.M. Arny to D.N. Cooley, 23 August 1866, BIA, M234, 553.

derstand each other,[9] and hostilities between them were often intense,[10] the shared similarities were so evident that many white observers were sure that the two tribes descended from a common ancestry. The Navajos (who inhabited the extreme southeastern portion of the territory), however, were recognized by all as a distinctly different culture.

Northern Utah was part of the traditional territory of the Northwestern Shoshonis, who gave allegiance to Washakie. Their lands, which extended north into Idaho and east into Wyoming, also included the fertile Cache and Bear Lake valleys and the northern portion of the greater Salt Lake Valley.[11] The Weber Utes lived just south of the Shoshonis, claiming the present locations of Ogden and Ogden Valley as their central homeland. To the southwest, near present-day Tooele, resided another hybrid group, the Goshutes. These Indians identified themselves as Shoshonis but were intermarried with and closely allied to the Pahvants, of Ute stock.[12]

The Northern Utes, who included the instigators of the initial raids of the Black Hawk War, were characterized by whites as extraordinarily handsome, courageous, and intelligent Indians. Described as "powerful and warlike,"[13] they were made up of such major bands as the Uinta, Yampa, Pahvant, Sanpitch, Shiberetch, Timpanogos, and White River Utes. By 1865, however, the remnants of the once powerful Timpanogos band were most often known simply as "Spanish Fork Indians." The Northern Utes' head chief was the ancient Sowiette, whose influence was faltering as a result of mental and physical infirmity incident to age. Collectively known as "Yutas, they who live on mountains,"[14] their territory extended from Utah Valley to the White River Plateau in Colorado. Bounded on the north by the Uinta Mountains, their lands also included the Juab, Sanpete, and lower Sevier valleys, the Wasatch Plateau, Castle Valley, and the San Rafael Desert and beyond.

---

[9] Huntington, *Vocabulary*, 31.

[10] The Utes and Shoshoni had a "deadly hatred between them" that was described by John W. Gunnison as "an eternal national war." See Henry R. Day to Luke Lea, 2 January 1852, in Sonne, *World of Wakara*, 130–33; and Gunnison, *The Mormons*, 150.

[11] For descriptions of the Shoshonis, who played little part in the Black Hawk War, see Brigham Madsen, *Shoshoni Frontier*; Thomas, et al., "Western Shoshone"; and Shimkin, "Eastern Shoshone."

[12] For general information on the Goshutes see Allen and Warner, "Gosiute Indians."

[13] For example, see Parley P. Pratt to Orson Pratt, 5 September 1848, in "History of Spanish Fork"; and J.F. Collins to William P. Dole, 8 October 1861, *RSI*, 1861:735.

[14] The Northern Utes reportedly had a "complicated sign which denote[d] 'living in mountains.'" Burton, *City of the Saints*, 136–37.

It is difficult to firmly delineate Northern Ute boundaries for a number of reasons. Among them, friendly relations with Ute bands not under Sowiette's direct control allowed them to move far into Colorado and northern New Mexico. The Capote, Tabaguache, and Mouache Ute bands of the Four Corners region had been formerly connected to the Northern Utes; however, because of tribal disintegration resulting from European settlement, these Indians (known today as Southern Utes) had broken away, forming a distinct though usually cooperative political entity. The Weeminuche, another Four Corners band (also now regarded as Southern Utes), in the 1860s apparently still maintained some allegiance to Sowiette, forming a connection through which, as shall be seen, Black Hawk gained recruits from other Southern Ute bands.[15] The importance of this Southern Ute connection cannot be overstated, and the Latter-day Saints early on noted that while the Northern Utes spent their summers fishing and trading in the Utah, Uinta, Sanpete, and Sevier valleys, in the fall they "hie away again to the south . . . frequently extend[ing] their visits to the Taos, and other Utes in the Territory of [New] Mexico.[16]

Another difficulty in defining the exact boundaries of Northern Ute territory is that by right of ancestral prerogative and military superiority (based on possession of horses and guns), the powerful conglomerate of Northern Ute bands maintained a hegemony over most other Indians in Utah, extending into eastern Nevada and northwestern Arizona. This allowed them to freely operate in lands claimed by several other major groups nominally connected to the Ute tribe—namely the Goshutes and Weber Utes, as well as the more numerous Paiutes and the Piedes in all their varieties. While the two last-named groups spoke dialects of the Ute language and all four shared a common Ute cultural heritage,[17] for generations the Northern Utes had captured Paiute, Piede, and Goshute children and sold them as slaves. Through intimidation Northern Utes, whom Mormons sometimes called "horse Utes," frequently directed the activities of these weaker and horseless groups whom they had driven in past generations from the fertile valleys of central and northern Utah to eke out scanty existences in the deserts and badlands to the south and west. This Northern Ute intru-

---

[15] J.F. Collins to William P. Dole, 8 October 1861.

[16] Brigham Young to Luke Lea, 13 August 1851, BYC.

[17] Brigham Young wrote that although the Shoshoni-speaking Goshutes and Weber Utes were "somewhat mixed with the snakes," they were both "really branches of the Utah tribe." Brigham Young to Luke Lea, 13 August 1851, BYC.

sion into the activities of other bands may in part explain Black Hawk's own stay with the Goshutes in 1859.[18] Tabby, Sanpitch, and Kanosh are all known to have temporarily "taken" leadership of Goshute, Paiute, and Piede bands.[19]

Kanosh's people, the Pahvants, were Northern Utes but enjoyed special relationships with the Goshutes, Piedes, and Paiutes, who were not. The Pahvants claimed the valleys and deserts from the Pahvant Mountains near Fillmore to the White Mountains of eastern Nevada, and their territory merged on the north with that of the Goshutes near the Deep Creek Mountains and on the south with that of the Paiutes near present-day Beaver.[20] Pahvant intermarriage provided important links between these groups and the Northern Utes. The Shoshoni-speaking Goshutes, for example, were led by Kanosh's younger brother Pi-an-ump. It was noted with interest that, "although speaking different languages," the two brothers' respective bands "affiliate socially, and often go on their hunting excursions in company." Despite their affinity for the Pahvants, however, the Goshutes, like their Shoshoni relatives, considered the rest of the Northern Utes bitter enemies.[21]

The Paiutes (often called Pah-Utes by the Mormons) and the Piedes (pronounced Pie-eeds) were so closely related that it is virtually impossible for the modern researcher to distinguish between the two. Mormons and representatives of the federal Indian Office sometimes recognized them as two distinct groups, although at other times they lumped them both together. Some came to believe the Piedes were descendants of California Indians who intermarried with the Paiutes after having been driven from their country by the Spaniards.[22] Their lands included most of present-day Beaver, Iron, Washington, Kane,

---

[18] Simpson, *Report of Explorations,* 51–52.

[19] For an example of Northern Ute chieftains dictating policy in areas of Paiute domain see Bleak, "Southern Mission," 1:22.

[20] Sevier Lake formed the center of their homeland, hence the name "Pah-vant," which means "close to water." Palmer, "Utah Indians," 40–41. Sevier Lake furnished an example of the impact of white settlement; by the time of the Black Hawk War this lake by which the Pahvants identified themselves was largely dried up due to Mormon irrigation practices.

[21] *RSI,* 1873:415.

[22] For general information on the Paiutes and Piedes (whose descendants, combined with those of most of the Pahvants and large numbers of Northern Utes, today comprise the Southern Paiute people) see Inter-Tribal Council of Nevada, *Southern Paiute History*; Holt, *Beneath These Red Cliffs*; Franklin and Bunte, *The Paiutes*; Martineau, *Southern Paiutes*; and Isabel Kelly and Fowler, "Southern Paiute." For examples of white perceptions of the relationships between Utah's Paiutes and Piedes see F.H. Head to D.N. Cooley, Commissioner of Indian Affairs, 4 August 1866, BIA, M234, 902; *RSI,* 1866:122; Erastus Snow to J.E. Tourtellotte, BIA, M834, 1; J.R.F[?]., "Utah Indian Tribes," 34; and Jimmie Pete, interview by Alva

Garfield, and Piute counties in south-central and southwestern Utah and included significant portions of eastern Nevada and northern Arizona as well. These Indians, often called "Diggers" by whites, were far more economically destitute than the Northern Utes and eked out an existence on the harsh semiarid badlands of the region digging for insects, roots, lizards, and snakes for sustenance.[23] Described by white sources as "the veriest slaves" to the Northern Utes, "who treated them very cruelly," they were, according to Brigham Young, "a constant prey to other more warlike bands," and "may be said simply to exist without either hunting or war, wikeup, or lodge, utensils, or clothing of any kind." Few had guns and fewer still had horses, facts compelling them generally to "remain in their localities."[24] This was in contrast to the Northern Utes, who collectively had hundreds of horses, which allowed them to venture out onto the plains and adopt certain Plains Indian cultural traits that the Piedes and Paiutes lacked.

Perhaps as a result of their more limited diet, the Paiutes and Piedes were generally smaller in stature than were the Northern Utes.[25] They were thought by whites to possess far less intelligence than their mounted kinsmen, though the agrarian Mormons rejoiced that prior to their own arrival some Piedes were already "farming in a rude manner," raising "patches of wheat, corn, squash, and melons."[26] In contrast to the proud and aggressive Northern Utes, Mormons found the Piedes and Paiutes "very timid," reporting that they actually "trembled" when they first encountered the white newcomers. This profound fear, the Mormons believed, "arose from the fact that bands of Utes and Mexicans had repeatedly made raids upon them and had taken their children to California and Mexico and sold them for slaves."[27]

The Latter-day Saints generally believed the Paiutes and Piedes were Northern Ute "outcasts,"[28] but rejoiced that they were much more "teachable" than their proud and warlike relatives. As a result, the

---

Matheson, 15 January 1968, in Western History Center, "American Indian Oral History," 329A.

[23] The Paiutes and Piedes were often called "Ute Diggers," while the Goshutes were called "Snake Diggers." Stansbury, *Exploration*, 148.

[24] Sidwell, "Reminiscences of Early Manti," 5; and Brigham Young to George W. Manypenny, 30 June 1855, Governor's Letter Book, BYC.

[25] Thomas Sale to O.H. Irish, 4 May 1865, BIA, M234, 901.

[26] Pettit, *Utes*, 12; and Bleak, "Southern Mission," 1:17.

[27] Bleak, "Southern Mission," 1:17.

[28] Stansbury, *Exploration*, 148.

church's greatest success in proselyting and civilizing Native Americans was among these Indians, the Piedes in particular, who were considered by many to be "the most degraded set of Indians in the Territory." Large numbers of the docile Piedes and Paiutes were taken into Mormon homes and raised as adopted children. Others worked on farms for food. Still others planted seeds given to them by the settlers, who were gratified by the native farmers' success.[29] Setting the example from the earliest period of settlement, Young and several of the church's apostles themselves raised such children, called "tame Indians" among the Saints. Wilford Woodruff, for example, "raised two of them nearly from Childhood up," but explained that they were "vary uncertain help," and "made me a good deal of trouble."[30] One of Young's Indian girls, Sally, by the time of the Black Hawk War had married Kanosh, thus helping cement an important union between the two leaders.[31]

By 1865 Kanosh was second in authority to Sowiette and was expected by whites to succeed the aged leader as head chief of the Northern Utes.[32] Partially a result of his connections with the Paiutes and Piedes, Kanosh's long-term response to Mormonism was far more like that of these humble tribesmen than was that of any other Northern Ute leader. Described as a "devout Mormon," by the time of the Black Hawk War Kanosh dressed like a Saint, wore his hair like a Saint, prayed and farmed like a Saint, and lived with Young's Indian daughter Sally (and other plural wives) in a house his white benefactors had built for him.[33] Since he was heir apparent to the faltering Sowiette, it is not surprising that the "cheerful acquiescence" of Kanosh would create a breach among the more militant Utes into which Black Hawk would step.[34] It is equally unsurprising that the Mormons would use Kanosh and other "tame Indians" against Black Hawk and other warlike leaders.

The portion of the Territory of Utah possessed by the Navajos was small; they occupied lands east of the Colorado River and south of the

---

[29] Carvalho, *Incidents of Travel*, 213, 223–24; *RSI*, 1857:598.

[30] Woodruff, *Journal*, 6:436–37.

[31] Gottfredson, *Indian Depredations*, 15–18, 272; Solomon Kimball, "Our Pioneer Boys," 734–36; and DUP, *Heart Throbs*, 1:108–15.

[32] *RSI*, 1865:313.

[33] Codman, *Round Trip*, 246; "Minutes [1853–57]," vol. 1, Edyth Romney Typescripts, b24; Gottfredson, *Indian Depredations*, 274; DUP, *Treasures of Pioneer History*, 4:28, 164; and *RSI*, 1865:313.

[34] *RSI*, 1865:313.

San Juan River. Mormons described the Navajos as large, healthy, and "fat" Indians. Their lifestyle, culture, and language had little in common with those of the Utes and Shoshonis. Settlers observed that they had "ranches" where they tended sheep and goats and raised gardens of beans, corn, and squash and cultivated thousands of peach trees. As a result, the Navajos were much less mobile than the Utes. The Navajos, it is believed, picked up this more sedentary lifestyle from Pueblo Indians, especially the Hopis, and from the Spanish and Mexicans, all of whom they had intermarried and traded with for generations. Just prior to the Black Hawk War, however, federal military incursions against the Navajos nearly destroyed their way of life and sent hundreds of them north towards the expanding southern border of the Latter-day Saints, naturally pulling some of them into the sphere of Black Hawk's influence.

In 1860 the powerful Navajo chiefs Manuelito and Barboncito, both of whom were later drawn into the Black Hawk War, commenced a war with the Americans by attacking Fort Defiance in northwestern New Mexico. In 1862 General James Carleton, commander of U.S. troops in New Mexico, having repulsed invading Texans in a series of Civil War skirmishes, turned his attention to the Navajos, who for generations had been raiding the former Spanish and Mexican colony. Employing the famous explorer and trapper Kit Carson, General Carleton directed the total destruction of hundreds of Navajo ranchos, farms, and orchards, as well as the rounding up and forced march of thousands of Navajos in the infamous "Navajo Long Walk" to the Bosque Redondo reservation at Fort Sumner on the Pecos River in eastern New Mexico. By 1864 most of the Navajos had been confined to the reservation, including Barboncito's band. Manuelito and others, however, refused to submit, and they were forced by the starvation resulting from Carson's destruction of their herds, farms, and orchards, as well as his constant incursions against them, to cross the Colorado River and join Black Hawk's raiders in plundering Mormons. Barboncito and his band eventually fled the appalling conditions of Carleton's reservation and along with his brother Spanshanks and hundreds of others joined Manuelito in raids on the Mormons.[35]

    [35] Lund and Lund, *Pulsipher Family*, 58; Underhill, *The Navajos*; McPherson, *Northern Navajo Frontier*; Sundberg, *Dinetah*, especially 13–14, 31–33, 38, 59–79; Loh, *Lords of the Earth*, especially 99–127; Roessel, "Navajo History"; Lawrence Kelly, *Navajo Roundup*; and Trafzer, *Carson Campaign*.

Northern Ute Political Structure and Lifeways

The best-informed whites estimated that at the time of the Black Hawk War the Northern Utes, Paiutes, Piedes, Goshutes, and Weber Utes were dispersed in "two or three hundred" constantly changing bands. These loosely organized bodies varied in size from "half a dozen" individuals to "two or three score" families and were kept in a constant state of flux as they came together or divided based on the abundance and accessibility of food sources at particular times in the year.[36] Hence, whites observed that Ute bands were in no way "permanent organizations." Indeed, they noticed that bands often split up over disagreements the European mind considered "very trivial" and that virtually any man could "become a chief" so long as he could convince even a handful of individuals to submit to his authority. Thus, whites noted that those they called "the legitimate aristocracy" were often challenged by others who gained power and influence by "being successful in stealing."[37]

Following ancestral practices going back generations and probably centuries before white contact, leaders of the various Ute bands demonstrated differing levels of allegiance to a complicated and dynamic political system nominally ruled by a head chief and a hierarchy of subchiefs.[38] At the opening of the Black Hawk War in 1865, this tribal system was still intact but was well on its way to disintegration as a result of European settlement. By the time the war closed in 1872, it had effectively ceased to exist, the "great chiefs" having "lost their power in the presence of white men."[39] In 1865 Sowiette was still head chief of what can be termed the Northern Ute tribe, a multiband confederation including major groups led by Kanosh, Tabby, Antero, Sanpitch, White-eye, Joe, An-kar-tewets, Mountain (Black Hawk's brother), and one band led by Sowiette himself with the help of his son Toquana.[40]

---

[36] John Wesley Powell, "Indian Life," 6–7; and idem, "Government," 1, in "Life and Culture of the Ute." For technical ethnohistorical analyses of the Utes see Jorgensen, "Ethnohistory of the Northern Ute"; Anne Smith, *Ethnology of the Northern Utes*; and Callaway et al., "Ute," 336–67.

[37] John Wesley Powell, "Government"; and Brigham Young to Luke Lea, 13 August 1851.

[38] John Wesley Powell, "Government," 3–4.

[39] *RSI*, 1873:8.

[40] It will be remembered that Joe, An-kar-tewets, and Toquana were present when John Lowry pulled Jake Arapeen from his horse on 9 April 1865. In January 1865 Sowiette and Toquana's band consisted of 200 people, Antero's 250, Tabby's 150, and White Eye's 300. The Sanpitches numbered about 1,000 in bands led by Joe, Sanpitch, and others. The largest

Each of these major bands was in essence a collection of smaller bands and clans that came together at various times during the year.

John Wesley Powell watched the collapsing Ute political system with great interest. An agent of the U.S. Bureau of Ethnology, Powell was not only the Utes' most astute observer (ethnologically speaking) but also the most prolific writer about them. Powell first entered Ute homelands in 1868 and spent portions of the next five years observing the Utes closely while acting as a government explorer and special agent for the Office of Indian Affairs. He observed that "the unit of political organization" among the Utes was "the family presided over by some patriarch, not always the oldest man of the family . . . but always the most powerful and most influential." Major bands under Sowiette each had an "Executive Chief, and a chief of the Council, and sometimes a War chief though usually the War chief and Executive Chief [were] one." The executive chief controlled the band's activities by directing them in their annual migrations in hunting and gathering seeds, fruits, berries, and other foodstuffs. While apparently possessing power within himself, the executive chief submitted for discussion all matters of importance to a council made up of the band's principal men; but in the end decision making was his alone.[41]

Sowiette was reportedly born near Utah Lake; his name meant "Man that picks fish from the water," though, as a result of environmental changes wrought by Mormon settlement, by 1865 he was telling whites that his name meant "Nearly Starved."[42] A very old man at the time the Black Hawk War began, Sowiette claimed to be 130 years old in 1866; when John Wesley Powell first saw him in 1869 he wrote that the ancient chief's "skin lies in wrinkles and deep folds on his limbs and body."[43] Sowiette apparently had long been head of the Northern Utes when the Mormons first arrived in 1847. In the years that followed, the old chief often raised his voice for peace and developed a deep friendship with Brigham Young, reportedly almost singlehandedly preventing war between the Latter-day Saints and his

---

Northern Ute band at the time was led by Black Hawk's brother Mountain (Quibits), whose band was made up of 500 individuals. See L.B. Kinney, Indian Agent, to O.H. Irish, Superintendent of Indian Affairs, 10 January 1865, BIA, M234, 901.

[41] John Wesley Powell, "Indian Life," 5–6, and idem, "Government," 1, 4–7.

[42] M.S. Marlenas, "Statement of M.S. Marlenas, Interpretor," 6 July 1853, BYC; and "Proceedings of a Council with the Utah Indians," 7–8 June 1865.

[43] *RSI*, 1866:123; and John Wesley Powell, "Journal," 2 July 1869.

people.[44] Representative of the limited nature of Sowiette's real power, however, Wakara and others occasionally eclipsed his authority and conducted short wars against the settlers.

By 1865 Sowiette was virtually incapacitated because of age and was unable to provide his people the kind of leadership necessary to enable them to successfully weather a time of incredible stress. Since they were generally pleased with his leadership, however, the Northern Utes determined to wait until his death to replace him.[45] In the meantime, one of Sowiette's wives and his son Toquana sought to speak for him.[46] This partial breakdown of tribal leadership is a factor of paramount importance in the Black Hawk War. As the war broke out, Sowiette, who was "exceedingly infirm," despite his desires for peace "virtually abandoned all claims to the chieftainship, so far as concerns the supervision and immediate control of his people." Indeed, as Utah's superintendent of Indian affairs summed it up, since the Northern Utes were functioning "without an efficient head chief," there was no leader powerful enough to "be held accountable for the depredations, or whose authority [could] punish the offenders."[47]

In describing the entire Ute "family of Nations," Powell noted that the daily life of the Indian was "one of much joy." Dancing, story telling, gambling, game playing, and physical sports appeared to have been almost constant activities. Despite an alarming winter mortality rate, during the warm months a Ute camp was "a scene of constant hilarity." Children built swings in trees, walked on homemade stilts, shot arrows at targets, made clay dolls, and engaged in "a great variety of athletic sports." Men and boys gambled day and night, and, among the Northern Utes, horse racing was a favorite sport. Even the women played ball and took time to gamble among themselves for beads and paint.[48]

As in most Native American societies, women did the bulk of the work around camp. When the men returned from hunting, the women

---

[44] For example, see Sidwell, "Reminiscences of Early Manti"; and Jennie J.[?], "Sowiette's Noble Act," 748–49.

[45] *RSI*, 1868:610.

[46] John Wesley Powell, "Journal," 2 July 1869.

[47] *RSI*, 1866:123, and 1868:610.

[48] John Wesley Powell, "Indian Life," 23–25, and "Games and Amusements," both in "Life and Culture of the Ute"; and Huntington, *Vocabulary*, 30. One Mormon wrote that the Utes "are great gamblers, often staking their all on the result of a single game." J.R.F.[?], "Utah Indian Tribes."

not only unloaded the game but also unsaddled the horses. The men reportedly then did "nothing more until the meat [was] gone, when the woman brings up the horse, saddles him, and he goes on the hunt [again]."[49] Women (especially married women) were responsible for all such tasks as cooking, curing meat and hides, making clothing, moving camp, tending children, collecting firewood, and gathering foods in the form of seeds, berries, roots, insects, and small reptiles. As a result, the joyful life described above was to a large degree over when a Ute woman married. In a less-than-tactful passage, Powell wrote that "when she becomes a wife she is soon broken down with the pains of motherhood and the heavy labors which fall to her lot, and she becomes wringled [*sic*] and ugly, garrulous, cross, scolding, in fact an old hag." Despite the overworked nature of their lives, Ute women treated their children "with great tenderness" and impressed Powell to write that "the love of a mother for her child is not greater among any people."[50]

The Utes were an extremely mobile people, forced by the rather harsh environment in which they lived to almost constantly be on the move in search of sustenance, firewood, and, in the case of the Northern Utes, pasturage for horses. A Navajo child who was captured and sold as a slave to Tabby's band later characterized the extent of Northern Ute mobility when she stated that the Uinta Utes were "always moving." "They would have dance and move," she said, "then they would have another dance. Pretty soon they would have a dance and move again."[51] Directed in their wanderings by their chiefs, Ute bands usually moved in "grand circuits" based on seasonal hunting and root, seed, and berry harvesting. So important was sustenance-driven migration to their existence that its direction was not only the main duty of the chief but also the determining factor in *who* the chief was and *whether* he retained his position.[52] Hence, Black Hawk's windfall of 125 head of cattle in his first raid transformed him overnight into an incredibly important leader among his people; and, as literally thousands of animals were run off by his warriors over the next three years, his importance increased dramatically.

The very identity of individuals and bands was based upon their

[49] Huntington, *Vocabulary*, 30.
[50] John Wesley Powell, "Indian Life," 42–43.
[51] "The Squaw Man."
[52] John Wesley Powell, "Migration," 1–3, in "Life and Culture of the Ute."

hereditary connections to specific geographic localities. The entire territory occupied by the Utes was subdivided into districts defined by natural landmarks, and clans originating in an area took its name as their own. Thus, Uinta Utes belonged to the Uinta Valley; Yampa Utes to the area near the Yampa River; the Timpanogos Utes to the Timpanogos Valley (Utah Valley); and so forth. "An Indian will never ask to what nation or tribe or body of people another Indian belongs," Powell noted, "but to what land do you belong and how [is your] land named." Bands desiring to hunt or gather on the land of other Utes could generally obtain permission, and friendly cooperation usually characterized relations between bands, although deadly feuds sometimes sprang up as result of migration or land-use disputes.[53] In fact, one of Sowiette's functions as head chief was to preside over "general councils," where land use and migration were coordinated.[54] As has been emphasized, however, the Northern Utes traveled well beyond their clan lands, and in fact they frequently left their own tribal territory for reasons of trade, hunting, and warfare, ranging from California to the Great Plains and from Montana to Mexico.[55]

Described as "a wandering people,"[56] the Utes based their entire lifestyle on their mobility. The shelters of the Paiutes and Piedes were simply brush wickiups created by inserting brush and branches into the ground in a circle, the leaves arching over the top forming a rude covering which was little more than a windbreak. When these groups moved, they simply walked away, constructing new shelters at their next camp.[57] The Northern Utes, long exposed to the horse and gun culture of the Plains Indians, used tepees made of elk and buffalo hides or of canvas provided by government agents. During the summer months they also constructed wickiups and boweries to shade themselves from the sun. A Northern Ute band could completely pitch or strike camp in a matter of minutes. Pack horses were loaded with what were described as "immense" burdens of buffalo robes and other gear,

---

[53] John Wesley Powell, "Indian Life," 7–8. Mormon settlement on Ute lands seriously disrupted this system.

[54] *RSI*, 1873:411.

[55] For these purposes Utes frequented the lands of the Sioux, Shoshoni, Arapaho, Cheyenne, Crow, Apache, Hopi, Navajo, and others. For examples see Bean, *Autobiography*, 70, 98, 105; Sonne, *World of Wakara*, 170, 184; and Brigham Madsen, *Exploring the Great Salt Lake*, 263.

[56] *RSI*, 1865:189.

[57] John Wesley Powell, "Home," in "Life and Culture of the Ute."

and lodge poles were dragged behind, making wide trails that were used year after year. Interestingly, these "lodge pole trails" were used as highways of invasion by Mormon settlers.[58]

Utah's severe winters prohibited any migration during the coldest months, and the happy camp life of summer was transformed into quite another scene. "During the inclement season," Powell wrote, "children huddle about the fire, coughs are prevalent, their eyes water, noses constantly running and altogether they present an appearance most abject and miserable."[59] Indicating the impact Utah winters had on Ute mortality rates, Brigham Young once stated that "if you give an indian plenty of beef, and keep him from freezing he will live to be 150 years old; there is nothing to kill them unless they freeze to death."[60]

Ute society was supported by an elaborate system of mythology based on stories of gods and demons governing virtually all facets of everyday life. The chief of the council usually was responsible for the perpetuation of this mythology. The Nar-i-gwi-nup, as these bards were called, whiled away long winter evenings with the entire band gathered around bonfires relating stories of the wonderful deeds of animals, birds, reptiles, fish, and insects. As the legends were told, the older members of the band acted them out, providing dialogue and action, mimicking the passions and emotions of the gods. Huddled closely around the fire, according to John Wesley Powell,

> all of the people listen and observe intently, laughing at the tricks of the gods and cheering at their triumphs until the rocks of the mountain region echo their shrill laughter, and wild shouts. But this is not all sport to them, for ever and anon their venerable Nar-i-gwi-nup stops to impress a moral, or implant a proverb, or teach a lesson; and when the young hunter goes out next day into the wilds he ponders on the doings of the gods, and the children tell the stories to each other and have their mimic religious plays.[61]

Powell took this body of stories to be the foundation of Ute society and was convinced it constituted their law. Indeed, he called it their "Bible." Explaining its impact on Ute society, he observed that the

---

[58] John Wesley Powell, "Migration," and "Home."

[59] John Wesley Powell, "Games and Amusements," 3.

[60] "Instructions by Pres. B. Young, Sunday, May 4, 1856," in "Minutes [1853–1857]," vol. 1.

[61] John Wesley Powell, "Religion of the Utes," especially 16–20, in "Life and Culture of the Ute."

Utes were free politically and socially "beyond the conception of the dreamiest philosopher" but were simultaneously "in a state of almost abject slavery to rules and regulations derived from their mythology." For example, "no one must whistle after sunset for SHIN-AU'-AV told his son not to open his mouth after the orb of day had gone down lest an U-NU'-PITS or evil spirit should enter therein."[62]

Few contemporary whites recognized the role Ute religion played in the events that started the Black Hawk War, and fewer still acknowledged its impact on the war's continuation. It is certain, however, that religion influenced the thought and action of the Utes at least as much as it did the actions and beliefs of the Latter-day Saints, and probably much more so. Since the Utes left no records, we must rely on the scant (and undoubtedly skewed) accounts left by whites to give us incomplete but significant insights into these religious notions that encouraged the Utes to commence and continue hostilities.

The Utes believed that air, rocks, water, and plants were inhabited by spirits. The afterlife was reached by way of a gloomy passage filled with ghostly demons and "horrid growlings" made by "monster" birds and animals.[63] While the Indians believed in no single almighty supreme being, "Shenob," a Satan figure, was a focus of worship and was served through fear. They believed in sorcery and witchcraft and that there was some kind of mystical (and deadly) charm in writing and drawing pictures. Pictographs and petroglyphs made by earlier native inhabitants of the area often terrified them, as did drawings and writings in books. For related reasons many were horrified of cameras and photography in general. Contemporary whites repeatedly referred to the Indians' conviction that Mormons caused Indian deaths simply by writing their names on paper.[64]

---

[62] John Wesley Powell, "Indian Life," 55.

[63] John Wesley Powell, "Religion of the Utes," 27, "Na-gun'-to-wip the Home of Departed Spirits," 1–2, "Indian Life," 46, and loose page numbered "8" directly following 51, all in "Life and Culture of the Ute."

[64] Dimick Huntington wrote that the Utes "were very much afraid of witches and crazy people, and believe in making medicine on paper to kill people." Huntington, *Vocabulary*, 30. Another settler wrote: "The Indians are superstitious and believe there is some kind of charm about writing and making pictures. They also believe in Satan (Shin-nob) who is always bent on doing harm, that he delights in seeing people do wrong. They do not serve God, because he is good and will not harm any thing; but they serve Satan through fear. . . . They believe that the white people can write to him and he will cause sickness or trouble to come onto others. And should you write the name of an Indian on a slip of paper and tell him that you was going to send it to Lucifer, the Indian would risk his life, if necessary to get possession of it." Gottfredson, *Indian Depredations*, 321–24. See also Bishop, "Journal," 178–79.

Among the Utes, disease was not understood to be a condition of the body; rather, it was seen as "an entity" which took "possession of the person" to do him harm. The sick were treated by shamans, who employed incantations, singing, and painful exorcisms which included steam treatments, kicking, beating, and scarification performed with special obsidian knives and red-hot coals.[65] Such exorcisms failed to save Indians encamped in and near Sanpete Valley who apparently died in large numbers from measles and other maladies during the winter of 1864–65. As a result, survivors accused the Mormons of sending death by writing Indian names to Shenob. According to some contemporaries, Black Hawk himself lost "wives and children" to the "evil diseases"; "burning for revenge," he incited the Indians to war upon the whites to placate the wicked god.[66]

The Utes were visionary people who sought direction in dreams and omens. Black Hawk himself was reportedly some kind of seer or prophetic dreamer. When he later made peace with the settlers, he allegedly informed them that from his youth his dead ancestors had come to him declaring the message: "Go-ahead-and fight-fight, kill-kill; Mormon cattle his cattle." Black Hawk's chief lieutenant, a Shiberetch Ute named Tamaritz, after having a horse shot out from under him in one of the war's most intense battles changed his name to "Shenavegan" (also "She-Na-Ba-Wiken" and "Chenowicket" in the sources), which meant "Saved by Almighty Power." Shenavegan continued fighting even after Black Hawk made peace, and reportedly ceased hostilities only when he was given "back his heart" in a vision that lasted three days and nights.[67] A dimension of history unattainable through the white record, this intriguing aspect of Ute motivation is in great part lost forever, although its shadow can be seen throughout the conflict.

Powell declared that "by his religious belief and by all the habits, customs, and superstitions of the race the [Ute] is urged to stealthy warfare." Howard Stansbury believed the Utes were more "warlike" than the Snakes, Sioux, Cheyenne, and Crow. Lieutenant John Gunnison was impressed that while the different bands of Utahs waged "eternal national war with the Shoshones," they still found time to

---

[65] John Wesley Powell, "Treatment of the Sick," in "Life and Culture of the Ute"; and Gottfredson, *Indian Depredations*, 335.

[66] Day, "History of Eli A. Day," 10.

[67] Rogerson, "Ending of the Black Hawk War," 3; Codman, *Round Trip*, 245; and Sloan, "White Horse Chief," 379.

"frequently [be] at war with each other."[68] To die in battle was to lose the right to live in "the loveliest portion" of the afterworld. The coward, however, forfeited his right to the world of spirits altogether. It was the brave man who wisely kept his life who obtained eternal happiness. Battle scars were badges of honor, and Wakara often displayed his, proudly stating that though he had fought the formidable "Sioux, the Snakes, the Arapahoes, and Cheyennes, and the Crow" his "scars were all in front, and not on his back."[69]

Notions of vengeance required the Utes to "fall upon the first possible [white person] after losing a friend" to "accompany the spirits of their dead and wait upon them" in the world of spirits. While the lives of Utes killed making raids solely for the purpose of stealing were not avenged, blood-for-blood retaliation was required when innocents were killed. Goods paid to the next of kin by offenders, however, could avenge the deceased without bloodshed if accepted by the injured family or band.[70] When innocent Indians were killed by way of reprisal shortly after Black Hawk's initial raid, Mormons effectively plunged themselves into a war of vengeance that was almost impossible to stop.[71]

In times of war the Utes artfully painted themselves with bright colors and fastened feathers to their hair as well as to the breechcloth strings they tied around their greased and nearly naked bodies. They "gorgeously decorated" their weapons, saddles, and bridles and similarly adorned their mounts with paint and ornaments. By 1865 many Northern Utes had owned "rifles of the first quality" for decades and in fact were generally better armed than their white counterparts. Despite their possession of and excellent ability to use guns, more traditional weapons such as bows and arrows, lances, war clubs, and tomahawks were also used during the Black Hawk War. "The best bows" were made of the horn of the mountain sheep. Black Hawk himself carried such a bow, which was "3 feet long" with arrows "barbed with iron."

---

[68] John Wesley Powell, "Religion of the Utes," 23–25; Brigham Madsen, *Exploring the Great Salt Lake*, 619; and Gunnison, *The Mormons*, 150. See also Winkler, "Ute Mode of War."

[69] John Wesley Powell, "Religion of the Utes," 23–25; Carvalho, *Incidents of Travel*, 190; and Bean, *Autobiography*, 98.

[70] Brigham Madsen, *Exploring the Great Salt Lake*, 263; John Wesley Powell, "Religion of the Utes," 23–25; Gottfredson, *Indian Depredations*, 26; and Dimick Huntington to E.S. Parker, 20 December 1870, BIA, M234, 902.

[71] George A. Smith to Orson Hyde, 22 October 1865, HOLB, 2:506–9; and "Proceedings of a Council with the Utah Indians."

Arrows were also commonly tipped with flint and obsidian heads and were sometimes dipped in a poison concoction made from rattlesnake venom to make them even more deadly. "Spearmen" carried lances "about ten feet long" decorated with eagle feathers and sometimes scalps. Utes also often carried beautifully decorated shields.[72]

Eveline Alexander, the wife of a gentile army officer, visited a camp of over a thousand Utes in southern Colorado in 1866, among whom were some of Black Hawk's raiders and perhaps even the war chief himself. She left this vivid description of their dress, weaponry, and war accouterments:

> . . . then came the Indians whooping to their ponies as they went, dressed in buckskin, bright blankets, gay beads, and feathers, their bows and arrows slung on their backs behind, encased in horse-skin, and their rifles in front.
>
> When we got to their village we found about a thousand wild Indians encamped there. They did not have skin wigwams like the Prairie Indians, but their wigwams were of drilling and looked like Sibley tents (which in fact were copied from these wigwams). In front of the warriors' tents were stuck up their spears, orna-mented with eagles' feathers and with their painted shields and head ornaments of feathers hanging on them. . . . I secured quite a valuable trophy . . . an Indian war shield. . . . General Carson told me the Indians valued them very highly and that a shield and head gear were worth a good horse. . . . It was an uncommonly handsome one, profusely ornamented with scarlet cloth and eagles' feathers, and had a fine cover of white buckskin. . . . I [also] bought a bow and six arrows. . . . The bow is very hand-some, and the arrows are "war arrows" painted and marked with deep lines along their length.[73]

The Utes often scalped their victims and, depending on time con-straints and levels of emotion, they sometimes mutilated their bodies. Scalps were taken as trophies of war and were the center of the war dance, which was performed by men and women. This dance appar-

---

[72] "Proceedings of a Council with the Utah Indians"; J.R.F.[?], "Utah Indian Tribes," 34–35; Carvalho, *Incidents of Travel*, 190; Burton, *City of the Saints*, 131–32; Simpson, *Report of Explorations*, 51–52; Ferris, *Life in the Rocky Mountains*, 346–47; Carvalho, *Incidents of Travel*, 222–23; Henroid, "Biography," 11; and Don Carlos Johnson, "Indians of Utah Valley," 5 March and 12 March 1908.

[73] Alexander, *Cavalry Wife*, 98, 102.

ently was used both to prepare for battle and to celebrate victory and was often engaged in just before a planned attack. Prior to the victory dance, men smeared their bodies with grease mixed with colored dirt and women mounted the scalps that were taken on poles. Forming a line, the women danced back and forth to singing and drum accompaniment while they waved the scalps in the air. Meanwhile the men "jumped around" performing war antics and brandishing weapons.[74]

It is important to emphasize the role raiding, and horse theft in particular, played as motivation for war, and, more importantly, as the chief means of making war. White observers made it patently clear that stock theft and war were virtually one and the same for the Utes. Gentile military officer William Waters, for example, who encountered a Ute war party going out against the Arapahos, wrote that their incursion amounted to little more than "a grand stealing expedition."[75] Another wrote, like other Indians in the region, the Utes "very seldom commit murder; but they consider theft one of the greatest human virtues, and no one is thought to be at all accomplished unless he can steal with adroitness."[76] As a result, for years before the Black Hawk War it was widely known throughout the West that "the Utahs are *very expert* horse-thieves" and generally killed whites only when necessary to the success of a stock raid.[77] With very few exceptions, the whites killed during the Black Hawk War were killed while a raid was in progress or while trying to retake stock the Indians had already stolen.

As has been pointed out, religion played a major role in Ute notions of warfare, and, like that of the Latter-day Saints, Ute religion justified in certain prescribed cases the taking of human life. "Walker will not kill a white man, nor go on a stealing expedition to California until he offers sacrifices to his God, then he thinks he is doing right," wrote Brigham Young during a lull in the Walker War in 1853. "The reason he has not done more in his war on the southern settlements," Young continued, "is because he could get no answer from his God." Since war was thus a religious act, to be a war chief was also to function in a certain prophetic role, which Black Hawk certainly did.[78]

---

[74] Ibid.; J. R. F.[?], "Utah Indian Tribes," 34–35; Sidwell, "Reminiscences of Early Manti," 6; Ronald Walker, "Gunnison Massacre," 153; and "The Squaw Man."

[75] Waters, *Life Among the Mormons*, 44.

[76] Davis, *El Gringo*, 412.

[77] *Los Angeles Star*, 25 December 1852, as quoted in Sonne, *World of Wakara*, 150. Italics mine.

[78] Brigham Young, as quoted in Sonne, *World of Wakara*, 180; and Rogerson, "Ending of the Black Hawk War," 3.

The extent and frequency of raiding was often commensurate with a perceived injustice committed by an enemy, and grievances sometimes were contrived to justify theft under the guise of war. Once justified, as Powell said, "by his religious belief and by all the habits, customs, and superstitions of the race," the Ute engaged in a "stealthy warfare" that was characterized both by indefatigable movement and energy as well as by a careful resolve not to expose himself to undue danger.[79] Thus, the Utes did not "count coup" as many Plains Indians did to demonstrate their courage.

Writing of Wakara's warfare, Gwinn Harris Heap wrote in 1854,

> Having an unlimited supply of fine horses, and being inured to every fatigue and privation, he keeps the territories of New Mexico and Utah, the provinces of Chihuahua and Sonora and the southern portions of California, in constant alarm. His movements are so rapid, and his plans so skillfully and so secretly laid, that he has never once failed in any enterprise, and has scarcely disappeared from one district before he is heard of in another. He frequently divides his men into two or more bands, which, making their appearance at different points at the same time, each headed, it is given out, by the dreaded Walkah [*sic*] in person, has given him with the ignorant Mexicans, the attribute of ubiquity."[80]

This "attribute of ubiquity," as we shall see, also characterized Black Hawk, who followed traditional Ute customs of warfare, "dividing his men" and keeping the Mormons in "constant alarm." Similarly, he modeled Wakara's tactic of rapid movement and laid out his plans with an eye to minimizing the danger to his men while they drove off thousands of horses and cattle.

Other Factors Contributing to the Outbreak of the Black Hawk War

From its very beginning, most Mormons blamed John Lowry for starting the Black Hawk War merely by pulling Jake Arapeen from his horse in a drunken rage. The Utes, however, did not hold this simplistic view. At a peace council held by Apostle Orson Hyde in 1868 the Utes emphatically declared that Lowry "was *not* the cause of the recent

---

[79] John Wesley Powell, "Religion of the Utes," 24.
[80] Heap, *Central Route to the Pacific*, 92.

Indian war." "So clearly was he exonnerated by the Indians" that Hyde felt obliged to announce the fact to local congregations "as a simple act of justice to Lowery [*sic*]."[81] Such disclaimers had little impact, however, and the Manti interpreter lived the rest of his life under the bane of accusation, all the while bearing (in his own words) "the stigma" of precipitating the Black Hawk War. Always quick to defend himself, Lowry ultimately swore out an official denial of guilt. The altercation in Manti "showed their hand," he wrote, "but the trouble would have come just the same."[82]

As early as the second week after Lowry pulled Jake Arapeen from his horse, Orson Hyde was told by Sanpete Valley Indians that they knew about the impending outbreak of hostilities "six weeks before it took place." Referring to Lowry's quarrel with Jake, Hyde wrote that the event obviously "did not load the gun, but might have been the match put to fire it off."[83] Informed Mormons and gentiles generally felt that Black Hawk and Jake came to Manti on 9 April 1865 seeking a "pretext" for war, as the Utes were loath to commence hostilities without first suffering some symbolic injustice, which Lowry quickly provided.[84] Whatever the meaning of the Lowry-Arapeen scuffle, it is clear that an exceedingly complex group of relationships and events involving Indians, Mormons, and gentiles set the stage for war. The remainder of this chapter examines them further.

The Mormons

The first company of Mormon pioneers began settling the Salt Lake Valley in 1847. Fleeing religious persecution in Nauvoo, Illinois, the Latter-day Saints hoped they were leaving the nation that had despoiled them and killed their prophet. In 1848, however, the conclusion of the Mexican War and the Treaty of Guadalupe Hidalgo placed the lands on which they settled in the possession of the United States. Mountain men and traders had long operated in what became the boundaries of the Territory of Utah, but with the Mormons came the first permanent white settlement. With every passing year, thousands of emigrants made their way to "Zion" in wagons, pulling handcarts,

[81] Robert L. Campbell to George A. Smith, 29 November 1868, GAS. Italics mine.
[82] Gottfredson, *Indian Depredations,* 335–38.
[83] Orson Hyde to Brigham Young, 23 April 1865, BYC.
[84] Ibid.; Gottfredson, *Indian Depredations,* 335–38; Andrew Madsen, "Personal History," 51; Kane, *Twelve Mormon Homes,* 35; and Brigham Young to Tabby, Sowiette, Toquer-ona, Jim, Joe and Anthoro, 18 May 1866.

or simply walking. Brigham Young viewed it as providential that the Latter-day Saints had been cast deep into Indian country where living among the Lamanites would facilitate their conversion as prophesied in the Book of Mormon. "The Lord could not have Devised a Better plan," he rejoiced, "than to have put us whare [*sic*] we are in order to accomplish this thing."[85]

Initially Mormons found little opposition to their presence expressed by the Indians of Utah. Shoshonis and Utes, at first oblivious to what it would mean for their collective futures, were happy for the trading opportunities settlement afforded. The Saints, however, had no intention of maintaining a weak colony or two to provide trading opportunities for Indians. Led by colonizer par excellence Brigham Young, they had in mind a "kingdom" that they were sure would expand to fill not only the Salt Lake Valley and adjacent country but eventually swallow up the Intermountain West, the continent, and ultimately the whole world.

Brigham Young had a systematic plan for colonization that was unparalleled in American history. From 1847 to his death in 1877 he personally planned and supervised the establishment of over three hundred settlements extending from Idaho to southern California. This system of settlement was supported by a well-organized proselytizing program, which enjoyed great success in Great Britain and Scandinavia, particularly in England and Denmark. Thousands upon thousands of foreign emigrants and American converts made their way to Zion using the Perpetual Emigration Fund, which allowed them to come to Utah with capital provided by the church, which they were to pay back later. By the beginning of the Black Hawk War, at least 58,000 Latter-day Saint converts had come to the territory in officially organized church emigrant trains. Perhaps as many more came on their own. Less than 20,000, however, made their homes in Salt Lake City; the majority were "called" to settle in outlying areas in order to "build up the Kingdom." By 1865 the Indians of Utah were probably outnumbered at a ratio of at least ten to one.[86]

---

[85] Woodruff, *Journal*, 4:25.

[86] Church Emigration Book; and Brigham Young to R.J. Moore, 13 February 1867, BYC. Because of the "bitter political controversies" existing between Mormons and many citizens and officials throughout the rest of the nation, Sir Richard Burton (who visited Salt Lake City in 1860) found it "impossible to arrive at a true estimate" of the white population. Complaining "the census is a purely party measure," he explained: "The Mormons, desiring to show the 100,000 persons which entitle them to claim admission as a State into the Union, are naturally disposed to exaggerate their numbers; they are of course accused of 'cooking up' schedules, of

Young's policy was to establish settlements on all rivers and streams throughout a tremendously large area and, by thus gaining control of important water resources in a semiarid region, he hoped to keep gentiles out and establish a huge empire where his people could practice their religion in peace. Unfortunately for the Indians, however, the very spots where Young placed settlements, often rich alluvial plains where rivers exited canyons, were the most productive components of the ecosystems upon which they depended for subsistence.

Almost overnight Mormon settlement transformed self-sufficient Indian groups into semidependent wards of the new society. As the territory's first superintendent of Indian affairs, Brigham Young showed sincere interest in the welfare of the Indians and from the beginning employed the maxim "It is cheaper to feed the Indians than fight them." Most of his people, however, were themselves struggling to subsist. In the months before the Black Hawk War, some settlements came dangerously near to exhausting their own food supplies and were in no position to provide for the Indians.[87] Stress created by the "cheaper to feed than fight" proposition was a source of constant tension between the two groups.

In the mid-1850s Superintendent of Indian Affairs Brigham Young established a number of small reservations called "Indian farms" near certain Mormon villages, including one in the Sanpete Valley not far from Manti. It was from there that Black Hawk would later launch his first raid. The farms were established as "near as practicible" to the settlements in order that the Indians might "raise their own food," "learn civilized habbits and [be taught] the gospel of Christ." The farms, however, simply drew hungry Indians to the settlements, and by 1860, with Young no longer in charge of the Utah superintendency, his "agricultural experiment" had been abandoned. The farms became "reservations" that were little more than campgrounds that Indians were allowed to use while visiting the settlements. Meanwhile, hundreds of Indians died of starvation.[88]

In their famished condition the Indians were especially susceptible

---

counting cattle as souls, . . . On the other hand, the anti-Mormons are as naturally inclined to underestimate. . . . The nearest approach to truth will probably be met by assuming the two opposite extremes, and by 'splitting the difference.'" Burton, *City of the Saints*, 325–27.

[87] Erastus Snow to Brigham Young, 19 June and 7 November 1864, and 11 April and 8 May 1865, BYC.

[88] "Gunnison Ward Record," 9; and Beeton, "An Experiment with Indian Farms."

to disease, and at the time of the outbreak of the war native populations were undergoing terrifying changes. In 1860 one Sanpete settler reported that "the aborigines in this part of the Territory seem to be wasting away very fast, and the band . . . has dwindled down to a mere handful of warriors."[89] The Indians themselves estimated that half their offspring died in infancy and that scarcely one-fourth reached maturity. While tribesmen of all ages succumbed to measles and smallpox, the most common diseases among adults were "scrofulous and syphilitic" in character. As early as 1861, Indian agent Jesse Bishop prognosticated that if something was not done to help the Indians, "the Gonorrhea or Clap," which was "almost universal" among them, would cause the Utes to "entirely disappear."[90]

As previously noted, by 1864 the Utes blamed the settlers for the diseases that had come upon them. They also were aware that the whites had taken their most productive lands and demanded payment in return. This, however, most Latter-day Saints refused to comply with. Hospitable themselves to whites who came hungry to their camps, the Utes expected no less of their neighbors, and often begged door to door. White women and children often were frightened to tears by natives pressing faces against windowpanes and looking in without warning. Hungry Utes often raided vegetable gardens, granaries, and smokehouses and sometimes forcibly entered homes and demanded food.[91] Repeatedly instructed by their leaders to feed the Indians, the settlers did make significant efforts to share. Manti, for example, reportedly expended $250,000 in fifteen years of feeding Indians.[92] While the figure is certainly a gross exaggeration, it does represent the fact that the settlers felt that feeding hungry Indians was a huge drain on their resources. It is certain, though, that in frontier communities where whites at times actually went hungry themselves, contributions to native neighbors were nowhere near enough.

Mormon records make it clear that begging put individuals from both cultures in situations that sometimes erupted into violence. A whole genre of folk stories sprang up among the settlers recounting how "helpless" white women chased "warriors" from their homes with

[89] JH, 22 January 1860, 1.
[90] *RSI*, 1867:175; and Jesse Bishop to Benjamin Davies, 16 January 1861, BIA, M234, 900.
[91] "Proceedings of a Council with the Utah Indians, especially 29–31."
[92] JH, 18 February 1865, 1.

rolling pins, brooms, red-hot pans, and fire pokers.[93] Frustrated Saints complained that it took "the patience of Job" to put up with Indian demands, "especially when it was about all they could do to live and support their own families."[94] Others felt that patience for Indian beggars was not a virtue. Indeed, John Lowry wrote:

> in those early days it was at times imperative that harsh measures should be used. . . . I threw an Indian out of my house and kicked him off the place, . . . We had to do these things, or be run over by them. It was a question of supremacy between the white man and the Indian.[95]

While Mormon sources record numerous incidents of kindness and restraint manifested towards the Indians, accounts of the dispensing of the kind of "harsh measures" Lowry referred to show up even more frequently. It is certain such treatment and the racism that provoked it figured significantly in bringing on the war. In fact, it is probable that as Black Hawk watched John Lowry assault Jake Arapeen, his own face still bore the marks of a Mormon "laying on of hands" he had recently received. Reportedly, about a week before the altercation in Manti, Black Hawk rashly pointed his rifle at a Sister Halliday for spooking his horse as she swept dust from her house with a broom. Bounding through the door, Halliday's husband jerked Black Hawk from his horse and allegedly pummeled the Indian's face with the heel of his boot. After "beating him good and plenty," "Brother Halliday" allowed the chief to leave.[96]

Another story was told about a similar beating Black Hawk allegedly received shortly before the commencement of the war. Black Hawk was said to have broken into the farmhouse at the Spanish Fork Indian Farm and helped himself to supplies and a brass bucket. Pursued and captured by several settlers, including one named Berry (whose sons were later killed in the Black Hawk War's Berry Massacre and whose stock was specifically targeted), Black Hawk was struck over the head with the stolen bucket. According to this story, he had been "a good Indian" up to this point, but reportedly "rode away with hatred for the

---

[93] For examples see Jacob Beacham, Pioneer Personal History Questionnaire, UWPA Historical Records Survey; and Morley, "Daniel & Amanda Henrie," 16.

[94] Wells, "Narrative," 132.

[95] Gottfredson, *Indian Depredations*, 338.

[96] Milas Johnson, Autobiography, 8.

whites in his heart to stir up strife among the Indians." From that time forth, it continued, "wherever he went, his name was known for cruelty and terror; behind him were ruin and death. The Black Hawk War was on!"[97]

Whether or not these stories in all their details are true, they demonstrate attitudes and actions that many Mormons were ashamed of, especially considering their beliefs concerning their responsibilities to the Lamanites. One Latter-day Saint described in his journal the murder of a "tame Indian" who was killed by her native husband in Gunnison as she attempted to rejoin her white family after the commencement of the Black Hawk War. Her body was treated by settlers as though the woman was nothing more than an animal; a chain was fastened about her neck and her body dragged "behind a wagon out to some place in the brush," where it was "deposited" in "some hole without decent burial." "This disgraceful spectacle" was understandably condemned by the writer, who could not believe that his coreligionists had become so hardhearted towards the Indians.[98]

Despite such accounts, many gentile observers wrote glowing reports of Latter-day Saint–Indian relations during the period. John Codman wrote, "The management of the Utah tribes by the Mormon government while it had supreme control, was greatly to its credit." The church, he continued, "imitated the humane policy of the Pennsylvania Quakers, rather than such a war of extermination as is advocated by Phil Sheridan."[99] Sir Richard Burton wrote that "the Mormons treat their step-brethren with far more humanity than other western men; they feed, clothe, and lodge them, and attach them by good works to their interests."[100] "For one thing," wrote Phil Robinson, "the Mormons are looked upon by the Indians in quite a different light [than] other Americans, for they consider them to be victims, like themselves, of Federal dislike, while both as individuals and a class they hold them in consideration as being superior to Agents in fidelity to engagements."[101] A California superintendent of Indian affairs passing through Utah wrote that "most" of the white families in southern Utah had "one or more Pah-Utah children," whom they had adopted and

[97] Versions of the story are found in DUP, *Heart Throbs*, 1:89–90; DUP, *Our Pioneer Heritage*, 3:423; Whitney, *History of Utah*, 4:348; and Barton, "Black Hawk War," 27.
[98] Dorcheus, "Memoirs," 29.
[99] Codman, *Mormon Country*, 53.
[100] Burton, *City of the Saints*, 268–69.
[101] Phil Robinson, *Sinners and Saints*, 163.

were raising in their homes. These "tame Indians" were "treated with kindness, and even tenderness" and were "taught to call their protectors 'father' and 'mother,' and instructed in the rudiments of education."[102]

Considering the immense Latter-day Saint emigration on the Overland Trail, one federal soldier was amazed that during "the Indian War of 1864" Mormon church trains "traveled along as if there were no such thing as Indians." "There was sort of a Masonic understanding of some kind between the Indians and the Mormons which we never understood," he reported, perplexed that the Saints "did not fear the Indians, and that the Indians never harmed a Mormon."[103]

In 1865 a California newspaper, the *Golden Era*, editorialized that "one thing speaks volumes for the Mormons. They have the friendship of all the Indian tribes between the two great ranges of mountains. The Mormons are always at peace with the race whose soil they have appropriated, while the Gentiles are at perpetual war." The paper went on to suggest that the entire "Indian problem" be turned over to Brigham Young, "giving him a certain sum to preserve peace." "Facts upset theories," the article continued, "Our clergymen preach a sublime religion, but whereever they go, there follows war, contentions and bickerings. No Christian community, with perhaps a single famous exception, has preserved the confidence and friendship of the aborigines of the country, so long as the Mormons."[104]

That same year, 1865, Orsemus Irish, Utah's new gentile superintendent of Indian affairs, found the Saints "very willing to co-operate as far as they could in . . . efforts for the relief of the Indians."[105] By that time, however, Brigham Young's Indian policy was increasingly challenged by local settlers. Within months of the outbreak of the Black Hawk War, Samuel Bowles, a visiting newspaper editor from the East, wrote that "the Mormons have exhausted the Quaker policy towards the Indians; have fed and clothed them for years, . . . but they are growing tired of it, both because it is expensive, and is not sure of success."[106] Young's policy, however, remained constant, and even after the war Elizabeth Kane wrote that "the patience of the Mormons with the

[102] Heap, *Route to the Pacific*, 91.
[103] Ware, *Indian War of 1864*, 101, 205–7, 398–99.
[104] *DN*, 8 October 1865, as copied into Manuscript History of Brigham Young, 1865:898–905.
[105] *RSI*, 1865:312.
[106] Bowles, *Across the Continent*, 69–70.

Indians surpasses anything we read of the Quakers or Moravians. You never hear the Mormon younkers boast of prowess at the savages' expense; their whole tone is different than ours."[107]

Gentiles, however, were not blind to the fact that "very often" members of the church did not follow Young's teachings. "It is true," Phil Robinson wrote, "individual Mormons have avenged the loss of a horse or a cow by taking a red man's life, but this was always in direct opposition to the teachings of the Church, which pointed out that murder in the white man was a worse offence than theft in the red, and in opposition to the policy of the leaders, who have always insisted that it was 'cheaper to feed than to fight' the Indians." Similarly, gentiles were not blind to the fact that "again and again" Mormons were compelled "to take the field" against the Indians, "but as a rule the extent of Mormon retaliation was to catch the plunderers, retake their stolen stock, hang the actual murderers (if murder had been committed) and let the remainder go after an amicable pow-wow."[108]

The "comparative fairness"[109] of the Latter-day Saints, however, was thought by many non-Mormons to be motivated by treasonous plans to use the Indians against the United States. "The humanity of the Prophet's followers to the Lamanite," wrote Sir Richard Burton, "has been distorted by Gentiles into a deep and dangerous project for 'training the Indians' to assassinate individual enemies, and if necessary to act as guerillas against the Eastern invaders."[110] Writing with some sarcasm, Jules Remy wrote of Brigham Young's Indian relations:

From the way in which he spoke of these people, of the fatherly relations he kept up with the Indians or Lamanites, there was not a syllable that could lead us to suspect he had any political object in view, so perfectly candid and disinterested did his anxiety about them appear to us to be. "They are children," he said; "we must treat them as such. We are their superiors only through the ripeness which civilization has given us; and we cannot, without forfeiting this superiority, let loose against them the avenging severity which we ought to reserve for our corrupt and apostate brethren. It was for the Indians Christ uttered this prayer: 'For-

---

[107] Kane, *Twelve Mormon Homes*, 120; and O.H. Irish to William P. Dole, Commissioner of Indian Affairs, 29 June 1865, in *RSI*, 1865:318.

[108] Phil Robinson, *Sinners and Saints*, 125–26.

[109] Ibid., 126.

[110] Burton, *City of the Saints*, 270–71.

give them, for they know not what they do.' " Noble words, well worthy of a more genuine prophet.[111]

Perhaps the most interesting example of gentile perceptions of Brigham Young's influence with Indians came from the aged artist George Catlin, a longtime observer and friend of Native Americans.[112] In 1870, after General Philip Sheridan had assumed command of "more than 5,000 miles of Indian frontiers" and had openly proclaimed that "the Indians are 'fiends'" who "must be removed by military force" or exterminated, Catlin wrote Young a truly significant letter. Catlin, who was perhaps as well informed on the views of Indians throughout all of North America as any white contemporary, said he had learned in conversations with even "remote tribes" of the "confidence" Young had gained by his "sympathies for, and kindness to" Indians. "Your people," he told the church president, "have been the friends of the poor Indians, who have now, no other efficient friends on the earth." He stated further that "the example which your people have shown to the world of Civilizing the Indians around you, is an honour to your Religion."

Having thus commended the Saints, Catlin got to the point of his letter, which embodied the prevalent gentile view of the Latter-day Saints' influence with Indians and articulated the similarly widespread contemporary belief that Brigham Young had it in his power to marshal the tribes of all of North America in a war against the federal government. Catlin suggested a "grand" Mormon-Indian alliance for their "mutual protection against the invading military forces which are entering the great Far West on every side." "I have visited nearly every tribe and remnant of the tribes now existing in North America," Catlin declared, "and if I were a younger man, I would go again to those tribes, *as your Emissary*, & show them that their deliverance from robbery and death was at hand." Offering Young his own influence with such tribes as the Cherokee, Choctaw, Creek, and Apache, as well as the Blackfoot, Crow, Sioux, and Pawnee, Catlin wrote that "the only chance" for

[111] Remy, *Journey to Great Salt Lake City*, 2:302.
[112] George Catlin to Brigham Young, 8 May 1870, BYC. Italics mine. Catlin, the famous "painter of Indians," left his Philadelphia home in 1830 with the goal of painting portraits of every Indian tribe in North America. Years of travel and portraiture took him throughout the West, and his gentle interaction with hundreds of tribes nurtured in him an intense love and concern for Native Americans. Keenly aware that they were vanishing before his eyes, Catlin hoped to preserve at least a part of their culture through his art. For further information on Catlin see Haverstock, *Indian Gallery*; and Ewers, *George Catlin: Painter of Indians and the West*.

survival of both the Indians and the Latter-day Saints lay in a pan-Indian–Mormon military alliance.[113]

Catlin's letter is far less important for what it shows us of reality than for what it reveals of contemporary gentile perceptions of that reality. Young knew the limitations of the Saints' real influence with Indians as well as anyone. Responding to Catlin's letter, Young brushed off the suggestion of a Mormon-Indian alliance and provided us a window into his soul by stating:

Notwithstanding the efforts of the Military commanders and their subordinates, who in response to the clamor of the border settlers and political demigogues [sic] of the great West, . . . make the extermination of the Indian one of their watch cries, I have no idea that they will succeed in their bloodthirsty and iniquitous designs. The "Great Spirit" has a future for the Red men, and that not in their grave, . . . but how much they may suffer, or how much they may be despoiled and wasted, before the tide of His providence turns fully in their favor is not for me to say. But I do know, and that in sorrow, that our country must answer for their bad faith, broken treaties, and great crimes in Indian matters, that they have perpetrated in the name of Christianity, civilization and progress, . . . The course the people of Utah have persued [sic] towards the Indians can be recommended not only on the score of humanity, but of economy. We *have* found it cheaper to feed than to fight them, . . . Thus we shall gain their love, and by keeping our word with them hold their respect. By this means we hope, with the help of the Lord to accomplish much good for the original owners of the soil of this continent.[114]

The "comparative" restraint many gentiles reported observing in Utahns' relations with the Indians, to the extent that it actually existed, was in great part the result of the leadership of Brigham Young and the teachings of the Church of Jesus Christ of Latter-day Saints. Young himself provided one of the best examples of Latter-day Saint kindness to Indians, and there is no question his actions won him great influence among Native Americans, though certainly not on the scale his non-Mormon contemporaries gave him credit for. Interestingly, even

---

[113] George Catlin to Brigham Young, 8 May 1870, BYC; also in Coates, "Catlin, Young, and the Indians." At the time he wrote this letter, Catlin was about seventy-four years old.

[114] Brigham Young to George Catlin, 27 June 1870, BYC; and Coates, "Catlin, Young, and the Indians." Italics mine.

during the war, most of Black Hawk's raiders viewed themselves at war with *certain Mormon communities* that had wronged them, not with Young personally or even with his church. Had the Latter-day Saints explicitly followed their leader's advice, the history of Mormon-Indian relations would have undoubtedly been significantly altered. As it was, however, Young was sure the "cupidity" and racism of his followers provoked the Indians to bloodshed.[115]

Despite how Mormon-Indian relations were viewed by non-Mormon countrymen, history is shaded with complicated dichotomies between what the Mormons believed regarding the Lamanites and how they actually treated them. This is true for Brigham Young as well as for his people. Young's idealism had its limits too, as will be evident in subsequent chapters. His sincere interest in the welfare and destiny of the Indians did not for a moment overshadow the callings he believed God had given him to preach the gospel to the four corners of the earth, to gather Israel, and to establish the Kingdom of God in Utah for the purpose of "making Saints."[116] But to make Saints the church must occupy the land, a process Young knew had disastrous effects upon native populations. While some Latter-day Saints believed they were fulfilling the curse of God upon the Lamanites by taking the land and despoiling Indians, their prophet's reconciliation of the dilemma was expressed this way:

> you are aware that we are settled upon their lands, (which materially interrupts their success in hunting, fishing, &c) that we are informed as to their origin . . . and the designs of the Almighty in their behalf; *for these reasons it behooves us to exercise toward them all possible kindness, liberty, patience and forbearance* . . . And inasmuch as we occupy their lands, . . . it is but right for us to give the well-behaved a horse or an ox now and again, and otherwise feed and help . . . [them, for] the Lord . . . has decreed the regeneration of that race.[117]

However, even this policy of giving natives token gifts as land payment caused some Indians to expect gifts, bringing increased tensions when Mormons failed to provide them.

---

[115] Coombs, Diary, 28 July 1866; Brvt. Col. O.E. Babcock to Maj. Gen. J.A. Rawlins, 23 June 1866, AGO, M619, 454; and JH, 28 July 1866, 3.

[116] Brigham Young said, "The idea may arise that this is a hard land in which to get a living. Now I am very thankful for the land just as it is. It is a splendid country to rear Saints in." Bleak, "Southern Mission," 2:126.

[117] Brigham Young to Orson Hyde, June 1864, BYC. Italics mine.

The outbreak of the Black Hawk War was in part the result of a tremendous burst of Mormon expansion. In 1864 alone Mormons commenced major settlements in northern and central Utah's Bear Lake, Ogden, Provo, Strawberry, and Sevier valleys. Simultaneously, villages sprang up along southern Utah's Virgin River and Kanab Creek as well as on the Muddy River in eastern Nevada. Settlers gave (or in some cases simply *promised* to give) token gifts for the right to occupy these areas.

As an example of how Brigham Young's policy was actually implemented, Apostle Orson Hyde invited Ute sub-chiefs Sanpitch and Joe to negotiate for the Sevier Valley late in 1864. However, settlers had *already* taken possession of the valley's most fertile areas, having established Monroe, Richfield, Glenwood, Salina, Circleville, and Panguitch earlier that year. Hyde proposed to give the Indians twenty or thirty animals for the entire valley, a rich strip of farming and grazing land nearly 150 miles long. Considering the substantial herds that ranged about each settlement, the chiefs were insulted and dictated their own terms, causing the apostle to grumble about Sanpitch's "extravigant notions as to the amount of pay he is to receive for the occupancy of . . . the Sevier."[118]

There can be no doubt that Mormon settlement of the Sevier Valley and Hyde's paltry offer were significant factors in the rise of Ute animosity on the eve of the war. Black Hawk and his compatriots undoubtedly watched with resentment as the Sevier Valley filled with cabins, plowed fields, and fences, as well as canals, ditches, and roads. Some whites came to view the war as a desperate attempt to drive the settlers from the Sevier; it and the Uinta Valley were the Northern Utes' last major food-producing valleys. Black Hawk undoubtedly felt the Mormons *owed* his people the stock the Indians killed during the winter of 1864–65, as well as the 125 animals he drove up Salina Canyon in compensation for lands *already* possessed by the Saints. Even Orson Hyde recognized the relationship between the settlement of the Sevier and the outbreak of hostilities, for when he heard of the initial raids he exclaimed that "the scamps have already got four times their pay" for the valley.[119]

Cattle played a central role in the starting of the war and became the

---

[118] Orson Hyde to Brigham Young, 29 October–3 November 1864, 12 November 1864, 13 February 1865, and 26 April 1865, all BYC.

[119] Orson Hyde to Bishop Bryan, 26 April 1865, BYC.

object of Black Hawk's raids. Shortly after settling Utah, Latter-day Saints discovered that they had stumbled upon magnificent stock raising country. Close proximity to overland trails gave them excellent opportunities to obtain stock, and thriving mining communities in California, Nevada, Colorado, Idaho, and Montana provided lucrative markets for beef. Stock raising was so important to their economies that central and southern Utah counties were called "cow counties," and observers noted that the area was "perfectly alive" with cattle.[120]

Brigham Young complained that the settlers had far more stock than they could take care of, yet, because they "want their stock to increase . . . they wont kill any," often letting them die on the range though people were hungry. This undoubtedly made little sense to starving Indians, who were constantly being told that the Saints had nothing to give them. "Cattle that are always roaming over the prairie don't do anybody any good," Young thundered, adding that "the way stock dies through neglect is a sin that will lay at the door of this people, if they do not repent."[121]

The tremendous expansion of Mormon settlement in 1864 was directly related to an explosion of the number of cattle in Utah. Young and certain apostles admitted that "the pressure to obtain the privilege of scattering into Small Settlements where a greed for land and stock could be gratified" had been "heavy and constant" and was *"the principal cause of the establishment of our small outer settlements."* The Sevier Valley itself, for example, was attractive to Orson Hyde, Barney Ward, and other promoters, because they saw it as "the finest country for wintering stock in Utah." By 1867 Young was preaching that the Black Hawk War was "caused" by the "unwise" and "selfish" course of such promoters, while Apostle George A. Smith asked, "is there any wonder the Lord allows the Indians to chastise us when we are so neglectful, & covetous[?] May the Lord help to wake us up!"[122]

The Gentiles

As has been shown, for years prior to the outbreak of the Black Hawk War an intense political struggle raged between the Mormons and the

---

[120] Gibbs, *Lights and Shadows*, 13; *DN*, 18 September 1867; and George A. Smith to John L. Smith, 22 May 1863, HOLB, 2:231.

[121] Miscellaneous Minutes, 23 August 1863, Edyth Romney Typescripts.

[122] Brigham Young to Brigham Young, Jr., 23 May 1866, BYC; Erastus Snow to Daniel H. Wells, 21 May 1866, TMR, #1526; DUP, *Heart Throbs*, 12:215; Peacock, Journal, 5 January 1867; and Miscellaneous Minutes, 13 July 1866. Italics mine.

United States. The Civil War and the slavery issue had done much to divert attention from Utah; however, as Union forces drove Robert E. Lee towards Appomattox in the spring of 1865, national interest again began to focus on Utah. Polygamy and "un-American" governmental practices were the main points of contention, but almost as important was Mormon Indian policy. The 1857 Mountain Meadows Massacre worked to convince the nation that the Mormon church made treaties with Indians to "destroy emigrant parties . . . who are not of their belief" and that the Intermountain West was "Swarming with Indians in the employ of the Mormons, who are taught to respect no person, unless he has a certificate signed by one of the 'Mormon Officers.'"[123]

Incensed by such rumors, local U.S. troops commander Patrick Connor vowed to destroy the theocracy. He organized an anti-Mormon cabal and established a system of espionage complete with agents and double agents hired "for secret service."[124] Meanwhile, he sought to wean the Indians from Mormon influence by furnishing them provisions and slandering the Latter-day Saints. Throughout the period he and other representatives of the military made it clear that the U.S. Army and the Mormon church were on the verge of actual warfare, and the natives were urged to fight with the United States *when* hostilities commenced.[125] Keenly aware of Connor's influence with the Indians, church leaders declared that the likelihood of war with the natives was not "in existence until [Connor] came and made it." Even Orsemus H. Irish, the gentile superintendent who took over Utah's Office of Indian Affairs in August 1864, noted Connor's deleterious influence on the Indians: "If the Military authorities will allow me to manage these Indians *without any further interference*," he wrote in November 1864, "I am satisfied . . . I can maintain peace."[126]

---

[123] Anonymous and undated statement found in Secretary of Utah Territory Papers, TEP, USA, document #73.

[124] George F. Price, Adjutant General, Head Quarters of the Plains, to Lt. Col. Milo George, 13 June 1865, District of the Plains, Register of Letters received, Jan–Sept. 1865, in vol. 326, District of the Missouri, 37, RUSA, RG 393, pt. II, entry 3257.

[125] For contemporary descriptions of Connor's policy, see C.D. Waudell to General Connor, 20 June 1865, District of the Plains, Register of Letters received, Jan–Sept. 1865, in vol. 781, District of Missouri, 525–26, RUSA, pt. 2, entry 3257; and P. Edw. Connor, Brig. Genl., to Major W.W. Barnes, A.A. Genl, U.S. Forces Kansas and the Territories, 30 November and 5 December 1865, District of Utah, 1865–1866, Letters Sent, Oct. 1865–June 1866, no. 345/1st 850 District of Missouri, 11–13, 18–19, RUSA, RG 393, pt. 3, entry 824, RUSA.

[126] George A. Smith to John F. Kinney, 15 December 1863, HOLB, 2:291; and O.H. Irish to William P. Dole, 9 November 1864, BIA, M234, 901. Italics mine.

Problems created by the Indian Department, however, probably had even greater impact in encouraging the Indians to fight the Mormons than did the feisty anti-Mormon general. As has been noted, Brigham Young had established four small reservations called Indian Farms in the mid-1850s while he served as ex officio superintendent of Indian affairs. When gentiles took control of Indian affairs after the Utah War in 1858, the farms almost immediately plunged into disarray, and hungry Indians turned to nearby Mormon settlements for food. By 1864 the results of the farm failures were serious. The collapse drastically increased begging and tempted the Indians to justify their theft of Mormon stock, vegetables, and grain. The begging and theft on the part of the Indians resulted in retaliatory measures on the part of the Mormons, and animosity between the two groups increased. Finally, the Latter-day Saints viewed the closing of the farms and the establishment of a *distant* reservation as the answer to "the Indian problem," and they petitioned President Lincoln to vacate the farms and open them for settlement.[127]

Assuming the Mormon request would be granted, gentile representatives of the Indian Office informed Indians that the farms would be sold and their inhabitants removed to a contemplated reservation in the Uinta Valley. Already aggravated that they were not involved in deciding their own fate, and resolving not to give up the farms, the Indians were even further excited when Mormon squatters began moving onto the farms. As a result of these tensions, Indians took shots at Mormons and wantonly killed cattle during the summer of 1864. Orson Hyde predicted that if things did not change "we must have an Indian War."[128] Some Mormons that summer actually called upon the troops at Camp Douglas to chastise the Indians, but acting superintendent Amos Reed viewed their requests as part of a Mormon scheme to stage an Indian war to keep gentile miners out of Utah. He therefore advised Connor "not to send out any soldiers."[129]

These problems were greatly increased by other factors. The unwarranted fear that the Indians were under the absolute control of the Mormons worked to encourage Congress to limit the size of appropri-

---

[127] Memorial for the Vacation of Indian Reservations to His Excellency Abraham Lincoln, President of the United States from the Utah Territorial Legislature, approved 11 January 1864, in Amos Reed to John F. Kinney, 13 January 1864, BIA, M234, 901.

[128] Extensive correspondence in BIA, M234, 901; and Orson Hyde to Brigham Young, 10–16 June 1864, BYC.

[129] Amos Reed to William P. Dole, 8 June 1864, BIA, M234, 901.

ations to the Indians. This reduction was made even more critical by the fact that funds already had been significantly diminished because of economic pressures imposed by the Civil War. Added to this, resources for the Indians of Utah were placed in New York banks to pay for drafts made in faraway Utah. Unfortunately for the Indians, however, the Latter-day Saints would not sell flour, beef, and other supplies to the Indian Office on credit. Past experience had shown that graft, poor Indian Office management, and anti-Mormon sentiment made it almost impossible to collect such debts.

As a result of these economic conditions, a devastating cycle was produced. First, Utah's superintendent requested money to ease actual starvation then in progress. The request, however, would sit until Congress was in session. Once the funds (which were often reduced) were appropriated, it often took months for the commissioner in Washington to notify the superintendent that they were available. Even more time then passed while the superintendent figured out how to get the cash to Utah, where its value plummeted by as much as 40 percent because of the territory's inflated frontier economy. By the time the money finally reached Salt Lake City, the winter months of starvation had passed and those Indians who had survived were able to sustain themselves by hunting and begging. The combined result of huge need, inadequate budgets, and (at least in some cases) malfeasance was a disastrous cycle for the Indians. By the time winter approached again, the money was usually gone and the cycle was repeated.

Thus, year after year the Indians of Utah were largely left empty-handed by the government superintendents and agents hired to feed them. Actual starvation was the result. Increasingly, the Indians were forced to depend upon settlers who were struggling to feed themselves. Mormon and gentile observers frequently noted, and with good reason, that the territory's natives were "unquestionably the poorest Indians on the continent."[130] As early as December 1862 one gentile Indian Office employee wrote that the Utes had only two options: "It is really a matter of necessity with these Indians that they starve, or steal."[131]

---

[130] See BIA, M234, 900–1 generally for documentation on these problems, especially Amos Reed to William P. Dole, Commissioner of Indian Affairs, 30 December 1862, and 6 March 1863; F.W. Hatch to William P. Dole, 14 March 1863, and 31 December 1863; and James Duane Doty to William P. Dole, 22 April 1863, 10 November 1863, and 20 January 1864. For references as to the extreme poverty of Utah's Indians see the last letter cited and *RSI*, 1861:741–42.

[131] Amos Reed to William P. Dole, 30 December 1862.

Financial problems were exacerbated by staff problems. In the five years immediately prior to the Black Hawk War, Utah's superintendents of Indian affairs often divided their time between other government assignments and their own private business interests. Perhaps the most egregious example of the problem is seen in the case of Amos Reed. For a time he simultaneously acted as Utah's governor, territorial secretary, superintendent of Indian affairs, and Indian Office clerk. Meanwhile, he still found time to pursue a busy mining career. Later, J. Duane Doty acted as both territorial governor and superintendent of Indian affairs for an extended period of time. As Orsemus Irish prepared to take over the superintendency just months before the Black Hawk War, he complained that the Indian Office in Utah had "been running for some time without a responsible head."[132]

No matter how noble their intentions might have been, such men as Reed and Doty were unable to even approach giving the time and energy that the Indian Office work demanded. Tied to Salt Lake City by other interests, they rarely ventured out among their Indian wards. As a result, Indians in the vicinity of the city received "by far the greatest portion of all presents," it was reported, while "the largest body of Indians . . . get but little." This had "the tendency of drawing all Indians to Great S L City" and other Mormon settlements, "the very place[s] they ought not to be," considering that the gentiles viewed Indian mingling with the Saints as being deleterious to government interests.[133]

The turnover among Indian Office personnel was a major problem; Indians complained that they hardly had time to meet a new superintendent or agent before he was replaced by another one. Graft and mismanagement also plagued the department. Amos Reed, for example, claimed to have used funds intended for one government office for another; this "seriously embarassed" his integrity. Similarly, Superintendent Doty was called upon to produce vouchers and receipts for monies he allegedly expended on behalf of the Indians of Utah. His valise full of vouchers was mysteriously "stolen" in a Washington hotel, however, after he had carried it safely all the way from Utah. The shoddy manner in which the Utah Indian Office was administered was characterized by Superintendent Irish when he arrived in Salt Lake City in 1864 to replace Doty, who was also serving as Utah's gentile governor:

[132] James Duane Doty to William P. Dole, 20 January 1864; Amos Reed to William P. Dole, 24 February 1864, 7 March 1864, and 19 July 1864; and O.H. Irish to William P. Dole, 7 July 1864, all in BIA, M234, 901.
[133] F.W. Hatch to William P. Dole, 18 February 1863, BIA, M234, 901.

"I have not yet taken possession of the Office," he wrote the commissioner of Indian affairs in Washington, "for in fact there is nothing to take possession of except a pair of Superanuated mules and an ambulance having only three wheels." Irish felt it was "absolutely necessary" to thoroughly clean house or risk an Indian war; but, by the time he had been in Utah one month, the funds for the department that he brought with him from the east were exhausted.[134]

While Mormons respected Superintendent Doty and generally believed him to be an honest man, it is clear that his Indian policy did not help the Utes and in fact contributed to the conditions that spawned the Black Hawk War. Most of the money Doty actually spent on the Indians of Utah was expended on the Shoshonis, who lived nearer to the Overland Trail. Doty understood the national importance of keeping the roads to California and Oregon open; therefore, paying the Shoshonis annuities and giving them gifts was his first priority. The Utes, like Indians throughout the West, held the common (and generally correct) belief that tribes engaged in hostilities at treaty time received much greater annuity payments than did those who were at peace.[135]

Even more than Doty, Superintendent Irish was anxious both to get along with the Latter-day Saints and make things right with the neglected Utes. He found Brigham Young and his followers to be cooperative and became so comfortable among them that General Connor and other vehement anti-Mormons turned on him and accused him of selling out to the Latter-day Saints.[136] In his enthusiasm, however, Irish himself made a blunder that significantly added to the hunger the Utes experienced during the winter of 1864–65 and thus inadvertently en-

---

[134] Amos Reed to William P. Dole, 16 and 19 July 1864; J. Duane Doty to William P. Dole, 20 January 1864; and O.H. Irish to William P. Dole, 26 August 1864, all in BIA, M234, 901.

[135] See BIA, M234, 901, especially James Duane Doty to William P. Dole, 10 November 1863, and 20 January 1864.

[136] "Imagine my surprise," wrote one anti-Mormon to General Connor, "to find our Superintendent of Indian [sic] making frequent visits to that man [Brigham Young], and appearing to be on good terms with him. So well, indeed, has he secured the good graces of the Polygamist that they are getting up a petition to have him appointed Governor in place of that good and true man Governor Doty." Connor immediately sent his views to his superiors that such federal officials as Irish should be replaced by men "who can resist either the threats or flatteries of Brigham Young and his Agents." See C.D. Waudell to General Connor, 20 June 1865, District of the Plains, Register of Letters received, Jan–Sept. 1865, in vol. 781, District of Missouri, 525–26, RUSA, pt. II, entry 3257; and P. Edw. Connor, Brig. Genl., to Maj. Genl. G.M. Dodge, 14 July 1865, District of the Plains, Register of Letters received, Jan–Sept. 1865, in vol. 326, District of Missouri, 130, RUSA, RG 393, pt. 2, entry 3257.

couraged the outbreak of hostilities. Aware of Utah's high prices, lack of credit, and other unique money problems, he opted to import supplies rather than purchase them locally. In good faith he gathered the Utes together to receive food and clothing in the fall of 1864, but Indian war on the plains and other problems waylaid his wagons traveling the long road from Nebraska. Meanwhile, deep snows prohibited the waiting Indians from dispersing to their wintering grounds, and, as a result, many more than usual wintered near the Mormon settlements during the 1864–65 season.[137]

In perhaps an even greater blunder, Irish added to already seething Indian-white tensions in Utah by energetically pushing the creation of the Uintah Reservation and by announcing to Indians the government's plan to extinguish Indian land title and to remove the natives from the area of Mormon settlement. Both Mormon and gentile sources abundantly record the terrific "anxiety" that the rumors of forced removal to the Uinta Valley engendered. Once the rumors were circulating, Irish "thought it dangerous to delay negotiations" with the Utes and invited their leaders to meet him in a grand treaty conference to be held late in the spring of 1865.[138] Leaders like Sowiette, Kanosh, and Tabby felt there was nothing they could do but accept the whites' proposals. Black Hawk and Jake Arapeen, on the other hand, spurned such fatalism, and the proposed reservation enlarged the growing fissure in the Ute system of leadership. As much as anything, the initial raids of the Black Hawk War were violent native reactions against the reservation system of the United States government.

As such, the Black Hawk War was part of the general Indian unrest and warfare that dominated the larger Indian society in the trans-Mississippi West during the 1860s. The Northern Utes were aware that their kinsmen and other Indian groups to the north, east, west, and south were fighting federal troops over similar issues. Superintendent Irish himself was certain that distant "Indian difficulties . . . were having a bad influence" on Utah's natives. He therefore rushed to extinguish their land title and establish an annuity-bearing treaty before

---

[137] Had they dispersed to their hunting grounds in time, Irish believed that the Indians could have subsisted on game, particularly beaver, which were still "abundant." During these years, the Indians trapped substantial numbers of beaver, eating the meat and trading the pelts to whites for meat, clothing, and other supplies. O.H. Irish to William P. Dole, 5 November 1864, and 30 January 1865, BIA, M234, 901.

[138] *RSI*, 1865:317–20.

they could be "drawn into alliances with other tribes hostile to the United States."[139]

As has been mentioned, the Northern Utes were part of a fluid, dynamic, and extended Indian community and were in communication with their Navajo, Apache, Shoshoni, Cheyenne, Arapaho, and Sioux neighbors and responded to white expansion as part of the larger group. As the Black Hawk war began, Irish notes that "Indian wars are raging on our immediate boundaries in Nevada, Idaho, Colorado, and Arizona." The effect was that the Indians of Utah were "anxious and excited," and runners from hostile tribes to the north, east, west, and south pled for their assistance in fighting the whites using the following arguments:

> . . . the Indians now in arms are contending for their homes; that
> if they are conquered and submit, they [the Indians of Utah] will
> be exterminated; that our Indians should join them *in this last
> struggle*, as the existence of all Indian tribes depends on their suc-
> cess; that our [efforts] . . . to concentrate and civilize them [on
> reservations] . . . is only to get them together where they can be
> slaughtered, and [all Indians] thus put entirely out of the way . . .
> [will leave the land] to the sole occupancy of the whites.

To men like Black Hawk and Jake and their followers, such arguments undoubtedly made good sense, and the Indian Department's sudden rush to "concentrate and civilize" them pushed them to join other hostiles.[140]

Indian Department graft during the period was very common, and the actions of Utah's single Indian agent and his employees in the years directly preceding the Black Hawk War provide a good example. Frederick W. Hatch operated the Spanish Fork agency, using the farmhouse at the Spanish Fork Indian Farm as his headquarters. Contrary to the wishes of his superiors, Hatch used funds and supplies intended for the Indians to feed and pay a retinue of unauthorized "employees," which included some of his own family members as well as female associates of his farmhands and interpreters. Even worse, Hatch and his son carried on a brisk mercantile business selling supplies intended for the Indians to Mormons in the nearby community of Payson. When hundreds of Northern Utes came to the farm to obtain provisions during

[139] Ibid, 316–20.
[140] Ibid., 310–16. Italics mine.

the winter of 1863–64, their agent required them to *pay* for the food, blankets, and clothing he had been hired to *give* them.

With no other recourse, the Indians turned to the Mormons, who themselves were "short of bread stuffs by [reason] of the drouth of last year." In exasperation, Apostle George A. Smith wrote Utah's delegate to Congress that he could "do a service to the Government by telling them the manner their Agents are causing the Indians to sponge and steal their living from the Inhabitants, while they [the agents] are speculating upon the Indians with the Government money."[141] Superintendent Irish dismissed Hatch and his employees immediately upon his arrival in Utah Territory in August 1864. Hatch's replacement, L.B. Kinney, however, turned out to be even more corrupt.

Indian Office graft was not confined to gentiles. Dishonest appropriating of Indian supplies by Mormon interpreters John Lowry, Jerome Kempton, and George W. Bean must be viewed in the same context. When Irish's Indian goods finally arrived from Nebraska late in 1864, Agent Kinney and Interpreter Bean went to check on large numbers of starving Indians in Sanpete Valley who could not come to Spanish Fork to get provisions because of deep snows. They found over two feet of snow on the valley floor and concluded that it was impossible for the Indians to get away to obtain game. Kinney apparently purchased quantities of flour, beef, and clothing in Manti and other Sanpete settlements and "arranged with John Lowry & Jerome Kempton to deal out these supplies as the Indians might need."

In one account, Bean remembered that the Indians accused Lowry and Kempton of "misapplying the funds & not feeding the needy." In another, Bean himself confessed that "in serving the Government . . . I became a little tricky" and got "my affairs mixed up, public and private [and] invested money that did not belong to me."[142] Thus driven to desperation, the Indians killed a number of Mormon cattle, including at least one animal owned by Lowry. Later, perhaps in an attempt to placate Lowry and thereby get access to the supplies left by Agent Kinney, Indians assembled in front of Kempton's house in Manti on 9 April 1865 and brought a horse "to pay for damages." According to Bean's account, it was then that the inebriated John Lowry attacked

---

[141] George A. Smith to Judge Kinney, 11 March 1864, HOLB, 2:345–46.

[142] Bean, Autobiography, 1897, 68–69; and George W. Bean to Brigham Young and Counselors, 28 July 1872, BYC.

and severely beat an Indian, whom Bean mistakenly identified as Black Hawk.[143]

It is therefore clear that John Lowry had more to do with the starting of the Black Hawk War than he acknowledged in his account of his altercation with Jake Arapeen. But, as the preceding pages point out, the Northern Utes were driven to violent acts by an extremely complex set of factors and events involving Indians, Mormons, and gentiles. Lowry's mistreatment of Jake, ill-advised as it was, was still basically only the symbolic pretext Black Hawk and Jake felt was necessary to open hostilities. As Orson Hyde would point out, the event did not create the explosive situation existing between Indians and whites in the Utah Territory; but it was indeed "the match" that finally ignited it.[144]

---

[143] Bean, Autobiography, 1897, 68–69.
[144] Orson Hyde to Brigham Young, 23 April 1865.

Above: Artist's rendition of Joseph Smith telling Native Americans that the Book of Mormon is the record of their forefathers, translated from plates of gold and brought forth in the "latter days" to bring them back to Christ. Courtesy of CHD.

Right: Brigham Young, successor of Joseph Smith, led the LDS church from 1844 until his death in 1877. Courtesy of CHD.

"Fort Utah on the Timpanogas"; 1852 drawing. Black Hawk and his family came to this fort (located near the present site of Provo) seeking protection on the eve of the Battle of Fort Utah early in 1850, in which as many as seventy of his people were killed and decapitated. Black Hawk and other Ute captives subsequently spent several winter months under the inadequate shelter of the fort's cannon platform. The whole experience transformed the Ute leader from what Brigham Young termed "the friendly Indian Black Hawk" into "the most formidable foe amongst the red men the Saints have had to encounter...." Courtesy of UUWA.

Black Hawk and other "Utah Indian Prisoners under the Common Platform" after the 1850 battle at Fort Utah; 1852 drawing. Courtesy of UUWA.

Above left: "Old Elk and his Squaw"; 1852 drawing. Both Old Elk and his wife died as a result of Mormon attacks on the Utes in which Black Hawk was forced to participate. Old Elk's head was taken as a trophy of war. Courtesy of UUWA.

Above right: A young Northern Ute poses in a Salt Lake City studio. Courtesy of CHD.

Right: Painted Northern Ute Warrior and his young wife. Courtesy of Smithsonian Institution.

Pahvants with their chief, Kanosh, front row, second from right. Courtesy of Smithsonian Institution.

"Pahute Boys." Courtesy of CHD.

Left: Ouray and other leaders of the Colorado and New Mexico Ute bands. Some of their people were drawn into Black Hawk's war on the Mormons. Courtesy of USHS.

Mormons baptizing Piedes and Paiutes. Courtesy of CHD.

"Pahute squaw & 1/2 breed son & daughter." Mormons took many Native Americans into their homes as wives, adopted children, and farm-hands. The Saints called these people "Tame Indians." Courtesy of CHD.

Black Hawk resented the fact that Kanosh, a high-ranking Northern Ute chief, dressed, worshiped, and farmed like the Mormons. Courtesy of CHD.

Antero, the Uinta war chief, led raids against the Latter-day Saints. Courtesy of Smithsonian Institution.

Tabby, chief of the Uinta band, initially sought to keep his band from Black Hawk's influence; but, as a result of Mormon military movements against his people, he eventually declared war on the Mormons himself. Courtesy of Smithsonian Institution.

Southern Utah Piede with wickiup in background. Courtesy of Smithsonian Institution.

Northern Ute family with lodge made of canvas provided by whites. Courtesy of Smithsonian Institution.

Right: "An-te-ro's encampment." Courtesy of Smithsonian Institution.

Northern Ute in winter dress.   Northern Ute in summer dress.
Courtesy of Smithsonian Institution.   Courtesy of Smithsonian Institution.

Left: Northern Ute
family. Courtesy of
Smithsonian Institution.

Tabaguache Utes with a pistol. Courtesy of USHS.

Northern Utes with a rifle and powder horn. Courtesy of Smithsonian Institution.

Right: Northern Ute with traditional weapons. Courtesy of Smithsonian Institution.

Left: Armed Utes with a scalp pole. Courtesy of Smithsonian Institution.

Below: Farmhouse at the Spanish Fork Indian Farm, where the Treaty of Spanish Fork was concluded in June 1865. This treaty, and its promise of forcing Utah's Indians to reservations, was a major factor in inducing Black Hawk to organize resistance to white settlement in Utah and the Four Corners region generally. Courtesy of CHD.

Apostle and LDS First Presidency member George A. Smith. Courtesy of USHS.

Apostle Orson Hyde. Courtesy of USHS.

Brevet Brigadier General Patrick Edward Connor, self-proclaimed archenemy of Brigham Young and the "one-man-power" of the Mormon theocracy. Courtesy of USHS.

Utah Superintendent of Indian Affairs Orsemus H. Irish. Courtesy of Nebraska State Historical Society.

John Lowry, Jr., credited with having started the Black Hawk War.
Gottfredson, *Indian Depredations of Utah*, first edition.

Brigadier General Warren S. Snow, Commander of the Sanpete Military District of the Nauvoo Legion and chief implementer of Brigham Young's Indian policy during the first years of the Black Hawk War. The Northern Utes held Snow personally responsible for the military offensives the Latter-day Saints launched against them, while they held Young virtually guiltless.
Original in author's possession.

Dimick B. Huntington, Brigham Young's brother-in-law and most-used Indian interpreter.
Improvement Era 11 (1908): 837.

CHAPTER FOUR

The Thistle Valley Massacre and the Treaty of Spanish Fork

San Pitch headed the war [the Black Hawk War] which devastated these settlements ten years ago. As in the difficulty that occurred at Eden, Troy, and thousands of other places, a woman was the cause of this trouble. Barney Ward, an old settler before the time of the Mormon occupation of the valley, was on such terms of friendship with San Pitch, that he promised him his daughter in marriage when she should become a suitable age. But when that time arrived, the young woman was found to have a will of her own. She rejected the advances of the swarthy Ute, and he took vengeance on the whites for the jilting he had received. The innocent people who had begun to settle in the valley were murdered or driven out, their habitations laid waste, their crops burned, and their cattle stolen. All this happened because of the obstinacy of Miss Ward.

—John Codman, 1879[1]

Sanpitch and the Daughters of Barney Ward

COMING JUST THREE DAYS after John Lowry assailed Jake Arapeen in Manti, the ambush of Colonel Reddick Allred's Nauvoo Legion troops in Salina Canyon on 12 April 1865 was a major blow to the Mormons. The deaths of William Kearnes and Jens Sorensen in the attack, added to those of Peter Ludvigsen, Barney Ward, and James Anderson, who were killed earlier as Black Hawk's raiders drove off stock, brought Latter-day Saint losses to five in the three-day-old war. Feeling responsible for the tragedy in the mountains, Allred resigned the following day, passing his command to Colonel Warren S. Snow. As we have

---

[1] Codman, *Round Trip*, 219–20.

seen, that same day Gunnison's LDS bishop, Hamilton Kearnes, sent messages apprising Brigham Young of the disaster and begging the gentile commander at Camp Douglas to send troops with howitzers to drive the raiders from their position in the canyon.

Convinced that the body of his son and the other slain legionnaire could not be safely retrieved by whites, Kearnes also sent a notice to Manti in an effort to get Sow-ok-soo-bet (Joe), to recover the bodies of the two dead men "for pay."[2] As this last dispatch was heading north, however, the settlers of Manti were in the process of alienating Joe, one of their greatest Indian allies. It will be remembered that at the 9 April 1865 council in Manti Joe defended the white position, reprimanded Black Hawk and his confederates for stealing cattle, and tried to secure peace. After the slaying of Peter Ludvigsen on 10 April, however, the settlers rounded up the sub-chief and held him at gunpoint in Manti. On the evening of the thirteenth Joe threw his buffalo robe over the head of his Danish guard and joined his offended band, who had already fled to the mountains.[3]

Since Joe was no longer available to go for the bodies, local militia leaders sent for Sanpitch, who was camped with his band near Nephi. This powerful Ute chief was a brother of Wakara and Arapeen, a nephew of Sowiette, an uncle of Jake Arapeen, and a "relative" of Black Hawk. Sanpitch was not only willing to fetch the bodies, he surprised the whites by eagerly volunteering to lead them in an attack on the raiders. It was not until the chief arrived in Salina on 15 April that militia leaders learned what he had in mind. As Warren Snow negotiated payment for bringing in the dead Mormons, Sanpitch claimed that the slain Barney Ward had promised to leave his two half-breed daughters to him when he died.[4] The chief offered to go up the canyon free of charge if he could take one or both of Ward's Shoshoni daughters to wife. Snow shrewdly informed him, however, that Brigham Young was the only man in the territory authorized to give women in marriage but said that he would take the matter up with the church president *after* the bodies were returned.[5]

---

[2] Reddick N. Allred to Major Tuttle, 12 April 1865, BYC; H.H. Kearnes to Brigham Young, 13 April 1865, BYC; and Warren S. Snow to Brigham Young, 22 April 1865, BYC.

[3] Peacock, Journal, 13 April 1865; and Weibye, Journal, 19 March 1868.

[4] Polly and Louisa Jane Ward were respectively seventeen and sixteen years of age. Both lived in Salina at the time of their father's death.

[5] Reddick N. Allred to Brigham Young, 13 April 1865, BYC; Orson Hyde to Brigham Young, 15 April 1865, BYC; C.H. Bryan, Bishop of Nephi, to Brigham Young, 18 April 1865, BYC; and Warren S. Snow to Brigham Young, 22 April 1865, BYC.

Miffed at not obtaining Ward's daughters outright, Sanpitch refused to bring down the bodies; but, under pressure, he at last agreed to go up the canyon to make sure the whites could safely retrieve their dead themselves. That evening he returned and reported that Black Hawk's band had crossed over the head of the canyon into Castle Valley. The following day, Colonel Snow and a command of militiamen went to the ambush site, suspecting duplicity on Sanpitch's part. While they found that the raiders had indeed vacated Salina Canyon, they were convinced by tracks and other signs that the Indians had left only after being sent away by Sanpitch. The body of Jens Sorensen "bore symptoms of the most cruel barbarism," having been "scar[r]ed with hot rocks" and tossed from a cliff, where his comrades later found him with his head "completely smashed." In contrast, the body of William Kearnes was not mutilated at all. They found the stiff body respectfully leaned against a boulder in a near-standing position with a grid of carefully woven willows around it to protect it from animals and birds.[6]

The deferential treatment Kearnes's body received was believed by Mormons to be in consideration for the kindness Kearnes and his family had shown to the Indians over the years. Having lived together as neighbors for nearly two decades, large numbers of Utes and Latter-day Saints knew each other intimately. Despite occasional differences, many of these relationships were positive. In the opening raids, as well as throughout the rest of the war, Indians consistently avoided hurting settlers who had been good to them, while they specifically targeted those with whom they had grievances. The young courier, for example, who took the news of Peter Ludvigsen's death to Gunnison, was later told by raiders that he was allowed to ride through a planned ambush because his stepfather was their "white brother."[7] The following day, however, Barney Ward was slain and mutilated, presumably to settle an old score dating back as far as the 1850 Fort Utah fight.

Along with Dimick Huntington and George W. Bean, Ward was one of the Indian interpreters most used by Brigham Young. He reportedly came to the West with Nathaniel Wyeth in 1834, helped build Fort Hall, worked for a time at Astoria, and "was a companion of Kit Carson, Jim Bridger, Baker, Smith and other prominent mountaineers." Ward married a Shoshoni woman and lived as a trapper and

---

[6] Kearnes, "Statement as to Indian Difficulties"; Warren Snow to Brigham Young, 22 April 1865; "Gunnison Ward Historical Record," 14–15; and *Memory Book*, 42.

[7] *Memory Book*, 42.

Indian trader until he was baptized a Latter-day Saint in 1850. As early
as 1837 he established a trading post in Utah Valley, apparently making
a living for over a decade trading with the Utes. He lost the tribe's good
will, however, long before his death on 10 April 1865. As we have seen,
Ward led frontiersmen in their first punitive strike against the Utes in
1849, in which it was alleged by some that Black Hawk was the only
male survivor.[8] A year later, a pacified Black Hawk watched as Ward
played a leading role in vanquishing Old Elk's Timpanogos at Fort
Utah, for which the Utes "ever after held a grudge against him."[9] It will
also be remembered that a band led by Black Hawk himself ransacked
Ward's home and killed his cattle in 1854 after a party of eighty Snakes
visiting Ward and his Shoshoni wife attacked them. Apparently, only
the intervention of other Mormons saved Ward's life at that time.[10] On
the eve of the Black Hawk War a decade later, Ward's role in encouraging the settlement of the Sevier Valley exacerbated old animosities.[11]
Considering Ward's unhappy history with the Utes and, in fact, with
Black Hawk himself, it is not surprising that whites eventually discovered his "tortured" and "terribly mutilated" body in Salina Canyon,
while they found William Kearnes's body carefully encased in its woven
willow shroud.[12]

To some degree, Ute considerations of friendship seem to have extended to certain settlers' livestock as well. Years after the war, for example, whites remembered that a certain raider "turned back [animals]
that had the brand of his special friends on them." During a lull in the
firing in the Salina Canyon fight, an Indian on the cliffs allegedly
shouted in English to a Mormon acquaintance below: "I am still your
friend. Tell Uncle Walter I turned back his black cow, and Shoe-
makers' red steer the other night."[13] Bishop Kearnes and his family
were generous, frequently killing beeves for the Indians and hiring
them to work for food. Black Hawk himself was said to have been a
beneficiary of their kindness, and hence William Kearnes was not

---

[8] See chapter two; LeRoy Hafen, "Elijah Barney Ward"; Elijah Barney Ward biographical sketch in Jenson, *Latter-day Saint Biographical Encyclopedia*, 3:552–54; and *Deseret Evening
News*, 6 June 1906, 10.

[9] Chapter two; Gottfredson, *Indian Depredations*, 31; and *Deseret Evening News*, 6 June
1906, 10.

[10] Alexander Williams to Brigham Young, 22 and 24 September 1854, BYC; and George
W. Bean to Brigham Young, 24 September 1854, BYC.

[11] DUP, *Heart Throbs*, 12:215–16.

[12] Gottfredson, *Indian Depredations*, 131.

[13] "Sketch of the Life of Abraham Washburn," 9–10; Lorena Larsen, "Black Hawk War";
and Benjamin Johnson, *My Life's Review*, 227–29.

scalped or mutilated and his body was protected with the willow covering, while the body of Jens Sorensen was "entirely cut to pieces."[14]

Following their return from the canyon with the bodies of Kearnes and Sorensen, Warren Snow put Salina's men "in a position of self defence" and sent the village's women and children to Gunnison. On 18 April Snow and the majority of the Sanpete men returned to their homes, hoping the "war" was over. Despite Brigham Young's wishes to the contrary, within days of the outbreak of hostilities J. Duane Doty (by now territorial governor), Superintendent of Indian Affairs Orsemus Irish, and Lieutenant Colonel William M. Johns,[15] temporary commander at Camp Douglas, all received requests from Mormon settlers that the Indians be chastised by United States troops. A dispatch was quickly forwarded to General Connor, who was leading a campaign against Indians on the Powder River in Wyoming and Montana. The general "refused," explaining that since the raids did not involve the Overland Trail or transcontinental telegraph lines, they were not under his jurisdiction. When Governor Doty heard of Connor's decision, he sent directly to Washington seeking authorization to deploy the local militia (the Nauvoo Legion) to chastise the Indians; however, considering the condition of political affairs in Utah, the request was "filed without action."[16] Hence, Brigham Young was left to deal with the situation on his own, the scenario he had hoped for all along. Eventually, in a provocative extralegal act, he would deploy the Nauvoo Legion without any federal or territorial authority.

Brigham Young Seeks Peace

As he had been both before and after the 1850 Fort Utah fight, Brigham Young was more interested in peace with the Indians than with chastising them, and before the fallen militiamen had even been removed from Salina Canyon he was working to pacify the raiders. First, he convinced Superintendent Irish that sending gentile troops would "only add a new element of bitterness to the strife." Then, on 16 April, he sent a letter to Orson Hyde chiding Sanpete and Sevier Saints not only for calling on the gentiles for military aid but also for failing to

---

[14] *Memory Book*, 41; and "Gunnison Ward Historical Record," 15.

[15] Lt. Col. William M. Johns was in command of Camp Douglas during the month of April 1865; see Camp Douglas post returns, Returns From U.S. Military Posts.

[16] *RSI*, 1865:314; U.S. Congress. House. *Memorial of the Legislative Assembly of Utah Territory*, 21 February 1868; William W. Belknap, Secretary of War, to House Committee on Military Affairs, 6 February 1873, in U.S. Congress. House. 42d Cong. 3d sess., Ex. Doc. 175; and JH, 26 February 1919, 9–11.

follow his directions over the years to properly prepare for such crises by building forts. The letter's main message, however, was one of reconciliation: "Better for us to feed [the raiders] and give them such necessaries as they may want than to fight them." The letter made it clear, however, that the church's political conflict with the government made peace with the Utes particularly imperative, and Young concluded that it was "no time for us to have an Indian war on our hands."[17]

The church president sent his son Joseph to hand deliver his letter and to see that the Latter-day Saints responded to the raids in such a way as would "result in peace instead of war." Simultaneously, he dispatched interpreters Huntington and Bean to smooth matters out with the estranged Indians.[18] By the time Young's emissaries reached Salina, however, Black Hawk and his men were nowhere to be found. Huntington and Bean subsequently visited "friendly" bands and declared the Saints' determination to maintain good relations with *all* the Utes.

Joseph Young remained in the area for several days investigating the cause of the outbreak and encouraging church members to sell their excess stock, gather together from scattered locations, and fortify their major settlements. Sanpete and Sevier Latter-day Saints ignored these last instructions, however, because many Indians, including women and children, were still begging in their settlements and they believed that as long as this was the case the raiders would not attack again.

Meanwhile, Sanpitch continued to clamor for the daughters of Barney Ward and promised to go after Black Hawk and the cattle *if* he could have the girls. His offers, however, simply raised suspicion. Within ten days of Ward's death, Orson Hyde was convinced that Sanpitch was "the Alpha and Omega" of the whole "disturbance." "Ward never promised Sanpitch his daughter," he reasoned in a letter to Young, but the chief "contrived this spurious and artful tale to gain the object of his brutal lust." "To execute [his] design," Hyde inferred, Sanpitch

> set Jake, Black Hawk and Topaddy to Kill Ward, and also some others to cover his mischief and as a reward to the murderous wretches that were to execute his plans, told them to drive off all

---

[17] Brigham Young to Orson Hyde, 16 April 1865, BYC; and Brigham Young to "President Orson Hyde and the Bishops of the various settlements between Great Salt Lake City and Sanpete Co., and in Sanpete and Sevier Counties," 17 April 1865, BYC.

[18] Brigham Young to "President Orson Hyde and the Bishops of the various settlements," 17 April 1865.

the stock they could into the Kanyon, . . . Then he, as the faithful ally of the mormons, would offer to make peace on condition that the girl or girls were given to him.[19]

Brigham Young at least partially accepted Hyde's conclusions and about 1 May brought the girls north from Gunnison under a heavy guard and placed them in his own household in Salt Lake City, where they remained until they married *white* Latter-day Saints.[20] The church leader had several reasons for not turning the girls over to the chief. Among them was the fact that the girls were baptized Mormons; however, evidently so was Sanpitch. A more compelling reason was that the chief had previously demonstrated his inability to properly care for a wife he had obtained from a white mountaineer. In the late 1840s or early 1850s Sanpitch married the Ute wife of deceased mountain man Miles Goodyear.[21] He treated Goodyear's two mixed-blood sons so brutally that to preserve their lives Young felt constrained to take them into his own care. It was not possible to save their mother, however, who reportedly died as a result of one of Sanpitch's beatings.[22]

Unable to obtain Ward's daughters, Sanpitch treated the Mormons with contempt for the next six or seven weeks, compounding the suspicions of Mormons, for which he would eventually pay with his life. Jake and Black Hawk were not heard from, and the settlers went about their business as if the trouble was over. Aware that more bloodshed could scuttle his plans for the Utes to cede title to their lands to the United States and settle on the Uintah Reservation, Superintendent Irish rushed to announce a treaty council to be held with the entire Northern Ute Tribe in the first week in June at the Spanish Fork Indian Farm. As hundreds of Utes under Sowiette, Toquana, Tabby, Antero, Kanosh, Mountain, and Joe made their way to the Spanish Fork council, however, Black Hawk struck again.

---

[19] Orson Hyde to Brigham Young, 23 April 1865, BYC.

[20] *Memory Book*, 24; and Milas Johnson, Autobiography, 11–12. For conclusive evidence that Brigham Young believed the basic story outlined by Orson Hyde see Brigham Young to "Tabby, Sowiett, Toquer-ona, Jim, Joe and Anthoro," 18 May 1866, BYC. For evidence that whites continued to believe the story even years after the war see Codman, *Round Trip*, 219–20.

[21] Goodyear came West as a youth of nineteen with the Marcus Whitman missionary party in 1836 and eventually established a ranch near the present site of Ogden, where the Mormons found him when they settled Utah in 1847. Goodyear sold out to the Mormons and apparently died shortly thereafter. See DeVoto, *Across the Wide Missouri*, 166, 246; and Sidwell, "Reminiscences of Early Manti," 8.

[22] Sidwell, "Reminiscences of Early Manti," 8.

The Thistle Valley Massacre

On the evening of 25 May, Jens Larsen was killed while herding sheep in Thistle Valley some five miles north of Fairview. Early the next morning a family of six was killed on Thistle Creek near the present site of Indianola. John Given, Sr., and his wife, Eliza, had recently moved into Thistle Valley from Spanish Fork with their nineteen-year-old son and three small daughters aged nine, five, and three. A major mountain thoroughfare and a favorite Ute hunting and camping area, Thistle Valley is actually a long, wide canyon connecting Sanpete Valley with Spanish Fork Canyon. Ignoring the warnings of local church leaders regarding the possibility of Indian attack, the Given family and several other disaffected Spanish Fork Latter-day Saints commenced dairy operations at several spots in Thistle Valley early in May. The inhabitants of Fairview claimed the valley as their own private herdground, and in mid-May the Fairview bishop unsuccessfully tried to run off the Spanish Fork squatters, who reportedly showed "signs of insubordination" to the priesthood. Described as "rather reckless" folks, the Givens allegedly boasted "that if the *white Indians* [Fairview Mormons] would let them alone they did not fear the *Black ones.*"[23]

On the morning of 26 May the Given family was still asleep in a rude temporary hut constructed of willows and mud; two other Spanish Fork men slept in a nearby wagon. Unaware of the men in the wagon, fifteen Indians surrounded the hut while four more crept inside. John Given was immediately shot through the heart, and his son had only time to yell "You d—d sons of B—s," before he was shot through the chest, leg, and arm. Simultaneously, Eliza was shot in the head. The firing awakened the three young girls, who screamed as the Indians clubbed their dying father and brother with tomahawks. At this point, the two startled white men jumped from the wagon, one of them brandishing a gun, momentarily chasing the attackers from the hut. Other raiders opened fire, however, forcing the pair into a patch of willows, leaving "the little girls weeping over the body of [their] mother." Armed with only one charge, the men watched helplessly from the willows as the Indians returned to the hut and shot one of the girls "in

---

[23] Andrew Peterson [Bishop of Fairview] to Brigham Young, 12 May 1865, BYC; A. Milton Musser to Brigham Young, 28 May 1865, BYC; Musser, Journal, 27–28 May 1865; undated *Salt Lake Daily Telegraph* article copied into Manuscript History of Brigham Young, 1865:322–26; Gottfredson, *Indian Depredations*, 140–44; and Culmsee, *Utah's Black Hawk War*, 44–47. Italics mine.

the face, another thro' the abdomen," tomahawking the last "in the face." They then watched them "finish" Eliza Given with a tomahawk.

The Indians stripped the bodies and buried them in feathers ripped from pillows and bedding as they ransacked the hut looking for guns, axes, and other valuables. As the two frightened whites in the willows watched, the raiders used tomahawks to break the backs of fifteen or twenty small calves in nearby pens so they would not slow their mothers, which the Indians subsequently drove north towards Spanish Fork Canyon. As the raiders pushed fifty dairy animals up the valley, they were apparently joined by others of their party, who helped them round up several hundred head of beef cattle and horses belonging to the people of Fairview and Mt. Pleasant.

Traveling Bishop A. Milton Musser, who happened to arrive in Fairview on the day following the massacre, noted in his journal that Jens Larsen's "sheep coming into Town without a Shepherd was the first intimation the people had of anything being wrong." Meanwhile, the two men who escaped the Givens' fate warned other scattered families in the valley to flee and came to Fairview with news of the killings. By the time Musser arrived on 27 May, Larsen was already buried, but the bishop poignantly described seeing the Given family "as they lay there . . . being washed, with the awful gashes made with the tomahawk[,] hair matted with blood[, and] eyes distended." Hardly able to express his emotions, Musser wrote that the "blood settled in the face of Bro. G. presented a specticle most horrible & ghastly to behold."[24] That the killings were the work of "the Notorious Blackhawk" was instantly assumed, as one of the survivors reported having visited with him the evening before the attack. As has been pointed out, within days of the murders, Black Hawk was identified in the *Salt Lake Daily Telegraph* as the leader of a band that had "been long known as a desperate gang of robbers and murderers."[25] Preceding the Spanish Fork conference by twelve days, the killings and stock thefts could well be seen as Black Hawk's message to Mormons, gentiles, and the leaders of his own people regarding the proposed treaty.

[24] See previous note and "Incidents in the Black Hawk Indian War," in Richfield Veterans, "Record," 301; Wakefield, "Life Story," 4; Day, "History of Eli A. Day," 10; Day, "Abraham Day III," 17; and Milas Johnson, "Life Review of a Mormon," 13–14.

[25] A. Milton Musser to Brigham Young, 28 May 1865; Musser, Journal, 27 May 1865; undated *Salt Lake Daily Telegraph* article copied into Manuscript History of Brigham Young, 1865:322–27, especially 322 and 325; and Benjamin Johnson, *My Life's Review*, 228–29.

On the morning of 28 May, the members of the Given family were "coffined separately" and buried together in a single grave. Later that day, as Bishop Musser preached in the Fairview meetinghouse, the assembly was interrupted by news that Indians had been discovered just outside town. The meeting broke up and a posse soon returned with four prisoners. Making special efforts to follow Brigham Young's peace policy, the settlers accepted the Indians' professions of innocence and dismissed them with a "*towidge ticaboo.*"[26]

The following day, however, David Jones was killed while searching for stock just three miles from town. On receipt of the news, Orson Hyde issued orders "to hunt the Indians & use them roughly." In all, thirteen Mormons had been killed by the raiders over a seven-week period, by far the worst figures up to that time in the Latter-day Saints' entire experience with the Indians. Despite Young's instructions to cultivate peace, local settlers were eager for blood.[27] Shortly after the new wave of killings, Hyde sent a letter to Young boldly announcing a change in policy he had mandated without waiting to consult the president. "I cannot see my Brethren shot down by the poor devils that we have fed and clothed without doing something to repel such agressions," he declared. "Immediate action" was "imperatively demanded," Hyde insisted, and he revealed that he was "raising forces to march *to night* in persuit of the murderous villains." Hyde still maintained that Sanpitch's "disappointment in [not] getting a girl is the principle cause of the whole affair," a point that was to be important to subsequent events.

To justify his decision, Hyde expressed his conviction that there was not a single "friendly Indian" in all of Sanpete County. In his mind, those that professed friendship were simply spies feeding information to Black Hawk. Therefore, he explained, "I have given instructions to capture every Indian that is seen . . . and those that cannot be captured [are] to be shot if within range. Those that are captured [are] to be tied fast so that they will not rest very easy, and kept safely in some cellar 'till further orders." As he concluded his letter, Hyde broached a sensitive subject. While he was very much aware of Young's determination not to involve gentile troops, the recent killings had convinced him that the time had come to reconsider that policy. "This war is on a scale that

---

[26] Ute for "a friendly good-bye." See Musser, Journal, 27–28 May 1865; and A. Milton Musser to Brigham Young, 28 May 1865.

[27] Musser, Journal, 30 May 1865; Peacock, Journal, 30 May 1865; and Gottfredson, *Indian Depredations*, 144.

cannot well be kept within ourselves," he wrote, though he promised he would "take no measures to disclose it outside the priesthood of God" until the president of the church agreed.[28]

Brigham Young continued to assert a restraining influence, however, though he concurred that the string of killings was the most foreboding sign of Indian trouble the Saints had ever experienced. He exclaimed that the Given massacre was "the first instance" in Mormon history of "women and children being killed in attempting to settle in any place!" To him it signified that something was seriously wrong.[29] Chastising Indians definitely known to have been involved in depredations was in line with his policy, but when he responded to Hyde's letter he stressed vigilance in self-preservation and not wanton killing. He also still viewed the coming talks at Spanish Fork as an opportunity to end the hostilities.[30] In the panic that swept central Utah in the aftermath of the Thistle Valley killings, however, it is clear that Orson Hyde's orders outweighed those of Brigham Young, and, as a result, "four lodges" of innocent Indians were apparently massacred near Manti. The exact nature of this incident and the date it occurred are not clear, though Indian leaders complained of it to Superintendent Irish at his treaty council early in June 1865. One Mormon, however, left a grisly memoir of firing on Indian women and children "at the mouth of Manti Canyon." Christian Anderson wrote:

> We were ordered to shoot; we came upon an Indian squaw lying on the ground dead, a little papoose lying by her side with four of her little fingers shot off. We were ordered to kill the baby, but by accident we saw another squaw running behind some willows. We shot in the air and rode on, leaving providence to bring the squaw back. Years after the papoose returned to Manti and visited at my home, showing me the fingers were gone. She was the baby left."[31]

According to one reminiscence writer, the Thistle Valley Massacre "thoroughly launched" the Black Hawk War.[32] The wave of fear these killings sent crashing over the Mormon frontier community unleashed

---

[28] Orson Hyde to Brigham Young, 29 May 1865, BYC.
[29] *MS*, 27:572–74.
[30] Brigham Young to Orson Hyde, 31 May 1865, BYC.
[31] "Proceedings of a Council with the Utah Indians," 38; and DUP, *Heart Throbs*, 6:493–94.
[32] Day, "History of Eli A. Day," 10.

pent-up frustrations and hatreds that Brigham Young's leadership and ideology had most often been able to hold in check. As Superintendent Irish and Brigham Young prepared for the 7 June council at the Spanish Fork Indian Farm, news of the murders in Thistle Valley spread. Rumors in Salt Lake City more than doubled the number killed, while certain gentiles started stories of their own. It was well known that the Given family and others settling Thistle Valley were unhappy with church authorities. Bishop Peterson of Fairview called them "saucy & impertinent," and Bishop Thurber of Spanish Fork affirmed that they were "an unruly set."[33] Gentiles, particularly those associated with the Connor clique, saw the killings as Mormon retribution upon dissidents unwilling to submit to Young's authority and sent word of the killings east by telegraph. The *New York Sun* told its readers that the Givens were murdered by Mormon vigilantes called "destroying angels" who disguised themselves as Indians and systematically put "obnoxious persons out of the way."[34]

The popular contemporary gentile notions that "Saints in the disguise of Indians" perpetrated the massacre or that Brigham Young or other church leaders set Indians on the family are totally without grounds. Bishops and concerned settlers wrote a number of letters requesting that the church president stop the settlement of Thistle Valley, specifically naming the Given family as "insubordinate" land jumpers. Two days before the massacre, however, Young sent pointed (and private) instructions that the families settling in Thistle Valley had "just as good a right to . . . make farms there, as the [Fairview and Spanish Fork] brethren had to settle the places which they now occupy." Young, in fact, was "pleased" that the valley was being settled and he hoped the Givens and others would make "a good Settlement in Thistle Valley as a stopping place, for, when the roads are made right, there will be quite a thoroughfare through there."[35]

As has been discussed, Indian attacks in Utah during the period, and, in fact, anywhere on the Overland Trail, were commonly laid at the feet of the Latter-day Saints. Based in part on Brigham Young's supposed involvement in the Mountain Meadows Massacre in 1857, these allegations were expressions of growing Mormon-gentile friction throughout the nation. With the coming of the Black Hawk War,

[33] Andrew Peterson to Brigham Young, 12 May 1865, BYC.

[34] JH, 6 September 1865, 3.

[35] Brigham Young to the "Bishops of San Pete and Utah Counties, and to all whom it may Concern," 24 May 1865, BYC; and Andrew Peterson to Brigham Young, 12 May 1865, BYC.

Young actually expressed some relief that the Saints too had their Indian troubles. "The cry has been raised in many quarters when the Indians have been hostile on the plains and have attacked trains," he complained,

> that we were in league with them and were inciting them to those deeds of violence. Were we to be at peace with them now, and were not suffering ourselves from their depredations and attacks, our enemies would be very likely to raise the old cry and reiterate the old charges, and a feeling of suspicion and hatred would likely be engendered against us. But as matters are now their anger is disarmed. We have Indian difficulties as well as they.[36]

Anti-Mormon sentiment in the United States was at an all-time high. Slavery had recently been expunged and the end of the Civil War allowed the nation to turn its attention to the surviving "relic of barbarism." The rallying cry in the eastern press was that polygamy must *now* follow slavery to its grave.[37] War between the United States and the Latter-day Saints was openly urged on the floors of Congress and preached from the pulpit in the Salt Lake Tabernacle. At the time of the murders in Thistle Valley, two congressional delegations, including Speaker of the House Schuyler Colfax and J.M. Ashley, the powerful chairman of the House Committee on Territories, were already making their way to Utah. Their purpose was not only to gather information but to threaten the rebellious territory.[38] Meanwhile, members of the Connor clique talked vituperatively of landing Brigham Young in "some secure Penitentiary for life" or, better yet, seeing to it that he was "casterated with a dull knife."[39] More realistically, Connor hoped to represent Utah affairs in such a light that additional troops would be placed at his disposal so that he could dismantle Young's "one man power" in Utah.[40] The church leader, on the other hand, feared that calling troops to go after the raiders would give his enemies the advantage they sought, and he continued to give strong orders for Sanpete and Sevier county settlers to keep quiet about their Indian troubles. For example, he wrote Orson Hyde,

---

[36] Brigham Young to Hiram B. Clawson, 18 June 1867, BYC.
[37] Ibid.
[38] Musser, Journal, 6 July 1865.
[39] William P. Sargent Affidavit, 31 July 1869, BYC.
[40] Long, *Saints and the Union*, 262–63; and Brigham Young to William H. Hooper, 21 February 1866, BYC.

Your letter and several others which I have received speak about
getting outside aid to quell this outbreak. I am surprised that you
should expect or ask for such a thing. You would find if this aid
were down there with you, it would be far better to have the Indians to war with and to deal with than to have to war with and deal
with them [that is, U.S. troops]."[41]

The Treaty of Spanish Fork

On 23 February 1865 Congress approved an act authorizing treaty negotiations with the Northern Ute confederation designed to extinguish
their title to the Territory of Utah and to provide for their removal to
a reservation in the Uintah Valley.[42] Extinguishment of native title and
removal to the reservation were considered necessary to accommodate
the flood of gentiles some federal officials hoped Connor's policies
would attract to Utah. When Superintendent Irish received orders to
commence negotiations, he was urged by the secretary of the interior
and the commissioner of Indian affairs to use Brigham Young to influence the Indians to agree to the proposed treaty. While Connor
thought it strange that "the arch traitor" Brigham Young would be
called upon for such a purpose, Irish explained that "the fact exists,
however much some might prefer it should be otherwise, that he has
pursued so kind and conciliatory a policy with the Indians, that it has
given him great influence over them."[43]

The extraordinary confidence the Indians had in the Mormon leader
should not be minimized, nor, for that matter, should it be exaggerated.
As hundreds of Indians under Sowiette, Kanosh, Toquana, Sanpitch,
Tabby, Ankawakits, Mountain, Joe, and other leaders began to gather
at the Spanish Fork Indian Farm in mid-May, the chiefs dictated a letter to the church president requesting that he represent them at the up-
coming council. Unacquainted with Superintendent Irish, the Utes
were fearful that they would be taken advantage of. Because Young
through the years had shown himself to be "the good father of the Indians" and "never promised anything" he "did not perform," the chiefs
pledged to agree to whatever Young felt was right.[44]

[41] Brigham Young to Orson Hyde, 16 April 1865, BYC; and George A. Smith to Orson
Hyde, 5 November 1865, HOLB, 2:510–11.
[42] Secretary of the Interior J.P. Usher to Commissioner of Indian Affairs, William P.
Dole, 15 March 1865, BIA, M234, 901.
[43] Ibid.; and O.H. Irish to William P. Dole, 29 June 1865, in *RSI*, 1865:317–20.
[44] Tabby representing Sowiette and others per George W. Bean to Brigham Young, 19
May 1865, BYC.

When Irish announced his intention to involve the church president in the treaty-making process, however, virtually all of the territory's non-Mormon officials and military leaders refused to attend. Connor repeatedly had instructed his officers not "to mix with Mormons" until "they cease to violate the laws of the land." Irish received word that, "rather than associate with Brigham Young on such an occasion," the bulk of Utah's federal officials would rather "have the negotiation fail"; they also favored the Indians keeping their land instead of letting it go to the Mormons. The one exception was Governor Doty, who agreed to participate in the talks; but an illness, which shortly proved to be fatal, prohibited him from joining Irish, Young, and the Indians at Spanish Fork.[45]

By the first week in June as many as 500 Indians set up their lodges near the dilapidated farmhouse on the defunct Spanish Fork Indian Farm. On the afternoon of 6 June a large party of whites with wagons loaded with presents and provisions approached the farm. The group included Brigham Young, at least five of the church's twelve apostles, Nauvoo Legion officers such as Colonels Robert T. Burton and Warren S. Snow, Indian interpreters Huntington and Bean, and Superintendent Irish, who apparently was the only gentile representative.[46]

After initial greetings, Young, Irish, and sixteen major Ute leaders retired to the farmhouse to discuss some alarming news just learned by native sentries: two companies of U.S. soldiers from Camp Douglas were approaching the farm from different directions. Still keenly aware of Connor's 1863 massacre at Bear River and his subsequent attack on a Ute encampment in Spanish Fork Canyon, and also aware that several hundred Cheyenne and Arapaho had been massacred in November 1864 by troops and militia on Sand Creek in neighboring Colorado, the Utes were naturally frightened and demanded to know the meaning of the sudden movements of the military. Young and Irish assured the Indians that they had nothing to fear, suggesting that the troops probably hoped to break up the negotiations by scaring the Indians away with the display of force.[47]

---

[45] Patrick Connor to Lieut. Col. Milo George, 7 June 1865, Register of Letters received, Jan–Sept. 1865, District of the Plains, in vol. 326, District of Missouri, 11, RUSA, RG 393, pt. II, entry 3257; and O.H. Irish to William P. Dole, 29 June 1865, *RSI*, 1865:317–20.

[46] "Articles of Agreement . . . concluded at Spanish Fork Indian Farm." A draft of this treaty is also found in BYC, r92, b58, f16. For additional information on the treaty talks see Gustive Larson, "Ute Treaty, 1865"; JH, 7 June 1865, 1; and Gottfredson, *Indian Depredations*, 151–56.

[47] *MS*, 27:572–74.

Accepting Young's assurances of their safety, native leaders listened while Irish read an abstract of the treaty. According to terms drafted in Washington, the Utes were to relinquish all rights to the territory with the exception of the Uinta Valley region, which would constitute a reservation that was to be settled within one year of the treaty's ratification. The Indians were to promise not to commit depredations on whites or make war on other tribes except in self-defense, and the government reserved the right to settle other Utah tribes with the Utes on the proposed reservation. Not surprisingly, the treaty also contained a clause in which the Utes were to "agree not to shelter or conceal" raiders, but rather to promise "to deliver them to the authorities for trial."

In exchange for these concessions, the United States would provide treaty annuities of "$25,000 annually for 10 years, . . . $20,000 annually for 20 years thereafter, and $15,000 annually for 30 years thereafter." Additionally, $30,000 would be expended to make initial improvements on the reservation and to procure cattle for Indian stock raising. Another $10,000 would be used to build and operate "a manual labor school," which children seven to eighteen years of age would be forced to attend. The Indians were promised grist- and sawmills, and personal homes were offered as perks for treaty signers. After the reading, Ute leaders, in another evidence of their confidence in Young, sought "private counsel" from the church leader on the course he thought they should pursue.[48]

The following morning Indian and white delegates met in the shade of a bowery erected especially for the purpose of the treaty talks. Sowiette (Nearly Starved), Toquana (Black Mountain Lion), and Tabby (the Sun) represented the Yampa and Uinta Utes. Kanosh (Man of White Hair), Ankawakits (Red Rifle), Pean-up (Big Foot), Eah gand (Shot to Pieces), and Nar-i-ent (Powerful) represented the Pahvants. Sanpitch (Bull Rush), Pan-sook (Otter), and Que-o-gand (Bear) represented the "Utahs." Joe, or Sow-ok-soo-bet (Arrow Feather), represented the Sanpitch Utes. An-kar-tew-ets (Red Boy) and Nanp-peads (Foot Mother) represented the Timpanogos Utes; Quibets (Mountain), who was Black Hawk's brother, represented the Spanish Fork Utes; and An-oosh represented the Weber Utes. Superintendent Irish alone represented the United States government.[49]

---

[48] See "Articles of Agreement . . . concluded at Spanish Fork Indian Farm"; JH, 6 June 1865, 1, and 16 June 1865, 3–4; and Gustive Larson, "Ute Treaty, 1865."
[49] "Proceedings of a Council with the Utah Indians," 1–2.

With Dimick Huntington and George Bean serving as interpreters, Irish officially opened the treaty negotiations by referring to the recent killings committed by Black Hawk and his band. He rewarded Joe and Toquana with blankets (and promises of special treatment in the future) for standing up for the whites at the failed council in Manti. He then delivered a protracted monologue designed to impress tribal representatives with the benefits of ceding their lands to the United States. "If you sign this treaty," he concluded, "you shall have farms and houses and goods." "Will your decision be such as will make your people happy and prosperous in the future," he asked them, "or will you decide to be poor, miserable and unhappy[?]"[50]

After reading the treaty again, Irish stepped aside and allowed the Indians to speak. They indicated that Sowiette, Kanosh, Sanpitch, and Tabby (unquestionably the most powerful Northern Ute leaders at the time) would speak for the rest. Kanosh spoke first, acknowledging the aged Sowiette as head chief. He further recognized that "Brigham is the great Captain of all, for he does not get mad when he hears of his brothers and friends being Killed, as the California Captains do." This was a blatant reference to the actions of General Connor and his California Volunteers at Bear River, Spanish Fork Canyon, and elsewhere. Kanosh declared that the land belonged to both the Mormons and the Utes and expressed the hope that "it all remain as it is, . . . let them all [Mormons and Indians] live here together." "The best thing," he concluded, "is for the Superintendent to give us our blankets and shirts, and not talk about trading the land."[51] For the Latter-day Saint Kanosh, the status quo was satisfactory.

Sanpitch also affirmed the position that the Mormons and Utes already "shared" the land on the basis of multiple verbal treaties and small purchases made over the years. He too felt that "the paper" was unnecessary. "If the talk is for us to trade the land in order to get the presents," he said, "I do not want any blankets or any clothing. . . . I would rather do without, than to give up my title to the land I occupy."[52]

The speeches of Kanosh and Sanpitch demonstrate that they were not mere puppets of Brigham Young, who had been urging them all along to accept the terms. Young then arose to encourage them again to accept the treaty, declaring he was only seeking their "welfare."

[50] Ibid., 1–7.
[51] Ibid., 7–10.
[52] Ibid., 10–12.

With the history of generations of Indian-white relations in mind, he implored them to give up their rights to the soil, arguing that if they did not sell their land to the United States, the government would "take it, whether you are willing to sell it or not." "They are willing to give you something for it," he counseled them, "and we want you to have it." The church president then lamented that the Mormons had not given the Indians more for the land they had shared for almost two decades. "We have not been able to pay you enough," he admitted,

> although we have helped you a good deal. We have always fed you, and we have given you presents, just as much as we could: but now the great father is willing to give you more: and it won't make one particle of difference whether you say they may have the land or not, because we shall increase: and we shall occupy this valley and the next, and the next, and so on till we occupy the whole of them: and we are willing you should live with us.[53]

To the pragmatic church leader, the treaty had nothing to do with land, for the whites would have the land one way or the other; it was an opportunity for a destitute and disintegrating people to obtain aid—*at the expense of the government.* For Young, the treaty shifted the burden of feeding the Indians from his own people to the government while legally throwing open for settlement lands that he and his people had been squatting on for nearly two decades. Besides, he believed that the Lord had an agenda for the land that could not be changed. "The land," he told the Indians again, "is the Lord's and we shall occupy it, and spread abroad until we occupy the whole of it." Accepting that fact as primary, Young looked for the second-best scenario as far as the Indians were concerned. "This treaty is just as liberal and does everything for you and for your people that can be done. If it were not so, I would not ask you to sign it."[54]

The native delegates became "excited" and argued among themselves as to the course the church leader advised them to follow, stark evidence that Young had nowhere near the degree of control over the Utes he was often given credit for. At last Tabby suggested that they return to their lodges to "talk and smoke over" what had been said. Before the meeting adjourned, however, Sowiette affirmed his friendship to both the Mormons and the people of United States. "When I met

---

[53] Ibid., 12–13.
[54] Ibid.

President Young," the ancient head chief said,"we talked and understood each other, me and my children the Utahs, and Brigham and his children. When some of my children stole horses and acted bad, did I break my friendship? No, never. . . . I never felt like breaking friendship. I do not want to see it. I am old: my heart is very weak now, but it is good." At this point, the Ute leaders returned to their lodges. Irish and his Mormon interpreters spent the afternoon and evening talking informally with various chiefs, while Young preached to hundreds of Latter-day Saints in nearby Payson.[55]

The following morning, 8 June, the talks under the bowery at the Indian farm resumed. Upset at the conclusion reached by his fellow leaders in the private council, Sanpitch refused to attend and defiantly remained in his lodge. Without further discussion, Irish asked the Utes for their decision. Speaking for his people, Sowiette simply said, "It is good. We will sign." Irish promised the aged head chief, "you are an old man, but if you live a year, you will live long enough to be glad of having signed this treaty." The fifteen chiefs then attached their marks to the prepared document, and Orsemus Irish signed as the sole representative of the U.S. government. Brigham Young then attached his signature, but only as a witness. Once the signing ceremony was over, Irish exultantly told the Indians that "the man who looks at you today, and will look at you a few years hence, would not think you the same people."[56] The superintendent's prophecy ultimately came true, but tragically not as he expected.

In what were intended as concluding remarks, Brigham Young told the Utes that he had "the same regard" for them as he had "for all who [would] be friends to God and righteousness." He assured them that he valued their welfare just as he did his own children's and that he had given them good advice. Promising that they were still welcome in the settlements, he blessed them in the name of the Lord. Kanosh then declared that it was "all good peace and good friendship" and eagerly announced that he was ready to receive his presents.[57]

The whites, however, carefully turned the conversation to the raiders, who naturally did not attend the Spanish Fork talks. Tabby affirmed that none of Black Hawk's men had come to his camp and that he had instructed his band to capture them if they did. Young urged the Indians not to "punish the innocent for the crimes of the guilty" and to

[55] Ibid., 14–15; and JH, 7 June 1865, 1.
[56] "Proceedings of a Council with the Utah Indians," 15–17.
[57] Ibid., 17–21.

"never [hurt] women or children." The church president reminded the Indians that by signing the treaty they had covenanted to deliver those who raided and murdered the settlers "to the authorities of the whites," for which they would "receive presents."[58]

The Indians then lined up in three long rows to receive the gifts the superintendent brought to distribute. The men sat in the first row, women and infants in the next, and children in the third. Whites described the "child-like eagerness" most of the impoverished Indians displayed on receiving blankets, clothing, knives, and tobacco. Several of the chiefs, however, received their gifts with "stoical apathy."[59] Sanpitch refused to attend the distribution of presents altogether, and when Irish visited him in his lodge he covered his face with his hands, determined not even to acknowledge the superintendent's presence.[60]

The following morning, apparently after Brigham Young and his entourage had left, Irish held more informal talks. Again the recent raids and killings were discussed. With Sanpitch still brooding in his tepee, Irish told the Utes that the chief's behavior suggested that he had something to be ashamed of and Irish confessed that he suspected the sullen chief was somehow involved in the killings. Toquana agreed that Sanpitch "acted ashamed." In discussing the Salina Canyon ambush, Tabby indicated that only forty-four Indians had participated; according to him, they were mostly Elk Mountain Utes assisted by "a few Manti Indians." While he generally declined giving names, he revealed that Sanpitch's father-in-law was among them.

Realizing that many of the assembled Indians had relatives and friends among the raiders, Irish warned them to stay away from Black Hawk or face serious consequences. The Mormons, he explained,

> are your friends. How long, however, will you be trusted, if they are to be thus murdered and destroyed? If you wish to assure them of your fidelity, of your truthfulness, you should not hide among you, nor let any man remain with you who is the friend of those who have been engaged in these murders.[61]

Irritated by Sanpitch's sullen behavior, Irish announced that the chief was acting like an enemy and that he would be treated as such if he did

[58] Ibid., 24–25.
[59] JH, 8 June 1865, 2.
[60] "Proceedings of a Council with the Utah Indians," 34–42.
[61] Ibid., especially 36–37.

not make greater efforts to demonstrate peaceful intentions. When the Indians heard Irish's tough talk, Douglas, the war chief of the White River band (who primarily resided in Colorado and therefore was not invited to sign the treaty), went to get Sanpitch to make things right with the superintendent. Old Sowiette wept like a child when Sanpitch refused to come. When Irish grew even more resolute, other messengers went to get the chief.

Succumbing to pressure from his peers, Sanpitch eventually shook hands with Irish but still refused to sign the treaty. "I will not put my name to the paper now," he insisted. "If it is a good paper, that is enough. This is my land. I shall stay here on this land till I get ready to go away, and then I shall go to the Snakes or somewhere else [and not to the reservation.]"[62] Irish tried to give the chief his share of the presents. Viewing the gifts as token payments for the land, Sanpitch still balked at accepting them, but he promised to visit the superintendent soon in Salt Lake City.

As Irish prepared to leave the following day, the chief finally came forth and received his presents, but nothing more was spoken concerning his signing the document.[63] On learning of Sanpitch's refusal to sign the treaty, Brigham Young said he was "glad," for, in his view, Sanpitch would "be the first to break it." Despite this, before a week had passed, Sanpitch came to Salt Lake City and put his mark to the paper. As he and his band traveled south from the city, however, they were accused of stealing a number of horses, which only added fuel to an already raging fire of white suspicion regarding the unsuccessful suitor of Barney Ward's daughters and the lone hold-out at the Spanish Fork talks.[64]

Ute Politics

Latter-day Saints were delighted with the outcome of the treaty negotiations and were especially gratified that Superintendent Irish witnessed first-hand that the Utes refused "to take any steps to make a treaty only as Pres. Young would advise." As Young summed it up, "the superintendent received evidence, if he needed any, to convince him

---

[62] Ibid., 34–35, 39–42.

[63] Ibid., 42.

[64] Ibid.; and *MS*, 27:572–74. Tabby and Sowiette and several Mormons were certain that Sanpitch was innocent and that the horses were taken by Goshutes. Aaron Johnson to Brigham Young, 27 June 1865, BYC.

that our humane and fatherly treatment of the Indians had had its effect, and given us justly grounded influence."[65] Most Mormons viewed the treaty as "very favorable" to the Utes, as it gave them "a million and a half of dollars in sixty years, in annual installments" and "builds them mills, houses, farms, and procures for them farming implements." "It will be a great blessing to the Indians," wrote Apostle George A. Smith, "if the Senate [will] ratify and the government carries [it] out." The treaty, however, was never ratified by the Senate. But for the next eight years both the government and the Latter-day Saints acted as though it had been, especially insofar as the Indian land cessions and obligations to remove to the Uintah Reservation were concerned.[66]

At first, many of the Indians appeared to be pleased with the treaty as well. Sowiette, Toquana, and Tabby and their bands were especially gratified because the Uinta Valley was their traditional homeland and the treaty prohibited white settlement there. Naturally, bands led by Kanosh, Sanpitch, Joe, and others were less than thrilled, because the treaty moved them to lands where they had no traditional rights. In fact, there is substantial evidence that the proposed removal of the various Ute bands en masse to Uinta Valley created political problems among the Indians that contributed to numerous individuals and entire bands joining Black Hawk's forces.

John Wesley Powell described the root of the problem when he wrote that the Utes were "subdivided into districts" and that individual bands not only "take the name of the land" upon which they lived but were also "fixed to this land" as far as their identity and political rights were concerned. To permanently leave their inherited country, Powell explained, not only caused them to give up their identity but also meant they "must join and become recognized as a member" of the band owning the land to which they moved. Catastrophically, as far as Ute society was concerned, this included giving allegiance to that band's leaders. "Thus it is that these Indians have contended so fiercely for the possession of the soil," Powell continued,

for a [band] to yield the district which it inhabits they must lose their nationality and become incorporated in other [bands]. . . . His national pride and patriotism, his peace with other [bands],

---

[65] Brigham Young to Daniel H. Wells and Brigham Young, Jr., 20 June 1865, in JH, 20 June 1865, 1; and George A. Smith to Daniel H. Wells, 20 June 1865, HOLB, 2:493–94.
[66] Ibid.; Musser, Journal, 12 June 1865; and Peacock, Journal, 11 June 1865.

his home and livelihood for his family, all his interests, everything that is dear to him is associated with his country.[67]

Mormon settlement in Utah had long disrupted Ute society, but the Saints' willingness to allow Indians to live among them on ancestral homelands permitted at least a semblance of traditional patterns to continue. The mass removal of Indians to the Uintah Reservation, however, posed insurmountable threats to Ute social organization. Whole bands with distinct heritages and customs would disintegrate, and the people belonging to them would be forced to enter bewildering new social relationships without status. While most whites present at the treaty negotiations were oblivious to Indian politics and social structures, Sanpitch's strained behavior at the proceedings undoubtedly had much to do with how the treaty impacted his position among his people.

Sanpitch's deceased brothers, Walker and Arapeen, had both undercut Sowiette's authority and successively established themselves as powerful and quasi-independent chieftains. Now their younger brother was trying to do the same thing, and the agreement to settle in the Uinta Valley undermined his power while strengthening the positions of such Uintah leaders as Sowiette, Toquana, Tabby, and Antero. Sanpitch's opposition to the treaty as well as his defiant declarations of his intention to go where he wished are perhaps best viewed against the backdrop of intricate political maneuverings among the Utes, as are also Sowiette's tears at Sanpitch's initial refusal to sign and Toquana's quick agreement with Superintendent Irish that Sanpitch "acted ashamed" and was probably in league with Black Hawk. Mormon apostle Wilford Woodruff seemed to grasp what was happening as well as any white when he noted in his journal that Sanpitch "Claims to be the main Chief" and "lay in his tent on his face for about 2 days on his dignity, Walker like, & would not speak to any one. The other Chiefs went on & done their business & paid no attention to him."[68] Kanosh had similar reasons to oppose the treaty, but repeated verbal assurances from Irish and Young that he and his band would be allowed to remain on their own lands in Millard County quieted his concerns.

---

[67] See John Wesley Powell, "Indian Life," 7–8, in "Life and Culture of the Ute."

[68] Woodruff, *Journal*, 6:227. The *Deseret News* correspondent who reported the treaty's proceedings partially discerned the reasons for Sanpitch's attitude when he wrote, "The only chief who was averse to signing the treaty was San-pitch, brother to Walker and Arrapeen, but subsequently it appeared more as if he were standing on his dignity as a 'big chief' than anything else, he being willing to sign on Saturday." *DN*, 9 June 1865.

Shortly after the meetings at the Spanish Fork Indian Farm, Sowiette, Toquana, and Tabby and their bands broke camp and immediately headed towards the Uintah Reservation. Others returned to their own traditional lands. Brigham Young, before leaving the area, preached to 3,000 Utah Valley Saints on the evils of having more stock than they could care for. Demonstrating his conviction that the treaty had not ended hostilities, he urged his people to sell their surplus stock and use the proceeds to purchase weapons and build forts as he had always counseled.[69]

Time for Retaliation

Immediately upon Brigham Young's return to Salt Lake City, gentiles noticed and articulated a change in the church president's attitude towards the Indians. Samuel Bowles, editor of the *Springfield Republican*, visiting from Massachusetts as a correspondent accompanying a congressional delegation investigating Utah affairs, penned the following on 12 June 1865:

> The Mormons have exhausted the Quaker policy towards the Indians; have fed and clothed them for years, paying them in all ways heavy subsidies, in consideration of being let alone; *but they are growing tired of it*, both because it is expensive, and is not sure of success. Only a few days ago some Indians attacked the Mormons at a settlement about eighty miles south of here, and killed eighteen or twenty persons. Brigham Young and other officials of Church and State went down to investigate the matter and restore peace; they have just come back, reporting success, and laying part of the blame on the whites, *but still with less of the old disposition to subsidize the barbarians.*[70]

What Bowles probably sensed was that Young's forbearance with Black Hawk's raiders was at a low ebb. He had repeatedly sent out overtures of peace, but Young was also governed by religious principles that under certain circumstances not only allowed violent retaliation but *required* it. An ardent believer in the Book of Mormon, Young believed God expected the Latter-day Saints to fight "for their homes, and their liberties, their wives, and their children, and their all; yea, for their rites

[69] JH, 10 June 1865, 1.
[70] Bowles, *Across the Continent*, 69–70. Italics mine.

of worship, and their church." The book declared that self-preservation was "a duty which they owed to their God"; it taught that God himself had decreed that "inasmuch as ye are not guilty of the first offense, neither the second, *ye shall not suffer yourselves to be slain by the hands of your enemies.*" Indeed, one of the book's most repeated themes was that God expected His people to defend their families "*even unto bloodshed.*"[71]

Far more than even most of his coreligionists were aware, Brigham Young based his Indian policy on religious principles he had received from Joseph Smith, the founder of Mormonism. While the "better to feed than fight" maxim was cited repeatedly by both Mormons and non-Mormons as being his guiding philosophy regarding Indians, a much more complete understanding is acheived when one becomes aware that both his Indian feeding *and* his Indian fighting were deeply rooted in Latter-day Saint scripture. Joseph Smith reported a revelation on war in 1833 that reiterated and amplified Book of Mormon teachings on the circumstances under which God expected his people to protect themselves militarily. Judging by Young's actions in regard to Native Americans for nearly four decades, this revelation lay very close to his heart and along with related Book of Mormon passages was the foundation philosophy upon which he based his relations with the Indians.

"Renounce war and proclaim peace," the revelation commanded the Latter-day Saints, and if attacked a first, second, or third time by their enemies, they were required "to bear it patiently and revile not against them, neither seek revenge." "If any nation, tongue, or people should proclaim war against them," the revelation continued, "they should first lift a standard of peace unto that people, nation, or tongue, and if that people did not accept the offering of peace, neither the second nor the third time, they should bring these testimonies before the Lord; then I the Lord would give unto them a commandment, and justify them in going out to battle against that nation, tongue, or people." Even when thus "justified" in rewarding the enemy "according to his works," the Lord urged restraint. "And then if thou wilt spare him, thou shalt be rewarded for thy righteousness," the LDS scripture read; "nevertheless, thine enemy is in thine hands; and if thou rewardest him

---

[71] The Book of Mormon (1830), 344. Compare with Alma 43:45–47 in modern editions. Italics mine.

according to his works [by killing him] thou art justified; if he has sought thy life, and thy life is endangered by him, thine enemy is in thine hands and thou art justified."[72]

Brigham Young's Indian policy has been described as a policy of contradictions and ambiguities, and indeed it was. Accused of sometimes alternating arbitrarily between what have been called policies of "open handed" benevolence and "mailed fisted" retaliation,[73] Young, it nevertheless can be argued, *continuously* applied Mormon religious notions regarding war and peace in his relations with the "Lamanites." His thinking, motivations, and actions, as well as the military measures he ordered, simply cannot be fully understood without some concept of these notions, and the Black Hawk War provides an excellent opportunity to observe them at work.

Having raised the "standard of peace" to Black Hawk and his men several times, and feeling that he had sufficiently warned them through Ute leaders at the negotiations in Spanish Fork, Brigham Young now determined to deploy the Nauvoo Legion against the raiders, a policy that would eventually escalate violence on both sides of the growing conflict and simultaneously raise the ire of the federal government.

---

[72] Joseph Smith, Jr. et al., *Doctrine and Covenants*, 216–17; compare with Section 98 of current editions of the *Doctrine and Covenants*.

[73] See Christy, "Open Hand and Mailed Fist."

Chapter Five

The War Escalates

. . . although the Lamanites [are the] see[d] of Israel, they are
against us . . . if [the] Saints had hearkened [to the council of their
leaders,] they would not need to have lost one man . . . when men
do as they are told, they will be healthy and strong. . . . When Israel [has been] obedient they always [have] had success & prosperity, but when disobedient [they have been] chastized . . . when
life [has been] sacrificed it was when counsel had not been observed, every instance if [we were] familiar [with it and] could
trace it[, we] would find disobedience at the bottom . . . God has
stirred up the indians to bring [the Saints] to their senses . . . we
are not going to have the sceptre of authority in our hands until
we are sanctified and our hearts made pure before God. . . . The
machinations of those that have plotted against us [are] over-
rulled. The clique against us in Salt Lake City [was] never more
powerless than now. They have been remembered in the prayers
of the servants of God. . . . Rather fall into the hands of God than
any one else, rather be chastized by the Lamanites than the
avowed enemies of the children of God . . . pray for the Lamanites that the Lord take away their wrath. . .
—Brigham Young et al., 1866[1]

Mormon Mobilization

IMMEDIATELY AFTER the treaty negotiations at Spanish Fork in mid-
June 1865, national developments convinced Brigham Young more
than ever that involving U.S. troops in Utah's Indian problems was
politically dangerous. General Connor, though temporarily removed

---

[1] Miscellaneous Minutes, preaching in Tooele County by Brigham Young, Heber C.
Kimball, George A. Smith, and George Q. Cannon, 13–15 July 1866, Edyth Romney Typescripts, b99.

from the territory, was making "every possible effort" to convince
America's highest-ranking government and military leaders "to have
more troops sent to Utah."[2] Simultaneously, officials throughout the
nation predicted that "within a year . . . there *must* be a collision of
more or less importance between the church and the government."[3] To
show their resolve, in early July, Speaker of the House Schuyler Colfax
and Chairman of the House Committee on Territories J.M. Ashley had
arrived in Utah to personally issue on behalf of Congress serious new
threats against polygamy and the Mormon theocratic system.

Ashley was especially direct. In a face-to-face interview, he told
Brigham Young that now that the Civil War was over, the "religious
element" that had led the successful crusade against slavery was demanding that troops be sent to Utah to abolish polygamy. Actual warfare "might come at any time," he prophesied to the prophet, and, if it
did, "it would be terrible," for the troops on hand were "the refuse of
Sherman's" army, the same soldiers who "ravished every female &
burnt every house" in a swath "50 miles wide" while humbling Georgia
the previous summer. Referring to Sherman's famous march from At-
lanta to the sea, Ashley swore that "that's what they intended to carry
out here!"

Upon hearing Ashley's intimidations, Young passively replied that
he "did not expect a war" with the United States. "The Lord [has] been
the trust of this people heretofore," he informed the congressmen,
"and He would still be." "They might get an army here," he allowed,
"but by and by it would go away again" without injuring the Latter-day
Saints. Always a firm advocate of what he called "practical religion,"[4]
however, Young and an entourage of apostles left the very next day on
a "missionary trip" to prepare Saints in Utah, Juab, and Sanpete valleys
to defend themselves against the Lamanites lest continued Indian
troubles draw more troops into the territory.[5]

There is no doubt whom the Latter-day Saints considered their primary enemies. Not long before the trip south to prepare the people,
Apostle George A. Smith pled in public prayer that the Lord would

---

[2] Capt. Geo. F. Price, A.A.A.G., Fort Laramie, D.T., to Lt. Col. Milo George, Salt Lake
City, 21 August 1865, District of the Plains, Register of Letters Received, Jan.–Sept. 1865, in
vol. 326, District of Missouri, 259, RUSA, RG 393, pt. II, entry 3257.

[3] McCormick, *Across the Continent*, 20–21. Italics mine.

[4] The notion that one should express faith by doing all in one's power to bring about a desired effect *before* depending on God to do the rest.

[5] HOJ, 5 July 1865; Musser, Journal, 6 July 1865; JH, 20 June 1865, 1–2, 5–7 July 1865,
and 24 July 1865, 1.

look down in His "great mercy upon the Lamanites" and bring them "to a knowledge of Thee and of their fathers" while he prayed God to "consume" in His "hot displeasure" those who had "shed the blood of the prophet" and "concocted schemes to bring mischief upon" the Saints.[6]

By 10 July 1865 Young and his party were in Utah Valley preaching that surplus cattle be sold or traded for weapons, that substantial forts be built, and that people living on outlying ranches move to larger, more defendable settlements. The visiting congressmen's threats were openly discussed. One settler reported the prophet and apostles told them, "It has been proposed by some Senator to send an army out to Utah to defile our wives and daughters as Sherman[']s soldiers did the Southern women in their triumphal march through Georgia & Alabama." The fiery orators thundered that "not a true hearted man in Utah would tamely submit to such outrages" and resolved that if federal troops "attempt to injure us we will send them to hell faster than they went to Petersburgh!" All Latter-day Saints "were advised to provide weapons of defense, plenty of ammunition & [to] be on the watch to defend themselves from an enemy."[7]

Over the next few days similar meetings were held in Nephi and the Sanpete Valley settlements of Moroni, Mount Pleasant, Spring City, and Ephraim. While the Saints were counseled not to injure innocent Indians, they were informed that the time had come to protect themselves, even if it meant killing the raiders. The message of the sermons was simple: "Let the guilty be punished and the innocent go free," and prepare to defend yourselves not only "from the Indians" but also the "*white devils*" from the States.[8] Significantly, the shift towards stronger action against Black Hawk's raiders was clearly rooted in the precarious state of Mormon-gentile relations.

While the meetings were in progress in Manti on 14 July, word arrived that Black Hawk and his men had killed two more Mormons near Salina and had driven 300 head of cattle into the mountains east of the Sevier Valley settlement of Glenwood. Anthony Robinson of Monroe was hauling wheat to Manti's mill and Robert Gillespie of Mount Pleasant was hunting lost stock when they were individually overtaken and killed by Black Hawk's raiding party in the vicinity of Salina. What

---

[6] JH, 24 June 1865, 4.

[7] Coombs, Diary, 10 July 1865.

[8] JH, 10–14 July 1865, especially 12 July, 3, and 14 July, 1; and Azariah Smith, Journal, 17 July 1865. Italics mine.

made matters worse was that just prior to the killings some of Black Hawk's men and their families had been hosted at a feast by the people of Salina and apparently had been given "paper" from the local bishop identifying them as "friendly Indians." It was significant to subsequent events that they were accompanied by an unknown white man. Quickly reacting to the news, Brigham Young called for one hundred well-armed men to immediately "seek out the Murdering Indians and slay them"; but in light of the political situation he commanded them "to keep quiet about it." "Do your duty & say nothing to any man," he ordered, "& Call upon Nobody to help you for you are able to help yourselves." In the heat of the moment, the "let the innocent go free" principle was replaced with harder doctrine. Considering the fact that a portion of Black Hawk's band had "innocently" mingled with the settlers just before these last killings, Young urged, "Use up thes [*sic*] wicked Indians who are killing the inhabitants," and "if these Indians who profess to be friendly will not help bring them to justice, do not let them stay with you but treat them as Enemies."[9]

The following day, by Young's mandate, Warren Snow was "elected" brigadier general of the Sanpete Military District of the Nauvoo Legion,[10] and that night he and detachments of militia from throughout Sanpete Valley rode to Glenwood under the cover of darkness. As a result of Young's new directive regarding "friendly Indians," Black Hawk's brother, Chief Mountain, was pressed into service as a guide. He quickly gave the Mormons the slip, however, and apparently went straight to his brother's camp.[11]

The Squaw Fight

Snow and his men spent 16 and 17 July hiding in the tiny settlement of Glenwood while their force expanded nightly. After dark on the seventeenth the new general led one hundred men up a canyon east of Glenwood through a drizzling rain in pursuit of Black Hawk, who they

[9] See "Incidents in the Black Hawk Indian War," in Richfield Veterans, "Record," 301; Gottfredson, *Indian Depredations*, 156–59; Martineau, *Southern Paiutes*, 55–57; Woodruff, *Journal*, 6:235; Weibye, "Journal," 15–16 July 1865, in Danish; Lingren, "Autobiography," 247–48; Seeley, "History," 4–5; and "Col Snow on the War Path."

[10] Warren Snow was forty-six years of age and had been deeply involved in Mormon military movements since his teens. He protected Joseph Smith and other Saints from apostates and non-Mormon vigilantes in Ohio and Illinois, and he also played leading roles in the Battle of Nauvoo and the Utah War. See John A. Peterson, "Warren Snow."

[11] Weibye, "Journal," 15 July 1865, in Danish; Peacock, Journal, 16 July 1865; and "Col Snow on the War Path."

believed was being assisted by Sanpitch.[12] Following a "rough" Indian trail over the mountains, they reached Grass Valley at dawn on 18 July. Near present-day Burrville, Snow allowed his wet and weary men to rest near a large grove of cedars in a beautiful meadow. Unbeknownst to the tired militiamen, six tepees were concealed in the trees. Snow's picket guards were sauntering towards suitable positions when the report rang out that the cedars were "full of Indians." Quickly mounting their horses, the Mormons surrounded the grove and began to close in. Although they were significantly outnumbered, thirteen Indian males fought desperately to defend their families. In a four-hour battle, ten of them were killed, two others escaped, and a third was captured.

Tragically, a number of women and children were also killed. Militiamen claimed that they unknowingly fired into a "bushy cedar" where women and children had taken cover. Later, a captive attacked her guard with a knife; he responded by shooting her, sending other female prisoners into a violent panic that ended only after even more of them were killed. As a result, this unfortunate battle was referred to as "the Squaw Fight."

Considering that Brigham Young had issued strict instructions that women and children not be harmed, Snow was shocked by the killings and angrily reiterated orders that females and youngsters be left alone. Similarly, he raged at the men who commenced plundering the bodies and the Ute camp following the battle. When some of his war-crazed men ignored his orders, he sent others to arrest them. Calling the entire company together, Snow harangued them, reiterating that "the expedition was only to punish the Indians for the depredations and that we were not out for plunder." In the Ute camp, however, booty seekers had already discovered items owned by the two slain Mormons, convincing the militia after the fact that they had attacked a portion of the guilty party. Tracks indicated that the missing cattle had been driven ahead some time before by other raiders, and, as a matter of strategy, Snow retreated to Salina.[13] Superintendent Irish later learned from Indian sources that the small band the Mormon militia had attacked represented "about one-third" of Black Hawk's band. Other native

[12] Warren S. Snow to Brigham Young, 16 July 1865, BYC; and "Col Snow on the War Path."

[13] Andrew J. Moffitt, Bishop of Manti, to Brigham Young, 23 July 1865, BYC; R.N. Allred to Bro. Stenhouse, 20 July 1865, BYC; "Col Snow on the War Path"; Seeley, "History," 4–6; Gottfredson, *Indian Depredations*, 159–61; Sylvester, "Indian Wars," 3; Farnsworth, "History of Manti," 50; Weibye, "Journal," 3 August 1865, in Danish; and Lingren, "Autobiography," 247–48.

sources evidently denied this, however, and maintained that those Indians were innocent.[14] Significantly, a newspaper article written to report the tragic affair to the readers of the *Deseret News* in Salt Lake City was pocketed by Brigham Young, who from this time forward largely succeeded in squelching press coverage of the Saints' war with the Indians lest it attract gentile attention and federal troops.[15]

Despite the cover-up, news of the massacre quickly spread through Ute society and was one of the few events of the Black Hawk War to survive to the present in Ute oral tradition.[16] While the story has several variations, and some of the details have changed over the years, it is still clearly recognizable and supplies significant elements of the incident that were probably purposely left out of white accounts. Walker Ammon, a son of Wakara, reportedly passed the story on in this form:

One time soldiers were sent down into Sevier Valley from the Mount Pleasant area. Some Paiutes were encamped at Glenwood at the time. The Bishop of Glenwood warned the Indians and told them to leave. They then broke camp and followed the horse trail over the mountain and down into Grass Valley where they stopped.

The next day or so, one of the Indians was out hunting and spotted someone in a white blanket standing on a point. He sneaked up close and saw that he had a white face. He went back to the camp and told his people. The Chief said, "Don't worry, I have a paper from the Bishop; they won't bother us." Feeling safe, they remained there that night.

Early in the morning, before the sun came up and while they

---

[14] *RSI*, 1865:314; and Martineau, *Southern Paiutes*, 55–57.

[15] The article, entitled "Col Snow on the War Path," was never published.

[16] Martineau, *Southern Paiutes* is an important source of Ute oral tradition relating to the Black Hawk War. The name "Paiute" in the title is misleading, because some of the descendants of Northern Utes such as Wakara, Arapeen, Kanosh, and Black Hawk's brother Mountain ended up being classified as "Southern Paiutes." Special Indian Agent G.W. Ingalls, an associate of John Wesley Powell, wrote that by 1873 Black Hawk's "She-be-reches" had been "completely broken up and scattered—some to the White River & some to Uintah Valley reservations and the bal[ance] have joined the Pai Utes." See G.W. Ingalls to E.P. Smith, Commissioner of Indian Affairs, 10 July 1873, BIA, M234, 904. Martineau, a Caucasian, was raised as the son of Edrick Bushhead, a Paiute, and subsequently married a Paiute woman; he married another after his first wife died. One of these women was a great-great-granddaughter of Kanosh. Living among the Southern Paiutes, Martineau recorded "Southern Paiute" oral tradition for several decades beginning in the 1940s. For a brief discussion of the fact that many "Southern Paiute" ancestors "were considered Utes in the last century," see Martineau, *Southern Paiutes*, 149–53.

were all sleeping, the soldiers attacked them and killed them all. Some were still sleeping in their blankets. One Indian ran up the side of the hill and was shot between the eyes from a long way off as he looked back down.

One very small boy who had on a sheepskin cloak was lying beside his dead mother and when the white men spotted him they picked him up and took him with them, as they started back north. They hadn't gone far when the boy got loose and ran away. The soldiers didn't bother to chase him figuring he would die of starvation.

The little boy . . . [eventually found another band of Indians and] told them what had happened. They then formed a war party and asked the little boy to show them where it had happened. They followed the horse trail down off Fish Lake Mountain to Cedar Grove, near Burrville, and there they saw the massacred Indians.

They said, "Let's go chase the soldiers." . . . [They] followed the trail for two days but couldn't catch up to them so they returned. The bones lay there for a long time until the white men took them.[17]

Florence Kanosh, the wife of a grandson of Chief Kanosh, said that the "Indian name for the massacre site" is "*Tawhoo'Kwechun or Toohoo'-wutsekai* meaning something like a 'Wail' or 'War Cry from a Ridge.' " She also said:

The Indians killed at the Burrville, Utah, massacre were from the Koosharem Band. When the soldiers attacked the Indians, a little old man went out with a piece of paper in his hand and showed it to the soldiers. He said, "We are not at war with you! We are at peace and have a treaty!" He was the first one killed. The soldiers cut his head off with a sword. There were no men in the camp, only old people, women, and children. My grandfather was a young boy and escaped and went and told the Indians at Fish Lake. They came and found the bodies of the Indians scattered around in the cedar trees.[18]

[17] Martineau, *Southern Paiutes*, 55–56. Walker Ammon was born "about 1854" and died in 1920 on the Koosharem Reservation near the massacre site (Martineau, *Southern Paiutes*, 273).

[18] Ibid., 56–57. Florence Timmican Kanosh was born in 1889 at Fish Lake, Utah, and died in 1986 at Richfield, Utah; see pages 282–84.

The Green River Expedition

The militia's return to Salina was designed as a feint to make the Indians think the expedition against them was over. Once in Salina, however, Snow's men prepared to ride to Castle Valley, where they hoped to overtake and destroy Black Hawk and his raiders.[19] Typical of subsequent expeditions, preparations involved entire families. While Snow and his command chased and engaged the Indians in "the Squaw Fight," men at home in Sanpete Valley slaughtered and dried beef for the Nauvoo Legion's rations. Women and girls made homemade hard tack they called "butter crackers," sometimes pricking "their names on the crackers as a loving message" to brothers and sweethearts in the militia. Children helped melt lead and mold musket balls. In all aspects Mormon military preparations and movements were amateurish and unpolished, since church members were by no means professional soldiers.[20]

From Salina, General Snow sent orders to Spring City to have Colonel Allred lead "60 or 70 Men" across the mountains east of Fairview and meet him on the Price River in Castle Valley.[21] Snow's command of one hundred men left Salina on the evening of 20 July and displayed their inexperience and unprofessionalism when they mistook the reflection of the moon on a mountain pond for Black Hawk's campfires. One Mormon recorded the incident in this manner:

> . . . the sky was full of floating clouds. A short distance down the canyon was a pond of water, and when the moon shone out on the water it looked like fires being replenished at intervals with brush. . . . The men thinking it was an Indian camp stood and held their horses all night, intending to surround the camp and make an attack at daybreak; but in the morning we found out our mistake.[22]

This delay, added to others of like nature, doomed the expedition to failure from the outset.

Once in Castle Valley, Snow's command struck the stolen herd's trail clearly heading towards the Green River following the general route of the Old Spanish Trail. As yet untouched by white settlement, the valley was familiar to a few Mormons, but none knew it well. Named by trappers for numerous rock formations that look like

---

[19] Peacock, Journal, 20 July 1865; and Gottfredson, *Indian Depredations*, 161.
[20] DUP, *Heart Throbs*, 11:349; and Clark, "John Haslem Clark," 87–89.
[21] R.N. Allred to Bro. Stenhouse, 20 July 1865.
[22] Gottfredson, *Indian Depredations*, 161–62.

fortresses, much of Castle Valley is incredibly rough desert country characterized by barren alkali flats broken by huge eroding shale and sandstone bastions. Immense rock formations, of which the San Rafael Swell, the "Wedge" (sometimes described as Utah's Grand Canyon), and Buckhorn Wash are characteristic, made a direct route across the valley impossible.

Castle Valley's badlands, together with the rugged terrain of the Wasatch Plateau, were key to the success of most of the cattle raids during the Black Hawk War. Stock in the Sanpete and Sevier valleys were easily driven into the many canyons in the huge mountain wall to the east of the Mormon settlements. As the Salina Canyon fight demonstrated, these passes were relatively easy to defend. Beyond the mountains, Castle Valley, the San Rafael Swell, Capitol Reef, and what was called the East Desert provided literally thousands of hiding places. By the 1860s, the region's rough canyonlands were already used successfully by white cattle thieves to conceal herds of stolen stock. A generation later, men like Butch Cassidy and the McCarty brothers would make "Robber's Roost" and other hideouts in the area infamous.[23]

The Indians were aware of numerous waterholes in the generally dry area. They also used Huntington, Ferron, and Cottonwood creeks, as well as the Muddy, San Rafael, Price, and Green rivers, to water the stock. If Mormons chased them into Castle Valley, the pursuers could be seen for great distances, allowing plenty of time for stock to be driven across the Green River at Gunnison Ford (near the present site of Green River, Utah). A few sharpshooters concealed behind cottonwood trees on the ford's east bank could easily keep the whites from following farther. Generally, however, the huge distances involved and the resulting logistical problems kept the Nauvoo Legion from pursuing the raiders through Castle Valley after this first expedition to the Green River.

As they made their way towards the prearranged rendezvous spot with Snow, Allred's command came across "three or four lodges of Tabby's Indians returning from a hunt." Fully aware that these Indians had nothing to do with the recent stock thefts, the militiamen still pled with Allred to attack. The leader "restrained them," but only "because they had their families with them."[24] When the Snow and Allred commands met on the flat lands between the Price River and the present

---

[23] See Charles Kelly, *Outlaw Trail*.

[24] Reddick N. Allred, "Diary of Reddick N. Allred," 349; and Gottfredson, *Indian Depredations*, 161–62.

location of Wellington, the combined force numbered 175 men. Taking stock of their supplies, the officers were disappointed to learn that they had only "three pint cups" of "cracker dust to the man."[25] Determined to push on and punish the thieves and retake the cattle, however, the officers carefully rationed the remaining provisions, urging the men to forage as best they could on weeds and other plants. The joint command then traveled southeast on "the grassy trail" to Gunnison Ford on the Green River.[26]

At the ford, the militiamen discovered that the Indians had only recently crossed with the stock. Anxious to attack the raiders, the men pressured their leaders to move onward. However, considering their famished condition, not to mention the possibility of an ambush, the officers decided to rest and then start the long trail home the following day. Disgruntled at the decision, most of the men spent the day gathering greens, fishing, and bathing in the river.[27] The determination not to cross the ford was apparently a good one, for the Mormons later learned that "there were 30 or 40 Indians on the other side" quietly waiting "in the willows." After the war, Jake Arapeen informed Thomas Caldwell that he saw him come to the river to get water and could have shot him. He also claimed that the Indians could have shot all the men who bathed in the river. "Why didn't you shoot them?" asked Caldwell. Jake's answer was that the raiders "wanted all the men to get into the river, then the water would have been red. He said they were ambushed and as soon as the white men all got into the stream they were going to open fire."[28]

The following morning, the hungry troopers started for home, traveling up the deep chasm known as Buckhorn Wash.[29] Famished, the men scattered out along the wash's towering rock walls searching for berries, roots, and greens to eat, but because they "knew so little about such things" most of them soon had "the cramps."[30] Meanwhile, driving

---

[25] The crackers so lovingly made by Sanpete Valley women did not fare well on the journey and were broken to pieces by the rigors of the pursuit of the Indians. Bodily, *Autobiography*, 21; Seeley, "History," 7; Gottfredson, *Indian Depredations*, 162; and Clark, "John Haslem Clark," 85.

[26] Seeley, "History," 7. The ford, named for John W. Gunnison, had long been a major Ute crossing and was an important landmark on the Old Spanish Trail.

[27] Gottfredson, *Indian Depredations*, 162–63; Clark, "John Haslem Clark," 85-87; and Andrew Madsen, "Personal History," 57.

[28] Bodily, *Autobiography*, 21; Sylvester, "Indian Wars," 3; and a similar but variant account in Gottfredson, *Indian Depredations*, 162–63.

[29] Andrew Madsen, "Personal History," 54.

[30] Clark, "John Haslem Clark," 87.

rains made them even more miserable; eventually they reached home safely, however. Aside from the geographic knowledge and experience it provided, the two-week expedition to the Green River was a failure. Establishing a precedent Mormon generals were loath to break, the troops started out so late that overtaking Black Hawk was virtually impossible.

The Second Glenwood Raid

Warren Snow was greeted with bad news when he arrived home in Manti on 3 August. While he and his men were away, the tiny settlement of Glenwood had been attacked again, this time in retaliation for the Indians killed in the "Squaw Fight." Consisting of fewer than forty families, the tiny settlement was imprudently built so close to the mountains to the east that Indians could fire down into it with ease. At daybreak on 26 July the shooting started when the village blacksmith arose to light his fire. Wounded in the chest, the old man staggered back to his dugout as several teenage boys and an adult named Solomon Chase emerged from nearby cabins and dugouts to return the fire. An Indian on the nearby hill shouted, "Sol Chase, shoot him," directing a volley of shots that rang out from the raiders' positions. The Indians kept up "a constant fire" while the families living closest to the hill ran to safety.

Despite their poor position, Glenwood's little force was determined to rout the Indians. Bishop James Wareham noticed an Indian casually sitting on a boulder, obviously convinced he was out of range. Handing his new Sharps rifle to a better shot, Wareham said, "There sits a beggar on a rock." Taking careful aim, the marksman rejoiced when he shot the Indian's jaw off with the bishop's long–range rifle. Knowing white reinforcements would soon be on hand, the Indians gathered up what was left of the Glenwood stock and fled up the same Grass Valley trail General Snow and his men had traversed the previous week.[31]

Mormon Animosity

As word of Latter-day Saint action in the "Squaw Fight" spread through the native society, virtually all Indians in the Sanpete and Sevier valleys were compelled by fear to flee from the settlements, even

---

[31] Nelson Higgins, Bishop of Richfield, to Brigham Young, 2 August 1865, BYC; Peacock, Journal, 26 July 1865; Gottfredson, *Indian Depredations*, 163–67; "The History of Glenwood," 2; and Sorensen and Bybee, *History of Glenwood*, 23.

though most had taken no part in Black Hawk's raids. One Sanpete diarist told only half the story when he wrote that local Indians "left for the mountains" because they were "mad."[32] The wholesale exodus was imperative, for local enmity towards Indians was intense and growing by the minute. On 6 August, just three days after the return of the Green River expedition, Orson Hyde preached in Manti, absolving the settlers of accountability for killing Indians by declaring "that only a few" of them were "of Israel" anyway. Most of Utah's Lamanites, he taught, were "the descendants of Cain or the Gadianton Robbers." Regarding "peaceful" Indians, Hyde announced that they were "first peaceful when they are dead."[33] Such teaching only compounded natural fears and frustrations spawned by five months of successful raiding.

Relations were further strained when Mormons badgered Indian neighbors in Utah, Juab, and Pahvant valleys for information regarding the raiders. On 16 August the presiding elder of Santaquin learned from native informants that two of Black Hawk's men were visiting a "peaceful" band encamped nearby. A force of Payson and Santaquin militiamen surrounded the small Ute village early on the seventeenth. Discovering that they were surrounded, and undoubtedly thinking of the recent slaughter in the "Squaw Fight," thirty warriors "drew their guns and [made] ready for battle."

Defusing a potential bloodbath, militia leaders informed the frightened Utes that they simply wanted the two raiders, who were soon turned over. These Indians allegedly "confessed" to participation in the raids, and one supposedly "acknowledged that he killed Barney Ward." The two were promptly executed and, as a result, the "peaceful" band became "wroth with the Payson people." The two may indeed have been guilty, but conscientious Latter-day Saints later admitted that innocent Indians were sometimes killed and that such "peaceful" bands "had a right to get mad." More representative of his community, however, one Utah Valley diarist objected to the Santaquin band's anger and wrote that he was "in favor of punishing" the offended Indians "in a manner that *the survivors* will remember to the end of their lives."[34]

---

[32] Weibye, "Journal," 3 August 1865.

[33] Ibid., 6 August 1865. The Gadianton robbers were a wicked group written about in the Book of Mormon who, like the raiders, plundered others and escaped to mountain strongholds.

[34] President David M. Holladay to Brigham Young, 18 August 1865, BYC; Daniel Jones, *Forty Years Among the Indians*, 173; and Coombs, Diary, 20 August 1865. Italics mine.

According to white sources, the leaders of this band, Guffick and Showan, took no part in the hostilities throughout the entire war. But, since Black Hawk was born near Santaquin and was perhaps more closely related to this band than any other, violent distrust on the part of their Mormon neighbors forced this group to find refuge in the mountains. Simultaneously, they were under considerable pressure from hostile bands to renounce the Saints and join the raiders. Caught in the middle, noncombatants were often threatened by violence from both sides. Guffick, who was a baptized Latter-day Saint (as were most of the Santaquin Indians) complained to a special Mormon friend of the difficulty his neutrality put him in. Benjamin F. Johnson wrote:

> . . . I saw someone moving in the brush at the foot of the mountains, and thinking it might be Guffick, I started in that direction. Seeing me, [Guffick] hurriedly came, clasped me in his arms and wept. I asked him with his family and friends, to come and live with me through the war [Johnson had a small private fort at Spring Lake], and I would give my life for his did anyone kill him or his. He said he could not, *for if the Mormons did not kill him the Indians would*, should he do so. His grief for the war then going on appeared extreme, and at parting he again hugged me and wept as before. Such was his integrity to me, and our mutual confidence and love for each other that to but few would I have entrusted my life sooner than with him.[35]

Sadly, other Mormons, who like Benjamin Johnson had been special friends and protectors of the Indians, were beginning to turn from their former associates as white casualties and the numbers of stock driven off in Black Hawk's raids mounted. Bishop Aaron Johnson of Springville, for example, had long been an advocate for Native Americans, and his home and table had formerly been centers of happy Indian-white interaction. In the choleric intensification of bad feelings during the summer of 1865, however, he too succumbed to the violent spirit of the times, sending Mormon troops against peaceful Indians in nearby mountains simply because the Springville Latter-day Saints had "stock in that vicinity." "Bring their scalps," the bishop's son remembered his father saying as he sent the Springville Nauvoo Legion out after Indians who had yet to commit any offense.[36]

---

[35] Benjamin Johnson, *My Life's Review*, 224, 229–30. Italics mine.
[36] Don Carlos Johnson, *History of Springville*, 66.

As his people's animosity grew, Brigham Young stepped up his efforts to keep reports of Indian trouble from reaching federal military authorities. After the gentile press alleged Danite involvement in the killing of the Given family in May, the *Deseret News* gave only casual notice of the Indian trouble to the south, consciously minimizing its scope and the Saints' reaction to it. Despite these efforts, General Connor and his staff were very much aware of the growing conflict and read subterfuge and conspiracy into the Mormon secrecy. The temporary commander of Camp Douglas wrote his superiors, "The Indians in Southern and Western Utah are also committing depredations, *instigated thereto by Mormon leaders.* They are doubtless attempting the same policy which they tried there, three years ago, . . . [that is, using staged Indian attacks] to force every man, woman, and child, not a Mormon to leave the Territory." As a result, the limited reports of Indian depredations in Utah that did reach U.S. military officials were largely ignored. Gentile Indian policy, like that of the Mormons, was overshadowed and dictated by their own conflict with the opposing group of whites. Interestingly, gentiles used the war as an opportunity to ask that "more troops" be sent to Utah, not to go after the Indians but to protect "Gentile life" and "interests" from Mormon schemes.[37]

The Fish Lake Expedition and Engagement at Red Lake
While Warren Snow chased Black Hawk in Castle Valley, Kanosh and Moshoquop, the Pahvant war chief, reported that the raiders had strongly urged the Pahvants to join them. The word among Kanosh's people was that Black Hawk was congregating his forces near Fish Lake preparatory to launching further attacks on Sevier Valley settlements. The attack on Glenwood seemed to confirm this report, and an increase of Indian signal fires on the mountains gave Mormons the impression that further attacks were imminent.[38] On 14 September Warren Snow and Colonel John L. Ivie left Manti with 111 men "to discover the whereabouts" of Black Hawk's band. Traveling first to Circleville, they learned from Paiutes that the chief raider was concentrating a force of "two or three Hundred" warriors near Fish Lake. The Paiutes themselves evidently had been recruited, but, eager to show their friendliness, they informed Snow of the location of Black Hawk's

[37] Captain George F. Price to Maj. Genl. Grenville M. Dodge, 21 August 1865, District of the Plains, Register of Letters Received, Jan.–Sept. 1865, vol. 326, District of Missouri, 258–59, RUSA, pt. 2, entry 3257. Italics mine.
[38] "Col Snow on the War Path."

"place of Gathering" as well as of his intention "to make an attack upon the settlement [of Circleville]."[39]

By 21 September Snow and his men had reached the Fish Lake region. In the process of reconnoitering the shore of Red Lake, two miles south of present-day Bicknell in Wayne County, Snow and Ivie halted the command and rode their horses up a ridge, hoping to get a better view of the area. By chance, the two men stumbled right into a hundred Indians who were concealed in the brush waiting to ambush the militiamen. The two officers wheeled their horses as their attackers discharged their first volley. Snow was hit in the shoulder and knocked from his horse. Rolling behind a large rock, he momentarily gathered his senses and then ran for his horse, mounting it "under a heavy fire." Miraculously, both officers made it back to the command.

Meanwhile, the evenly matched native force opened fire on the 111 militiamen; but, firing downhill, they overshot, "the bullets singing over the heads of the soldiers," striking the lake behind them, "fairly making it boil." Despite this, two more men were wounded and the entire Mormon patrol retreated in disarray. Once out of range, they quickly selected an advantageous site and used pack horses to form a bulwark to protect themselves from the Indians, who were making their way down the ridge. Well matched in size and firepower, the two groups fought intermittently throughout the remainder of the day. No more white casualties were reported, though Indian deaths were variously estimated at four and seven. The Indians disappeared into the hills near dark and the militiamen limped back towards Glenwood, where Snow and his wounded compatriots received medical attention thirty-six hours later.[40]

Ute oral tradition relates the Battle of Red Lake in this manner:

These white soldiers were discovered accidentally while an Indian was out hunting. He spotted a man in a white blanket and being curious, he sneaked closer to get a better look. When he saw that

---

[39] Warren Snow (by George Peacock) to Brigham Young, 24 September 1865, BYC.

[40] A major landmark in Rabbit Valley at the time of the Black Hawk War, Red Lake, once located in "Bicknell Bottoms," has ceased to exist due to changes wrought by white settlement. Interview of Clifford Mangum by the author, Bicknell, Utah, 13 September 1997, notes in author's possession. For information regarding the expedition and the battle see Weibye, "Daybook," 50; Warren Snow (by George Peacock) to Brigham Young, 24 September 1865, BYC; Peacock, Journal, 21 September 1865; Farnsworth, "History of Manti," 52; *Juvenile Instructor* 13 (15 July 1878): 165; Andrew Madsen, "Personal History," 60; Sarah Milner, various historical sketches of Warren S. Snow; Gottfredson, *Indian Depredations*, 167–69; and Jenson, *Encyclopedic History*, 929.

he had a white face the Indian ran back to his camp on Pine Creek south of Bicknell. He told his people of what he saw and they decided to evacuate the women. The women all left their camp that night and started up O-aw'Kaiv, a nearby mountain while the men waited behind to fight the soldiers.

Early that morning the soldiers spotted the women through their telescope going up the last of the trail near the top of the mountain. They also saw the men down in the valley sitting around at the camp.

The Indians meanwhile had concealed some men in the brush where the soldiers would approach so they might ambush them. As the soldiers approached and were starting into the ambush, the lead man spotted one of the Indians who was probably wearing a red blanket. The lead man whirled around dashing past one other concealed Indian and out into the clear. The soldiers then ran up onto the point of the hill the Paiutes called Pachu Tahng-kun'evuhts and commenced firing down on the Indians. The Indians and soldiers were not too close to each other so they were firing from long range. The Indians at this time had good rifles.

There were two Indians concealed behind a rock, somewhat closer to the hill, that almost got hit. One of these Indians spotted a man on the hill who was firing these shots. He told the other that he saw where the shots were coming from and that he was going to aim and wait for him to stick up again. When he stuck up, the Indian shot him between the eyes.

[One white] hollered down from the hill in Paiute, as he spoke good Indian, and he said "Tahnunk'wu evun'ee, kwou tuhkaw kwaivadum. Kaw yavawhaisump!" Come up here; let's smoke. Don't be afraid! In the battle two white men were killed and no Indians.[41]

Last Chance for Peace

Upon learning of the Red Lake engagement, Brigham Young issued orders for Nauvoo Legion operations against the Indians to cease. Though he alone was responsible for the policy that resulted in the Squaw Fight and the battle near Red Lake, it appears that the killing of Indians, and more particularly the wounding of Warren Snow, convinced Young that his original peaceful approach was best after all.

---

[41] Martineau, *Southern Paiutes*, 54–55.

Understanding something of native notions of vengeance, the church leader was aware that killing Indians would probably result in even more depredations and concluded that chasing Lamanites through the mountains exposed Mormon lives to more danger than it was worth.

Accordingly, on 1 October the church president charged interpreter Dimick Huntington to find Sanpitch and inform him that orders were being sent to Sanpete and Sevier county militia units "to cease their hostilities against the Indians" at once. Furthermore, Huntington was to ask Sanpitch to send runners to the raiders to "tell them to stop their waring and fighting and make peace with the whites." Young promised to send presents when Black Hawk and his men were ready to receive them, but he stipulated that they were to "return the Stock they have stolen."[42]

That same day, Young sent an epistle to Orson Hyde and the Latter-day Saints in Sanpete and Sevier counties reinstating the "cheaper to feed than fight" policy. "The correctness of this maxim," he dictated, is "fourced [*sic*] upon us when we consider the great risk the brethren run of losing their lives in endeavoring to whip or kill the marauders." The plan he now proposed was "to stop fighting altogether . . . and endeavor to make peace with them by means of presents." Although formerly he had withheld information, Young now invited Superintendent Irish to write a formal peace treaty, thus shifting the cost of his policy to the federal government.

The epistle then addressed a serious and growing problem in the war counties, a problem fueled by the teachings of Orson Hyde. "We have learned the brethren of Sanpete and up the Sevier are much exasperated against the Indians . . . and feel like slaughtering them indiscriminately," it read. "Such a course would be most injudicious and cruel, and will never do," Young dictated. Instructions were given that the contents of his letter be made known to all the Saints "in the disturbed district," with emphasis on its special caution that the Saints "not feel relieved" by the new peace policy "from the necessity of continued vigilance in guarding against depredations."[43]

Two days later, the epistle was hand-delivered to Warren Snow by Joseph Young, who came to Manti to make sure his father's policy was implemented. That same day, two special "peace missionaries" were

---

[42] Brigham Young to Dimick B. Huntington, 1 October 1865, BYC.

[43] Brigham Young to "President Orson Hyde and the Bishops and Presidents, Elders and brethren in San Pete Co. and up the Sevier River and all others whom it may concern," 1 October 1865, BYC; and JH, 6 November 1865, 2.

called to present and explain the policy change to local settlers. Significantly, one of them was the father of Peter Ludvigsen, the war's first
casualty.[44] A rush of optimism attended the epistle and the war-frazzled
Saints immediately rejoiced as if peace already existed. "TheBreatheren
[*sic*] will be most Happy at once more enjoying Peace," Warren Snow
dictated from his bed in Manti the very day he learned of the shift in
strategy. Chronicling some of the economic challenges the war imposed, Snow complained that for fear of Indians the Saints were unable
to go to the mountains for lumber to finish their homes and granaries
or to fence their fields. Even prohibited from getting firewood, they
had been forced "to use fencing &c for fuel." "We find by Experiance
[*sic*] your Council to be true," Snow assured Young, "'better feed the
Indians than fight them' *and far Cheaper!*"[45]

As soon as Young's new peace policy was announced, scores of
Sanpete Saints recklessly rushed to the canyons after wood as though
the war were over. Meanwhile, Sanpitch sent a runner with news of
the prophet's peace proposals to Black Hawk. The courier returned
sometime later with word that the war chief flatly rejected Young's
overtures, defiantly declaring that he would fight to the death.[46] Unfortunately for some Sanpete Latter-day Saints, word of Black Hawk's
response was not quickly disseminated, and they learned from the
raiders themselves in the most daring raid to date that the war was far
from over.

The Ephraim Massacre

On the morning of 17 October, sixteen men from Ephraim took work
teams and wagons up a canyon east of town. Spreading out some distance on the road, they spent the morning gathering firewood and
fence poles, and felling large trees for lumber. About 2:00 P.M. twenty
mounted Indians led by Black Hawk, "who carried a big shield," attacked a group of six woodsmen, immediately killing one of them. The
dead man's comrades scattered, frantically warning other whites as they
started a desperate five-mile footrace back to town. The raiders

[44] Warren S. Snow to Brigham Young, 3 October 1865, BYC; and Weibye, "Journal," 4
October 1865. George Peacock was the senior Ludvigsen's traveling companion. "Our mission," Peacock noted, "was one of peace, and the good Spirit was with us." Peacock, Journal,
6 October 1865.

[45] Warren S. Snow to Brigham Young, 3 October 1865. Italics mine.

[46] M.D. Hambleton to Brigham Young, 22 October 1865, BYC; Weibye, "Journal,"
22–26 October 1865; and JH, 6 November 1865, 1.

stopped long enough to brutalize a Danish convert, viciously dismembering him with his own axe. Luckily for the whites, the Indians stopped at each wagon long enough to slash harnesses and free the oxen, inadvertently giving most of the sprinters time to reach the safety of a local gristmill. The slowest runner, however, was overtaken and killed on the flats near the mouth of the canyon.

On emerging from the canyon, the Indians saw a covered carriage with three riders approaching Ephraim on the road from Manti and dashed towards the vehicle. Seeing the raiders from a distance, the three Mormons speculated as to whether or not they were in danger. A Danish woman blurted out, "they are going to hurt us." The American driver tried to calm her by suggesting that it was "Chief Sanpitch bringing the Indians down to make peace." The third occupant of the carriage, another Dane, nervously pointed out that the Indians were "riding very recklessly."

Black Hawk's men stopped and readied their weapons as the carriage approached them. The driver, who had calmly walked his horses to this point, now gave them free rein. As the carriage passed the waiting Indians at full gallop, the raiders stoically "leveled their guns" and fired. The horses reportedly were a pair of trained racing animals; one was mortally wounded but ran on as though no damage had been done. Filling the air with war whoops, the Indians gave chase, but most of their exhausted ponies could not catch up with the fresher animals pulling the carriage. Mounted on a superior horse, though, Jake Arapeen rode adjacent to the whites and emptied his revolver at them. The woman buried her face in her lap as her countryman scrambled over the dashboard and crouched on the carriage tongue between the horses. Meanwhile, the driver courageously urged his animals on with a whip. Unsuccessful with his pistol, Jake shot arrows point blank into the carriage, sinking one six inches into the driver's back. Finally the carriage outdistanced Jake and the others, who chased it right to the edge of the settlement.

The raiders then turned their attention to a number of frightened Latter-day Saints who were running in from fields where they had been digging potatoes. Falling in behind two women and a man carrying a baby boy (all Danes), they waited before shooting until the group was within a few yards of the first row of Mormon homes. Morton Kuhre, the man with the child, was allegedly shot in the back with bullets and arrows by Black Hawk himself. Kuhre's wife grabbed the child as she passed her husband's body but after running a few more yards was shot in the back herself. Kuhre's seventeen-year-old sister-in-law was then killed with arrows. Men, women, and children watched with horror from nearby Ephraim windows and streets as an Indian reached down from his horse and picked up the screaming infant. Thoughtfully observing the child for a moment as if deciding whether or not to kill it, the Indian at last set the boy "gently" on the breast of his dying mother and rode off to join his associates.

The raiders next collected a herd of about a hundred cattle ranging south of town. A good number of Ephraim's men were away, and, as Orson Hyde later pointed out, those who remained were "frightened and paralyzed even to stupidity." Most of Ephraim's males were Scandinavian converts who had ignored Young's instructions to buy guns; they armed themselves with pitchforks and axes and watched from the village's southernmost street as the Indians ran off their cattle. A few Danes recklessly ran towards the herd with only one load in their guns, forgetting to take ammunition with them. Fortunately for them, the Indians were so occupied with driving away their booty that they paid the unseasoned foreigners little heed.

Better armed and more experienced, the few American men on hand moved towards the gristmill to try to keep the Indians from driving the herd into the canyon. Thwarted by Indian sharpshooters, the few Mormons brave enough to do anything at all followed the animals towards the canyon, taking scattered shots as they went. Near "Guard Knoll" (so called because prior to their newfound "peace" the people of Ephraim generally posted picket guards there to warn them of just such a raid) the Indians made a stand against their pursuers. During the shooting a seventh settler was killed and badly mutilated. Put to flight, the defenders returned dejectedly to the settlement and sent word of the attack to General Snow, who was still convalescing in Manti.[47]

Shortly after the Indians escaped into the canyon with the cattle, Orson Hyde arrived from Spring City totally unaware of the tragedy. The apostle was shocked at the lack of courage demonstrated by the Scandinavians; for, although there were Americans willing to lead a

[47] JH, 18 October 1865, 1–2; Gottfredson, *Indian Depredations*, 169–75; Weibye, "Journal," between entries for 22 and 26 October 1865, in Danish; Peacock, Journal, 18 October 1865; Canute Peterson, Bishop of Ephraim, to George A. Smith, 11 September 1867, GAS; Orson Hyde to Brigham Young, 18 October 1865, BYC; Kuhre, Interview; Samuel Pitchforth to George A. Smith, 30 November 1865, GAS; DUP, *Treasures of Pioneer History*, 2:463; and DUP, *Our Pioneer Heritage*, 9:179, 11:281.

force against the Indians, they "could hardly induce a man to follow them." What made it worse, Hyde observed, was that "never was there a better opportunity" to destroy Black Hawk's "whole squad." According to Hyde, the Scandinavians were "good to raise wheat, cattle, and horses but seem[ed] totally inadequate for an emergency of that kind."[48]

Fearing another attack, the Mormons waited until the following day to bring in the remains of their seven slaughtered friends. The bodies, one without arms, legs, and head, were laid out in the meetinghouse for all to see. The sight of the mutilated corpses and the loss of most of Ephraim's livestock fueled the burgeoning hatred for Indians felt by the Sanpete Saints. Afraid even to venture out of town as far as the local cemetery, the settlers temporarily interred their dead in a shallow grave near their meetinghouse. That day Elder Hyde sent word of the massacre to Salt Lake City, tersely noting that "this is the evidence [the raiders] give us of their disposition to make peace!" Viewing the bodies filled Hyde with "chagrin and mortification," and the angry apostle threatened to excommunicate the negligent Latter-day Saints if they did not immediately sell their "new chicago wagons" and buy guns and ammunition.[49]

Church authorities in Salt Lake City were equally upset over the calamity. "The proposals for peace were accompanied with instructions to the Settlements to in no ways relax their vigilance," thundered George A. Smith. "Really, was there no horses kept up ready to mount in Ephraim?" he asked in disbelief. "Was there no Serjeant or Corporal who could follow out and recover the cattle without sending to Manti to find if bro. Snow was at home?" Brigham Young himself was appalled at the "stupidity of our settlements and their recklessness of life," especially after "the many years of counsel" he had given them to build forts, buy guns, and not unwisely expose themselves to Indian attacks. Like Apostles Hyde and Smith, however, he was resigned to the fact that "the architects of Zion" had to "work with such material as the Lord has provided, stupidity, wooden shoes, and cork brains thrown into the bargain."[50]

Black Hawk Escalates the War

Within days of the Ephraim Massacre, Mormons became aware that the killings were the expression of an almost universal anger against

[48] Orson Hyde to George A. Smith, 29 October 1865, GAS.
[49] Ibid.
[50] George A. Smith to Orson Hyde, 22 October 1865, HOLB, 2:506–9.

them on the part of the Indians of Utah. Killings of Indians in military movements like those ordered by Orson Hyde in Sanpete Valley and those ordered by Brigham Young in official Nauvoo Legion expeditions such as those which resulted in the Squaw Fight and Red Lake engagement, as well as the executions of the raiders captured near Santaquin, all called for vengeance. Perhaps even more serious were the individual, unauthorized, and often unrecorded murders of innocent Indian men, women, and children by angry Mormons that increasingly took place throughout central Utah as feelings between the two groups further polarized. George A. Smith identified a major problem when he wrote that "every Indian that is killed . . . has friends who expect to kill two for him—some lone traveller—some person keeping mill or digging potatoes has to be killed by way of retaliation."[51]

In the wake of the killings at Ephraim, Brigham Young and other leaders were inundated with reports that Black Hawk's messengers were stirring up anger among the Shoshonis, Pahvants, Piedes, and Paiutes; also, the first reports of Black Hawk's emissaries exciting Indians "as far south as our Dixey"[52] began to pour in. Previously friendly Ute bands, including Mountain's, officially "declaired alliance" to Black Hawk. Indians under Sowiette, Antero, and Tabby at the Uintah Reservation were "frequently urged" to join the raiders, and Black Hawk "was joined by wild spirits and outlaws from various bands." Even Kanosh was momentarily "disaffected by rumors from Black Hawk's camp" and informed his trusted friend, Bishop Callister of Fillmore, that "*all* the Utah nation are mad" and that leaders had called "a grand war council" to coordinate wholesale operations against the Mormons in the spring. While Callister succeeded in calming Kanosh, the Pahvant chief indicated that he could hardly restrain his men and that a significant number of them had already followed his father-in-law, an Indian named Ungowguitch, to Black Hawk's camp. Meanwhile, Sanpitch and his band fled to Camp Floyd (the federal military base west of Utah Valley) because "Some of the San Pete Brethren has threatend to Com and Kill [them]." After receiving promises of protection from the soldiers, Sanpitch and his people became "saucey" toward Mormons and boasted of "what they would do" the following spring.[53]

---

[51] Ibid.

[52] The region of southwestern Utah around St. George, commonly spelled "Dixie." See Andrew Larson, *"I Was Called to Dixie."*

[53] M.D. Hambleton to Brigham Young, 22 October 1865, BYC; *RSI*, 1866:10, 124; *RSI*, 1867:181; Thomas Callister to Brigham Young, 22 October 1865, BYC; Erastus Snow to

Frightened southern Utah Piedes came to Apostle Erastus Snow in St. George with reports of "Black Hawk's threats" to come south to "corall the Mormons in and about Washington and St George" and to "capture Piede women and children," presumably because these weaker Indians would not join the raiders against the Saints.[54] As a result of such reports, Snow sent ranchers living in Long Valley, Kanab, along the Paria River, and other spots near the Arizona border an epistle with orders to build forts as protection "against hostile Utes, who . . . are liable to beat South and prey upon the herds of Kane County, during the winter."[55] Meanwhile, regular Piede reports that hostile Utes were gathering east of Circleville caused so many settlers to leave that community that Orson Hyde, fearing the settlement would be totally deserted, ordered the people back on threat of excommunication.[56]

What church leaders did not fully grasp (and, in fact, would not grasp for years to come) was the extent to which Black Hawk exported his anger beyond the territory's boundaries on all sides.[57] This explosion of Black Hawk's influence was in part the result of the notoriety that his military exploits engendered. Apostle Erastus Snow wrote that Black Hawk's "success driving off stock" gave the raiders "great prestige with the surrounding bands and tribes."[58] Even more important than the chief raider's "prestige" was the power his huge herd of stolen stock gave him over hungry Indians of many bands and tribes throughout the region. However, a big part of the expansion of his influence was brought on by his own efforts to replenish and expand his raiding party. Black Hawk's original party reportedly consisted of only forty-four men, though "his numbers were constantly on the increase" throughout 1865; but his losses that season were also staggering. Indian sources revealed that "forty of his warriors were killed by the settlers in

---

Brigham Young, 4 November 1865, BYC; Charles H. Bryan, Bishop of Nephi, to Brigham Young, 6 November 1865, BYC; Lewis Robison to Daniel H. Wells, 5 March 1866, TMR, #817; and Robison, "Journal," 25–27 February 1866. Italics mine.

[54] Erastus Snow to Brigham Young, 4 November 1865.

[55] Erastus Snow "to the Saints in Long Valley, . . . Kanab, . . . and all others in that region of the country," 12 November 1865, in Bleak, "Southern Mission," 1:207.

[56] Orson Hyde to Brigham Young, 19 November 1865, BYC.

[57] The boundaries of the Territory of Utah changed many times during the period covered in this study, as the federal government systematically diminished the sphere of Brigham Young's dominion. Within a year of the inauguration of the Black Hawk War, however, the territory had been essentially reduced to the area embraced by the State of Utah today, and these 1866 borders will be used here. See Greer et al., *Atlas of Utah*, 160–65.

[58] JH, 3 May 1866, 3.

repelling his different attacks" that year.[59] His success was costly in terms of Indian lives, yet, in order to continue, he must have recruits. It is clear that he desired to turn his movement into a pan-Indian crusade that would drive the whites from the entire region; therefore, his emissaries were wide-ranging.

Black Hawk's influence, while perhaps only of minor importance in Idaho and Nevada, was truly significant in southwestern Wyoming and even more substantial in southwestern Colorado, northwestern New Mexico, and in northern Arizona. Nevada was arguably impacted less than any other bordering state or territory, though Black Hawk's runners clearly encouraged Indians there to make raids of their own on Mormon settlements along the Muddy River. Also, some of the stock stolen by Black Hawk's raiders was sold or traded to white middlemen supplying beef to the Nevada mines. Black Hawk's own Goshute intermarriage and his close ties to Tintic, who a decade earlier had led Nevada recruits against the Mormons, undoubtedly worked to his advantage in exporting his war to the west.[60]

As for the north, sometime in 1865 Black Hawk himself evidently visited the Shoshonis in southern Idaho to solicit their support. Still suffering from the tremendous losses they suffered at General Connor's hands in the Bear River Massacre in 1863 and anxious to retain their treaty annuities (which potentially would be lost if they joined Black Hawk en masse), Washakie's people for the most part refused his overtures. Scores of "renegade" Shoshonis and Goshutes, however, still broke from Washakie and joined the Ute's ranks. His plans for a wholesale Ute-Shoshoni alliance foiled, Black Hawk and a small retinue of his men reportedly stayed long enough in Shoshoni country to collect gentile scalps on the Idaho stretch of the Overland Trail.[61] Still the main route across the nation, the Overland Trail provided a significant market for stolen horses and cattle, especially near Fort Bridger. The raiders' tremendous success in marketing cattle there and

[59] Franklin H. Head to Commissioner of Indian Affairs D.N. Cooley, 30 April 1866, in *RSI*, 1866:128.

[60] Erastus Snow to Daniel H. Wells, 18 March 1866, TMR, # 824; Bleak, "Southern Mission," 1:220, 2:108; Andrew Larson, *Red Hills of November*, 151; DUP, *Heart Throbs*, 11:335. See also discussion of a Nevada arms and stock dealer named Patterson later in this chapter.

[61] Benjamin Johnson, *My Life's Review*, 228–29; Henroid, "Biography," 11; Cropper, "Life and Experience," 57; and McBride, "Journal," 59. In the summer of 1866 Apostle Lorenzo Snow wrote that the Shoshonis "continue to assure us they will not join the south against us. . . . they acknowledge that some emisaries of the southern Indians have been endeavoring to exercise [bad influences] over them." Lorenzo Snow to Brigham Young, 10 July 1866, BYC.

in other areas in southwestern Wyoming will be discussed later in this chapter.

Black Hawk's most successful recruiting ground by far was the Four Corners region, the area traditionally inhabited by the Shiberetches, who made up the largest portion of his original raiding band. It will be remembered that for decades before the Black Hawk War, Wakara had marshaled the Shiberetches and other Four Corners Indians into an effective raiding force. Wakara and his "Chiveretches" ran off stock from California to Sonora, Mexico, driving their hoofed plunder over the Old Spanish Trail that ran through the heart of the region, which allowed him to develop a formidable reputation among Indians, Hispanics, and whites of the Southwest.

From the very start of the Black Hawk War, Mormons and Indian leaders identified the raiders as mostly "Elk Mountain Utes," or "Shiberetches," assisted by "a few Manti Indians." Just before the initial raids in April 1865, a band of Shiberetch Utes came to the Mormon settlements in the Sevier Valley "because they were hungry." After the first wave of stock thefts, the Shiberetches, with "Black Hawk . . . at there head" were immediately identified as the guilty party.[62] By the spring of 1866, Utah's gentile superintendent of Indian affairs had learned through native informants that Black Hawk had wintered east of the Elk Mountains (now known as the La Sal Mountains near Moab), "having gone [there] to endeavor to procure recruits from among the Elk Mountain Utes, the most powerful tribe in the Territory," and that he had "secured a sufficient number" to "swell his force to three hundred warriors."[63] As the war went on, Mormons became more acquainted with such Elk Mountain raiders as Augavorum and Tamaritz, who along with Jake Arapeen and Mountain were among Black Hawk's chief lieutenants.[64]

Even before the end of 1865, however, Indian Office employees in Colorado, New Mexico, and Arizona were aware that "Asavaritches" (Shiberetches) or "Green River Utes—driven from Utah by the troops—or Mormons," along with Mexican accomplices, were aggressively enlisting Navajos, Hopis, Jicarilla Apaches, and Utes of the Weeminuche, Capote, Mouache, and Tabaguache bands to join them

---

[62] Reddick N. Allred to Brigham Young, 11 and 12 April 1865, BYC.

[63] Franklin H. Head to Commissioner of Indian Affairs D.N. Cooley, 21 June 1866, in *RSI*, 1866:129–30.

[64] Weibye, "Journal," 4 July 1869; *DN*, 26 August 1868; Sloan, "White Horse Chief"; and Gottfredson, *Indian Depredations*, 259, 289, and supplement, 3–4.

in raids against the settlers of Utah, and, in fact, against all whites.[65] Black Hawk's movement apparently was intertribal in nature from the very first, for, as Utah's superintendent of Indian affairs soon learned from native sources, his original band "consisted at first of but forty-four men, who were mostly outlaws and desperate characters from his own *and other tribes*."[66] Black Hawk's intertribal action came as no surprise to whites most closely connected with the Indians of the Four Corners region, for, as one New Mexican superintendent of Indian affairs warned his commissioner,

> there is a regular communication kept up between the various tribes which inhabit the central portion of the continent, . . . each one is cognizant of the affairs and doings of the others. How combinations might be formed among them can be easily conceived, and how dangerous these combinations might become can easily be understood by those who have the least knowledge of the Indian character.[67]

The truth is, there was so much intermarriage between the different groups living on the periphery of Navajo, Hopi, Apache, and Ute lands, which all came together in the Four Corners region, that these tribes were "so mixed up by marriage" that one Indian Office employee was certain that when one "will begin the war it will involve all."[68] It is clear that Black Hawk enlisted warriors from each of these major tribal groups, and by the spring of 1866 he not only had replenished his lost raiders but had expanded his raiding band to "three hundred warriors . . . one-half of whom are Navajoes from New Mexico."[69] Hence, when John Wesley Powell encountered Black Hawk's Shiberetches after their leader's death, he learned that "in their raids they have been

[65] Major Alb. H. Pfeiffer to Don Felipe Delgado, Supt. of Indian Affairs, Sante Fe, New Mexico, 22 December 1865, in "No. 11, Resolutions, Correspondence, &c. New Mexico, Report of J.K. Graves, U.S. spl. comr., 1866," BIA, M234, 553; Felipe Delgado to D.N. Cooley, 10 December 1865, and 7 January 1866, BIA, M234, 533; Felipe Delgado to J.K. Graves, U.S. Special Indian Commissioner, 9 January 1866, BIA, M234, 553; Correll, *Navajo History*, 5:298–99; *Santa Fe New Mexican*, 27 October 1866; CR, 229; and Bleak, "Southern Mission," 2:10, 65.

[66] Franklin H. Head to D.N. Cooley, Commissioner of Indian Affairs, 30 April 1866, *RSI*, 1866:128. Italics mine.

[67] J.L. Collins to William P. Dole, Commissioner of Indian Affairs, 10 October 1862, *RCIA*, 1862:241.

[68] W.F.M. Arny, Santa Fe, New Mexico, to D.N. Cooley, Commissioner of Indian Affairs, 23 August 1866, BIA, M234, 553.

[69] *RSI*, 1866:128–30.

associated with the Nav-a-jos and Utes, who inhabit the country to the east of the Colorado River."[70] Another gentile, Phil Robinson, wrote of "Black Hawk and his flying squadron of Navajos and Piutes."[71]

Perhaps because of the sparse white population in the area, for some time only Indian Office employees, mountaineers, and miners knew of Black Hawk's intertribal "alliance." Newspapers in Santa Fe and Denver, however, soon chronicled an immense burst of Ute animosity in southwestern Colorado and northwestern New Mexico that coincided precisely with Black Hawk's movement into the area. In October 1866, for example, the *Denver Rocky Mountain News* reported that "the miners in the Southern mines . . . and many of our mountainmen have noticed the anxiety the Indians have displayed, *for a year past*, to obtain firearms, and ammunition, trading for them at the most extravagant rates. By this the Indians have secured quite a stock of the desired arms, which, should the present trouble continue, will undoubtedly be used against the whites."[72]

While Mormons generally ignored Kanosh's warning that "*all* the Utah nation were mad" and had called "a grand war council," the *Denver Rocky Mountain News* affirmed that Indians normally "at peace" were suddenly "ripe for an outbreak," stating that "there is a perfect understanding existing between the different bands of the Ute nation in our mountains, and a war with one of them, if continued for any length of time, will be almost certain to bring [in] the whole nation."[73] It is well documented that Black Hawk played a vital role in this rise of Ute animosity in southern Colorado and northern New Mexico. The *Santa Fe New Mexican*, for example, described that "most of the Wemunuche Utes and all the Asavaritches or Green River Utes are together on the Rio Dolores [in the Elk Mountain country]" and had "been up to the Mormon settlements, and returned with a large amount of stock they stole there." "These are the same Indians," the *Santa Fe New Mexican* reported, who some time since stole the stock at Tierra Amarilla and killed the herders."[74]

This is significant, for it confirms that Black Hawk's band not only was at war with the Mormons but also raided stock and killed

---

[70] Ibid., 1873:410.

[71] Phil Robinson, *Sinners and Saints*, 162.

[72] *Denver Rocky Mountain News*, 12 October 1866. See also *Santa Fe New Mexican*, 6 October 1865, 22 June 1866, and 27 October 1866.

[73] *Denver Rocky Mountain News*, 12 October 1866.

[74] *Santa Fe New Mexican*, 27 October 1866.

non-Mormon white and Hispanic settlers on New Mexico's northern frontier. New Mexico's superintendent of Indian affairs made extensive trips into the Four Corners region for the express purpose of encouraging the Capote and Mouache bands of Utes not to "engage with . . . the Asavaritches or Green River Utes," who he had learned were in the area again "making preparations to attack the settlements in the northwestern portion" of his territory.[75] That Black Hawk's war was not just with Mormons, and that his killings were not just incident to cattle raiding, is confirmed by the correspondence of Indian Office employees in Colorado, who learned from Colorado Utes of "hostilities going on between the Salt Lake Utes . . . and the Mormon settlers *and miners* in the Great Basin."[76]

Although they were almost totally unaware of the extent of Black Hawk's movements beyond Utah's borders, rumors of an impending and colossal war with local Indians were more than enough to infuse the Latter-day Saints with an almost unprecedented martial spirit. Annual Nauvoo Legion musters held near the first of November 1865 were grand successes and boasted the largest turnouts in the militia's history. Even in the smaller villages, musters were extraordinarily serious and well attended, causing a resident of Parowan, for example, to exult that "the martial appearance of our militia would justify a stranger in presuming that a portion of Sherman's troops had settled in Utah."[77]

As November progressed each settlement established "military schools" where men commenced to study the newly published *Rifle and Light Infantry Tactics . . . Prepared Expressly for the Use of the Militia of the Territory of Utah, by Colonel Wm B. Pace, Nauvoo Legion* and competed for prizes of revolvers and swords awarded to those demonstrating the greatest military "proficiency." Wealthier Nauvoo Legion detachments in cities like Salt Lake, Provo, and Ogden selected regimental uniforms and more than ever before attempted to "fit themselves out" as real soldiers. As one Gunnison resident summed up the military spirit among the Saints, "All was war, war preparations, war outfits, and war duties."[78] A similar spirit clearly rested upon Black Hawk and many Indians throughout Utah and beyond. Perhaps as a prelude to what

---

[75] Ibid.

[76] Daniel C. Oaks, U.S. Indian Agent (for Grand River and Uinta bands) to A.C. Hunt, 10 June 1867, BIA, M234, 199. Italics mine.

[77] Hyrum Coombs to Isaiah Coombs, 15 November 1865, Isaiah Coombs Papers.

[78] Coombs, Diary, 4 December 1865; "Gunnison Ward Historical Record," 15–16; and Pace, *Rifle and Light Infantry Tactics*.

they intended to do the following spring, the raiders closed the 1865 season by attacking Circleville and driving off much of that village's stock.

The First Circleville Raid

About noon on 26 November 1865, a dozen raiders shot the Circleville herd's Danish guard and commenced rounding up the settlement's cattle. In the process, they killed two boys out hunting stock. Others chased a handful of settlers who barely made it to town, where the frightened townspeople gathered in the public square with pitchforks and homemade shotguns. Led by a rising young Shiberetch chief named Tamaritz, who was quickly becoming one of Black Hawk's most important lieutenants, the raiders drove the cattle east towards a canyon passage leading to Grass Valley. A few hardy settlers rode after the herd, but Tamaritz turned them back with his Henry repeating rifle because they had "no modern arms."

As the Indians neared the canyon, they encountered two young families in wagons and a man driving a small herd of steers, the last of a substantial contingent of Circleville deserters who had been ordered back by Orson Hyde. The wagons and steers were spread out for a distance of several miles on the road, and the closest wagon was about three miles from town. Leaving their captured herd, a few raiders shot the best horse of the team drawing the first wagon but were momentarily scared off by a Dane named Mads Nielsen who pointed an unloaded and "broken" pistol at them. This move gave Nielsen, his wife, and a two-year-old child time to escape to a nearby swamp and be concealed by willows. The Indians ransacked the wagon, breaking dishes, spilling flour, and ripping open bedding, while Ellen Nielsen prepared to drown both the child and herself. After setting the wagon on fire, the Indians moved towards the willows, but Nielsen's worn-out pistol again turned them back.

Farther up the valley, the raiders found a "Brother Froid" driving a few steers. Froid might have escaped had he abandoned his stock and fled, but instead he insisted on trying to save them from the Indians, who soon killed him, robbing him of all his clothing but his socks. The family in the second wagon came upon Froid's body and saw the Nielsens' rig burning in the distance and hurried to town with the news. After spending the day in the swamp, the frightened Danes walked to Circleville after dark, their wet clothes freezing stiff in the late November air. The next day, the Circleville Saints went out to recover the four bodies, which they found "stiff and naked" and "filled full of arrows." Mads Nielsen and a few armed friends went out to his charred wagon. His wife Ellen remembered that "everything had been destroyed but one large platter and it had fell in the sand and was not broken. When my Dear Husband got back we set in our little log home without anything, we were broke, our team and wagon and four of our cattle and all our supplies were gone, my darling husband took me in his arms and we had a good cry."[79]

Arms Race

In terms of lives lost, for the whites the 1865 season of the Black Hawk War was by far the most costly. Twenty-five Latter-day Saints were dead, as the Mormons counted, and eight had been wounded.[80] As the attacks on Ephraim and Circleville both illustrated, the pitchforks and "broken" firearms of the immigrants were no match for the superior arms of the Indians, who from the time of settlement were described as possessing "rifles of the first quality" and as being "most expert in their use."[81] Up to this point, it was well known that despite Brigham Young's preachings, only "the prosperous brothers" in frontier settlements even owned guns, let alone ample supplies of ammunition. Finally convinced that the war was more than a few isolated depredations (and urged on by Orson Hyde, who in the wake of the Ephraim Massacre was threatening "disfellowshipment from the church" for those not obtaining arms[82]) central and southern Utah Mormons worked during the winter of 1865–66 and beyond to trade their surplus cattle for weapons. At the same time, Black Hawk's raiders worked even more actively to replenish their own supplies of guns and ammunition. Significantly, this was only the beginning of an unprecedented expansion of firearms among both groups that accelerated as time went on.

Responding to Young's explicit instructions, each settlement, usually under the direction of local bishops, sent droves of cattle to Salt Lake City and other northern communities, where they were ex-

---

[79] Those killed in the first raid on Circleville were Orson Barney, Ole Heilersen, Hans Christian Hansen, and the above-named Froid, whose name is also given as Floyd, Flygare, or Flygard. Eunice Larsen, "Biography," 5–7; Munson, "Questions Concerning Black Hawk War"; Oluf Larsen, "Biographical Sketch," 46–47, and variation in DUP, *Our Pioneer Heritage*, 9:208–10; and Gottfredson, *Indian Depredations*, 176–79.

[80] "Memorandum of Killed and Wounded with an approximate amount and Value of Stock Stolen and Loss of Property during the 3 years Indian War," 1868, TMR, #1565.

[81] S.N. Carvalho, as quoted in DUP, *Treasures of Pioneer History*, 4:25.

[82] Nielsen, "A Short History," 17; and Orson Hyde to George A. Smith, 29 October 1865.

changed for rifles, muskets, cartridges, lead, caps, and powder. One such company from the Sevier Valley in May 1866 traded fifty head of cattle for "eighteen rifles, eleven revolvers and one hundred and forty pounds of ammunition," complaining that they had to pay such "an enormous price" because the Black Hawk War had made "these articles . . . indispensible." In Gunnison, Bishop Hamilton Kearnes, whose son William died in the opening battle of the war, joined with his business partner to purchase $2,500 worth of weapons and ammunition, which they apparently "scattered amongst the people" gratis.[83]

Mormon and gentile entrepreneurs saw the "weapons for cattle" market as an opportunity to turn a quick profit, and soon the *Deseret News* and other papers were running advertisements for "cases" of new repeating rifles. Visiting gentile newspaperman Charles Dilke noted these "warlike advertisements" with fascination, reporting one in which "fourteen cases of Ballard rifles" were offered "in exchange for cattle."[84] Almost immediately traveling munitions vendors coursed through the territory, using the fear of "certain Indian war next season" as their prime marketing tool. In the farthest-flung outposts of Utah, cattlemen and farmers suddenly became arms dealers. John D. Lee of Mountain Meadows Massacre fame, for example, bought hundreds of dollars worth of weapons from a gentile passing through the southern settlements with wagonloads of arms; Lee then in turn sold them to his co-religionists at a profit. The gentile arms peddler, whose name was Patterson, in one pass through southern Utah accumulated a herd of "700 head of cattle" in addition to a large amount of cash and produce. A beef supplier for the Nevada mines, Patterson also found the Indian side of the weapons trade to be as profitable as the white side, and Mormons eventually heard that he "instigated" raids on their stock.[85]

This impressive firearms traffic came as the U.S. War Department began to sell as surplus thousands of Civil War weapons, including late-model Sharps, Henry, and Spencer repeating rifles. Soldiers stationed in Utah were allowed to keep such firearms when they were mustered out of service, and, despite injunctions against it, discharged soldiers often financed trips home by selling guns and sabers to Mormons.[86]

---

[83] "Gunnison Ward Historical Record,"16, 19–20; and Gottfredson, *Indian Depredations,* 226.

[84] Dilke, *Greater Britain,* 1:165.

[85] Lee, *Diaries,* 2:39–40, 49, 53, 63, 93, 98; and Bleak, "Southern Mission," 2:108.

[86] Mormon merchants "openly" offered soldiers "twenty dollars for carbines, & twenty five Dollars when accompanied by five rounds of ammunition." For example, see Statement

The new Civil War repeaters were expensive, however, and since the Latter-day Saints in frontier settlements tended to be the poorest, few of the late-model weapons ended up where they were needed most, thus perpetuating an already uneven distribution of arms. The influx of war surplus weaponry did, however, allow wealthier Mormons in northern Utah cities and towns to obtain the new firearms and sell off their older and sometimes broken-down muskets to impoverished frontier Saints who generally had never owned guns.

Illustrative of the disproportionate distribution of firearms, by the spring of 1866 the First Division of the Salt Lake Nauvoo Legion was totally fitted out with guns, "a large portion" of them being new Springfield and Enfield rifles. On the other hand, the militia of the two-year-old Sevier Valley settlement of Panguitch had only twenty-two guns for forty men, and "one half" of these weapons "were scarcely fit for service being thin barrelled fowling pieces" which were mostly "out of repair."

A survey of weapons in Richfield, Monroe, and Glenwood in July 1866 not only illustrates the unequal concentration of weapons but also the great progress frontier Mormons were making in obtaining arms as a result of the war. Of 112 men residing in the three settlements, ninety-one had guns, most of whom the previous summer had simply depended on knives, axes, pitchforks, and other tools to protect themselves and their families from Black Hawk's raiders. In July 1866, however, only six of the 112 had the new Sharps, Henry, or Spencer repeating rifles that so many Salt Lakers could afford. Ten had Smith and Wesson, Joslyn, and Yauger rifles, while twenty-one had pistols. Seventy-five, however, almost 70 percent of the total number, had acquired old muskets.[87] Aware of the situation, Salt Lake City militiamen smugly ridiculed new-settlement Mormons as possessing weapons which were "not much better than a good club." Throughout 1866 and 1867, however, Sanpete and Sevier county gunsmiths were kept busy repairing the older guns, while Civil War repeating rifles slowly spread

---

of Lieut. William H. Tucker, Co. E. 1st Mich. Cav. Camp Douglas, U.T., Register of Letters Received, Oct. 1865–June 1866, No. 355, District of Missouri, 463, RUSA, pt. 3, entry 827.

[87] William B. Pace to General Daniel H. Wells, 30 July 1866, TMR, #946; George A. Smith to General Wells, 2 April 1866, TMR, #829; and "Report of arms ammunition &c Richfield and Glenwood and Alma," 30 July 1866, TMR, #1541. John Bohman, like many other Sevier Valley settlers during the war's first season, "had no gun so he would take his axe in the house at night in case of Indian attacks." DUP, *Treasures of Pioneer History*, 4:161.

southward. The result was that, by 1867, "Ballards, Spencers, and Henrys" were "plentiful" even in some of the frontier settlements. Still, Nauvoo Legion leaders found it "hard knocking to get some of the Saints to buy arms so as to be able to defend their families" and threatened to confiscate property and sell it to purchase arms for the "disobedient" settlers.

Good weapons were obtained at great sacrifice on the part of most frontier Mormons. One Circleville Dane purchased a Colt revolver and a Spencer rifle to replace "an old shotgun barrel" that was "little better than a broom stick." To get them, he described, "took about all I owned." For the two guns he traded "two young cows, three head of young stock, twenty bushels of wheat and some furniture."[88] The effect the Black Hawk War had on encouraging Mormons to obtain and upgrade weapons was so dramatic that many became convinced that God had sent the war for this very purpose. "If we do not come out of this war a well armed people I shall be much mistaken," wrote Isaiah Coombs in 1866, "and I am satisfied that that is what it is sent upon us for."[89]

The Utes' drive to improve the quality and numbers of their arms and to replenish their supplies of ammunition even exceeded that of the Latter-day Saints, and it eventually became clear that they traded off much of their stolen stock to this end. Like the above-mentioned gentile trader Patterson, some Mormons obliged weapon-hungry Indians despite Brigham Young's strict orders to the contrary. To stop this clandestine trade, the church leader instructed bishops to watch for and turn in the names of such offenders, who in turn were threatened with excommunication. Cattle thieves and other outlaws, who abounded both in and out of the church, were a major source of arms and ammunition for the Indians, as were soldiers, trappers, miners, and emigrants, as well as other Native Americans, especially those in adjacent territories.[90]

As has been pointed out, in southern Colorado and northern New

---

[88] Blythe, Journal, 27 April 1867; Clara Allred, Pioneer Personal History Questionnaire; Warren S. Snow to General Wells, 1 April 1866, TMR, #1522; *DN*, 8 May and 12 June 1867; and Oluf Larsen, "Biographical Sketch," 45, 48.

[89] Coombs, Diary, 2 July 1866.

[90] M.D. Hambleton to Brigham Young, 22 October 1865, BYC; Charles H. Bryan, Bishop of Nephi, to Brigham Young, 6 November 1865, BYC; Brigham Young to George Wilkin, 27 October 1865, BYC; and Brigham Young to Bishop Charles H. Bryan, 27 October 1865, BYC.

Mexico, the areas of Black Hawk's greatest recruiting success, miners and mountaineers reported an extreme burst of "anxiety" on the part of the Indians "to obtain firearms, and ammunition" that coincided with Black Hawk's recruiting efforts in the area and resulted in the Indians "trading for them at the most extravagant rates."[91] Meanwhile, the *Denver Rocky Mountain News* ran articles "censuring merchants for selling powder, lead, arms, etc. to the Ute Indians," warning that although the Utes were currently "friendly" to Colorado's gentiles they were probably "furnishing munitions of war to the other bands of Utes who are committing depredations" elsewhere.[92] Throughout the period, the *Denver Rocky Mountain News* frequently reported on the constant flow of guns and ammunition from Colorado whites to Utes "in exchange for furs, &c.," editorializing that men "who would furnish these Indians, lately so hostile, with means to renew their warfare, ought to be hung."[93]

Army officers farther west corroborated these reports, sometimes connecting the flow of arms directly to the Ute war in Utah. William E. Waters, traveling to Camp Douglas "under orders of Major-General Pope" early in 1866, wrote to the *New Orleans Advocate* from the Overland Trail that the entire Ute Tribe, most of whom did not even live in Utah, were angry with the Mormons and "were exceedingly anxious to trade for weapons and ammunition." "The Utes," he wrote, "have not been hostile to emigrants generally, but are unfriendly toward the Mormons, and have commitied [*sic*] depredations upon their trains and other property, and charge the 'Saints' with deceitfulness and treachery. A queer charge coming from an Indian!"[94] A queer charge, indeed, considering that a year and a half before, army officers were writing about the strange "masonic" relationship between Mormons and Indians that made the Saints the only whites able to safely traverse the plains.[95] The distinction between gentiles and Mormons that Indians had made for years, usually in favor of the Latter-day Saints, was now turned on its head, especially among those tribes who lived nearest to the Utah settlements. Mormons, however, were quick to see this change as the result of their enemies' "meddling with the Indians." "It is well understood," wrote Traveling Bishop A. Milton Musser in 1866,

[91] *Denver Rocky Mountain News*, 12 October 1866.
[92] *Denver Rocky Mountain News*, 11 August 1866.
[93] *Denver Rocky Mountain News*, 2 January 1866.
[94] Waters, *Life Among the Mormons*, 44–45.
[95] Ware, *Indian War of 1864*, 206–7.

"that our 'Christian' friends have furnished Black Hawk & his band with guns & ammunition to use against us."[96]

Indian Markets and White Middlemen

Franklin H. Head, who replaced Orsemus Irish as Utah's superintendent of Indian affairs early in 1866, estimated that during the 1865 season the raiders ran off "upwards of two thousand cattle and horses."[97] In terms of the Native American economy, this figure was a windfall of almost inconceivable proportions. In the years just prior to the war, the wealthiest Northern Ute bands boasted herds of less than thirty cattle. Over a period of just a few months, Black Hawk's military and accompanying economic success catapulted him to incredibly important positions of wealth, status, and power as far as his own society was concerned. In April 1866 Superintendent Head wrote that Black Hawk "has never yet met with a serious reverse, having always attacked small settlements or unprotected families. *He has thus acquired a considerable reputation among the various Indian tribes.*" "I am very apprehensive," he continued, "that unless Black Hawk is severely chastised, an Indian war of considerable magnitude may be inaugurated."[98] While little understood by contemporary whites, Black Hawk became a figure the likes of which the region had not seen since the 1840s when Wakara plundered California ranchos and marketed stolen stock in Santa Fe.[99] Indeed, the Black Hawk War in one sense can be viewed as the grand finale of the glory days of Ute raiding.

What became of Black Hawk's stock is a simple question, the answer to which is as complex as it is incomplete; nonetheless, it provides important insights into the raiders' motives, strategies, and operations. The raiders and their families and the large number of hungry Indians that quickly collected around them obviously consumed some of the stolen animals. Indeed, beef was Black Hawk's most important tool of recruitment. Superintendent Head wrote that Black Hawk's "success in stealing . . . *enabled him to feed abundantly and mount all Indians who joined him*, and the prestige acquired by his raids was such that his numbers were constantly on the increase, despite his occasional losses of

---

[96] Musser, Journal, 14 August 1866.

[97] F.H. Head to D.N. Cooley, Commissioner of Indian Affairs, 30 April 1866, *RSI*, 1866:128.

[98] Ibid. Italics mine.

[99] See Bailey, *Walkara*; Sonne, *World of Wakara*; and LeRoy Hafen and Ann Hafen, "Horse Thieves," in *Old Spanish Trail*.

men." Head soon learned from native informants that Black Hawk and his raiding band drove much of their booty east of the "Elk Mountains," where they "spent the winter near where the Grand and Green rivers unite to form the Colorado."[100]

It is clear that Indians of several tribes flocked to the area to trade or beg for Black Hawk's beef. The Elk Mountain region had long been a Ute wintering ground where various bands from throughout Utah, Colorado, and New Mexico traditionally came together to trade. In addition to the Tabaguache, Weeminuche, Capote, Mouache, and Shiberetch bands, white sources indicate that during the period of the Black Hawk War, portions of the Uinta, Grand River, and Yampa Ute bands wintered in the general vicinity of Black Hawk's camp "on the banks of Grand river above its confluence with Green river . . . about sixty miles distant from the Elk mountains."[101] These multiband Ute gatherings were often visited by Navajos, Apaches, and Hopis, as well as by mountain men and by Mexican and American traders. Attracted by the milder climate and these intertribal "trading fairs," Sowiette's Northern Utes spent so many winters near the Elk Mountains that Colorado whites often referred to them as "Elk Mountain Utes." Wakara too had often used the area as a winter camp, as it provided a ready marketplace for his stolen stock. It is only natural therefore that Black Hawk, himself a Northern Ute and a close "relative" of Wakara, chose the intertribal nexus of the Four Corners region as his central market and prime source of recruits.[102]

While Utahns were as yet unaware of Black Hawk's exact location and were just getting their first reports of his efforts to draw others to his standard, army officers and Indian agents from New Mexico and Colorado described an intertribal gathering 3,500 strong centered around "the Green river utes" lately "driven from Utah by the troops— or Mormons." The intertribal gathering reportedly included 1,200 Weeminuche, 1,500 "Pah Utes,"[103] 800 Navajos, as well as "some few

---

[100] Franklin H. Head to Commissioner of Indian Affairs D.N. Cooley, 30 April 1866, *RSI*, 1866:128. Italics mine.

[101] James, Journal.

[102] "Report of H.M. Vaile, on his expedition from Denver, Colorado to Great Salt Lake City, and back, under instructions from Wm. Gilpin, Governor, and ex officio superintendent of Indian Affairs, Colorado Territory," 5 July 1862, in BIA, M234, 197.

[103] "Pah Ute" is an enigmatic term in the history of Utah and the Four Corners region. It was sometimes used to delineate the Piede-like Paiutes who lived in southern Utah. It was also used, however, especially by gentiles, to refer to Utes called "Fish Utes" ("Pah" means "water" in the Ute language) because they primarily subsisted on trout. For similar reasons

Mexicans" and "renegade whites." A small band of Capote Utes and their Jicarilla Apache relatives were also connected to Black Hawk.[104] The power of meat to draw hungry Indians to Black Hawk was perhaps best exemplified after the second season of the war, when the raiders tried to duplicate the numbers of cattle stolen the previous year and again returned to the Elk Mountain region. That fall (1866) one government agent from Santa Fe on a tour through northern New Mexico in an attempt to treat with Utes visited all their regular "camping places" but "did not find a single Utah, they had [all] gone up to Colorado Territory."[105] About the same time, the *Santa Fe New Mexican* announced that "most of the Wemunuche Utes and all the Asavaritches or Green River Utes are together on the Rio Dolores [in the Elk Mountain Country]," and "have been up to the Mormon settlements, and returned with a large amount of stock they stole there."[106]

A major use of Black Hawk's cattle, then, was clearly feeding the Indians of different bands and tribes that gathered about him. The cattle also provided the raiders with a powerful medium of exchange to trade for goods, weapons, and ammunition among their own people. White sources make it clear, however, that there were other outlets for Black Hawk's stock on all four sides of the Utah settlements and apparently even within the Mormon communities themselves. As has been pointed out, white and Hispanic outlaws, shady cattle merchants, and traders played increasingly important roles in Black Hawk's operations. Tracking the movements of these rustlers and illicit traders, who worked hard to obscure their activities from their contemporaries, is no easy

---

Mormons initially called the Timpanogos and other Northern Utes "Pah Utes" but in time ceased that usage, while gentiles, particularly in Colorado, kept it up. It appears that the "Pah Utes" referred to here were a band of Utes associated with the Shiberetches, probably the Weeminuche, who were sometimes called "Poruches" or "Pah Utes." In 1870, for example, Utah's gentile superintendent of Indian affairs wrote that "the Elk Mountain Utes, Fish Utes, Shiberetches, and Yam Pah-Utes, are the most wild and disorderly Indians of this superintendency." *RSI*, 1870:606–7. For evidence of Weeminuche Utes being called "Poruche" or "Pah Utes" see *RCIA*, 1865:163.

[104] Major Alb. H. Pfeiffer to Don Felipe Delgado, Superintendent of Indian Affairs, Sante Fe, New Mexico, 22 December 1865, and "Conference with the Utahs," 2 January 1866, both in "No. 11, Resolutions, Correspondence, &c. New Mexico, Report of J.K. Graves, U.S. spl. comr., 1866"; Felipe Delgado, Superintendent of Indian Affairs, Santa Fe, to D.N. Cooley, Commissioner, 7 January 1866, BIA, M234, 553; Felipe Delgado to J.K. Graves, 9 January 1866, *RSI*, 1866:138; and *Denver Rocky Mountain News*, 6 July 1866, and 1 August 1866.

[105] W.F.M. Arny to Col. A.B. Norton, Supt. Indian Affairs, New Mexico, 18 October 1866, BIA, M234, 553.

[106] *Santa Fe New Mexican*, 27 October 1866.

task after more than 130 years, but certain evidence gives at least some insight into their involvement with Black Hawk's raiders.

The fact that Mexican traders and "renegade whites" were attending Black Hawk and his stock in the Elk Mountain Country is significant. In the early 1850s, Brigham Young had outlawed the Mexican trade in Utah, an act which provoked the 1853–54 Walker War. Pushed to the periphery, however, Mexican traders, operating from such centers of Spanish culture as Colorado's San Luis Valley and the New Mexican cities of Taos and Santa Fe, continued to trade among Utah's Utes. Often exchanging whiskey, guns, ammunition, and other factory goods for furs, skins, stolen stock, and Indian captives to be sold into slavery, the Mexican traders generally lured Utah Utes to Colorado and New Mexico, but sometimes ventured close enough to the Mormon settlements to be captured and prosecuted in Utah.[107]

White traders in violation of the Indian trade and intercourse acts, which prohibited any trade among the Indians without a license, operated similarly. Throughout the period, Salt Lake, Denver, and Santa Fe newspapers ran stories about "the white renegades that have fled from the law, and hide" among the Utes. The papers described these "renegade whites . . . sojourning with the Utes" as "outlaws of the worst character," and the general public in Utah, Colorado, and New Mexico believed these men were "almost sure to cause trouble between the Indians and the whites."[108] Much of the trouble they feared came in the form of Indian raids on the settlers' cattle directed by these outlaws.

The emerging cattle boom of the post–Civil War era brought a huge upsurge of illicit livestock trade to the Southwest generally, as incredibly profitable new beef markets caused traders to entice Indians to steal stock from settlers by promising them trade goods. Building on the tradition of generations of successful raiding in former Spanish and Mexican colonies, an increased focus on stock theft quickly

---

[107] That the Ute slave trade was still strong at the beginning of the Black Hawk War is well documented. It was so widespread in the Mexican settlements of southern Colorado and New Mexico that the president of the United States took special notice of it and ordered its destruction. See John Evans, Governor of Colorado and ex officio superintendent of Indian Affairs, to "U.S. Indian Agents and all those in the employ of the Indian service," 28 June 1865; John Evans to Commissioner William P. Dole, 28 June 1865; and "List of Indian Captives, acquired by purchase, and now in the service of the citizens of Conejos County, C[olorado]. T[erritory]., as taken, and rendered by Lafayette Head, U.S. Indian Agent, for the Tabaguache Utah tribe of Indians, July 1865"; all in BIA, M234, 198. The last document referred to shows that most of these Indian slaves were purchased by Mexicans from the Utes, though some were also obtained from the Navajos.

[108] For example, see *Denver Rocky Mountain News*, 6 July 1866 and 1 August 1866.

spread among Native Americans from Texas to New Mexico and north into Colorado. Considering the strength of the burgeoning American cattle market of the period and its successful use of Indians to raid settlers' stock, it is not surprising that the Utes were soon drawn into the action.

Interestingly, a huge, lively, and profitable market for cattle presented itself at the precise time Black Hawk commenced his raids. Indeed, it can argued that this expanding national market for livestock was a prime motivation for Black Hawk commencing his raids in the first place. As one gentile military officer visiting Utah summed it up, "The resident Indians of Utah have been hostile to the Mormons, but I think are so *because it is profitable to be*, and not because of any unfair dealing with them, as they charge upon the settlers." "I am of the opinion," he continued, "that a population of Gentiles would be subjected to exactly the same annoyances and depredations."[109] The question now arises whether Black Hawk was an Indian patriot fighting for his peoples' rights and lands or whether he was simply a thievish opportunist seeking to enrich himself. The fact that his raiding band renamed him "Nu-ints," the name of the Ute people themselves, gives some insight into how the Utes of his time might have answered the question.[110] On the other hand, Brigham Young called Black Hawk and his associates a "predatory band of outlaws." "The success of Black Hawk... in murder and robbery," he wrote, "has enabled him to collect a band of renegade Indians, who hope under his leadership, to gratify their murderous and thievish propensities. They are not a tribe, neither is Black Hawk a recognized Chief; but they are banded together for purposes of plunder."[111] Whether Black Hawk was champion of native rights or chief of a band of robbers depends on one's perspective; in actuality, he was probably both.

The role Mexican traders played in Black Hawk's market in the Four Corners region is significant. A.B. Norton, New Mexico's superintendent of Indian affairs, reported that Mexican traders with trains of as many as "sixty or seventy" donkeys "loaded with merchandise... whiskey and ammunition" coursed through the New Mexican frontier, often visiting Indians in the states and territories on her borders. "These traders," he wrote, "exchange goods for Cattle & horses—

---

[109] Waters, *Life Among the Mormons*, 83. Italics mine.

[110] John Wesley Powell, "Government," 2–3, in "Life and Culture of the Ute," and "Indian Life," 4–5; and *RSI*, 1873:424.

[111] Brigham Young to Brigham Young, Jr., 15 June 1866, BYC.

thereby giving a market and encouraging the [Indians] to steal from the inhabitants of those states [and territories]." "This trade has been really immense of late," he wrote in 1866. Providing insight into the huge profits to be made by middlemen in such traffic, Norton wrote, "I know of one man here in Santa Fe who took about $150.00 worth of goods there, and came back with one hundred head of Texas Cattle for his goods." Considering that cattle were selling for forty dollars per head in Santa Fe at the time, the trade represented a profit of more than 2,500 percent![112] So many stolen cattle were imported by Indians and their Mexican and American allies that the Santa Fe beef market was eventually glutted, causing prices there to tumble.[113] Though the fact was hardly grasped by the Mormons, throughout the Black Hawk War Mexican traders aided and abetted the raiders, sometimes even participating in their sorties; most often, however, they were simply observed hovering around Black Hawk's stock. Significantly, after the largest raid of the 1866 season, Indian reports were that Black Hawk's band "had gone to Sante-fee to trade off the stolen Cattle & Horses and recruit their supplys of amunition to carry on the War."[114]

In actuality, Black Hawk's connection to Mexican traders was part of a much larger Hispanic–Native American trade involving Indians throughout the southern plains, especially the Kiowas and Comanches, who, like the Utes, were pulled into the large and profitable New Mexican stock market. New Mexico's superintendent of Indian affairs described "an unrestrained commerce" carried on between the Comanches and "hundreds" of Mexican traders. "Thousands" of "Texas cattle bartered for from these Indians are being scattered all over the Territory," he wrote, adding, "When no cattle or horses are found in the Comanche camp by the Mexican traders, they lend the Indians their pistols and horses and remain at the camp until the Comanches have time to go to Texas and return, and get the stock they desire." "What a disgrace that our government should permit this plundering of the people on the frontiers," Norton wrote in frustration, in view of the

---

[112] A.B. Norton, Supt. Indian Affairs, Santa Fe, New Mexico, to D.N. Cooley, Commissioner of Indian Affairs, 31 July 1866, BIA, M234, 553.

[113] The *Santa Fe New Mexican* for 14 July 1866 read in part: "A large trade has been carried on with the Commanches for the past few months, and parties of traders are coming into the settlements almost daily. They have been more successful than common, and large numbers of cattle have been brought into the territory, which accounts for the low prices of beef."

[114] Peter Maughan to Brigham Young, received 31 August 1866, BYC, r59, b30, f17.

fact that the local government winked at the trade, freely giving "the Indians a market for their booty." "But how can it be stopped?" he asked.[115]

Finally succumbing to pressure from Texas, the governor of New Mexico issued a proclamation acknowledging the extent of his territory's traffic in stock run off from its neighbors by Indians "instigated by traders." "It is believed," the proclamation read, "that the largest share of the traffic herein complained of, is in cattle stolen from our fellow citizens in the State of Texas," implying that he was aware it was going on elsewhere. The proclamation closed by warning that the New Mexico government was now prepared to prosecute to the fullest extent of the law traders operating in Indian country without permits.[116] While other significant factors were also at work, it is interesting to note that the end of full-scale Ute raids on the Mormon settlements coincided with the publication and promised enforcement of this proclamation.

The immense profits to be taken by trading for stock stolen by Indians also attracted whites of questionable character to Black Hawk and other raiders. Special Indian Agent H.T. Ketcham, in a letter to Colorado governor John Evans, described several different types of white thieves operating with Indians in the region. "There are Vagabond white men living among the Indians," he wrote, "who are meaner, more degraded & more despicable than the meanest [Indian]." Describing their tactics, he explained that these whites "make [the Indians] drunk, cheat them out of their robes & peltry, swindle them out of their ponies and seduce their women. If they seek redress, they are often knocked down & beaten." However, according to Ketcham, "besides the above named Knavish scums of society, there is a more respectable class of swindlers in the Indian Country; who not only cheat the Indians but steal systematically from freighters, Emigrants & drovers."

Reciting the activities among the Indians of this "more respectable class of swindlers," Ketcham linked cattle theft to Uriah Curtis, an influential Indian agent for the Grand River Utes and the Colorado

---

[115] A.B. Norton, Superintendent, Santa Fe, New Mexico, to N.G. Taylor, Commissioner of Indian Affairs, 24 August 1867, *RCIA*, 1867:191–95.

[116] "A Proclamation by the Governor of New Mexico, Santa Fe, New Mexico, Rob't B. Michell, Governor New Mexico," 12 September 1867, BIA, M234, 554.

branch of the Uinta Utes, two bands having very close ties to Black Hawk. Ketcham wrote:

> They do not always steal *directly* . . . but in an *indirect* & civilized way; by getting Indians to run off . . . stock at night, . . . The animals are then brought in & branded; and the Indians paid a few brass buttons, beads & other trinkets for their trouble. —A Mr. Fenton of Denver bought $500 head of cattle . . . his cattle were stampeded at night, and over a hundred of them driven off. After having hunted several days for them, he learned that a Mr. Curtis, formerly Post Interpreter, had *some how* come into possession of a number of them: but before Fenton could reach his ranch, he had sold them! And refused to pay for them! It can be proven that Curtis knew they were Fentons cattle before he got them! He found 25 or 30 more of his cattle being branded in the enclosure of another respectable swindler; who claimed to have got them of Indians, & refused to give them up. . . . I mention these facts to show how the Indians . . . are being civilized. Is it strange that they steal, when they are instructed & encouraged to do so? And ought they to be killed for stealing, while the whites who have set them the example go unpunished?[117]

Interestingly, such illegal trading seemed to be contagious, and Fenton, the victim in the above account, apparently joined in the profiteering and got the Utes to steal for him too.[118] More important for a study of the Black Hawk War, though, Uriah Curtis, the above-mentioned "Post Interpreter" turned cattle thief, was the only white to attend a multiband council in Spanish Fork Canyon in 1863 where Black Hawk allegedly first sought to organize a pan-Ute alliance against the whites.[119] While it can only be inferred, it is possible that Curtis attended Black Hawk's council in 1863 to capitalize on the growing Ute animosity towards the Mormons by offering to market Utah beef in Colorado.

Throughout the war, other Indian Office employees, both in Utah and in Colorado, were accused of encouraging Indians to steal from the Mormons and were believed to be middlemen in the marketing of the

---

[117] H.T. Ketcham, Special Agent, Conejos, Colorado, to John Evans, 1 July 1864, BIA, M234, 197. Italics in original.

[118] Bleak, "Southern Mission," 2:108.

[119] O'Neil, "History of the Ute Indians," 56.

raiders' stock.[120] Even Utah Superintendent of Indian Affairs Franklin H. Head was accused by other gentiles of such shady trading. Gentile informants in Salt Lake City postulated that Superintendent Head "has built him a fine house out of Indian goods, [while] the Indians in the Southern part of Utah are starving and forced to steal the settlers stock to live on."[121] More seriously, others accused Head of employing known cattle thieves as interpreters and agents. "Supt. Head," read one complaint, "employed as interpreter for the Uinta reservation one Richard James known to be a bad and dangerous man. The Indians for which said James was interpreter stole some stock and when the owners demanded it, James told the Indians not to give it up." James was known to have been involved in Black Hawk's operations, and the fact that Head hired him and refused to fire him when Mormons complained evidently was taken by some to be tacit evidence of the superintendent's own involvement. According to one document, Dimick Huntington requested that James be removed or the thieving interpreter would be "hurt" by the settlers. Head allegedly responded by threatening that "if James was hurt, . . . he [Head] would be damned if he would restrain the Indians from falling on and butchering women and children in the [Mormon] settlements."[122]

So many charges of Head's "malfeasance in office" were sent to Washington that President Andrew Johnson himself ordered an investigation.[123] Overwhelmed by answering all the charges against him, in his correspondence to the U.S. Commissioner of Indian Affairs Head essentially gave up trying to inform Washington of Black Hawk's activities, and thus posterity lost from that point on what had been the most detailed non-Mormon source relating to the war.

Partially because he suited their purposes, Latter-day Saint leaders used their influence to defend Head's integrity. The Secretary of

---

[120] For examples see George A. Smith and Warren Snow to Thomas Callister, 28 March 1866, in JH, 28 March 1866, 2–3; and Alexander Cummings, Governor and ex officio Superintendent of Indian Affairs, Colorado Territory, to D.N. Cooley, Commissioner of Indian Affairs, 10 October 1866, in *RSI*, 1866:156.

[121] Austin A. King, Richmond, Mo., to Commissioner N.G. Taylor, 8 April 1867, BIA, M234, 902.

[122] Dimick B. Huntington to Secretary of the Interior, O.H. Browning, 12 December 1866, BIA, M234, 902. Other documents in this collection indicate that Huntington may not have authored this letter. More detailed documentation of Richard James's involvement in native stock theft is presented below.

[123] See endorsement, W.T. Otto, Acting Secretary of the Interior, to N.G. Taylor, Commissioner of Indian Affairs, 15 June 1867, BIA, M234, 902.

the Interior eventually concluded that the evidence presented in a mammoth stack of charges and countercharges was not sufficient to indict Head.[124] Interestingly, Lafayette Head was the Indian Agent at Conejos, Colorado (the closest Ute agency to Black Hawk's headquarters in the Elk Mountain Country), located in the San Luis Valley, the heart of the Mexican community in Colorado. Lafayette Head was repeatedly accused of "complicity" in the Ute slave and stolen cattle trade, and both he and Franklin Head were accused of "stealing" Indian goods "and substituting spoiled provisions, and selling the original goods at a profit.[125] Considering their given names of Franklin and Lafayette, both obviously commemorating Revolutionary War heroes, the two Heads very likely were brothers and may even have had an illicit arrangement where Indians ran cattle from one's jurisdiction and marketed them in that of the other. Though both were repeatedly accused of malfeasance in office, however, conclusive evidence of any collusion between them has not been found.

Franklin Head's Indian interpreter, Richard James, though, is known to have carried on a brisk trade in stolen cattle, sometimes using the Overland Trail market based at Fort Bridger as an outlet. Again, Head's involvement cannot be conclusively documented, though he later admitted that he knew that James, an apostate Mormon and former Indian missionary, "had been guilty of theft some 6 or 8 years before I employed him."[126] Latter-day Saints visiting Fort Bridger actually observed James's illicit sales, while others used circumstantial evidence to identify him as one of several whites allegedly seen directing Ute raiding activities.[127] By the end of 1866, enraged Utahns apparently pressured Head to "discharge" Richard James; they then ran him out of the territory, but as late as 1872 they believed Indian Office employees were still selling Mormon cattle at Fort Bridger.[128]

Significantly, after he was "discharged" by his embattled superin-

---

[124] O.H. Browning, Secretary of Interior, to N.G. Taylor, Commissioner of Indian Affairs, 6 February 1868, BIA, M234, 902.

[125] For examples see Samuel F. Tappan to D.N. Cooley, 27 January 1866, BIA, M234, 198; and P. David Smith, *Ouray*, 54, 61.

[126] Franklin H. Head to Commissioner J.G. Taylor, 24 June 1867, BIA, M234, 902.

[127] CR, 82; Thomas Callister to George A. Smith, 13 May 1866, GAS; C. Wilken to Robert T. Burton, 27 July 1866, TAS; Aaron Johnson to Brigham Young, 3 July 1866, BYC; and "Gunnison Ward Historical Record," 17.

[128] The going price was ten dollars for cattle and fifteen dollars for horses. For example, see Erastus Snow to Brvt. Col. J.E. Tourtellotte, Superintendent of Indian Affairs, 4 July 1870, BIA, M834; and JH, 18 February 1872, 1.

tendent, James went straight to the Elk Mountain country, where he spent the second winter of the Black Hawk War (1866–67) encamped with a large band of Uinta, Grand River, Yampa, Tabaguache, and Shiberetch Utes, and presumably with Black Hawk himself.[129] The following spring, Richard James and Chief Antero led a large band of Utes from the Elk Mountain country to Denver. These Indians told Colorado's governor and ex officio superintendent of Indian affairs "that a war had begun between their relatives and the Mormons of the Great Basin." "They seem to have no errand here," Governor A.C. Hunt wrote of the Utes and the "young white man named James [who] arrived with them from the West." Considering that they had just been with Black Hawk, however, it is likely that their "errand" was to arrange for the disposal of Mormon stock in the Denver area.[130]

That white and Hispanic traders, and not the Utes themselves, were taking most of the profits from the sale of the raiders' cattle seems to be supported by Governor Hunt, who wrote, "I visited their camp today and a more thorough manifestation of squalid poverty I never saw."[131] Bands of "Salt Lake Utes" visited Denver all summer long, telling Hunt "their relations were at war with the Mormons, whom they, the Indians, seemed to regard as a different people from other White men, and not desiring to fight have moved over to this region." Though these Utes represented themselves as being "unwilling" to return to their country lest they "risk a collision with the Mormons," Governor Hunt was suspicious of their connection to mysterious "vagabond whitemen" who freely supplied them with whiskey.[132]

The Indian Office did not have a corner on this sort of dishonesty. Isaac Potter, also known as Ike Potter, along with Richard James, provides one of the best-documented examples of a white outlaw associated with Black Hawk's raiders. Potter was a Mormon polygamist with five wives from Springville, Utah. In the mid-1850s he served as an Indian interpreter at the Spanish Fork Indian Farm and won the natives' friendship by his determination to look out for their interests.[133] In 1857, however, his brother was mysteriously killed by Springville

[129] James, "Journal"; and A.C. Hunt, Governor and Ex Officio Superintendent of Indian Affairs, Denver, Colorado, to N.G. Taylor, Commissioner of Indian Affairs, 20–22 June 1867, BIA, M234, 199.

[130] A.C. Hunt to N.G. Taylor, 20–22 June 1867; and *RSI*, 1867:185.

[131] A.C. Hunt to N.G. Taylor, 20–22 June 1867.

[132] A.C. Hunt to N.G. Taylor, 7 June and 4 August 1867, BIA, M234, 199; Daniel C. Oaks, U.S. Indian Agent, to A.C. Hunt, 10 June 1867, BIA, M234, 199; and James, "Journal."

[133] HOJ, 17 June 1863.

churchmen in what were called the "Parrish-Potter murders"; this undoubtedly played a role in Isaac's disaffection from the Mormon
faith.[134] By the early 1860s he was using his influence to employ Indians in a well-organized cattle-rustling ring. The leader of "a gang of
thieves" based in Utah Valley, Potter was believed to be "the Captain
of [an] organization reaching through the Territory." Potter and Indian accomplices were arrested frequently before the opening of the
Black Hawk War and accused of murder and grand larceny for cattle
theft. "More than forty criminal charges had been brought against him
in the courts," but because the disaffected Mormon held the sympathy
of gentile federal judges, he was "honorably acquitted" from all of
them. When "Potter the horse and cattle thief, and confederate of Indians [and] thieves" was released for such charges in 1863, church authorities considered it an attempt on the part of gentiles "to involve the
settlers in bloodshed with the Indians." That same year, Potter warned
Northern Utes of a planned surprise attack on their villages in Spanish
Fork Canyon and foiled the designs of Connor's troops, furthering his
reputation of being one of the few whites, Mormon or gentile, in whom
the Indians had full confidence.[135]

Sometime after the beginning of the Black Hawk War, Indians told
Mormons that Potter and his men instructed them

> to go down to Sanpete, and gather up a large lot of the Horses and
> cattle there and drive them down East, and they would be there,
> and trade the Horses and Cattle to Emigrants, and get them
> money, Tobaco, Whiskey, and Horses, that would be their own,
> So they went and got the Horses and Cattle, and drove them
> where the men wanted them, and the men sold them the way they
> said.[136]

The following summer, Potter was described by whites at the Uintah Agency as having been drafted as "war chief" by angry Utes, and
along with a handful of white ruffians he was frequently seen with Black

[134] Alan Johnson, *Aaron Johnson*, 560–63.

[135] Utah County, Utah, "Probate Doc[k]et 'A,'" 80, 87–91; William E. Higby, "Affidavit
of William E. Higby," DUP, *Treasures of Pioneer History*, 4:383–84; Thurber, "Journal,"
302–3; U.S. Congress, House Committee on Elections, *McGrorty vs. Hooper*, 21; George A.
Smith to John L. Smith, 24 June 1863, HOLB, 2:242; JH, 11 September 1867, 2; and U.S.
Department of War, *War of the Rebellion*, series 1, vol. 50, pt 1: 207.

[136] Eldridge, "Biographical Sketch," 103–4. One Sanpete resident recorded that the Indians sold the stolen stock to "wicked" white men "who paid them in powder and lead to shoot
Mormons with." Hansen, *Autobiography*, 147.

Hawk's brother Mountain and sometimes with Black Hawk himself. That same year, the extent of Potter's involvement with the raiders began to come clear, as Mormons learned that "four whites" were "coleaging" with the raiders. By 1867 Mormons living nearest the Uintah Reservation were convinced "the notorious renegade" Isaac Potter was the leader of a band of Ute raiders who were assisted by fifteen whites.[137]

Like James, Potter more than likely funneled his stock through Fort Bridger, or perhaps even through Brown's Hole. Located on the Green River north and east of the Uinta Mountains, Brown's Hole was a well-known refuge for outlaws, and in the 1860s and 1870s an enormous illicit stock trade flourished there. While its boom years occurred after the arrival of the transcontinental railroad, the Hole's superb cattle country, close proximity to the Overland Trail, and early reputation as an outlaw "den" made it a natural outlet for stolen Mormon stock.[138] Fort Bridger, Brown's Hole, and similar spots on or near the Overland Trail provided lucrative markets for stolen stock. Describing "a small trading settlement on 'Ham's Fork,' a stream emptying into [the] Green River," one gentile wrote:

A few white men, and a larger number of Indians and half-breeds, all living in lodges, earn a livelihood at this place by buying and selling cattle. When an ox becomes foot-sore and exhausted on his long journey, the alternative with the owner lays between abandoning his animal or selling him for what he can get, and under these circumstances such traders purchase for a mere nominal sum, and after a few weeks' rest the ox is sold again for a high price. The Amount of money made in this way on the plains is by no means insignificant. These men also trade with the Indians, after they return from their yearly hunts, for robes and skins, which they obtain at a mere trifling cost, and then sell them on the spot for a higher price than the same articles would command in St. Louis.[139]

Horace Greeley, who visited the area a few years before the Black Hawk War, described the stock trade in the Black's Fork and Ham's

---

[137] A.F. MacDonald to William B. Pace, 24 May 1866, WBP; Eldridge, "Biographical Sketch," 96–100, 105, 108–9; JH, 11 September 1867, 2; Aaron Johnson to Daniel H. Wells, 3 July 1866, TMR, #1536; Aaron Johnson to Brigham Young, 3 July 1866, BYC; and Summit Stake Manuscript History, 1867, no pagination.

[138] Charles Kelly, *Outlaw Trail*, 61–68.

[139] Waters, *Life Among the Mormons*, 54.

Fork areas of southwestern Wyoming near Fort Bridger: "On these streams live several old mountaineers, who have large herds of cattle which they are rapidly increasing by a lucrative traffic with the emigrants, who are compelled to exchange their tired, gaunt oxen and steers for fresh ones on almost any terms." He described one trader, who "is said to have six or eight hundred head," and another one, "who has been here some twenty-odd years, began with little or nothing, and has quietly accumulated some fifty horses, three or four hundred head of neat cattle, three squaws, and any number of half-breed children. He is said to be worth seventy-five thousand dollars."[140]

That hundreds of head of Black Hawk's stock ended up at such outlets is certain. Before Black Hawk's second season of raiding began, the Mormon hierarchy attributed "the fine fitouts" of "the Blackhawk raiders to trades in stock made with employees on the overland road and others, *some of them connected with the Indian Department.*"[141] They were about to learn, however, of Black Hawk's Four Corners connection and that the chief raider had enlisted a powerful new ally, the Navajos. Significantly, Northern Ute recruiting efforts in the south helped inaugurate a Navajo-Mormon war that started as part of the Black Hawk War but eventually took on a life of its own and outlived the war that spawned it.

---

[140] Greeley, *Overland Journey*, 194–95.

[141] George A. Smith and Warren Snow to Thomas Callister, 28 March 1866, in JH, 28 March 1866, 2–3. Italics mine.

CHAPTER SIX

The Navajo War and Brigham Young's Hostage Plan

I am sorry to say that there are some Indians, in these mountains, that are very bad. I should be sorry to learn that any of you have got mixed up with them or in any way connected with them. I advise you, and you will do well to take my advice and act upon it, to keep away from them. Can you expect the people to be your friends when you are the friends of those who are killing them and destroying their property[?] I tell you now to be careful about having anything to do with those Indians. When you leave here, hunt, fish, go to your homes, but be careful and keep away from where those Indians are. I may hear of your getting into very serious trouble if you do not remember what I say.
—Superintendent Orsemus H. Irish, 1865[1]

The Beginning of Utah's Navajo War

As HAS BEEN SHOWN, during the winter of 1865–66, when snows in northern and central Utah prohibited raids, Black Hawk withdrew to the Four Corners region where, in addition to trading off his cattle, he worked to raise recruits where Ute, Navajo, Hopi, and Apache lands met. Due to the area's high frequency of intertribal marriage, Brigham Young described Indians living there as being "Utahs, or rather *a mixture of that tribe with the Navajoes, and Moqui* [that is, Hopis]," adding that it was an area with which the Northern Utes themselves maintained "considerable intercourse."[2] The abundant intermarriage and trading connections between these four major tribal groups allowed

---

[1] "Proceedings of a Council with the Utah Indians," 31–32.
[2] Brigham Young to George W. Manypenny, Commissioner of Indian Affairs, 27 May 1856, Governor's Letter Book, BYC. Italics mine.

Black Hawk's recruiting efforts to quickly surmount intertribal barriers. A Piede chief the Mormons called Panguitch John, himself the son of Wakara and a Piede woman, told church officials that Black Hawk was "collecting all he can to join him" and that he had "already" enlisted "8 or ten small bands" and that even more "were deliberating upon the matter, and most likely would follow the example of the others."[3]

By May 1866, Mormons had learned from Tabby on the Uintah Reservation that Black Hawk had recruited "three tribes from the South East."[4] Black Hawk himself later described these recruits as "three bands or tribes of Indians [residing] east of the Moquici."[5] Just who the groups were that joined Black Hawk is difficult to determine. His alliance was in no way a permanent organization in the first place, and individuals, families, and whole bands came and went as it suited their immediate personal interests—thus the constitution of his raiding band was constantly changing. Also, independent bands and individuals were inspired by Black Hawk's success to commence raids of their own without submitting to his authority. Credit for their deeds, no doubt, in some cases went to Black Hawk.

Despite the paucity of sources regarding Black Hawk's operations in the south, evidence warrants that the following sketch of his Four Corners confederation be put forth. The Shiberetches, described as living "north of the Spanish trail and west of Green River," had been with him all along, and he was soon considered the head chief of the entire band. Piede bands living in the same area, some probably intermarried with the Shiberetches, also gave him allegiance.[6] The Weeminuche Utes, seemingly the closest relatives of the Shiberetches, apparently joined Black Hawk en masse, eventually becoming "a terror, not only to the whites, but also to the different tribes of the Utes."[7] While a large

---

[3] Robert Gardner to Brigham Young, 22 January 1866, BYC; Erastus Snow to Brigham Young, 12 February 1866, BYC; and Bleak, "Southern Mission," 1:215, 221.

[4] A.F. Macdonald to William B. Pace, 24 May 1866, WBP.

[5] A.K. Thurber to Brigham Young, 26 July 1869, BYC

[6] *DN*, 25 May 1869.

[7] Major Albert H. Pfeiffer to Don Felipe Delgado, Superintendent of Indian Affairs, Santa Fe, New Mexico, 22 December 1865–?? January 1866, in "No. 11, Resolutions, Correspondence, &c, New Mexico, Report of J.K. Graves, U.S. spl. comr., 1866," BIA, M234, 553; C.T. Speer, Lieut., U.S. Army, and Indian Agent, Office of Southern Ute Agency, Colorado Territory, to His Excellency E.M. McCook, Governor and ex. off. Supt. of Indian Affairs, Colorado, 5 February 1870, *RCIA*, 1870:173; and Major Wm. Redwood Price, Los Pinos Agency, Colorado, to Lieut Wm. J. Sartle, A.A.A. Genl., District of New Mexico, 1 and 7 September 1872, BIA, M234, 202.

faction of the Capote Utes balked at first, it appears they ultimately united with the raiders.[8] Ankatash and Keneache, both war chiefs of the Mouache Utes, were at various times suspected of having joined with Black Hawk's hostile "western bands."[9] And, though Ouray, chief of the Tabaguache Utes, appears to have worked hard to keep his people from Black Hawk's influence, he summed up the situation correctly when he prognosticated that, despite his own and others' efforts, "some young men [from] *all the bands* will probably go on the war path."[10]

That Black Hawk found recruiting successful among the Utes of Colorado and New Mexico was clearly fostered by the fact that the Treaty of Conejos, concluded between the United States and Ouray's Tabaguache Utes in 1863 (and expanded in 1864 to include most of the Southern Utes), had been almost entirely ignored by the whites.[11] As a result, "great dissatisfaction" existed among Four Corners Utes, who reportedly made "almost continuous complaints . . . of the wrongs and hardships which they endured, claiming that treaties were disregarded, obligations slighted, and pledges unfulfilled." According to Kit Carson, the commander of U.S. troops in the Four Corners area, because of their "destitution, that great incentive to Indian outrage," the region's Utes were like "a powder magazine," waiting for "a spark."[12]

Since the Jicarilla Apaches considered themselves "as one family and one blood" with the Utes because of exceptionally close "matrimonial ties," it is not surprising that some of them joined in Black Hawk's aggression.[13] Considerably more surprising, unless viewed in the context of the mixed nature of the area's Native American

---

[8] DUP, *Our Pioneer Heritage*, 9:254; and Gottfredson, *Indian Depredations*, 294, 302.

[9] For examples see Christopher Carson, Brvt. Brig. Gen. U.S. Vols., Comdg. Head Quarters, Fort Garland, to his Excellency the Governor of Colorado, 8 October 1866, BIA, M234, 198; and J. Francisco Chavez, Santa Fe, to D.N. Cooley, Commissioner of Indian Affairs, 9 October 1866, as quoted in the *Santa Fe Weekly Gazette*, 1 December 1866.

[10] Telegram of A. Cummings, Gov. & Supt. Indian Affairs, Denver, Colorado, to D.N. Cooley, Commissioner of Indian Affairs, 9 October 1866, BIA, M234, 198. Italics mine.

[11] See Treaty Between the United States and the Tabeguache Band.

[12] Felipe Delgado, Superintendent of Indian Affairs, Santa Fe, New Mexico, to D.N. Cooley, Commissioner, 10 or 12 December 1865, BIA, M234, 553; and Christopher Carson, Brevet Brig. Genl. U.S. Vols., Comdg., Fort Garland, Colorado Territory, to His Excellency, Governor of Colorado, 1 October 1866, BIA, M234, 198, and 15 December 1866, BIA, M234, 199.

[13] W.F.M. Arny, Acting Governor of New Mexico, to D.N. Cooley, Commissioner of Indian Affairs, 23 August 1866, BIA, M234, 553; and *Santa Fe New Mexican*, 15 and 25 August 1866. This last source states: "The Utah Indians of New Mexico and Colorado, *with the Jicarilla Apaches* are on the war path, and unless judicious measures are adopted for their pacification, they will lay waste the entire frontier." Italics mine.

society, was that Black Hawk's emissaries also made inroads among the Hopis, some of whom eventually joined in raiding the Mormon settlements.[14]

Throughout the war Mormons had little inkling of the involvement of Hopis and Apaches, or, for that matter, of even that of the various bands of Four Corners Utes. But before the end of 1865 they learned with great alarm that Navajos "in considerable force" were "in with him [Black Hawk] and intend to fight!" That same month, "friendly Indians" reported that Black Hawk, accompanied by "some Navajos and eight or ten small bands of other Indians, all very hostile," had crossed the Colorado River and was encamped on southern Utah's Paria River preparatory to initiating new assaults on Mormon stock in the south.[15]

As has been discussed, Black Hawk enlisted so many Navajos that for the next two years they made up at least half of his raiding band.[16] His success in raising Navajo recruits in part resulted from circumstances created by the 1863–64 campaigns of Kit Carson, the devastating forced march of the "Navajo Long Walk," and the wretched conditions at the Bosque Redondo reservation at Fort Sumner, New Mexico.[17] Carson's operations nearly destroyed Navajo status systems by decimating huge herds of the tribe's cattle and sheep and by displacing thousands of Indians, many of whom were pushed into southern Utah. Since the Navajo social system was much more closely tied to stock ownership than was that of the Utes, it is not surprising that some displaced and indigent Navajos who were anxious to rebuild destroyed herds fell in with Black Hawk.[18]

---

[14] Aaron Johnson to General William B. Pace, 29 July 1867, in CR, 220; Bleak, "Southern Mission," 2:10, and 65; and Erastus Snow to Brigham Young, telegram, 20 November 1869, BYC.

[15] Robert Gardner to Brigham Young, 22 January 1866, BYC; Erastus Snow to Brigham Young, 12 February 1866, BYC; and Bleak, "Southern Mission," 1:215, 221.

[16] By April 1866 Black Hawk's raiders consisted of "one hundred warriors, one-half of whom are Navajoes." Franklin H. Head to D.N. Cooley, Commissioner of Indian Affairs, 30 April 1866, RSI, 1866:128. That this ratio continued well into 1867 is evident in Lewis Simmons to Franklin H. Head, 9 July 1867, RSI, 1867:184–85.

[17] "The Navajo Long Walk" refers to the forced march of nearly 10,000 Navajos from their traditional homelands in the Four Corners region to a reservation at Fort Sumner, in eastern New Mexico. Located in the Staked Plains (described by one modern historian as "one of the most desolate expanses of desert on the continent"), the reservation was centered in a huge grove of cottonwood trees along the Pecos River called the Round Grove, or "Bosque Redondo." Horrible living conditions and successive crop failures decimated Navajo populations and forced hundreds of survivors to flee; some of whom eventually joined Black Hawk. See Loh, *Lords of the Earth*, especially 99–127.

[18] Mormon Indian interpreter Thales Haskell, after noting Kit Carson's campaigns against the Navajos attempting to force them to the Fort Sumner reservation, wrote, "A large

While Black Hawk himself was not personally named in them, letters of New Mexico military officers and Indian Office employees offer rare insight into the exportation of his conflict to the Four Corners region. Additionally, they document further the role Mexican traders played in his movements. Even more importantly, though, these letters give some picture of the impact Black Hawk's solicitations had on native groups. Some erupted into internecine violence as they argued as to whether or not they should participate in Black Hawk's raids, which, of course, potentially could bring very serious consequences upon them. Before the end of December 1865, Major Albert H. Pfeiffer, military officer, Indian agent, and adopted member of the Ute tribe,[19] wrote that in the fall of that year, "when all the Utes were at peace with the whites," a mysterious group of Utes "*driven from Utah by the troops—or Mormons*" were involved with "some Mexicans" in forming "an alliance" between the Pah, Capote, Weeminuche, and Shiberetch bands to raid Tierra Amarilla, Abiquiu, and other settlements in northwestern New Mexico.[20]

These Utes sent word to the Hopi villages "and beyond" inviting all Navajos then in violation of federal orders to locate on their new reservation in eastern New Mexico to join them on the San Juan River, preparatory to commencing their raids. As details of the proposed alliance were being worked out, a dispute over whether or not to involve their traditional enemies the Navajos occurred between the Weeminuche and a portion of the Capote band, which resulted in the killing of a Weeminuche chief named Cabeza Blanco. It must be remembered that the Navajos in question were then at war with the United States, and large numbers of troops were pursuing them through the wilderness. During the previous two years literally hundreds of Navajos had been tracked down and killed by U.S. soldiers, who were often assisted by Ute scouts. Associating with the Navajos was therefore very serious

number of [Navajos] escaped into the wild, rough Colorado River country and formed themselves in small groups of raiding parties which came across the Colorado River [to the Mormon settlements] to steal provisions and livestock, especially horses which they moved back into rough country where it became almost impossible to track them down." Wixom, *Hamblin*, 253–54.
    [19] Correll, *Navajo History*, 6:267–72.
    [20] Major Albert H. Pfeiffer to Don Felipe Delgado, Superintendent of Indian Affairs, Santa Fe, New Mexico, 22 December 1865–?? January 1866, in "No. 11, Resolutions, Correspondence, &c, New Mexico, Report of J.K. Graves, U.S. spl. comr., 1866," BIA, M234, 553, portions also published in Correll, *Navajo History*, 5:298–99. Italics mine.

business. Utes favoring the Navajo alliance, including Cabeza Blanco's adult sons, chased the chief's Capote killers, who fled to the protection of the gentile settlers in the neighborhood of Tierra Amarilla in northwestern New Mexico. Here the intertribal alliance party retaliated by entering the plaza of Tierra Amarilla, killing a Mexican child and three Indian slaves belonging to settlers, and driving off fourteen head of stock. The affair caused Weeminuche attacks on Capote bands and Capote retaliation for some time.

"The whole party of Wymin [Weeminuche] and Pah Utes and Navajos then left that region and went to the neighborhood of the Rio Dolores, Sierra Satiar, and Sierra Oregos, about one hundred miles from the settlements of Abiquiu and Tierra Amarilla in northwestern New Mexico—the exact area Black Hawk had chosen for his winter headquarters. According to Pfeiffer, these Indians, now joined by a large contingency of "hostile" Navajos, threatened "as soon as the snow goes off," to "come down in force on the Tierra Amarilla and destroy the entire settlement." The major also made it clear that Jicarilla Apaches had joined the alliance.[21]

Significantly, before snowy mountain passes allowed Black Hawk's raiders to return to northern Utah, these Indians pillaged frontier settlements from Abiquiu and Tierra Amarilla in New Mexico to those on the Rio Grande in Colorado. "There is scarcely a town on the Rio Grande that has not lost stock," the *Santa Fe New Mexican* complained, chronicling, without mentioning his name, that since Black Hawk's arrival with his first droves of stock to the Elk Mountain country, "depredations" were "fast becoming the order of the day." Indians who had recently been peaceful, now "had full and undisputed possession" of gentile settlements bordering Black Hawk's Elk Mountain retreat. The settlers complained that the Indians belligerently entered their towns and ranches, "making off with whatever pleased their fancy."[22] In great

---

[21] Major Albert H. Pfeiffer to Don Felipe Delgado, Superintendent of Indian Affairs, Santa Fe, New Mexico, 22 December 1865–?? January 1866, in "No. 11, Resolutions, Correspondence, &c, New Mexico, Report of J.K. Graves, U.S. spl. comr., 1866," BIA, M234, 553, portions also published in Correll, *Navajo History*, 5:298–99; Felipe Delgado, Superintendent of Indian Affairs, Santa Fe, New Mexico, to D.N. Cooley, Commissioner of Indian Affairs, 7 January 1866, BIA, M234, 553; Felipe Delgado to J.K. Graves, U.S. Special Indian Commissioner, 9 January 1866, *RCIA*, 1866:138; Correll, *Navajo History*, 5:290; and W.F.M. Arny, U.S. Indian Agent, Rio Arriba County, New Mexico, to Luther E. Webb, Superintendent of Indian Affairs, New Mexico, 31 August 1868, *RCIA*, 1868:166–68.

[22] *Santa Fe New Mexican*, 6 October 1865.

alarm, the settlers sent a messenger to Santa Fe with word that "the Utes have contracted an alliance with the Navajos" intending to "drive off the settlers of Tierra Amarilla."[23]

It is interesting to note that after the three Indian slaves and the Mexican child were killed by Black Hawk's confederates calls were made for U.S. troops to protect the settlers from the intertribal alliance forces they knew were gathering in the Elk Mountain country.[24] In contrast to the Utah situation, where nearly thirty settlers had been killed and over 2,000 head of stock had been run off, and where for reasons already discussed *soldiers were not sent in*, the deaths of the child and three slaves and fourteen head of cattle stolen from Tierra Amarilla were enough to immediately activate the troops in the New Mexican theater of the Black Hawk War. On the soldiers' arrival at Tierra Amarilla, the raiders immediately left the area and headed back to Utah, the Santa Fe papers actually reporting that the intertribal confederation had "gone north to the Mormon settlements."[25]

Several important points emerge in this narrative of the early Four Corners arena of the Black Hawk War. First, Black Hawk clearly stepped into the Southern Ute "powder magazine" at an auspicious moment and provided the "spark" Kit Carson feared. Second, while few whites understood it at the time, Black Hawk's war was not just waged against Mormon Utah but also extended to other European settlers in the widening sphere of his domain. Third, while Black Hawk brought large amounts of stock into the area, many of which undoubtedly went to Mexican and American settlers, his raiders also helped themselves to animals owned by gentiles on the Colorado and New Mexican frontier. Fourth, Black Hawk's invitations, for various reasons (including the fear of military retaliation—especially in areas outside of

[23] Correll, *Navajo History*, 5:346.

[24] Over a hundred settlers of Tierra Amarilla formally petitioned General James Carleton, the highest ranking U.S. military officer in New Mexico, to establish a military post in their area. Correll, *Navajo History*, 5:294. See also Felipe Delgado, Santa Fe, New Mexico, to J.K. Graves, U.S. Special Indian Commissioner, 9 January 1866, *RCIA*, 1866:138; and Felipe Delgado, Superintendent of Indian Affairs, Santa Fe, New Mexico, to D.N. Cooley, Commissioner, 10 or 12 December 1865, BIA, M234, 553.

[25] While formal petitions were first drawn up in January 1866, it appears the federal military did not take these reports seriously until "Henry Mercure, former agent of the Utes" came to Santa Fe in June to make verbal requests for troops. Within three weeks "2 companies of Infantry and 2 companies of Cavalry" were ordered to establish "Fort Plummer" near Tierra Amarilla. See Correll, *Navajo History*, 5:294, 356–57; and *Santa Fe New Mexican*, 10 November 1866.

Mormon domain), caused major fissures in native society, sometimes erupting in internecine violence.

A fifth salient point arises from the fact that after comparatively slight provocation, and even though most of the affected settlers were "Mexicans," federal military and civil authorities responded to the raiders with "prompt action" in deploying troops and otherwise working to "save our country from the devastations of these savage bands."[26] While the Hispanics of southern Colorado and northern New Mexico had their own special political problems with white civil and military authorities, the facts presented here confirm that the "uneasy triangle" of the Utah situation described in previous chapters was indeed an anomaly. Similarly, these facts strongly suggest that the depth of religious and political prejudice held by gentiles against Mormons even surpassed the tensions of Hispanic-white racial relations on the American frontier.

One last point relative to Black Hawk's alliance with the Navajos must be reiterated and strengthened here. Manuelito, the most important Navajo chief refusing to go to the Navajo Reservation and the single most important Navajo raider of the period, responded to Black Hawk's invitations; early in January 1866 he and others of his people joined the Utes in a series of raids on Mormon cattle in southern Utah. A major figure in Arizona and Navajo history, Manuelito was the unquestioned leader of Navajo resistance to the reservation policy of the United States government during the 1860s. Since Black Hawk played a similar resistance role for the Utes, it is perhaps only natural that the two would seek each other out. According to Santa Fe newspapers, Manuelito was "the most stubborn of all the Navajo Chiefs," declaring that he "would suffer death rather than go to the Reservation," and hence was the leader of "the last organized band of Navajos that remained in their country and refused to give up after the surrender of the main portion of the tribe."[27] At least symbolically, Manuelito was

---

[26] *Santa Fe New Mexican*, 25 August 1866.

[27] *Santa Fe Gazette*, 15 and 29 September 1866, as quoted in Correll, *Navajo History*, 5:368. John C. Cremony left this description of Manuelito: "Manuelito was the finest looking Indian man I ever saw. He was over six feet in height, and of the most symmetrical figure, combining ease, grace, and power and activity in a wonderful degree. He was a great dandy, and was always elaborately dressed in the finest Indian costume. His leggings were highly ornamented, and his buckskin jacket fitted without a wrinkle. A splendid bunch of many colored plumes, surmounted by two eagle's feathers, adorned his head, while his shapely feet were incased in elegantly worked moccasins. Navajo blankets have a wide and merited reputation for

the leader of all Navajos who refused to go to the reservation as well as the hundreds who escaped once they experienced its deplorable conditions.

Before being drawn into Black Hawk's alliance, Manuelito hid in the fastnesses of the Four Corners region from the numerous military campaigns launched against him by the federal government. For a time he hid near the Hopi villages, where he traded with Hopi allies to meet the needs of his band. But sometime in 1865 Cabeza Blanco, the Weeminuche chief discussed above, led a Ute raid against Manuelito's band, killing some of the Navajos. Cabeza Blanco eventually captured Manuelito, and then, in November 1865, his Navajo captive's status suddenly changed from prisoner to ally when "some of the Utahs proposed an alliance with the Hostile Navajo."[28] Another contemporary source, however, indicates that "two Navajoes came over to Black Hawk last fall and proposed to him to come over the river this winter and [together] they would drive off the stock of Kane County."[29] Despite this account, it is certain Black Hawk masterminded the alliance, and that he along with Manuelito and Cabeza Blanco (who promptly lost his life for it) were the original kingpins of the Ute-Navajo alliance. Perhaps it was Manuelito's connection with the Hopis that would draw some of this people to raid Mormon stock.

It should be made clear that while some Navajos submitted to Black Hawk's authority and actually joined his band, others, like Manuelito, simply accepted the opportunity to collaborate in raiding. Acknowledging the influence of the Northern Utes in initiating their raids on the Latter-day Saints, Manuelito and other Navajos conducted their own spirited assaults on southern Utah herds well into the 1870s. Even after Black Hawk withdrew from the area, and continuing long after his surrender, a Northern Ute named Patnish repeatedly led mixed bands of Utes, Paiutes, Piedes, Navajos, "and a few Hopis" across the

---

beauty and excellence, some of them being worth a hundred dollars a piece in the New Mexican market, and over his shoulders was one of superior character, worn with the grace and dignity with which a Roman Senator might be supposed to don his toga. So vain a man could not be well otherwise than brave, and he was noted for his gallantry. But he was also esteemed one of the wisest counselors in his tribe, and had headed many a bloody and destructive inroad until compelled to yield to the Californian troops." Cremony, *Life among the Apaches*, 305–6.

[28] See Correll, *Navajo History*, vol. 5, especially 290, 295–96, 298–99.

[29] Erastus Snow to Brigham Young, 12 February 1866, BYC.

Colorado River to plunder Utah's Dixie. Similarly, another of Black Hawk's recruits was Banashaw, an important Navajo sub-chief known to southern Utah Mormons as "Spanshanks" or "Spanish Hank," a brother of the period's secondmost-noted Navajo raiding chief, Barboncito. When Spanshanks was killed while attacking three Mormons in the Berry Massacre of April 1866, Barboncito and other Navajos seeking vengeance and livestock commenced their own raids on the Mormon settlements.[30]

Contemporary whites and subsequent historians have most often viewed these Navajo raids as part of the Black Hawk War, though they actually *in time* came to constitute a distinct war I will call "Utah's Navajo War." Because it heavily influenced the course of events farther north, the beginning of the Navajo War will be treated here, but only as it sheds light on Black Hawk's war that gave it birth.[31]

The Pipe Springs Murders and Mormon Retaliation

Ecclesiastical warnings of Black Hawk's expected raids frightened southern Utah Mormons for nearly two months before the first stock thefts on the west side of the Colorado River actually took place. Before the end of December 1865 "friendly Indians" averred that Black Hawk had finally crossed the Colorado River into Mormon country and was "on the Pahreah with some Navajos, and eight or ten small bands of other Indians, all very hostile."[32] Immediately, Black Hawk's combined force of Northern Utes, Paiutes, Navajos, and Apaches, perhaps already assisted by the Hopis, ran off a herd of cattle ranging near the Paria River and besieged the Mormon family that owned the stock in their well-built rock house.[33] Later that month a raid was made on the

---

[30] Ibid.; Brigham Young to Erastus Snow, 15 August 1866, BYC; Aaron Johnson to General William B. Pace, 29 July 1867, in CR, 220; Bleak, "Southern Mission," 1:215, 2:10, 28, 61, 65, 66, 71–73; Dellenbaugh, *A Canyon Voyage*, 167; Telegram of Erastus Snow to Brigham Young, 20 November 1869, BYC; "Council at Fort Defiance"; JH, 4 December 1870, 1, and 10 December 1870, 1; Ivins, "Forgotten Trails," 352; and DUP, *Kane County*, 8–9, 28.

[31] For general information regarding the Navajo War see DUP, *Kane County*, 7–57; and Bleak, "Southern Mission."

[32] Bleak, "Southern Mission," 1:215; and Robert Gardner to Brigham Young, 22 January 1866, BYC.

[33] The home belonged to Mormon frontiersman Peter Shirts. Because the roof of the stone house was "covered with flat Rock," virtually rendering it "impregnable against fire," and because it was ingeniously built in such a manner that water from the river actually came into its walls, members of Shirts's family survived attempts to fire or smoke them out of the house as well as a three-month-long siege. Robert Gardner to Brigham Young, 22 January 1866, BYC; Erastus Snow to Brigham Young, 12 February 1866, BYC; Brigham Young to William H. Hooper, 13 February 1866, BYC; James Andrus to George A. Smith, 3 April 1866,

Kanab herd, but because ranchers there had followed Brigham Young's counsel to corral and guard their stock, the raiders succeeded only in running off eight horses. On 5 January, however, a Piede runner appeared in St. George with news that a huge herd of cattle, horses, and sheep had been driven from the James Whitmore ranch at Pipe Springs, just south of the Utah-Arizona border.[34]

A wealthy Texas cattleman, Whitmore had embraced Mormonism and immigrated to Zion with other Lone Star State converts. Settling in Utah's Dixie, he soon learned that his large herds of extraordinarily "fine" cattle, sheep, and horses required ranges that the Virgin River towns of southwestern Utah could not provide. As a result, in 1863 he took up squatter's rights on grazing lands surrounding Pipe Springs. The arid land was far from lush, however, and his stock barely managed "to pick up a living" from the desolate desert terrain. By 1865 Whitmore had at least 400 head of cattle and perhaps as many as 1,000 sheep and an unknown quantity of horses ranging near Pipe Springs under the supervision of a hired hand. While maintaining a residence in St. George, he built a number of crude log and stone ranch houses at Pipe Springs as well as several corrals enclosing about fifty dairy cows. Similarly, he fenced and cultivated eleven acres on which he planted "about a thousand grapevines" and a number of fruit trees.[35]

Aware for months that Black Hawk was moving in his direction, Whitmore and ranchers in similarly exposed locations were counseled by Brigham Young to move their animals to the safety of St. George and other towns on the Virgin River. In the meantime, they were urged to carry firearms at all times. Confident of his abilities to deal with Indians, however, Whitmore ignored the directives, and when he left St. George to see if his herd had indeed been run off as reported by the Piedes, he carried no weapons at all.[36]

As the combined force of Ute, Navajo, and Apache raiders moved west into southern Utah, they undoubtedly viewed Whitmore's huge herd as easy pickings, and near the end of December they drove off

GAS; George A. Smith to William H. Hooper, 5 April 1866, HOLB, 2:525; and Lee, *Diaries*, 2:138.

[34] Bleak, "Southern Mission," 1:209–10.

[35] Ivins, "Forgotten Trails," 350–51; George A. Smith, "Journal," 14 November 1871; Bleak, "Southern Mission," 1:190; and Walter Powell, "Journal," 400.

[36] George A. Smith sermon in Grantsville, 13 July 1866, in "Minutes," vol. 3, BYC; and Erastus Snow to George A. Smith, 19 November 1865, GAS.

most of the wealthy Mormon's stock.[37] "Friendly Indians"confirmed that Black Hawk was responsible for the raid, without specifying whether or not he directed it personally.[38] Contemporary whites used circumstantial evidence to convince themselves that at least Black Hawk's brother Mountain was present.[39] Settlers ultimately came to believe that Patnish, Spanshanks, and a combined force of Ute and Navajo raiders had compelled a band of Kaibab Paiutes to lead them to Whitmore's herds and to help them drive the animals across the Colorado River.[40] What the settlers were not aware of, but that gentile records make clear, however, is the fact that Manuelito was personally present and played a leading role in the raid.

When Whitmore arrived at Pipe Springs, his ranch hand, Robert McIntyre, was unaware the grazing herds were missing, because the dairy cows, sheep, and horses in corrals under his direct surveillance near the ranch house were as yet unmolested. Whitmore's herds were in fact so large that the raiders had "been coming back and forth for the last month" and were not yet finished with their systematic spoiling of the wealthy Mormon's stock when local Piedes reported their actions to the Saints. On 8 January 1866 Whitmore and McIntyre left Pipe Springs to see if their herds were still on the range, telling the former's nine-year-old son that they would be back "for dinner." The two men never returned, and the frightened boy hid that night in a rock dugout while Indians raided and burned his father's corrals and shot arrows into the barricaded door that saved his life. After he was convinced they were gone, the youngster set out on foot for St. George and was eventually picked up by other stockmen. Word of the raids reached St. George on the evening of 11 January, while the settlers (including the families of both Whitmore and McIntyre) met for a party in the community's social hall. The festivities ended dramatically as an excited call was made for an expedition to start "at once" for Pipe Springs.

Forty-four men responded and left early the next morning.[41] Travel-

[37] Andrew L. Siler to George A. Smith, 27 December 1865, GAS.

[38] Bleak, "Southern Mission," 1:215.

[39] George A. Smith and Erastus Snow to Brigham Young, 4 February 1866, BYC; and George A. Smith and Erastus Snow to Daniel H. Wells, 7 February 1866, TMR, #804.

[40] Bleak, "Southern Mission," 2:71–72; *DN*, 10 December 1870; Ivins, "Forgotten Trails," 352; Woolley, "Indian Story," 12; and DUP, *Kane County*, 8–9, 28.

[41] Erastus Snow to Brigham Young, 12 February 1866; Walter Powell, "Journal," 400; Ivins, "Forgotten Trails," 350–56; JH, 12 January 1866, 1; and Bleak, "Southern Mission," 1:211–12.

ing through a snowstorm made their journey arduous, but on 16 January 1866 they reached Whitmore's ranch, where they were joined by thirty men from Grafton and Rockville. Prohibited from tracking the raiders by snow so deep their "stirrups dragged," the seventy-four militiamen split up and searched for local Indians to interrogate. On 18 January a dozen militiamen came across two Kaibab Paiutes skinning a beef. Both denied having any knowledge of the raid. Despite the fact that Captains James Andrus and John Pierce, the two commanders of the Nauvoo Legion force, were both "good Indian talkers," it still reportedly took "three days of talking to get anything out" of the captured Kaibabs. Apparently, the natives' memories were finally jogged when Andrus threw a rope over a beam in the ranch house the militia occupied as a headquarters and threatened to hang them if they did not talk. On 20 January one of the captives led half the soldiers to the bodies of Whitmore and McIntyre while his companion directed the rest to the Kaibab camp.

The stripped bodies of the two missing stockmen were found beneath a foot of snow four miles southeast of the springs. Whitmore had a single gunshot wound but had also been shot with eight arrows. Similarly, McIntyre had been shot once with a gun and sixteen times with arrows.[42] Meanwhile, the other group was led to the Kaibab camp, where seven or eight men, three women, "and a couple of children" were huddled under some ledges in a ravine trying to keep warm.

Surrounding the camp, the militia searched it for evidence. They found fresh rawhide, several sheepskins, large numbers of "Navajo arrows" and a "peck" of newly made "flint arrowheads." Sitting on some gear, one Paiute refused to move and defiantly set an arrow to his bow. Without hesitating, Captain Andrus shot him dead. Under the dead man they discovered "Whitmore's old fur collared over coat and McIntyre's trowsers." In addition to the clothing, they found some gold coins and a wad of greenbacks amounting to "several hundred dollars." It was well known that Whitmore had been "receiving money to buy goods in San Francisco on commission."

Convinced they had found "evidence enough," the troopers dis-

---

[42] James G. Bleak to George A. Smith, 15 and 26 January 1866, GAS; Henry Lunt, Bishop of Cedar City, to George A. Smith, 17 January 1866, GAS; John Steele to George A. Smith, 22 January 1866, GAS; Robert Gardner to Brigham Young, 22 January 1866; Woolley, "Indian Story"; and idem, "Notes on Fathers Life"; and other miscellaneous papers in Edwin Woolley, Jr., and Erastus Snow Family Collection, BYUA&M, b1, f13.

armed the Kaibabs. The Indians protested, claiming the Utes and Navajos had threatened to kill them if they did not help murder the two white men and assist in driving away the stock. The arrows, sheepskins, and rawhide, they averred, were gifts from the raiders. When the whites doubted the story, one Indian "made three attempts to wrest a gun" from his captors and was finally killed. In the excitement, an old Indian was accidentally shot in the thigh, shattering his femur. The four remaining able-bodied Paiute males were then marched off "as prisoners."

They reached the other Nauvoo Legion detachment just as its members were loading the slain white men into a wagon. "Seeing the bodies of their dead brethren," the combined force "lost their patience" and shot the five prisoners on the spot. In all, seven Indians were killed that day, though Pierce and Andrus spared the life of one of their Kaibab guides. This was not the end of the expedition's killing, however; the following day, a small detachment came upon a woman dragging the old man wounded in the thigh the day before. Convinced her last hour had come, the "terror stricken" woman unleashed a piercing cry her captors described as a "death yell." Attempting to speak to the Kaibabs, the Mormons reported "the old Indian was sullen [and] didn't seem to care whether he was [killed] or not." At first the troopers left the couple and rode ahead two or three miles, when the men convinced their officers that the company's safety "demanded" the old man's death.

While some protested the killing as useless, volunteers were called to go back and do the deed. Tom Clark said, "Damned if I wouldn't like to kill an Indian before I go," and he raced a man named Ward back to the wounded old Paiute to see who got to "blow his brains out." Clark and Ward left the woman "wailing over her dead husband" and "rode triumphantly back." At least one trooper, however, looked on the event with remorse. Edwin D. Woolley, Jr., who had argued on behalf of the old man's life, declared, "I never was so ashamed of anything in all my life—the whole thing was so unnecessary."[43]

Several accounts of the Kaibab killings have survived in Southern Paiute folklore. One of them follows:

After the Navajos had killed Whitmore they gave some of his clothes to one of the members of a band of Paiutes. When the

[43] Ibid.; and George A. Smith and Erastus Snow to Daniel H. Wells, 7 February 1866, TMR, #804; and Musser, Journal, 23 January 1866.

white men found these clothes among the Paiutes they killed them all including men, women, and children. The only survivors were Georgey George's father and his brother who ran away because they were young men and could run fast, while those who were killed were mostly old people.

One of the white men in the killing party recognized one old lady who used to do his washing for him in St. George and he didn't want her killed. James Andrus, however, wanted to kill her. In order for this man to save her, he had to grab her and lift her up to the side of his horse and hold her weight by having her stand on his foot in the stirrup. James Andrus, meanwhile, was trying to grab her but this white man kept spinning his horse around to keep her out of the reach of Andrus. Andrus finally decided to let her live. The friendly white man gave her some money to try to make her feel better. She threw the money on the ground feeling that it was not worth the lives of her loved ones they had just killed. The money is still there.[44]

The massacre near Pipe Springs gave rise to a surname still found among the Southern Paiutes. According to the modern tribal members, a female child survived the killings, though neither of her parents did. Left an orphan, she "received the name *Tuhduh'heets*," a word meaning orphan and derived from a root signifying "desolate, barren, or naked." The name was anglicized as "Tillahash," and modern Southern Paiutes hold that its "general meaning" is "The Beginning and the End of a Family" and that it is used "in referring to the desolation of this family caused by the massacre."[45]

An important sequel to the raids on James Whitmore's stock at Pipe Springs adds insight not only into Black Hawk's operations but also into the danger and social turbulence his activities brought to native cultures over a wide region. Whitmore's cattle, horses, and sheep were driven across the Colorado River by the raiders at the Crossing of the Fathers (now under Lake Powell) and at "the mouth of the Pahria" (present-day Lee's Ferry),[46] where Black Hawk's Mexican allies, "with wagons" evidently full of trade goods, were waiting for them. "Dividing

[44] Martineau, *Southern Paiutes*, 62–63.
[45] Ibid., 63, 304.
[46] Crampton and Miller, "Journal of Two Campaigns against the Navajo," 160–62; and Walter Powell, "Journal," 400–401.

up their plunder," the sheep "and a few Beeves were driven south toward the San Francisco Peak [present-day Flagstaff, Arizona] while the Horse[s], mules, and bulk of the Cattle were driven to the East," towards Black Hawk's Elk Mountain market. "The Oribees" (Hopis from the village of Oraibe) learned of these movements. Gathering up "20 or 30 old guns" Mormon missionaries had given them to protect themselves from the Navajos, they ambushed a party of sixteen raiders led by Manuelito. The Moquis killed "11 out of 16 Navajoes," and captured "all the horses, and cattle, and returned home without loss."[47]

While there is no evidence contemporary Mormons ever learned it, Manuelito himself was severely wounded in the Hopi raid on his small contingent of Black Hawk's confederation. His stock lost and his band dispersed, Manuelito, who even after months of convalescence had "almost entirely lost the use of his left arm," eventually surrendered to federal authorities at Fort Wingate in August 1866.[48] Subsequently, when Black Hawk's combined forces had returned from another successful season raiding the Mormon settlements in the north, it appears they joined with eighty Mexican "bandits" and an unknown number of "whites" from the Elk Mountain region and took vengeance on the Hopis. In December 1866 they entered the offending Hopi village of Oraibe, killing and scalping seven Moquis, carrying away "one woman, and eleven children," and driving off all the Hopis' stock, which by now consisted of only "seven hundred head of sheep and goats." Undoubtedly revealing the original intended destination of Manuelito's herd (and simultaneously giving insight into where much of the Mormons' stock ended up as well), the Mexicans involved in the punitive strike against the Moquis were from such settlements as Tierra Amarilla, Abiquiu, and Taos in northwestern New Mexico, and Conejos in southwestern Colorado—the closest European settlements to Black Hawk's Elk Mountain headquarters.[49]

---

[47] Captain L.H. Roundy to Major Maxwell, received in St. George, 5 January 1866, in Erastus Snow to Brigham Young, 12 February 1866, BYC; and Jacob Hamblin and John R. Young, Kanab Mission, to George A. Smith, 12 September 1869, GAS.

[48] It was originally reported that Manuelito died from serious wounds to the left forearm and side. Correll, *Navajo History*, 5:344, 347, 352–53, 363, 368; and Lawrence Kelly, *Navajo Roundup*, 167.

[49] N.M. Davis, Chief Clerk, Indian Department, New Mexico, to L.V. Bogy, Commissioner of Indian Affairs, 19 January 1867, BIA, M234, 554; *Santa Fe New Mexican*, 26 January 1867; John Ward, Special Agent for the Pueblos, Santa Fe, New Mexico, to L.V. Bogy, 4 April 1867, BIA, M234, 554; and Correll, *Navajo History*, 5:417.

Brigham Young's Hostage Plan

When reports of the Paria, Kanab, and Pipe Springs raids and the murders of Whitmore and McIntyre reached Salt Lake City, Brigham Young and other top-level Mormon church officials were distressed. The raids in the south confirmed their fears that Black Hawk had expanded the conflict to other tribes. This along with the threat of wholesale war on the part of the Northern Utes convinced them to take a hard line with the Indians.

On 2 February 1866 Apostles Erastus Snow and George A. Smith left on a tour of the settlements that would take Apostle Smith over a course of 800 miles in two months. Armed to the teeth, the churchmen each carried a new Spencer repeating rifle and a brace of pistols, and between them they had more than 400 rounds of ammunition. Their mission was to "put an end" to Indian "outrages" by ordering "vigorous measures," which included a secret and dangerous plan to force Black Hawk to make peace by taking certain key native leaders hostage. Using hostages as bargaining chips had proved effective before, especially during the Walker War, when the holding of a son of Chief Peteetneet helped bring that conflict to a speedy conclusion. Visiting each of the major settlements in Utah, Juab, Sanpete, and Millard counties, as well as the Virgin River settlements in southern Utah, the church leaders advised Warren Snow and other Nauvoo Legion leaders of the hostage plan. Similarly, they reorganized military districts and continued the familiar counsel to build forts, obtain weapons, move herds to safer locations, and establish cattle-guarding procedures. Laying the groundwork for what was to follow, they instructed the settlers to carefully watch the movements of "friendly Indians" still living near the settlements.[50]

Latter-day Saint leaders had long suspected that Sanpitch was an accessory to Black Hawk's raids. Their suspicions dated back to the very first raid of the war, when Sanpitch refused to retrieve the bodies of fallen militiamen from Salina Canyon unless he was given the

---

[50] There can be no doubt the leaders anticipated "a general Indian war," for they said as much as they preached in various Mormon settlements as they traveled in February and March. For example, see Coombs, Diary, 4 February 1866. See also Brigham Young to William H. Hooper, 13 February 1866, BYC; Brigham Young to Thomas Callister, 21 February 1866, BYC; George A. Smith to William H. Hooper, 5 April 1866, HOLB, 2:525; George A. Smith to Bathsheba W. Smith, 6 February 1866, GAS; and JH, 25 March 1866, 2. For information regarding the role Indian hostages played in ending the Walker War see "History of Spanish Fork," 156–57.

daughters of the murdered Barney Ward. His anger at not obtaining the girls, his surly mood at the Spanish Fork treaty conference, and the testimonies of his own people there convinced Orson Hyde and for a time even Brigham Young that Sanpitch was the mastermind behind the whole war.[51] As time went on, some settlers believed that Sanpitch actually took part in the raids, while others felt he only funneled information and ammunition to the raiders.[52] After investigation, even Utah's new gentile superintendent of Indian affairs was convinced Sanpitch "was a bad Indian" and "had been for a long time furnishing Black Hawk with ammunition, and also advising him as to the most feasible points for stealing cattle."[53] Added to this, in signing the Treaty of Spanish Fork, Sanpitch and other native leaders had pledged to capture the raiders and turn them over to white authorities. As Black Hawk's activities continued, Brigham Young saw no efforts taken by the treaty signers to bring the war chief to justice. With the spread of hostilities to the south, and rumors of an imminent and "general war" involving the Utes, the church president's confidence in the noncombatants waned, and the charges against Sanpitch made him the prime candidate for Young's hostage program.[54]

As the apostles traveled south, they spread new suspicions regarding "friendly Indians" throughout the territory. Even Kanosh was suspect, and orders were given to Fillmore Mormons to see that the raiders and the Pahvants "have no communication" and that runners "do not go from one band to the other." The First Presidency viewed the apostles' work as "perilous business" and urged that they go about it as "quietly" as possible. This last directive was undoubtedly added to avoid attracting the attention of federal military authorities and exacerbating an already tense situation.[55] As the Mormons planned this new and dangerous phase of their military operations against the Indians, bills were introduced in Congress calling for the dismantling of the Territory of

[51] Orson Hyde to Brigham Young, 23 April 1865, BYC; and Brigham Young to "Tabby, Sowiett, Toquer-ona, Jim, Joe and Anthoro," 18 May 1866, BYC.
[52] "Col Snow on the War Path"; and Gottfredson, *Indian Depredations*, 187.
[53] *RSI*, 1866:125.
[54] Brigham Young to Thomas Callister, 21 February 1866; and Brigham Young to John D. Lee, 6 March 1866, BYC.
[55] Daniel H. Wells to George A. Smith, 3 February 1866, in JH, 3 February 1866, 2–3; Brigham Young to Thomas Callister, 21 February 1866; George A. Smith and Erastus Snow to Daniel H. Wells, 7 February 1866; and George A. Smith to Daniel H. Wells, 19 February 1866, TMR, #808.

Utah.[56] Simultaneously, Utah's gentile chief justice passionately pled before the House Committee on Territories that 5,000 troops be sent to Utah to enforce anti-polygamy laws. The secretary of war summoned General Connor and his bitterly anti-Mormon chaplain to Washington to testify as to whether or not such a significant massing of troops was really necessary. When Brigham Young heard of the summons he wrote, "They had better send for Nero to give testimony against the Christians," and "for Herod" to ask "about the character of John the Baptist and whether Jesus is the Christ. This would be in keeping with what they wish to do for us."[57]

A spirit of deep apprehension settled in over Utah's cities and villages; it was reflected in the journal of Isaiah Coombs:

The last dispatches from the East show that there is a greater outside pressure against this people than has existed for a long time. Resolution after resolution is being introduced in congress concerning the polygamy of the Mormons. One honorable gentleman thinks that all polygamists should be prohibited from holding any office. . . . Well, let them work while they may but the more they oppose polygamy the more it will increase and become popular and the time will come soon when those who practice it will rule this continent from sea to sea and ultimately the whole earth."[58]

Brigham Young wrote that communications from the nation's capital indicated "that the feeling at Washington was very intense against us, and [that] there was a deep seated, sullen determination manifested on all hands to strangle the remaining 'twin' as early as possible." Considering the proposed dissolution of the territory, Young threatened to organize a state without the approval of Congress. "We have the State Machinery all ready to put in motion," he wrote Utah's delegate to Congress, "and we shall not hesitate to use it, should such a bill pass." If a hostile body of troops were actually sent to Utah, he promised the Mormon church would fight, as it had a decade earlier during the Utah War. "When they commence a war with the Almighty and his

---

[56] One of these bills, typical of the others, was designed to "extend the boundaries of the State of Nevada, thereby wiping out the Territory of Utah." Brigham Young to William H. Hooper, 21 February 1866, BYC.

[57] Ibid.

[58] Coombs, Diary, 20 January 1866.

purposes," Young wrote, "they will find" that they "have a power to contend with in the presence of which they are but as vile worms."[59] With martial fervor on the increase both in Utah and Washington, Young resolved with more determination than ever to bring the Black Hawk War to a close, the more serious threat in the East demanding an increased firmness in Mormon–Indian relations.

In Fillmore the traveling apostles learned that a mysterious Indian messenger had just crossed the mountains on snowshoes bringing some sort of news to Kanosh, and that some of his Pahvants were killing stock, poisoning their arrows, and declaring their intentions "to fight the citizens." "Kanosh too seems to act somewhat strangely," wrote a third traveling church leader. To the apostles, however, the Pahvant chief remained at least outwardly pacific and apparently had just re-turned from St. George, where he told the settlers that he was "Sorry any of the Mormons [had] been killed" in that region and that the Kaibab killings committed by the Pierce and Andrus companies "served the Indians right."[60] Most Native Americans were not so placid about the killings, however, and word quickly spread among them that the seven Kaibab Paiutes the militia killed were not the murderers of Whitmore and McIntyre.

Enraged Piedes and Paiutes reported the affair to John D. Lee in southern Utah, and Lee relayed the information that "the NavaJoes" killed the whites and gave the Kaibabs "their clothes & 3 oxen & 5 sheep, & because they had Whitmores & Bro. Mackintires clothes, . . . [the] mormons killed seven of the Pieutes, & they are mad about it, & say that we do Just as the Indians do; kill the first that we find—whether they are guilty or not."[61] Such killing could not help but provoke hos-tility, and Indian notions of vengeance called for retaliation. Brigham Young, who demonstrably deplored the killing of innocent Indians, was convinced, however, that "if those Indians upon whom the things were found were not guilty of murdering the brethren they certainly were accessory, and had evidently justified the proceeding by sharing in the plunder."[62]

---

[59] Brigham Young to Brigham Young, Jr., 27 February 1866, in Manuscript History of Brigham Young of that date; and Brigham Young to William H. Hooper, 21 February 1866.
[60] George A. Smith and Erastus Snow to Daniel H. Wells, 7 February 1866; Musser, Journal, 16 February 1866; and James G. Bleak to George A. Smith, 27 January 1866, GAS.
[61] John D. Lee to Brigham Young, 8 February 1866, BYC.
[62] Brigham Young to John D. Lee, 6 March 1866; and Brigham Young to George A. Smith and Erastus Snow, 5 March 1866, in Manuscript History of Brigham Young, 1866: 174–77.

Indian Hostages

Realizing the danger that Latter-day Saint attitudes posed to himself and his band, Sanpitch spent the winter encamped near gentile soldiers at Camp Floyd. Large numbers of Connor's troops were discharged in February, however, and by the end of the month the military base was virtually vacated. By the first week in March, Latter-day Saints in Nephi notified their leaders that Sanpitch and "about a Dozen of his men" had reappeared at their usual winter camp near that settlement and were "quite saucey & making threats [of] what they would do when [the] snow is gone." Meanwhile, an Indian informant reportedly confirmed Sanpitch's secret intention of raiding Nephi.[63]

These and similar threats expressed by "friendly Indians" in Millard, Juab, and Sanpete counties convinced Brigham Young that the time had arrived to implement his secret hostage strategy. On 20 February Warren Snow wrote the church leader that three Utes camping near the tiny Sanpete Valley settlement of Wales belligerently threatened that any Mormons who ventured into the canyon to dig coal would be killed. Snow was convinced the men were spies and had been with Black Hawk. He indicated that he had been ordered to destroy the three "bucks" *and their families* (most likely by Orson Hyde), but he was reluctant to do so without instructions from the church president.[64] Though Young's response has not been found, subsequent events make it clear that he ordered Snow to capture and incarcerate the three Indians in Moroni and let their families go free. Also, the command was issued that Sanpitch and other "friendly Indians" suspected of duplicity be rounded up and "comfortably" hidden in cellars and jails until Black Hawk was brought to terms. Young hoped the plan would induce Indian leaders like Sowiette, Kanosh, Tabby, Toquana, Antero, and even Sanpitch himself to send their men out after Black Hawk to forcibly bring him in to make peace.[65]

Threatened by a potentially large-scale Indian war while fighting for Zion's very political life, Brigham Young felt his back was up against the wall. "We do not want to injure innocent Indians," he wrote just days before implementing the plan, "but we cannot submit to the murder of our brethren." He felt that Indians who were truly "friendly" were obligated to "give us an evidence of their friendship by warning us

[63] Robison, "Journal," 25–27 February 1866; Lewis Robison to Daniel H. Wells, 5 March 1866, TMR, #817; and McCune, "Biography," 28–29.

[64] Warren S. Snow to Brigham Young, 20 February 1866, BYC. Italics mine.

[65] Daniel H. Wells to Warren Snow, 19 March 1866, TMR, #1521.

of the wicked plots of bad Indians, so that we may guard against them, and valuable lives be saved." Too often, he complained, such "friendly" Indians "are treacherous, and, while professing friendship for us, are conniving with the murderers to aid them in their schemes of plunder and murder." Resolutely, he declared, "It is time that such things were ended; we have been here now long enough to show to the Indians that we are their true friends, and that we will not injure an hair of an innocent Indian. They should be satisfied of this by this time, if they ever can be satisfied upon such a point."[66] Young's risky plan backfired, however, erupting in a new wave of Mormon Indian killing. Tragically, despite Young's words, the Lamanites would soon have more reason than ever to question the friendship of the Latter-day Saints.

On 11 March Utah's new governor Charles Durkee and new superintendent of Indian affairs Franklin H. Head[67] met with Brigham Young and were encouraged, as the only public officials legitimately authorized to direct Utah's Indian affairs, to send runners to Sanpitch, arranging for an immediate meeting "for the purpose of making a treaty." The offer to hold treaty talks seems to have given the chief a false sense of security that caused him to relax his guard, for the talks evidently were part of Young's clandestine plan to capture Sanpitch.[68]

Before the new superintendent and governor could reach Nephi for the proposed talks, Warren Snow, clearly acting under Young's orders, surrounded Sanpitch's camp with Nauvoo Legion detachments and captured the chief and eight other Indians, arresting them on charges of harboring raiders and supplying Black Hawk with ammunition.[69] In addition to Sanpitch, the prisoners taken on 14 March 1866 included at

---

[66] Brigham Young to John D. Lee, 6 March 1866.

[67] Durkee replaced J. Duane Doty, who died in June 1865. He prevailed upon Washington authorities to appoint Head, his niece's husband, to replace Orsemus Irish, who resigned his post as superintendent of Indian affairs late in 1865.

[68] Robison, "Journal," 11–12 March 1866; Franklin H. Head to D.N. Cooley, Commissioner, 12 March 1866, BIA, M234, 902; Captain George F. Price to Captain E.B. Grimes, 12 March 1866, District of Utah, Letters Sent Oct.–June 1866, 354/1st 850, District of Missouri, 79, RUSA, RG 393, pt. 3, entry 824; and Col. O.E. Babcock, Salt Lake City, to Maj. Gen. J.A. Rawlins, Chief of Staff United States Army, Washington, D.C., 23 June 1866, RG 94, AGO, M619, 454, frame 961A.

[69] Warren S. Snow to George A. Smith, 14 March 1866, GAS; Charles H. Bryan to Brigham Young, 22 March 1866, BYC; JH, 14 March 1866, 5; Clark, "John Haslem Clark," 91–94; Sanpete Stake Manuscript History, 14 March 1866; Henroid, "Biography," 11; Peacock, Journal, 12 March 1866; Harley, Journal, 14 March 1866; and Coombs, Diary, 22 March 1866.

least one other major Ute leader, Ankawakits, who was a signer of the Treaty of Spanish Fork and, significant to subsequent events, was Tabby's brother-in-law. The surprised Indians protested as they were shackled and loaded into a wagon. Following instructions received from his superiors, Snow informed the Utes they would be jailed until their people turned Black Hawk over to the whites. "If Hostilities continued," Snow told them, "they would be shot to begin with and so on until the last Indian was distroyed that could be found" for the Saints "could not Put up with Killing and stealing eny longer."[70]

When the First Presidency learned of the captures, Daniel H. Wells wrote Warren Snow that the leaders "were pleased to learn that every thing passed off so well." General Wells sardonically urged Snow to see that similar steps be taken to make "a general invitation" to provide "the chiefs and principal men of the Indians" with "comfortable quarters in your settlements until they can have a visit from Black Hawk." "Should they see that you are so very pressing, and determined that they shall share your hospitality," Wells continued his satire, "they may be induced to send for Black Hawk and Jake and their distinguished friends to come and visit and have all differences adjusted so that we can live together in peace."[71]

By 16 March Snow's prisoners were in Manti, where they were put "in irons" in a makeshift jail on the second story of the Sanpete County Courthouse. Once confined, Sanpitch panicked and agreed to "confess all if they would let him go free." The chief admitted that he had "furnished Blackhawk with provisions" but denied further involvement in the raids. Sensing the seriousness of the new Mormon resolve, he agreed to identify Indians pretending to be noncombatants but who in reality had taken some part with Black Hawk, and he stated that five raiders were still at his camp in Nephi. Simultaneously, he ordered Kanosh and "all the head men of the nation" to "to unite together and take Black Hawk so that the prisoners might be liberated from confinement." Since he knew the chief raider had already moved into the central Utah region, Sanpitch expressed his confidence that Black Hawk could be brought in within "three weeks." But as Kanosh's Pahvants and other Indians gathered "for the avowed purposes" of taking Black Hawk by force, Mormon leaders put the settlements on alert, surmising that the

---

[70] Warren S. Snow to George A. Smith, 14 March 1866.
[71] Daniel H. Wells to Warren S. Snow, 19 March 1866.

Ute gathering could just as well "eventuate in an attempted rescue" of the hostages or even in "retaliation" for their capture.[72]

Acting on Sanpitch's admission that some of Black Hawk's men were in his camp, Warren Snow and twenty-five militiamen returned to Nephi under the cover of darkness on the evening of 17 March. They were accompanied by John Kanosh, sent by his father, the Pahvant chief, who was doing all he could to convince his white coreligionists of his loyalty. Before daybreak the following morning, Snow's detachment, joined by additional men from Nephi, surrounded Sanpitch's camp a second time and quietly waited for light. At length an old woman emerged from a tepee and began gathering brush for her fire. John Kanosh shouted something "in [a] shrill Indian tongue" and the woman warned the sleeping men. At this, a teenager burst from a tepee "coiling a Lariet round his body as he ran." Snow commanded his men to fire, and the youth fell dead. With the help of John Kanosh, three other accused raiders were identified, shackled, and led to Nephi. A hasty court martial was held. General Snow acted as judge and Kanosh's son as the only witness. One of the captives allegedly helped Black Hawk kill the Given family, and all reportedly "had been with Chief Black Hawk at Ephraim the year previous where many depredations were committed by them." In a matter of minutes all three were condemned to die and shot before empty graves. The Indians were said to have faced their executioners with "arms crossed, eyes and attitude defiant," displaying "not a sign of fear, nor the motion of a muscle."[73]

Not surprisingly, native reaction to these killings, along with botched attempts to take more captives and word of yet another Nauvoo Legion slaughter of Kaibab Paiutes in the south, convinced not only Kanosh and Sanpitch, but eventually even Warren Snow, that Brigham Young's hostage scheme could not succeed.[74] The three Indian men

[72] *RSI*, 1866:125; Sanpete Stake Manuscript History, 14 March 1866; JH, 27 March 1866, 8; and Warren Snow to Brigham Young, 22 March 1865, BYC (this letter is misfiled under "1856" on current CHD microfilm).

[73] For information regarding the second raid on Sanpitch's camp and the resulting Nauvoo Legion court martial see Warren S. Snow to George A. Smith, 18 March 1866, TMR, #823; Warren S. Snow to William B. Pace, 18 March 1866, TMR, #822; Charles H. Bryan to Brigham Young, 22 March 1866; Peacock, Journal, 17 March 1866; Coombs, Diary, 22 March 1866; Weibye, "Journal," 8 March 1866; Sanpete Stake Manuscript History, 14 March 1866; Clark, "John Haslem Clark," 91–93; Andrew Madsen, "Personal History," 62; Pay, "History," 11; and Henroid, "Biography," 11.

[74] Coombs, Diary, 31 March–4 April 1866. In late February, James Andrus's Nauvoo Legion detachment attacked another band of Kaibab Paiutes suspected of killing Whitmore and McIntyre and three more Indians were killed. James Andrus to Daniel D. McArther, 9 March 1866, TMR, #1518.

Warren Snow had imprisoned in Moroni learned of the executions at Nephi and the continuing seizure of hostages through their families, whom their guards allowed to bring food each day. Understandably fearing for their lives, the prisoners and their wives planned an escape. A sub-chief named Wanrodes (apparently in the valley to confer with Warren Snow, Kanosh, and Sanpitch about the Mormon plan to have Ute leaders bring in Black Hawk) smuggled in several knives and a chisel to the three prisoners.

On the night of 20 March "a dance was given to the soldier boys" in Moroni. "Hearing the sounds of music and revelry," the Indians "thought it a good time to make their escape." The wife of one of the Utes brought the inmates some food. As one of the two guards opened the door, the woman knocked him down. The three prisoners sprang through the door armed with the knives and chisel, attacking the second guard. The man with the chisel knocked the guard's front teeth out and beat him "terribly." The battered guard somehow managed to raise his pistol, however, and killed two of the freed captives; but the third fled into the night.

Apparently in town for the dance, Warren Snow quickly dispatched a group of mounted men with lanterns in hopes of "overhauling" the hostage. Somehow following the Indian's trail through the darkness for ten miles, the posse closed in on the escapee. Writing a letter that night, Snow described that the Indian "still showd fight" and made at the militiamen with a knife. As a result, "the boys . . . put an end to his carreer so their is three more good indians." Snow concluded by discussing his plans to capture "more Hostyle Indians" in Utah Valley.[75]

The tragic affair was not yet over; the following day a Ute woman and little boy involved in the jailbreak were ruthlessly tracked down and murdered by Moroni settlers. "I have fought against harming women and children," Snow justified himself in a letter to Brigham Young. Not only had the church president issued strict orders that juveniles and females be left alone, but Snow had personally guaranteed Sanpitch as much. "For this to happen at this excitement," Snow confided to his leader, jeopardized the success of the entire hostage strategy.[76] Snow's fears were well founded. The murders of the woman and

---

[75] Warren S. Snow to Major Sutton and Col. Pace, 20 March 1866, TMR, #826; and Clark, "John Haslem Clark," 93–95.

[76] Warren Snow to Brigham Young, 22 March 1865.

little boy, added to the seven other deaths resulting from the hostage program, convinced Sanpitch and the other prisoners that their lives were in serious danger and they began plotting an escape of their own. Similarly, the hostage strategy and related killings exponentially multiplied Northern Ute animosity towards Sanpete Mormons in general and Warren Snow in particular.[77]

Because of Sanpitch's apparent cooperation, Snow allowed the inmates in Manti to receive visits from other "friendly Indians," and they saw their wives almost every day. But shortly after the Moroni killings Snow noted a change in the countenances of the prisoners. "Sanpitch and his associates are very low spirited [and] they do not have much to say," he wrote General Wells on 1 April, adding his suspicion that they were contemplating an escape. The cause for the sudden change in attitude was probably due to Black Hawk's refusal to negotiate and the fact that none of the other Ute chieftains had the power to bring him in. Hence, Sanpitch was stuck in jail and feared, with good reason, that Warren Snow would make good his threat to kill the hostages one by one if hostilities continued. By 1 April Snow himself had clearly lost his zeal for the hostage plan, and Sanpitch's fallen visage and the movements of other Indians convinced him that the raiders still "calculate on a general war this season."[78]

As the Mormons "ordered" Sanpitch to send out runners to all Ute headmen including Black Hawk, it is not surprising that the two chiefs were in communication with each other and apparently orchestrated a plan to free the incarcerated Indians. Native women smuggled a file and several knives in to the captives, who used the file to etch teeth into a knife which they in turn used to saw through the shackles around their ankles. The tedious work could be done only while they were not under the direct observation of their guards, and the cuts were hidden by rags given to pad their skin from the coarse irons that held them fast.[79]

Meanwhile, other events transpired to strengthen the growing war hysteria among both Utes and Mormons, further setting the stage for

[77] "Tabby and other Chiefs" per L.B. Kinney to Brigham Young, 12 May 1866, BYC; A.F. MacDonald to William B. Pace, 24 May 1866, WBP; and George W. Bean to William B. Pace, 29 July 1867, CR, 223.

[78] Warren S. Snow to Daniel H. Wells, 1 April 1866, TMR, #1522; and Warren S. Snow to George A. Smith, 14 March 1866.

[79] Fowler, "Diary," 4–5.

the tragedy that occurred when Sanpitch and his fellow prisoners escaped from their confinement in mid-April. Near 1 April, Utah County militiamen followed orders to take more hostages; in the process, they wounded a Ute named Jim Minto, a son-in-law of Guffick and a close relative of Showan, both headmen of the peaceful Goshen band. Convinced he was dying, and held hostage in a "vacant house" in Payson, Jim Minto gave the names of other Utah Valley Indians who allegedly had participated in Black Hawk's raids, and the militia vigorously tried to find them. Eventually, Jim Minto was murdered by an unknown assailant in his makeshift prison in the Mormon town.[80]

"Terribly frightened" by the movements of the Mormon troops, several peaceful bands fled up Spanish Fork Canyon. Because of the hostage program and the deaths of Jim Minto and the captives and their relatives at Moroni, Showan, whom white sources make clear had been amicable to this point, understandably sent word to the Latter-day Saints that he had lost all confidence in their peaceful intentions. He called for all Utes still around the settlements to join him in the mountains, and he and the others then slipped off into Spanish Fork Canyon. A party of Payson settlers went up the canyon bearing "presents" to seek to conciliate the noncombatants, but they "found the camp deserted and the Indians gone and no trace of their destination." The nearly total withdrawal of Indians from Utah and Juab valleys would last more than two years, and because of the establishment of the Uintah Reservation most of these Indians would never return for more than short visits.[81]

Meanwhile, there was further evidence that Black Hawk had exported his war to the Navajos. On 2 April, a band of thirty Navajos, Utes, and Paiutes took vengeance for Nauvoo Legion killings of Kaibab Paiutes by murdering Joseph and Robert Berry and the latter's wife Isabella about twelve miles west of Pipe Springs. As the three Mormon travelers futilely fought for their lives, they killed a Navajo subchief named Spanshanks. As has been mentioned, Spanshanks was the brother of Barboncito, who next to Manuelito was the most important

[80] Coombs, Diary, 31 March–3 April, and 22 April 1866; and William B. Pace to Daniel H. Wells, 5 April 1866, TMR, #1523.

[81] Coombs, Diary, 3 and 24 April 1866; William C. McClellan to William B. Pace, 13 April 1866, TMR, #833; and William B. Pace to Daniel H. Wells, 15 April 1866, TMR, #836.

Navajo raider. Kanosh was soon anxiously reporting that "six thousand [Navajo] warriors" planned to avenge Spanshanks's death.[82]

The Manti Jailbreak

The first reports of the Berry killings shocked Sanpete Valley Mormons as Sanpitch and Black Hawk made their final preparations for the jailbreak. To make matters worse, Superintendent Head, Governor Durkee, and interpreter Richard James had recently made a mysterious trip to Kanosh's camp. Church leaders took the visit for "Federal interference" intended to obtain "the release of Sanpitch and the chiefs confined with him." Because they felt that Sanpitch's release without Black Hawk's surrender "would be equivalent to sacrificing the lives of many helpless persons," church officials viewed the superintendent, the governor, James, *and Kanosh* with suspicion. When Kanosh appeared in Nephi around 11 April with a company of armed Indians and asked that Sanpitch be brought there so he could "see him" before he took to the mountains to capture Black Hawk, Warren Snow was certain the Pahvant chief was up to no good. Refusing to comply, Snow immediately notified General Wells of the request and suggested that "if Kanosh does not show His friendship in a Proper shape He had better be *dealt with* at once."[83]

Kanosh's request probably was part of a scheme to free Sanpitch, but it is unknown whether it originated with the Pahvant chief, Superintendent Head, Governor Durkee, Richard James, the hostages, or Black Hawk himself. In any case, it should be remembered that Head's interpreter, the cattle-thieving, ex-Mormon Richard James, would soon *openly* join the raiders and was even then *covertly* associated with them; during the time of the governor's and superintendent's visit he was observed communicating with Kanosh in "a sneaking way." Spies were set on James by Bishop Thomas Callister of Fillmore, who, as a result of "hints that were dropped" at the Pahvant camp, became "very suspicious that this man has something to do with Black Hawk and his moves."[84] No matter what James's various clandestine communications

---

[82] For general information regarding what some called the "Berry Massacre" see Henry Eyring to Erastus Snow, 8 April 1866, TMR, #831; JH, 8 April 1866, 3, and 9 April 1866, 2; A.P. Winsor, Bishop of Grafton, to Brigham Young, 9 April 1866, BYC; Walter Powell, "Journal," 407–8; and Gottfredson, *Indian Depredations*, 181–83. For the threat of Navajo retaliation for the death of Spanshanks see Brigham Young to Erastus Snow, 15 August 1866.

[83] George A. Smith to Thomas Callister, 28 March 1866, in JH, 28 March 1866, 2; and Warren Snow to Daniel H. Wells, 13 April 1866, TMR, #832. Italics mine.

[84] Thomas Callister to George A. Smith, 13 May 1866, GAS.

with Kanosh may have been, on 13 April Black Hawk initiated a chain of events that was clearly part of an orchestrated attempt to free the hostages. His design, as immediately recognized by Warren Snow, was to attack Salina in order to draw the militia out of Manti so that the prisoners, who by now had all sawed through their irons, could be more sure of a safe and easy escape.

Accordingly, on the morning of 13 April Black Hawk and a band of fifty raiders emerged from Salina Canyon and began gathering cattle grazing near the village he had assailed almost exactly a year before in the first raid of the war. Less than a mile from town they intercepted four wagons loaded with wheat. Chasing the drivers to the settlement, they pilfered clothing and other valuables and feasted on the teamsters' lunches while their horses ate and "trampled" wheat dumped from the wagons. Frightened settlers watched from an only partially built fort, hoping they and several herdsmen out tending stock would be safe.

Shortly an old sheepherder and a boy were killed. The latter apparently was killed while trying to cross the Sevier River, and family members reported that the body "was never found, but one foot with the shoe on was found down the river during the [following] summer." The dead youth's brother was also attacked, but he saved his life by feigning death as an Indian boy shot him with arrows at point-blank range. Seven settlers tried to retake the herd as Black Hawk's band pushed it towards the canyon. In "a sharp skirmish" they succeeded in killing one raider and knocking a horse out from underneath another. At last, however, the whites were overpowered and forced to retreat. Four hours after the raid commenced, Black Hawk reentered Salina Canyon with 150 animals. As was their typical practice in such raids, the Indians shot calves and intractable cattle and horses—in this case leaving thirty-two dead or wounded animals behind them. Interestingly, several times during the raid Black Hawk and other raiders stood "on a round mound above the town" and baited the Saints in plain English, daring them "to come to the Indians now for milk" as their children "would soon cry for milk."[85]

Reports of the raid reached Manti later that evening. Writing a

---

[85] Hamilton Kearnes to George A. Smith, 15 April 1866, BYC; JH, 15 April 1866, 3–4; Peter Rasmussen to Warren S. Snow, 13 April 1866, TMR, #833; JH, 24 April 1866, 1; Gottfredson, *Indian Depredations,* 185–87; Nuttall, Campaign Records, 21 August 1866; and Rasmussen, "Life of Peter Rasmussen." This last source garbles chronology and at times mixes several events together.

dispatch to inform General Wells of the incident, Snow expressed his belief that Black Hawk made "this move so as to draw our forces frome [*sic*] this Point so as to make a Break on manti and if Possible obtain those in charge from their confinement." Snow resolved to keep his command in Manti and suggested that if the Indians "still commit their deprations [*sic*] we head better get [rid] of what we have on hand [that is, kill the hostages] and prepare for the worst." Snow suggested a similar fate for Kanosh if he did not show more convincing signs of friendship. Concluding his message, the Sanpete commander informed Wells, "I have sent to Kanosh if he is our friend to send some of his men and Bring back the stoke [*sic*] taken from Salina and then we shall Know that he wants to live in Peace."[86]

Instead of mustering the Nauvoo Legion and chasing the Indians up Salina Canyon, where the militia had been ambushed the year before, Snow increased the guard around the courthouse jail to twenty well armed men and went to bed. Indian women attending the prisoners probably informed Sanpitch that the militia had failed to take the bait by chasing Black Hawk and that the guard around the courthouse prison had been increased. The desperate hostages apparently decided to make the break anyway, for the following evening they escaped just after dark. Guards watching the jail had gathered on the street in front of the building, where they passed the time telling jokes. Unobserved, an Indian woman crept up the stairs along the side of the building and unlatched the door to the second-story cell. Pulling off their sawed-through shackles, the prisoners sprang over the stair rail and scattered as an alarmed passerby on the street reportedly shouted to the guards, "There go your damned Indians!"

Shots were fired as the hostages fled into the darkness, wounding (but not stopping) Sanpitch and at least one other Ute. The startled guards hurried after their escaping wards while someone sounded the alarm by beating a big bass drum kept on hand to notify the community of Indian trouble. Andrew Van Buren saw an Indian running east and followed him. Jumping a stone wall then under construction to protect Manti from the Lamanites, both men picked up large rocks and prepared to attack one another. Van Buren threw his rock first, breaking the Indian's jaw in two places and bringing him to his knees. Pulling "an old jack knife with a broken backspring" from his pocket, the

[86] Warren S. Snow to Daniel H. Wells, 13 April 1866, TMR, #832.

Mormon grappled with the escapee, seizing him by the neck. As they struggled, Van Buren succeeded in opening the blade with his teeth and slit the Indian's throat, holding him down while he bled to death. Meanwhile, William Cox looked for Indians in the darkness and thought he saw something move under a pile of fence posts. Unable to see clearly, he kicked a dark object and a Ute jumped up "with a loud 'wah.' " Stepping back, Cox shot him in the stomach with his pistol. The man still came forward until Cox shot him in the heart.

By now the whole town was filled with excitement. Nervous men scoured the streets with lanterns cautiously looking in barns, sheds, and privies. Their frightened families locked and barricaded doors and lay on floors breathlessly listening to the shouting and occasional firing of weapons. All suspected Black Hawk was close by to rescue the hostages. Warren Snow himself found Ankawakits hiding in a shed, and the chief lunged at him with a knife. Snow knocked the chief down twice with the butt of his rifle, hitting him so hard he split the stock. At last the general drew his revolver and shot Ankawakits, "which put an end to the fight with him."[87] One Mormon wrote this vivid description of the night's activities in his memoirs:

> What a wave of excitement and suspicion swept over Manti that night, when bullets were flying[,] lights were flashing and people expecting to see the painted faces and hear the terrible war hoop of the rightly named Black Hawk. It was the uncertain where-abouts of this cruel Chief, all thought them near to rescue the fleeing Chiefs[.] Twas few who closed their eyes in slumber that night.[88]

Before the night was over, Snow hastily drafted a letter to inform Wells of the jailbreak. "I cannot express my feelings of Regret at the affair," he wrote, describing his exasperation that "the guard should be so careless as to let them escape." Filled with despair, he predicted that "San Pich, will doubtless make war with a vengence" and explained that

---

[87] Warren S. Snow to Daniel H. Wells, 14 and 21 April 1866, TMR, #835, #839; Warren S. Snow to Brigham Young and Daniel H. Wells, 21 April 1866, BYC; Fowler, "Diary," 4–5; Coombs, Diary, 18 April 1866; Peacock, Journal, 15 April 1866; Clark, "John Haslem Clark," 95–97; Cox, "Biographical Sketch," 19–20; Manti Centennial Committee, *Song of a Century*, 143–44; Farnsworth, "History of Manti," 53; Keeler, *Cheney Van Buren*, 147–48; and Gottfredson, *Indian Depredations*, 187–88.

[88] Clark, "John Haslem Clark," 95–97.

he was sending men to "retake the Prisoners" and guard the trails to Spanish Fork Canyon, which he was convinced would be Sanpitch's natural escape route.[89]

The Death of Sanpitch

Sanpitch and the other four surviving escapees headed north to Moroni, where they stole two horses and found food, blankets, and knives in a "Sheep Herders Shanty." Hiding a comrade wounded so badly he could go no farther, they traveled north until they were spotted by a man from Fountain Green who "raised the Alarm." Leaving the horses at the base of the Sanpitch Mountains, the four climbed the elevation with the militia "in hot persuit." Darkness forced the whites to retire to Fountain Green on the night of 17 April, but early the next morning they again "took up the track."

Slowed by his wound, Sanpitch was overtaken first and killed at Birch Canyon on the mountain that now bears his name on the west side of Sanpete Valley. Near the top of the mountain two more Indians were overhauled and killed. The last of the fleeing Indians buried himself with leaves "in a patch of oak brush" but was spotted by a militiaman named Bennett. As the troopers closed in, the Indian "jumped up and came at Bennett with a large butcher knife." The white man "emptied his revolver" at the Indian but did not bring him down. When the native was "within a few feet," Bennett hit him with the empty pistol and "wrenched the knife from his hand and cut his throat."[90]

The injured Indian who was hiding near Moroni was finally discovered on 19 April riding a stolen horse. Warren Snow wrote that, since "he refused to surrender," the last of the hostages "was shot dead, and buried." "Thus Ends the lives of the Eight Prisoners, San Pich included," Snow wrote to Brigham Young and Daniel Wells a few days later. Concerned that the church presidency would not approve of the killings, Snow expressed the hope that he and his men had "not been to[o] fast in the matter." He justified the actions by stating that the prisoners "would not be retaken alive" and that he "was not with the boyes at the time they came up with them" and that if he had been he would have "Cept Sanpitch alive and took him home." As it was, he explained,

---

[89] Warren S. Snow to Daniel H. Wells, 14 April 1866.

[90] Ibid., Warren S. Snow to Brigham Young and Daniel H. Wells, 21 April 1866; and Gottfredson, *Indian Depredations*, 188–89.

it was "far better" the escapees were killed "than to let them go into the indian Camp."[91]

Young's private response to Snow, the chief implementer of his Indian policy, is significant and illustrates his feelings regarding the brutal actions taken by his people. "I do not know that any better course could have been taken in relation to Sanpitch and the others than has been," he wrote, though he added that Snow "could not feel any worse about their escape" than he did. "We do not want to kill the Indians; it is painful and repugnant to our feelings to have to recourse to violence against them," he attested, "but it will not do for us to sit down and see our brethren and Sisters killed by them, and not take measures to prevent such occurrences."

Young explained that he had just had a "long talk" with Kanosh "and reasoned the case with him." The church leader asked the chief, "What could we do?" and vented his frustration that the "professedly friendly Indians never tell us where the hostile Indians are; but they can go to them and tell them all about us." Young wrote Snow that he had threatened Kanosh that if the Indians "did not cease" such practices the Saints "would have to cut them *all* off." The terrified Kanosh "agreed" and said his white coreligionists "could do no less."[92] The sorrow of this exchange must have been poignant for both leaders, who, it will be remembered, enjoyed a sort of father-son relationship because Young had given an adopted native daughter to Kanosh in marriage. For Kanosh and his people the tragedy is obvious. Even for the generally optimistic Young the conversation must have evoked an overwhelming sense of his people's failure to fulfill Latter-day Saint prophecy by helping the Lamanites to "blossom as the rose."[93] Instead of fulfilling the sacred obligation to bring the Lamanites to Christ, which was unquestionably his sincere and heartfelt desire, he found himself threatening to utterly destroy them. The declaration was not lost on Kanosh, who quickly spread it to other Ute leaders such as Sowiette, Toquanna, Tabby, and Antero, who understandably, especially in light of the recent rash of Indian killings, got the "idea . . . that the Mormons were designing to make war upon them."[94]

---

[91] Warren S. Snow to Brigham Young and Daniel H. Wells, 21 April 1866; and Warren S. Snow to Daniel H. Wells, 21 April 1866, TMR, #839.

[92] Brigham Young to Warren Snow, 25 April 1866, BYC. Italics mine.

[93] [Joseph Smith, et al.], *Book of Commandments*, 118; and Section 49:24–25 in current editions of the *Doctrine and Covenants*.

[94] *RSI*, 1866:130.

After the killing of Sanpitch, fear of Indian war reached fever pitch among Utah's settlers. Sanpitch had allegedly boasted to his captors that "You may kill Black Hawk and all his band; but if you kill me, you will never have peace!" and many settlers believed it. Nauvoo Legion leaders prepared for all-out war, while settlers throughout Utah expressed their conviction that "the prospect for an Indian war was never more flatering than now" and prayed for "their sake as well as ours" that "a kind Providence [would] avert such a calamity."[95] War hysteria, distrust, and vengeful desires among Indians and Mormons, however, subsequently pushed both groups towards even more catastrophic outbursts of violence.

[95] DUP, *Heart Throbs*, 6:483; Culmsee, *Utah's Black Hawk War*, 81; and Coombs, Diary, 18 April 1866.

Chapter Seven

The Circleville Massacre and the Battle of Gravelly Ford

Every endeavor should be made and every precaution used to protect yourselves and your settlements against the attacks of such treacherous foes. . . . It is only by being constantly vigilant that you can ensure the safety of the people and the preservation of their property against these surprises and sudden attacks.

—Brigham Young[1]

War Hysteria and Indian Killing

Upon learning of Sanpitch's death, Orson Hyde put Sanpete and Sevier county militia companies on alert. Certain the botched hostage plan would provoke "the whole Utah nation [to] unite with Black Hawk," he and other Latter-day Saints anticipated "hot times."[2] Therefore, Hyde issued orders for the total evacuation of Salina, Glenwood, and Monroe. Once it was reinforced with Mormons from the evacuated settlements, Hyde deemed Richfield to be strong enough to repulse the vicious attacks he expected. Similarly, he considered Circleville and Panguitch relatively safe because of the construction then in progress of a Nauvoo Legion garrison called Fort Sanford that was strategically located between the two settlements.[3] Hyde sent wagons and teamsters from the Sanpete settlements to carry the evacuees away. He also

---

[1] Brigham Young to Orson Hyde, 31 May 1865, BYC.

[2] Warren S. Snow to William B. Pace, 15 April 1866, WBP; Orson Hyde to George A. Smith, 26 April 1866, GAS; and George A. Smith to Brigham Young, Jr., May 1866, HOLB, 2:535–39.

[3] Located on the Sevier River near the mouth of Bear Creek, Fort Sanford was established in March 1866. Mormon military leaders deemed it of great strategic value not only because it provided protection for Panguitch and Circleville but also because it guarded a spur of the Old Spanish Trail that potentially could be used to drive off stock from Parowan, Paragonah, and Beaver.

dispatched herds of Sanpete and Sevier valley cattle to Salt Lake City to be traded for weapons and ammunition as well as for tents, saddles, and other accouterments necessary for Indian fighting.[4]

On 21 April 1866, militiamen chasing stock stolen from Monroe were ambushed within two hundred yards of the tiny fort at Marysvale. Four whites were shot, one dying instantly, while a second died a month later. The soldiers retreated while their attackers escaped with the animals.[5] The same day, frightened militiamen near Fort Sanford initiated a chain of events that shortly would result in the worst massacre of the entire war. Following the raid on Salina and the jailbreak at Manti, "friendly" Piedes residing near Circleville told settlers that Black Hawk was gathering his forces at Fish Lake preparatory to attacks intended to drive the whites from the Sevier Valley. Nervous Mormons from Circleville, Fort Sanford, and Panguitch observed small squads of unfamiliar Indians with painted faces mysteriously traveling up and down the Sevier. Orders were issued to apprehend and question the strangers in an attempt to learn the meaning of their movements.

On 22 April, militiamen at Fort Sanford noticed two Indians "bedaubed with paint" coming up the opposite side of the Sevier River and sent two men to bring them to the stockade for questioning. Fearful because of the recent killings, the Indians refused to come to the fort. When the soldiers became adamant, the natives shot a militiaman in the shoulder and attempted to flee. In the process, one Indian was killed and the other wounded as he made good his escape. The two whites returned to the fort with word that the Indians "were on express from Black Hawk's band."[6]

It was assumed that the messengers were enlisting support for Black Hawk, and dispatches were sent to Panguitch and Circleville "advising that the Indians encamped near the two settlements be immediately disarmed." The following day, 23 April, a small detachment of Nauvoo Legion men surrounded a band of Piedes near Panguitch. They discovered the camp all "packed and tied up, ready for a move." The militia noticed that most of the men were away and concluded the braves had already joined Black Hawk at Fish Lake. Four adult males re-

---

[4] JH, 24 April 1866, 1; Warren S. Snow to Brigham Young and Daniel H. Wells, 21 April 1866 TMR, #839; Weibye, "Daybook," 47–48; and Gottfredson, *Indian Depredations*, 226.

[5] John W. Peterson, Autobiography, 4–7; Zebulon Jacobs, "Journal," 10–12 May 1866; and Gottfredson, *Indian Depredations*, 193–95.

[6] Erastus Snow to Daniel H. Wells, 25 April 1866, TMR, #1524; Gottfredson, *Indian Depredations*, 190–93; JH, 22 April 1866, 1, and 5 May 1866, 2; and Fish, "Diaries," 24.

mained with the women and children, however, and when the soldiers attempted to take their weapons they commenced firing with muskets and arrows. One white was struck with an arrow and two Piedes were killed, including an old shaman the Mormons called "Doctor Bill." According to one Nauvoo Legion report, "the killing of Old Bill (the medicine man) cowed the Indians more than the loss of twenty warriors would, [for] their tradition made him Bullet proof." The Mormons concluded that "this must also have been his own belief for he commenced firing when surrounded by a party of 14 well armed men." Stores of guns, powder, and lead, "many new arrows, and about a peck of new arrow points" convinced some Latter-day Saints the Panguitch band was indeed preparing for war.[7]

The Circleville Massacre

Meanwhile, orders to disarm "friendly" Piedes near Circleville reached that community. Just days before, raiders made off with "twenty-five head of cattle, two mules and two horses," and "unfamiliar" Indians were seen visiting the local Piede encampment. Before light on 23 April, militiamen surrounded the camp and forcefully "invited" several Indians to come to town for a "talk." Once they were in Circleville, the Piede's were informed that since they were suspected of aiding Black Hawk they were now considered prisoners.

Later that day, Circleville militiamen intercepted two Lamanite "strangers" near the Piede camp and killed one of them when they tried to escape. Local Mormons were afraid the Piedes still in camp would take word of the killing to Black Hawk; therefore, the surviving "strange Indian" and the entire Piede band, including women and children, were rounded up and taken at gunpoint to Circleville. The terrified Indians allegedly "confesed to [carrying] ammunition to the hostile Indians." They also announced that Black Hawk was at nearby Fish Lake, where Utes, Paiutes, Piedes, Pahvants, and Navajos were gathering "to unite against us," and threatened that soon Circle Valley would "be full of them."

Realizing their exposed position and their proximity to Black Hawk's forces and fearing they had just killed one of the war chief's "emissaries," the settlers determined to place the entire band under guard while they sent to church leaders in Beaver for instructions. In

---

[7] Erastus Snow to Daniel H. Wells, 25 April 1866; Gottfredson, *Indian Depredations*, 191–92; JH, 22 April 1866, 2; and Silas S. Smith to George A. Smith, 29 May 1866, GAS.

all, twenty Piedes were incarcerated: nine men in the community's meetinghouse, and five women and six children in a nearby cellar. After just one day in confinement, on 24 April, six of the nine males "severed the thongs binding their hands" and were in the process of freeing their friends when "one of the guards discovered what was going on." "A brief, and fatal fight ensued between the guards and the liberated prisoners," and, since "the former [had] the advantage of their 'arms,' " they soon "dispatched the Indians and sent them into Eternity." The remaining males were confined with their women and children in the cellar.

Having suffered repeated attacks at the hands of the raiders in which some of their own people had been brutalized, and fully expecting their tiny settlement to be destroyed if word of these latest killings of Indians reached Black Hawk (who they were sure was camped with his whole force at nearby Fish Lake), the Circleville Saints held a "hearing." One settler remembered that "a few men in the community exhibited great hatred for the Indians," and it seems they now seized control, for the consensus was to destroy every Indian old enough to tell. The Piede males, the five women, and the two oldest children were "taken up one at a time" from their cellar prison and had their throats slit. The four remaining youngsters were "saved and adopted by good families."[8] Tradition among some of Circleville's descendants is that one Indian climbed up the meetinghouse chimney during the escape attempt and survived the carnage. Returning to the settlement sometime later, he apparently boasted of his escape to a Mormon, who then hired him to "dig a pit in [the] bottom of his orchard." When the pit was finished, the Circleville "Saint" allegedly "hit him in the head and killed him," burying the last of Circle Valley's Piedes in a grave dug by his own hands.[9]

Paiute oral tradition remembers the Circleville Massacre in this manner:

There used to be a big old log house in Circleville, Utah, beside the road where it curves near where the potato cellars are. Years

---

[8] William J. Allred, Bishop of Circleville, to George A. Smith, 5 May 1866, GAS; Erastus Snow to General Wells, 25 April 1866, TMR, #1524; Oluf Larsen, "Biographical Sketch," 47–48, and variation in DUP, *Our Pioneer Heritage*, 210–12; Jacobs, "Journal," 10–12 May 1866; Reddick N. Allred to Major Seeley, 27 April 1866, in Andrew Madsen, "Personal History," 63–64; Culmsee, *Utah's Black Hawk War*, 90–91; Tolton, "Memories," 9–10; and Winkler, "The Circleville Massacre."

[9] Alton Blackburn, interview by Charles S. Peterson, Sunnyside, Utah, 1966, notes in author's possession.

ago the white men at Circleville locked up in that house all the Indians who were living nearby and told them they were going to cut their throats. They began doing this by taking them outside one at a time and cutting their throats.

There were two young men inside who decided they were going to escape. One said to the other "We will have to dash through them and run just as they open the door." They did this and ran through the white men who were gathered all around, some on horseback. They opened fire on these two Indians but couldn't hit them. They ran towards the cemetery on the hill to the north and as they were going over it, one of the pursuing white men on horseback shot one of the Indians in his side by his ribs but it was only a flesh wound. From there they ran up into the mountains and then the wounded Indian put some Indian medicine on his wound and wrapped it in part of his shirt. The white men didn't follow them far so from there they went on over to Parowan or Beaver.[10]

The Circleville Massacre was the greatest single tragedy of the Black Hawk War. At first it appears the Circleville Saints sought to cover up the full extent of their involvement, representing that "all but the papooses" were killed *while attacking their guards.*[11] On hearing this sanitized report, Daniel Wells wrote that, considering the circumstances, he "could not well see how the brethren there . . . could have done less." Brigham Young, however, was immediately disgusted, and fully a decade after he learned the complete story he still publicly deplored the affair, noting that he believed the curse of God rested upon Circle Valley and its inhabitants because "a band of our Lamenite [*sic*] brethern and their families, were here cruely slain." As he then sized it up, the settlers of Circleville "excused" their "cruel act," claiming it was a "necessity of war."[12]

On the other hand, Orson Hyde was pleased when he learned of the killings. "Sanpitch and his Braves and the Piutes of Circleville have received that kind of gospel which they merit," he wrote his fellow apostle George A. Smith. "I do not know but that there are friendly Indians in Utah," he stated, "but I must confess I know not where they

[10] Martineau, *Southern Paiutes,* 58–59.
[11] For example, see Colonel R.N. Allred to Major William Seeley, 27 April 1866, in DUP, *Our Pioneer Heritage,* 9:180.
[12] Daniel H. Wells to Erastus Snow, 3 May 1866, in JH, 3 May 1866, 3–5; and "Gunnison Ward Historical Record," 18.

are." Reflecting the spirit of war hysteria that precipitated the killings in the first place, he continued:

> You will learn of their uniting for the purpose of using us up. The Utes, Piutes, Pauvantes and Navahoes in the South . . . and there is said to be a heavy force of Utes in Spanish Fork Kanyon, probably far up enabling the Indians of Uinta Valley to join them. Thus on our North a Strong force of the enemy, and likewise on the South who contemplate no doubt simultaneous action. You will see that we are threatened with extermination.

Hyde closed his letter by praying that God would "soon strike a blow that will make his people free from the miserable clans and hordes that fight against Mt. Zion."[13]

These sentiments were typical of those expressed in Hyde's correspondence and recorded addresses throughout the period. The apostle's attitudes are significant because they give some insight into how Sanpete and Sevier county Latter-day Saints could take the brutal and violent measures they did when Brigham Young most often urged the opposite course. Many settlers felt that Young, living as he did in his mansions in Salt Lake City, was far removed from the problems and issues they faced. On the other hand, Hyde, the top-ranking local authority, actually lived in Sanpete County and, losing substantial numbers of his own stock to the raiders, he shared their troubles. Throughout the war, the Sanpete apostle provided leadership to central Utah Saints that was often diametrically opposed to the more peaceful policies Young sought to pursue. Long known to other Mormons for their extraordinary penchant for violence, the Saints under Hyde's jurisdiction were quick to put aside Young's peace policy for their local leader's more malignant rhetoric.[14] The Indians themselves could sense the difference, and before the 1866 season was over it became clear that many of them considered themselves at war specifically with Sanpete and Sevier valley settlers and not with Mormons generally.[15]

Another Shift in Strategy

Despite the growing hatred for Indians nurtured in Sanpete and Sevier counties, Brigham Young reverted to a more peaceful strategy after his

[13] Orson Hyde to George A. Smith, 26 April 1866, GAS.

[14] For example, see Charles Kelly and Hoffman, *Holy Murder*, 188.

[15] A.F. MacDonald to William B. Pace, 24 May 1866, WBP; Brigham Young to Orson Hyde, 16 May 1866, BYC; and CR, 223.

hostage plan failed. Afraid Sanpitch's death would cause reservation Indians to join Black Hawk, Young sent a courier on snowshoes with a letter addressed "to Tabby and Toquer-oner [Toquana], my good Friends in Uinta Valley." The letter was a significant gesture. The preceding winter had brought "double" the usual amount of snow, causing extreme suffering among Indians who had removed to the Uintah Reservation; all of their cattle, most of their ponies, and many of their kinsmen perished of starvation, cold, and disease. Enraged that the federal government did not honor its promise to feed them on the reservation, Tabby usurped the peaceful Sowiette's leadership and his warriors chased the Indian agent, his employees, and a platoon of federal soldiers from the newly established Uintah Agency. When the exhausted whites stumbled into the Mormon settlements in the middle of the winter, they reported that Tabby had replaced Sowiette as head chief and that his warriors promised to join Black Hawk as soon as the snow melted.[16]

"We have heard of the cold weather you have had this Winter, and how you have suffered and lost your horses," Young's letter to the reservation chiefs began. "Our hearts have been very sorry at this news," he wrote, avowing that he would have sent help but was prohibited by the deep snows. He urged Tabby and Toquana to come to Salt Lake City and visit him. "We want to say Peace to you, and have you say Peace." He assured the chiefs that "the Mormons are the friends of the Indians and do not want to hurt them," and declared that "this fighting and killing ought to be stopped."[17]

Young's messenger was Lot Huntington, who like Dimick was known and trusted by the Utes. Unfortunately, Huntington arrived with Young's letter just as reservation Indians learned of the deaths of Sanpitch and the other native leaders. Huntington reported that despite his former friendship, the Utes circled about him in frenzied anger. He tried to read them the letter, but they called for his death instead. Convinced they would kill him, he sat down and cocked his pistols. Huntington allegedly said that while he was surrounded Sanpitch's wife "came up crying & asking them to kill the Mormon quick so she could eat his heart while it was warm." Huntington was reportedly saved from certain death by the "old & blind" Sowiette, who chided his people for seeking to kill a white man brave enough to come

---

[16] Brigham Young to Tabby and Toquer-oner, 21 April 1866, BYC; Lyman S. Wood to Brigham Young, 6 February 1866, BYC; O.H. Irish to D.N. Cooley, Commissioner of Indian Affairs, 1 February 1866, BIA, M234, 902; and *RSI*, 1866:122–30.

[17] Brigham Young to Tabby and Toquer-oner, 21 April 1866.

and "talk peace" under such circumstances. At last the Indians "cooled down" and Huntington escaped, but only after expressing "sincere thanks to brave old Sowiet." Huntington apparently returned to the church president with the news that Tabby and the other reservation chiefs "had thrown [Young] away" and planned to join Black Hawk.[18]

Meanwhile, word of the jailbreak killings and the slayings at Fort Sanford, Panguitch, and Circleville spread through native populations. Kanosh's Pahvants were "uneasy hearing so many reports of cruelty to friendly Indians." Even Kanosh declared he finally had "sufficient cause to lose confidence" in the Saints. Simultaneously, frightened Shoshonis reported they were warned by Ute runners that "the Mormons were killing the various tribes off . . . by wholesale."[19]

The *Deseret News* gave a watered-down version of the latest rash of Indian killings; however, it reiterated Brigham Young's policy "to treat the friendly Indians well, to let those who are 'mad' feel that [the Settlers] mean to protect themselves and can punish aggressions; and that when the savages cease their depredations they will be treated with that kindness which they have uniformly received in the past."[20] In the excitement of that turbulent spring, Superintendent Head, highlighting Black Hawk's recent success in his raid on Salina, appealed to federal military authorities to send "one or two companies" to chastise the raiders. Major General John Pope's reply was that "there were no troops to be spared for such service" and that "the Supt. of Indian Affairs will have to depend for the present on the militia to compel the Indians to behave at Selina [*sic*]." Upon learning of Head's request, Daniel Wells wrote, "I don't think they have time to attend to such matters, and very much doubt if any [troops] will go. The regeneration business [that is, the reformation of Utah] keeps them all busy."[21] Military records make it clear that a huge downsizing of the army was then in progress, and

[18] Ibid.; Lindsay, "Autobiography," 282; DUP, *Heart Throbs*, 1:104; and Brigham Young to Tabby, Sowiette, Toquana, Jim, Joe and Antero, 18 May 1866, BYC.

[19] Thomas Callister to George A. Smith, 13 May 1866, GAS; and Peter Maughan to Brigham Young, 29 May 1866.

[20] JH, 22 April 1866, 2–3.

[21] F.H. Head to D.N. Cooley, Commissioner of Indian Affairs, 30 April 1866, in *RSI*, 1866:128; Col. Carroll H. Potter, comdg. District of Utah, Salt Lake City, to Capt. Sam. E. Mackey, A.A.A.G., Fort Leavenworth, 29 April 1866, Telegrams Sent, Oct. 1865–June 1866, 354/4th 850 District of Missouri, 34–35, RUSA, pt. 3, entry 826; Sam. E. Mackey to Col. C.H. Potter, 2 May 1866, Register of Telegrams Received, Oct. 1865–June 1866, 343/854, District of Missouri, 169, RUSA, pt. 3, entry 828; Daniel H. Wells to Erastus Snow, 3 May 1866 in Bleak, "Southern Mission," 1:231; and George A. Smith to Brigham Young, Jr., May 1866, in HOLB, 2:535–39.

serious shortages of troops throughout the West reached their nadir just as Pope denied Head's request. It is important to note, however, that Pope granted a similar request made by Kit Carson on behalf of New Mexico and Colorado gentiles at the same time. Carson, it will be remembered, asked that troops be stationed in the Four Corners region. He did not base his request on a recent major raid such as the one Head reported at Salina but simply noted that the troops were needed because "a blow *might* be struck" by Indians "hanging in the vicinity of the settlements."[22] In the case of Utah, however, as one sympathetic gentile remembered it, Pope, "acting under the orders of General Sherman, refused to help the settlers, telling them in a telegram of twenty words *to help themselves.*"[23]

In truth, Pope's response was just what Brigham Young hoped for, as he was still convinced that involving federal soldiers would be disastrous for Latter-day Saint interests. Not only was Connor still in Washington seeking troops to use against the theocracy, but Congress continued to debate splitting the territory as a means of destroying the church's political power.[24] To make matters worse, on 10 April exaggerated reports of Salt Lake City murders caused Major General William T. Sherman to telegraph Young that the country was full of "tried and experienced soldiers, who would be pleased . . . to avenge any wrongs" the Saints dared commit.[25] On 8 May the commander of Camp Douglas visited Young in his home and defiantly declared that "the Mormons should know that the U.S. were only wanting a pretext to wipe them out of existence."[26]

Meanwhile, the *Deseret News* reprinted excerpts from articles published throughout the nation disparaging the "mad leprosy of Mormonism" for its "crime[s] against civilization." Latter-day Saint polygamy, "the other barbarism," was depicted as a "monstrous abomination," an "offshoot of Turkish sensuality," and a "degrading system" of "physical and spiritual bondage." Newspapers all over the country

---

[22] See Bvt. Brig. Genl. Christopher Carson to Major C.H. De Forrest, 1 June 1866, John P. Sherburne to Bvt. Brig. Genl. J.H. Carleton, 9 July 1866, and related correspondence, in AGO, M619, 496. Italics mine.

[23] Phil Robinson, *Sinners and Saints*, 180. Italics mine.

[24] Brigham Young to William H. Hooper, 21 February and 3 March 1866, BYC; and T.B.H. Stenhouse to Brigham Young, 5 May and 19 June 1866, BYC.

[25] Telegram of Major General William T. Sherman to Brigham Young, 10 April 1866, in W.T. Sherman, Maj. Gen. Comdg. to Genl. E.D. Townsend, 13 April 1866, AGO, M619, 494, 573M; and Brigham Young to William H. Hooper, 14 April 1866, BYC.

[26] George A. Smith to William H. Hooper, 7 May 1866, HOLB, 2:532–33.

called for the removal of the "festering pollution [of Mormonism] from our body politic."[27] The belief that warfare between Utah and the nation was imminent was so widespread that a number of recently defeated Confederate military leaders offered their expertise to Brigham Young should the church actually fight "the so called U S."[28] Responding to deep-seated tensions, Orson Hyde expressed a prevalent Utah attitude when he wrote, "If United States troops should consent to make an effort to quel the Indians, they would probably never find them & if the[y] did the[y] would probably make a sham treaty with them & give them plenty of guns & ammunition & tell them to go ahead."[29]

In light of these tensions, Brigham Young was understandably relieved when Superintendent Head received word the first week in May that eastern generals chose not to send United States troops after Black Hawk's forces. Instead, Superintendent Head and Governor Durkee were empowered "for the present" to mobilize the local militia.[30] The truth is, Young had illegally employed the Nauvoo Legion against Black Hawk for over a year, and days before the receipt of this official authorization to the governor and superintendent, he dispatched 100 Salt Lake and Utah Valley militiamen to the troubled region and ordered 100 more to prepare to go.[31]

This arrangement of Young directing the militia continued, and in December 1866 Charles Durkee, like other gentile governors before and after him, registered a formal complaint in his "Governor's message to the Territorial Legislature." He stated what all knew: that Utah's militia practices were "not in accordance with the Territorial Organic Act," especially in "the provision therein, that the Governor shall be commander-in-chief of the militia." Mormon military practices constituted a serious breach of law that was openly "ignored." Pointing to a fact that later would cause Black Hawk War veterans much consternation, the governor predicted that claims for reimbursement for time and expenses fighting Indians "would be much more favorably considered by the General Government were [the] militia

---

[27] JH, 1 May 1866, 1.

[28] For example, see Thomas B. Brantley to Brigham Young, 14 April 1866, BYC.

[29] Orson Hyde to George A. Smith, 20 May 1866, GAS.

[30] Telegram of Capt. Sam E. Mackey to Col. C. H. Potter, 2 May 1866, Register of Telegrams Received, Oct. 1865–June 1866, 343/854 District of Missouri, RUSA, pt. 3, entry 828, 169.

[31] Orders no. 4, 28 April 1866, TMR, #842.

called upon . . . by the *recognized superior of the organization.*[32] During his tenure as governor, Durkee made "repeated efforts to have this militia disbanded, or its control turned over to him," but he at last concluded it could not be done without military force mandated by a special act of Congress.[33]

Like gentile governors before him, Charles Durkee was forced to acknowledge that he was simply "the Governor of the *Territory*," while BrighamYoung was "the Governor of the *People.*" But he added a new twist to this long-standing colloquialism which his predecessors would have agreed with when he exclaimed, "A Gentile Governor in Utah is the biggest farce on Earth!"[34] In Durkee's judgement, the Nauvoo Legion was nothing less than "a standing menace to [U.S.] authority in Utah, and would make us trouble yet."[35] As gentile observers almost with one voice reiterated, "Brigham Young is still governor *de facto* . . . of the State of Deseret, no matter whom the President may send out as governor *de jure* of the Territory of Utah."[36]

It must be remembered that during this period, the so-called "State of Deseret" operated behind the scenes in the Territory of Utah. The legislature of this Latter-day Saint "ghost state" continued to meet annually, Brigham Young delivering speeches as "governor" and the legislature officially "re-enacting" the laws it had passed acting in its dual role as territorial legislature. As special U.S. investigator Brigadier General James F. Rusling correctly summed it up, the Mormons "decline to recognize the United States territorial organization any further than they have to, and would reject it altogether if they had the power to." "My conclusion was and is," he continued, "that there is no substantial liberty of speech or of the press in Utah, and no safety for Gentile life or property without a tacit acquiescence in the existing order of things there. . . . The *vital fact* remains, unfortunate as it may be, that *the Mormons are a lawless and seditious community of people, hostile to persons not of their faith and practice, and that they live boastingly in defiance of the public laws of the Union!*" The Mormon army, Rusling wrote, "carries the flag of the 'State of Deseret' and of the old Nauvoo legion," but only bore "the United States standard *ex necessitate.*"[37]

[32] See "Governor Charles Durkee's Address to Utah Territory's Legislative Assembly, December 10, 1866," in "Governor's Messages, 1851–1876," 118. Italics mine.
[33] Rusling, "Report," 26.
[34] As quoted in Jarman, *Uncle Sam's Abscess,* 161. Italics mine.
[35] Charles Durkee, as quoted in Rusling, *Across America,* 173–74.
[36] Rusling, "Report," 26.
[37] Ibid., 25–27. Italics in original.

It was clear to Rusling, Durkee, and other leading gentiles that the existence of the Nauvoo Legion and Brigham Young's personal control of it were the ultimate expression of Mormon power and therefore had to be curbed. Responding to reports presented by Rusling and others regarding Young's and Wells's leadership of the Legion, even U.S. President Andrew Johnson declared it was "high time something was done to *clean out* such scoundrels." Rusling later lamented Johnson's re-solve, however: "It was a generous impulse, while it lasted, and he meant it, too. But subsequently, when I saw him again, in the winter, he had become embroiled with Congress, and dismissed the Utah ques-tion with the curt remark, that there was 'practical polygamy in Massa-chusetts too, as well as Utah.' "[38]

LDS church control of the Utah Territorial Militia had long been a major source of gentile-Mormon friction. The changing of the militia's official name to "the Nauvoo Legion" was the least of gentile worries but was symbolic of the whole problem. The Mormon militia was orig-inally organized under the 1840 "Nauvoo Charter," a most unusual in-vestiture of power granted by the Illinois Legislature at a time when that state's Whigs and Democrats were falling over each other trying to oblige Joseph Smith in order to respectively secure the bloc vote of the Latter-day Saints. Both Whigs and Democrats soon awakened to the fact that they had virtually empowered a huge military force to be "ex-clusively under the control of the authorities of [the church] and in no way subject to the Militia Laws of the State." "A large portion" of the gentile population eventually came to believe the Legion "would be wielded for the conquest of the country; and for their subjection to Mormon domination."

Not surprisingly, the Nauvoo Legion's very existence played a major role in the death of Joseph Smith, who in 1844 was murdered in a Carthage, Illinois, jail while answering charges of using the Legion to destroy an opposition press and for the "treasonous act" of levying war "against the State" by "ordering out the Legion to resist the posse comitatus" sent to arrest him. As the Latter-day Saints sought to pro-tect themselves and their leaders, according to Illinois governor Thomas Ford, Nauvoo was transformed into "one great military camp." Consequently the charter was revoked; despite the destruction of its legal foundation, though, the Nauvoo Legion continued to func-tion, and this played a significant role in the final expulsion of the

---

[38] Rusling, *Across America*, 190. Italics in original.

Latter-day Saints from the state of Illinois. Not surprisingly, Brigham Young and his vanguard rolled out of Illinois early in 1846 under the banner of the Nauvoo Legion.[39] Transplanted in Utah, the Legion continued to be the physical protector of the Latter-day Saint "Kingdom" ideal.

During the period of the Black Hawk War, the *Salt Lake Union Vedette* kept up an unrelenting attack against the Nauvoo Legion, constantly pointing to its illegality and mocking with military smugness its awkward and amateurish appearance and organization. "The militia of this Territory hoist over their heads the flag of our Union, and yet they are arrayed in open opposition to the laws passed by the General Congress of the States, which those stars and stripes represent," the paper stated. Noting that, while the Legion was "ostensibly a Territorial militia organization," the newspaper declared it was no secret that it was "under the entire control of the Church authorities, and has on several occasions been used in open opposition to the United States . . . once during the administration of President Buchanan and twice during the command of General Connor at Camp Douglas." "The peculiar feature of this organization," it continued, "is that every man, with scarcely a single exception from high private to lieutenant general, holds some office in the Mormon priesthood. It may with propriety be termed an army of ecclesiastics, who believe literally as well as figuratively in fighting the good fight of faith." Mocking the 270-pound George A. Smith, the *Vedette* jeered that "quite a number of Apostles, both north and south, answer to the title of Brigadier General . . . even our fat friend, whose plethoric proportions remind us forcibly of a Dutch alderman of 'ye ancient tyme.' "[40]

Concerning the Legion's frequent musters and drills, the *Vedette* asked, "But, why is a constant system of drill kept up throughout the Territory? Once, and sometimes twice a week men are ordered to report for drill, and twice a year for general muster. . . . Tactics can not be used in Indian warfare, and this is well known to the militia officers. Whether they can be used with success against an army sent to enforce the laws of the Union remains to be seen."[41] Reporting one such drill,

---

[39] For specific quotations used here see Hallwas and Launius, *Cultures in Conflict*, 104, 209–10. For detailed information on Mormon Nauvoo's last years see Flanders, *Nauvoo*; and Hallwas and Launius, *Cultures in Conflict*. For information regarding the role the Nauvoo Legion played in the early stages of the exodus from Nauvoo see John A. Peterson, "Warren Snow," 54–70.

[40] *Salt Lake Union Vedette*, 1 November 1867.

[41] Ibid.

the *Vedette* lampooned, "the Mountain has labored and brought forth a mouse.... [The Legion's] perfect drill and martial appearance was much admired—by little boys."[42] But even prominent Utah gentiles were forced to admit that "this was the formidable army of half clad, half starved ragamuffins that whiped out our army under Johnson, sent by Buchanan to conquer the Mormons in 1857, which expedition cost our government twenty millions of dollars."[43]

The scorn U.S. military officers had for the Nauvoo Legion can be seen in Brigadier General Rusling's report of visiting Salt Lake County's "annual militia muster" in 1866. It "was a great gala-day at Salt Lake . . . the whole country-side apparently turned out," he wrote. But of the militia itself, he disparaged that there

> was not much of the military about it, except in name. The officers were mainly in uniform, but the men generally in civilian dress, and many without either arms or accouterments.... Of course, there were many awkward squads, but the so-called officers were the awkwardest of all. In many instances, they were unable to drill their men in the simplest evolutions; but stood stupidly by, in brand-new coats, resplendent with brass-buttons, while some corporal or private, in civilian dress, 'put the men through!' . . . The personnel of the force was certainly good; but everything betrayed an utter lack of discipline and drill. Nevertheless the Mormon officials seemed greatly elated by the martial array, and much disposed to exaggerate its numbers.... No doubt this militia from its Lieutenant-General commanding, down, is a mere creature of Brigham Young's—Mormon in composition and organization—Mormon in spirit and purpose—Mormon in body, brain, and soul—and what Brother Brigham proposes to *do* with it, . . . in case of a future collision in Utah, between United States and Mormon authority, we shall probably soon learn.[44]

Brigham Young's Vigilance Policy

The calling up of 200 Salt Lake, Utah, and Davis county militia was part of a renewed program of "vigilance" in guarding stock, building forts, abandoning weaker settlements, and concentrating the Latter-day

---

[42] *Salt Lake Union Vedette*, 2 November 1867.
[43] Waite, *Adventures*, 102–3.
[44] Rusling, *Across America*, 171–74. Italics in original.

Saints in the strongest ones. In the first Nauvoo Legion "general order" of the Black Hawk War, issued on 25 April 1865, the Saints were reminded of the "old maxim that 'eternal vigilance is the price of liberty.' " (Making the maxim their own, during the war church leaders changed it to "*eternal vigilance is the price of safety.*")[45] Fully a year later, on 28 April 1866, Brigham Young dictated a lengthy "General Epistle" to Mormons in exposed positions that encapsulated the basic policy of "vigilant defense" he would seek to implement for the rest of the war.[46] For the most part it was simply a new presentation of the policy he had expounded for years. This time, however, it was tendered and followed up with such resolve that it revitalized the settlers' defense system. Eventually the plan submitted in "the Epistle" diminished Black Hawk's success and ultimately was a major factor in his surrender.

The Epistle demanded that "thorough and energetic measures of protection" be implemented immediately. The most staggering directive was mentioned first. A force of 150 "well armed men" was considered the *minimum* capable of offering adequate protection, and all settlements with less than that number were ordered to be vacated *post haste*. The decision was significant, for, as a result, dozens of settlements throughout Utah were abandoned. Though smaller in scope, it was an operation similar to the "Move South" of the entire northern Utah population during the Utah War, and it was ultimately even more devastating because the evacuation in many cases lasted for years.[47] Instructions followed regarding the dismantling of homes and fences in the sites to be abandoned, including directions to bury logs, doors, and fencing to prevent the Indians from burning them. This unusual directive undoubtedly was inspired by the fact that when Spring City was deserted during the 1853–54 Walker War, the Utes reduced it to ashes.[48] Similar guidelines were given as to what should be done with crops already planted near villages slated for abandonment. Settlers in smaller communities were advised to band together to create larger

---

[45] General Orders No. 1, Head Quarters Nauvoo Legion, Adjutant General's Office, GSLCity, by Daniel H. Wells, 25 April 1865, TMR, #761; and *DN*, 26 August 1868. Italics mine.

[46] Brigham Young, Heber C. Kimball, Daniel H. Wells, George A. Smith to President Orson Hyde and the Bishops and Saints in Sanpete, Sevier and Paiute Wasatch & Summit Cos. and Pres. E. Snow and the Saints in Iron, Kane and Washington Counties, 28 April 1866, BYC. See also Christy, "Walker War."

[47] For information regarding the Move South see Arrington, *Great Basin Kingdom*, 182–94.

[48] Gottfredson, *Indian Depredations*, 83.

ones, but Young made it clear that "at *all* points where Settlements are maintained good and substantial forts, with high walls and strong gates" must be built "*and the people moved into them!*"

Directives concerning corralling and herding of livestock came next, underscoring the necessity of employing armed herdsmen in sufficient numbers to "insure their own safety and the safety of the herds placed in their care." Similarly, the Saints were reminded to dispose of excess stock and to cease traveling in small groups or without adequate weaponry. Predicting that these measures must be taken *immediately* or whole counties would be wiped out, Young also made this prophecy (which demonstrates the rationale behind his entire policy): "Adopt such measures . . . that not another drop of your blood . . . be shed by the Indians, and keep your stock so securely that not another horse, mule, ox, cow, sheep or even calf shall fall into their hands, *and the war will soon be stopped.*" "Put yourselves and your animals in such a condition that the Indians will be deprived of all opportunity of taking life and stealing stock," the prophet promised his people, "and you may rest assured that . . . they will soon cease their hostilities."

Young then spoke of the Indians, reminding his followers that they were "human beings and the descendants of Abraham" and that they must always be treated "with proper kindness and consideration." "We have had revealed unto us of their origin and the Lord's purposes concerning their future," he stated, but he resolutely declared that the Saints could not "allow them to murder our brethren and sisters . . . without doing our best to check them, *even if we have to resort to strong measures in doing so!*" Regarding "friendly Indians," his teaching reverted back to his earlier position. They were to be treated kindly, but once shown to be "our secret enemies" by "giving aid and comfort to those who are openly hostile" they were to be "treated as foes." Their "friendship" was to be demonstrated by their giving the Latter-day Saints information regarding the hostiles.

Finally, he noted that one hundred militiamen from the north would soon be sent "to strengthen and assist" Sanpete and Sevier Latter-day Saints "in the defence of [their] lives, homes and property." The church president closed his epistle with the warning that Zion could not be built, nor the Kingdom of God carried forward, if the Saints were not "diligent" in performing these duties.[49]

---

[49] Brigham Young et al., to President Orson Hyde and the Bishops and Saints, 28 April 1866. Italics mine.

The policies outlined in Young's epistle were inspired by an amazingly similar situation chronicled in the Book of Mormon, a significant example of the role Latter-day Saint scripture played in directing Mormon military thought throughout the Black Hawk War. The book tells of a time when God's people, the Nephites, were plundered by a band of raiders called the Gadianton robbers. Like Black Hawk's band, after their raids these robbers escaped to the mountains, where because of "their holds and their secret places" they could not be captured and thus they "did do much slaughter among the people." The leader of God's people "sent a proclamation among all the people, that they should gather together their women, and their children, their flocks and their herds, and all their substance . . . unto one place. And he caused that fortifications should be built round about them, . . . And he caused that there should be armies . . . placed as guards round about, to watch them, and to guard them from the robbers, day and night." Once their families were ensconced in their fortifications, the armies of the Nephites "were compelled, for the safety of their lives . . . to take up arms against those Gadianton robbers." Marching out against the raiders, the Nephites "cut them off" by "thousands and by tens of thousands" until the Gadianton band began "to withdraw from their design, because of the great destruction which had come upon them."

In an ideological precursor to Brigham Young's own capture and incarceration of Sanpitch and other suspected raiders, the Nephites "cast" all non-repentant robbers "into prison" in an attempt to force them to repent. However, an example of the disparity between scriptural idealism and reality, the Gadianton robbers had "the word of God . . . preached unto them; and as many as would repent . . . were set at liberty," while Sanpitch, who pledged to behave, continued to be held and threatened.[50] The fascinating point here, though, is the degree to which Brigham Young looked to Mormon scripture for strategical precedents upon which to base his policies.

Feeding Reservation Indians

Although Brigham Young's "better to feed than fight" policy was not mentioned in his epistle, his subsequent actions demonstrate that it remained a standard pillar of his master plan, as was the scriptural injunction to "raise the standard of peace" upon which his feeding policy was based. Even before he initiated his hostage strategy, he announced

[50] Book of Mormon (1830), 454–63. Compare with 3 Nephi 2–4 in current editions.

his intent to send $5,000 worth of food to Tabby's starving Indians on the Uintah Reservation. The decision was most likely prompted by reports of native destitution brought back by the employees and soldiers Tabby's band had chased from the reservation during the winter. Young's resolve to send supplies to Uintah to keep Indians there from joining Black Hawk was dramatically increased by the violent events of the spring of 1866. Hence, about the time he issued his epistle, the church president prepared to send seventy beeves and several wagonloads of flour and other supplies to the reservation once the snow had melted enough to make travel possible.[51] In addition, he dispatched special missionaries to preach the points of his epistle to Sanpete and Sevier county settlers, emphasizing the need to feed friendly Indians *"and not be so stingy as to disgust them."*[52]

Meanwhile, Indians attached to Tabby continued to raid stock and shoot at settlers near Spanish Fork and Heber City. On 29 April they killed a guard and wounded another near Fairview. About that same time, they convinced one of Kanosh's wives to leave her peace-minded husband while he was visiting Brigham Young in Salt Lake City. She escaped to a camp of hostile Utes in Spanish Fork Canyon with four of her husband's horses, along with most of his clothing and money. Soon after Kanosh returned to his camp near Fillmore, Utes from "the North" raided the Pahvant horse herd. Local settlers considered the raid on Kanosh's horses a punishment for Pahvant neutrality. While it is clear that Kanosh and his band were under considerable pressure to leave the Mormons, Bishop Callister noted that the chief "continues friendly as usual, and is, I believe, a grand exception among our red brethren."[53]

Superintendent Head and Governor Durkee viewed Kanosh's friendship towards the whites as the key to establishing peace. Hence, they borrowed several tons of flour and other supplies from Brigham Young and distributed them at the chief's camp on 11 May. Head and Durkee requested Kanosh to send runners to plead with Black Hawk to

---

[51] The only road to the reservation was impassable to wagon travel from November to June. Manuscript History of Brigham Young, 1866:180; Brigham Young to Tabby, Sowiette, Toquana, Jim, Joe and Antero, 18 May 1866; Brigham Young to Stephen Moore, 22 May 1866, BYC; and F.H. Head to D.N. Cooley, Commissioner of Indian Affairs, 21 June 1866, *RSI*, 1866:130.

[52] Brigham Young to Canute Peterson, 16 May 1866, BYC. Italics mine.

[53] Orson Hyde to George A. Smith, 20 May 1866, GAS; JH, 29 April 1866, 7; Gottfredson, *Indian Depredations*, 196; and Thomas Callister to George A. Smith, 6 May 1866, GAS.

come in and "meet" with the superintendent. Happy to comply, the Pahvant leader sent "strong recommendations" that Black Hawk "make a permanent peace." Similarly, Head asked Kanosh to go to the Uinta Valley with him to visit Tabby and the other reservation chiefs. As has been pointed out, the "idea had become prevalent" among those Indians "that the Mormons were designing to make war upon them," and Head hoped that Kanosh could convince them otherwise. Having recently pursued hostiles up Spanish Fork Canyon in search of stolen Pahvant horses and a runaway wife, and perhaps uneasy about threats made by some Utes against noncombatants, the chief declined. He did agree, however, to send his son John and three other Pahvant subchiefs to the Uintah Reservation with the superintendent.[54]

While Brigham Young, Superintendent Head, and John Kanosh waited for snows in mountain passes to melt, Young's vigilance policy went into effect. Settlers in southern Idaho, eastern Nevada, and throughout Utah dismantled and evacuated dozens of smaller settlements and commenced building forts in the larger ones. Orson Hyde, who personally directed the disassembling of Spring City, complained that the work of burying the village's "poles, posts & houselogs" would "require as much time as it [would] to bury the Slain at the battle at armaggedon; to wit. 6 months." Furthermore, he grumbled that the added guard duties, travel restrictions, and fort-building requirements were "more than any but saints" could endure.[55]

Throughout May rumored and actual accounts of stock thefts and killings continued to rage through frontier communities, where patience and resources were stretched to the limit by the requirements of Young's epistle. Interestingly, predictions of total war seemed to be confirmed by the demanding edict. Unfortunately, the excitement it produced actually worked against the attitude of peace Young sought to cultivate, and some Mormons openly displayed desires to fight. In Panguitch, Fort Sanford, and Parowan, for example, Colonel William H. Dame, the highest-ranking local militia officer, was "censured terribly" by local Latter-day Saints for enforcing Young's orders to treat neighboring Piede bands with kindness. Settlers under Dame's military jurisdiction described his policies as "white livered" and went so far as

---

[54] Thomas Callister to George A. Smith, 6 May 1866; F.H. Head to D.N. Cooley, 21 June 1866; and *RSI*, 1866:130.

[55] Orson Hyde to George A. Smith, 20 May 1866.

to threaten to "hold him responsible for the lives of their families" should they be hurt by any of these Indians. Simultaneously, they vowed that local Indians would "have to be very cautious, or furloughs [from this life] will be granted them *indiscriminately*."[56]

By mid-May, hostile attitudes of rank and file Mormons threatened to scuttle their president's efforts to make peace with Tabby and other leaders at Uintah. On 12 May the reservation chiefs dictated a letter to Young in which they responded negatively to the prophet's invitation to come to Salt Lake to negotiate and receive presents. With justified prudence, they reported they "dare not visit the Settlements" because some of Young's followers would "cut their throats" if they did. The chiefs claimed that they themselves were peacefully disposed but that their people were so infuriated it was "almost impossible to restrain them." Urging that the superintendent come to the reservation, they pledged he would be "perfectly safe" in spite of the fact that their men swore they would "not be friends until they Kill[ed] Col Snow," whom they personally blamed for the whole hostage fiasco. The gentile Indian agent who dictated the letter wrote that the reservation Indians looked "upon the Killing of their Brother Sand Pitch [*sic*] in no other light than murder *as they know he was inocent*." Describing their resolve to take vengeance upon Warren Snow, he cautioned Young that "if you do not bring him to Justice they will."[57]

Throughout the remainder of the war it is clear that the Utes held Warren Snow personally responsible for the killings of Sanpitch and at least sixteen other Indians in March and April 1866. They also knew that during the previous summer he led expeditions in which a similar number of natives were killed. Brigham Young, who for all intents and purposes was commander of the Nauvoo Legion, was well aware that Snow in each of these instances was simply implementing his policy. While shrewdly letting Snow take the blame for his own tactics, Young would not allow him to be punished for them, and he ignored this and subsequent native demands that the Manti general be brought "to justice." As early as the spring of 1866 Warren Snow was coming to personify Mormon violence in the minds of many Northern Utes, just as Black Hawk had earlier come to personify Indian violence in the

---

[56] Hyrum S. Coombs to Isaiah Coombs, 19 May 1866, Isaiah Coombs Papers. Italics mine.

[57] "Tabby and other Chiefs" per L.B. Kinney to Brigham Young, 12 May 1866, BYC. Italics mine. The text makes it clear that Sowiette, Toquana, and Joe joined Tabby in dictating this letter.

minds of most Mormons. The Northern Utes and the Latter-day Saints respectively clamored for and actively sought the lives of Warren Snow and Black Hawk, their respective archenemy figures. One gentile military officer wrote the chief of staff in Washington that "Black Hawk demands the men that killed [Sanpitch] or blood, and is taking blood." A year later, feelings towards the opposing leaders had crystallized to the point that Tabby predicted that when "Bp Snow . . . & Black Hawk are dead he [could] settle the war in ten days."[58]

Interestingly, one of the few reports to leak out of Utah and get picked up by the national press obliquely publicized Ute demands that Snow, the former bishop of Manti and other white leaders be turned over to them to be killed. Originating with the *Vedette* and sent abroad by telegraph, the short article read:

> The Ute Indians, now engaged in hostilities against the residents in the Southern and South-eastern portions of Utah, give as a reason for their conduct that the Mormons killed San Pitch, their head chief, while he was in their power—that he went to them upon promises made that he should not be molested. We are not prepared to say how much of this is true, aside from the fact that San Pitch was killed. It is, however, authoritatively stated that the Utes demand the bodies of six Mormon Bishops as a "blood atonement" for the killing of their chief—and they declare that nothing but blood will avenge his death. We rather think the Utes will wait some time before their demand is satisfied; nevertheless it serves to show the intensely hostile feeling now animating the Ute tribes.[59]

About the time Brigham Young received the chiefs' letter, startling news from the Uintah Reservation reached his settlements that Tabby's patience had at last run out. The Uinta head had "effected a union of some seven tribes or branches of tribes," and, although resolving to "take no part with Black Hawk," he was determined to make his own war with Sanpete and Sevier valleys settlers to retaliate for the deaths of Indians killed there. Presumably the seven tribes referred to were the seven major bands of the Ute tribe living in Colorado,

---

[58] Ibid.; and A.F. MacDonald to William B. Pace, 24 May 1866, WBP; Bvt. Col. O.E. Babcock, Salt Lake City, to Maj. Gen. J.A. Rawlins, U.S. Army, Chief of staff, Washington, D.C., 23 June 1866, AGO, M619, 454; and George W. Bean to William B. Pace, 29 July 1867, CR, 223.

[59] See previous footnote; and *Denver Rocky Mountain News*, 30 May 1866.

so Tabby's disaffection was no small matter. Sending word through Latter-day Saint employees of the Indian Department, the new Uinta head chief declared that "the only conditions on which 'Tabby' will commence to make [a] treaty for peace . . . [is that] Genl Snow must be delivered up to him, then he *might talk!*" He also issued the warning that "Mormons between [Nephi] and Salt Lake better stay out of the Kanyons and Mountains lest stragglers from his band should kill [them, for] he proposes to clean out all sanpete and the country south." Perhaps most startling of all was the report that the cattle thief Isaac Potter was so involved in Ute affairs that he was considered "War Chief" of the operations that promised to "commence as soon as the rivers lower."[60]

Near the last week in May, twenty-five Mormon militiamen drove a herd of seventy cattle towards the Uintah Reservation, a symbolic "standard of peace" raised by Brigham Young to Tabby's exasperated Utes. Traveling with them was Superintendent Head, who borrowed several wagonloads of flour and other supplies from Young to give the Utes on behalf of the government. Head sent John Kanosh and three other Pahvants along with Richard James to gather Tabby's Indians at the Uintah Agency for a conference.[61] As has been mentioned, some settlers already suspected James of being in league with Black Hawk, and within weeks it was discovered he was selling stolen Mormon stock at Fort Bridger.[62]

John Kanosh and his fellow travelers found the agency virtually deserted, for the reservation bands had moved to the southeast to hide their women and children preparatory to making "war upon the settlements."[63] The Pahvant delegation and Richard James, however, pushed on to bring them back to parley with Head.

Once he was at the agency, the superintendent learned firsthand of Tabby's determination to fight the Latter-day Saints. Told by his employees to expect bloodshed should the Utes return and find Mormons on the reservation, Head tried to buy Young's cattle on credit and send the militia home. Misinterpreting the move as a plan to betray them

---

[60] A.F. MacDonald to William B. Pace, 24 May 1866. Italics in original.

[61] Brigham Young to Stephen Moore, 22 May 1866; Brigham Young to Joseph S. Murdock, Bishop of Heber City, 22 May 1866, BYC; Crook, Record of the Wasatch Militia, 2; Lindsay, "Autobiography," 281; F.H. Head to J.R. Doolittle, undated, BIA, M834, 1, frames 1021–22; and F.H. Head to D.N. Cooley, 21 June 1866.

[62] Thomas Callister to George A. Smith, 13 May 1866; and C. Wilken to Robert T. Burton, 27 July 1866.

[63] F.H. Head to D.N. Cooley, 21 June 1866; and DUP, *"Under Wasatch Skies,"* 45.

and ally the Indians to the government, the Mormons barricaded themselves in one of the agency's log structures. Stockpiling food and water in case of a siege, they prepared to defend themselves against Tabby's forces by drilling numerous loopholes in the walls with an auger. Looking upon the drilling as needless destruction of government property (and noticing that some of the portholes allowed them to shoot directly into the building he occupied), Head chastised them. Now fully estranged from the gentile official, the militia threateningly replied that should hostilities break out the superintendent would be "the first Indian" they shot.[64]

Exactly what caused this temporary breach between Legion members and Head is not entirely clear. The superintendent's correspondence demonstrates that native grievances with the federal government were at least as great as their complaints against the Mormons. While citing the anger Sanpitch's death provoked, Head blamed most of the Indians' dissatisfaction on starvation and the failure of Congress to ratify the Treaty of Spanish Fork and appropriate the necessary funds to keep government promises. These problems were greatly compounded by frauds perpetrated by L.B. Kinney, the reservation's gentile Indian agent.[65] While Young and other church leaders generally looked favorably upon the superintendent's efforts to placate the Indians, the militiamen at Uintah reported that Head "acted as a traitor at that time rather encouraging the Indians in their warlike actions." It appears they felt that Head made alleviating the Indians' rage against the United States a higher priority than establishing peace between the Utes and the Latter-day Saints.[66]

When Tabby and several hundred Indians returned to the agency a few days later, they found the whites there still divided. Tabby met with Head while 300 of his men angrily surrounded the Mormons' position. The chief informed the superintendent that he would *not* make peace, and it looked like an attack was imminent. At last, William Wall, the militia's commander, left his stronghold and walked boldly into the cabin where Tabby and Head were meeting. For some time Tabby harangued him for the killings of Sanpitch and the others and said that he refused to consider peace until Warren Snow paid with his life. Once

---

[64] F.H. Head to D.N. Cooley, 21 June 1866; Crook, Record of the Wasatch Militia, 2; Lindsay, "Autobiography," 281; DUP, *"Under Wasatch Skies,"* 46–48.

[65] F.H. Head to D.N. Cooley, 21 June 1866.

[66] Lindsay, "Autobiography," 281.

the chief had vented his feelings, however, Wall persuaded him to listen to the letter Young sent with the cattle.[67]

Written 18 May, and addressed to Tabby, Sowiette, Toquana, Antero, Jim, and Joe, the letter affirmed Young's friendship: "I have fed and clothed you and done you good, and, if you will let me, will still be your friend." "Why do you want to kill any of the whites?" Young asked rhetorically. Answering his own question, Young guessed that it was because of Sanpitch's death; but he asked further:

> Do you not know that the cause of the war was Sanpitch's wanting Barney Ward's girls to be his squaws, and Barney Ward was killed. Who killed him? Do you not know that Sanpitch got some men and went and killed Barney Ward that he might get the girls? Had Barney Ward or any of our people spilled the blood of the red men that they had to be killed? You all know there was peace between your people and ours, and we were not expecting difficulty when the stock was driven off and Barney Ward and others were murdered. Did not Sanpitch encourage this war, and has he not furnished powder and lead to help Black Hawk carry on the war?[68]

Young pointed out instead of helping Black Hawk, that Sanpitch should have "fulfilled the Treaty" by bringing in the war chief. The settlers "did not want to kill Sanpitch," he explained, "and had his ears been open to the talk of General Snow, he might have been alive now, and had his wife and children with him; but his ears were closed, and he could not think good, and he got killed *and we could not help it.*" In defense of the killings, Young asked, "What else could we do?" and added that Kanosh "does not blame us for what we have done."

Referring to the gift of cattle, Young wrote, "We want you to have plenty to eat and fill yourselves and get fat, so that if you come over to fight Mormons you will be strong and able to do it." "But we wish you to know," he cautioned, *"that if your young men come over to fight and kill our people, we shall defend ourselves, even if we have to kill the Indians. They cannot kill our people and we sit tamely by and not defend ourselves."* He ended the letter by again reaffirming Mormon friendship towards the

---

[67] Crook, Record of the Wasatch Militia; DUP, *"Under Wasatch Skies,"* 46–48; DUP, *How Beautiful upon the Mountains,* 110–12; and DUP, *Heart Throbs,* 1:96–97. The two last-named sources mistakenly identify Warren Snow as "a man in Sanpete County named Sloan."

[68] Brigham Young to Tabby, Sowiette, Toquana, Jim, Joe and Antero, 18 May 1866, BYC. Italics mine.

Indians and repeating his invitation for them to come over the mountains for a "visit."[69]

Tabby at first rejected Young's letter and the cattle. Considering his people's starving condition, though, after again venting his frustrations he accepted the stock, agreeing at least to "not fight until they heard from 'Brigham.' " Official Nauvoo Legion correspondence indicates its officers viewed the settlement as tenuous at best, noting that "there seems to[o] much 'Head' in all this matter and we have little or no confidence in the supposed peace."[70] On the surface, however, it appeared that Young's "better to feed than fight" policy had worked; but Tabby made it abundantly clear that he could not restrain his "young men" from killing Latter-day Saints. To the shock of the militiamen, as soon as they turned the cattle over to Tabby, hungry Indians shot the whole herd down like buffalo and "cut pieces from them to eat raw dripping with blood."[71] The cattle having been delivered, Tabby urged the Mormon troops to leave before his men became unmanageable and attacked them.

Despite this warning, the militia lingered while Superintendent Head (who apparently made his own peace with the militia by working to calm Tabby) distributed presents and held treaty councils with the Indians. Among other things, he disbursed blankets, hats, shirts, metal cups, and butcher knives. Head exultantly wrote the commissioner of Indian affairs that these gifts, along with Young's beef and flour, allowed him to pacify "all the Utes except Black Hawk & his band who are still hostile." The superintendent's euphoria was short-lived, however, for as he left Uintah, runners came in from the south with reports that Black Hawk and a band of 300 Elk Mountain Utes and Navajos were moving towards Manti bent on attacking the hometown of Warren Snow.[72]

The Scipio Raid

When word of Black Hawk's plans reached Salt Lake City, the First Presidency responded by ordering an additional 125-man force from the northern settlements to strengthen the hundred men already put on

[69] Ibid. Italics mine.

[70] Alexander F. MacDonald to Brig. Genl. William B. Pace, 11 June 1866, in "Brigade Record."

[71] DUP, *"Under Wasatch Skies,"* 48–49; and Lindsay, "Autobiography," 281.

[72] F.H. Head to Luther Mann, Jr., undated, BIA, M834, 1, frame 1023; Reddick N. Allred to Maj. Bradley and Capt. Robertson, 10 June 1866, TMR, #867; and F.H. Head to D.N. Cooley, 21 June and 24 October 1866, BIA, M234, 902.

active duty in Sanpete and Sevier counties. General Daniel H. Wells himself prepared to lead this second group of northern reinforcements, who were to leave Salt Lake on 11 and 12 June.[73] Meanwhile, dispatches carrying news of Black Hawk's approach on the Old Spanish Trail reached Sanpete Valley about the same time the war chief's forces reached the mountains just east of the settlements. As early as 16 May Brigham Young warned Orson Hyde that the raiders had "a particular antipathy" against Manti and had made "many threats against it and its inhabitants."[74] Responding to such warnings, the Sanpete Nauvoo Legion was put on alert, now having been reinforced with the first installment of troops from Utah, Davis, and Salt Lake counties, who had arrived in May. Finding the Sanpete and Sevier settlements prepared to defend themselves, Black Hawk's warriors decided to attack Scipio in Millard County some twenty miles northwest of Salina.

The selection of Scipio illustrates the raiders' skill in locating weakness in the Mormon defense system as well as their keen understanding of local topography. It also gives insight into the role Ute concepts of vengeance played in the selection of raiding targets, a major factor that operated behind the scenes during the entire conflict. While Sanpete and Sevier valley settlers feverishly worked to implement Young's directives by raising walls around their villages, Scipio's residents flatly refused to build a fort. Also, because of their unusually large horse and cattle herds, they ignored instructions to concentrate in large settlements and jealously guarded their rights to grazing lands by forbidding others to consolidate with them in "Round Valley." Although Young's epistle required that there be a force of 150 well-armed men to maintain a settlement, Scipio's tiny brigade of twenty-five men and boys boasted only "12 gunns and 5 pistols," yet the inhabitants declined to abandon their position. In like manner, they ignored Young's "vigilance" policy by neglecting to post guards to watch their stock.[75]

About noon on 10 June, a cold and drizzly Sunday, more than 100 raiders under Black Hawk's leadership quietly gathered 350 cattle grazing near the settlement. Additionally, they drove off a herd of about seventy-five horses, including large numbers of fine Kentucky-bred

[73] JH, 11 June 1866, 1; and Brigham Young to Lorenzo Snow, 14 June 1866, BYC.

[74] Reddick N. Allred to Maj. Bradley and Capt. Robertson, 10 June 1866; and Brigham Young to Orson Hyde, 16 May 1866, BYC.

[75] Thomas Callister to George A. Smith, 17 June 1866, GAS; and Jesse B. Martin to Brigham Young, 7 May 1866, BYC.

mares and a magnificent white stallion. In the process, they killed a fourteen-year-old herd boy and an old Mormon soldier named James R. Ivie, who, along with his relatives, owned much of the stock.[76]

With the exception of Warren Snow's Manti, Scipio was at the very top of the Utes' list in terms of grudges held against Mormons, and significantly the old man killed in the raid was the kingpin in a longstanding feud between the Utes and members of the Ivie family. In this context it must be strongly emphasized that avenging real or supposed mistreatment was *the* single most powerful motivation for Ute warfare, and despite Indian hunger and the drive to obtain cattle to exchange for trade goods, retaliation for wrongs still continued to play a significant role in the Black Hawk War. We have seen how John Lowry's personal affront to Jake Arapeen was used as a "pretext" to start the war in the first place, how Barney Ward was killed and mutilated in the war's first raid because of a grudge the Utes had nursed against him for nearly two decades, and how the body of William Kearnes, who was accidentally killed in the war's first battle, and for whom the Utes had good feelings, was carefully protected with a grid of woven willows. The Utes' antipathy towards Manti in general and Warren Snow in particular continued, and on at least one occasion, as shall be seen, they made an unusual frontal attack on a Mormon village simply because they knew Snow was there. Symbolic of the role Ute vengeance played during the entire conflict, in the Black Hawk War's very last raid William Miller was killed because he was mistaken for Bernard Snow, another Mormon with whom the Utes had a longstanding quarrel.[77]

James R. Ivie and his relatives formed the nucleus of the village of Scipio and together owned large numbers of livestock.[78] Various members of the Ivie family had played major roles in starting *all three* of the Mormon-Indian conflicts large enough to be termed "wars" that occurred before Black Hawk commenced his own.[79] Richard Ivie, James's oldest son, it will be remembered, provoked the outbreak of the 1850 Fort Utah War when he, with two other Mormons, killed "Bishop" in

---

[76] James R. Ivie had been a member of the 1834 "Zion's camp" expedition, one of the first Mormon paramilitary operations. He also allegedly served as a "bodyguard to the Prophet Joseph Smith in Nauvoo days." See Joseph Smith, Jr., [et al.,] *History of the Church*, 2:184, and DUP, *Our Pioneer Heritage*, 9:216. For general information on the raid, see Ivie, "Statement"; Robert G. Frazer to Warren S. Snow, 10 June 1866, TMR, #865; and Gibbs, "Black Hawk's Last Raid," 99–101.

[77] Gottfredson, *Indian Depredations*, 312.

[78] Foote, "Autobiography," 1:174–76.

[79] All of these, including the Ivies' involvement, are discussed in greater detail in chapter 2.

a squabble over a shirt and tried to hide the deed by filling the dead Indian's abdominal cavity with rocks and sinking the body in the Provo River. This event was viewed by the Utes as "the first blood shed" between Mormons and their people, and since as many as seventy Timpanogos Utes died in the subsequent fighting (which Antonga Black Hawk witnessed first-hand), it was never forgotten.[80] James R. Ivie himself was credited with starting the Walker War in 1853 by hitting an Indian over the head with a gun. He played a less violent but equally effective role in precipitating the 1856 Tintic War, which resulted in the killing of Black Hawk's comrade Squash-Head and in the wounding of his friend and ally Tintic.[81] It is therefore understandable that, since the large force of raiders found Warren Snow's hometown of Manti "forted up," well guarded, and reinforced with militia from the north, Black Hawk would turn his attention to James Ivie's poorly defended Scipio. Finding Ivie tending to "a favorite milk cow" in a pasture within earshot of his door, the raiders raised the "war whoop," filled the old man with arrows, and stripped him of all but his boots.[82]

Alarmed by the "war hoops" of Ivie's murderers, thirteen whites moved out towards the herd of 350 cattle and seventy-five horses the raiders had already gathered. They retreated, however, when fifteen Indians made a feint back towards the tiny village where the settlement's women and children were defended by five poorly armed men. Executing what was obviously an ambitious and well-conceived plan, Black Hawk drove the stock into a pass to the southeast. Called "the Scipio Gap," the pass provided a natural trail through rough mountainous and broken hill country to the Sevier Valley and Black Hawk's oft-used escape route from there to Castle Valley and beyond via the Old Spanish Trail through Salina Canyon. Prepared to ambush and otherwise slow pursuers, as many as fifty Indians (who did not participate in the initial raid) were concealed on the trail near Scipio Lake to keep anyone from following. Similarly, another sixty warriors guarded the crossing at "Gravely Ford" on the Sevier River. Since it would take at least twenty hours to drive the stolen herd to the Sevier River, commanding the ford was necessary to keep Nauvoo Legion troops from cutting off the raiders' retreat.[83]

---

[80] Daniel Jones, *Forty Years Among the Indians*, 213.

[81] See George W. Armstrong to Brigham Young, 31 March 1856, BIA, M234, 898.

[82] Robins, "James Russell Ivie," 3–4; and DUP, *Our Pioneer Heritage*, 9:216.

[83] John Memmott to Daniel H. Wells, 11 June 1866, TAS; Thomas Callister to George A. Smith, 17 June 1866, GAS; Ivie, "Statement"; "Gunnison Ward Historical Record," 20–21;

The Battle of Gravelly Ford

Once the raid was over, Scipio townspeople sent riders with calls for help to Nauvoo Legion brigades stationed at Fillmore and Gunnison. By 10:00 P.M. on 10 June Brigadier General William B. Pace left Gunnison with all the troops he had at his disposal—a meager force of twenty northern volunteers supplemented by four or five local men. Assuming that the Indians would head the stock towards Salina Canyon, they traveled all night "through Mud and rain," reaching the deserted settlement of Salina about daybreak on 11 June.

Expecting reinforcements from Manti, Pace's command was disappointed to learn from five Sanpete couriers that help from the north was not forthcoming. Because Warren Snow and others viewed the raid as a feint "to attract attention from Manti," where "more serious depredations are contemplated," the Sanpete general opted not to weaken that settlement's defenses by sending additional men after Black Hawk; instead, he ordered his men to attend a military ball.[84] Strengthened by only the five couriers, Pace's command saw about thirty Indians who were driving the stolen herd emerge from "the gap" just as the morning sun began to shine upon the west mountains. Ascertaining that the raiders were headed towards Gravelly Ford, which lay three or four miles farther up the Sevier River near the present site of Vermillion, Pace and his thirty men quickly made their way to the ford. When they found it already in the possession of a force of sixty warriors, Pace "provoked an engagement."

Aware that his force was outnumbered at least three to one (counting the thirty Indians approaching the ford with the stock), Pace hoped to stall the herd on the west side of the river while he sent to Richfield for reinforcements. A three-hour gun battle ensued in which Pace and his men knocked "six or seven" Indians from their horses and "badly hurt" Black Hawk's "foot corp." Although bullets "fairly rained down" on them, the Mormons suffered only one minor casualty. At last Pace realized that his supply of ammunition could not sustain the battle much longer and he ordered his men to retreat to a point just out of the Indians' range.

Gibbs, "Black Hawk's Last Raid," 99–108; Warren S. Snow to Col. Kimball, 10 June 1866, TMR, #866; and Gottfredson, *Indian Depredations*, 201.

[84] William B. Pace to Warren S. Snow, 11 June 1866, TAS; Warren S. Snow to Col. Kimball, 10 June 1866; and Robert T. Burton to Daniel H. Wells, 12 June 1866, TMR, #869.

Realizing that the cattle could not pass until the whites were chased from the ford, "two or three" bold native horsemen sought to complete Pace's withdrawal by repeatedly riding close enough to fire at the militia. One of these horsemen, riding the white stallion formerly owned by the slain James Ivie, was clearly one of the raiders' head men. As the "white horse chief" swept by the Mormons again and again firing from behind his mount, Pace ordered his men to kill the beautiful animal. The horse was shot down at full gallop, but its body served its rider as a bulwark from which the determined Indian continued to fire. At last a Mormon sharpshooter hit the warrior in the stomach, and the militiamen cheered as he retreated on foot "pressing his hands to his abdomen." A short time later, the militiamen left the Indians in possession of the ford and retreated.[85]

As they withdrew, Pace's men noticed thirty distant riders emerging from "the gap" to the west. Unknown to Pace, the horsemen were Fillmore militiamen hurrying to come to his aid. The newcomers, strung out on the trail for a distance of two miles, looked like Indians to some of Pace's "Utah County boys." Even with telescopes the retreating troops could not make out whether the riders were Indians or whites. Aware that a force of thirty reinforcements with more ammunition could allow them to secure the ford and save the cattle, Pace's men debated for some time regarding the identity of the distant force. At last the general concluded that they must be Indians, believing there was no "man Holding office in the Legion so stupid" as to allow his men to spread out for such a distance while chasing a hostile force. Hence, he continued his retreat while the Fillmore troops watched in astonishment as the opportunity to save the large herd and punish the raiders slipped away.[86]

For the Latter-day Saints, Pace's miscalculation was perhaps the greatest tactical error of the Black Hawk War. From the beginning white strategists predicted that the conflict would immediately end if the raiders could only be cornered and soundly routed in a major

---

[85] William B. Pace to Warren S. Snow, 11 June 1866; Thomas Callister to George A. Smith, 17 June 1866; Brigham Young to Lorenzo Snow, 14 June 1866; Brigham Young to Brigham Young, Jr., 15 June 1866, BYC; Howard, Diary, 11 June 1866; Coombs, Diary, 13 June 1866; Ivie, "Statement"; "Gunnison Ward Historical Record," 20–21; Gottfredson, *Indian Depredations*, 201–3; Woolley, "Dictation During Declining Years," 6–7; and Gibbs, "Black Hawk's Last Raid," 103–4.

[86] William B. Pace to Warren S. Snow, 11 June 1866; and Gibbs, "Black Hawk's Last Raid," 104.

battle. Two Nauvoo Legion companies converging on Black Hawk's force at Gravelly Ford provided the perfect opportunity for such a defeat. But with Pace's withdrawal, the opportunity was lost. Furthermore, Young's vigilance policy was stymied by the Indian victory at Gravelly Ford. The whole notion of the church leader's epistle was to compel Black Hawk's forces to cease raiding by convincing them that there was "no chance of getting a single hoof without first getting a bullet." As it was, the large herd of cattle and horses gained was sufficient motivation to encourage them to continue raiding for at least another year. Following Pace's blunder, Nauvoo Legion leaders mourned the lost opportunity that could have "ended Blackhawks career" and "closed the war." Instead, they were constrained to acknowledge that Black Hawk's men were "gaining strength [with] every raid" and that their "every move . . . Indicates *Smartness* and *ability* to carry on a *long war* in these *rough & rugged mountains.*"[87]

Pace's men, however, actually did more to end the war than their leaders originally gave them credit for. Although they did not know it at the time, they "severely wounded" both Black Hawk and his most influential lieutenant, an "active and daring" Shiberetch youth named Tamaritz.[88] There is some confusion in Mormon sources regarding the identity of the Ute leader unseated from James Ivie's white stallion. Arising in part because this was the first raid in which he was identified, the confusion regarding "the White Horse Chief" was enhanced by the fact that most of the whites involved in the fight were Utah County youths who did not know Black Hawk or Tamaritz personally. As a result, some believed the rider of the stallion was the head raider himself. This view was so strong among some that it has persisted for generations.[89]

A journal account written only forty-eight hours after the fight

---

[87] Daniel H. Wells to Erastus Snow, 1 June 1866, in JH, 1 June 1866, 1–2; Robert T. Burton to Daniel H. Wells, 14 and 27 June 1866, TMR, #873 and #884; and John R. Winder to Robert T. Burton, 25 June 1866, TAS. Italics in original.

[88] *DN*, 26 August 1868; and Gottfredson, *Indian Depredations*, supplement, 3.

[89] *DN*, 26 August 1868. One of the most prominent sources for Black Hawk being the rider of the white horse is Gibbs, "Black Hawk's Last Raid," 103–4. Gibbs did not witness the battle, but he arrived at Gravelly Ford later that day, and for the rest of his life he had ready access to comrades who were present. As late as 1931 Gibbs was widely publishing that Black Hawk was "the White Horse Chief." For evidence that Gibbs played some role in the events surrounding the battle see "Black Hawk's Last Raid," 106; Gibbs, *Lights and Shadows*, 14; and Utah State Press Association, "The Utah Newspaper Hall of Fame," 1970, USHS, Pam, #14621.

contains a key to understanding why some whites came to believe that the Indian wounded in the abdomen while shooting behind the body of the slain white horse was Black Hawk. Isaiah Coombs wrote that initial reports of the battle were that "quite a number of the red skins were killed *including their two leaders.*" Later, Indian interpreter George W. Bean wrote that both "Chief Black Hawk . . . and Chief White Horse, or 'Tamaritz' " were only wounded by "Gen. Pace's long range guns."[90] Since both Indians fell at Gravelly Ford while obviously playing leading roles, it is only natural that some confusion would enter accounts. There is conclusive contemporary evidence, however, that Tamaritz was the bold rider of James Ivie's white stallion. Dimick Huntington, who was *the* best-informed Mormon on Ute affairs, reported to the *Deseret News* only days after meeting with both Black Hawk and Tamaritz at an 1868 peace council that Tamaritz "was the chief who was riding the white horse in one of the battles with the Indians, who was severely wounded, and was supposed to be Black Hawk, at the time it was reported that Black Hawk was killed."[91] After a remarkable recovery, Tamaritz changed his name to "Shenavegan" (also rendered by whites as "She-Na-Ba-Wiken" or "Chenowicket"), meaning "Saved by Almighty Power."[92]

In a less dramatic but even more significant occurrence that day at Gravelly Ford, Black Hawk was shot by the twenty-year-old nephew of Warren Snow. Throughout the battle Black Hawk reportedly "was stationed on one of those red mounds south of Salina, commanding his forces," while "General Pace was in the valley below." In a lull in the fighting, Black Hawk rode down to the battlefield to bring back a wounded man. Meanwhile, James E. Snow crept through a wash, and hiding behind a "large sage-brush" tried to draw a bead on the chief. Black Hawk's horse acted as a shield, however. Peter Gottfredson wrote that Snow

> . . . could not see the body of the Indian, but judging from the position of his feet and legs, he decided that by shooting the horse through the body in the region of the heart the same shot would get the red man. The aim proved true, for at the report of the rifle

---

[90] Coombs, Diary, 13 June 1866; and Bean, *Autobiography*, 251. Italics mine.

[91] *DN*, 26 August 1868.

[92] Ibid.; Codman, *Round Trip*, 245; Sloan, "White Horse Chief," 379; and Gottfredson, *Indian Depredations*, supplement, 3–4. Modern Paiutes render Tamaritz' name as "*Tosaw'Kuvaw Neahv*," which was "anglicized to Shenavegan." See Martineau, *Southern Paiutes*, 58.

the horse fell and the Indian was wounded. He was picked up by two of his braves and spirited away. The wounded Indian was none other than the famous Black Hawk, though at the time it was not known.[93]

Contemporary sources indicate that Black Hawk "got an ounce ball through his loins" and later became "a cripple; misserable and unhelply [*sic*]."[94] The injury was so serious that rumors spread throughout Utah's native population that he "died from his wounds received in fighting the Mormons."[95] The *Deseret News* eventually reported, however, that Black Hawk was still very much alive; but the paper stated he was "wounded" and that "he received his most spirited repulse from the command of General Pace."[96]

Paiute oral tradition has preserved an account of the battle that has striking resemblance to the white sources yet reverses a number of key points:

> Soldiers from up north came down to Sevier Valley to fight the Indians. The Indians laid an ambush for them at Rocky Ford near Sigurd, Utah. As the soldiers approached, the lead man spotted one of the Indians sleeping in a red blanket. This alerted the soldiers who then retreated. After this retreat they returned and attacked and the Indians retreated to the hillside. One Indian was shot through the leg just above the knee, not hitting the bone. The bullet went on through his leg killing his horse. Another Indian came back after him and pulled the wounded warrior up behind him on his horse and took him to safety.
>
> These two, or two others, took refuge in a wash below the hill and were the closest to the soldiers. One white man who had no shirt on and who had painted his body would charge at them on his horse and tempt them by coming very close before retreating. One of the Indians had an old muzzle loader and the other had a bow. None of the Indians were well armed, some having bows and the others muzzle loaders.

---

[93] Woolley, "Dictation During Declining Years," 6–7; and Gottfredson, *Indian Depredations*, 202–3. James Erastus Snow was the son of Warren Snow's brother James Chauncy Snow.

[94] See "Gunnison Ward Historical Record," 21, 54–55; *DN*, 8 May 1867; Gibbs, "Black Hawk's Last Raid," 104; Woolley, "Dictation During Declining Years," 6–7; and Gottfredson, *Indian Depredations*, 203, 227–29.

[95] Peter Maughan to Brigham Young, received 31 August 1866, BYC, r59, b30, f17.

[96] *DN*, 8 May 1867.

These two men tried to hit the white man on horseback but couldn't. They both tried several times. One time he came close and almost hit them. The Indian with the muzzle loader then loaded it very careful with a quartz crystal. He painted his rifle with war paint and prayed. When the white man came close again, he fired and killed him. In this fight the Indians lost two horses and suffered one wounded man. They killed two white men.

The white men claim that they killed White Horse Chief in this battle by shooting him in the belly from a great distance as he was standing on top of the hill. This is not true. All during the fight, they never got very close to each other, always firing at a distance.[97]

Both Ute leaders recovered to fight again; but, in Black Hawk's case, the injury ultimately played a role in his surrender and contributed to his death four years later. Interestingly, as Black Hawk's health faltered, some of the mystique formerly attributed to him by Mormons began to be transferred to Shenavegan, "the White Horse Chief." While Black Hawk was clearly still "the leading spirit" and mastermind in the raids, many Mormons came to believe that Tamaritz was "the prime mover in several of the raids made on our settlements, and in the murder of whites, which have been beforetime accredited to Black Hawk." The latter was said to be the "cunning and cruel being" that "planned all the raids," but it was "She-na-ba-wiken . . . who lead [*sic*] the warriors and carried out the plans of the wily chief." Hence, in the minds of some Latter-day Saints, Tamaritz was becoming "a much worse man than 'Black Hawk' himself," and even "more feared." As it turned out, in fact, he continued fighting long after the chief raider made peace.[98] At the time, with both Black Hawk and Tamaritz temporarily unable by reason of their wounds to lead the raiders, others came forward, including Mountain, Isaac Potter, and Richard James, to lead the ever-increasing number of angry Utes in assaults on Mormon militia and herds.

[97] Martineau, *Southern Paiutes*, 58.

[98] JH, 22 April 1866, 3; *DN*, 26 August 1868; DUP, *Our Pioneer Heritage*, 13:10; Sloan, "White Horse Chief"; and Gottfredson, *Indian Depredations*, supplement, 3.

Above left: Hijo Cabeza Blanca, a
Weeminuche sub-chief whose father
(Cabeza Blanca) was killed by other
Weeminuche leaders for supporting a
Ute-Navajo alliance put together by
Black Hawk. Hijo Cabeza Blanca and
large numbers of Four Corners area
Utes, Navajos, Hopis, and Jicarilla
Apaches were recruited by Black
Hawk to help make raids on Mormon
livestock in central and southern
Utah. Courtesy of UUWA.

Above right: Manuelito, Arizona's most
influential Navajo raider, was drawn
into Black Hawk's confederation.
Courtesy of Smithsonian Institution.

Right: Manuelito Segundo, son of
Manuelito, was representative of
scores of young Navajo raiders who
joined forces with Black Hawk to
make war on the Mormons. Courtesy
of Smithsonian Institution.

Left: Daniel H. Wells, LDS First Presidency member, mayor of Salt Lake City, and lieutenant-general of the Nauvoo Legion. Courtesy of CHD.

Below left: "Lieutenant-General Joseph Smith," founder of the Church of Jesus Christ of Latter-day Saints, was killed in Carthage, Illinois, in 1844, while awating a hearing on charges of "treason" for deploying the Nauvoo Legion against state troops called out by the governor of Illinois. Courtesy of CHD.

Below right: "Lieut.-General Brigham Young," commander in chief of the Nauvoo Legion from 1844 until his death in 1877. *Contributor* 9 (December 1887): 40.

LIEUTENANT-GENERAL JOSEPH SMITH.
[Prophet, Seer, and Revelator.]

Right: Franklin H. Head, who replaced Orsemus H. Irish as Utah's Superintendent of Indian affairs early in 1866. George Brooks Shepard, ed., *Untrodden Fields in History and Literature and Other Essays by Franklin Harvey Head* (Cleveland, OH: The Rowfant Club, 1923), Vol 1: frontispiece.

Below: Regimental flag of the First Battalion, Third Regiment, Nauvoo Legion Infantry. Courtesy of CHD.

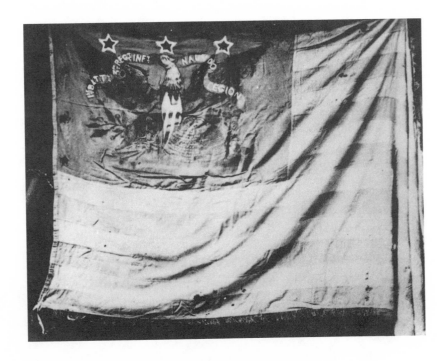

"Third Regiment Martial Band." Nauvoo Legion annual regimental muster, 1865. Dimick Huntington is the man in front left wearing a plumed black hat and holding a sword in his right hand. Note Nauvoo Legion regimental colors. Courtesy of CHD.

"Officers of the 3rd Regiment of the Nauvoo Legion." Regimental muster, 1865. Courtesy of CHD.

Nauvoo Legion militiamen at regimental muster, 1865. Courtesy of CHD.

Nauvoo Legion militiamen in camp, at Regimental Muster, 1866. Courtesy of CHD.

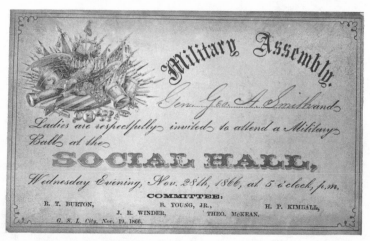

This invitation to an 1866 Nauvoo Legion ball highlights some peculiarities of Mormon society. George A. Smith held the rank of general because he was a senior apostle in the Mormon hierarchy. As the highest-ranking LDS ecclesiastical/military leaders were generally also polygamists, the embossed invitations requested Smith and other Nauvoo Legion officers to bring their "Ladies." Courtesy of CHD.

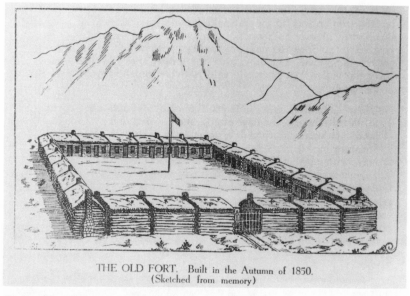

An example of an early Mormon fort. Caption, "The Old Fort. Built in the Autumn of 1850. (Sketched from Memory)." Emma N. Huff et al., *Memories that Live: Utah County Centennial History*, 304.

Above left: "Group of Black Hawk Soldiers ... taken on the day they returned from the Black Hawk Campaign, July, 1866." The Nauvoo Legion detachments most often sent out against Black Hawk and his raiders were generally made up of impoverished young recruits who were poorly uniformed and equipped. *Improvement Era* 11 (September 1908): 846.

Above right: "Wm. B. Dougall, Jasper Conrad, and S. F. Kimball, just returned from Black Hawk War, July, 1866." *Improvement Era* 11 (July 1908): 680.

Right: William B. Pace, Commander of the Utah County Military District, who eventually replaced Warren S. Snow as commander of the Sanpete Military District. Courtesy of CHD.

WHITE HORSE CHIEF, (Shenavegan)
Notorious in Black Hawk War

Tamaritz, also known as She-na-
vegan, Chenowicket, and "the White
Horse Chief." Gottfredson, *Indian
Depredations of Utah*, first edition.

"Tabiyuna or One who wins the race."
Sometimes confused with Tabby,
Tabiyuna, whose name is also
interpreted as "Bright Sunshine," was
one of Black Hawk's chief raiders.
Like his leader, he displayed a special
antipathy towards Warren Snow and
James A. Ivie.
Courtesy of Smithsonian Institution.

"Fort Union." Courtesy of USHS.

"Spanish Wall" around Brigham Young's mansions in Salt Lake City. Such walls were constructed around many Mormon settlements during the Black Hawk War. Courtesy of CHD.

"Old Fort at Deseret Built in 1866." Courtesy of USHS.

Cove Fort, built in central Utah during the Black Hawk War, is now an LDS visitor's center. Courtesy of USHS.

Fort Pearce near St. George, Utah, was built to guard an important Indian trail. Photograph by the author.

"Windsor Castle," originally constructed to protect Mormon herds during the Black Hawk War, is now preserved as Pipe Springs National Monument in northern Arizona. Courtesy of UUWA.

"The Moyle Indian Tower" was built by the John R. Moyle family in Alpine, Utah, and is the last known survivor of numerous private family fortifications which were built outside village forts or in exposed ranch locations during the Black Hawk War. Reportedly there was a tunnel running from the house in the background to the turret, which then was protected by a secure wooden door. Photograph by the author.

Utes posing for a photographer in Salt Lake City while en route to Ghost Dance ceremonies in Shoshoni country in 1870. Courtesy of CHD.

Chapter Eight

The Battles of Thistle Valley and Diamond Fork

[President Young] had a longe talk with Beaverits, chief of Beaverite Indians through me, an Interpeter, relative to the killing of Indian John by our Brethren at the Iron Springs. The Prest. expressed his disapprobation to the course of some of our Brethren & said that they were Guilty of cold blooded murder & that the Indians were more honest according to their training than we were [to ours].

—John D. Lee, 1870[1]

Black Hawk's Escape

LIEUTENANT GENERAL Daniel H. Wells was already on his way to Sanpete Valley with 125 reinforcements from the north when he received word of the Scipio raid and the battle at Gravelly Ford. He also learned that the day following the fight General Snow started out after the raiders with a force of nearly one hundred men. Wells drafted yet another hundred Utah Valley legionnaires to bolster his small army and moved towards Salina to support Snow, though he confided in a letter to Brigham Young that he had "but little confidence" in Snow's "overtaking the Indians on account of their late start."[2]

Snow's force reached Salina on 13 June, fully forty-eight hours after the battle. Surprised to find the stock had *not* been driven up Salina Canyon, they struck the trail a few miles to the south heading towards Grass Valley by way of "Lost Creek Canyon." Implementing instructions from the First Presidency regarding caution and safety, Snow proceeded slowly, halting frequently to examine the terrain with a telescope.

---

[1] Lee, *Diaries*, 2:134.
[2] This brought the number of troops from the northern settlements to more than 300. Daniel H. Wells to Brigham Young, 14 June 1866, BYC; and JH, 11 June 1866, 1.

Meanwhile, his men sat impatiently "in their sadles makeing sad complaints" about their leader's "slow and tardy movements." Anxious to overtake and rout the raiders, many lamented that they had already delayed "to[o] long to be sucsesfull." About noon the following day, however, the frustrated militiamen found warm embers, scraps of hide, and beef bones in campfires where the Indians had just breakfasted. The deserted campsite was located in a small canyon in a "very rough and dangerous" mountain region just east of Grass Valley some thirty miles southwest of Salina. On examining the area, Snow's men found "fresh fortifications" where some of the raiders had waited in ambush expecting their pursuers "to blunder through and be mowed down by cross fire." It seems the Indians abandoned their position when scouts learned the size of Snow's ninety-four-man force.

Worried by the well-laid ambush site and sure he was within hours of overhauling the herd, Snow called a "council of war" to ask his officers if the Nauvoo Legion force should proceed. Shocked at the suggestion of abandoning the expedition just as they were closing in on Black Hawk, Snow's officers listened in dismay as he explained that "he thought it unwise to follow any farther." Snow guessed that the Indians were heading for the rugged country around Fish Lake and stated that he "would not attempt" to follow them there "with less than 4 or 5 Hundred men." Apparently none of Snow's officers dared speak against his decision; one confided to his journal, however, that most of the men were "quite disapointed" and had lost their patience with Snow "long before they reached that point." Dejectedly, the command "took the back track" towards Salina.[3]

Snow's decision to call off the expedition ranks with Pace's retreat at Gravelly Ford as one of the war's greatest tactical blunders, for the militia later learned that they gave up the chase only twelve miles from the wounded Black Hawk and his stolen herd.[4] Some of Snow's contemporaries and at least one modern historian disparaged the general's decision, suggesting it resulted from cowardice.[5] Snow's nerve may well have been weakened by failing health and the rigors imposed by the war, for in his official correspondence he frequently complained of

[3] Daniel H. Wells to Brigham Young, 15 June 1866, BYC; Dewey, "Journal," 11–15 June 1866; Howard, Diary, 13–14 June 1866; Gottfredson, *Indian Depredations*, 205–6; and Woolley, "Father Tells His Experience," 2.
[4] Gottfredson, *Indian Depredations*, 206.
[5] Heber P. Kimball to Robert T. Burton, 20 June 1866, TAS; and Metcalf, "A Reappraisal of Utah's Black Hawk War," 95.

an ongoing degeneration of his physical constitution. In June 1866 Warren Snow was forty-seven years old; his vitality continued to ebb such that by the spring of 1867 his condition was deemed so critical that church leaders actually feared for his life. As a result, he was relieved of his command in the spring of 1867, William B. Pace taking his place as head of the Sanpete Military District.[6] That he had been wounded himself in an ambush in the same general locale only nine months earlier and that his life was so energetically sought by the Utes may also have influenced his judgment. So too may the fact that the weather was extremely cold, actually snowing in the middle of June.[7]

It is more likely, though, that Snow's decision was based on orders to protect the lives of his men.[8] From the first months of the war, Snow had received repeated instructions to chase raiding Indians to "get back the property they have stolen," but these orders always included the directive for Snow's command to "not risk their lives in so doing." From the start, Brigham Young's mandate to Warren Snow was to "follow them *only* where you can inflict punishment upon them" and never "suffer them to decoy you into a position where they will have every advantage." Having chased the raiders through the Fish Lake region before, and having been "taught by experience" in that very area the dangers of "rushing recklessly into a possible ambuscade," Snow opted to withdraw.[9]

The very fact that Snow called a "council of war" rather than simply making the decision himself, highlights a problem of Nauvoo Legion leadership that worked against the military success of the Latter-day Saints. Officers of the Legion were by no means trained military men; most were farmers, ranchers, and businessmen pressed into service by a man they believed to be a prophet of God. These amateurs were forced to make decisions that, considering the superb hit-and-run tactics of their adversaries, most often resulted in failure. Since Black Hawk's larger raids economically devastated entire communities, literally overnight wiping out the fortunes of hundreds of individuals, serious

---

[6] Brigham Young, Heber C. Kimball, and Daniel H. Wells to Orson Hyde, 2 April 1866, BYC; and Orson Hyde to Brigham Young, Heber C. Kimball, and Daniel H. Wells, 9 April 1867, BYC.

[7] H.P. Kimball to J.R. Winder, 12 June 1866, TAS.

[8] Warren Snow was no coward. As experienced in military affairs as any Mormon, Snow was known for his courage before, during, and after the Black Hawk War. See John A. Peterson, "Warren Snow."

[9] Brigham Young to A.J. Moffatt, Bishop of Manti, 13 May 1865, BYC; Brigham Young to Orson Hyde, 31 May 1865, BYC; and Gottfredson, *Indian Depredations*, 205. Italics mine.

animosity was often expressed towards the very officers who were wearing themselves out trying to prevent and recoup such losses. Since Brigham Young himself officially held no office in the Nauvoo Legion (and since Mormons were under religious obligation to find no fault with "the Lord's Anointed"), he was generally shielded from the condemnation that men like Snow and William Pace endured. To protect themselves individually from this excruciating social pressure, Snow and other Mormon military leaders often tried to involve as many officers as possible in decision making. As a result, as one Mormon general complained, "There is a great lack in the officering of post commandants and company officers, hence nearly everything has to go through a General 'Town meeting' System, which frequently causes a total failure, and in some instances, the worst confusion immaginable."[10]

The predicament in which Warren Snow found himself is demonstrated in Nauvoo Legion correspondence. General Wells, on the one hand, wrote letters expressing anxiety "for the safety of Genl Snow and command" and, on the other, complained of Snow's caution. Meanwhile, Snow's careful response to Wells's own orders for caution caused his officers to gossip about his "slow and tardy movements" in their official reports. "You should of seen the Genral when he met us," one wrote of Wells meeting Snow's retreating command. "When he [Wells] met us he said nothing but he cept a thinking I know not what. But I know what he had ought of thought, 'Boys you have showed your asses.' "[11] Increasingly, Brigham Young came to see that the answer to his Black Hawk dilemma lay not in endless military campaigns against the raiders in Utah's mountain fastnesses, but, rather, in vigilantly guarding stock around the settlements so they were not taken in the first place. Interestingly, a song was written by Black Hawk War veterans regarding this particular botched expedition, the frustration of slow-moving and cautiously officered Nauvoo Legion campaigns, and Young's vigilance policy:

Black Hawk Times
Song and Chorus by F. Christensen, Fairview
Tune: Ta-ra-ra-Boom-de-ay.

---

[10] "Brigade Record," 11; also in CR, 72.
[11] See notes 2 and 3, above; and Daniel H. Wells to Brigham Young, 15 June 1866, BYC; and H.P. Kimball to General Burton, 20 June 1866, TAS.

Black-hawk and his red-skin band,
    Was a terror in the land;
Proud he was, the Indian chief,
    Who could live on Mormon beef.

Chorus:
Singing heyeh, heyeh, yah,
Singing heyeh, heyeh, yah,
Heyeh, heyeh, heyeh, yah.

Every "Hawk" has piercing eyes—
    From the hills his prey he spies—
Waits till Mormons pray and sleep,
    When he takes their cows to keep.
    Chorus
I have always heard folks say
    Men should watch as well as pray.
True, they did quite early rise,
    Scratch their heads and rub their eyes.
    Chorus
Then they find their cattle gone—
    Beat the drum and sound the horn;
"Get yer guns and don't bewail,
    But git on that Indian trail."
    Chorus
Up the Canyon, big and wide,
    Watching every mountain side,
While ahead some twenty mile
    Black-hawk and his red-skins smile.
    Chorus
After hours continuous tramp
    Strike they Black-hawk's breakfast camp;
Scraps of hide and roasted bone,
    But the "Hawks" have long since gone.
    Chorus
Hungry and with weary feet,
    Turn about and make retreat;
Having learned this truth that day,
    "Better watch as well as pray."
    Chorus

Black-hawk then was all the dread,
 Now he's good, for he is dead;
When he left us he was bound
 For the "Happy Hunting Ground."[12]

The Killing of Panikary

As Warren Snow and his men made their way back towards Salina on
15 June, an event transpired near Scipio that would have some bearing
on Brigham Young's Indian policy. James A. Ivie, the son of the old
stockman killed in the Scipio raid just five days before, was enraged at
his father's death and, according to his own account, determined "to revenge the blood of my father." Panikary, one of Kanosh's "friendly Indians," apparently came to Scipio to visit and beg from his Mormon
friends. The Pahvant medicine man was described as "an inoffensive"
old Indian with a "peaceful disposition."

Thomas Callister, the bishop of Fillmore and the presiding ecclesiastical and military authority in the area, also happened to be in Scipio
at the time. Callister warned Panikary "that some of the Mormons were
very mad" and that he was not safe in the settlement. He was advised to
go to Kanosh's camp and stay there. Following the bishop's instructions, the Indian ran off across a sagebrush flat in the direction of
Kanosh's camp. In the meantime, James A. Ivie learned of Panikary's
presence and started out after him. In addition to losing his father in
the recent raid, Ivie personally lost "27 head of as good American mares
as can be found in the country, 2 span of mules, and 80 head of cowes
of different ages," the equivalent of a wealthy Utah cattleman's life
savings. When Ivie overtook Panikary, he promptly murdered him.
Within minutes, Bishop Callister appeared on the scene and found the
dead Indian lying in his gore with Ivie and another man gloating over
the body. When Callister asked who shot Panikary, Ivie proudly confessed that "he was responsible for it, —that his father had been killed
and he was going to avenge his blood."[13]

Callister was appalled. Noted for his fairness and generosity to
Lamanites, the kind-hearted bishop had almost single-handedly secured Kanosh's friendship and the Pahvants' neutrality. Aware that

[12] *Utah Indian War Songster*, 21–22.
[13] Ivie, "Statement"; Thomas Callister to George A. Smith, 17 June 1866, GAS; "Synopsis of the People vs James A. Ivie"; Thomas Callister to Hiram B. Clawson, 15 July 1866,
TMR, #926; Gottfredson, *Indian Depredations*, 227–29; and Peacock, Journal, 24 June 1866.

Kanosh had struggled desperately to keep his band from uniting with Black Hawk, Callister feared that Panikary's murder would upset the delicate Pahvant peace for which he had worked. In an action typical of his straightforward and honest approach in dealing with Indians, Callister hurried back to Fillmore to inform Kanosh of the tragedy. The Pahvant chief was ill at the time but said that he was "very glad" his friend "had not kept anything back," though he bluntly pointed out that Panikary was "the first indian that had been killed by the mormons in [Pahvant country] and that [his people] had killed no mormon." Moshoquop, the Pahvant war chief, and twenty-seven of his men angrily visited Callister at his home in Fillmore, but after the bishop exerted his influence they left speaking "very reasonably." Callister freely admitted that the killing was a breach of faith on the part of the Mormons but convinced the Pahvants to leave the punishment of the offenders to President Young.

After the Pahvants left, Callister wrote a letter to church headquarters describing the killing, and, in frustration, he noted that he found it necessary to "order all the scattered indians into Kanosh's camp" for their own protection. As the bishop well knew, the killing of Panikary was no anomaly, and he bitterly complained to authorities in Salt Lake City that "if I find we have men that cannot live without shooting friendly indians I am going to order them into the field where the hostile indians are."[14]

Brigham Young's response to Callister's letter is significant. He wrote that he was "grieved" to hear of the shooting of yet another Indian "by a man *professing* to be a Latter-day Saint." How a man so recently bereaved of his own father by "an act of barbarity" could inflict "a similar deed of cruelty on the person of an unoffending Indian" was beyond him. To Young's way of thinking, James A. Ivie was "as much guilty of murder as if he had stepped up and killed a white man," and the church leader declared that Ivie "be arrested and tried for murder!" Regarding Callister's suggestion that such men be sent "into the field to fight the hostile Indians," he wrote, "you may depend upon it that a man who would shoot down a friendly, inoffensive Indian in cold blood, is not the man to stand up on equal terms and defend himself against a foe. Such an act is too dastardly for a brave man to perpetrate [but] is the deed of a coward."

Young closed his letter by declaring that the Latter-day Saints "must be just" and "secure the confidence of the Indian" by acting consistently with their professions; to "permit such an outrage as this killing of that Indian to go unnoticed, every Indian who hears of the occurrence will set us down as untrue to our principles."[15] As a result, James A. Ivie was arrested and tried for murder. In the court proceedings that followed, however, Warren Snow's brother acted as attorney for the defense, and local Mormons, who for the most part identified with Ivie, made up the jury. Despite Callister's and Young's stated wishes to the contrary, Ivie was cleared and discharged. The acquittal was based on the argument that Panikary was a spy for Black Hawk and that Scipio military authorities in the wake of the raid had ordered local militiamen "to know no friendly Indians until peace was made." Bishop Callister felt the court was a farce, and, since Panikary's killer could not be punished through the civil courts, he eventually excommunicated both Ivie and the militia officer who issued the extermination order.[16]

Fort Building

The same day James Ivie killed Panikary (15 June 1866), Daniel Wells and his men met Warren Snow's retreating command at Salina. Frustrated that Snow had failed to chastise the Indians or recover the stock, Wells could do nothing but attempt to prevent additional raids. Hence he dispersed the 350 Salt Lake, Davis, and Utah county recruits at his disposal among the various Sanpete and Sevier valley settlements. He also made personal visits to each village to see that fort building and other defensive measures outlined in Young's epistle were put into effect. Prior to 10 June 1866 many settlers had questioned the necessity of implementing Young's directives, but Black Hawk's success in the Scipio raid changed their minds, and the summer of 1866 saw the greatest flurry of fort building in Utah history.

Brigham Young had urged his people to build forts from the time of their first arrival in Utah. He felt the Walker War occurred because his people did not follow his instructions "to fort up," and in 1853 he prophesied that if the people did not build the protective structures, "in twenty years they would be driven out of the Settlements" altogether. By 1866, church leaders were teaching that "God has stirred up the

[15] Brigham Young to Thomas Callister, 21 June 1866, BYC. Italics mine.
[16] "Synopsis of the People vs James A. Ivie"; Thomas Callister to Hiram B. Clawson, 15 July 1866, TMR, #926; and Thomas Callister to Brigham Young, 15 July 1866, BYC.

indians to bring [the Saints] to their senses & [to] fort up the people."[17] With renewed dedication, the settlers divided up into teams to build forts, fortified corrals, and guard towers.

Rocks set in mortar were the most common materials used, but in some places log, adobe brick, or even mud stockades were constructed. Forts varied in the size of enclosure from less than an acre for the smallest villages to about ten acres for larger settlements like Manti. While there was substantial variation from settlement to settlement, the typical Mormon fort consisted of a large square or rectangle enclosed by fourteen-to-twenty-foot-high walls, with towers erected in at least two diagonal corners and sometimes in all four. Walls and towers were generally equipped with loopholes and simple catwalk systems. Depending on the fort in question, one to four heavy wooden doors provided access.

Mormon villages were constructed on a plat grid of square city blocks, and the typical fort was simply an enclosure surrounding one or more existing city blocks. Homes situated outside the proposed fort area were sometimes relocated and set in line with others to form the fortification's perimeter. Spaces between these dwellings were then simply walled with rocks. Thus, the back walls of dwellings often actually formed a portion of the fort's outer wall.[18] With living quarters thus along the inside perimeter, stock could be turned out in the enclosure at night or during times of emergency. It should not be understood, however, that the center grounds of most forts were devoid of structures, since, as has been pointed out, walls were often erected around existing village blocks that already contained homes, barns, corrals, pig sties, privies, and meetinghouses. When stock was guarded within such forts, animals generally ran loose in streets, vacant lots, unfenced dooryards, and garden plots.

In some cases, individuals whose homes lay within easy running distance of forts were allowed to maintain their residences outside. Similarly, rock and pole corrals were sometimes built outside the forts, but they were usually located close enough to be covered by rifle fire from inside. Such allowances were made because the plan was eventually to completely encircle each settlement with a high wall the

---

[17] Miscellaneous Minutes, preaching en route to and in Grantsville, 13–15 July 1866, Edyth Romney Typescripts, b99.

[18] "Gunnison Ward Historical Record," 20; Daniel H. Wells to Brigham Young, 15 July 1866, BYC; and Yates, "Thomas Yates," 2.

Latter-day Saints called "Spanish walls." By the fall and winter of 1866 most Sanpete and Sevier settlements had working forts and their residents had at least commenced building "Spanish walls" and some had even completed them.[19]

Fort and wall building were arduous tasks that involved both men and boys for extended periods of time. In some cases the tasks were performed by military order, with militia brigades receiving assignments for certain segments of walls and bastions. Other communities, however, sought to relieve the rigor and monotony of the labor with competitions. Residents of the Millard County settlement of Deseret, for example, erected a two-acre mud-and-adobe-brick fort in nine days by having two thirty-two-man teams race to see who could complete their half of the fort first. The losers were to provide the winners with a dinner and a dance. The contest ended in a draw, however, when part of the winners' wall collapsed. Both sides enjoyed the dinner and dance inside their new fort, but only after shoring up the sagging wall.[20]

Originally viewed as one of the shoddiest forts constructed during the Black Hawk War, Fort Deseret is one of the few Mormon forts still standing today. Most stone forts were dismantled shortly after the war, as they provided a ready source of building materials.[21] For this reason no major rock fort built in a Mormon village in 1866 has survived. A number of forts built to protect individual families, herdsmen, or to guard crucial trails and telegraph lines are still extant, however, and give some insight into Mormon fort building in the 1860s. Cove Fort, for example, was commenced in 1867 "for the protection of the telegraph line" and to guard a major spur of the Old Spanish Trail that crossed through "Sevier Pass."[22] Fort Pearce was commenced in December 1866 to guard a similar trail leading to the Colorado River. It was built on a prominence overlooking an important source of water, and eventually a stone corral that could easily be defended from the

---

[19] Daniel H. Wells to Brigham Young, 15 July 1866.

[20] Cropper, "Life and Experience," 51–53; and "The History of Christian Overson," 32–33.

[21] For example, see Longsdorf, *Mount Pleasant*, 117.

[22] The site for Cove Fort was selected by Brigham Young on 29 April 1867 specifically "for the protection of the telegraph line at this point." See "A Diary of President Young's Trip South," 29 April 1867; Codman, *Round Trip*, 243–44; Kane, *Twelve Mormon Homes*, 76; Porter, "Cove Fort,"; and The Church of Jesus Christ of Latter-day Saints, "Cove Fort Historic Site: The Church of Jesus Christ of Latter-day Saints," CHD.

fort's loopholes was built below it.[23] Brigham Young himself selected the site for "Winsor Castle" (now Pipe Springs National Monument) in September 1870 to protect Mormon herds and guard an important Indian trail. Enclosing "a fine spring of good water," Young planned this impressive structure "to be 152 by 66 feet, [and] to be so arranged as to accommodate a number of persons in case of an Indian attack."[24] These few Mormon forts survive today primarily because they were not close enough to settlements to be plundered for building materials after they were no longer needed for defensive purposes. An example of the quality and strength of the finest Mormon forts, Cove Fort has been restored by the Church of Jesus Christ of Latter-day Saints and is presently operated as a historic site. Equally impressive, the fort at Pipe Springs is operated as a historical monument by the National Park Service.

While significant fortifications were built in some of these communities prior to 1866, major fort construction took place that year in such central Utah towns as Lehi, Springville, Spanish Fork, Payson, Santaquin, Nephi, Scipio, Fillmore, Deseret, Moroni, Mt. Pleasant, Ephraim, Manti, and Richfield. Smaller forts were constructed in such places as Marysvale and Spring Lake, and some construction took place in Fairview, Spring City, Glenwood, Monroe, and Salina before they were abandoned and after some of them were resettled in the fall of 1866. Additional fort construction took place in southern Utah settlements like Beaver, Parowan, Panguitch, Cedar City, St. George, Glendale, and Kanab. Special Nauvoo Legion garrison forts were built at Fort Sanford and Gunnison, the latter designed to be the strongest fort in central Utah. Forts were also erected in settlements along the Muddy River in eastern Nevada. Other forts went up in the Shoshoni country of northern Utah in such areas as the Kamas, Ogden, Box Elder, Cache, and Bear Lake valleys.[25] While the Shoshonis continued

[23] The order to build Fort Pearce was issued 29 November 1866. Orders no. 16, Brigade Headquarters, Iron Military District, 29 November 1866, TMR, #1548. For additional information regarding this fort see Charles Walker, *Diary*, 1:274, 302–4; Andrew Larson, *Red Hills of November*, 177–78; and U.S. Department of Interior, "Old Fort Pearce."

[24] Brigham Young to Horace S. Eldredge, 4 October 1870, in Alter, "The Mormons and the Indians," 66; Walter Powell, "Journal," 400–401; and Stephen Jones, "Journal," 107–8, n. 89.

[25] For general information on Mormon fort building see Rosenvall, "Mormon Fortifications," 195–212. Other measures required by Brigham Young's epistle were followed in these areas as well. In Bear Lake Valley, for example, the Saints deserted seven settlements while concentrating the population in four. JH, 26 July 1866, 2.

to assert their friendship, church leaders were convinced that fort building worked to maintain that tribe's "good intentions." Apostle Lorenzo Snow wrote that the forts preserved the Shoshonis "from being overcome by bad influences" exerted by "emisaries of the southern Indians," who the northern tribe acknowledged *continually* came among them soliciting support for Black Hawk.[26]

Living in the forts posed major inconveniences for the settlers of Utah. Correspondence, journals, and reminiscences make it clear that cramped conditions made life frustrating and caused fort dwellers to look wistfully back upon their former living arrangements. Pig sties, sheep pens, and cattle and horse corrals "clustered so close to the streets and to the fronts of their houses" made fort life "disagreeably filthy." Fearing to let their children wander outside fort walls because of the Indians, parents were pestered by bored and peevish children who could not understand why they were confined to the fortifications.[27] Establishing an idiom that would continue to be used for generations, mothers warned children not to wander off or "Old Sanpitch will get you!"[28]

As has been shown, while General Daniel H. Wells personally supervised fort building in central Utah in late June 1866, he also deployed over 350 militiamen recruited primarily from the larger population centers in the north.[29] He detailed groups of from ten to fifty men to strengthen weaker settlements, where they helped build forts and guarded stock. Other groups of similar size were strategically positioned on important Indian trails, while still others were sent out as scouts to discover the movements of the Indians.

The call for Salt Lake, Utah, and Davis county troops to protect central Utah communities from Indians was viewed as a "mission," as one expressed it, as "honorabile as if we had bean called to go forth Amongst the nations of the earth to preach the gosple." Many were even "set apart" for such callings.[30] Northern recruits were required to

---

[26] Lorenzo Snow to Brigham Young, 10 July 1866, BYC.

[27] Hamilton H. Kearnes to Daniel H. Wells, 12 July 1866, TMR, #918; and DUP, *Treasures of Pioneer History*, 4:207.

[28] Folklore Society of Utah, *Lore of Faith & Folly*, 6.

[29] The vast majority of these recruits came from Salt Lake, Utah, and Davis counties, though a few also came from Millard, Iron, and Kane counties. Gottfredson, *Indian Depredations*, 199–200.

[30] Blythe, Journal, 26 April 1867; Lambert, "Autobiography"; and DUP, *Heart Throbs*, 6:493. "Setting apart" is a blessing pronounced with the laying on of hands by a priesthood holder for the bestowal of spiritual gifts to help a church member fulfill a calling, mission, or other assigned task or duty.

provide their own horses, saddles, weapons, and ammunition, although few were equipped with official Nauvoo Legion uniforms. Most were lower-class youths in their late teens or early twenties who viewed the few dollars military service brought as a godsend. Hence, they entered the service poorly outfitted. Nauvoo Legion officers complained that all too many were "transient hirelings, . . . p[i]ck'd up at 15.$ per month." As a result, the militia detachments from the north tended to attract a breed of young men their officers described as "ignorant indifferent 'Radicals' many of whom [were] disaffected or disfellowshiped [from the church] for their meanness prior to leaving home." General William B. Pace complained that such recruits were "sent out half fed" and "without cloths [*sic*]." According to him, some were essentially "pantless," while others were without "shoes Shirts or hats." [31] Sanpete and Sevier settlers freely provided the northern troops with large quantities of beef and "Danish beer" and shared what little grain they had with the legionnaires' horses.[32]

The Battle of Thistle Valley

Designed to reduce the prospects of a general Ute war, the reinforcement of Sanpete and Sevier counties with Nauvoo Legion detachments from northern Utah actually exasperated reservation Utes and played into the hands of the war factions. It will be remembered that in May 1866, Tabby and other leaders had apprised Brigham Young that the hostility their bands felt was aimed at Warren Snow and other Sanpete and Sevier settlers and not at the Latter-day Saints generally. They warned the church leader not to send help from the north, for that would expand the conflict to settlers with whom they had no quarrel.[33] But when mounted brigades of Salt Lake, Utah, and Davis county scouts pushed bands who were loyal to Tabby from Thistle Valley, large numbers of Tabby's men finally gave in to the raiders' petitions to join them in forays against Sanpete.

According to whites at the Uintah Agency, Mountain and Isaac Potter played key roles in this decision. Hailed as "War Chief" by large numbers of reservation Utes, Potter himself evidently accompanied the raiders at this time; that he certainly did later will be shown. Circumstantial evidence also convinced Latter-day Saints that Richard James

---

[31] CR, 77 and 72.

[32] Zebulon Jacobs, "Journal," 1–23 May 1866.

[33] "Tabby and other Chiefs" per L.B. Kinney to Brigham Young, 12 May 1866; and A.F. MacDonald to William B. Pace, 24 May 1866.

personally took part in raids on Mormon stock. Sowiette and Toquana had already moved east to keep their young men away from the settlements. Similarly, Tabby, Joe, and Showan "preached peace" and, in a move designed to keep their people away from the Mormons, announced their intention to take all who would follow them to Fort Bridger, where Superintendent Head promised to distribute presents. Before the peace chiefs could get away, however, Mountain left the agency on 20 June with a large party of "young bucks," telling agency employees "they were going on a hunt." Two days later another war party led by Tabby's brother and son-in-law left "under similar pretences." Participants later told whites that the two reservation groups were joined by "some of Black Hawks Party" and together they attacked a Nauvoo Legion detachment near the present site of Indianola in Thistle Valley on 24 June.[34]

As part of his effort to protect Sanpete Valley, Wells had ordered a force of fifty-seven men under Captain Albert Dewey to build a fortified blockhouse to guard the "principal trails coming in to the North End of San Pete [valley]" from the Uintah Reservation by way of Spanish Fork Canyon.[35] Hence, a combined force of cavalry and infantry entered Thistle Valley on 20 June with about thirty horses and five or six baggage wagons. On the twenty-second they pitched camp in a "beautiful grassey plain" about 600 yards from the cedar-skirted foothills that form the eastern boundary of the valley.[36] On the night of 23 June, while the men amused themselves with a "stag dance," picket guards heard sounds resembling dogs barking and wolves howling and suspected it was Indian scouts calling to each other as they prowled about the camp. During the night, sentries fired at a wolflike animal which immediately "ran on two legs to the creek and disappeared."

Finding no tracks the following morning, the militiamen deter-

[34] Aaron Johnson to Daniel H. Wells, 3 and 8 July 1866, TMR, #1536 and #913; Aaron Johnson to Brigham Young, 3 July 1866, BYC; Dimick B. Huntington to Brigham Young, 11 August 1866, BYC; Eldridge, "Biographical Sketch," 88–89, 96–109, especially 103–5; A.F. MacDonald to William B. Pace, 24 May 1866; Brigham Young to Bishop W.W. Cluff, 5 July 1867, BYC; "The People Vs. Isaac Potter," 28–42; Weibye, "Journal," 11 August 1867; Summit Stake Manuscript History, 1867; and CR, 81–83.

[35] Daniel H. Wells to Brigham Young, 25 June 1866, BYC; Robert T. Burton to Daniel H. Wells, 2 July 1866, TMR, #897; Peter Sinclair to Franklin D. Richards, 2 July 1866, TMR, #4729; and Dewey, "Journal," 15 June 1866.

[36] Dewey's camp was pitched south of Thistle Creek just a few hundred yards east of the present site of Indianola and a little over a mile from the site of the Given family massacre that had occurred the year before.

mined they had overreacted in the darkness and laughed at the mysterious animal they thought was an Indian. Relieved, the youthful soldiers concentrated on enjoying a relaxing Sabbath. Some bathed in a nearby hot spring while others played games or lay about camp talking and reading. Two men lazily guarded the grazing horse herd while Charles Brown and a comrade walked to the cedars "to gather gum." About 11:00 A.M. shots rang out in the trees and Brown's companion ran from the cedars screaming that his friend had been killed by Indians. Thirty warriors followed, "yelling like demons and swinging their blankets" in an attempt to drive off the militia's horses. Opening fire on the camp, the Indians succeeded in stampeding twenty-six of the whites' thirty-two horses.

As the raiders drove the bulk of the horses into a side canyon, militiamen secured six strays and sent two riders to Mount Pleasant for reinforcements. With the remaining animals they hurriedly maneuvered baggage wagons into a circle and pulled down tents, piling canvas, bedding, saddles, "and anything else that would form a barricade" beneath the vehicles. Meanwhile, Captain Dewey and three others ventured into the cedars in search of Brown's body but were chased back by Indians.

Before the militia's makeshift breastwork was completed, the Indians returned with reinforcements of their own, the band now numbering more than seventy. Lashed to their mounts, the warriors circled the wagons on the run, firing "from under their horses." Simultaneously, native footmen concealed by sagebrush slithered towards the wagons. Because most of his troops were equipped with antiquated weapons, Dewey ordered his men to hold their fire while he and another man, each armed with Spencer repeating rifles, took carefully aimed shots. After the Indians in the grass opened fire, however, the militia's antique Kentucky long rifles and muskets proved effective.

Three different times the Indians attacked and each time they were repulsed. Dewey himself fired more than seventy-five rounds and hit a number of Indians, including "one that seemed to be giving orders." While Dewey reported that "inside the wagons the lead flew thick all around," miraculously, only one militiaman was seriously wounded (not counting Brown, who was killed earlier in the cedars). Throughout the afternoon Dewey's sharpshooting kept the Indians at bay, but as evening came on it became clear the native force was preparing to assault the militia's position after nightfall. Aware they could not ward off their attackers in the dark, the Mormons prepared for the worst and prayed that their couriers had reached Mount Pleasant and were returning with help.

An hour before sundown Dewey noticed a force of riders approaching from the south. The Indians tried desperately to keep thirty Mount Pleasant and Fairview men under Colonel John L. Ivie (a brother of James A. Ivie) from reaching their besieged comrades. A daring Indian leader who the militiamen thought was Tabby himself rallied the native force, but when Ivie knocked him off his horse with a Henry repeating rifle, the warriors fell back. Once Ivie's command reached the circled wagons, the Indians attacked again. At length Mormon sharpshooting convinced the Utes that their attack on Dewey's wagons had become too dangerous and they drew off into the foothills.[37]

The following morning, another force of Latter-day Saint reinforcements (this one numbering eighty-five men) reached Dewey's camp. As plans were made to retaliate, dispatches were sent to General Wells informing him that the attacking force was from Tabby's band. Not only had the Indians come from the north, but "they had on new hats, shirts & blankets, supposed to be the Presents recently received from Superintendent Head" at Uintah. A number of militiamen including Colonel Ivie were sure they had seen Tabby himself directing the raiders' movements. The confidence Wells placed in Tabby's declarations of peace, however, was such that he refused to believe the Uinta leader was involved in any way and he concluded that his officers had mistaken Tabby's brother Jim for the chief.[38]

Dewey and other militia leaders examined the battle site and found "pools of blood" that convinced them they had inflicted serious wounds on some of their attackers. Following the Indians' track a short distance, they found a blood-laced trail that seemed to be heading back towards Spanish Fork Canyon. Afraid to follow farther, they returned to camp and waited for Warren Snow to arrive and take up the trail.

---

[37] Albert Dewey to Heber P. Kimball, 25 June 1866, TAS; Dewey, "Journal," 19–26 June 1866; Heber P. Kimball to Daniel H. Wells, 24 June 1866, TMR, #878; Reddick N. Allred to Daniel H. Wells, 25 June 1866, TAS; Daniel H. Wells to Brigham Young, 25 and 26 June 1866, BYC; Brigham Young to Charles C. Rich, 5 July 1866, BYC; Peacock, Journal, 24 June 1866; Lambert, "Autobiography"; Seeley, "History," 3–4; Woolley, "Dictation During Declining Years," 6; Gottfredson, *Indian Depredations*, 208–11; and DUP, *Treasures of Pioneer History*, 5:350.

[38] John R. Winder to Robert T. Burton, 25 June 1866, TAS; Reddick N. Allred to Daniel H. Wells, 25 June 1866, TAS; Warren S. Snow to Daniel H. Wells, 26 June 1866, TMR, #881; and Daniel H. Wells to Aaron Johnson, 1 July 1866, TMR, #895.

The following day Snow and a 130-man force followed tracks a distance of fifty miles to Soldier Summit at the head of Spanish Fork Canyon. Here the Indians had separated in different directions, only the ones trailing blood heading back towards the reservation. Snow was satisfied the "main party" intended to double back, regroup, and attack some settlement in Sanpete or Utah counties. Abandoning the chase, he found isolated tracks in Thistle Valley heading towards Utah Valley, but because they were of "small magnitude" he paid them little attention and led his men back towards Sanpete Valley.[39]

The Battle of Diamond Fork

Early on the morning of 26 June, a war party led by Mountain stole thirty-eight cattle and fifteen horses near Spanish Fork, specifically targeting the pasture of William Berry, whom Black Hawk and his brother apparently had begrudged ever since Berry was involved in an incident in which Black Hawk was battered with a brass bucket sometime before the war began.[40] Mountain's take was sparse considering the 3,000 head of Payson, Spanish Fork, and Springville stock safely guarded west of the Spanish Fork River. Finding Utah County in a high state of defense, as Young's "vigilance policy" had been fully implemented, the raiders barely escaped the brigades of militiamen guarding the huge herd and the major trails to the mountains. Because groups of legionnaires were bivouacked in the mouths of Hobble Creek and Spanish Fork canyons, the Indians drove their booty into Maple Canyon and up a trail the Mormons left undefended because they considered it impassable to stock.

By 4:00 A.M. guards had discovered the theft, and bass drums and church bells summoned Springville and Spanish Fork militiamen to the chase. Hesitant to allow precious time to elapse while a large force assembled, Major William Creer and fifteen men from Springville started after the stock. Trusting reinforcements would follow, they tracked the Indians up Maple Canyon, traversing an almost insurmountable trail leading over the top of Maple Mountain and down the other side to Little Diamond Creek, a course obviously heading to the reservation. They overtook the herd not far from the confluence of the Little Diamond and Diamond Fork River. Obviously not expecting

to be followed, the raiders had set up camp and turned their animals out
to graze in a meadow surrounded by steep canyon walls. Mountain and
his men had killed several head of cattle and were hanging out slices of
meat to dry on rocks and brush as Creer's small force apparently rushed
past them to block the escape route farther down the steep-sided
canyon.

Disturbed that they had been outflanked, Mountain's men knew the
captured stock was lost unless they could drive the Springville men
from the trail, and they moved in to attack at once. Hardly prepared
for battle, Creer's sixteen-man force carried only a few pistols and
shotguns. Two men, in fact, had no weapons at all, and their leader
lamented that there was not a single "breech loading gun in the outfit." Praying that reinforcements were close at hand, Creer's men took
refuge behind trees and opened fire, initiating a gun battle that was variously reported as lasting from two to four hours.

At times there were lulls in the fighting when the Indians taunted the
white men, calling them "all kind of names" and daring them to come
out in the open. One Indian who knew some of the whites personally
was particularly "abusive," swearing at Albert Dimmick by name and
calling him "a squaw and a coward." Young and inexperienced, Dimmick jumped to his feet and "brandished his rifle with a shout of defiance." Shots instantly rang out and Dimmick fell mortally wounded. As
the firing continued both groups spread out and sought shelter in the
dense scrub oak that covered the mountainside. Meanwhile, a group of
eight Spanish Fork militiamen who had followed Creer's force heard
the shooting and rushed to reinforce their comrades. Three foolhardy
Spanish Fork youths anxious for Indian blood recklessly attempted to
ride through the raiders' position to reach Creer. When the Indians
fired at them, two rushed back up the canyon, but eighteen-year-old
Jonathan Edmiston, a nephew of Warren Snow, continued his impru-
dent ride, disappearing in the brush only fifty yards from the raiders.

Pinned between two tiny Nauvoo Legion units, the raiders hun-
kered down and the firing stopped. At length a mounted Indian appeared on a ridge above them and with "excited gestures" urged his
tribesmen to continue their attack. Creer's force commenced "volley
firing at the chief" and on their fifth try the native leader "fell upon the
neck of his horse, which ran behind the hill and out of sight." At this,
the foiled Indians deserted their stolen cattle and retreated over the
steep canyonside, carrying their dead and wounded with them.

Once they were gone, the whites fanned out to look for Edmiston and to gather stock. Failing to locate the missing man, they plundered Mountain's camp, capturing buffalo robes, lariats, and other native gear, including new blankets, hats, butcher knives, and tin cups recently handed out as presents by Superintendent Head to Tabby's reservation Indians. These last items were gathered up to present to the superintendent with an official request that the reservation Utes be chastised by federal troops.

As they had done at Thistle Valley, Mormons found blood at various spots on the battlefield and later learned from native sources that "5 or 6 Indians were killed and several wounded." Fearing a night counterattack, Creer and his men drove the recovered stock back over the mountain to Spanish Fork, carrying the wounded Albert Dimmick on a litter. Dimmick, however, died before they reached home. The following morning, another force was summoned to search for Edmiston. The young man's stripped body was found in a thicket of scrub oak with two bullet holes in his heart. He had been scalped and his left hand had been severed from his body and taken as a trophy of war. The searchers also found two Indian ponies that day, one of which "was covered with blood all over his neck and shoulders"; they presumed it had belonged to the Indian they had shot at by volley.[41]

Immediately following the battle, the captured blankets, knives, cups, and hats were turned over to Brigham Young so he could give Franklin Head "official Notice" that Tabby's Indians were responsible for the attacks. Though Young as usual distanced himself from federal soldiers by keeping quiet, some of his followers informed the superintendent, who promised to "order out Government Troops on Tabbies renegades." Most local Mormons, however, continued to view the superintendent and his department with distrust, especially since it was reported that "white men were Seen directing the movements of the

---

[41] William Creer to George A. Smith, 16 March 1869, GAS; *Deseret Evening News*, 12 July 1866; Aaron Johnson to Daniel H. Wells, 27 and 29 June, 3 and 8 July 1866, TMR, #1533, #1534, #1536 and #913; Aaron Johnson to Brigham Young, 27 June 1866, BYC; Aaron Johnson to "the Bishops or Commanders of Posts on the Route," 28 June 1866, BYC; C. Wilken to Robert T. Burton, 16 July 1866, TAS; Daily Log of unidentified Nauvoo Legion unit stationed in Utah Valley, 26 June 1866, TMR, #1532; Brigham Young to Charles C. Rich, 5 July 1866, BYC; CR, 82; Coombs, Diary, 27 June 1866; JH, 26 June 1866, 1; Gottfredson, *Indian Depredations*, 213–20; *William Jex*, 40–44; Don Carlos Johnson, "The Indians of Utah Valley," 11 and 18 June 1908; and Farnsworth, "History of Manti," 55. Jonathan H. Edmiston was the son of Warren Snow's sister Martha Jane.

Indians" and that the horse of Head's interpreter Richard James was found dead on Diamond Fork's battleground.[42] As a result, rumors spread "that a certain Indian Agent . . . bought the horses and cattle that the Indians robbed from the Mormons, and paid them with arms and amunition, that they might so much more effectually raid on, and fight the Mormons." Significantly, it was further rumored "that this same Indian Agent was backed by his superiors in the government in this his dastardly acts."[43]

Meanwhile, gentiles at the Uintah Agency reported that Tabby's son-in-law and other Indians were returning to the reservation with wounds. Accounts of high numbers of Indian casualties reassured Nauvoo Legion officials that the fights in Thistle Valley and Diamond Fork had been tremendous moral victories for the Latter-day Saints.[44] Thus far, in fact, with the single exception of the 1865 "Squaw Fight" in Grass Valley, they were the only instances in which the raiders had been met with any degree of military success. The battles at Thistle Valley and Diamond Fork were significant turning points in the Black Hawk War for both Mormons and Indians. For the Latter-day Saints, the Indian defeats demonstrated that Brigham Young's vigilance policy could work, and they confirmed the First Presidency's assertion that only when the Indians were convinced that there was "no chance of getting a single hoof without first getting a bullet" would the raiding cease.

For the raiders, the Mormon victories crippled the move to enlist the major Northern Ute bands in the fighting. The killing and wounding of significant numbers of Tabby's men also strengthened their head chief's pacifistic position. Tabby reportedly harangued the whipped warriors in disgust, telling them "that he was glad that [they] got wounded for they had no business to goe and fight." He conceded, however, that the blood of Warren Snow's nephew and the other two whites killed at Diamond Fork and Thistle Valley was sufficient "to pay for the killing of Sandpitch."[45]

Within weeks of the battles, word came in from Uintah that most of Tabby's young men were "tired of fighting," and Tabby and Sowiette sent "a deputation of the principal men of the Ute tribe" to Salt Lake

---

[42] Aaron Johnson to Brigham Young, 27 June 1866; CR, 82; and A.F. MacDonald to William B. Pace, 3 July 1866, in "Brigade Record," 21.

[43] "Gunnison Ward Historical Record," 17.

[44] Aaron Johnson to Daniel H. Wells, 8 July 1866.

[45] C. Wilken to Robert T. Burton, 27 July 1866, TAS.

City to assure Brigham Young of their "anxiety for peace." Significantly, the head envoy was Tabby's brother Jim, who was a major figure in the Thistle Valley fight. Despite Jim's known participation in the fighting, Young heartily accepted the reservation Indians' plea for peace. Though small raiding parties would continue to be launched from the reservation for years to come, until the war's final conflagration in 1872 the Mormons had little fear of Tabby's Indians joining the conflict en masse.[46]

Even more important than the effect the Mormon victories had on Tabby's Indians was the impact they had on Black Hawk's band itself. Since the beginning of the war, Latter-day Saint strategists had prognosticated that Indian depredations would continue until the raiders were defeated in battle. While there is no evidence that Black Hawk was present at either the Thistle Valley or Diamond Fork fights (indeed, he was probably convalescing from the wound he received at Gravelly Ford), there is no question that large numbers of his men were present. They likely suffered similar casualties to those of the reservation Indians who had joined them. Although Black Hawk's band succeeded in driving off one more large herd in July 1866, it is clear the Mormon victories seriously weakened the raiders' solidarity; from that point on, Black Hawk's band began to disintegrate, as did their war chief's military success.

Still Better to Feed than Fight

Brigham Young obviously believed the initial reports that Tabby himself had led the attacks made by reservation Indians. Even so, he continued his policy of feeding Indians to maintain peace. Within days of learning of the battles, and before he was visited by the Ute delegation, Young dispatched William Wall to deliver "twenty sacks of flour to Tabby, though he does fight us and tries to kill us." Along with the flour Wall carried yet another offer of peace from Young to the reservation Indians. "When you get tired of fighting," it read, "you will recollect that we were your friends. We did not commence fighting you. We have wanted peace." Young chided Tabby for not honoring his pledge to "not steal from or kill white men" made when he signed the Treaty of Spanish Fork, and the church leader urged the chief to "live

---

[46] C. Wilken to R.T. Burton, 16 July 1866; Brigham Young to Erastus Snow, 21 July 1866, BYC; Brigham Young to Brigham Young, Jr., 30 July 1866, BYC; Brigham Young to Tabby and Sowiette, 31 July 1866, BYC; and Dimick B. Huntington to Brigham Young, 11 August 1866, BYC.

according to that treaty." As for himself, Young characteristically declared, "I have always talked and acted straight with the red men," and in an obvious jab at Tabby he added, "when *I* make a promise and agree to do any thing, *I* keep my word."[47]

Wall eventually tracked Tabby, Sowiette, Toquana, Joe, Jim, and several "little chiefs" to Fort Bridger, where their bands were trading with whites and over a thousand Shoshonis. He learned firsthand that "Taby himself had not been in either of the engagements, but that Mountain (Black Hawks brother) had been the leader." Sowiette and Toquana also convinced Wall that they were innocent of any involvement. Still somewhat disgruntled, Tabby reluctantly concluded that there "had been done enough now to pay for the killing of Sandpitch." Washakie joined in the discussion and at the request of the Mormons sternly told the Utes that if they wanted peace with the Shoshonis they had "to quit steeling and murdering." At this, Tabby declared that if President Young "was willing to make a permanent peace, he was." Young's offers of peace and his twenty sacks of flour (backed up by the Mormon victories and Washakie's threats) succeeded in bringing Tabby to terms and resulted in the visit of the Ute delegation to Salt Lake City described above. Significantly, though, Wall wrote his superiors in the militia that he found Richard James at Fort Bridger with Tabby's Indians selling horses stolen from Mormons to emigrants for "$15 a piece" and "doin[g] all the mischief he [could]" among the Utes.[48]

Expeditions

Captain Wall's mission to deliver flour and make peace with Tabby and other reservation chiefs represented only one prong of Young's Indian policy following the victories at Thistle Valley and Diamond Fork. Taking his cue from Book of Mormon accounts of the people of God *aggressively* going after the Gadianton robbers, the church president ordered Daniel H. Wells to launch major Nauvoo Legion expeditions through the mountains, with the goal of breaking up Black Hawk's band once and for all. The plan was to "hunt them to their den" by converging with several large militia detachments on supposed raider hideouts in Castle Valley, Grass Valley, and in the Fish Lake country. Wells instructed his church troops "not to go forth seeking vengeance and

---

[47] Brigham Young to "Tabby and other chiefs and the men who are with him," 2 July 1866, BYC; and Brigham Young to Daniel H. Wells, 2 July 1866, BYC. Italics mine.

[48] C. Wilken to R.T. Burton, 16 and 27 July 1866.

retaliation" but rather in the spirit of "Humility and faithful discharge of a Duty." In addition to finding the raiders, the militiamen were to do all they could to locate and reclaim the stock run off in the Scipio raid and in scores of smaller forays that season. The hierarchy believed that recovering the stock on the heels of the Indian setbacks at Thistle Valley and Diamond Fork would cause Black Hawk's band to stop raiding whether they were militarily chastised or not. Unfortunately for Latter-day Saint militiamen, after at least 200 men had departed on lengthy and tiresome mountain expeditions, church leaders learned from Indian sources that the bulk of the raiders "had gone to Sante-fee to trade off the stolen Cattle & Horses and recruit their supplys of amunition to carry on the War."[49]

Two distinct 100-man detachments left Salina on 8 July after a massive "general preparation" which involved many local Sanpete Latter-day Saints in "drying Beef, Baking Bread & Crackers [and] fitting up Pack Saddles." One group, under Colonel Heber P. Kimball, traveled through Salina Canyon and explored Castle Valley. Although it found no Indians and only a handful of stray cattle, Kimball's command did make an important discovery. Following trails made by Indians driving stolen cattle through the rugged San Rafael Swell country, they came upon an impressive network of fortified corrals and stone "batteries" complete with loopholes, which some took as evidence the raiders were in league with significant numbers of white men. The Indians had only recently deserted this hideout, and tracks made it clear they were heading towards Gunnison Ford on the Green River using the Old Spanish Trail.[50]

Meanwhile one hundred men under William B. Pace reconnoitered Grass Valley, Fish Lake, and Rabbit Valley,[51] following the Fremont River as far east as the present site of Fruita, where gigantic "perpendicular Rocks" on either side of the river with "no trail through" stopped their advance. The towering cliffs that brought Pace's force to a standstill are now popular tourist attractions in Capitol Reef National

---

[49] William B. Pace to Robert T. Burton, 1 July 1866, TAS; Unknown correspondent writing from the camp of Daniel H. Wells to Brigham Young, 8 July 1866, TMR, #911; and Peter Maughan to Brigham Young, received 31 August 1866, BYC, r59, b30, f17.

[50] John R. Winder to Brigham Young, 8 July 1866, BYC; Brigham Young to Erastus Snow, 21 July 1866, BYC; Brigham Young to Brigham Young, Jr., 20 July 1866; and Howard, Diary, 9 July 1866.

[51] Rabbit Valley, later the home of such settlements as Fremont, Loa, Lyman, and Bicknell, was named by Pace's command because of the large numbers of rabbits they found there. DUP, *Treasures of Pioneer History*, 4:166.

Park. Also tracking small herds of recently stolen cattle, Pace's command was amazed at the "impenetrable Rocks" the Indians maneuvered their hoofed booty through, and they declared in their official report that the Indians had successfully negotiated "the worst looking country immaginable."[52]

Had Pace's command spent more time exploring Grass Valley, they might have discovered a second complex of Indian corrals and stone fortifications built in a canyon on the eastern border of the valley. As it was, however, the easily defensible stone compound, camp, and natural stockyard was found deserted over a month later by a third Nauvoo Legion expeditionary force. Launched from St. George in mid-August, this eighty-man force led by James Andrus made the longest and most difficult military excursion of the Black Hawk War. As a follow-up to the Kimball and Pace expeditions, Andrus's men rode an estimated 440 miles through the heart of Utah's canyon country, covering some of the most rugged and breathtakingly beautiful terrain in all of North America. Traversing the northern reaches of the Grand Canyon's north rim, they passed the Vermillion Cliffs, skirted the area that would become Zion and Bryce Canyon national parks, and overlooked parts of the modern Glen Canyon National Recreation Area as well as portions of Capitol Reef and Canyonlands national parks.

Ordered to "make as thorough an examination as possible" of a huge stretch of badlands extending from the Arizona Strip to the confluence of the Green and Colorado rivers, Andrus's purpose was twofold: first, he was to learn if there were any major Indian trails crossing the Colorado River that the Mormons were unaware of; second, he was to locate "the places of rendezvous or retreat of the hostile Indians, who have so long been making raids upon our Eastern borders." In accordance with Brigham Young's peace policy, Andrus was instructed to "take especial pains to conciliate the Piedes and Ki-babbits," but he was also ordered to "inflict such chastisement" as he could upon Black Hawk's band of cattle thieves should he come upon them.[53]

---

[52] Report of William B. Pace's expedition to Daniel H. Wells, 16 July 1866, WBP; variation also found in William B. Pace to Daniel H. Wells, 15 July 1866, TMR, #1539; and "Expedition to Fish Lake, July 15 1866, W.B. Pace," holograph map, TMR, no number, photocopy in author's possession.

[53] "Order no. 14, Brigade Head Quarters, Iron Mil. Dist., Erastus Snow Brig. Genl. Comdg. to Capt. James Andrus, 15 August 1866," TMR, #1543; Fish, "Diaries," 24–29; and James Andrus and Franklin B. Woolley to Erastus Snow, 18 September 1866, TMR, #967.

While Andrus lost one man in an ambush, he and his men saw few Indians.[54] They did, however, confirm the previous Mormon belief that the two "Ute Trail crossings" at Lee's Ferry and the Crossing of the Fathers were the only major Indian fords on the Colorado River below Gunnison Ford at Green River. As was the case with other Nauvoo Legion expeditions to the north, Andrus's expedition took Latter-day Saints into areas they were unfamiliar with and actually paved the way for future settlement.[55] One of the war's greatest ironies was that Indian efforts to halt Mormon colonization actually resulted in extensive Nauvoo Legion reconnaissance that put the settlers in possession of geographic knowledge that at the close of the war greatly facilitated a burst of expansion into the very areas in which Mormons had pursued the raiders. The longevity of names given to numerous geographic features by militiamen chasing Indians during the Black Hawk War is but a small indication of the impact the expeditions had on the settlement of Utah.[56]

Besides confirming that the raiders used only the three major fords, the most immediate contribution of Andrus's exploration was the discovery of the deserted fortified Indian hideout in a Grass Valley side canyon. Even before Warren Snow tracked a herd of stolen animals into the valley and attacked a portion of Black Hawk's band there in June 1865, Latter-day Saints suspected Grass Valley and the adjacent Fish Lake country to be the war chief's "headquarters." Subsequent expeditions and Andrus's discovery of the fortified Indian camp and stockyard confirmed the fact that Grass Valley was indeed a major "runway of [the] marauders."

Named for luxuriant meadows produced by Otter Creek and its tributaries, Grass Valley provided a natural pasture several miles wide and about forty miles long. The valley and surrounding country was the

---

[54] Elijah Averett, Jr., was killed near the Paria River on or about 26 August 1866. George Isom received an arrow wound in the shoulder in the same engagement. See James Andrus and Franklin B. Woolley to Erastus Snow, 18 September 1866; Gottfredson, *Indian Depredations*, 222–24; and Charles Walker, *Diary*, 1:268.

[55] For general information regarding this expedition see James Andrus and Franklin B. Woolley to Erastus Snow, 18 September 1866; Erastus Snow to Daniel H. Wells, 20 September 1866, TMR, #967; Bleak, "Southern Mission," 1:242–43, 245–47; Fish, "Diaries," 24–29; and Gottfredson, *Indian Depredations*, 221–25.

[56] For a brief discussion of the impact Mormon military expeditions had on Latter-day Saint settlement see Crampton and Miller, "Journal of Two Campaigns Against the Navajo," 149–51.

principal homeland of a band of Indians the Mormons called "the Red Lake Utes," who along with their close relatives, the Shiberetches, or Elk Mountain Utes, constituted the core of Black Hawk's Ute supporters. Bordered on the west by the Sevier Plateau and on the east by the Parker Range and the Fish Lake Mountains, Grass Valley provided the Indians with a strategically secure mountain sanctuary. Grazing their stolen herds in the valley, Indian guards could alert their tribesmen in plenty of time to drive stock up canyons to the east that led to numerous escape routes. Militiamen would be loath to follow because of the almost infinite number of potential ambuscade sites the rugged terrain afforded.

The abandoned camp Andrus stumbled across in September 1866 had obviously harbored stolen cattle. The troopers could clearly discern places where cattle had been tied to trees for days at a time, and Indian meat-jerking racks were still standing as their builders had left them. Andrus noted in his official report that there were a number of "rude breast works" scattered about, but they formed no organized "system of defence so far as [he] could discern." Instead, the rock Indian forts seemed to have been "thrown up in a hasty manner [at] points widely seperated from each other." The raiders had obviously occupied the camp "for some time."[57] Interestingly, when Black Hawk made peace in a series of verbal treaties from 1867 to 1870, he reportedly told Latter-day Saints that the Andrus command unwittingly passed within three miles of another camp inhabited at the time by some of the raiders' families. Fortunately for the Indians, the Nauvoo Legion company was unaware of both the camp and the "old men and squaws" the raiders had left there.[58]

Even before Andrus's impressive journey, the mid-July failure of the Pace and Kimball expeditions to locate Indians or significant numbers of stolen stock seemed to confirm native reports that the raiders had left the area. As a result, General Wells released 200 northern troops, replacing them with only 100 fresh recruits. The tired soldiers arrived in Salt Lake City on 21 July, having been engaged in "fighting Indians" for almost three months. Brigham Young took one look at the "outfit" that was dismissed before his balcony and declared that it was clear they had had "rough, hard times."[59]

[57] James Andrus and Franklin B. Woolley to Erastus Snow, 18 September 1866.
[58] Gottfredson, *Indian Depredations*, 223.
[59] Daniel H. Wells to Brigham Young, 15 July 1866, BYC; and Brigham Young to Erastus Snow, 21 July 1866.

Preaching Peace

With Black Hawk's band ostensibly out of the country and Tabby and other reservation chiefs voicing desires for peace, Brigham Young and the church's apostles began preaching a renewed policy of reconciliation. On 28 July the church president assembled a huge congregation of Latter-day Saints in an open-air meeting in Springville. Speaking to settlers gathered from many central Utah settlements directly involved in the fighting, the church president's sermon provides important insights into his Indian policy and some of the fundamental beliefs that shaped it. Indeed, the sermon sheds more light on Young's thinking on the war and his related policy than does any other single document that has survived.[60] It therefore will be considered here in some detail.

Brigham Young opened his remarks that day by imploring his followers to treat the Indians with kindness. Aware that many under the sound of his voice felt "like wiping out the Lamanites in these regions, root and branch," he called upon the Saints to subject such feelings to "the law of Christ." Unwilling to dismiss his people's culpability in provoking the Indians to bloodshed in the first place, Young charged that "If the Elders of Israel had always treated the Lamanites as they should," they would have had no "difficulty with them at all." According to Young, the Lord sent the war upon the Saints to convince them "to overcome the vindictive feelings which we have harbored towards that poor, down-trodden branch of the house of Israel." As long as the Saints held "such feelings," he promised, "so long they will be our enemies, and the Lord will suffer them to afflict us." Young prophesied that the people of Utah would see the "end of this Indian War," but he taught that kind treatment of Indians was a prerequisite.

He announced that various bands on the reservation with Tabby had expressed desires to return "and live as they formerly did" as neighbors to the Latter-day Saints. "Let the Lamanites come back to their homes, where they were born and brought up," he urged. The prophet reminded his listeners:

> This is the land that they and their fathers have walked over and called their own; and they have just as good a right to call it theirs to-day as any people have to call any land their own. They have buried their fathers and mothers and children here; this is their

---

[60] Minutes of this important sermon can be found in various sources, including JH, 28 July 1866, 3–5; and *JD*, 11:263–66.

home, and we have taken possession of it, and occupy the land where they used to hunt the rabbit and, not a great while since, the buffalo, and the antelope . . .

Addressing the apparent contradiction between the Indians' right to the land and that of the settlers, Young reassured his followers that "The Lord has brought us here and it is all right. We are not intruders, but we are here by the providence of God." Young's vision of the Indians' and Saints' dual ownership of the land, however, brought special obligations to the Mormons, and it was their "duty to feed these poor ignorant Indians."[61]

Very much aware of the risks involved in inviting the Indians to come back among enraged Mormons, the church leader repeatedly admonished his people to see that "all feelings of vengeance" were "banished" from their hearts. "Were they to come back again without the minds of the people being prepared," he acknowledged, "probably some of the Indians might get killed."[62] Censuring violence against "innocent Indians," Young condemned such acts as that perpetrated against Panikary by James Ivie and obliquely reiterated his position that Ivie was "just as much a murderer through killing that Indian, as he would have been had he shot down a white man." He referred to the biblical penalty of death for murder and ordered that if Indians returning to the settlements in friendship were killed by any Mormon, the Saints were to "take that man and try him by law and let him receive the penalty."

He then quoted Genesis 9:6, which states: "Whoso sheddeth man's blood, by man shall his blood be shed: for in the image of God made he man." According to Young's theology, capital punishment for such crimes was necessary because Christ's atonement did not cover murder; as a result, the murderer must pay for the sin himself by allowing his own blood to be shed. Young taught that this applied to the killing of innocent Indians, saying, "Those who shed the blood of the innocent . . . will have to pay the penalty here, or come short of receiving the glory and the peace which they anticipate receiving hereafter." Referring to the wanton killing of Indians some of his followers had engaged in, he asked, "Shall we do as the Lamanites do?" An emphatic

[61] *JD*, 11:263–66.
[62] Ibid., 264.

"No!" was his answer, and he forcefully thundered this command and accompanying curse:

> I forbid it in the name of the Lord Jesus Christ—I forbid any elder or member in this church slaying an innocent Lamanite! When a man undertakes to shoot an ignorant Indian, except in defence of life and property, he degrades himself to the level of the red man, and the portion of that Indian shall be his, and his generations shall be cut off from the earth.[63]

The curse invoked by the Mormon prophet upon the heads of Indian killers demonstrates that, while some of his ideas differed radically from those held by the majority of whites in the West, others were more in line with those of his gentile contemporaries. Despite his desire to protect and treat Indians kindly, to Brigham Young, Native Americans were "poor," "degraded," "ignorant," and "wild," clearly existing on a "level" inferior to that of the white man. Implicitly trusting the Book of Mormon, though, it was his firm belief that the Lamanites could and would be lifted from their "fallen condition" to inherit all the blessings of Abraham, Isaac, and Jacob.

Instructed as they had been in Book of Mormon teachings regarding the origin and destiny of the Lamanites, in Young's view it was incumbent upon the Latter-day Saints to "set an example for all mankind" of how Indians should be treated. "We could circumscribe their camps and kill every man, woman and child of them," he hypothesized. "This is what others have done." However, if the Saints did so, he questioned, "What better are we than the wicked and the ungodly?" Setting forth the policy he had preached throughout the war, and, in fact, since 1846, he stated, "It is our duty to be better than [the gentiles] in our . . . conduct toward the Lamanites. It is not our duty to kill them; but it is our duty to save their lives and the lives of their children."[64]

Notwithstanding their problems with the Indians, Brigham Young and his followers prided themselves on treating the Indians better than their gentile neighbors did. As has been shown, contemporary Americans believed that the Latter-day Saints wielded great influence with

[63] Ibid., 263–66.
[64] Ibid., 264–65.

Indians throughout the West because of their extraordinary benevolence and generosity towards them. While their influence with the Native Americans was significantly less than was generally presumed, and despite the bloodshed of the Black Hawk War, it cannot be denied that Mormon doctrine, and particularly Brigham Young's insistence that it be implemented, tended to make Latter-day Saints more humane in their treatment of Indians than were most of their neighbors.

In truth, however, rank and file Latter-day Saints were often moved more by traditional American values in their treatment of Indians than by their prophet's passionate rhetoric. Mormon views of their own benevolence and equally complimentary gentile opinions on the subject were sometimes more a reflection of Brigham Young's *wishes* than of the Latter-day Saints' *actual behavior*. There is no question that from even before the time of Mormon settlement in Utah, Brigham Young forcefully urged his followers to be kind to Indians. The Black Hawk War, however, demonstrated that Young's voice, like those of certain compassionate religious leaders before and after him, was sometimes more "a voice crying in the wilderness" than the followed policy of his people. Young was, however, very much aware that his restraining influence made a significant difference, and he told his people that were "the spirit of war . . . let loose among the Elders of Israel," they would "become as wild as unbroken colts on the prairie."

In this sermon Young also chided the Mormons for waiting for the outbreak of hostilities to induce them to implement his instructions on fort building and for neglecting other "salutary counsels" that he had "continually" given them. Obviously now aware of the roles Richard James, Isaac Potter, and other whites were playing in the war, he condemned all those "who supply the Lamanites with powder and lead, and foster and encourage them in killing the Saints" and prophesied that "their iniquity" would "turn upon their own heads." Alluding to growing frictions between the church and the United States, Young also prophesied that the Indians "would see the time they would rather defend this people than slay them."

Allying the Indians militarily to the Latter-day Saints was never Brigham Young's principal goal; there is no doubt, however, that he considered it an advantageous side benefit. From the start his belief was that Mormons and Indians should have a mutually beneficial relationship, and even at that date he prophesied that the war would end to "the benefit of the Latter-day Saints, *and* the exaltation of the . . . Laman-

ites." As a result, the burden of Young's message to his people continued to be one of peace. "We should now use the Indians kindly, and
deal with them so gently," he urged them, "that we will win their hearts
and affections to us more strongly than before; and the much good that
has been done them, and the many kindnesses that have been shown
them, will come up before them, and they will see that we are their
friends."

As might be expected, Young closed his remarks by underscoring the
need for the people to continue his vigilance policy, a policy he maintained would quickly restore peace when it was fully implemented.[65]

[65] Ibid., 263–66; and JH, 28 July 1866, 3–5. Italics mine.

CHAPTER NINE

———————— ≫ ————————

The Triumph of Vigilance

During the summer the Indians made several attempts of driving off stock, but the people having placed themselves in a more safe and guarded position . . . little was effected by the Indians. Strong guards are kept up day & night and whenever the Indians prowl about they find the herds strongly guarded and themselves badly pursued.

—George Peacock, 28 April 1867[1]

WHILE BRIGHAM YOUNG preached peace in Springville, the raiders pulled off their last major central Utah raid of the 1866 season. This time they succeeded in taking some long-awaited vengeance on Warren Snow's Manti. In one of the most impressive raids of the war, nearly 200 cattle (mostly expensive work oxen) were driven into canyons east of Ephraim and Manti towards Castle Valley. The oxen had just been turned out to pasture after spending the day hauling poles to be used in a telegraph line being built to apprize the militia of just such an attack.[2] Although Snow himself led more than 100 militiamen in a spirited but typically belated pursuit, the Indians and their prizes escaped beyond the Green River with little problem. The loss of the oxen constituted a major blow to the Sanpete agricultural economy, and the raiders could hardly have found a better way to pour salt into the wounds of their chief antagonists.[3]

The raid undoubtedly overrode much of the salutary effect Brigham Young's sermons may have produced, and Orson Hyde fumed not only

[1] Peacock, Journal, 28 April 1867.
[2] A. Milton Musser and Joseph F. Smith to Brigham Young, 29 July 1866, BYC.
[3] Ibid.; George Peacock to Daniel H. Wells, 30 July 1866, TMR, #944; Reddick N. Allred to Daniel H. Wells, 1 August 1866, TMR, #947; Daniel H. Wells to Brigham Young, 29 July 1866, BYC; and Peacock, Journal, 28 July–4 August 1866.

at the Indians but at the federal government, which he held responsible for the war generally, and especially for this latest raid, which threatened to entirely cripple Sanpete County. In a letter to Daniel H. Wells he raged against Governor Durkee, who, according to the apostle, was very much aware that the territory's "citizens are shot down like beasts by cruel and merciless savages, and their stock stolen and driven off by the hundreds . . . and that white men are furnishing them with arms and amunition to kill us and even planning their expeditions and aiding to execute them." Notwithstanding all this, the governor had failed to call in federal troops! As far as Hyde was concerned, "by his silence" Durkee gave the raiders "encouragement" if not actual "aid and comfort." "Is it possible," Hyde rhetorically asked President Wells, "that we are cursed with rulers who, like Herod, desire our destruction, and who, unlike Herod, have not the moral courage to do it openly?"[4]

In reality, however, at this point federal noninterference was probably more the result of Brigham Young's wishes and army personnel problems than it was an expression of anti-Mormon rancor. In 1866 the United States Army was in the midst of a massive personnel crisis that resulted from the mustering out of hundreds of thousands of soldiers as peace came to the nation following the Civil War. By August of that year, "army regulars" had replaced Civil War volunteers like Patrick Connor and his men. Despite Hyde's grumbling and the fact that Young found the career officers much easier to work with than the California volunteers, the church president's policy of keeping the federal government out of the Black Hawk War did not change. Shortly after the raid on Manti and Ephraim stock, however, Young turned to another outside source to pressure the Utes to end hostilities.

Help From Washakie

Washakie, the Shoshoni head chief, visited President Young and Superintendent Head in Salt Lake City during the second week in August. No record of their conversations has been found, but the Shoshoni leader left the city wearing a peace medal presented on behalf of the president of the United States about his neck and proceeded to move with more than 1,000 tribesmen towards the Uintah Reservation. Local Mormons reported that Washakie "promised his aid in repeling the hostile Utes" and was apparently prepared to make good on his

---

[4] Orson Hyde to Daniel H. Wells, 9 August 1866, TMR, #1542.

warning made to Tabby earlier that summer that if the Utes wanted to have peace with the Shoshonis they "had to quit steeling and murdering."[5]

There is no record that any major Ute-Shoshoni altercation occurred at this point. To the contrary, in fact, within days of Washakie's appearance near Coalville in eastern Utah, a Ute promise of peace was delivered to Heber City. A delegation that included Toquana, one of Tabby's sons, and Ankawakits's widow brought church leaders there a letter dictated by Tabby. According to the native leader, the reservation Utes were finally "anxious to make Peace and abide by it." The Shoshoni threat did not keep Tabby from speaking his mind, though, and he complained that some of Brigham Young's people still wanted to "kill Indians whare ever they see them." Tabby made it clear that his band "Blame[d] Bishop Snow for all [the] trouble" and promised that if Young would have Warren Snow killed he would "do the same with Black Hawk." Remembering that the Mormon president had declined to give Snow up in the past, Tabby tersely added: "I think as much of my Flesh & Blood as you do of yours and if you dont chastise Snow[,] Black Hawk will go unharmed by me." Toquana and the other envoys were fed and sent back to the reservation with five "small Beef Cattle."[6]

Apparently, just before the Shoshonis moved back to the north a few weeks later, Tabby himself and a retinue of sixty Utes visited Heber City to again demonstrate their peaceful intentions and to obtain gifts of provisions to see them through the coming winter. Antero, Douglas, Toquana, Showan, and Dick were among the group's leaders. They made no secret of their people's hungry condition and promised to visit Heber City again when the Latter-day Saints had harvested their grain. Tabby called a meeting to "Shake hands and talk" with local Latter-day Saints. Large tables were placed under a bowery used for the village's Sunday services and Heber City's women prepared a huge "picnic" complete with a beef barbecued over an open fire. After the feast, Tabby told the assembled whites that he "felt bad" about the "Death of Sanpich," but in light of the number of Mormons killed by his men he was ready to "let the past be forgotten." He indicated that Black Hawk

---

[5] F.H. Head to D.N. Cooley, Commissioner of Indian Affairs, 13 August 1866, BIA, M234, 902; Summit Stake Manuscript History; Tullidge, *Tullidge's Histories*, 2:133; Eldridge, "Biographical Sketch," 94; DUP, *Our Pioneer Heritage*, 8:108; and C. Wilken to R.T. Burton, 27 July 1866.

[6] Joseph S. Murdock, Bishop of Heber City, to Brigham Young, 25 August 1866, BYC; and Tabby per Thomas Carter to Brigham Young, 25 August 1866, BYC.

was "in the Elk Mountain Country" and that he had sent runners to urge the war chief to "quit his fighting" too. His desire was for his people to come to terms with the Mormons so that they could visit the settlements with safety as they had done before the war.[7]

Word of Tabby's peace overtures spread through the settlements, as did reports that even Black Hawk was tired of fighting. These reports, combined with the fact that no more major raids occurred during the remainder of 1866, gave some whites hope that the period of hostility was over. Near the end of September, Saints from certain evacuated settlements, some of whom were "almost crazy to get back to their homes," were allowed to return, and on 21 October the last of the militia detachments from northern Utah were released.[8]

The Deseret Telegraph and the Navajo War

Confident that the war was not yet over, throughout the fall and winter of 1866 Brigham Young vigorously pushed forward a new telegraph line, which he was sure would play a significant role in ending the "Indian difficulty." Clearly part of Young's vigilance policy, the Deseret State Telegraph line extended 450 miles from Logan to St. George, with an ancillary line running sixty miles from Nephi to Manti. Already conceptualized before the outbreak of the Black Hawk War in 1865, Young's plans for the wire were expedited after the conflict's opening weeks.[9] The new line was completed in January 1867 at a cost of $80,000 and caused Young to exult:

A new era is inaugurated in Zion by the erection of this wire . . . I can now sit in my office and communicate with Bros. Benson, Snow and Hyde in their several settlements . . . to give counsel, warning or instruction *or to ask information from any of them concerning the Indians,* . . . [10]

---

[7] Joseph S. Murdock, Bishop of Heber City, to Brigham Young, 12 September 1866, BYC; DUP, *Heart Throbs,* 1:97; and Gottfredson, *Indian Depredations,* 254. The August 1867 date for the feast in Gottfredson is in error.

[8] Lyman S. Wood to Brigham Young, 19 December 1866, BYC; JH, 23 November 1866, 1; Orson Hyde to Daniel H. Wells, 6 September 1866, TMR, #961; Weibye, "Journal," 20 and 27 September 1866.

[9] The very day the first killing of the war took place, but before Brigham Young could have known of the outbreak of hostilities, he instructed one of his eastern agents to ascertain the price of 500 miles of telegraph wire, insulators, and shipping. Brigham Young to William S. Godbe, 10 April 1865, BYC.

[10] Arrington, *Great Basin Kingdom,* 228–31; Brigham Young to George Nebeker, 13 March 1867, BYC; and JH, 23 November and 1 December 1866. Italics mine.

Significantly, one of the first messages sent across the completed line contained information regarding a Nauvoo Legion expedition that had killed a dozen Navajo raiders near Pipe Springs in the wake of a major flare-up of the Navajo war.[11] After Spanshanks was killed by three Mormons attempting to defend their lives during the Berry Massacre on the Arizona Strip in April 1866, southern Utah ranchers braced themselves for Navajo reprisals. Aware that Spanshanks, a minor chieftain, was the brother of Barboncito (one of the most powerful of Navajo chiefs), the whites were surprised that retaliatory raids were so late in coming. Not long after the Berry Massacre, Piedes told Kanosh that the dead sub-chief's sons were "raising the tribes to avenge their father's death." Kanosh excitedly told Brigham Young that the Navajos "count on having six thousand warriors ready in six weeks . . . to make a descent upon [the] Settlements and clean them out from St. George to Beaver." Characteristically, the church leader took the news to be "an Indian story"; nonetheless, he urged the southern Saints to "be prepared to ward off any attack that may be made."[12]

Fear fed hostility among the inhabitants of St. George to the extent that Apostle Erastus Snow felt constrained to remind them that "no man (unles justified before God [in accordance with LDS scriptural principles discussed above]) had the right to shed the Blood of his fellow man, . . . and because a man is an Indian or an Hottentot, Chinamen, or Laplander or any other color or nation no man is justified before the Lord in taking away his life." In September, missionary trips to ascertain "the attitude and doings of friendly Indians" on the Kaibab Plateau and in the Hopi country appear to have been designed to enlist native help in keeping raiding Navajos from crossing the Colorado River that winter.[13] Not until late October did the first of another series of Navajo raids occur. On 23 October Navajos allegedly inspired Paiutes to attack and set fire to the home of a family living eight miles southeast of Beaver while the Navajos gathered up and drove away their cattle.[14] On 11 November one Mormon was wounded and a hundred animals driven away by Navajos near the Long Valley settlements on the Virgin River.[15] In late November fear of more Navajo incur-

---

[11] JH, 15 January 1867, 1.

[12] Brigham Young to Erastus Snow, 15 August 1866, BYC.

[13] Charles Walker, *Diary*, 1:267; and Bleak, "Southern Mission," 1:244–45.

[14] Daniel Tyler to Brigham Young, 25 October 1866, BYC; and Gottfredson, *Indian Depredations*, 229–44.

[15] J.E. Johnson, Nephi Johnson, A.P. Winsor, and A.P. Hardy to Erastus Snow, 11 November 1866, TMR, #1547; and Charles Walker, *Diary*, 1:272.

sions induced Nauvoo Legion authorities in St. George to order the construction of two stone garrisons to guard the main trails the Navajos used in coming to the settlements.[16]

Despite these efforts, on 28 December fourteen Navajos stole thirty horses and thirteen head of cattle from settlers at Pine Valley north of St. George and made a dash for the Colorado River. A Nauvoo Legion force led by James Andrus and John Pearce overtook the raiders near Pipe Springs. In a running battle that raged over "one of the roughest[,] rockyest[,] worst cut up pieces of ground . . . that could be imagined," the militia routed the Indians and recaptured the animals. No white was injured in the fighting, but the number of Indians killed in the Mormon victory was estimated at twelve.[17] Part of a Navajo war just getting under way, by this time these raids may have had little to do with Black Hawk; but, then again, Black Hawk continued to move stock into Navajo country, and New Mexico newspapers continued to run stories about a Ute-Navajo alliance operating out of the Four Corners region.[18]

Black Hawk's participation in a huge stolen cattle market involving Indians, Hispanics, and whites has been discussed. However, to put it in chronological context, it is important to point again to the fact that after Black Hawk's raid on Scipio in June 1866, he and "about 40 lodges of the hostile Utes" moved their stolen cattle to the Elk Mountain country of southwestern Colorado and, according to native sources, took some of it all the way to Santa Fe.[19] He was joined by another contingent of his band after the raid on Manti and Ephraim late in July, and by October the *Santa Fe New Mexican* reported that "most of the Wemunuche Utes and all the Asavaritches [Shiberetches] or Green River Utes are together on the Rio Dolores [in the Elk Mountain Country], and are making preparations to attack the settlements in the northwestern portion of the territory [of New Mexico]." "These are the same Indians," the *New Mexican* continued, "who sometime since stole the stock at Tierra Amarilla and killed the herders. *Since then they have been up to the Mormon settlements, and returned with a large amount*

---

[16] The most prominent of these was Fort Pearce, which is still partially standing some sixteen miles southeast of St. George. Orders no. 16, Brigade Headquarters, Iron Military District, 29 November 1866, TMR, #1548; and Charles Walker, *Diary*, 1:273–74.

[17] J.T. Willis, Bishop of Toquerville, to Brigham Young, 14 January 1867, BYC; James Lewis to George A. Smith, 24 January 1867, GAS; John Steele to George A. Smith, 22 January 1867, GAS; Bleak, "Southern Mission," 255–57, 259; and JH, 4, 8, and 26 January 1867.

[18] For example, see the *Santa Fe New Mexican*, 22 June 1866.

[19] Peter Maughan to Brigham Young, received 31 August 1866, BYC, r59, b30, f17.

of stock they stole there."[20] By this time Superintendent Head was aware that Black Hawk's "She-be-retches" were "much visited by Spanish traders from New Mexico," and that, "for the purposes of trade, they usually travel" to Taos and Santa Fe.[21]

Meanwhile, authorities in Colorado were also becoming aware of the roles Richard James, Isaac Potter, and other whites were playing among the Utes. Apparently without having learned James's name as yet, Colorado's governor and ex-officio superintendent of Indian affairs complained of "a man who had formerly been engaged in the service of the government as an interpreter" who was living with the Utes, endeavoring "to incite them to raids upon the settlements, using as a pretext the failure of the government to fulfil its treaty stipulations."[22] Suspicion against James evidently became so strong that he published a journal of his whereabouts in Colorado newspapers the following spring. It was a belabored attempt to create an image of "his gentlemanly deportment and honest expression" in order to win "the esteem of the citizens" of that state, some of whom already acknowledged that he commanded "the respect *and obedience* of the savages with whom it has been his fate to be cast for the last seven months."[23]

Claiming he spent more than half a year with the Utes on the orders of Superintendent Head and an agent from Colorado, Richard James indicated that he had followed "the Old Spanish Trail" and wintered in the Elk Mountain country at a time that coincided exactly with Black Hawk's efforts to trade off his stock.[24] Interestingly, James stated that he accompanied "a large camp of Tabaguache, or Nevava Utes and *Shirerites* [Shiberetches] . . . on the banks of Grand river above its confluence with Green river, about . . . sixty miles distant from the Elk Mountains," the precise area of Black Hawk's headquarters. James's journal and Indian Office correspondence make it clear that large numbers of Tabaguache, Mouache, Capote, Uinta, Grand River, and Yampa Utes, as well as some Jicarilla Apaches, joined Black Hawk's Shiberetches, Weeminuches, Paiutes, and Navajos in the Elk Mountain country during the winter of 1866–67. Ute leaders mentioned as having wintered with James include Antero, Douglas, and Shivano,

---

[20] *Santa Fe New Mexican*, 27 October 1866.
[21] *RSI*, 1867:174–75.
[22] *Denver Rocky Mountain News*, 6 July and 1 August 1866; and *RSI*, 1866:156.
[23] *Denver Rocky Mountain News*, 12 June 1867. Italics mine.
[24] Ibid.

thus tacitly indicating they may have had at least some involvement with Black Hawk.[25]

Black Hawk's alliance apparently planned to again raid Tierra Amarilla and other New Mexico settlements until the federal troops Kit Carson called for pushed them back north towards "the Mormon settlements."[26] It appears that some of them (as was discussed in chapter six) joined their Mexican allies in avenging the Moqui attack on Manuelito's contingent of Black Hawk's raiders earlier that year by attacking the Hopi village of Oraibe. This positioned them to make incursions into southern Utah's Dixie by way of the Colorado River crossing at Lee's Ferry, not far from the Hopi pueblos. Whether the Navajos and other Indians who made raids in southern Utah during the winter of 1866–67 were associated with Black Hawk may never be known. Settlers throughout Utah, however, saw the raids as part of the Black Hawk War, and reports of the incursions unnerved Mormons hundreds of miles from Navajo lands.

Other rumors unnerved central Utah Latter-day Saints even more. As the spring of 1867 approached, predictions were rampant that "when the snow is gone the Indians are *all* going to get mad, east, west and south." While it was well known that Tabby had made peace, the word was out that many of his braves were still after Warren Snow and other Sanpete Saints. Orson Hyde predicted that Tabby would stay on the reservation "under the profession of friendship but secretly instigate his young men to go forth and plunder and shed blood." Characteristically, Hyde's solution was to send "a moderate force of United States troops" to the reservation to "make them pay the penalty of their evil intentions."[27]

The Glenwood Massacre

Tabby's "young men" were not the only Utes seeking the life of Warren Snow, and it appears the ailing Nauvoo Legion general nearly fell into Black Hawk's hands in the first raid of the 1867 season. Sometime near the middle of March, Snow and an adult son brought several wagonloads of merchandise to Glenwood to trade for stock and produce. They planned the trip early in the year when they were confident snow-filled mountain passes would keep Indians from interfering.

[25] For examples see ibid.; and A.C. Hunt, Gov. and Ex Officio Supt. of Ind. Affrs. to N.G. Taylor, Commissioner of Indian Affairs, 20 June 1867, and 4 August 1867, BIA, M234, 199.

[26] *Santa Fe New Mexican*, 10 November 1866.

[27] Orson Hyde to the Editor of the *Deseret News*, in *DN*, 7 March 1867. Italics mine.

While in Glenwood, however, Snow's health failed and he was confined to bed with a life-threatening lung ailment.[28] On the night of 20
March a large body of raiders "under command of the Indian Rover,
Blackhawk" gathered some eighty head of stock ranging near the settlement and quietly drove them into the mountains.[29] Then, in a rare
move suggesting they knew Warren Snow was in Glenwood, the
raiders returned to assault the tiny village.

Throughout the Black Hawk War, with this single exception, the Indians attacked a settlement only if it somehow strategically aided them
in stealing stock. In this instance, their booty already safely driven
away, whites were convinced "that the driving off of the Stock . . . was
not the extent of their purpose." Their plan, rather, was to destroy "the
whole of the inhabitants of Glenwood," including their archenemy,
Warren Snow.[30]

During the night of the twentieth, in an interesting turn of events,
thirty-five Indians took up positions in a new fort the settlers were
building about a mile from town. The settlers had been advised to
move the location of their town because it was within shooting range of
mountains to the east. It appears the raiders planned to ambush Glenwood's men as they arrived for their day's labor at the new fort. A series
of crude camouflaged rock bulwarks were strategically built by the Indians at various locations between the old settlement and the new fort
where native sharpshooters waited to fire at any workers who should
escape the band at the fort and attempt to run back towards town. With
the village's men thus out of the way, Warren Snow could easily be captured or killed.

Fortunately for Snow and the people of Glenwood, two youngsters
out hunting cattle before dawn discovered the Indians and sounded the
alarm. Their plans foiled, the raiders were easily chased into nearby
hills, where the two groups exchanged shots for about two hours.
Allegedly led by a chief mounted on another white horse, the raiders
tauntingly challenged individual Mormons by name in broken English.
At last the Indians withdrew and joined their companions and the
stolen herd in the mountains.

---

[28] Orson Hyde to Brigham Young, Heber C. Kimball, and Daniel H. Wells, 9 April 1867,
BYC; George Peacock to Brigham Young, 28 March 1867, BYC; Peacock, Journal, 21 March
1867; and "J.P. Petersen, Wife and Mary Smith Killed Near Glenwood."
[29] A.J. Moffitt to Brigham Young, 26 March 1867, BYC; and Hamilton H. Kearnes to
George A. Smith, 30 March 1867, GAS.
[30] Hamilton H. Kearnes to George A. Smith, 30 March 1867.

At some point that morning Black Hawk's party came across a Danish couple accompanied by a sixteen-year-old American girl traveling by ox team from Richfield to Glenwood to trade with Warren Snow. Jens Peter Petersen's face was beaten terribly with his own wooden shoes before he was killed. His wife, Caroline, "was scalped and cut up in a most brutal maner[,] a portion of the lower part of her body was cut out and laid upon her face." The teenaged Mary Smith was found "scalped and badly cut up with a stick run up about 10 inches into her privates." In what was perhaps the most brutal attack of the entire war, the threesome probably reaped the wrath the Indians had hoped to unleash on Warren Snow.[31]

More Evacuations

News of this massacre shocked Utah. Brigham Young, who had hoped to be able to allow settlers in Sevier Valley villages to remain in their homes, immediately telegraphed Orson Hyde that the Sevier settlements must be evacuated again posthaste. In a follow-up letter he ordered the Sanpete settlers to help the refugees move and announced that Warren Snow was temporarily relieved "owing to his ill health" and that William B. Pace would take his place as commander of the Sanpete Military District. That Snow was deathly ill is well documented, but Young may have finally gotten the message that Ute feelings against the Mormon general, not to mention those of rank and file militiamen (who still complained Snow was much too cautious), were so strong that Snow's continued leadership was counterproductive.[32] Though his health eventually improved, Warren Snow did not resume his command.

During the next three weeks hundreds of wagons from such Sanpete settlements as Manti, Ephraim, Mt. Pleasant, and Moroni rolled out to aid in the total evacuation of Sevier County. Nauvoo Legion detachments guarded the settlers of Glenwood, Monroe, Richfield, and other places as they loaded what they could into wagons and headed north driving cattle, sheep, swine, and chickens. Despite the fact that some 130 vehicles showed up to evacuate Richfield, grain, potatoes, lumber,

[31] Ibid.; A.J. Moffitt to President Brigham Young, 26 March 1867; George Peacock to Brigham Young, 28 March 1867, BYC; Peacock, Journal, 21 March 1867; "J.P. Petersen, Wife and Mary Smith Killed Near Glenwood"; JH, 22 March 1867, 1; Williams, "Life Sketch," 106–7; and Sorenson and Bybee, *Founded on Faith*, 25.

[32] Peacock, Journal, 1 and 28 April 1867; and Brigham Young, Heber C. Kimball and Daniel H. Wells to Orson Hyde, 2 April 1867, BYC.

and many household items were left behind because there was not enough wagon space to transport them.[33]

A result of the Black Hawk War (and part of Brigham Young's vigilance policy), from 1866 to 1871 the First Presidency of the LDS church ordered the closure of dozens of major settlements and hundreds of ranches. This impacted to varying degrees Sanpete, Sevier, Piute, Beaver, Iron, Kane, Washington, Juab, Millard, Utah, Summit, Wasatch, Weber, Box Elder, and Rich counties in Utah, as well as the areas of Mormon settlement in southern Idaho and eastern Nevada. The list of settlements evacuated at some point during the conflict includes Fairview, Spring City, Wales, Salina, Glenwood, Richfield, Monroe, Marysvale, Circleville, Panguitch, Glendale, Ash Creek, Pinto, Shoal Creek, Mountain Meadows, Gunlock, Grafton, Duncan's Retreat, Dalton, Mountain Dell, Shooensburg, Northrop, Springdale, Clover Valley, Beaver Dams, Simonsville, and St. Joseph. Governor Durkee, noting only the more substantial settlements that had been deserted, wrote that "six flourishing settlements in Piute and Sevier Counties, four settlements on the borders of Sanpete County, and fifteen settlements in Iron, Kane and Washington Counties, were entirely abandoned." But the "out settlements" and "most exposed" ranches of virtually all of Mormondom, even those in the Shoshoni country of the Box Elder, Cache, and Bear Lake valleys, were also compelled to "move in & consolidate."[34]

Some of these settlements never recovered from the upheaval. This was no minor population disturbance, for John Wesley Powell estimated that as many as "eight or ten thousand white people were driven from their homes" by "a chief named Nu'-ints, known to the white man as Black Hawk."[35] Although Powell's figure is probably excessive, because this forced abandonment involved "an almost total loss" of improvements, frontier Mormons felt it profoundly. One more episode in what they must have felt was a never-ending pattern of dispossession, this last eviction took its place in the Latter-day Saint psyche next to their banishment from Jackson County, Missouri, and Kirtland, Ohio,

---

[33] See Weibye, "Journal," 10–27 April 1867.

[34] Gottfredson, *Indian Depredations*, 278; Bleak, "Southern Mission," 1:257, 271–72, 231–34, 237, 239; *Laws, Memorials, and Resolutions*, 167–68; Brigham Young to the Bishops and Saints of Ogden, Cache, Malad & Bear Lake Valleys, BYC; and Lorenzo Snow to Brigham Young, 10 July 1866, BYC.

[35] *RSI*, 1873:424.

their later ouster from northwestern Missouri, and the forcible expulsion of church members from Illinois that brought them to Utah in the first place. Journals, memoirs, and other writings resonate with the pathos that this last "forced removal" provoked. The incredible irony of their predicament is that this last Mormon dispossession was caused by a people that they themselves were then in the process of dispossessing in much more destructive ways than they had or would ever experience. As accounts of these last Latter-day Saint evacuations are reviewed, perhaps echoes of an unrecorded but even more devastating Native American "forced removal" from the very same locations will also be heard.

After hearing Washington County church leaders report on a "mission up the Virgin River" encouraging settlers "to carry out the Counsel of the 1st Presidency in respect to consolidating the Settlements," Charles L. Walker of St. George confided to his journal that he was touched by the faith expressed by the people in exposed locations who manifested their "willingness to leave their homes and possessions." He was equally impressed by those in the larger villages who "were ready to divide their lands with those of their Brethren that had to move in from the minor settlements." "I[t] seems rather hard after battling the sand and alkali and rocks of this desert reigion [*sic*] for four years and just beginning to eat the fruits of there labor to have to pull up stakes and make a new home in another place," he wrote, continuing, "Yet they do it willingly, choosing to abide the counsel of the Holy Prie[s]thood rathr than enjoy the fruits of these hard earnd toils. God bless them is my desire."[36]

Not all were as compliant. Manomas Andrus, for example, the wife of Captain James Andrus, was "ordered" by priesthood leaders to move to Rockville while her husband was away, he having been "called back into Salt Lake for ammunition." As both of her children were sick with scarlet fever at the time, she protested, saying she "would rather take her chances with the Indians" than endanger their lives by moving them in their weakened condition. "Forced to comply," however, she was transported to Rockville, where arrangements had been made for her to stay in the home of a Sister Dennett. Perhaps due to the fever, when Sister Andrus arrived with her children in Rockville, Sister Dennett's house "was all filled up," but she "offered to let us use her cow

<hr>

[36] Charles Walker, *Diary*, 1:260.

shed for a dwelling." "We cleaned it out good and called that our home," Manomas later wrote. But unfortunately both of her children soon died.[37]

On the last Sunday before Glenwood was evacuated in April 1867, James Wareham, the leader of the local congregation, called his people together and sermonized that "the saints always have had trials," passing their impending exodus off as "proof" of the truthfulness of the church. "I do not think we will see each other again in this life as we see each other this morning," he correctly predicted, "for we are going to be scattered in different settlements, and it is no ways likely we will all meet in this life again." "Some think it hard to leave all they have here," he continued, "but it is of little consequence what we do if we keep our eye on the Kingdom of God." Two babies were born as the inhabitants journeyed away from their village.[38]

Jesse N. Smith, the Nauvoo Legion officer who supervised the evacuation of Panguitch, wrote:

> It was interesting to note the changing emotion of the people as they left their homes and commenced the difficult and dangerous march. The young mother turned involuntarily to seek out with tearful eyes the roof that had sheltered her infant's cradle. Nor could the husband pass unmoved by the broad acres redeemed from the desert by his toil, now putting forth the young crop, a crop that should never know a harvest. . . . The lot of these settlers had been one of peculiar hardship. They came out here that they might farm their own lands and no longer work land in shares for their more fortunate brethren. Many had expended nearly all their little property in opening their farms; . . . It was hard to thus give up all for which they had toiled and suffered. What wonder the women wept at the parting. What wonder strong men turned away to hide their swimming eyes.[39]

Describing the orderly relocation of these white refugees of the Black Hawk War, Reddick Allred wrote that "Spring City moved to Ephraim, Fairview to Mt. Pleasant, and Fountain Green and Wales to Moroni."[40] But the demographic realignment sometimes caused

[37] Manomas Andrus, Pioneer Personal History Questionnaire; and "Pioneer, Near Century Mark, Recalls Early Utah Days," in *Salt Lake Tribune*, 10 March 1938.

[38] Sorensen and Bybee, *Founded on Faith*, 24, 26–27; and DUP, *Heart Throbs*, 9:43.

[39] Jesse Smith, "Our Indian War," 20–21.

[40] Reddick Allred, "Diary," 350.

serious frictions. Most of those asked to move did so out of loyalty and obedience to "the Priesthood" and *not* because they wanted to, or even felt it was necessary. Decisions made by priesthood leaders relative to which settlements were evacuated and which were fortified sometimes caused bad feelings for residents of smaller communities, who felt that such rulings showed undue favoritism. Reacting to some supposed injustice, when the people of Monroe were ordered to move to Richfield in 1866, some of them balked, saying "that they was willing to obey council, in anything . . . *but living in Richfield*[;] they would move to camp, move out of the county, or stay in their own settlement, but *they could not live in Richfield!*" As it was, Richfield and the other settlements selected for consolidation that year were already bursting at the seams, and serious tension was created as displaced settlers snatched up every available house, dugout, chicken coop, and shed, until every conceivable "place for cover was occupied."[41] Stresses between the established villagers and the refugees sometimes were expressed in fights between the youngsters of the respective groups. Also, some settlers complained that the refugees boarded with them for months at a time "without paying any Interest."[42] Despite all this, one Sanpete County resident remembered, "Many pleasant acquaintances were made between the people of Fountain Green and those who came to live there during the war period." For him, "mirth and amusement" characterized the time they spent together.[43]

The evacuees ultimately found Brigham Young's mandate to dismantle and bury their homes and fences impractical, if not impossible, and most of the deserted settlements "remained the same" as when they were occupied, except for the grass and weeds, which grew "a foot high in the streets," creating "lonesome" scenes many whites never forgot. For example, gentile Walter C. Powell, a brother of John Wesley Powell, passed through Circleville in 1872 after it had stood vacant for four years. "The place seemed haunted with its vacant adobes, with staring doors and windows," he wrote, explaining that as he traveled down the Sevier Valley he passed "here and there" many "a lonely ranch" left similarly desolate.[44] Most settlements had already planted crops when

[41] L. John Nuttall to Daniel H. Wells, 2 October 1866, TMR, #1545; and Nuttall, Campaign Records, 23 August 1866. Italics mine.

[42] Day, "History of Eli A. Day"; and Weibye, "Daybook," 1 July 1866.

[43] Joseph Johnson, "A History," 3.

[44] Fish, "Diaries," 24; Nuttall, Campaign Records, 21 August 1866; and Walter Powell, "Journal," 476.

their residents were called upon to leave. While some simply opted to donate the crops as "a free will offering to the friendly indians,"[45] most sent work crews back to irrigate and harvest them. "We would go back every couple weeks to take care of things," one Spring City evacuee wrote, remembering lonely times sleeping "on the floor" of that town's forlorn church house. Settlers performing a similar duty at Glenwood "found the silence of the place so eerie" they "could hardly stay long enough to accomplish their mission" and therefore "loaded up their wagon and hurried out as quickly as they could."[46]

Brigham Young's mandated evacuations exacted a very high toll on both the finances and the emotions of his people. As frontier populations shifted, for example, Levi Savage lost rights to hundreds of acres of prime grazing lands in the Kanab area, and for years he harbored feelings against local churchmen who he felt had used Young's abandonment policy to jump his claims. Writing Young on the subject in 1871, Savage invited the church leader to visit the hovel in Toquerville to which he had been banished, stating "you are more than wellcom to such as I have[,] but cream is not as flush with me as it used to be."[47] On returning to Circleville with a company of other Saints "to gather what we had left," Oluf Christian Larsen found "most of the wheat I had left in the bin was stolen as well as doors, windows, and other things." "With a sad heart," he wrote, "I looked upon the remains of what I had expected would be a good home with my hopes badly shattered."[48] After being "ordered to leave" Glenwood in 1866, Robert W. Glenn despaired that already most of his stock had "gone to Black Hawk's herd." Continuing, he wrote:

My losses since the war commenced is about ($1700.00) Seventeen Hundred dollars. I still own a good farm, hayland, house, etc. but all of that is of no use and cannot now be sold for one dollar. I see but a gloomy prospect before me to make a living for my family. . . . I have . . . nothing to keep me here only I can't get away. . . . If I had a wagon and team sufficient to get away with I would start the first company that leaves and not stop in San Pete either![49]

[45] Bleak, "Southern Mission," 1:239.
[46] Watson, *Under the Horseshoe*, 15; Sorensen and Bybee, *Founded on Faith*, 27.
[47] Levi Savage to Brigham Young, 2 February 1871, BYC.
[48] Oluf Larsen, "Biographical Sketch," 48.
[49] Robert Wilson Glenn to Bro. R.G. Clark, 8 July 1866, Manti Ward Record, as quoted in Sorensen and Bybee, *Founded on Faith*, 24–25.

Though some of the evacuees eventually repossessed their towns and farms, many a Black Hawk War refugee returned several years later to rodent-infested dwellings that had been "severely damaged by weather" and were filled with "layers and layers of dust and dirt."[50] When Peter Rasmussen returned to Salina in 1871, he wrote Brigham Young, "When we came back we found most of the houses in ruins, the floors and [doors] carried of[f] by the miners and the last stick of fence burned up by shephurds men and trapers, that staid here in the winters. The dams has all been washed away with the high waters and the old ditches in many places useless, the farming land worse to Grub than it was in the beginning."[51]

While Young's evacuations exacted a high price, they clearly saved lives, and when fully implemented with the rest of his vigilance policy in the late spring of 1867, they almost immediately ended the extensive, frequent, and costly raids that characterized the war up to that point. Oluf Larsen's reaction when he wrote of losing virtually all he had in the world to either Indian raids or Young's evacuation plan can be viewed as representative of the general attitude of the Mormon people; he only half-grudgingly stated that he "gradually got over it and pressed onward anew."[52] As James Wareham prophesied that last Sunday morning before his Glenwood congregation abandoned their village, "The breaking up of this valley will not break us up."[53]

White Cattle Thieves and an Attempt to Treat with Black Hawk

As had been the case the previous year, in the spring of 1867 hundreds of militiamen from population centers in Salt Lake, Utah, and Davis counties were sent out to protect Sanpete County settlers. By mid-April, Kanosh, who by that time had totally given himself to maintaining the interests of the whites, confirmed that the Indians responsible for the Glenwood Massacre "belonged to Black Hawk's band." The peace chief indicated that the raiders contemplated further hostilities, and he agreed to scatter his scouts to watch Black Hawk's movements and "warn the settlers of his approach." Expecting the worst, throughout April and May the settlers carefully protected their stock with the help of the militia. No major raids occurred, however, though tracks

---

[50] Sorensen and Bybee, *Founded on Faith*, 27.
[51] Peter Rasmussen to Brigham Young, 7 August 1871, BYC.
[52] Oluf Larsen, "Biographical Sketch," 48.
[53] Sorensen and Bybee, *Founded on Faith*, 26.

and signal fires made it clear that Black Hawk's own spies were prowling about the settlements. The truth is, the raiders found Mormon stock so well guarded that they had little opportunity to run it off. The Latter-day Saints at last were beginning to fully implement Brigham Young's vigilance policy set forth in the April 1866 epistle—and it was working.[54]

Interestingly, Latter-day Saint vigilance in guarding stock netted more white cattle thieves than it did Indians, and the role rustlers were playing in the Black Hawk War began to emerge even more plainly. Anglo rustlers were so frequently captured stealing cattle on "Indian credit," that newspapers joked about "*White* Hawk's band of Cattle thieves" and encouraged vigilance to keep animals from being stolen by "Indians—both red and white." Reports pointed to the "existence of an organized band of thieves" so large that it operated throughout the entire territory.[55] Perceptive Latter-day Saints increasingly began to suspect white involvement in Black Hawk's raids. Even Washakie acknowledged the influence lawless whites had on the region's Indian depredations. "Great numbers of white men, thieves and murderers, who were outlaws because of their crimes," he explained to Superintendent Head, "had taken up their residences among the Indians, and were always inciting them to outrages; *often leading in their stealing raids.*"[56]

Franklin Head hired just such a man to locate Black Hawk in another attempt to invite the chief raider to make peace with the federal government. Ironically, the last man of this stripe Head sent out to "find Black Hawk" (that is, Richard James) actually joined the chief

---

[54] F.H. Head to N.G. Taylor, 19 April 1867, BIA, M234, 902; and Telegram of Brigham Young to "all the Operators," 18 May 1867, BYC.

[55] CR, 76; David Candland, "The Sanpitcher," (a handwritten newspaper "published every Saturday at Mount Pleasant,") 6 May 1867, CHD; F.G. Robinson, "Manti Herald and Sanpete Advertiser," (also a handwritten newspaper), 4 and 11 May 1867, CHD; *DN*, 29 May and 26 June 1867; and "A Diary of President B. Young's trip South," 26 April 1867. Italics mine.

[56] F.H. Head to N.G. Taylor, Commissioner of Indian Affairs, 30 July 1867, *RSI*, 1867:187. Italics mine. In the spring of 1867, for example, Daniel H. Wells sent a letter warning Latter-day Saints near the reservation that "white men were in communion with the Indians, in the Uintah Reservation." Eldridge, "Biographical Sketch," 96. But such activities were occurring throughout the territory. Erastus Snow, for example, wrote Brigham Young from St. George in February 1867 that he was convinced from "accumulating evidence that a large herd of stolen horses and cattle are gathered west of this valley about the severe Lake . . . [by] a band of thieves who . . . aim to market their stock in Nevada. This county is suffering from them, and Marshall, Hughs and other noted characters now here are closely watched. . . . Salt Lake Police I doubt not are on the look out, if not[,] they should be." Erastus Snow to Brigham Young, 15 February 1867, BYC.

raider and did not return. Head now hired mountain man Lewis Simmons, a son-in-law of Kit Carson who had killed a man in California and lived among other fugitives in the Brown's Hole area near the Uintah Reservation in order to avoid prosecution.[57] Head wrote that he was attracted to Simmons because he had lived in the mountains "for upwards of 35 years," was "known favorably by almost all the Indians in the Territory," and allegedly was "more familiar with the mountain roads & passes than even the Indians themselves."[58] As has been suggested (and as many Mormons believed), however, Franklin Head was possibly involved in Black Hawk's deeds himself; and since it is known that some of the raiders' stock ended up in the Brown's Hole–Fort Bridger cattle market, the superintendent's selection of employees like James and Simmons should at least raise serious questions.

On 20 April Simmons embarked on a journey that took him over 1,200 miles of "Indian trails" in about twelve weeks. He reported that he did not find Black Hawk but had learned that the war chief was "encamped a short distance east of the eastern terminus of the Elk mountains, and directly south of South Park, in Colorado Territory."[59] Black Hawk at the time was said to have had with him "60 men, about one-half of whom are Navajoes, and the balance renegades from various bands of Utah Indians." As further evidence that Brigham Young's vigilance policy was working, Simmons reported that Black Hawk's raids were temporarily stymied because Navajos attached to the Ute chief were now balking at "coming to Utah to steal horses," claiming they could get them elsewhere *"with less trouble and risk."* As a result, Simmons's Indian sources "thought it doubtful whether Black Hawk would return the present summer."[60]

While Mormons did not yet realize it, their defense system was succeeding in breaking the solidarity of Black Hawk's confederation. Stock theft in Utah was becoming hard, dangerous, and profitless work. Mormons continued to perfect complex guarding practices and signal systems and dispatched "spy corps" that carefully watched major Indian trails day and night. Scores of settlements had completed substantial forts and fortified corrals, and, most importantly, they were using

---

[57] Guild and Carter, *Kit Carson*, 193, 196; and Charles Kelly, *Outlaw Trail*, 65–66.

[58] F.H. Head to N.G. Taylor, 19 April 1867, BIA, M234, 902.

[59] Lewis Simmons to F.H. Head, 9 July 1867, *RSI*, 1867:184–85. That Black Hawk was out of the area in June 1867 was confirmed by John Kanosh and other Indians at the Uintah Reservation. See CR, 183.

[60] Lewis Simmons to Franklin H. Head, 9 July 1867. Italics mine.

them. Military drills and target practices were performed frequently in each settlement and substantial numbers of weapons, including surplus Civil War breechloaders, continued to spread throughout the territory. Even Sanpete's Scandinavian population, most of whom two years before did not know how to shoot a gun, much less own one, had progressed to the point that their leaders were convinced "the Indians *Could* not now do the deeds of the past with impunity."[61]

The Fountain Green and Twelve Mile Creek Murders

According to Superintendent Franklin Head's native sources, frustrated raiders who a year earlier found stock theft in Sanpete and Sevier counties an almost effortless enterprise, now were compelled to go north to Cache, Weber, and Bear Lake valleys or south to St. George and the other Virgin River settlements in hopes of better opportunities. Unhappily for them, as a result of Young's vigilance policy, they found these outposts equally well defended. On 18 May, for example, a telegram was sent to "give the Bishops and leading men" of the northern settlements the message that Superintendent Head had learned that "Black Hawk and a party of Braves are on there way north with the intention of makeing Raids on Settlements there, *the Settlements South being too well prepared for them to attack.*"[62] Their work becoming increasingly dangerous and unprofitable, some raiders simply gave up. As early as May 1867 Daniel H. Wells elatedly announced that some of them were finally "desirous of living in peace."[63]

The most persistent raiders, however, earnestly watched the settlements, hoping a moment of carelessness would give them the break they needed to make off with some of the Saints' livestock. As it turned out, some of them did not have long to wait. Keeping up with all the measures Young's defense system required was not easy, and Nauvoo Legion leaders identified a serious problem when they complained that "if any settlement is blessed with peace for a short time, [the People] act just as if there never had been [any] difficulty."[64] But such negligence was hazardous, for, as Orson Hyde put it, "if there is a day's lull or slackness on our part, the Indians seem to know it."[65] Apparently herdsmen at Fountain Green in northern Sanpete Valley and a handful

---

[61] CR, 168. Italics in original.
[62] Telegram of Brigham Young to "all the Operators," 18 May 1867, BYC. Italics mine.
[63] *DN*, 8 May 1867.
[64] R.T. Burton to William B. Pace, 11 June 1867, CR, 162–64.
[65] Orson Hyde to the *Deseret News*, 30 June 1867, in *DN*, 10 July 1867.

of Nauvoo Legion officers stationed at Gunnison were among the first to drop their guard, and on 1 June 1867 two separate incidents occurred that proved fatal for three Latter-day Saints.

That morning, the Fountain Green herd, usually guarded by ten men, was tended by only half that number since their leader was in town "getting his horse shod." Three of the remaining five guards left sight of the herd to clean some rabbits they had killed to pass the time. Within minutes twenty-one raiders (later identified by other Indians as being from Tabby's band) descended on the unwary guards' herd and drove off forty head of cattle and horses. Sweeping the stock off towards Thistle Valley, they killed one of the rabbit-hunting guards as they passed. The new telegraph wire paid off, however, and within a short time militiamen from three different settlements converged to retake the herd. Aware they had failed, the disappointed raiders callously killed as many animals as they could before mounting fresh horses and fleeing towards the reservation empty handed.[66]

That night, four Nauvoo Legion officers carelessly riding from Manti to Gunnison in violation of Brigham Young's instructions (and Nauvoo Legion regulations) about traveling only in large numbers, were ambushed on Twelve Mile Creek. Finding stock nearly impossible to run off, "a small scouting party" led by Tamaritz became frustrated by the Mormon's high state of defense and secreted themselves behind brush barricades from which they attacked the whites. Major John W. Vance, a popular Nauvoo Legion officer from Utah Valley, was shot in the heart and died instantly. Heber Houtz was shot from his horse and unsuccessfully fought for his life while the other two men raced back to Manti.[67]

The deaths of Vance and Houtz caused more attention in Salt Lake City newspapers than any other single event of the Black Hawk War, and some grief-stricken Latter-day Saints passionately insisted that it was time federal troops were sent to punish the raiders. Public outcry, particularly from war-weary Sanpete County residents, caused Brigham Young to once again reiterate his oft-spoken position regarding the United States Army. To Orson Hyde, his chief antagonist on the issue, he wrote:

---

[66] Brigham Young to Erastus Snow, 11 June 1867, BYC; Hamilton H. Kearnes to George A. Smith, 9 June 1867, GAS; CR, 132–33, 144–45, 224; JH, 3 June 1867; Adams, Autobiography, 32–33; and Gottfredson, *Indian Depredations*, 262–66.

[67] Lewis Simmons to Franklin H. Head, 9 July 1867; Musser, Journal, 27 January 1869; Brigham Young to L.D. Rudd, 8 June 1867, BYC; and CR, 148–50.

Our policy has been to say as little to the troops, or to the officers of Government respecting our Indian difficulties, as we could possibly help. We prefer settling them ourselves, for their interference would very likely be hurtful, and might precipitate a general Indian war. The troops that are here could not check the depredations of the Indians if they were to abandon the camp in our vicinity and go in a body to Uinta. We must manage these Indians ourselves, put our trust in God and use the means he has placed in our power.[68]

The Fountain Green and Twelve Mile Creek murders perplexed Young, but his response was typical: "greater care must be exercised by the Saints!" Despite Hyde's conviction that the settlers were "about as well organized for protection and defence as we well can be," Young demanded more, and "Eternal Vigilance" continued to be the watchword.[69]

Black Hawk's Final Raid

As Latter-day Saints throughout Utah intensified their defensive measures to their highest state of effectiveness, Black Hawk and the main body of his band apparently left Colorado and again approached the Mormon settlements. By the first week in July Indian scouts employed by the Nauvoo Legion brought word that Black Hawk was encamped in Grass Valley seeking to bolster his war party with new recruits preparatory to making another attack. Signs of "Indian Spies" and signal fires in the mountains seemed to confirm Black Hawk's return.

Having spent the previous winter with Black Hawk, Antero, the Uinta war chief, apparently broke from Tabby, determined "to take the War path." Perhaps Tabby was not the "peace chief" he represented himself as being, for gentiles at Fort Bridger reported that "two chiefs of the Utes" there were publicly announcing that they were "just about to go down in San Pete to give the Mormons hell."[70] Indicative of a thaw in relations between Brigham Young and the new commander at Camp Douglas and his officers, however, Antero "got chained up" because he said "too much" at Fort Bridger about his plans.[71] Tabby was

---

[68] Brigham Young to Orson Hyde, 11 June 1867, BYC.
[69] Brigham Young to Carl C. Asmussen, 14 June 1867, BYC; Orson Hyde to the *Deseret News*, 30 June 1867, in *DN*, 10 July 1867; and CR, 188.
[70] Jackson, *Diaries*, 185–86.
[71] CR, 193, 206, and 183.

at least outwardly peaceful and continued to tell Mormon interpreters "his spirit has got right [now] and he can visit as formerly all but Bp Snow." Tabby still saw the conflict personified in Warren Snow and Black Hawk and claimed that when they were both dead he could "settle the war in ten days."[72]

On the night of 21 July 1867, in what was to be the last *major* raid of the Black Hawk War, an attempt was made to run off at least 700 animals in Iron County. In terms of the numbers of stock (if contemporary estimates are reliable), had the raid been successful it would have been the largest single raid of the war.[73] Significantly, the raid's failure played a major part in convincing Black Hawk to yield to Brigham Young's vigilance policy and make peace with the Mormons.

On the evening of 21 July 1867 at least three different groups of Indians, each of them numbering "about thirty," entered Parowan Valley and began gathering stock in separate but obviously coordinated forays.[74] There is no doubt that Black Hawk's band supplied the bulk of the raiders, but they were also joined by a considerable number of Tabby's warriors and local Piedes.[75] Guards near the mouth of Little Creek Canyon east of Paragonah discovered one band, recaptured the stock, and engaged the thieves in an all-night battle. Meanwhile, other Mormons similarly foiled the plans of the other parties. In a major coup, one group of Mormon guards chased a second raiding party driving a stolen herd into a canyon, where the pressure of their pursuit forced the Indians to abandon even their own ponies. The following day, another battle took place in Little Creek Canyon, but at last the settlers dislodged the Indians, who then fled in full retreat.[76]

The Paragonah raid was a complete Mormon victory. The raiders were "defeated on all points" and lost "about 50" of their own "saddle

---

[72] Ibid., 223.

[73] One of the guards hired to watch Parowan Valley herds (and hence presumably well informed as to their numbers) noted in his journal that the Indians actually "gathered about 700 head of stock." Fish, "Diaries," 32.

[74] Ibid., 31–32.

[75] After the raid, but before news of it spread to reservation Indians, "An Indian from 'Showan's band confirm[ed] the report of An intended 'Raid' on some of the Southern Settlements by Black-hawk strengh [*sic*] reinforced from Tabbys tribe." CR, 224. That local Piedes were involved is evidenced in Silas S. Smith to George A. Smith, 25 July 1867, copied in Jesse N. Smith to George A. Smith, 13 August 1867, GAS.

[76] For information regarding the Paragonah, or "Little Creek," raid see Brigham Young to Orson Hyde, 23 July 1867, BYC; Brigham Young to Erastus Snow, 24 July 1867, BYC; Jesse N. Smith to George A. Smith, 13 August 1867; Weibye, "Journal," 21 July 1867; JH, 22 July and 13 August 1867; Fish, "Diaries," 31–32; Rogerson, "Bear-Valley Fight"; DUP, *Paragonah*, 90–93; Bate, *Ebenezer Hanks*, 63–65; and DUP, *Heart Throbs*, 6:492.

horses." Not a single Mormon life or animal was lost. As one participant recorded in his journal, the resounding defeat of Black Hawk's
raiders "pleased Brigham Young very much."[77] Indeed, the church
president was elated. "A few such affairs as this, [will] probably induce
them to come to terms!" he rejoiced. Then, reiterating the very foundation philosophy of his vigilance policy, he wrote: "If they find they
cannot make a raid without endangering their lives, they [will] cease
their depredations, or they will at least learn that they cannot commit
them with impunity."[78]

The Mormon victory at Paragonah and the vigilance policy that
produced it stopped Black Hawk cold. Prior to receiving news of the
raiders' defeat, Tabby had repeatedly told Mormons that Black Hawk
was planning to attack Manti. In fact, Tabby declared that the war chief
and his Shiberetches were intent on doing "Mischief to Manti as long
as Snow lives there."[79] However, on 10 August, less than three weeks
after the Paragonah raid, Black Hawk showed up at the Uintah Agency
and told whites there that he and "two other chiefs besides him Who
lead the fighting Utes" were ready to make peace.[80]

In addition to Brigham Young's vigilance policy, there were other
important factors that probably had some bearing on Black Hawk's capitulation. The war chief, it will be remembered, had been seriously
wounded in the Battle of Gravelly Ford. White sources indicate that
complications related to the wound, combined with tuberculosis and
venereal disease, gradually reduced him to a "living skeleton" and eventually took his life in 1870. Although he was still capable of raiding in
1867, Black Hawk's failing heath probably played some role in his decision to stop fighting.[81] The death of cattle thief Isaac Potter may also
have had some influence.

The Death of Isaac Potter

Not long after Black Hawk's band returned from Colorado near the
end of June 1867, Isaac Potter and Mountain requested "some 10 or 15

---

[77] Fish, "Diaries," 32.
[78] Brigham Young to Orson Hyde, 23 July 1867, BYC.
[79] CR, 222.
[80] Ibid., 239.
[81] "Gunnison Ward Historical Record," 21, 54–55; Bate, *Ebenezer Hanks*, 65; Orson Hyde
to Brigham Young, 9 August 1870, BYC; Pay, "History," 11–12; Woolley, "Father tells his
Experience," 1; and Gibbs, "Black Hawk's Last Raid," 107.

Beeves, and a lot of Flour" from Coalville's bishop, William W. Cluff, claiming they represented Tabby, Sowiette, and other reservation Indians. Aware of Potter's reputation, and convinced he was somehow tied in with Black Hawk, the bishop and other Coalville settlers rejected the petition out of hand. The bishop wrote Brigham Young that Potter was part of an "organized band of thieves who steal stock from the residents, travelers and . . . coal haulers." The band, which had "infested" the area for a "long time," all apparently "call[ed] themselves Latter-day-Saints" and, according to Cluff, had "frequently been arrested but hitherto thro' their craft and cunning they evaded the law." The bishop viewed the request for supplies simply as "a Scheeme of Potters, to give him greater influence" with the Indians.[82] About this time, Potter allegedly led Indians in a raid on a sawmill fifteen miles from Coalville, "in which two Indians were killed and two citizens slightly wounded." Charges of "Grand Larceny" were subsequently filed against Potter and two white associates over the seemingly insignificant theft of a single cow. The local sheriff, who had had considerable trouble with Potter in the past, obtained a warrant and attempted to bring the outlaw in. The apostate Mormon refused to be taken and threatened to "call on Black Hawk to [wipe] out coalville."

Taking the threat seriously, the settlement's militia leaders put their men on alert. Meanwhile, they intercepted a letter from Potter to his father (who lived in the area) claiming the younger man had secured a promise from the commander at Fort Bridger that if the Mormons "hurt him [the troops] would come down and clean out the G-d Damed Mormons, and expecialy Coalville."

On 27 July Mormon scouts learned of Potter's whereabouts, and the following day the militia, in a stroke of luck and strategy, captured the rustler, two of his partners, and sixteen native accomplices. The Indians were placed under guard in Coalville's rock fort while the three whites were incarcerated in the local schoolhouse. After dark on the night of 1 August, Potter and his two partners allegedly attacked their guard and broke out of their makeshift prison. In a tragedy that later caused much friction between Mormon Utah and her gentile judges, unknown gunmen filled Potter with buckshot and slit his throat "from ear to ear." One of his associates escaped with a wound while the other was found

---

[82] William W. Cluff to Brigham Young, 2 and 30 July 1867, BYC; and Brigham Young to William W. Cluff, 5 July 1867, BYC.

the following morning face down in a nearby river, his body riddled with bullets.[83]

The exact nature of the relationship between Isaac Potter and Black Hawk will probably never be known. Some sources indicate that before his capture, Potter "was camped on Bear River with a large party of Indians, *among whom was Black Hawk.*"[84] Leading Mormons were well aware that whites were furnishing the raiders with arms and ammunition and "even planning their expeditions and aiding to execute them." As has been shown, before the war Potter employed Indians in an organized stock-rustling operation, causing the Mormon hierarchy to brand him as a "horse and cattle thief, and confederate of Indians." Having lived near and worked on the Spanish Fork Indian Farm in the late 1850s and early 1860s, Potter was well known among the very Indians Black Hawk was most closely associated with during that period. Because of his use of Indians in stock theft, his release from the territorial penitentiary by federal officials in 1863 was seen by some Mormons as an attempt "to involve the settlers in bloodshed with the Indians."

By 1866 gentiles and Mormons employed at the Uintah Agency confirmed that Potter was still "meddling" with the Utes and that certain Indians went so far as to draft him as their "war chief" in raids against the settlements. Mormons living near the reservation were constantly harassed by Potter's thefts and believed he was the leader of "an organized band of thieves" that inspired raiding throughout the entire territory. Some of these settlers were allegedly even told by Indians that Potter inspired the Black Hawk War in the first place by promising Indians "money, Tobaco, Whiskey, and Horses" for driving off Mormon cattle, which were in turn sold to emigrants. In light of these charges, the fact that Potter was frequently seen with Black Hawk's brother Mountain is significant.[85]

---

[83] "The People Vs. Isaac S. Potter," 28–42. For other cases and information regarding Potter and his gang see also Summit County, Utah, Probate Court Records. Offenses, Book A., 3, 21–25, 45–46; William W. Cluff to Brigham Young, 2 and 30 July 1867; Eldridge, "Biographical Sketch," 85–113; JH, 11 September 1867, 2; DUP, *Treasures of Pioneer History,* 4:383–84; Summit Stake Manuscript History; Tullidge, *Tullidge's Histories,* 2:133; Weibye, "Journal," 11 August 1867; *Salt Lake Union Vedette,* 23 August 1867; and "The People etc. Vs. Jacob Hoffman, et al."

[84] Tullidge, *Tullidge's Histories,* 2:133. Italics mine.

[85] Orson Hyde to Daniel H. Wells, 9 August 1866; HOJ, 17 June 1863; George A. Smith to John L. Smith, 24 June 1863, HOLB, 2:242; A.F. MacDonald to William B. Pace, 24 May 1866; Aaron Johnson to Daniel H. Wells, 3 July 1866, TMR, #1536; William W. Cluff to Brigham Young, 30 July 1867; Eldridge, "Biographical Sketch," 103–4; and DUP, *Treasures of Pioneer History,* 4:383–84.

While Brigham Young's vigilance policy and the war chief's failing health played major roles in Black Hawk's capitulation, it may nonetheless be a significant fact that within ten days of Potter's death, the Ute raider appeared at the Uintah Agency announcing to whites there that he was ready to make peace. On 10 August 1867 word was sent to Superintendent Head that Black Hawk, attended only by his family, was eager to meet with him to discuss "a cessation of hostilities."[86] It is significant that Black Hawk sent word of his desire to surrender to Head rather than to Brigham Young. Head and other gentiles learned that Black Hawk was afraid of Mormon "treachery," for, from his perspective, Sanpitch had been "placed in jail, . . . and killed" when he came in to treat with the Mormons.[87]

By 12 August Head was on his way to the reservation, where he obtained a long sought meeting with Black Hawk. Not surprisingly, word of the war chief's change of heart had already spread among the Indians, and Head found that Kanosh, Sowiette, Tabby, Antero, and other Indian leaders had already gathered for talks at the agency, presumably the first time all (with the exception of Black Hawk) had been together since signing the Treaty of Spanish Fork just after the war's opening raids.

According to the superintendent, Black Hawk "was saucy at the opening of their interview" but eventually "toned down" and admitted that he and his men were "tired of fighting, and desirous of a permanent peace." When questioned regarding the number of Indians in his raiding band, Black Hawk responded that there were "28 lodges under his sole control" but that he was also "assisted" by "3 Elk Mountain chiefs, who have each 10 or 12 lodges with them." No mention was made of his Navajo associates, who appear to have left him by this time, and Head was given to understand that Black Hawk had "never had above 100 men" at his disposal. The chief's supporters, Head was told, were scattered throughout Utah still "watching opportunities to make raids."

These Indians, Black Hawk explained, "looked to him as head chief." Giving some insight into the limited nature of his power, however, he stated that he could only be "answerable for his band" but that he "believed" he could get the other "Elk Mountain chiefs" to stop raiding as

---

[86] Bishop Aaron Johnson and Lyman S. Wood to Generals Burton and Pace, 13 August 1867, CR, 239.

[87] Bvt. Col. O.E. Babcock to Maj. Gen. J.A. Rawlins, Chief of Staff, U.S. Army, 23 June 1866, AGO, M619, 454, #961A.

well. This would take some time, considering how they were scattered, but Black Hawk promised to do what he could not only to end the war but also to gather all the raiding bands together "to have a talk" with Franklin Head.

Black Hawk then asked Superintendent Head to cut his hair as a symbol of his capitulation. The chief explained "that he had made a covenant, when he commenced to fight, that he would not have his hair cut, and [that] he had spoken strong of Tabby and Kanosh who had theirs cut like white men; but now that he was going to have peace, he wished to have it cut." Head obliged the war chief's request and "short-ened his locks for him," after which Black Hawk started off "to put an end to hostilities among his followers."[88]

There can be no doubt that Brigham Young credited Black Hawk's reconciliation and ultimately the end of the war to his vigilance policy. In looking back over the previous spring and summer, on 19 September 1867 he concluded:

> We have very peaceful times in the Territory at present. The In-
> dians are manifesting an inclination for peace. Black Hawk has
> had an interview with Superintendent Head and wishes peace.
> *The vigilance which our people have maintained this season in San Pete*
> *has had a salutary effect upon the Lamanites.* They have been foiled
> in several of their attacks and have lost some of their men. It is not
> profitable to rob and plunder under such circumstances. It pays
> better to have peace & have the run of the settlements to beg what
> they want.[89]

Five years later, in a letter to the U.S. Secretary of the Interior, Young still credited the Latter-day Saints' extraordinary Indian rela-tions to "a wise policy" of "kindness" and "redoubled vigilance."[90] From his time to our own, the church leader's Indian policy has been simplistically summed up and characterized by the "better to feed them than fight them" maxim. A much more accurate summation of his In-dian policy lies in his much-used watchwords "kindness," "peace," and "vigilance." His was a policy that demanded vigilance in building forts,

---

[88] Ibid.; Lyman S. Wood to Brigham Young, 14 August 1867, in CR, 243; F.H. Head to N.G. Taylor, 22 August 1867, *RSI*, 1867:178–79; *DN*, 28 August 1867; Brigham Young to Moses Thatcher, 29 August 1867, BYC; Brigham Young to John Brown, 19 September 1867, BYC; and Brigham Young to Henry Boyle, 21 September 1867, BYC.

[89] Brigham Young to John Brown, 19 September 1867. Italics mine.

[90] Brigham Young to C. Delano, Secretary of the Interior, 18 July 1872, BYC.

guarding stock, training settler soldiers, and in treating Indians kindly. "We have had Indian difficulties this season in the southern part of our territory," he wrote shortly after the victory at Paragonah, "but by being *vigilant*, the unfriendly Indians have gained no advantages, while they who were friendly have been kept so by *Kindness*."[91]

In his rejoicing following the foiling of the Paragonah raid, the Mormon leader ranked the relative success of "vigilance" versus simply feeding Indians when he wrote: "Where the brethren are vigilant, they can ward off these attacks with great advantage and teach the Indians a lesson that will do more toward bringing about a peace than any amount of presents."[92] In short, the "better to feed than fight" policy was simply part of a much broader policy—a policy of kindness and vigilance that succeeded in restoring peace without incurring the bloody assaults on Indian populations by United States troops so characteristic of the era.

[91] Brigham Young to William Woolley, 23 July 1867, BYC. Italics mine.
[92] Brigham Young to Erastus Snow, 24 July 1867, BYC.

CHAPTER TEN

The Ghost Dance and
the End of the War

The citizens feel jubilant over the prospects of peace with the Indians. "Black Hawk" and his brother, and "the Indian with the
white horse," and others had been there, and Black Hawk said he
had buried the hatchet and meant to keep it buried. He had found
his heart and it was good. The leading men of the settlement
had a talk with them and treated them kindly, and good feelings
prevailed.

—W.K. Barton, Manti, 1869[1]

Messenger For Peace

NEWS OF BLACK HAWK'S settlement with Superintendent Head was met
with mixed feelings in Salt Lake City, for the report from Uintah arrived simultaneously with word of yet another attack in Sanpete Valley.
On 13 August raiders killed two herdsmen and wounded another as
they ran off forty horses from Spring City.[2] Figuring it would take
Black Hawk some time to spread word of his capitulation, Mormons
waited anxiously for any sign of a change in attitude among the raiders.
On 4 September, however, militiamen engaged in obtaining materials
for a new fort at Gunnison were ambushed and one of their number
was killed. Then, on 16 September, 200 head of stock were driven off
from Beaver.[3] Clearly, three seasons of raiding and the violent Mormon
response to it had spread the conflict beyond Black Hawk's control.
While it was he who commenced the war and was the leading spirit

---

[1] *DN* as quoted in JH, 4 July 1869, 1.
[2] CR, 236–43; *DN*, 28 August 1867; Weibye, "Journal," 13 August 1867; Gottfredson, *Indian Depredations*, 270–75; and Watson, *Under the Horseshoe*, 15–17.
[3] *DN*, 11 September 1867; Gottfredson, *Indian Depredations*, 275–78; and Weibye, "Journal," 16 September 1867.

behind the confederation that kept it going, the fact that the conflict failed to stop when Black Hawk surrendered demonstrates that the raids had become more the general expression of native solidarity and discontent than the machinations of one man.

As usual, Ute raiding activities subsided as winter approached. As they did, Brigham Young was bombarded with requests from the exiled Sevier Valley Latter-day Saints that they be allowed to return to their abandoned settlements. Concerned that Black Hawk was either insincere or incapable of stopping the raids, the church president was reluctant to allow the settlers to return. But when reports reached him that hundreds of gentile miners responding to rumors of gold discoveries on the Sevier River were inhabiting the empty villages and threatening to jump Mormon claims, he reconsidered. He instructed that armed men, but no women or children, would be allowed to return to the evacuated villages in the spring.[4]

In March 1868, Joe and a few other Indians who formerly inhabited the Sanpete Valley nervously returned to the settlements, first making a treaty with Orson Hyde to obtain assurances that they would not be killed by vengeful Saints.[5] Taking Joe's return as evidence that the war had ended, a wagon train escorted by twenty-five heavily armed men started for the evacuated settlements about 1 April. South of Salina, however, the returnees learned firsthand that native hostility had not yet played itself out. On 5 April eleven Indians led by Tamaritz forced the returning refugees to corral their wagons and then fired at them for several hours, killing two whites and wounding another.[6] The defeated settlers returned to their exile in Sanpete villages and Brigham Young decreed that "Sevier County will not be settled this year." In fact, it would be nearly three more years before the Sevier settlers would be allowed to return.[7]

As the spring and summer of 1868 wore on, minor raids and occasional killings continued, but it was clear they were of much smaller

---

[4] Brigham Young to Nelson Higgins, 13 November 1867, BYC; Weibye, "Journal," 12 April 1868; Reddick N. Allred to Brigham Young, 13 March 1868, BYC; and Joseph S. Wing to Brigham Young, 22 March 1868, BYC.

[5] Weibye, "Journal," 19 March 1868; idem, "Daybook," 30 March and 5 April 1868; Andrew Madsen, "Personal History," 72–73; and JH, 30 March 1868, 1.

[6] Hamilton H. Kearnes to George A. Smith, 11 April 1868, GAS; Peacock, Journal, 6 April 1868; Weibye, "Journal," 6–12 April 1868; "Gunnison Ward Historical Record," 23–24; JH, 5 April 1868, 2–3; and Gottfredson, *Indian Depredations*, 279–84.

[7] Weibye, "Daybook," 9 April 1868; and William Morrison to Brigham Young, 27 March 1871, BYC.

magnitude than they had been while Black Hawk led his confederation. In the 1866 Scipio raid, for example, over a hundred raiders drove off 300 head of cattle and horses. By contrast, however, another raid on that same settlement in May 1868 netted "four Indians" only "fifteen head of horses."[8] "Other chiefs with their warriors went on fighting, so the war continued," one settler remembered, *"but hardly so bad as under Blackhawk."*[9] Mormons eventually learned that Black Hawk had in fact done what he promised in August 1867 at the Uintah Agency. But, as he intimated in his talks with the superintendent, he could control only his own band. By the end of May 1868, Mormons learned from native sources that Black Hawk's allies leading the other Shiberetch, Elk Mountain, and Red Lake bands refused to be reconciled.[10]

That some of his associates continued fighting put the ex-war chief in a dangerous position. Eager to demonstrate his peaceful intentions, Black Hawk brought his own band of "thirty warriors" and their families, totaling nearly a hundred individuals, to Mt. Pleasant to meet with Brigham Young near the end of June 1868. The church president appears to have been unavailable, but Orson Hyde met with the Indians in the settlement's "social hall," where they "signed a treaty of peace." Mounted on a new saddle, a gift from Young and Head, Black Hawk left the conference committed to try again to get the other members of his confederacy to come to terms.[11]

Exhibiting strong evidence of the powerful skills of persuasion and diplomacy that had made him a leader in the first place, on 19 August 1868 Black Hawk led a delegation of three Elk Mountain and Shiberetch chiefs (Augavorum, Tamaritz, and Sowahpoint) and about thirty of their men to Strawberry Valley, where they held treaty talks with Superintendent Head and Dimick Huntington. The *Deseret News,* which until Black Hawk's surrender had published very limited coverage of the fighting, suddenly used every opportunity to show that peace had been restored. Reporting that Black Hawk had "faithfully observed the treaty made last year," the *News* jubilantly called attention to the fact that Black Hawk had "not been engaged in any raid on the whites since." The paper similarly announced that "Tam-a-ritz" had been "the prime mover in several of the raids . . . which have been before-

---

[8] Gottfredson, *Indian Depredations,* 284.
[9] Day, "History of Eli A. Day," 11–12. Italics mine.
[10] Reddick N. Allred to Brigham Young, 31 May 1868, BYC.
[11] Telegram of Orson Hyde to Brigham Young, 28 June [1868], BYC, r38, b16, f1; and Day, "History of Eli A. Day," 11–12.

time accredited to Black Hawk. He was the chief who was riding the white horse in one of the battles with the Indians, who was severely wounded, and was supposed to be Black Hawk, at the time it was reported that Black Hawk was killed."

The Indians at the conference "recited their wrongs from the time John [Lowry] abused them in Manti, and told deliberately about their killing this one and that one." The "big talk" consumed an entire day, but in the end Black Hawk succeeding in convincing Tamaritz and the others to "bury the hatchet." In reporting the treaty, however, the *Deseret News* reminded the "brethren in the settlements who are exposed to [the raiders'] incursions" that "eternal vigilance is the price of safety," and, following Brigham Young's old line, exhorted the Latter-day Saints to "keep themselves ever ready to guard their lives, their families and property from Indian attacks."[12]

While the Elk Mountain Utes and Shiberetches met with Franklin Head, similar meetings that Black Hawk had helped orchestrate took place elsewhere. Orson Hyde presided over peace talks in Ephraim; Bishop Charles H. Bryan received the ancient Sowiette, Toquana, and their men in Nephi. Mountain and his band were given beef by the bishop of Coalville, while Heber City residents prepared a feast for Tabby and his Indians. After the Strawberry Valley talks, Dimick Huntington met with other Indians in Thistle Valley. Gunnison's ex-bishop Hamilton Kearnes, father of one of the war's first casualties, took "a good will offering of flour and tobacco" to the deserted settlement of Salina. There he smoked "the peace pipe" with Jake Arapeen, who had rarely been seen since John Lowry yanked him from his horse at the beginning of the war in April 1865.[13] In reporting the peace talks to the Commissioner of Indian Affairs in Washington, Superintendent Head wrote that Black Hawk "aided greatly in finding the Indians and inducing them to make peace."[14]

In the minds of some Mormons, these treaties ended the Black Hawk War. As a result of the conflict's decreased intensity after 1867, white contemporaries disagreed on the exact time of its conclusion. Some felt that the war ended when Black Hawk settled with Franklin

---

[12] *DN,* 26 August 1868; JH, 19 and 22 August 1868; *RSI,* 1868:612–13; Orson Hyde to Brigham Young, 12 July 1869, BYC; and Gottfredson, *Indian Depredations,* 289.

[13] *DN,* 19, 21, and 26 August 1868; William B. Pace to John R. Winder, 12 August 1868, TMR, #1131; *Memory Book,* 45; Gottfredson, *Indian Depredations,* 254; Daniel Jones, *Forty Years Among the Indians,* 168; and DUP, *Heart Throbs,* 6:485–86.

[14] *RSI,* 1868:613.

Head in 1867. Others used the 1868 Mormon-Ute treaties to mark its cessation. Since raiding continued even after these treaties, however, still others variously recorded each successive year from 1869 to 1872 as the year of conclusion.[15] While there are reasonable arguments for some of these interpretations, the evidence makes it clear that related raiding continued until 1872 when federal troops were called in. Mormon Indian interpreter Daniel W. Jones wrote, "About the year 1868 or 1869 there was some little effort made to bring about a peace. Brother D.B. Huntington had a talk with some in Thistle valley who wished peace, *but many thefts and small raids were made after this, continuing from time to time.*" Brigadier General William B. Pace, one of the best-informed Mormons regarding the conflict (as he served as commander of the Sanpete and Utah military districts and, with the exception of Warren Snow, played a greater role in the fighting than any other Nauvoo Legion general), reminisced that the *"Black Hawk War was prolonged from July 1865 until 1872* when a Treaty was finally made with the last [raiding] band of Utah Indians at Fish Lake."[16]

After the August 1868 peace councils Black Hawk returned to the Uintah Reservation, where, according to Superintendent Head, he conducted himself "in an exemplary manner," becoming "one of the most industrious Indians in labors connected with the farm" there.[17] His efforts at the reservation as well as his work to restore peace were part of a calculated program of penance prescribed by Brigham Young. Convinced by his deteriorating health that he would probably not live long, Black Hawk believed he had done wrong in killing so many Latter-day Saints and, as will be seen, he turned to the Latter-day Saint prophet for spiritual advice.

Immediately following the 1868 peace councils, Black Hawk visited his old friend Bishop Aaron Johnson in Springville and had him telegraph Brigham Young asking if he (Black Hawk) was "at liberty to travel as usual" in the Mormon settlements.[18] Obviously answered in

---

[15] For examples of different views on when the war ended see Gottfredson, *Indian Depredations*, 293; "Gunnison Ward Historical Record," 13; Cox, "Biographical Sketch," 24; *Salt Lake Tribune*, 4 July 1897, 27; William B. Pace to "Dear Comrades," no date, but text indicates the letter was read "on this the 12th Annual Anniversary of the Veterans of 'Utah Indians Wars,'" probably after 1910, in Pace, "Autobiography," unpaginated.

[16] Daniel Jones, *Forty Years Among the Indians*, 168; and William B. Pace to "Dear Comrades." For persuasive evidence that 1872 should be considered the end of the Black Hawk War, see Daniel Jones, 166–214. Italics mine.

[17] *RSI*, 1868:612.

[18] Telegram of Bishop Aaron Johnson to Brigham Young, JH, 8 September 1868, 2.

the affirmative, Black Hawk visited Young in Salt Lake City in May 1869. An account of what passed between them has not been found, but Black Hawk left the capital city on yet another "peace mission" to bring in some raiding Piedes "who live on Gunnison's trail and the Spanish trail, west of Green River" to enter yet another peace agreement.[19] Giving additional insight into the nature of his former confederacy, as well as Young's role as the director of his program of repentance, Black Hawk corresponded with the church president regarding his plans to visit "three bands or tribes" living "east of the Moquci [Moqui]" in order to "talk peace" with them. This was an obvious reference to the Weeminuche, Capote, and Mouache bands of "Southern Utes," each of whom had participated to some degree in his confederation. Black Hawk promised to make arrangements to see them, but only if Young wished him to.[20] As part of his penance program, Black Hawk took on the role of protector of the Mormons. In this capacity he warned Utah County Saints that "more vigilance" was "necessary in that neighborhood," because Tabiona, one of his former raiding partners, was on the prowl and had already "stolen six horses from the vicinity of Payson."[21]

On 3 July 1869 Black Hawk and Tamaritz led another 120 raiders to Ephraim to meet with Dimick Huntington. In an article entitled "*Repentant Indians*," the *Deseret News* reported that Black Hawk and four other "principle men" expressed themselves "very humbly and penitently over their past bad deeds, *asking what they must do to be saved.*" Black Hawk said that "for four years they had had no heart, but now they had got heart, eyes and ears, and could both see and hear" and would do as Brigham's spokesman directed. During the talks, Black Hawk and the others asked the whites "who was making bad medicine and killing all the rabbits in the valley, as they are dying off in great numbers." Huntington told them it was simply "a disease."[22]

Black Hawk's question regarding the rabbit epidemic is significant and gives some insight into his "repentance," for, at the same time, smallpox was decimating his Shiberetches. As they had on the eve of the war, the Utes still believed that Mormons used supernatural powers to punish them by sending evil spirits who brought death in the form of diseases. Black Hawk remembered well that Wakara died in the aftermath of the Walker War shortly after he trampled a letter from

[19] *DN*, 2 June 1869.
[20] A.K. Thurber to Brigham Young, 26 July 1869, BYC.
[21] *DN*, 2 June 1869; and A.K. Thurber to Brigham Young, 26 July 1869.
[22] JH, 5 July 1869, 6, and 20 June 1869, 1. Italics mine.

Young under his feet which allegedly threatened that "if he troubled the Lord's people any more, he would . . . suffer for it."[23]

Mormons often used the Utes' beliefs regarding disease and death against them. Benjamin F. Johnson, for example, wrote that he led Indians to believe he killed former raiders with " 'Pokent,' or medicine," expressed in the form of white man's writing. Even the faithful Showan believed that Johnson "had shot him with [his] words," and simply went "home to die." "I was a little fearful the Indians would hold me responsible for his death," Johnson wrote, "but it was the reverse, so much so that they would . . . do nothing without my sanction or advice."[24] Interestingly, as Indians continued to die in droves from various diseases, whites reported that native survivors clamored for "paper," or "what might be termed letters of introduction[;] . . . they insist upon having a signed document to the effect that they are 'good Injun.' "[25]

Brigham Young had on many occasions threatened the Utes that if they did not cease to kill and rob they would "continue to decrease until they become extinct, until there is no man of them."[26] Black Hawk, like most of his tribesmen, never lost his respect for the Mormon leader and took such threats seriously, coming to believe that the loss of tribesmen to disease was God's punishment for Indians who had hurt His chosen people.[27] By 1869 Black Hawk's "consumptive look and hollow cough" convinced all who saw him that he could not "last long."[28] Described that year as being in "the last stages of consumption" and as having wasted away to little more "than bone, hide and sinew," Black Hawk allegedly said, "You need not be afraid of [me] any more. I am sick of blood. Look at me, the great Chief. Brigham Young told me if I shed the Mormon's bloo[d], I would wither and die. I am going up to see the

---

[23] Bean, *Autobiography*, 98, 106.

[24] Benjamin Johnson, *My Life's Review*, 230–33.

[25] Anonymous letter written from Echo City to the Editor of the *Deseret Evening News*, 6 August 1868, in JH, 6 August 1868, 3.

[26] For example, see Brigham Young to Isaac Morley, 7 May 1853, Edyth Romney Typescripts, b18, f1.

[27] John Wesley Powell and G.W. Ingalls, both special commissioners for the Indian Department, visited the Shiberetches several times in the early 1870s. They reported that the Shiberetches (whom they called Seu-a-rits) "stated that their people had been dying very fast of late years, so that their numbers were greatly reduced, and they were specially terrified on account of some disease which had carried off more than twenty of their number in less than a week. . . . Some of their people attributed this to sorcery practiced by other Indians, others to sorcery practiced by the white inhabitants of Utah, but the great majority seemed to consider it a punishment for the petty wars which they had waged of late years." *RSI*, 1873:415.

[28] For example, see JH, 22 December 1869, 1–2.

great chief Brigham once more and then I am going to the place where I was born and die."[29]

Unfortunately, the multiple peace conferences and treaties Black Hawk helped bring about could not instantaneously root out the deep-seated malice existing between the Indians and the settlers of Utah. In fact, hatred fed by the fighting would linger for generations, actually remaining long after the events of the war had faded from the collective memories of both groups. Brigham Young and his bishops preached reconciliation so aggressively that some whites both in and out of the church openly criticized them for it. Gentile Elizabeth Kane, for example, wrote during this period that she "found the Mormons disposed to justify and excuse the Indians" more than she "thought the hideous creatures deserved." Based on Young's reaction to the Black Hawk War, she concluded, "the patience of the Mormons with the Indians surpasses anything we read of the Quakers or Moravians. . . . their whole tone is different from ours."[30]

Typical of a certain class of Latter-day Saints, though, James A. Ivie and some of his relatives maintained a vendetta against Black Hawk and hoped to take his life for killing their father in the Scipio raid. Conversely, a raider named Tabiona (not to be confused with Tabby) also had lost a father in the fighting and sought the life of James A. Ivie. Jake Arapeen himself was killed near Ephraim by some "young" and "revengeful" whites, though the exact date of his murder cannot be determined.[31] While such killing could be concealed from Brigham Young, it could not be from the Indians, and Shiberetches and Paiutes who only recently had been induced by their war chief to stop fighting excitedly sent messengers to Kanosh to ascertain whether the Mormons had resumed hostilities.[32]

Black Hawk himself telegraphed Brigham Young from Fillmore that "Jim Ivie" had "threatened his life." Through the telegraph operator, Black Hawk solicited "paper" from Young "so that he can carry it with him certifying that he made peace agreeable to your approval and if he is killed he may have the certificate on his person."[33] Young responded

[29] Rogerson, "Ending of the Black Hawk War," 3; and Pay, "History," 12.
[30] Kane, *Twelve Mormon Homes*, 40, 120.
[31] Rogerson, "Ending of the Black Hawk War," 2; Gottfredson, *Indian Depredations*, 228, 284–85; *Salt Lake Daily Tribune*, 2 July 1872; Telegram of Black Hawk to Brigham Young, 28 December 1869, BYC, r39, b16, f8; Tabby per Thomas Carter to Brigham Young, 25 August 1866, BYC; and JH, 29 September 1919, 11.
[32] JH, 12 June 1869, 1.
[33] Telegram of Black Hawk to Brigham Young, 28 December 1869.

by telegraph, promising that if the chief and his followers would honor their treaty with Superintendent Head, he would continue to command the Latter-day Saints not to "molest or harm him or any of his Indians." A true believer in "Brigham's medicine," Black Hawk wore the prophet's telegraph message in a leather pouch about his neck so as to hang "over his heart so that if any one of the Mormons shot and killed him, they would have to shoot through the message" first.[34]

Even before Black Hawk formally complained of such Mormon animosity, Brigham Young, who was very much aware of the vengeful feelings of James Ivie and a host of others, directed the ailing chief to visit each of the settlements involved in the conflict to ask forgiveness and convince the Saints that he and his people desired to live in peace. The church president gave Black Hawk special instructions to meet with Warren Snow and others in Manti in an effort to ensure that all things "done in the war be forgotten."[35] In an interesting turn of events, from July to December 1869 Black Hawk, accompanied by Mountain and sometimes by Tamaritz, visited every major Mormon settlement from St. George to Spanish Fork. He had never fully recovered from the gunshot wound he had received in the Battle of Gravelly Ford, and Mormons reported he also suffered from syphilis and tuberculosis. Looking "very feeble" and "seekly of health," and wearing a specially constructed "buckskin belt" to protect his festering stomach wound, the crippled chieftain rode his "peace path." Under the direction of priesthood leaders and Nauvoo Legion officers, "Martial Bands" welcomed the war chief to the settlements, playing "lively tunes for him," which "seemed to please him very much." Repeatedly appearing before Mormon congregations who had once viewed him as their archenemy, Black Hawk now "expressed sorrow" at the raiding and killing but still maintained that the war was "*forced* by [the] starvation of his people."

Demonstrating Brigham Young's control over his people, congregations voted "unanimously" to forgive the former raider, convinced "the Lord had punished [him enough] for the bad deed[s] of which [he] was gilty." Unofficially, though, some angry Latter-day Saints objected, telling the broken chief to his face that he was a "*black murderer*" and "*black devil*," and that they would *not* forgive nor forget! Throughout such attacks, the dying Indian reportedly "personified dignity

---

[34] Ibid.; and Rogerson, "Ending of the Black Hawk War," 1–3.
[35] Weibye, "Journal," 4 July 1869.

in every movement and gesture" and "never batted an eye." Recognizing the danger such visits put him in, church leaders provided the ailing warrior with an armed escort for this, his last tour through the settlements.[36]

From 1868 to 1872 and beyond, such racism and hatred tainted Mormon society and occasionally expressed itself in bloodshed—as it did in Fairview in 1870 when an Indian girl raised by a white family was found in the street with her throat slit. At first the murder was attributed to Indians, but shortly a "Brother Stuart" boasted that he was responsible. In what can be seen as a consequence of Brigham Young's efforts to stop such acts, Stuart was tried six weeks later and condemned to die. However, in a demonstration of the prevalent local feeling regarding the matter, and ultimately the power of the people to countermand Young's will, the murderer was apparently allowed to escape "out of a Window in the Manti jail."[37]

Although they are much harder to document, it is certain that similar attitudes and actions existed among Utah's Indians. Mormons who dared visit the reservation were run off by angry natives who threatened to kill them. Indian Office employees noted that, "with the exception of the old men round the Agency," most of the reservation bands were still "inclined to be hostile."[38] Although he continued to maintain he "never had been at war with the Mormons," as late as 1871 Tabby was still smarting over the deaths of Sanpitch and others he felt were unjustly slaughtered.[39] While aware that a number of their tribesmen had been "killed in, and about San Pete" since the 1868 peace councils and that "some of the Indians wanted to fight in consequence," Tabby and the other chiefs still "said no," and, like Brigham Young, they used their influence to bring the killing to a stop.[40]

But Tabby and his peers were at least as unsuccessful at controlling

---

[36] Ibid.; Manti Ward Manuscript History, 1869; Charles Walker, 1:302; Pay, "History," 12; *DN*, 8 May 1867; Abram Hatch to Brigham Young, 17 April 1870, BYC; Woolley, "Father Tells His Experience," 1; "Gunnison Ward Historical Record," 21, 54–55; Gottfredson, *Indian Depredations*, 227–28; Bate, *Ebenezer Hanks*, 65; Lorena Larsen, "Black Hawk War"; Fillmore Ward Minutes, 26 December 1869; M.J. Shelton to J.E. Tourtellotte, 22 and 29 December 1869, 28 February 1870, and 20 March 1870, BIA, M834, 1; Culmsee, *Utah's Black Hawk War*, 153–55; and Gibbs, "Black Hawk's Last Raid," 107–8. Italics mine.

[37] Weibye, "Journal," 18–25 June 1870; and Peacock, Journal, 24 May–27 June 1870.

[38] Daniel Jones, *Forty Years Among the Indians*, 171–72; and Frank V. Goodman et al. to J.E. Tourtellotte, undated but written around April 1870, BIA, M834, 1, frame #824.

[39] Five years after Sanpitch's death Tabby still maintained that his deceased relative had been "a friend and not an enemy" of the Mormons. Daniel Jones, *Forty Years Among the Indians*, 173.

[40] Albert K. Thurber to William B. Pace, 18 May 1872, WBP.

hot heads among their followers as Brigham Young and his bishops were among theirs. When one of John Wesley Powell's expeditions visited the Uintah Reservation in 1871, an expedition member noted that while "the old men of the tribe are quiet and peaceably disposed," the "young ones chafe at restraint" and "think it an act of bravery to kill a defenseless white man, and glory in stealing horses." A raider named Yank proudly showed the gentile explorers "a wound in his hip received recently while trying to steal horses in Utah Valley."[41] Interestingly, considering the vendetta James Ivie maintained against Black Hawk, Tabiona repeatedly accosted various members of the Ivie family, only letting them go when he was sure they were not James, who along with Warren Snow had become infamous among the natives. On one such occasion in 1872, Colonel John Ivie, while traveling through Nephi Canyon with his wife and children, "was surrounded by a dozen Indians, headed by Tabbona, [*sic*] a well known Ute chief." Readying an arrow, Tabiona "demanded if he was Jim Ivey," but several of the Indians convinced him "that it was not the Ivey in question." John Ivie was convinced "that if it had been his brother they would have killed him, or attempted it, on the spot." [42]

White Against White

Mormons and Indians did not have a corner on rancor. As Black Hawk made his 1869 tour through the settlements, he brought news that soldiers at Fort Bridger were telling Indians that the troops still intended "fighting the Mormons." A few months later, other tribesmen reported that Indian agents in Idaho had "proposed to hire the Bannacks, Snakes, Shoshones and Digger Indians to commence war against the Mormons" in return for "blankets, guns, ammunition[,] Mormon cattle and all the houses and farms."[43] Indicative of renewed Mormon-gentile tension associated with the completion of the transcontinental railroad and an unprecedented influx of non-Mormons to Utah, these rumors signaled an intensification of the attempted manipulation of Indians as the two groups of whites grappled for political control of the territory. In an incredibly complex turn of events, however, by 1872 competition between the two white communities caused both to unite militarily against the Indians. The result was that for the first time since the 1850

---

[41] Stephen Jones, "Journal," 49.

[42] *Salt Lake Tribune*, 2 July 1872; and Gottfredson, *Indian Depredations*, 284–85.

[43] A. Milton Musser to Brigham Young, 25 August 1869, BYC; and Peter Maughan to Daniel H. Wells, telegram, 1 March 1870, TMR, #1201.

Fort Utah fight, the Latter-day Saints and the United States Army co-operated in a major way to put a stop to Ute raiding. The occasional raids leveled at the settlements by Utes, Paiutes, and Navajos (the latter were then aggressively raiding southern Utah ranches) gave the Mormon church the excuse to polish the Nauvoo Legion to the highest degree of discipline and efficiency in its history. Frequent musters, drills, and sham battles were held, and thousands of uniforms were purchased. More importantly, surplus Civil War weapons were aggressively acquired by Nauvoo Legion officers. The simple fact was that Mormon militarization designed to protect the church from national persecution was doggedly pressed forward under the guise of preparation for defensive operations against the Indians. Mormon watchers in and out of Utah were not fooled, however, and many were convinced that the Nauvoo Legion and the federal troops stationed at Camp Douglas would soon test each other in battle.

As part of President Ulysses S. Grant's "get-tough" policy towards the Mormons, Utah's new gentile governor, J. Wilson Shaffer (formerly a successful Reconstruction "war governor" in the South), outlawed the Nauvoo Legion in 1871. "Never after me," he exclaimed soon after his appointment in 1870, "shall it be said that Brigham Young is governor of Utah." Attacking the ultimate expression of Young's power, Shaffer's dismantling of the Legion was an important component of an intricate federal plan to arrest the Mormon prophet, Second Counselor in the First Presidency Daniel H. Wells, and other members of the hierarchy on charges of "unlawful cohabitation" and "murder in the first degree" for their supposed involvement in the Mountain Meadows Massacre. Attempts to prosecute Young on these charges had been made before but had always been frustrated by the Nauvoo Legion. Disbanding the Mormon militia, therefore, was viewed as the first step in capturing (and holding) the church president in order to try him. In preparation for these contemplated proceedings, Camp Douglas was reinforced with hundreds of additional troops, and finally both Young and Wells were arrested and held in custody during the winter of 1871–72.[44]

By official proclamation Governor Shaffer prohibited musters, drills,

[44] Gustive Larson, *Americanization of Utah*, 72–73; Bancroft, *History of Utah*, 658; George L. Woods, Governor of Utah, to His Excellency, U.S. Grant, President of the United States, 2 October 1871, AGO, M666, 32, 1871, 3311–40, #82–89; and copy of telegram of C.C. Augur, Brigadier General Commanding, Headquarters Department of the Platte, Omaha, Neb. to Adjutant General U.S. Army, 2 October 1871, AGO, M666, 32, 1871, 3311–40, #48.

and movements of armed men except by his own order. Furthermore, he decreed that all public weapons be turned over to General Connor, whom Shaffer symbolically appointed major general of the new gentile-controlled "Utah Territorial Militia." Connor, who left the army in 1866, had returned to Utah to pursue mining and business interests. Still considering Connor an archenemy, Mormon officials ignored the order, and for a time an armed clash seemed imminent.[45] The governor's edicts were tested in July 1871 when the Nauvoo Legion prepared to march in the Fourth of July parade in Salt Lake City. Acting Governor George Black forbade the Legion's participation in the celebration and ordered three companies of soldiers and a section of artillery from Camp Douglas to prevent it. Correspondence between the acting governor and the post commandant reveals that government forces had every intention of attacking the Nauvoo Legion had it marched in the parade. Fortunately, the militia backed down, but not before a number of its officers were arrested.[46]

Federal proscription of the Nauvoo Legion left the Mormons in a difficult position as far as the Indians were concerned. When the raiders struck, settlers were *in each instance* required to obtain permission from the governor before they could legally send armed men out to recover stock. Such requests were a major point of contention and in 1871 and 1872 *the governor* often ignored them. The LDS church suddenly had no way of protecting its settlers from the Indians short of calling on the troops at Camp Douglas, which they still viewed as a hostile army of occupation.[47] Early in 1872, however, alarming developments among native populations throughout Utah and neighboring territories transformed the dilemma into a major political crisis that captured the attention of the president of the United States, his cabinet, and the nation's highest-ranking military officers.

The Ghost Dance Religion and the 1872 Crisis

From 1865 to 1872 Indian populations in Utah continued to undergo the catastrophic demographic changes that led to the Black Hawk War

[45] Proclamations of J. Wilson Shaffer, Governor of Utah Territory, 15 September 1870, Secretary of Utah Territory, TEP.

[46] Proclamation of Acting Governor George A. Black, 30 June 1871, Secretary of Utah Territory, TEP; Col. R. DeTrobriand, Commandant, Camp Douglas to George A. Black, 2–3 July 1871, Secretary of Utah Territory, TEP; and JH, 7 July, 1–2, 10 July, 1, 12 July, 1, and 14 July, 1, all 1871.

[47] Brigham Young to William Belknap, Secretary of War, 21 May 1872, AGO, M666, 32, 1871, 3311–44, #150–54.

in the first place. Starvation, disease (including several smallpox epidemics that literally destroyed an entire band of Shiberetches), and the war itself, reduced Utah's Indian population by as much as 50 percent in eight years.[48] War with the Mormons not only had interrupted annual subsistence migrations and thrown social organization into further disarray but also drove the Indians from the settlements where they had formerly eked out meager existences by begging. More and more Indians were concentrated at the Uintah Reservation where federal neglect and agent fraud left them with less and less food.[49] Bewildered by the government's failure to live up to the terms of the 1865 Treaty of Spanish Fork, and cast out by their former Latter-day Saint friends, the Indians of Utah simply had nowhere to turn—except to the supernatural.

In 1870 the Ghost Dance religion, in part produced by the teaching of Latter-day Saint missionaries and embracing an amalgamation of Indian and white beliefs, was exported by Nevada Paiutes to the Uintah Reservation and beyond. Believed by some scholars to be an effort to "revitalize" disintegrating native populations through the process of ceremonially petitioning God to allow the dead to return to their former tribes, "the 1870 Ghost Dance" was a precursor of the more widely known "1890 Ghost Dance" that played such a major role in the Sioux disaster at Wounded Knee.[50]

In the spring of 1870, "three strange Indians" came to the Northern Utes with news that "word is being carried to all the indians, east, south, west and north to not fail to come as they intend to reserect their

---

[48] Utah's Indian population when the Black Hawk War started in April 1865 was estimated at 23,000. By 1872 the number had fallen to 10,000. While these figures are questionable, they reflect an undeniable and tragic demographic trend that continued throughout the entire period examined in this study. See Huntington, "Tribes of Indians in Utah reported by Dimick Huntington," 26 April 1865, BYC; and *RSI*, 1872:439. For information regarding large numbers of Shiberetch deaths see *RSI*, 1873:415, 424; and George W. Bean and Albert K. Thurber, "Report of an Exploration of a portion of South-Eastern Utah, made June AD 1873 . . . an examination of the country with a view to making new settlements," BYC, b34, f16.

[49] Even Franklin Head may have been guilty of malfeasance in office. For information regarding charges of fraud against Head, see numerous letters in BIA, M234, 902, particularly those written during the winter of 1866–67.

[50] Wovoka, the prophet of the 1890 Ghost Dance, is thought to have been a son of either the Paiute prophet who originated the 1870 Ghost Dance or of one of his disciples. See Thornton, *1870 and 1890 Ghost Dance Movements*, especially xi, 1–5, 17–19; and Jorgensen, *Sun Dance Religion*, especially 6, 28. For additional information regarding the 1890 Ghost Dance see Barney, *Ghost Dance Religion*; Dobyns and Euler, *Ghost Dance*; Miller, *Ghost Dance*; and Utley, *Last Days of the Sioux Nation*.

Forefathers and all indians who wish to see them must be there." The messengers said that the huge intertribal gathering would take place "in the vicinity of Wind river—northwest of Washake's Reservation" and that it was "the command of the Indian God and if they do not go they will sicken and die."

Black Hawk, Tabby, Toquana, Antero, and their people joined with Kanosh's Pahvants and headed north, leaving word with a new super-intendent that "the Whiteman has nothing to do with this" and that they had "no evil intentions" but would simply engage in "religious ceremonies." The Northern Utes met with several thousand Shoshonis and Bannocks in their first Ghost Dance near Soda Springs, Idaho, later that spring.[51] Rumors of the huge gathering were misinterpreted by federal officials and even by some Mormons as "a big council . . . preparatory to making a raid of extinction on the whites."[52]

In 1872 the Northern Utes hosted the Ghost Dance, announcing that it was to be held at a sacred Ute site near Fountain Green in San-pete Valley. By May of that year, more than 2,000 Utes from various Utah, Colorado, and New Mexico bands, augmented by hundreds of Navajos, had gathered in Sanpete County.[53] Meanwhile, 2,000 Sho-shonis under Washakie and Pocatello prepared to join them. Added to this, exaggerated reports were sent from other territories that "6,000 Sioux, Cheyenne, and other Indians from the North East," were on their way to the huge intertribal powwow.[54]

While gentiles and Mormons at first suspected each other of insti-gating the unusual native rendezvous, the Indians repeatedly assured both groups that they came simply "to dance[,] sing—pray and offer their ceremonies to Shenob or Great Spirit." They made it clear that

---

[51] M.J. Shelton to J.E. Tourtellotte, Superintendent of Indian Affairs, no date, but re-ceived 23 May 1870, BIA, M834, 1, #843–44; and Abram Hatch to Brigham Young, 13 May 1870, BYC. The Ute-Shoshoni Ghost Dance in 1870 was part of a pan-Indian movement that eventually spread from Nevada to California and Oregon, throughout the Intermountain re-gion, and apparently to the western portion of the Great Plains. See Thornton, 4–5; and George W. Dodge to Charles Delano, Secretary of the Interior, 24 July 1872, BIA, M234, 903.

[52] Peter Maughan to Brigham Young, 24 May 1870, BYC.

[53] Northern Ute bands led by Tabby, Toquana, Antero, Joe, Yank, Tabiona, Kanosh, and several bands of White River Utes under Douglas from Colorado's White River Agency con-stituted roughly one thousand Native Americans. Another thousand was made up of "Nava-jos, Kapotas, Elk Mtn. Utes, and Shiverets" from the Four Corners Region. George W. Dodge to Charles Delano, Secretary of the Interior, 21 June 1872, BIA, M234, 903; George W. Dodge to F.A. Walker, Commissioner of Indian Affairs, 16 August 1872, BIA, M234, 903; and *Denver Rocky Mountain News*, 15 May 1872.

[54] George W. Dodge to Charles Delano, Secretary of the Interior, 24 July 1872.

their visit was "friendly" and that they did not "want to fight any body, *not even San Pete.*" Informed Mormons and non-Mormons were aware that the gathering was inspired by a new native religion which bore the trappings of Latter-day Saint and other Christian doctrines mixed with traditional native beliefs.[55]

The Indians said they had been directed by dreams and visions to the Sanpete Valley where they were to meet the "Voice from the West," a Paiute prophet from western Nevada, who would "foretell the future of all the Indians in America." Clearly inspired by Mormon teachings regarding the future of the "Lamanite," the Utes also told both Mormons and gentiles that the "Indians of America are the descendents of the 'Lost Tribes of Israel,' and lineal descendents of Manasseh, the son of Joseph; and, therefore, they are to be taken under the supervision of the Mormon Church."

Disturbed gentile Indian agents were told that the Utes had "had a revelation from the Great Spirit, through the 'Voice from the West,' that a 'Great White Prophet' [was] soon to appear to . . . reveal to them both their origin and destiny, and tell them what they must do." Many Indians and whites immediately suspected that Brigham Young was the "Great White Prophet" that the "Voice of the West" had in mind. With claims obviously reminiscent of Book of Mormon prophecies that the Lamanites would one day become "white and delightsome," the Indians said further that the purpose of their ceremonies was to ask Shenob "that their skin of blackness may be taken from them and they become white."[56]

An example of the fascinating phenomenon of syncretism, where different religious forms merge, the Ghost Dance religion clearly borrowed heavily from the religion of the Latter-day Saints. Demonstrating the eclectic nature of Ute beliefs, Chief Ouray reportedly once said that "if one religion is good, two religions are much better."[57] But the essence of the new religion had been around for some time and its origins were deeply rooted in Ute tradition. Years before the Ghost

---

[55] George W. Bean to George A. Smith, 1 July 1872, GAS; and Albert K. Thurber to William B. Pace, 18 May 1872, WBP. Italics mine.

[56] The Utes, like other native societies, fashioned the Ghost Dance religion to meet their own needs and to correspond with their own surroundings and beliefs. Considering their proximity to the Mormon people, it is not surprising that the Ute variation of the nativistic movement was riddled with Latter-day Saint teachings. See George W. Dodge to Charles Delano, Secretary of the Interior, 24 July 1872; George W. Bean to George A. Smith, 1 July 1872; and Bean, Autobiography, 1897, 79.

[57] P. David Smith, *Ouray*, 35.

Dance gatherings of the early 1870s, Keneatche, a major chief of the Mouache band, told Kit Carson that the Utes "would all gradually disappear" from their country but would "assemble, immortal, in another world." The chief told Carson "in that country there would be some Mexicans, but no white people, *not one*," adding that

> All the game which the Indians had killed from the earliest periods of time would there reappear; the Indians who had died natural deaths would wear the same appearance they formerly did on earth but the warriors who had fallen in battle would be pale and bloody. And after a while, when all the Indians had been gathered into that other country, they would then come again to this world and dwell here supreme forever.[58]

Subsequently decked with Latter-day Saint trappings, this traditional Ute belief and especially the mammoth native gatherings it provoked were viewed by federal officials to be part of a Mormon conspiracy. To some, it was simply a plot to obtain authorization to reactivate the Nauvoo Legion.[59] But most had more grandiose visions of the significance of the huge concentration of Indians in the Mormon heartland. Special Indian Agent George W. Dodge, a gentile who became a significant actor in breaking up the gathering, wrote that the absence of Tabby, Toquana, and Antero's bands from the reservation was "*ostensibly* because they do not like the Agent," but was "really because the Mormons wish to *drill them!*" The Latter-day Saints, he explained, "fear a conflict with the United States" and "*are preparing for it*" by training Indian troops.[60]

Meanwhile, General Henry A. Morrow, the post commander at Camp Douglas, reported that he and other gentiles (including President U.S. Grant's secretary of the interior) were convinced that the Mormons were staging the conflict as part of "a wild scheme" to have Brigham Young "appointed Superintendent of Indian Affairs for Wyoming, Colorado, Nevada and Utah." According to this theory,

---

[58] Alexander, *Cavalry Wife*, 97, 152. Italics in original.

[59] One officer at Camp Douglas expressed his belief that "the Indians have been brought into the Territory by the Mormon leaders . . . that they might commit some depredations which would enable them to again call the Nauvoo Legion into service." Captain Robert Nugent to Lieut. J.C. Chance, 19 July 1872, AGO, M666, 73, 1872, 2748–2841, #55–62.

[60] George W. Dodge to Charles Delano, Secretary of the Interior, 21 June 1872. Italics in original.

Young planned to "surround his territory" with "a cordon of Indian Reservations," giving him "the absolute Command of the heart of the continent."[61]

The truth is, however, that the Latter-day Saints were at least as alarmed by the huge influx of Indians into the central Utah valley as were gentile government officials, but obviously for different reasons. Initially unaware of the religious nature of the intertribal assembly, many local Mormons thought that their gentile governor was "trying to bring on a fuss between us and the Indians in order to get us destroyed."[62] Others assumed the Indians had at last come to take vengeance on Sanpete County residents. They soon learned from defiant native beggars, however, that although the Indians had grievances, open warfare was not their purpose.

Present in sufficient numbers to enable them to assert themselves, hundreds of hungry Indians descended on the Sanpete settlements belligerently demanding food. Whites were given to understand that, since the Treaty of Spanish Fork was never ratified by the U.S. Senate, native title to the land was *not* extinguished and, as a result, the Indians had "a right to come in and levy contributions on the settlers for rentage."[63] Throughout the late spring and summer, local citizens complained that they were totally overwhelmed by wild demands for presents and sustenance. The secretary of the interior was informed that the Indians had become

> so insolent and hostile, that the citizens were compelled to go armed to their fields and about their villages. No hour of either day or night, [are] the people free from them. Food and presents they must have. Women must rise at midnight, or be ready at any time, to prepare these despotic savages food which they often [require] most imperviosly, and with weapons in hand to enforce their demands.

The panhandling problem was exacerbated by the fact that dozens of unscrupulous white entrepreneurs saw in the Indians a ready market for wagonloads of whiskey and "hundreds & probably thousands of dollars [worth of] Ammunition." What had started as a religious

---

[61] General Henry A. Morrow to General E.O.C. Ord, 20 July 1872, AGO, M666, 73, 1872, 2748–2841, #64–66.

[62] Coombs, Diary, 16 July 1872.

[63] George W. Dodge to Charles Delano, Secretary of the Interior, 24 July 1872.

gathering took on riotous dimensions as liquor-inflamed natives became "so insubordinate that the Chiefs were utterly unable to control
them."[64] As a spirit of drunken revelry and near anarchy overtook the
Indians, the Shiberetches announced their intention "to make war" on
the Mormons "on account of the loss of some of their leading chiefs"
who died of the diseases described above, which they believed the
Latter-day Saints sent to punish them for their involvement in the
Black Hawk War. The Shiberetches, recognized by many as "the remnants of Blackhawks band of out laws," moved off into Grass Valley
with all who would follow them and prepared for battle.[65]

Under such circumstances it was inevitable that interracial violence
would occur, and on 16 June a young Danish herdsman was killed by
Shiberetches. That same week, reports of renewed stock raids came in
from Monroe, Glenwood, Salina, Gunnison, and Manti.[66] With enmity
spawned by years of confrontation still common in their communities,
some local church members were described by a new batch of Young's
peace missionaries as being "very blood thirsty." George W. Bean complained that even certain ecclesiastical authorities "including Orson
Hyde" manifested "such a hatred towards all Indians that it seemed to
me they were cultivating a bloodthirsty spirit while Prest Young and
many of us were doing all we could to reconcile difficulties and exercise
a forgiving spirit towards those ignorant sons of Lamans curse."

Typical of many central Utah Saints, the bishop of Monroe defiantly
told Young's messengers that "he wanted peace if he had to kill every
Indian to get it." He insolently asserted that he was "tired of acting the
squaw with indians any longer and the people generally was opposed
to the policy that has been persued in the past [that is, Young's peace
policy]." Symptomatic of a major weakening of Brigham Young's control over his own people that coincided with the coming of the railroad,
the end of Mormon isolation, and the dismantling of the Nauvoo
Legion, the Monroe bishop declared, "It is no use for men in G S L City
to dictate for [the settlers of central Utah] on Indian Matters!" He closed
by tersely stating "that he never wanted to see a Mormon General in the

<hr />

[64] George W. Dodge to Charles Delano, Secretary of the Interior, 17 September 1872,
BIA, M234, 903; George W. Bean to George A. Smith, 1 July 1872, GAS; and Daniel Jones,
Forty Years Among the Indians, 203–6, 212.
[65] William Holden to Brigham Young, telegram, 19 June 1872, BYC; Daniel H. Wells to
General Henry A. Morrow, draft, 21 June 1872, TMR, #1590; *RSI*, 1873:415, 424; and Bean,
Autobiography, 1897, 80.
[66] Peacock, Journal, 18 June 1872.

Country and there was no power on Earth to get him to follow one into the field as he had done."[67]

As the bishop's comments indicate, the 1872 Ghost Dance crisis actually contributed to a major rift in the Mormon authority system, and in open defiance of church policy a substantial number of Sanpete residents determined that "the People North dont care a dam for the People of Sandpitch," and, bucking Brigham Young's long-standing instructions, they "sent for [federal] soldiers" on their own. Meanwhile, they killed an undisclosed number of Utes to let the Indians know that the days of Young's peace policy were over. Simultaneously, they falsified reports of depredations and otherwise "used their influence to bring about a collision hoping thereby to get the Indians killed by setting the troops upon them."[68]

Quite aware of sentiments in Sanpete County, and conscious that the church was facing one of the greatest physical threats in its history without the Nauvoo Legion to fall back upon, Mormon leaders reversed the long-standing policy regarding the noninvolvement of U.S. troops in the territory's Indian troubles. On 21 June 1872, Daniel H. Wells requested General Henry Morrow of the United States Army to aid the Latter-day Saints "in the present emergency" with "two or three companies of cavalry or such other force" as the gentile commander might "deem proper." Anxious that the Indians not be used by the Mormons against the United States, Morrow cheerfully complied, requesting that "two companies" of the ostensibly defunct church militia aid him in driving the Indians out of Sanpete Valley.

Distrustfully eyeing each other, but forced by circumstances to work together, Utah's federal officials, army representatives, and LDS church leaders joined to orchestrate the dispersal of the huge intertribal Ghost Dance assembly. Though five companies of Morrow's troops guided by Mormon militiamen actually took the field to drive the Indians from Sanpete and Grass valleys, to the credit of careful Indian, gentile, and Latter-day Saint negotiation, a potentially

---

[67] George Halliday to William B. Pace, 4 September 1872, TMR, #1235; Bean, Autobiography, 1897, 81; and extract of letter of George Halliday to [?], 30 August 1872, WBP. See also Ronald Walker, "The Godbeite Protest."

[68] See preceding footnote; Bean, Autobiography, 1897, 79; and Daniel Jones, *Forty Years Among the Indians*, 211. Regarding the falsifying and exaggeration of reports from Sanpete County, George Peacock admitted that "Matters have been bad enough, but nothing to what has been represented." George Peacock to William B. Pace, 22 August 1872, WBP. Also see Daniel Jones, 207. For a graphic example of brutal Indian killing by Sanpete Latter-day Saints see Daniel Jones, 212.

monumental bloodbath was avoided.[69] Lamentably, however, before the 1872 crisis was totally over, at least two more Mormons and an undisclosed number of Indians fell victim to interracial hatred.[70]

The End of the Black Hawk War

As they made their way out of Sanpete Valley en route to the Uintah Reservation, a small band of Northern Utes stopped at the Fairview home of Mormon Indian interpreter Daniel W. Jones. The empathetic white man listened as the Indians told of the recent killing of one of their kinsmen by "six or eight" Fairview youths who chanced upon the Indian while gathering wood several miles from town. "Feeling very badly" about the murder, they expressed their intention to "seek blood for blood." In an attempt to dissuade them, Jones recited "a great deal of the Indian history from the earliest settling of Utah" to his friends, acknowledging that "the first blood shed" between the two groups "was that of an Indian." Admitting that his people had wronged the Indians and that he "fully sympathized with them," Jones gently suggested that "Some one has to be the last or this killing will never cease." Reasoning with the grieving natives, he pointed out that if they killed

a Mormon to pay for it, won't some bad Mormon kill another Indian? Then when am I ever to see good peace? If you will pass this by and let this be the last, I don't believe there will be any more killing; for when the Mormons know that an Indian was last killed they will be ashamed, and the men who killed your friend will be despised by all good people."

Probably motivated more by fear of federal troops than by the Mormon's reasoning, the Indians agreed not to retaliate, and Jones later recorded that he "never heard of their breaking this promise."[71]

Though few contemporaries clearly understood it at the time, the

[69] Daniel H. Wells to General Henry A. Morrow, draft, 21 June 1872; Henry A. Morrow, Comdng Dist. of Utah, to Daniel H. Wells, 23 June 1872, TMR, #1222; Daniel H. Wells to William B. Pace, 17 August 1872, TMR, #1225; and extensive military correspondence in Letters Received, AGO, M666, 73, 1872, and in TMR.

[70] On 10 August three Mormons were fired upon near Fairview. Nathan Stuart was killed, while his companions escaped with wounds. Then, on 26 September, Daniel Miller was killed and his young son wounded east of Spring City by Tabiona and several other Indians. See Andrew Madsen, "Personal History," 79; Gottfredson, *Indian Depredations*, 303, 306–12; and "Killing of Danial [*sic*] Miller," in Richfield Veterans, "Record," 304–9. For some insight into Indian deaths during this same period see Daniel Jones, *Forty Years Among the Indians*, 212–13.

[71] Daniel Jones, *Forty Years Among the Indians*, 212–14.

Black Hawk War had come to an end. The Northern Utes returned to the Uintah Reservation with renewed but largely empty promises of better treatment by the federal government, which included an opportunity for a Ute delegation to personally lay their grievances before President Ulysses S. Grant. The Utes were led to believe the delegation's purpose was to obtain better treatment through personally speaking to the president; the objective of the whites who organized the trip, however, was to give Ute representatives the "opportunity to see the magnitude of the country and the number of our people" so they would "realize fully the utter hopelessness of armed resistance to the wishes of the Government." Government agents originally desired Tabby, Toquana, and Kanosh to make the trip, but the two Uinta chiefs refused to go. As a result, in October 1872, four other leaders, including two former raiders (Tabiona and Antero), boarded a train for Washington. The tour apparently provided the Utes little more than a photo opportunity in a Washington studio.[72]

In the aftermath of the Ghost Dance crisis, the Utes also obtained renewed promises of friendship from the Mormons. But it turned out to be a distant friendship, for the Mormon-gentile alliance on Indian matters ensured that the bulk of the Northern Utes would be forced by the military to stay on the reservation in the future.

Utah's federal officials were delighted with the settlement. Special Indian Agent George Dodge wrote the secretary of the interior that "the Indians, both fear and respect, Government authority and power, better than at any former period." Dodge also was convinced that the Mormons were left with "a more wholesome respect for the Government which has so heartily and promptly come to their relief." In view of "the powerful combination" that he believed had existed between the Indians and the LDS church, Dodge exulted to the commissioner of Indian affairs that "the spell is virtually broken." Looking to the future, he enthusiastically wrote: "I have no doubt but a brighter day has dawned for the Indians *and* the Government in Utah."[73]

The Latter-day Saints came out of the 1872 crisis with their military power essentially obliterated, and the new dependence on federal forces marked the end of an era. No longer would the Utes raid the

---

[72] Henry A. Morrow to Charles Delano, Secretary of the Interior, 24 August 1872, BIA, M234, 903; Gottfredson, *Indian Depredations*, 312–14; and *MS*, 34:756–57.

[73] George W. Dodge to F.A. Walker, Commissioner of Indian Affairs, 16 August 1872; and George W. Dodge to Charles Delano, Secretary of the Interior, 17 September 1867. Italics mine.

settlements without fear of the hard-fisted federal reprisals other Indians in the West had known for over a decade. No longer would Nauvoo Legion detachments made up of settler-soldiers chase Indians through the mountains and seek to keep the conflict to themselves. Compared with the coming of the railroad and the incessant flow of miners into the territory, though, the introduction of troops into the Mormon heartland had little effect in breaking up the isolation Brigham Young had so tenaciously protected.

On the contrary, inviting the army to take charge of checking raids and pushing Indians onto reservations opened a new era for Mormon expansion. In 1873, employing former raiders as guides, Mormon interpreters and cattlemen sent by Brigham Young moved into Black Hawk's former strongholds in Grass and Rabbit valleys and the nearby Fish Lake country. Simultaneously, Latter-day Saint cattlemen followed well-used raiding trails into Castle Valley and streams of new Mormon settlers reinforced old settlements and created new ones in the Sevier Valley.[74] With the army collecting and holding Indians on the reservation, the Saints used knowledge obtained while chasing raiders to storm the barriers to expansion that Black Hawk and his men once fought so desperately to maintain. Of equal importance, the psychological backing the army provided allowed the Latter-day Saints to attempt to tackle another barrier to expansion, and in 1873 Brigham Young launched his first major effort to colonize northern Arizona.[75]

With one eye on the future and the other on the past, Jacob Hamblin analyzed the history of Mormon-Indian relations in a letter to Brigham Young on the eve of the settlement of Arizona in 1873. "When the white man settles the country," he wrote,

> as a matter of course it is where it is the most productive, the same where the red man & his forefathers have subsisted for generations unnumbered. The white man's cattle crop the vegetation that produces the seed from early spring to late winter, from valley to mountain, . . . The game also disappears. Grievances are talked over at the campfire, the women & children beg at the door of the white man, [and finally] necesity drives the Indian to steal. The white man wants to bring the Indian to his standard of civi-

---

[74] For example, see Bean and Thurber, "Report of an Exploration of a portion of South-Eastern Utah, made June AD 1873 . . . an examination of the country with a view to making new settlements."

[75] Charles Peterson, *Take Up Your Mission.*

lization, they are both driven to despiration all for the want of a little understanding. All these evils we have had to contend with, from the Early settleing of this Territory.

At an early day I herd a White man bo[a]st of fattening his horses on seeds taken from an Indian cache. This called my attention to listen to both sides of the question—the Indians & White-man's. I anticipate better results in the future, with our Arizona red men, because of our expirience.[76]

With their invasion of Arizona, the Latter-day Saints would have a new chance, with different Indians, to put Book of Mormon teachings regarding the Lamanites into practice.[77]

[76] Jacob Hamblin to Brigham Young, 19 September 1873, BYC.
[77] See Charles Peterson, *Take Up Your Mission.*

CHAPTER ELEVEN

Conclusion

The Territories around us are involved in Indian difficulties, and they are strenuously in favor of the exterminating policy. It is a cruel policy and a very expensive one. The costliest way of managing the Indians, in blood and treasure, is to exterminate them. We have Indian troubles to contend with, yet they are caused by a comparatively small number of the savages in this Territory. If we were to adopt the policy advocated and urged by many of our surrounding neighbors, offer a scalp bounty, of $20 each, as the citizens of Central, Colorado, have done, and seek to "wipe out" the Indians, innocent and guilty, all the friendly savages in our Territory would soon be numbered with Black Hawk and his outlaws, and we would have an Indian war of dimensions sufficiently large to make the existence of many of our settlements an impossibility.

It will not do to give way to feelings of revenge, and, stooping to the level of the savage, make war upon him according to his own barbarous code. The policy that has characterized our settlement of these valleys up to the present, with the Indians, has enabled us to live in an Indian country and have less difficulty with the aborigines, than the history of the settlement of any other State or Territory in the Union can show, except the settlement made by Penn and his followers.

Because of the humane policy which we have adopted, we have been at peace with the Indians when others around us have been at war with them, and we have been falsely charged with complicity in their outrages on whites in consequence; and there are men today, here in our midst and elsewhere, reckless enough to charge us with complicity in every outrage committed by Indians between this city and the Missouri. If we were not actually in conflict with the savages ourselves, were such charges made, they would be as false now as they have ever been, but wisdom inculcates that, as a people, we should hold to the policy which we have proved to be so good, and act according to the counsel of our leaders, who have, by the wisdom of God, turned aside many a threatening evil.

—Deseret News, 1867[1]

The Uneasy Triangle

IN THE FALL OF 1871 Mormon Indian interpreter Daniel W. Jones risked his life on a special mission of peace assigned by the church's First Presidency to disgruntled Indians on the Uintah Reservation. Though warned away on the threat of death, Jones courageously stayed and eventually obtained an interview with fourteen admitted raiders. After giving details of their personal involvement in the fighting, the men acknowledged that "hunger" forced them to steal cattle so they could "eat." "Each taking his turn in talking," the raiders complained that gentile "agents stole what 'Washington' sent them [and] that Mormons helped the agents to steal." Furthermore, the Latter-day Saints "had stolen their country and fenced it up," turning the lands where their fathers were buried into "wheat fields." Worst of all, when the Indians asked "for some of the bread raised on their [own] lands" the settlers "insulted them, calling them dogs and other bad names."[2]

The Black Hawk War in reality was much more complex than the raiders articulated. As part of a fluid, dynamic, and extended Native American community, the Indians of Utah were in close communication with other western tribes and were responding to white expansion as part of the larger group. As has been shown, however, factors unique to Utah made the war an anomaly in western history. An intricate set of political conditions enabled Black Hawk and others to carry on their raiding for almost eight years with little threat of the bloody federal military reprisals that other Native Americans experienced on all sides of the Mormon heartland during the same period. In large measure, the war erupted and was sustained as the result of an uneasy, dynamic, and oftentimes volatile triangle that formed as Mormons, gentiles, and Indians maneuvered for position in the Territory of Utah.

It was a credit to Black Hawk's political acumen that he and his raiders exploited these conditions so adroitly that they enjoyed a degree

---

[1] *DN*, 12 June 1867; also in JH, 12 June 1867, 4–5.
[2] Daniel Jones, *Forty Years Among the Indians*, 169–94, especially 190–92.

of raiding success unattainable anywhere else in the region, as a result driving thousands of stolen cattle and horses over the Old Spanish Trail towards the Santa Fe market. Not surprisingly, when the 1872 Ghost Dance crisis forced a greater degree of Mormon-gentile cooperation (essentially collapsing the triangle—at least as far as Indian relations were concerned), Northern Ute raiding was immediately brought to a standstill. "The Mormons are too glad to be protected in person and property now," wrote one gentile that year, "to call 'Americans'— the loyal citizens of the country—'No good.' "[3] Until then, the federal military had largely left the Mormons to deal with their Indian troubles on their own, but the army's 1872 success in quelling the Ghost Dance crisis brought a new commitment to employ troops against the Indians in Utah, if for no other reason than to keep the Nauvoo Legion from having an excuse to function. As General Henry Morrow wrote in an 1873 request for more troops that ended up on the desk of the secretary of war, "an Indian Scare in Utah leads . . . to Political [and] Military complications. It always brings up *the question of the local Militia* upon which the General Government has expressed itself *decidedly*."[4]

Mormon-Indian Relations

The unique religious beliefs of the Latter-day Saints regarding Indians added other anomalous and intriguing dimensions to the conflict. Even before their arrival in Utah in 1847, Mormons believed their relations with Indians to be superior to those of *all* other groups of whites. "History does not show that a colony was ever settled, either in North or South America," Brigham Young boasted on the eve of the Black Hawk War, "that had so little difficulty with the Indians as we have had." Even at the height of the fighting, Mormons exulted that the raids involved only *"a comparatively small number* of the savages in this Territory." For years the church leader and his associates insisted that "better conduct and a more perfect walk ought to be expected from us" because of Book of Mormon teachings regarding the history and destiny of the Lamanite.[5]

At the close of the 1872 Ghost Dance crisis that ended the Black

---

[3] George W. Dodge, U.S. Special Indian Agent, to F.A. Walker, Commissioner, 16 August 1872, BIA, M234, 903.

[4] General Henry A. Morrow, Camp Douglas, to A.A. General, Dept. of the Platte, 27 April 1873, and attached endorsements, BIA, M234, 904. Italics mine.

[5] *JD*, 10:336, 3:287–88, and 11:263; *DN*, 12 June 1867, also in JH, 12 June 1867, 4–5. Italics mine.

Hawk War, like so many gentiles before him, General Morrow wrote, "I think I may say with truthfulness, that there is not another American community in the nation which would have endured half the [Indian] outrages these people endured, before rising up as one man to drive out the savage invaders at the point of the bayonet." Elizabeth Kane, also a gentile, wrote that same year, "I really think the patience of the Mormons with the Indians *surpasses anything we read of the Quakers or Moravians.* You never hear the Mormon younkers boast of prowess at the savages' expense; *their whole tone is different from ours.*"[6] Like gentile Superintendent of Indian Affairs Orsemus Irish, Kane and Morrow affirmed that "the fact exists, however much some might prefer it should be otherwise, that [Brigham Young] has pursued so kind and conciliatory a policy with the Indians, that it has given him great influence over them."[7] What these gentile observers were noting was an actual and perceivable difference in how Mormons treated Indians *in comparison* with how the general American population treated them.

Unfortunately, however, this was simply a matter of *degree.* As this study has shown, despite Mormon doctrine and the constant goading of the church's leaders, it took "very little to rouse in some [Latter-day Saints] a disposition to kill and destroy" their native neighbors in much the same spirit and manner as did non-Mormons throughout the West during the same period. The truth is, the failure of the settlers of Utah to put their beliefs into practice was a major factor in both precipitating the Black Hawk War and in ensuring its continuation. Brigham Young repeatedly admitted that "if the Elders of Israel had always treated the Lamanites as they should" the Saints would have had no "difficulty with them at all."[8]

As it was, Brigham Young was forced to concede that it was much easier to "gather the people" to Zion through preaching the gospel than "to make Saints" of them once they got there.[9] In the end, the failure of the Mormon people to live up to their religious ideals relating to Indians is perhaps the most provocative evidence that can be found of the limitations of Brigham Young's actual power over his people. Gentile John Codman expressed a notion held almost universally by

[6] Henry A. Morrow to George W. Dodge, 7 September 1872, in *DN,* 25 September 1872. Kane, *Twelve Mormon Homes,* 120. Italics mine.
[7] O.H. Irish to William P. Dole, 29 June 1865, in *RSI,* 1865:318.
[8] *JD,* 11:263, 3:287–88.
[9] Coombs, Diary, 10 June 1865.

Young's contemporaries both in and out of the church when he wrote
that the prophet had his people's

> confidence not only in everything pertaining to heaven above, but
> on the earth beneath.
>   He is a priest and king, bishop and farmer, minister and manu-
> facturer—theoretical in religion and practical in all the affairs of
> life. When he has a revelation of a new doctrine, the people be-
> lieve it. When he counsels a new mode of irrigation, they dig the
> ditch. When he preaches morality, they practice it, and when he
> wants woollen-mills and railroads, they build them.[10]

Though touted by Mormons and gentiles alike, Brigham Young's
influence, despite his unusual theocratic power, at least when it came to
restraining the hatreds of his people, resembled more that of Tabby
and Black Hawk after they made peace than that of the absolute spiritual and temporal dictator he is often made out to have been. As we
have seen, neither Young, Tabby, nor Black Hawk had anything
approaching absolute control over their people when it came to
squelching hatred or mandating peace.

Instead, Young's conciliatory policies towards the Indians during the
Black Hawk War actually weakened his influence in Sanpete County
and other areas affected by the fighting and even caused some of his
people to leave the church. Bernard Snow, for example, described by
gentiles as "a seceder from the Mormon church," circulated a petition
among Sanpete Valley Latter-day Saints in 1873 condemning Young's
Indian policy and calling for tough federal military action against
Utah's native inhabitants should they ever step out of line again. In a
significant show of disobedience in theocratic Utah, 175 "residents of
Ephraim, Spring City, Mt. Pleasant, Fairview, and Fountain Green"
flaunted Young's injunctions against settlers dealing directly with
Camp Douglas's military officers by signing a petition addressed to
General Henry A. Morrow, the post commandant. Snow wrote that he
obtained the signatures "by barely passing through" each settlement,
"presenting it to such as I chanced to meet." With a little work he was
sure he "could obtain four times this number."

Snow and his fellow petitioners cited the "uniform kindly mode of
treatment" Brigham Young had forced them to show the Indians over

---

[10] Codman, *Mormon Country*, 142.

the years and complained that "long time, and close observation" had taught them that the Indians "mistake our deeds of mercy and kindness" for "servile acts, prompted only by our fear." They reasoned that hostilities during the Black Hawk War were designed to increase this fear: "It is a very necessary conclusion with [the Indians], that the more horrible their deeds[,] the greater will be our fear, and correspondingly large our gifts, as the alternative of fighting them." Striking directly at Young's policy, Snow wrote that it was "easy to perceive that the present mode of [kind] treatment aggravates" the situation. "We are fully convinced," the packet of signatures and letters sent to General Morrow read, "that all attempts to bring the indian to permanent terms of peace, and wean him of his thieving and murdering propensities, without first giving him a sound and thorough drubbing, . . . will prove futile." Hence they petitioned Morrow to reverse Young's peace policy.

Snow wrote that this was "the universal feeling" of Sanpete, if he excepted "a few spiritual heads, who are bound to follow the pet ideas of Brigham Young, or loose their offices" in the priesthood. Snow wrote that even most local ecclesiastical leaders supported his petition but that he had "studiously avoided" asking for their signatures to keep from "placing their necks upon the block of the priestly guillotine." Significantly, the petition and accompanying papers were reviewed by the nation's highest-ranking military leaders, including Generals Edward O.C. Ord, E.D. Townsend, Philip H. Sheridan, William T. Sherman, and even Secretary of War William W. Belknap, most of whom agreed that despite the claims of "(Brigham Young, to the contrary notwithstanding) the Indians grow worse the better they are treated."[11]

Though he did not sign the petition, these sentiments doubtless were shared by Orson Hyde, the president of the Quorum of the Twelve Apostles, who, after Brigham Young and his counselors in the First Presidency, was the highest-ranking Latter-day Saint ecclesiastical leader. Of the feelings exhibited in Sanpete County against Young's policies at the end of the Black Hawk War, George W. Bean wrote:

> I was surprized and really offended at the hostile spirit of the parties and of certain authorities in Sanpete, including Elder Orson Hyde [who] manifested such a hatred towards all Indians that it seemed to me they were cultivating a bloodthirsty spirit while Prest Young and many of us were doing all we could to reconcile

[11] See Lt. Col. Henry A. Morrow, Head Quarters Camp Douglas, to A.A. General, Dept. of the Platte, 27 April 1873, and accompanying petition and papers, in BIA, M234, 904.

difficulties and exercise a forgiving spirit towards those ignorant sons of Lamans curse. Shortly after, I was with Prest Young on a free excursion on the U[tah] C[entral] R[ail] R[oad] to Ogden and I gave him a chapter of my experience in those lines and he felt quite sad to learn of the Sanpete spirit still being cultivated but remarked that while Elder Hyde lived it was likely to remain.[12]

From the start, Brigham Young saw something divine in his people's troubles with the Indians. "I certainly believe that the present affliction, which has come upon us from the Indians," he said at the height of the Black Hawk War, "is a consequence of the wickedness which dwells in the hearts of some of our brethren."[13] To him the war was a providential punishment challenging his people "to repent" and take the obligations more seriously that were put upon them by the Book of Mormon and the revelations of Joseph Smith regarding the Lamanites. "Let the Indians live," he thundered again and again, and let the Saints "help them to live!"[14]

Brigham Young's Indian Relations

No matter how one judges Brigham Young's controversial Indian relations, it cannot be denied that his deportment towards the Indians, from the way he doggedly raised "the standard of peace" to how he waged war against them, was in close harmony with religious principles revealed by Joseph Smith in the Book of Mormon and the *Doctrine and Covenants*. Nearly a third of the Book of Mormon deals with the principles of war, and Young clearly used it as his handbook. His policies of colonization, expansion, fort building, abandonment, consolidation, quick chastisement followed by offers of peace, and even his hostage policy, can all be found in the Book of Mormon, as can also his policy of unbegrudgedly forgiving past wrongs. Similarly, the *Doctrine and Covenants* contains significant instructions on war. As has been pointed out, Young's thinking, motivations, and actions, as well as the military maneuvers he ordered, simply cannot be fully understood or adequately assessed without some concept of unique Latter-day Saint religious notions relative to war and peace. Significantly, the Black Hawk War provides the best opportunity available to observe these principles at work.

[12] Bean, Autobiography, 1897, 81. Italics mine.
[13] *JD*, 11:263.
[14] Ibid., 265.

While Brigham Young may not have been totally true to late-twentieth-century notions of fairness to Indians, he was true to his own religious ideals. "If they repent," he repeatedly told his people regarding the Indians, "according to the revelations given to us we are bound to forgive them." The fact that men like Black Hawk and Tamaritz were not hung or imprisoned, as their counterparts often were following conflicts outside of Mormon country, is significant (and in total harmony with Latter-day Saint scriptural teachings). Former raiders were welcomed by Young into his settlements, and, as has been shown, he did his best to protect them from the most vengeful of his people. This notwithstanding, however, probably more than the record shows met the same fate as Jake Arapeen, who was vindictively killed *after* he made peace.

"The feeling, which is too common under such circumstances, is one of vengeance," Brigham Young told the legislature of the ghost state of Deseret after the war's first season. The "merciless policy" of a "vengeance that does not distinguish the innocent from the guilty, but visits all of the same nation and color with indiscriminate punishment" would "always be discarded" if the Saints "were true to themselves and [their] common humanity." The church leader continued: "We have proved that the pacific, conciliatory policy is in every sense the better course for us to pursue. Experience has taught us that it *is* cheaper to feed Indians than to fight them—a statement that has been so often repeated that it has become a recognized axiom among us."[15]

Black Hawk himself affirmed the doctrine Mormons preached but did not always practice. While making his "peace path" tour through the Mormon settlements in 1869, the dying chief arrived in Parowan just after Navajo raiders had made off with some of the villagers' horses. "He told us to catch the Navajoes, if we could, when they came to steal," one settler wrote to the *Deseret News*. But Black Hawk warned them *not to kill* the raiders, "but talk to them and show that we do not desire to shed blood; send them back to their home and friends to tell what was said to them." Based on experience, Black Hawk emphatically stated that such a course "would do *far more good* than killing them." "This is good advice," the *Deseret News* editorialized, "but comes with rather a bad grace from such a quarter."[16]

[15] "Governor's Message to the General Assembly of the State of Deseret [1866]," in Alter, "The Mormons and the Indian," 65.

[16] JH, 22 December 1869, 1–2. Italics mine.

For the president of the Mormon church, nurturing Indians in the gospel of Jesus Christ, and more particularly getting his people to do so in love, were matters that required great patience. "We cannot come to a knowledge of the truth in one year," he said; "neither can we bring them to a knowledge of God all at once. It will take time and a great deal of patience to accomplish this great work." In fact, he prophesied that it would "take the patience of Job," and he repeatedly emphasized that "we cannot hurry these matters."[17] Filled with the indomitable optimism for which he was known, at the very zenith of the Black Hawk War's interracial violence he enthusiastically urged his people: "Let us set an example" in Indian relations "for all mankind to follow in the high road to peace, love, union, fellowship, and confidence."[18]

While some of his people may have failed to treat the Indians kindly, Brigham Young's own Indian relations were extraordinary. Acknowledging from the outset that he was settling Latter-day Saints on Indian lands, Young went to great lengths to see that his people treated the Lamanites kindly and shared with the Indians their own limited resources. When Latter-day Saint blood was shed in the war's initial raids, he repeatedly sought peaceful solutions. Driven to desperation by continued killings, stock thefts, and major displacement of his own people, at times he took a hard line against the Indians, though throughout the war he held out an undeviating offer to "square off" and unbegrudgingly end the fighting. Despite the fact that the intense challenges he faced sometimes tainted his humane goals and actions with ambiguity, Brigham Young was certainly an anomaly in a nation awash in a sea of Indian bloodletting.

The Hungate and Thistle Valley Massacres Compared

A case-in-point comparison may be helpful. In May 1865 Black Hawk and his raiders killed six members of the Given family in what became known as the Thistle Valley Massacre. Less than six months before, a similar event known as the Hungate Massacre transpired in Colorado; it was named for a family of four murdered near Denver by Arapaho and Cheyenne raiders. Brigham Young responded to the Utah situation by sending Dimick Huntington and his own son Joseph to make peace with the Indians while he dispatched special peace missionaries

---

[17] James W. Cummings, "A Journal of the Travels of Prest. B. Young and Company from Great Salt Lake City, U. T. to Fort Limhi in Oregon Territory, on Salmon River, April 24, 1857," in "Minutes," vol. 1., Edyth Romney Typescripts, b24.
[18] *JD*, 11:265.

to encourage the Latter-day Saints to lay aside their vengeful feelings. In Colorado, on the other hand, the scalped and bloated bodies of the Hungates were paraded through the streets of Denver, and the leaders of both church and state, including "the fighting parson" John Chivington, worked the people up to *demand vengeance*. In contrast to Brigham Young's sending out offers of reconciliation and quieting his people, Chivington (a former missionary and important minister in the largest Protestant church in America and, when he first volunteered for military service, the presiding elder of Denver's First Methodist Episcopal Church and the Methodist district superintendent in Denver) led an attack in which a band of several hundred Cheyenne and Arapaho *noncombatants* were brutally massacred in what became known as the Sand Creek Massacre. Subsequently, as Young's *Deseret News* worked to allay vengeful feelings and threatened Indian killers with excommunication, the *Denver Rocky Mountain News* exonerated the actions at Sand Creek and its readers elected Indian killers to high office.[19]

The Squaw Fight in Utah's Grass Valley that followed the Thistle Valley Massacre can be viewed as a small-scale corollary to the Sand Creek Massacre, since ten Indian men and an undisclosed number of women and children were killed. But, in the Utah setting, Warren Snow, knowing he would have to answer to Brigham Young, stopped his war-crazed men (whose orders were "to let the innocent go free"). During the fight, but after all the Indian males had been silenced, Snow ordered his men to form "a hollow square," where he harangued them, forbidding them to continue injuring women and children. When some of his men refused to submit to these orders, he had them forcibly arrested.[20] In contrast, "previous to the slaughter" at Sand Creek, Chivington "addressed his command, *arousing in them by his language all their worst passions*," saying himself that he longed *"to be wading in gore."*[21] Eyewitnesses repeatedly affirmed that as Chivington worked up the feelings of his men moments before the attack at Sand Creek, he told

---

[19] See Burkey, "Murder of the Hungate Family," 139–42; Tinker, *Missionary Conquest*, 5; Svaldi, *Sand Creek*; Berthrong, *Southern Cheyennes*; Hoig, *Sand Creek Massacre*; Scott, *Blood at Sand Creek*; and U.S. Congress, *Evidence taken at Denver, 1864*. "John Milton Chivington was a preacher. He was an ordained minister in the largest Protestant church in America, the Methodist-Episcopal Church with its more than three million members. But he was more than merely a minister, he was a respected church leader; a senior Elder who began to have a tremendous impact on the church very early in his career." Scott, *Blood at Sand Creek*, 31. For other references to Chivington's ecclesiastical positions see Svaldi, 281; and Tinker, 5.

[20] Seeley, "History," 4–6.

[21] U.S. Congress, *Evidence taken at Denver, 1864*, 123, 117. Italics mine.

them, "I don't tell you to kill all ages and sexes, but look back on the plains of the Platte, where your mothers, fathers, brothers, sisters have been slain, and [think of] their blood saturating the sands."[22] In contrast to Snow's efforts to check the brutality of his men, in the Colorado setting Chivington and other militia and federal military leaders did nothing as their men scalped, disemboweled, and hacked to pieces the dead, "the most horrible" types of mutilation becoming "very near a general thing."[23] Hearings in Denver gathered testimony that ears, fingers, noses, and "private parts" were cut from the dead warriors and children, "while the dead bodies of females [were] profaned in such a manner that the recital is sickening; *Colonel J.M. Chivington all the time inciting his troops to these diabolical outrages.*"[24]

The purpose of this comparison is not to suggest that all gentiles were like the Sand Creek murderers or that all Mormons followed the teachings of Brigham Young, for ample evidence to controvert both notions is easily obtained. It is, rather, to demonstrate the positive influence that a man with the theocratic power Young held could and did have in *ameliorating* the traditional white response to the Indian dilemma in the American West. There were certainly others, coming from a host of different religious, cultural, and social backgrounds, who had similar or even more benign attitudes and behaviors towards Indians than did the Mormon prophet, but no one in the West was in the position to exercise them in such a powerful way, or over such an extent of country, or for such a duration, as was Brigham Young.

Significantly, there was no comparable extended war like Black Hawk's in Colorado, or in any other neighboring territory or state for that matter, because when Indians got out of line there, they were quickly destroyed by federal forces. With Sand Creek and similar demonstrations of federal and territorial power in mind, at the very pinnacle of his people's bad feeling for Indians, Brigham Young declared:

> We could circumscribe their camps and kill every man, woman and child of them. This is what others have done, and if we were to do it, what better are we than the [gentiles]? It is our duty to be better than them in our administrations of justice and our general conduct toward the Lamanites. It is not our duty to kill them; but it is our duty to save their lives and the lives of their children. . . .

---

[22] For example, see ibid., 68–69.

[23] Ibid., 112, 122.

[24] Ibid. in its entirety, but especially 113, 117, 122–24, 129–30, 139–40, 145. Italics mine.

We should now use the Indians kindly, and deal with them so gently that we will win their hearts and affections to us more strongly than before; and the much good that has been done them, and the many kindnesses that have been shown them, will come up before them, and they will see that we are their friends.[25]

These words are perhaps best seen when viewed in comparison to those of gentile ecclesiastical leaders in the Denver area on the eve of the Sand Creek Massacre. Representative of Chivington and others, the Reverend William Crawford, "a circuit-riding preacher representing the American Home Missionaries," wrote that among the Christians of Colorado there was but "one sentiment in regard to the disposition of the Indians; let them be exterminated, men, women and children!" "They are regarded [here] as a race accursed like the ancient Canaanites, devoted of the Almighty to utter destruction," he continued. "The grace of God may be sufficient for them, but humanly speaking, there seems no better destiny ahead [for the Indians] than to fade away before the white man.[26]

In an interesting twist, it was only Brigham Young's peace policy, and his related strategy of keeping federal soldiers out of the conflict, that ever allowed such a war as Black Hawk's to occur in the first place. In this sense it can be argued that Young's policies, though designed to produce the opposite effect, actually helped cause the war and worked to protract it once under way. Representative of more blatant ambiguities that characterized his Indian relations, the killings Brigham Young directed through the Nauvoo Legion also played significant roles in the war's escalation and continuation.

A Tinker's Damn

Among the many ambiguities characterizing Mormon Indian relations is that in the end, despite Brigham Young's desire to "help and bless" the Lamanites, his policies were almost as disastrous for native society as were the extermination policies he so heartily condemned. Some gentiles credited Young as saying, "with his wonted shrewdness, 'I can kill more injuns with a sack of flour, than a keg of gunpowder.' " They concluded that he was "no doubt . . . correct," since a result of Latter-day Saint "kindness" was that the Utes "were fast disappearing, and

---

[25] *JD*, 11:264.
[26] As quoted in Scott, *Blood at Sand Creek*, 119.

would soon become extinct."[27] In an 1866 article entitled "Flour as an Indian Exterminator," the *Denver Rocky Mountain News* correctly reported that "contact with the Mormons and Mormon flour has nearly destroyed" the entire "Uintah Ute Tribe." "The idea advocated by Brigham Young that a sack of flour will kill more Indians than a keg of powder, seems to be correct," the article contended, "at least so far as the experience of the tribes about Salt Lake goes."[28] In a statement that has caused some twentieth-century scholars to question his sincerity altogether, near the end of the Black Hawk War Brigham Young said,

> I will say to our government if they could hear me, "You need never fight the Indians, but if you want to get rid of them try to civilize them." How many were here when we came? At the Warm Springs, at this little grove where they would pitch their tents [near the site of Salt Lake City], we found perhaps three hundred Indians; but I do not suppose that there are three of that band left alive now. There was another band a little south, another north, another further east; but I do not suppose there is one in ten, perhaps not one in a hundred, now alive of those who were here when we came. Did we kill them? No, we fed them.... We brought their children into our families, and nursed and did everything for them it was possible to do for human beings, but die they would. *Do not fight them, but treat them kindly. There will then be no stain on the Government, and it will get rid of them much quicker than fighting them.*[29]

While this can be seen as an example of Brigham Young's frequent use of hyperbole and sarcasm, this statement demonstrates that despite his concern for and theological duty towards the Lamanites the Mormon leader was nonetheless keenly aware of what his colonization processes were doing to Indians both individually and collectively. Writing just after the Black Hawk War, gentile John Codman obliquely compared the missionary work of Young and the Mormons to that of John Eliot, the seventeenth-century Puritan missionary and first translator of the Bible into a Native American tongue. Codman allowed that "all attempts" to proselytize, "domesticate and elevate" the Indians had been "failures." "It has been thus from the first settlement of New Eng-

---

[27] Rusling, *Across America*, 213.
[28] *Denver Rocky Mountain News*, 20 October 1866.
[29] *JD*, 14:86–87. Italics mine.

land," he wrote. Referring to "the enthusiastic Elliot," who, "after spending years in acquiring the language of some of the Massachusetts tribes, devoted other years to translating the Bible into their tongue," Codman sarcastically wrote that, by the time "the task was accomplished and the book was printed," nearly all of the Massachusetts Indians were dead. As a result, "there was never a demand for the second edition."[30] Tragically, so it was with Young and the Latter-day Saints. By the time the Mormon "Kingdom" (whose primary goal was to bring the Indians to Christ) was firmly established in Utah, most of the native inhabitants were gone.

This brings us to the caustic but provocative ideas of Native American George E. Tinker, presented in his recent *Missionary Conquest: The Gospel and Native American Cultural Genocide.* An Osage/Cherokee, Protestant minister, theologian, and Indian historian, Tinker argues that "Christian missionaries—of *all* denominations working among American Indian nations—*were partners in genocide.*" Acknowledging that it "happened with the best of intentions," Tinker nonetheless concludes that the very missionaries Catholics and Protestants hold up as their best examples of "Christian benevolence" to Indians were key players in the "conquest and enslavement of native peoples, the exploitation of their labor and . . . natural resources, and the genocidal destruction of whole cultures and peoples."[31]

According to Tinker, such denominational heroes as John Eliot, Roger Williams, Junipero Serra, Pierre-Jean De Smet, Henry Benjamin Whipple, and the churches with which they were associated, despite their benevolent intentions to bring Indians to Christ, inadvertently destroyed them. "The religious institutions of the 'West' (that is, the churches of Europe and then the immigrant churches of the Americas)," writes Tinker, "have been closely associated with [the] history of colonialism and conquest and have consistently lent legitimacy to those acts." He argues that "at some level the church has ultimately functioned to provide theological justification for acts of conquest" by viewing "immigrant America as the New Israel" and by "overtly" building "the theological base for the doctrine of Manifest Destiny."[32]

None of these Christian missionaries, he continues, "could possibly foresee the long-term demoralizing effects his missions would have on

[30] Codman, *Mormon Country*, 53–54.
[31] Tinker, *Missionary Conquest*, especially vii–viii, and 4. Italics mine.
[32] Ibid., especially vii–viii, 4, and 24–25. Italics mine.

Indian people" nor have "understood his role in a process of pacification that enabled, simplified, and enhanced the ultimate conquest
of [the] tribes. Thoroughly blinded by their own inculturation and
their implicit acceptance of the illusion of European superiority, these
apostles of the church, and indeed virtually every missionary of every
denomination, functioned one way or another as a participant in an un-
intended evil."[33] Although it is profound in its implications, Tinker's
work unfortunately has a self-declared acerbic and imbalanced tone
that ultimately works against the "healing process" he advocates, due
to its want of understanding and compassion for the positions of *both*
Indians and whites.

     While Brigham Young and the Mormons are mentioned only curso-
rily in *Missionary Conquest*,[34] the issues Tinker explores deserve explicit
and detailed application to Young and the extraordinary Lamanite missionary impulse of the Church of Jesus Christ of Latter-day Saints. A
comprehensive discussion of these ideas lies outside the scope (and
space) of this book, but the following pertinent concepts should be
noted. Although it was clearly not his intention, Young's settlement of
his people among the Indians of Utah *did not* substantially result in
bringing the Lamanites to Christ; it *did* instead substantially contribute
to the processes of cultural and physical extermination that Indians
experienced throughout North America. This Young himself acknowledged when he speculated that only three of the three hundred Indians
he met on his arrival in the Salt Lake Valley in 1847 were still living in
1871. What Young was noting was a *catastrophic* decrease in the numbers of Native Americans in Utah. While Young's musings about the
Indians he saw near "the warm springs" in 1847 (pointing to a 99 percent decrease) probably can be taken as hyperbole, more realistic (but
still flawed) figures point to a demographic tragedy nearly as appalling.
As the Black Hawk War opened in 1865, the Indians of Utah were
already well on their way to extinction; Black Hawk's own Timpanogos
Utes, for example, had already essentially ceased to exist as a band.
That year, as has been pointed out, the best-informed white man in
Utah estimated that there were still 13,000 Utes *in Utah alone*.[35] By
1880, just fifteen years later, the combined number of Utes in Colorado, Utah, and New Mexico was estimated at only 3,975; by 1930,

---

[33] Ibid., viii–ix.
[34] Ibid., 7, 128 n. 18.
[35] Dimick B. Huntington, "Tribes of Indians in Utah reported by Dimick Huntington,"
26 April 1865, BYC. Problems with these figures were discussed in Chapter 3.

the nadir of Ute population, this number stood at 1,771.[36] While there are serious questions regarding the accuracy of all these figures, they do point to a result similar to Tinker's "genocide" (though modern dictionaries usually define that powerful and bias-drenched word as "the *deliberate* and *systematic* destruction of a racial, political, or cultural group").

Continuing the application of Tinker's ideas, Brigham Young and the Mormon church certainly viewed "immigrant America as the New Israel" and "overtly helped build the theological base for the doctrine of Manifest Destiny." In light of Latter-day Saint beliefs that the church fulfilled Daniel's prophecy of an expansive kingdom that would eventually *fill the whole earth*, it can be argued that the Indians of Utah were assailed by *the most potent form* of manifest destiny any group of Native Americans ever encountered. Young's key role in persuading the Utes to sign the Treaty of Spanish Fork is a classic example of Tinker's contention that "even missionaries of the most revered memory regularly fell into complicity" with the federal government's seizure of native lands by treaty.[37]

Also, as Tinker demonstrates with regard to the missionaries to the Indians he studies, Brigham Young and his coreligionists "ultimately functioned to provide theological justification for acts of conquest," (though they used a significantly different theology than that of other European/immigrant Americans to do it). Even within Mormonism, theological approaches to the "Indian dilemma" differed, as the comparison between Orson Hyde and Brigham Young has shown. As this study has made abundantly clear, though, Young and other Mormons, no matter where they stood on the theological spectrum, applied principles revealed by Joseph Smith in the Book of Mormon and the *Doctrine and Covenants* to justify appropriating native lands to themselves and to absolve themselves in certain cases for taking Indian life.

There are elements in Tinker's thinking that need to be tempered, however. His stated purpose is not only to "chastise" and "punish the memory" of the missionaries but also "to expose the illusion, the overt 'lie,' of white 'pseudoinnocence.' "[38] This he does "unabashedly and without apology from an American Indian point of view." But, as Ronald Walker has so aptly written, "too often revisionist passion hinders *thorough* and *balanced* analysis. Indeed, some . . . authors only

---

[36] Sturtevant, *Handbook of North American Indians*, 11:357, 359.
[37] Tinker, *Missionary Conquest*, 6–7.
[38] Ibid., 9, 4, 2.

reverse the roles of previous heroes and villains, creating fresh stereo-
types in their wake."[39] Thus Tinker and other radical revisionists can
create an Indian "pseudoinnocence" just as misleading as the one they
attack.

The fact that the Mormons had been forcibly driven from Missouri
and Illinois in their own "wars" with local settlers, as some earlier
Protestant groups had been driven from Europe before them, adds crucial dimensions to Tinker's discussion. To put his attack on European
expansion in context, if the truth were known, most Native American
groups probably occupied their "ancestral lands" in the first place because their forefathers had been driven there at some point in the past,
in the process driving out or eliminating other native peoples they
found there on their arrival. The Navajos, for example, are believed to
have come into the Four Corners region from Canada as late as 1300
A.D., barely anticipating the European invasion by two centuries. Originally settling in a relatively small area, they responded to pressures
from the advancing Shoshonean, or Yumic-speaking, peoples to the
north by expanding southward and westward, and they may well have
contributed to the Anasazi abandonment of the area that occurred
about the same time. The Navajos exported their culture to the indigenous groups of the area, finally overwhelming them and "absorbing"
the survivors of cultures they helped smother.[40]

And what Native American group did not have its expansive border
wars with its neighbors? The "eternal national wars" between the Utes
and the Shoshoni, Navajo, Cheyenne, and Arapaho were often wars
over territory, as population pressures or religious, political, economic,
or other factors caused each group to seek to expand its "ancestral"
homeland.[41] Where these native cultures met (to use Tinker's term), a
"cultural genocide" of sorts occurred as old cultures were swallowed
up and new ones forged, as demonstrated by the distinctive hybrid
groups of the Goshute, Weber Ute, and mixed Ute-Navajo-Paiute-
Hopi-Jicarilla Apache bands of the Four Corners region. The exportation of religion by the white newcomers is condemned, but Native
Americans could be aggressive missionaries too, as the rapid spread of
the Ghost Dance religion demonstrates. First carried to the Northern

[39] Walker, "Toward a Reconstruction of Mormon and Indian Relations, 1847–1877," 27.
Italics mine.

[40] See Brugge, "Navajo Prehistory and History to 1850"; and Sundberg, "Dinetah," 8–16.

[41] Brigham Madsen, *Exploring the Great Salt Lake*, 619.

Utes by Nevada Paiutes, in an incredibly short period it engulfed native groups from the Pacific Coast to the Great Plains.

While Tinker castigates whites for enslaving native groups and appropriating their resources to themselves, the Northern Utes participated in the killing, raiding, and enslavement of weaker native groups around them and similarly exploited those peoples' natural resources and sought to control them. In 1855, for example, Brigham Young wrote that "the Diggers" were "a constant prey to other more warlike bands who steal their children," and, since they possessed "no means of defence," they were pushed from the more productive lands into the deserts where they barely survived on "roots[,] insects, and seeds"—a development that could be seen as a prefiguration of the reservation system.[42] Tinker's thesis attacks whites for using their religion to justify the killing of Indians, implying that Indians did not use their own religious values to condone the reverse. As we have seen, though, Wakara would not "kill a white man, or go on a stealing expedition . . . until he offers sacrifices to his God, *then he thinks he is doing right.*"[43] Black Hawk himself used his religion to justify killing Mormons and help himself to their stock, just as they used their own to help themselves to his land and justify themselves in fighting back.[44]

According to the school of thought Tinker represents, whites are castigated out of hand as aggressors, while raiding, slaving, and killing on the part of native groups are passed without comment because "it was their cultural heritage to act in this way." It is time we stop viewing these injustices as simply *white processes* and begin viewing them as *human processes*. It is time to apply the same yardstick to both groups—compassionately seeking to understand human actions in the past without flailing old wounds by "unabashedly" taking sides.[45] Tinker was right when he wrote, "Without confronting and owning our past, as white Americans, as Europeans, as American Indians, as African Americans, we cannot hope to overcome that past and generate a constructive, healing process, leading to a world of genuine, mutual respect among peoples, communities, and nations."[46] But that "mutual respect"

[42] Brigham Young to George W. Manypenny, Commissioner of Indian Affairs, 30 June 1855, BIA, M234, 896.
[43] Brigham Young, as quoted in Sonne, *World of Wakara*, 180. Italics mine.
[44] Rogerson, "Ending of the Black Hawk War," 3.
[45] See Tinker, *Missionary Conquest*, 4–5.
[46] Ibid.

must begin by seeking to understand the history and human motivations of all these same "peoples, communities, and nations" with a spirit of equity, balance, and compassion.

As was stated in the introduction, despite the modern tendency to brand whites as aggressors and to continually represent Indians as innocent victims, the setting in Utah calls for understanding and compassion towards the positions of *both* groups. Two honorable peoples were trapped by their own cultures, goals, and interests, as well as by the larger political and national forces of their time. Both were victims of demographic and political changes that threatened their very existences as communities. While religious issues usually get the credit, Mormons were pushed to Utah by the same surging North American population system that eventually drove Indians in Utah and throughout the West onto reservations. Part of an even larger demographic tragedy, a considerable number of the whites involved in the Black Hawk War were poverty-stricken emigrants cast from exploding European population systems. Their lands invaded by over 100,000 Latter-day Saints, the Indians themselves became part of a vicious demographic catastrophe that forced men like Black Hawk to take desperate action or starve. At the same time, Mormons were forced to fight back by contingencies nearly as desperate.

This said, there *is* a tragic past for *both* the Latter-day Saints and the Indians of Utah to "confront" and to "own." As late as 1905 Colorado newspapers ran vitriolic headlines pointing to an abiding "Hatred of Utes for the Mormons" and telling of "Alleged Atrocities of Early Days" when "Cruelty Was Practiced by the Church Apostles and Disciples."[47] As was cited previously, John W. Gunnison, writing in the early 1850s, was one of the first to note the tragic irony of the Mormon position when he wrote, "It is a curious matter of reflection, that those whose *mission* it is to convert these aborigines by the sword of the spirit, should thus be obliged to destroy them—but they stoutly affirm that these people will yet, under their instruction, . . . listen to the truth and become 'a fair and delightsome people.' "[48]

Brigham Young sincerely grieved over the impact Mormon settlement had upon the Indians and often consoled himself with the notion that "there will be a remnant of them saved" to fulfill Book of Mormon prophecies that "the Lord God will not suffer that the Gentiles will

---

[47] *Denver Daily News*, 14 September 1905, 6. Capitalization in original.
[48] Gunnison, *The Mormons*, 147.

utterly destroy" them.[49] Even after all that had passed between the Utes and the Latter-day Saints, though, the Indians themselves still largely gave "the Mormons credit for all they get" from the whites. This was not much, however, and gentiles continued to describe the Indians of Utah as unspeakably poor, "notwithstanding the boast of the Mormons that they have done so much for them."[50]

The Gentiles

From the start, Brigham Young clearly believed the main burden of feeding Indians was the responsibility of the federal government.[51] While never absolving the Saints from their culpability in provoking the war, he and other church leaders were always quick to attach much of the blame to what they called "the interference of outsiders."[52] There is no question that the neglect of Indians by the federal government and the graft and mismanagement practiced by many of its agents played as big a part in the war's origin and longevity as any Mormon provocation. Similarly, the opposition of federal military leaders to Young's theocracy, as well as their failure to stop the raiding with customary procedures, no doubt went far to encourage Black Hawk both to commence and then to continue his plundering. Usually representing what little news they reported of the war to their superiors as simply staged "depredations, instigated . . . by Mormon leaders" to "force every man woman and child, not a Mormon to leave the Territory," Patrick Connor and his California and Nevada volunteers basically were too busy trying to topple Young's "one-man power" in Utah to concern themselves much about Black Hawk. Connor and other officers often denied outright that there was any disturbance among the Indians at all, and they commonly viewed fort building and Nauvoo Legion exercises as Mormon military build-up preparatory to waging war on the United States.[53]

---

[49] *JD*, 14:87; 1 Nephi 13:30. Italics mine.

[50] George W. Dodge to C. Delano, Secretary of the Interior, 21 June 1872, BIA, M234, 904.

[51] In his "Governor's Message" to the legislature in 1857, for example, Brigham Young stated that it was "the Parent Government" that was responsible for the "general supervision over the Aborigines within its borders." See Alter, "The Mormons and the Indians," 59.

[52] *JD*, 17:98.

[53] Capt. George F. Price (in absence of Genl. Comdg.) to Maj. Genl. G.M. Dodge, 21 August 1865, District of the Plains, Register of Letters Received, Jan–Sept., in vol. 326, District of the Missouri, 258–59, RUSA, RG 393, pt. II, entry 3257; and Telegram of Roberts to Col. C.H. Potter, 14 May 1866, District of Utah, Letters and Telegrams Received and Retained Reports, 1865–1866, RUSA, RG 393, pt. III, entry 829.

Camp Douglas commandants shortsightedly failed to use the Indian war as a "pretext" to bring in additional soldiers to use against the Latter-day Saints (as Brigham Young feared they would from the beginning), and, when occasional calls for troops did slip past the prophet, the officers simply telegraphed their superiors in the east that they had "too few troops" to get involved and suggested that the Nauvoo Legion was "sufficient to chastise all the Indians in that country."[54] Later, when army regulars were stationed in Utah, they too viewed the Mormons as hostile rebels and generally ignored the calls for help that slipped past Young's information moratorium. Significantly, one of the few federal military officers who ever recommended that troops be called in against Black Hawk callously wrote, "*I do not care much how many Mormons are killed,* but to protect the [western] settlements generally and the new [gentile] mining interest in the country, . . . I deem it very necessary that a military post be established in the Ute country."[55]

Certainly the lack of action on the part of the United States was significantly enhanced by Brigham Young's efforts to repress and minimize the information passed on to federal officials. Even more intriguing was Young's not-so-secret role as commander in chief of a major church military force only ostensibly connected with any grant of federal or territorial authority—a significant anomaly in the post–Civil War era. Young's exercise of military power during the Black Hawk War gives rich insight into the extent and use of his actual power through instrumentality of the Nauvoo Legion.

Noonch

Notwithstanding theocratic power or the might of the federal government, the Indians of Utah were not mere pawns employed in a "whites only" contest. Just as the Iroquois and Cherokees had for a time successfully played opposing European empires off against each other, the Utes exploited the political situation with remarkable success. Although almost totally ignored by modern Indian historians, Antonga Black Hawk himself was a Native American leader of prime significance. His people, however, understood his importance and, in a move

---

[54] Carroll H. Potter, Colonel Comdg. Head Qrs. Dist. of Utah, Salt Lake City, to Capt. Samuel E. Mackey, A.A.A.G., U.S. Forces, Fort Leavenworth, 29 April 1866, Telegrams Sent, Oct. 1865–June 1866, in vol. 354/4th 850, District of the Missouri, 34–35, RUSA, RG 393, pt. III, entry 826.

[55] Bvt. Col. O.E. Babcock, Salt Lake City, to Maj. Gen. J.A. Rawlins, Chief of Staff, Washington, D.C., 23 June 1866, AGO, M619, 454, #961A. Italics mine.

perhaps symbolic of what his resistance meant to them, changed his name to "Nu-ints," or "Noonch," the very word by which the Northern Utes knew themselves.[56] Ultimately a historical victim of Brigham Young's policy of withholding information, the military's lack of involvement, and the resulting nearly nonexistent coverage of the Black Hawk War in the national press, Noonch's name (in any of its forms) has not appeared on the list of key Indian leaders where it rightly belongs. Amazingly, Brigham Young was able to restrict direct reference to Black Hawk in the national press to a single line, *and that was to announce his surrender!* Buried in a long list of other "Indian News" just weeks after Black Hawk made peace with Superintendent Head in 1867, the *Denver Rocky Mountain News* gave its longest story of the whole conflict in these ten words: "Black Hawk, a chief of the Utah Indians favors peace."[57]

The leading Native American figure in the war that bears his name, the Timpanogos Ute Black Hawk lived a life characterized by desperation, courage, and utter agony. While some have viewed him as springing directly from obscurity to chieftainship with the war's opening raids, he actually had long experience with Mormons that both started and ended in reconciliation. Hoping to avoid bloodshed, Antonga Black Hawk had brought his family to Fort Utah in 1850 but was forced to take part in a winter campaign against his own people. Compelled to explore Old Elk's bombed and evacuated camp, he saw firsthand the effect that "ball and chain" shot from his captors' cannon had on his tribesmen.

Pressed further to guide the Mormons into Utah Valley's Rock Canyon, he found the bodies of Old Elk and others frozen in their tepees and witnessed the killing of additional Indians there, perhaps including the forced suicidal leap made by Old Elk's beautiful wife from Provo's "Squaw Peak." He may even have watched Bill Hickman sever Old Elk's head from his body. From his confinement under the Fort Utah cannon platform he later undoubtedly saw the heads of scores of other decapitated family members and friends. These experiences understandably brought him unspeakable anguish; thus "the friendly Indian Black Hawk" lost faith in reconciliation. Along with his "relative" Wakara and his friends Tintic and Squash-Head, Antonga became one of the four most noted native opponents to white settlement in Utah

---

[56] John Wesley Powell, "Government," 2–3, in "Life and Culture of the Ute"; idem, "Indian Life," 4–5; and *RSI*, 1873:424.

[57] *Denver Rocky Mountain News*, 2 September 1867.

during the 1850s. But it was in the second half of the 1860s, after his festering personal agony was compounded by the sickness and deaths of loved ones and by continued abuse from Mormons and Indian agents alike, that Black Hawk commenced his war.

Building an imposing war machine and masterminding a sophisticated and impressive strategy, the Ute war chief demonstrated a striking grasp of the economic, political, and geographic contexts within which he operated. Like Cochise, Geronimo, Sitting Bull, and Chief Joseph, Black Hawk displayed and exploited an extraordinary pan-regionalism that enabled him to operate in a huge stretch of country and establish a three-front war. In travels that were reminiscent of Northern Ute exploits under Wakara more than two decades earlier, Black Hawk and his associates covered enormous distances and marketed stolen livestock in a complex Native American trading system that involved white and Hispanic middlemen and embraced most of Utah and parts of six neighboring states and territories. Like Tecumseh before him, Black Hawk sought to export his resistance to white expansion to other native groups. The war chief's efforts not only succeeded in drawing significant numbers of Navajos, Paiutes, Apaches, Hopis, Shoshonis, and Utes from virtually every band into the conflict but also contributed to the outbreak of a Navajo-Mormon war that eventually took on a life of its own. Like Tecumseh's brother, the Shawnee prophet Tenskwatawa, Black Hawk was inspired by dreams and visions, and his entire movement was colored by mystical and nativistic nuances barely recognized by the whites he confronted. In the end it was the Ghost Dance religion, an amalgamation of Native American, Mormon, and gentile beliefs, that created the circumstances that ended his war.

Black Hawk established a temporary barrier to white expansion and even pushed back the line of Mormon settlement, forcing dozens of villages to be abandoned. Characteristic of other defenders of Indian rights, though, Black Hawk could not hold his position indefinitely, and the onslaught of white expansion eventually overwhelmed him as it did the others. Antonga Black Hawk was just the kind of Native American leader Wilbur Jacobs had in mind when in 1973 he expressed his hope that

> at some future time it may be that . . . Tecumseh, Pontiac, Black-hawk, Sitting Bull, and Chief Joseph, will be recognized as truly national figures in our history. As much as the heroic figure of the scout, the plainsman, the mountain man, and the cowboy

himself, these courageous Indians deserve our respect and admiration. For they and all their Indian brethren may have made contributions to our life-style which may ultimately bring about a better America.[58]

For Antonga–Black Hawk–Noonch perhaps that time has come.

In September 1870, almost two years before the war he engineered would finally end, Black Hawk returned to the place of his birth at Spring Lake and prepared to die. Accompanied by his brother Mountain, Joe, and other surviving members of his raiding band, the broken war chief was afflicted with syphilis and tuberculosis and tormented by the stomach wound he had received in the 1866 battle at Gravelly Ford. Previous to arriving at Spring Lake, Black Hawk had prepared to return to the Great Spirit by touring the Mormon settlements seeking forgiveness, as instructed by Brigham Young.

By 23 September, Antonga, his physical agony now nearly complete, had lost his sight as well as his ability to speak. That day Brigham Young and his entourage passed just below Black Hawk's lodges pitched at Spring Lake near the main road through the settlements. Mountain and Joe suddenly appeared beside Young's carriage and informed the church president that Black Hawk was in the last throes of death and implored him to pay their dying leader a visit. The aging church leader was returning from a month-long tour of southern Utah, where he had just selected the site for yet another fort, this time "Winsor Castle" at Pipe Springs. Worn out, and perhaps thinking a visit useless since the former war chief was now delirious, Young hurried on to Salt Lake City, leaving Black Hawk to face death without his shaman. Three days later, on 26 September 1870, Antonga Black Hawk died. Upon learning of his death, Young reflectively wrote that Black Hawk "was the most formidable foe amongst the red men that the Saints have had to encounter for many years."[59] Considering the length, intensity, and effect of his opposition to their settlement, history bears out that Black Hawk was indeed *the* "most formidable" Native American adversary the Mormons ever faced. The morning after his death, the war chief's body was dressed in a blue U.S. military jacket and loaded onto his favorite horse and carried up the side of the mountain. There, in accordance with Ute custom, Black Hawk was buried with his saddle and

---

[58] Wilbur Jacobs, "The Indian and the Frontier," 54.

[59] *Deseret Evening News*, 26 and 27 September 1870; and Brigham Young to H.S. Eldredge, 4 October 1870, BYC.

bridle and a bundle of supplies necessary for his journey into the world of spirits.[60]

Black Hawk's stand against white expansion was over. Less than three years after his death, Mormon Indian interpreters and former Nauvoo Legion troopers used geographic knowledge obtained chasing the chief raider through the mountains to launch staggering new incursions into the lands he once fought to defend. As if their victory was not enough, nearly a half century later, in 1917, a new generation of whites exhumed Black Hawk's bones and displayed them for decades in an LDS church museum, along with the war chief's saddle, bridle, spurs, pipe, and faded pieces of his blue burial jacket.[61]

As has been pointed out, in accordance with the Native American Graves Protection and Repatriation Act of 1990, Black Hawk's remains were reinterred in a new grave at Spring Lake, Utah, on 4 May 1996 by his closest living relatives, the descendants of his brother Mountain.[62] The grave, ironically located in a small park owned by the LDS church, was blessed in a traditional Ute ceremony by a modern Ute medicine man—a great-great-great-grandnephew of Black Hawk. On 27 September 1997 (the 127th anniversary of his original burial), the Mountain family dedicated a new monument over the grave and another Ute

---

[60] Benjamin F. Johnson, a resident of Spring Lake, wrote the following to the editor of the _Deseret News_ the day after Black Hawk died: "—Sept 27th 1870. Dear Sir—I hasten to tell you that Black Hawk, the Indian desperado, is dead. He has been living here in camp with his brother 'Mountain', together with 'Joe' and his band for some days. We knew he was sick, but did not think of so sudden a demise. This morning, before sun up, the Indian wail was heard in their camp, and soon was seen one Indian squaw with two horses heavily packed, on their way towards the foot of the mountain. Stopping at a small ravine within sight of our door, they killed one of the horses and proceeded to put away the body of the great Black Hawk. This is the place of his birth. Here he commenced his depredations, and here he came back to die. Showan, a friendly Indian, the head of the camp about here, died at Goshen a few days since, and Queant, another good Indian, lies in camp about to die. Really, our Indian neighbors are fast passing away! Indian 'Joe,' the present head of the Indians about here, is here, telling me about the death of Black hawk, and many other things that I cannot so well understand. He wants me to tell Brigham and Bro. Hyde not to let the Green river Indians have any powder, for they lie and steal, and they must be watched or they will take more horses this fall. He wishes the Mormons to know that Black Hawk is now dead and that he died in his camp." _Deseret Evening News_, 30 September 1870; also in JH, 26 September 1870, 1. For information about what was reportedly buried with Black Hawk see JH, 22 September 1917, 2; 29 September 1917, 5; 20 September 1919, 3–4, and 21 September 1919, 4.

[61] JH, 22 September 1917, 2; 29 September 1917, 5; 20 September 1919, 3–4, and 21 September 1919, 4.

[62] Black Hawk was originally buried high on the mountain east of Spring Lake on land now owned by the U.S. Forest Service. His relatives agreed to relocate the grave to a small park in Spring Lake to make the site accessible to visitors.

ritual was performed to bring Antonga Black Hawk to rest. Significantly, descendants of Warren S. Snow, James A. Ivie, and other participants of the Black Hawk War—both Indian and white—joined with the Mountain family in honoring Black Hawk. At the unveiling of the monument, several conciliatory speeches were made by representatives of both groups. Richard Mountain told of the Ute belief that, until their remains are buried, the spirits of the dead cannot rest but must wander in anguish and agony.[63] For those who looked for it, a grizzled red and white hawk flew over the gathering in the park and headed for the top of the mountain.

---

[63] See *Provo Daily Herald,* 28 September 1997.

Selected Bibliography

See List of Abbreviations, page x.

Adams, William Henry. Autobiography. CHD.

"A Diary of President B. Young's Trip South." Edyth Romney Typescripts, b99. CHD.

Ahlstrom, Mary Larsen. "Biography of Mary Larsen Ahlstrom." CHD.

Alexander, Eveline M. *Cavalry Wife: The Diary of Eveline M. Alexander, 1866–1867: Being a Record of Her Journey from New York to Fort Smith to Join Her Cavalry-Officer Husband, Andrew J. Alexander, and Her Experiences with Him on Active Duty Among the Indian Nations and in Texas, New Mexico, and Colorado.* Edited by Sandra L. Myres. College Station: Texas A&M University Press, 1977.

Allen, James B., and Ted J. Warner. "The Gosiute Indians in Pioneer Utah." *UHQ* 39 (Spring 1971): 162–77.

Allred, Clara Alice Robinson. Pioneer Personal History Questionnaire. UWPA Historical Records Survey. USHS.

Allred, Reddick N. "Diary of Reddick N. Allred." *Treasures of Pioneer History,* 5:297–372.

Alter, J. Cecil. "The Mormons and the Indians: News Items and Editorials, from the Mormon Press." *UHQ* 12 (1944): 49–67.

Andrus, Hyrum L. *Joseph Smith and World Government.* Salt Lake City: Deseret Book Company, 1963.

Andrus, Manomas. Pioneer Personal History Questionnaire. UWPA Historical Records Survey. USHS.

Armstrong, Perry A. *The Sauks and the Black Hawk War, with Biographical Sketches, etc.* Springfield, IL: H.W. Rokker, 1887.

Arrington, Leonard J. *Great Basin Kingdom: Economic History of the Latter-day Saints, 1830–1900.* Lincoln: University of Nebraska Press, 1958.

"Articles of Agreement and convention made and concluded at Spanish Fork Indian Farm, in the Territory of Utah, this eighth day of June, Eighteen hundred and sixty five, by O. H. Irish, Superintendent of Indian Affairs for said Territory, . . . and the undersigned Chiefs, head men and delegates of the Utah, Yampah Ute, Pah-vant, Sanpete Ute, Tim-p-noogs and Cumum-bah Bands of the Utah Indians occupying the lands within Utah Territory, . . ." Documents Relating to the Negotiation of Ratified and Unratified Treaties with various Tribes of Indians, 1801–1869. BIA, T494, 8.

Bailey, Paul D. *The Armies of God*. Garden City, NY: Doubleday & Company, Inc., 1968.

———. *Holy Smoke: A Dissertation on the Utah War*. Los Angeles: Westernlore Books, 1978.

———. *Walkara, Hawk of the Mountains*. Los Angeles: Westernlore Press, 1954.

Bancroft, Hubert Howe. *History of Utah*. San Francisco: The History Company, 1890.

Barney, Garold D. *Mormons, Indians and the Ghost Dance Religion of 1890*. Lanham, MD: University Press of America, Inc., 1986.

Barton, William G. "The Utah Indian War Known as the Black Hawk War of 1865–6–7." Master's thesis, Columbia University, n.d.

Bate, Kerry William. *The Ebenezer Hanks Story*. Provo, Utah: M.C. Printing, 1982.

Beacham, Jacob. Pioneer Personal History Questionnaire. UWPA Historical Records Survey. USHS.

Bean, George Washington. Autobiography, 1897. CHD.

———. *Autobiography of George Washington Bean, A Utah Pioneer of 1847, and His Family Records*. Compiled by Flora Diana Bean Horne. Salt Lake City: Utah Printing Co., 1945.

Bean, George Washington, and Albert K. Thurber. "Report of an Exploration of a portion of South-Eastern Utah, made June AD 1873 . . . an examination of the country with a view to making new settlements." BYC.

Beeton, Beverly. "Teach Them to Till the Soil: An Experiment with Indian Farms, 1850–1862." *American Indian Quarterly* 3 (1977-1978): 299–319.

Bennett, Richard E. *Mormons at the Missouri, 1846–1852: "And Should We Die."* Norman: University of Oklahoma Press, 1987.

Berthrong, Donald J. *The Southern Cheyennes*. Norman: University of Oklahoma Press, 1963.

Bishop, Francis Marion. "Captain Francis Marion Bishop's Journal." Edited by Charles Kelly. *UHQ* 15 (1947): 159–238.

Blackburn, Abner. *Frontiersman: Abner Blackburn's Narrative*. Edited by Will Bagley. Salt Lake City: University of Utah Press, 1992.

Bleak, James G. "Annals of the Southern Utah Mission." CHD.

Blythe, John L. Journal. John L. Blythe Papers. BYUA&M.

Bodily, Robert. Journal and Autobiography. USHS.

The Book of Mormon. 6th European ed. London: Brigham Young, Jr., 1866.

Bowles, Samuel. *Across the Continent: A Stage Ride Over the Plains, to the Rocky Mountains, the Mormons, and the Pacific States, in the Summer of 1865, with Speaker Colfax*. Springfield, MA: Samuel Bowles & Company, 1869.

"Brigade Record, First Brigade, Second Division Nauvoo Legion, Organized May 8ᵗʰ 1866." L. John Nuttall Collection. BYUA&M, MSS 188, b7, f9.

Brooks, Juanita. "Indian Relations on the Mormon Frontier." *UHQ* 12 (January–April 1944): 1–48.

———. *Mountain Meadows Massacre*. Palo Alto, CA: Stanford University Press, 1950.

Brown, Dee. *Bury My Heart at Wounded Knee: An Indian History of the American West*. New York: Holt, Rinehart & Winston, 1970.

Brown, John. *Autobiography of Pioneer John Brown, 1820–1896*. Edited by John Zimmerman Brown. Salt Lake City: Stevens & Wallis, Inc., 1941.

Brugge, David M. "Navajo Prehistory and History to 1850." In Alfonso Ortiz, ed. *Southwest*. Vol. 10 of *Handbook of North American Indians*, edited by William C. Sturtevant, 489–501. Washington, D.C.: Smithsonian Institution, 1983.

Burkey, Elmer R. "The Site of the Murder of the Hungate Family by Indians in 1864." *Colorado Magazine* 12 (July 1935): 139–42.

Burton, Richard F. *The City of the Saints: and Across the Rocky Mountains to California*. Edited by Fawn M. Brodie. New York: Alfred A. Knopf, 1963.

Bushman, Richard L. *Joseph Smith and the Beginnings of Mormonism*. Urbana: University of Illinois Press, 1984.

Callaway, Donald, Joel Janetski, and Omer C. Stewart. "Ute." In Warren L. D'Azevedo, ed. *Great Basin*. Vol. 11 of *Handbook of North American Indians*, edited by William C. Sturtevant, 336–67. Washington, D.C.: Smithsonian Institution, 1986.

Candland, David. "The Sanpitcher." CHD.

Carson, Lynn R. *The Tintic War and the Deaths of George and Washington Carson*. Salt Lake City: George Carson and Ann Hough Family Organization, 1979. CHD.

Carvalho, S.N. *Incidents of Travel and Adventure in the Far West; with Col. Fremont's Last Expedition Across the Rocky Mountains: Including Three Months' Residence in Utah, and a Perilous Trip Across the Great American Desert to the Pacific*. New York: Derby & Jackson, 1857.

Christy, Howard A. "Open Hand and Mailed Fist: Mormon-Indian Relations in Utah, 1847–52." *UHQ* 46 (Summer 1978): 216–35.

———. "The Walker War: Defense and Conciliation as Strategy." *UHQ* 47 (Fall 1979): 395–420.

Church Emigration Book. Vol. 1, 1830–1848. CHD.

Clark, Therissa E.C. "The Life Histories of Therissa Emerita Cox Clark and John Haslem Clark, written by Therissa E.C. Clark." CHD.

Clayton, William. *An Intimate Chronicle: The Journals of William Clayton*. Edited by George D. Smith. Salt Lake City: Signature Books/Smith Research Associates, 1995.

Coates, Larry C. "Cultural Conflict: Mormons and Indians in Nebraska." *Brigham Young University Studies* 24 (Summer 1984): 275–300.

————. "George Catlin, Brigham Young, and the Plains Indians." *Brigham Young University Studies* 17 (Autumn 1976): 114–18.

Codman, John. *The Mormon Country: A Summer with the "Latter-Day Saints."* New York: United States Publishing Company, 1874.

————. *The Round Trip by Way of Panama Through California, Oregon, Nevada, Utah, Idaho, and Colorado with Notes on Railroads, Commerce, Agriculture, Mining, Scenery, and People.* New York: G.P. Putnam's Sons, 1879.

"Col Snow on the War Path." 22 July 1865. BYC. R92, b58, f16.

Cook, Lyndon W. *The Revelations of the Prophet Joseph Smith: A Historical and Biographical Commentary of the Doctrine and Covenants.* Provo, UT: Seventy's Mission Bookstore, 1981.

Coombs, Isaiah M. Diary. CHD.

————. Isaiah Coombs Papers. CHD.

Correll, J. Lee. *Through White Men's Eyes: A Contribution to Navajo History: A Chronological Record of the Navajo People From Earliest Times to the Treaty of June 1, 1868.* 6 vols. Window Rock, AZ: Navajo Heritage Center, 1979.

"Council at Fort Defiance, N.M. with the Navajos. 5 November [1870]." National Anthropological Archives, Smithsonian Institution, Washington, D.C.

Cox, Margaret M. "A Biographical Sketch of William Arthur Cox by his Wife." Clare Christensen Papers. CHD.

Crampton, C. Gregory, and Steven K. Madsen. *In Search of the Spanish Trail: Santa Fe to Los Angeles, 1829–1848.* Salt Lake City: Gibbs Smith, 1994.

Crampton, C. Gregory, and David E. Miller, eds. "Journal of Two Campaigns by the Utah Territorial Militia Against the Navajo Indians, 1869." *UHQ* 29 (April 1961): 149–76.

Cremony, John C. *Life among the Apaches.* 1868. Reprint. Lincoln: University of Nebraska Press, 1983.

Crook, John. Record of the Wasatch County Militia. CHD.

Cropper, Thomas Waters. "The Life and Experience of Thomas Waters Cropper." BYUA&M.

Culmsee, Carlton. *Utah's Black Hawk War: Lore and Reminiscences of Participants.* Logan: Utah State University Press/Western Text Society, 1973.

Daughters of Utah Pioneers. *A Memory Bank for Paragonah.* Provo, UT: Community Press, 1990.

————. *Daughters of Utah Pioneers Lessons.* 38 vols. Edited by Kate B. Carter. Salt Lake City: Daughters of Utah Pioneers, 1936–1978.

————. *Heart Throbs of the West.* 12 vols. Salt Lake City: Daughters of Utah Pioneers, 1939–1951.

————. *History of Kane County.* Compiled and edited by Elsie Chamberlain Carroll. Salt Lake City: Utah Printing Company, 1960.

———. *Our Pioneer Heritage.* Compiled by Kate B. Carter. 20 vols. Salt Lake City: Daughters of Utah Pioneers, 1958–1977.

———. *Treasures of Pioneer History.* Compiled by Kate B. Carter. 6 vols. Salt Lake City: Daughters of Utah Pioneers, 1952–1957.

———. *"Under Wasatch Skies": A History of Wasatch County, 1858–1900.* Salt Lake City: Deseret News Press, 1954.

———. Wasatch County Chapter. *How Beautiful upon the Mountains: A Centennial History of Wasatch County.* Compiled and edited by William James Mortimer. Salt Lake City: Deseret News Press, 1963.

Davis, W.W.H. *El Gringo: New Mexico and Her People.* 1857. Reprint. Lincoln: University of Nebraska Press, 1982.

Day, Eli A. "History of Eli A. Day, Written by Eli A. Day, Commenced July 22, 1936 in Mt. Pleasant, Utah." USHS.

———. "Abraham Day III." USHS.

Dellenbaugh, Frederick S. *A Canyon Voyage: The Narrative of the Second Powell Expedition down the Green-Colorado River from Wyoming, and the Explorations on Land, in the Years 1871 and 1872.* New Haven, CT: Yale University Press, 1962.

Denver Daily News. Various issues.

Denver Rocky Mountain News. Various issues.

Deseret Evening News. Various issues.

Deseret News. Various issues.

DeVoto, Bernard. *Across the Wide Missouri.* New York: Bonanza Books, 1948.

Dewey, Albert. "Albert Dewey's Journal, 1866." CHD.

Dilke, Charles Wentworth. *Greater Britain: A Record of Travel in English-Speaking Countries During 1866 and 1867.* 2 vols. London: Macmillan and Co., 1868.

Dillon, Richard H. *North American Indian Wars.* New York: Facts on File, Inc., 1983.

Dobyns, Henry F., and Robert C. Euler. *The Ghost Dance of 1889 among the Pai Indians of North Western Arizona.* Prescott, AZ: Prescott College Press, 1967.

Dockstader, Frederick J. *Great North American Indians: Profiles in Life and Leadership.* New York: Van Nostrand Reinhold Company, 1977.

Dorcheus, John T. "Memoirs of John T. Dorcheus." BYUA&M.

Driggs, Howard R. *Timpanogos Town: Story of Old Battle Creek and Pleasant Grove, Utah.* Manchester, NH: Clarke Press, 1948.

Duncan, Clifford H. "Official Memorandum of Clifford H. Duncan, Native American Consultant, Roosevelt, Utah to Charmaine Thompson, Archaeologist, Uinta National Forest, Provo, Utah, regarding 'Black Hawk - Antenguer,' " 17 February 1995. John A. Peterson, Black Hawk Collection. UUWA.

Dwyer, Robert Joseph. *The Gentile Comes to Utah: A Study in Religious and Social*

Conflict (1862–1892). Washington, D.C.: Catholic University of America Press, 1941.

Eby, Cecil. *"That Disgraceful Affair," the Black Hawk War*. New York: W.W. Norton & Company, Inc., 1973.

Edmunds, R. David, ed. *American Indian Leaders: Studies in Diversity*. Lincoln: University of Nebraska Press, 1980.

Egan, Ferol. *Sand in a Whirlwind: The Paiute Indian War of 1860*. Reno: University of Reno Press, 1972. Reprint, 1985.

Eldridge, Alma. "A Biographical Sketch of the Life and History of Alma Eldridge written with his own hand." CHD.

Ewers, John C. *George Catlin, Painter of Indians and the West*. Reprinted from the Annual Report of the Smithsonian Institution for 1955. [Washington, D.C.]: Smithsonian Institution, [1957]. UUWA.

F[?]., J.R. "Utah Indian Tribes." *Juvenile Instructor* 20 (1 February 1885): 34–35.

Farnsworth, M.F. "History of Manti." CHD.

Ferris, Warren Angus. *Life in the Rocky Mountains: A Diary of Wanderings on the sources of the Rivers Missouri, Columbia, and Colorado, 1830–1835*. Edited by LeRoy R. Hafen. Denver: Old West Publishing Company, revised edition, 1983.

Fielding, Robert Kent. *The Unsolicited Chronicler: An Account of the Gunnison Massacre, Its Causes and Consequences, Utah Territory, 1847–1859*. Brookline, MA: Paradigm Publications, 1993.

Fillmore Ward Minutes. In Millard Stake Minutes. CHD.

Fish, Joseph. "Diaries of Joseph Fish." BYUSC.

Flanders, Robert Bruce. *Nauvoo: Kingdom on the Mississippi*. Urbana: University of Illinois Press, 1965.

Folklore Society of Utah. *Lore of Faith & Folly*. Edited by Thomas E. Cheney, assisted by Austin E. Fife and Juanita Brooks. Salt Lake City: University of Utah Press, 1971.

Foote, Warren. "Autobiography of Warren Foote, Son of David Foote a Descendant of Nathaniel Foote the Settler who came from England about 1633 and was one of the First Settlers of Weathersfield Conectticut [*sic*]." CHD.

Ford, Thomas. *History of Illinois, from the Commencement as a State in 1818 to 1847: Containing a Full Account of the Black Hawk War, the Rise, Progress, and Fall of Mormonism, the Alton and Lovejoy Riots, and Other Important and Interesting Events*. Chicago: S.C. Griggs & Co., 1854.

Fowler, Henry Ammon. "Diary of Henry A. Fowler, Sketch of My Life." USHS.

Franklin, Robert J., and Pamela A. Bunte. *The Paiute*. Edited by Frank W. Porter III. New York: Chelsea House Publishers, 1990.

Furniss, Norman F. *The Mormon Conflict: 1850–1859.* New Haven, CT: Yale University Press, 1960.

Gibbs, Josiah F. "Black Hawk's Last Raid—1866." *UHQ* 4 (October 1931): 99–108.

———. *Lights and Shadows of Mormonism.* Salt Lake City: Salt Lake Tribune Publishing Co., 1909.

Gottfredson, Peter. *Indian Depredations of Utah.* 1919. Reprint. Salt Lake City: Merlin G. Christensen, 1969.

"Governor's Messages, 1851–1876." SA.

Greeley, Horace. *An Overland Journey from New York to San Francisco in the Summer of 1859.* New York: C.M. Saxton, Barker & Co., 1860.

Greer, Deon C., et al. *Atlas of Utah.* Provo, UT: Brigham Young University Press for Weber State College, 1981.

Guild, Thelma S., and Harvey L. Carter. *Kit Carson: A Pattern for Heroes.* Lincoln: University of Nebraska Press, 1984.

Gunnison, John W. *The Mormons or Latter-day Saints, In the Valley of the Great Salt Lake: A History of their Rise and Progress, Peculiar Doctrines, Present Condition, and Prospects, Derived from Personal Observation, During a Residence Among Them.* 1852. Reprint. Brookline, MA: Paradigm Publications, 1993.

"Gunnison Ward Historical Record—Utah—1859—Oct. 1891." CHD.

Hafen, LeRoy R. "Elijah Barney Ward." In LeRoy R. Hafen, ed. *The Mountain Men and the Fur Trade of the Far West, Biographical Sketches of the Participants by Scholars of the Subject.* 10 vols. Glendale, CA: Arthur H. Clark Company, 1965-1972. 7:343–51.

Hafen, LeRoy R., and Ann W. Hafen. *Old Spanish Trail: Santa Fe to Los Angeles, With Extracts from Contemporary Records and Including Diaries of Antonio Armijo and Orville Pratt.* Glendale, CA: A.H. Clark Co., 1954.

Hallwas, John E., and Roger D. Launius. *Cultures in Conflict: A Documentary History of the Mormon War in Illinois.* Logan: Utah State University Press, 1995.

Hansen, Peter O. *An Autobiography of Peter Olsen Hansen, 1818–1895: Mormon Convert and Pioneer, Missionary, Translator of Book of Mormon into Danish.* Compiled by Leland Hansen Ashby. N.p., 1988.

Hanson, Klaus J. *Quest for Empire: The Political Kingdom of God and the Council of Fifty in Mormon History.* East Lansing: Michigan State University Press, 1970.

Harley, Edwin. Journal. CHD.

Haverstock, Mary Sayer. *Indian Gallery: The Story of George Catlin.* New York: Four Winds Press, 1973.

Heap, Gwinn Harris. *Central Route to the Pacific, from the Valley of the Mississippi to California: Journal of the Expedition . . .* Philadelphia: Lippincott, Grambo, and Co., 1854.

Henroid, Gustave Louis Edward. "Biography of Gustave Louis Edward Henroid." CHD.

Hickman, William. *Brigham's Destroying Angel: Being the Life, Confession, and Startling Disclosures of the Notorious Bill Hickman, the Danite Chief of Utah.* Salt Lake City: Shepard Publishing Company, 1904.

Hill, Marvin S. *Quest for Refuge: The Mormon Flight from American Pluralism.* Salt Lake City: Signature Books, 1989.

Historian's Office Journal. CHD.

Historian's Office Letter Book. CHD.

"The History of Christian Overson." Floyd Bradfield Collection. CHD.

"The History of Glenwood, Utah." FHL.

"History of Provo City." *Tullidge's Quarterly Magazine* 3 (July 1884): 233–85.

"History of Spanish Fork." *Tullidge's Quarterly Magazine* 3 (April 1884): 137–70.

Hoig, Stan. *The Sand Creek Massacre.* Norman: University of Oklahoma Press, 1961.

———. *The Western Odyssey of John Simpson Smith, Frontiersman, Trapper, Trader, and Interpreter.* Glendale, CA: Arthur H. Clark Company, 1974.

Holt, Ronald L. *Beneath These Red Cliffs: An Ethnohistory of the Utah Paiutes.* Albuquerque: University of New Mexico Press, 1992.

Howard, William. Diary. CHD.

Hoxie, Frederick E., ed. *Indians in American History: An Introduction.* Arlington Heights, IL.: Harlan Davidson, Inc., for the D'Arcy McNickle Center for the History of the American Indian, Newberry Library, 1988.

Hunting, Uel. Collection. CHD.

Huntington, Dimick B. "Tribes of Indians in Utah reported by Dimick Huntington." 26 April 1865. BYC.

———. *Vocabulary of the Utah and Sho-sho-ne or Snake Dialects, with Indian Legends and Traditions, Including a Brief Account of the Life and Death of Wah-ker, the Indian Land Pirate.* 3rd. ed. Salt Lake City: Salt Lake Herald Office, 1872.

Inter-Tribal Council of Nevada. *Nuwuvi: A Southern Paiute History.* Salt Lake City: University of Utah Printing Service for the Inter-Tribal Council of Nevada, 1976.

Ivie, James A. "Statement of James A. Ivie given in President Young's Office in G.S.L.City Aug 13th (monday) 1866." BYC.

Ivins, Anthony W. "Traveling Over Forgotten Trails." *Improvement Era* 14 (February 1916): 350–56.

"J.P. Petersen, Wife and Mary Smith Killed Near Glenwood . . ." CHD.

J[?]., Jennie. "Sowiette's Noble Act." *Juvenile Instructor* 27 (15 December 1892): 748–49.

Jackson, William Henry. *The Diaries of William Henry Jackson: Frontier Photog-

rapher. Edited by LeRoy R. Hafen and Ann W. Hafen. Glendale, CA: Arthur Clark Company, 1959.

Jacobs, Wilbur R. "The Indian and the Frontier in American History—A Need for Revision." *Western Historical Quarterly* 4 (January 1973): 43–56.

Jacobs, Zebulon. "Journal of Z Jacobs." CHD.

James, Richard W. "Excerpts from the Journal of Richard W. James." *Denver Rocky Mountain News*, 1 June 1867.

Jarman, William. *Uncle Sam's Abscess, or Hell Upon Earth... by W. Jarman, Esq., ... who Suffered Twelve Years in The Mormon Hell on Earth, ... Where Polygamy, Incest, and Murder are Taught and Practiced as Religion Under the "All Seeing Eye," and the sign "Holiness Unto the Lord."* Exeter, England: H. Leduc's Steam Printing Works, 1884.

Jennings, Warren A. "The First Mormon Mission to the Indians," *Kansas Historical Quarterly* 38 (Autumn 1971): 288–99.

Jenson, Andrew. *Encyclopedic History of the Church of the Church of Jesus Christ of Latter-day Saints*. Salt Lake City: Deseret News Publishing Company, 1941.

———. *Latter-day Saint Biographical Encyclopedia, a compilation of Biographical Sketches of Prominent Men and Women in the Church of Jesus Christ of Latter-day Saints*. 4 vols. Salt Lake City: Andrew Jenson History Company, 1920.

Johnson, Alan P. *Aaron Johnson: Faithful Steward*. Salt Lake City: Publishers Press, 1991.

Johnson, Benjamin F. *My Life's Review*. Independence, MO: Zion's Printing & Publishing Co., 1947.

Johnson, Don Carlos. *A Brief History of Springville, Utah, from its first settlement* ... Springville, UT: William F. Gibson, 1900.

———. "The Indians of Utah Valley: Incidents in their History and Wars with the White Invader." *Springville Independent*, 6 February 1908 to 18 June 1908.

Johnson, Joseph E. "A History of Joseph E. Johnson, Pioneer of 1879, In Castle Valley, Whose 100th Birthday Anniversary is January 31, 1958 ..." CHD.

Johnson, Milas E. Autobiography. CHD.

———. "Milas Edgar Johnson: The Life Review of a Mormon." Edited by Rolla Virgil Johnson. BYUA&M.

Jones, Daniel W. *Forty Years Among the Indians: A True yet Thrilling Narrative of the Author's Experiences among the Natives*. Salt Lake City: Juvenile Instructor Office, 1890.

Jones, Stephen V. "Journal of Stephen Vandiever Jones, April 21, 1871–December 14, 1872." Edited by Herbert E. Gregory. *UHQ* 16–17 (1948–49): 11–174.

Jorgensen, Joseph Gilbert. "The Ethnohistory and Acculturation of the Northern Ute." Ph.D. diss., Indiana University, 1964.

———. *The Sun Dance Religion: Power for the Powerless*. Chicago: University of Chicago Press, 1972.

Josephy, Alvin M., Jr. *The Patriot Chiefs: A Chronicle of American Indian Resistance.* New York: Viking Press, 1961.

Journal of Discourses by Brigham Young, President of the Church of Jesus Christ of Latter-day Saints, His Two Counselors, and the Twelve Apostles, and Others. Compiled by George D. Watt. 26 vols. Liverpool: The Church of Jesus Christ of Latter-day Saints, 1854–1886. Reprint. Los Angeles: General Printing & Lithograph, 1961.

Journal History of the Church of Jesus Christ of Latter-day Saints. CHD.

Kane, Elizabeth Wood. *Twelve Mormon Homes Visited in Succession on a Journey through Utah to Arizona.* Edited by Everett L. Cooley. Salt Lake City: Tanner Trust Fund/University of Utah Library, 1974.

Kearnes, Hamilton H. "H.H. Kearnes Statement as to Indian Difficulties in Manti & San Pete & Sevier Counties." BYC.

Keeler, Virginia C. *Cheney Garrett Van Buren and his Family.* Provo, UT: J. Grant Stevenson, 1962.

Kelly, Charles. *The Outlaw Trail: A History of Butch Cassidy and His Wild Bunch.* New York: Bonanza Books, 1938; revised 1959.

Kelly, Charles, and Birney Hoffman. *Holy Murder: The Story of Porter Rockwell.* New York: Minton, Balch & Company, 1934.

Kelly, Isabel T., and Catherine S. Fowler. "Southern Paiute." In Warren L. D'Azevedo, ed. *Great Basin.* Vol. 11 of *Handbook of North American Indians,* edited by William C. Sturtevant, 368–97. Washington, D.C.: Smithsonian Institution, 1986.

Kelly, Lawrence C. *Navajo Roundup: Selected Correspondence of Kit Carson's Expedition Against the Navajo, 1863–1865.* Boulder, CO: Pruett Publishing Co., 1970.

Kimball, James LeRoy, Jr. "A Study of the Nauvoo Charter, 1840–1845." Master's thesis, University of Iowa, 1966.

———. "The Nauvoo Charter: A Reinterpretation." *Journal of the Illinois State Historical Society* 64 (Spring 1971): 66–78.

———. "A Wall to Defend Zion: The Nauvoo Charter." *Brigham Young University Studies* 15 (Summer 1975): 491–97.

Kimball, Solomon F. "Our Pioneer Boys." *Improvement Era* 11 (August 1908): 734–42.

Kuhre, William D. Interview by John A. Butterfield and Wallace E. Malmstrom, 31 January 1958. CHD.

Lambert, George Cannon. "Autobiography." CHD.

Larsen, Eunice D. "Biography of Ellen Aurelia Allred Nielsen, Written by mu [*sic*] Daughter Eunice D. Larsen, Marysvale, Utah, Alunite Mill, June 15, 1919." CHD.

Larsen, Lorena Eugenia Washburn. "Black Hawk War." Jean R. Bradfield Collection. CHD.

Larsen, Oluf C. "A Biographical Sketch of the Life of Oluf Christian Larsen

Dictated by himself and written by his son Oluf Larsen, Dedicated to his posterity who might desire to read it." 1916. CHD.

Larson, Andrew Karl. *"I Was Called to Dixie," The Virgin River Basin: Unique Experiences in Mormon Pioneering.* N.p., 1961; second printing, 1979.

———. *The Red Hills of November: A Pioneer Biography of Utah's Cotton Town.* Salt Lake City: Deseret News Press, 1957.

Larson, Gustive O. *Americanization of Utah for Statehood.* San Marino, CA: Huntington Library, 1971.

———."Uintah Dream: The Ute Treaty—Spanish Fork, 1865." *Brigham Young University Studies* 14 (Spring 1974): 361–81.

———. "Walkara's Half Century," *Western Humanities Review* 6 (Summer 1952): 235–59.

Laws, Memorials, and Resolutions of the Territory of Utah, passed at the Twenty-third Session, of the Legislative Assembly, Held at the City of Salt Lake, . . . 1878. Salt Lake City: Star Book and Job Printing Office, 1878. UUWA.

Lee, John D. *A Mormon Chronicle: The Diaries of John D. Lee, 1848–1876.* 2 vols. Edited by Robert Glass Cleland and Juanita Brooks. San Marino, CA: Huntington Library, 1955.

LeSueur, Stephen C. *The 1838 Mormon War in Missouri.* Columbia: University of Missouri Press, 1987.

Lincoln, Abraham. Abraham Lincoln Papers. Library of Congress. Washington, D.C.

Lindsay, William. "Autobiography of William Lindsay, 1847–1932." USHS.

Lingren, John. "Autobiography of John Lingren." DUP. *Treasures of Pioneer History,* 1:233–71.

Loh, Jules. *Lords of the Earth: A History of the Navajo Indians.* New York: Crowell-Collier Press, 1971.

Long, E.B. *The Saints and the Union: Utah Territory during the Civil War.* Urbana: University of Illinois Press, 1981.

Longsdorf, Hilda Madsen. *Mount Pleasant, 1859–1939.* Salt Lake City: Steven & Wallis, Inc., 1939.

Lund, Terry, and Nora Lund. *Pulsipher Family History Book.* Salt Lake City: Terry and Nora Lund, 1963.

Lyman, Edward Leo. *Political Deliverance: The Mormon Quest for Utah Statehood.* Urbana: University of Illinois Press, 1986.

Madsen, Andrew. "The Personal History of Andrew Madsen and the Early History of Sanpete County and Mt. Pleasant, Utah." CHD.

Madsen, Brigham D. *Exploring the Great Salt Lake: The Stansbury Expedition of 1849–50.* Salt Lake City: University of Utah Press, 1989.

———. *The Shoshoni Frontier and the Bear River Massacre.* Salt Lake City: University of Utah Press, 1985.

Malinowski, Sharon, and Simon Glickman. *Native North American Biography.* 2 vols. New York: Gale Research, 1996.

Manti Centennial Committee. *Song of a Century*. [Manti, UT: Centennial Committee, 1949].

Manti Ward Manuscript History. CHD.

Manuscript History of Brigham Young. CHD.

Martineau, LaVan. *The Southern Paiutes: Legends, Lore, Language, and Lineage*. Las Vegas: KC Publications, 1992.

McBride, Heber Robert. "Journal of Heber Robert McBride." BYUA&M.

McCormick, Henry. *Across the Continent in 1865: As Told in the Diary of the Late Colonel Henry McCormick*. Harrisburg, PA: Patriot Company, 1944.

McCune, Henry F. "Biography Of, Henry, F, &, Elizabeth, Grace, McCune, of Salt Lake City, State of Utah, U, S, A [*sic*]." CHD.

McPherson, Robert S. *The Northern Navajo Frontier, 1860–1900: Expansion through Adversity*. Albuquerque: University of New Mexico Press, 1988.

Meline, James F. *Two Thousand Miles on Horseback, Santa Fe and Back: A Summer Tour through Kansas, Nebraska, Colorado, and New Mexico in the Year 1866*. New York: Hurd and Houghton, 1867.

"Memorandum of Killed and Wounded with an approximate amount and Value of Stock Stolen and Loss of Property during the 3 years Indian War." 1868. TMR, #1565.

Memory Book to Commemorate Gunnison Valley's Centennial. Compiled and edited by Centennial Committee. N.p., [1959].

Merrill, H.R. "A Veteran of the Black Hawk War." *Improvement Era* 29 (November 1925): 58–60.

Metcalf, R. Warren. "A Precarious Balance: The Northern Utes and the Black Hawk War." *UHQ* 57 (Winter 1989): 24–35.

———."A Reappraisal of Utah's Black Hawk War." Master's thesis, Brigham Young University, 1989.

Millennial Star. 132 vols. Manchester, Liverpool: The Church of Jesus Christ of Latter-day Saints in Great Britain, 1840–1970. Various issues.

Miller, David Humphreys. *Ghost Dance*. New York: Duell, Sloan and Pearce, 1959.

Milner, Sarah Ellen Kinsman. Papers. CHD.

Morgan, Dale L. *The State of Deseret*. Logan: Utah State University Press/Utah State Historical Society, 1987.

Morley, Callie O. "Daniel & Amanda Bradley Henrie." CHD.

Munson, Eliza M. "Questions Concerning Black Hawk War Answered by Eliza M. Munson." UWPA Historical Records Survey. USHS.

Musser, A. Milton. Journal. CHD.

Neff, Andrew Love. *History of Utah 1847 to 1869*. Edited by Leland Hargrave Greer. Salt Lake City: Deseret News Press, 1940.

Nichols, Roger L. *Black Hawk and the Warrior's Path*. Arlington Heights, IL: Harlan Davidson, Inc., 1992.

Nielsen, Lars. "A Short History of the Life of Lars Nielsen & Sidsel P. Nielsen." CHD.

Novak, Shannon A. "Skeletal Analysis of the Remains of Black Hawk." May 1996. U.S. Department of Agriculture, Uinta National Forest, Provo, Utah. Copy available in John A. Peterson, Black Hawk Collection, UUWA.

Nuttall, L. John. Campaign Records. L. John Nuttall Collection. Mss 188, b7, f9. BYUA&M.

Nye, Wilbur Sturtevant. *Plains Indian Raiders: The Final Phases of Warfare from the Arkansas to the Red River with Original Photographs by William S. Soule.* Norman: University of Oklahoma Press, 1968.

Olsen, Livy. "Life Story." USHS.

O'Neil, Floyd A. "A History of the Ute Indians of Utah until 1890." Ph.D. diss., University of Utah, 1973.

O'Neil, Floyd A., and Stanford J. Layton. "Of Pride and Politics: Brigham Young as Indian Superintendent." *UHQ* 46 (Summer 1978): 236–61.

Pace, William B. "Autobiography." CHD.

———. Papers. CHD.

———. *Rifle and Light Infantry Tactics; for the Exercise and Maneuvers of Troops When Acting as Light Infantry or Riflemen . . . Prepared Expressly for the Use of the Militia of the Territory of Utah, by Colonel Wm B. Pace, Nauvoo Legion.* Great Salt Lake City: Deseret News Print, 1865. TMR, b3, f36.

Palmer, William R. "Utah Indians Past and Present, An Etymological and Historical Study of Tribes and Tribal Names from Original Sources." *UHQ* 1 (April 1928): 35–52.

Pay, Mary G. "History of Mary (Goble) Pay." CHD.

Peacock, George. Journal. CHD.

———. "[Statement] in relation to Indian difficulties in Sanpete County during the past summer." JH, 6 November 1865.

Peterson, Charles S. *Take Up Your Mission: Mormon Colonizing Along the Little Colorado River, 1870–1900.* Tucson: University of Arizona Press, 1973.

Peterson, John A. Black Hawk Collection. UUWA.

———. "Mormons, Indians, and Gentiles and Utah's Black Hawk War." Ph.D. diss., Arizona State University, 1993.

———. "Warren Stone Snow, A Man in Between: The Biography of a Mormon Defender." Master's thesis, Brigham Young University, 1985.

Peterson, John W. Autobiography and Journal. CHD.

Pettit, Jan. *Utes: The Mountain People.* Colorado Springs, CO: Century One Press, 1982.

Poll, Richard D., and Ralph W. Hansen. " 'Buchanan's Blunder': The Utah War, 1857–1858." *Military Affairs* 25 (Fall 1961): 121–31.

Porter, Larry C. "A Historical Analysis of Cove Fort, Utah." Master's thesis, Brigham Young University, 1966.

Powell, John Wesley. "Indian Life." Papers of the Bureau of American Ethnology. National Anthropological Archives. Washington, D.C.

———. "Journal of Canion Trip of 1869." Papers of the Bureau of American Ethnology. National Anthropological Archives. Washington, D.C.

———. "The Life and Culture of the Ute." Papers of the Bureau of American Ethnology. National Anthropological Archives. Washington, D.C.

Powell, Walter Clement. "Journal of Walter Clement Powell, April 21, 1871–December 7, 1872." Edited by Charles Kelly. *UHQ* 16–17 (1948–49): 257–478.

"Proceedings of a Council held by O.H. Irish Superintendent of Indian Affairs with the Utah Indians for the purpose of negotiating a treaty with them for the extinguishment of their title to the lands within Utah Territory . . ." 7–8 June 1865. Documents relating to the Negotiation of Ratified and Unratified Treaties with various Tribes of Indians, 1801–1869. BIA, T494, NA.

Quinn, D. Michael. *The Mormon Hierarchy: Origins of Power*. Salt Lake City: Signature Books/Smith Research Associates, 1994.

Rasmussen, Peter. "A Life Scetch [*sic*] of the life of Peter Rasmussen who was born in the village of Manti Sanpete county . . ." CHD.

"Record of Provo Military District Command 1857–1858 and Campaign Record of Expedition to Sanpete and Piute Military District 1866–1867 Under Command of William B. Pace." BYUSC.

Records of California Men in the War of the Rebellion, 1861–1867. Sacramento: State of California, 1890.

Records of the Adjutant General's Office. NA.

Records of the Bureau of Indian Affairs. NA.

Records of U.S. Army Continental Commands, 1821–1920. NA.

Remy, Jules. *A Journey to Great Salt Lake City*. 2 vols. London: W. Jeffs, 1861.

Report of the Commissioner of Indian Affairs [1860–1875]. Washington, D.C.: Government Printing Office, 1860–1875.

Report of the Secretary of the Interior [1860-1875]. Washington, D.C: Government Printing Office, 1860–1875.

Returns From U.S. Military Posts, 1800–1916. NA.

[Richards, Franklin D., ed.] *The Pearl of Great Price: Being a Choice Selection from the Revelations, Translations, and Narrations of Joseph Smith, First Prophet, Seer, and Revelator to the Church of Jesus Christ of Latter-Day Saints.* Liverpool: F.D. Richards, 1851.

Richfield Indian War Veterans. "Record of the Richfield Post (Sevier County) of Utah Indian War Veterans, 1891–1914." CHD.

Roberts, Brigham H. *A Comprehensive History of the Church of Jesus Christ of Latter-day Saints, Century I.* 6 vols. 1930. Reprint. Provo, UT: Brigham Young University Press, 1965.

Robins, Hettie M. "The History of James Russell Ivie and Wife Eliza McKee Faucett." John A. Peterson Collection, UUWA.

Robinson, F.G. "Manti Herald and Sanpete Advertiser." CHD.

Robinson, Phil. *Sinners and Saints: A Tour Across the States, and Round Them, with Three Months Among the Mormons.* London: Sampson Low, Marston & Company, 1892.

Robison, Lewis. "Journal of Lewis Robison, 1863–1866." CHD.

Rockwell, Wilson. *The Utes: A Forgotten People.* Denver: Sage Books, 1956.

Roessel, Robert A., Jr. "Navajo History, 1850–1923." In Alfonso Ortiz, ed., *Southwest.* Vol. 10 of *Handbook of North American Indians,* edited by William C. Sturtevant, 506–23. Washington, D.C.: Smithsonian Institution, 1983.

Rogerson, Josiah. "The Black-Hawk War in Utah. 1867. Bear-Valley Fight, Iron-County, Utah." Josiah Rogerson, Sr., Collection. BYUA&M.

———."The Ending of the Black Hawk War in Utah." CHD.

Romney, Edyth. Typescripts. CHD.

Rosenvall, Lynn A. "Mormon Fortifications in Western North America," *Historical Archaeology in Northwestern North America.* Edited by Ronald M. Getty and Knut R. Fladmark. N.p., n.d. 195–212. CHD.

Rusling, James F. *Across America: or, The Great West and the Pacific Coast.* New York: Sheldon & Company, 1874.

———."Report of Brevet Brigadier General James F. Rusling, Inspector, &c. For the year ending June 30, 1867." In "Letter from the Secretary of War." U.S. Congress. House. *Affairs in Utah and the Territories.* 40th Cong., 2d sess., H. Misc. Doc. 153. Serial set 1350.

Salt Lake Daily Tribune. Various issues.

Salt Lake Union Vedette. Various issues.

Sanpete Stake Manuscript History. CHD.

Santa Fe New Mexican. Various issues.

Santa Fe Weekly Gazette. Various issues.

Schroeder, Theodore Albert. Papers. CHD.

Scott, Bob. *Blood at Sand Creek: The Massacre Revisited.* Caldwell, ID: Caxton Printers, 1994.

Seeley, Orange, Sr. "History of Orange Seeley, Sr., Told by Himself." CHD.

Shimkin, Demitri B. "Eastern Shoshone." In Warren L. D'Azevedo, ed., *Great Basin.* Vol. 11 of *Handbook of North American Indians,* edited by William C. Sturtevant, 308–35. Washington, D.C.: Smithsonian Institution, 1986.

Sidwell, A.B. "Reminiscences of Early Manti." Manti Ward Manuscript History. CHD.

Simpson, Captain James H. *Report of Explorations Across the Great Basin of the Territory of Utah for a Direct Wagon-Route From Camp Floyd to Genoa, In Carson Valley, in 1859.* 1859. Reprint. Reno: University of Nevada Press, 1983.

"Sketch of the Life of Abraham Washburn." Jean R. Bradfield Collection. CHD.

Sloan, Robert W. "She-na-ba-wiken, 'The White Horse Chief.' " *Juvenile Instructor* 18 (15 December 1883): 379.

Smith, Anne M. *Ethnology of the Northern Utes*. Santa Fe: Museum of New Mexico, 1974.

Smith, Azariah. Journal. CHD.

Smith, George A. Collection. CHD.

———. "Extracts from the Journal of George A. Smith." Edyth Romney Typescripts. CHD.

———. Sermon in Grantsville, 13 July 1866. "Minutes." Vol. 3. BYC.

Smith, Hyrum. "A Dayly [*sic*] Record of H Smith." Edyth Romney Typescripts. B101. CHD.

Smith, Jesse N. "Scenes of Our Indian War." *Juvenile Instructor* 10 (23 January 1875): 20–21.

Smith, Joseph, Jr. The Book of Mormon. Palmyra, NY: E.B. Grandin for Joseph Smith, Jr., 1830.

[Smith, Joseph, Jr., et al.] *A Book of Commandments for the Government of the Church of Christ, Organized According to Law, on the 6th of April, 1830*. Zion [Independence, MO]: W.W. Phelps & Co., 1833. Reprint. Independence, MO: Herald House, 1972.

———. *Doctrine and Covenants of the Church of the Latter Day Saints: Carefully Selected from the Revelations of God*. Kirtland, OH: 1835. Reprint. Independence, MO: Herald House, 1971.

Smith, Joseph, Jr., [et al]. *History of the Church of Jesus Christ of Latter-day Saints, Introduction and notes by B.H. Roberts*. 2nd ed., rev. 7 vols. Salt Lake City: Deseret Book Company, 1976.

Smith, P. David. *Ouray Chief of the Utes: The Fascinating Story of Colorado's most famous and controversial Indian Chief*. Ouray, CO: Wayfinder Press, 1986.

Snow, William J. "Utah Indians and Spanish Slave Trade." *UHQ* 2 (1929): 67–75.

Sonne, Conway B. "Royal Blood of the Utes." *UHQ* 22 (Summer 1954): 271–76.

———. *World of Wakara*. San Antonio, TX: Naylor Co., 1962.

Sorensen, Iva Lee, and Kaye S. Bybee, comps. and eds. *Founded on Faith: A History of Glenwood, 1864–1984*. N.p.: Glenwood Camp Daughters of Utah Pioneers, 1984.

Spencer, Deloy J. "The Utah Black Hawk War 1865–1871." Master's "report," Utah State University, 1969.

"The Squaw Man." Uel Hunting Collection. CHD.

Stansbury, Howard. *Exploration and Survey of the Valley of the Great Salt Lake of Utah Including a Reconnaissance of a New Route Through the Rocky Mountains*. Philadelphia: Lippincott, Grambo & Co., 1852.

Stout, Hosea. *On The Mormon Frontier: The Diary of Hosea Stout, 1844–1861*. Edited by Juanita Brooks. 2 vols. Salt Lake City: University of Utah Press, 1964.

Sturtevant, William C., ed. *Handbook of North American Indians.* 17 vols. Washington, D.C.: Smithsonian Institution, 1978– .

Summit County, Utah, Probate Court Records. Offenses, Book A., 1866–1880. FHL.

Summit Stake Manuscript History. CHD.

Sundberg, Lawrence D. *Dinetah: An Early History of the Navajo People.* Santa Fe: Sunstone Press, 1995.

Sweeney, John, Jr. "A History of the Nauvoo Legion in Illinois." Ph.D. diss., Brigham Young University, 1974.

Svaldi, David. *Sand Creek and the Rhetoric of Extermination: A Case Study in Indian-White Relations.* Lanham, MD: University Press of America, 1989.

Sylvester, Joshua. "A Sketch of My Life During the Indian Wars." TMR, #1298.

"Synopsis of the Proceedings of the Probate Court M[illard]. Co on the Case of the People vs James A. Ivie Indictment—Murder [of] an Indian, July 12th 1866." TMR, #1538.

Taylor, Colin F., and William C. Sturtevant, eds. *The Native Americans: The Indigenous People of North America.* London: Salamander Books Ltd., 1991.

Territory of Utah. Secretary of Utah Territory Papers. TEP. USA.

———. Territorial Executive Papers. USA.

———. Territorial Militia Records, 1849-1877. USA.

"The People etc. Vs. Jacob Hoffman, Jackson Redding, William Smith, Charles Livingston, Dick Eldridge (Whose real name is to the Grand Jurors unknown) and Joseph Brim, Indictment for Murder in the First Degree." Secretary of Utah Territory Papers. TEP, reel 6, #6195–6201.

"The People Vs. Isaac S. Potter[,] John Walker[, and] Charles Wilson for Grand Larceny," in Summit County, Utah, Probate Court Records. Offenses, Book A., 1866–1880, 28–42. FHL.

Thomas, David H., Lorann S.A. Pendleton, and Stephen C. Cappannari. "Western Shoshone." In Warren L. D'Azevedo, ed. *Great Basin.* Vol. 11 of *Handbook of North American Indians*, edited by William C. Sturtevant, 262–83. Washington, D.C.: Smithsonian Institution, 1986.

Thornton, Russell. *We Shall Live Again: The 1870 and 1890 Ghost Dance Movements as Demographic Revitalization.* London: Cambridge University Press, 1986.

Thurber, Albert K. "Journal and Diary of Albert King Thurber." *Treasures of Pioneer History*, 3:253–319.

Tinker, George E. *Missionary Conquest: The Gospel and Native American Cultural Genocide.* Minneapolis, MN: Fortress Press, 1993.

Tolton, John Franklin. "Memories of the Life of John Franklin Tolton, also a Brief Record of the Family and Other Matters commenced August 23 1887." CHD.

Trafzer, Clifford E. *The Kit Carson Campaign: The Last Great Navajo War.* Norman: University of Oklahoma Press, 1982.

Treaty Between the United States of America and The Tabeguache Band of Utah Indians: Concluded October 7, 1863 as Amended. Ratifications Advised, with Amendments, by Senate, March 25, 1864. Amendments Accepted October 8, 1864. Proclaimed December 14, 1864. N.p. BIA, M234, 199.

Trennert, Robert A., Jr. *Alternative to Extinction: Federal Indian Policy and the Beginnings of the Reservation System, 1846–1851.* Philadelphia: Temple University Press, 1975.

Tullidge, Edward W. *Tullidge's Histories, Containing the History of all the Northern, Eastern and Western Counties of Utah; Also the Counties of Southern Idaho, with a Biographical Appendix of Representative Men and Founders of the Cities and Counties; also a Commercial Supplement, Historical.* Salt Lake City: Juvenile Instructor, 1889.

U.S. Congress. House. Committee on Elections. *Report of the Committee of Elections upon the Contested Election Case of McGrorty vs. Hooper, Sitting Delegate from the Territory of Utah, . . .* 1868. 40th Cong., 2d sess., 1868, H. Rept. 79. Serial 1358.

U.S. Congress. House. *Memorial of the Legislative Assembly of Utah Territory to the Honorable the Senate and House of Representatives of the United States in Congress assembled, praying for an appropriation to pay for Indian depredations and expenses incurred in suppressing Indian hostilities.* February 21, 1868. 41st Cong., 1st sess., H. Misc. Doc. 19.

U.S. Congress. Senate. *Report of the Secretary of War, communicating, In compliance with a resolution of the Senate of February 4, 1867, a copy of the evidence taken at Denver and Fort Lyon, Colorado Territory, by a military commission, ordered to inquire into the Sand Creek massacre, November, 1864.* 39th Cong., 2d sess., S. Ex. Doc. 26.

U.S. Department of the Interior. Bureau of Land Management. Cedar City District [Utah] Dixie Resource Area. "Old Fort Pearce." N.d. CHD.

U.S. Department of War. *War of the Rebellion: a compilation of the Official Records of the Union and Confederate Armies.* Series 1. Vol. 50. Part 1. Washington: Government Printing Office, 1897.

U.S. State Department Territorial Papers. USA.

Uintah-Ouray Tribe. *The Ute System of Government.* Salt Lake City: University of Utah Printing Service for the Uintah-Ouray Ute Tribe, 1977.

Underhill, Ruth M. *The Navajos.* Norman: University of Oklahoma Press, 1956.

Utah County, Utah. Probate Court Records. "Probate Doc[k]et 'A.' " USA.

Utah Stake Manuscript History. CHD.

The Utah Indian War Veteran's Songster. Salt Lake City: Skelton Publishing Co., 1907. Special Collections, Merrill Library, Utah State University, Logan, Utah.

Utley, Robert M. *The Indian Frontier of the American West 1846–1890.* Albuquerque: University of New Mexico Press, 1984.

———. *The Last Days of the Sioux Nation.* New Haven, CT: Yale University Press, 1963.

UWPA Historical Records Survey, USHS.

"Vital Records of the Ute Indians to 1946." Uintah and Ouray Agency. BIA, film #1714, FHL.

Waite, Catherine Van Valkenburg. *Adventures in the Far West; and Life Among the Mormons.* Chicago: C.V. Waite and Company, 1882.

Wakefield, John F., Jr. "Biography or Life Story of John F. Wakefield." CHD.

Walker, Charles Lowell. *Diary of Charles Lowell Walker.* 2 vols. Edited by A. Karl Larson and Katherine Miles Larson. Logan: Utah State University Press, 1980.

Waldman, Carl. *Who Was Who in Native American History: Indians and Non-Indians From Early Contacts through 1900.* New York: Facts on File, 1990.

Waldman, Harry, et al. *Dictionary of Indians of North America.* 3 vols. St. Clair Shores, MI: Scholarly Press, 1978.

Walker, Ronald W. "The Godbeite Protest in the Making of Modern Utah." Ph.D. diss., University of Utah, 1977.

———. "President Young Writes Jefferson Davis about the Gunnison Massacre." *Brigham Young University Studies* 35 (1995): 47–170.

———. "Toward a Reconstruction of Mormon and Indian Relations, 1847–1877." *Brigham Young University Studies* 29 (Fall 1989): 23–42.

Ware, Eugene F. *The Indian War of 1864, being a Fragment of the Early history of Kansas, Nebraska, Colorado, and Wyoming.* Topeka, KS: Crane & Company, 1911.

Washburn, J.N. "Black Hawk: A True Short Story of Pioneer Times." *Improvement Era* 50 (1947): 154 ff.

Washburn, Wilcomb E. *The Indian In America.* New York: Harper & Row, 1975.

Waters, William E. *Life Among the Mormons, and a March to Their Zion: To Which is Added a Chapter on the Indians of the Plains and Mountains of the West by An Officer of the U.S. Army.* New York: Moorhead, Simpson & Bond, 1868.

Watson, Kaye C. *Life Under the Horseshoe: A History of Spring City.* Salt Lake City: Publishers Press, 1987.

Weibye, Jens C.A. "Jens C.A. Weibye 1st Daybook from September 26th 1824 to July 19, 1871." CHD.

———. "Journal of Jens Christian Andersen Weibye." CHD.

Wells, Daniel H. "Daniel H. Wells' Narrative." *UHQ* 6 (October 1933): 124–32.

Western History Center. University of Utah. "American Indian Oral History: The Duke Collection." UUWA.

Whitney, Orson F. *History of Utah*. 4 vols. Salt Lake City: George Q. Cannon and Sons, 1892–1904.

Whittaker, David J. "Mormons and Native Americans: A Historical and Bibliographical Introduction." *Dialogue: A Journal of Mormon Thought* 18 (Winter 1985): 33–64.

William Jex: Pioneer and Patriarch. Spanish Fork, UT: Spanish Fork Press, n.d. UUWA.

Williams, James Van Nostrand. "Life Sketch of James Van Nostrand Williams." USHS.

Winkler, Albert. "The Circleville Massacre: A Brutal Incident in Utah's Black Hawk War." *UHQ* 55 (Winter 1987): 4–21.

———. "Justice in the Black Hawk War: The Trial of Thomas Jose." *UHQ* 60 (Spring 1992): 124–36.

———. "The Ute Mode of War in the Conflict of 1865-68." *UHQ* 60 (Fall 1992): 300–318.

Wise, William. *Massacre at Mountain Meadows: An American Legend And a Monumental Crime*. New York: Thomas Y. Crowell Company, 1976.

Wixom, Hartt. *Hamblin: A Modern Look at the Frontier Life and Legend of Jacob Hamblin*. Springville, UT: Cedar Fort, Inc., 1996.

Woodruff, Wilford. *Wilford Woodruff's Journal, 1833–1898*. 9 vols. Edited by Scott G. Kenney. Midvale, UT: Signature Books, 1983–85.

Woolley, Edwin D., Jr. "Autobiography of Edwin Dilworth Woolley Jr.," USHS.

———. "Father Tells His Experience in the Black Kawk [*sic*] War to daughter Elizabeth." Edwin Woolley, Jr., and Erastus Snow Family Collection, BYUA&M.

———. "The following excerpts are taken from dictation during his declining years." Edwin Woolley, Jr., and Erastus Snow Family Collection, BYUA&M.

———. "Notes on Fathers Life." Edwin Woolley, Jr., and Erastus Snow Family Collection. BYUA&M.

———. "A True Indian Story." Edwin Woolley, Jr., and Erastus Snow Family Collection. BYUA&M.

Workers of the Writers' Program of the Work Projects Administration for the State of Utah. *Provo: Pioneer Mormon City*. Portland, OR: Binfords & Mort, 1942.

Yates, Thomas J. "Thomas Yates, Written by his son Thomas J. Yates." CHD.

Young, Brigham. Collection. CHD.

Young, Richard W. "The Nauvoo Legion." *The Contributor Representing the Young Men's and Young Ladies' Mutual Improvement Associations of the Latter-day Saints* 9 (1888): 1–8, 41–49, 81–89, 121–27, 161–68, 201–12, 241–51, 281–86, 321–32, 361–73, 401–13, 441–54.

Index